THE COLLAPSE OF A COLONIAL SOCIETY

PUBLISHED

UNDER THE AUSPICES OF

Nederlands Instituut
voor
Oorlogsdocumentatie

NETHERLANDS INSTITUTE FOR WAR DOCUMENTATION

AND

KONINKLIJK INSTITUUT

VOOR

TAAL-, LAND- EN VOLKENKUNDE

VERHANDELINGEN
VAN HET KONINKLIJK INSTITUUT
VOOR TAAL-, LAND- EN VOLKENKUNDE

206

L. DE JONG

THE COLLAPSE OF A COLONIAL SOCIETY

The Dutch in Indonesia during the Second World War

With an introduction by
JEROEN KEMPERMAN

KITLV Press
Leiden
2002

Published by:
KITLV Press
Koninklijk Instituut voor Taal-, Land- en Volkenkunde
(Royal Institute of Linguistics and Anthropology)
P.O. Box 9515
2300 RA Leiden
The Netherlands
website: www.kitlv.nl
e-mail: kitlvpress@kitlv.nl

Translated by: Jennifer Kilian, Cornelia Kist and John Rudge

Cover: Creja Ontwerpen, Leiderdorp

ISBN 90 6718 203 6

© 2002 Koninklijk Instituut voor Taal-, Land- en Volkenkunde

Printed in the Netherlands

Contents

List of maps

Acknowledgements

The translation and publication of this book were made possible by the financial support of the Historical Research Program. In 1996 the government of Japan awarded a grant to the Netherlands Institute for War Documentation (NIOD) for the implementation of research and documentation projects which are representative of the long history of relations between Japan and the Netherlands.

The following people have generously contributed to the appearance of this book:

Cornelia Kist, Elisabeth Broers, Elly Touwen-Bouwsma, Harco Gijsbers, Harry Poeze, Hinke Piersma, Jennifer Kilian, Jeroen Kemperman, John Rudge, José Nederend, Marco Keurentjes, Mariska Heijmans-van Bruggen, Marjan Groen, Peter Romijn, Remco Raben, René Kok, Ria van Yperen, Rita DeCoursey, Sirtjo Koolhof, Tom van den Berge.

And, of course, above all: Louis de Jong.

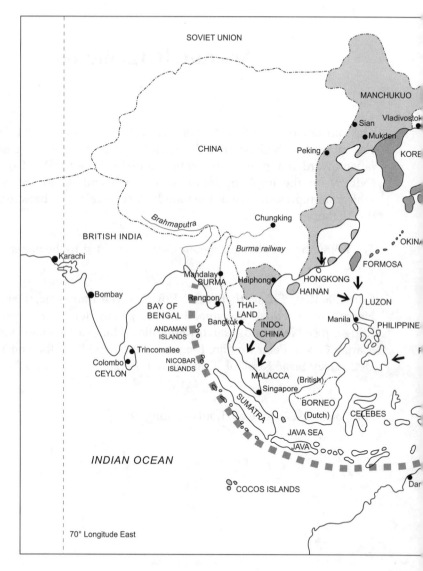

Japanese plan of attack.
The arrows indicate the first planned landings.

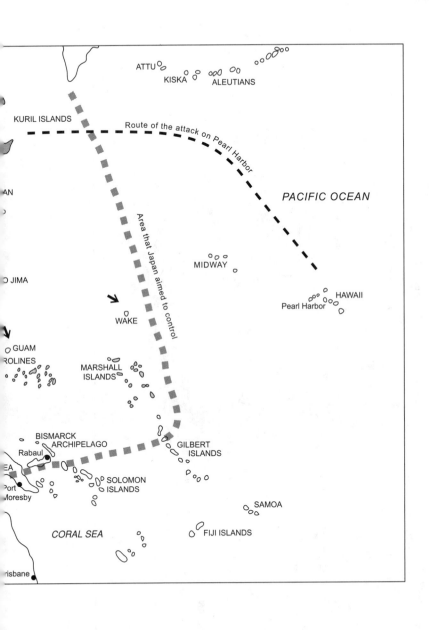

ATTU
KISKA
ALEUTIANS

KURIL ISLANDS
Route of the attack on Pearl Harbor

AN

PACIFIC OCEAN

JIMA

MIDWAY

HAWAII
Pearl Harbor

Area that Japan aimed to control

WAKE

GUAM
ROLINES

MARSHALL
ISLANDS

BISMARCK
ARCHIPELAGO
Rabaul

GILBERT
ISLANDS

EA

Port
Moresby

SOLOMON
ISLANDS

SAMOA

CORAL SEA

FIJI ISLANDS

risbane

Indonesia

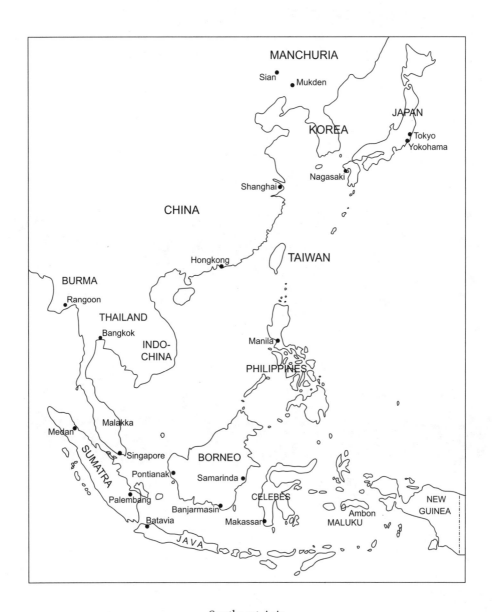

Southeast Asia

JEROEN KEMPERMAN

Introduction

Dr L. de Jong: his life and work

Louis de Jong was born in Amsterdam on 24 April 1914.[1] He studied social geography and history at the University of Amsterdam from 1932 to 1937. He was the foreign editor of the left-wing weekly *De Groene Amsterdammer* from 1938 to 1940. In May 1940, as the German army overran the Netherlands, he and his wife managed to escape to England. In London he became director of Radio Oranje, which broadcast to the occupied Netherlands. In October 1945 he was appointed head of the Rijksinstituut voor Oorlogsdocumentatie (RIOD, Netherlands Institute for War Documentation), which had been founded in May of the same year with the task of assembling an accessible collection of historical documents about the Netherlands in the Second World War. Eight years later he was awarded his doctorate cum laude for a thesis on the German Fifth Column in which he demonstrated that – contrary to the generally held view – secret underground operations by the Germans had not played a significant role in their military triumphs of 1939-1940. This study was translated into English, German and Russian. In 1963 De Jong became a member of the Koninklijke Nederlandse Akademie van Wetenschappen (KNAW, Royal Netherlands Academy of Arts and Sciences).

De Jong is one of the few nationally renowned Dutch historians. He acquired this status thanks to his appearance in the television series *De Bezetting* (The Occupation), which he wrote and presented in 21 instalments between 1960 and 1965. In 1962, the television critics awarded him their annual prize for 'the best television achievement on screen'.

In 1955 De Jong was commissioned by the Ministry of Education and Science to write a comprehensive history of the Netherlands in the Second World War. It was estimated that this would take about six years to complete. Aided and supported by the staff of the RIOD, De Jong set to work. The first part – entitled *Voorspel* (Prelude) – of *Het Koninkrijk der Nederlanden*

---

[1]   The information in this paragraph is taken from the articles in Madelon de Keizer (ed.), *'Een dure verplichting en een kostelijk voorrecht'; Dr. L. de Jong en zijn geschiedwerk* (Den Haag, 1995).

in de Tweede Wereldoorlog only saw the light of day in 1969, and stayed on the bestseller list for months. By then it was clear that completion of the series was likely to be a protracted affair. De Jong steadily produced volume after volume and in 1988, 19 years after the publication of the first part and nearly 10 years after his retirement, the 12th part – *Epiloog* (Epilogue) – finally appeared. The task was at last complete, although a 13th part containing appendices and corrections and a 14th one – edited by J.T.M. Bank and P. Romijn – with reactions to the series would be published later. It may rightly be described as a mammoth endeavour. De Jong's 13 parts are published in 27 volumes and together add up to almost 15,000 pages.[2]

De Jong did not want his work to be read only by historians and thus consciously strove to reach a broad public. And he succeeded. For a historical work, the volumes of *Het Koninkrijk der Nederlanden in de Tweede Wereldoorlog* were issued in large editions and reached a wide audience. The average print run for each volume was 75,000 copies. An estimated 74,000 readers even own the entire series. The work was greatly admired and showered with prizes. Its success may have been linked to the subject of the study. The experiences of the Second World War had deeply marked the collective memory of the Dutch population. No period in the history of the Netherlands has given rise to – and still gives rise to – as many Manichean controversies and affairs as the German occupation. The war has become a moral gauge, a source of lessons of relevance to contemporary society. Much weight was given to De Jong's opinion – both as the author of *Het Koninkrijk* and as director of the RIOD – concerning countless questions arising from the issues of resistance and collaboration.

De Jong's magnum opus has become the standard work. Which is not to say that it remained uncriticized. Quite possibly, no Dutch historian has been discussed, commented upon and condemned as much as De Jong. And no subject in *Het Koninkrijk der Nederlanden in de Tweede Wereldoorlog* elicited so much controversy as the volumes devoted to the Japanese occupation of the Dutch East Indies and the subsequent decolonization.

---

[2]   L. de Jong, *Het Koninkrijk der Nederlanden in de Tweede Wereldoorlog. Deel 1. Voorspel* (1969); *Deel 2. Neutraal* (1969); *Deel 3. Mei '40* (1970); *Deel 4. Mei '40-maart '41* (2 vols, 1972); *Deel 5. Maart '41-juli '42* (2 vols, 1974); *Deel 6. Juli '42-mei '43* (2 vols, 1975); *Deel 7. Mei '43-juni '44* (2 vols, 1976); *Deel 8. Gevangenen en gedeporteerden* (2 vols, 1978); *Deel 9. Londen* (2 vols, 1979); *Deel 10a. Het laatste jaar I* (2 vols, 1980); *Deel 10b. Het laatste jaar II* (2 vols, 1981); *Deel 11a. Nederlands-Indië I* (2 vols, 1984); *Deel 11b. Nederlands-Indië II* (2 vols, 1985); *Deel 11c. Nederlands-Indië III* (1986); *Deel 12. Epiloog* (2 vols, 1988); *Deel 13. Bijlagen* (1988). J.Th.M. Bank and P. Romijn (eds.), *Deel 14. Reacties* (2 vols, 1991).

The East Indies volumes

The first part on the Dutch East Indies appeared in 1984. This was part 11a, which in almost 1,200 pages addresses its history from the beginning of the Dutch presence in the archipelago to the capitulation of the Koninklijk Nederlands-Indisch Leger (KNIL, Royal Dutch East Indies Army) in March 1942. The work unleashed substantial criticism, on the part of both the general readership and historians. In the preface, De Jong even allowed two of his critics, Prof. I.J. Brugmans and R.C. Kwantes, who were personally familiar with colonial society and had therefore been called in as advisers by him, to express their views. Brugmans and Kwantes believed that part 11a 'focused in particular on the negative aspects of the Dutch presence in the Indonesian archipelago, while in contrast the favourable results of the activities developed by the government and business (partly for the benefit of the indigenous population) received scant attention' (De Jong 1984, 11a:xiv). Above all, the extensive attention De Jong devoted to the clashes between the colonial government and the Indonesian national movement resulted in the accusation that he harboured an 'anti-colonial bias'. A group of Dutch from the former colony even instigated lawsuits against the Dutch state as the commissioner of the work, demanding – without success – that the chapters on colonialism be rewritten by an 'impartial' historian.

The sequel, part 11b, appeared one year later. In approximately 1,100 pages it describes the occupation of the Dutch East Indies, ending with the proclamation of the Republic of Indonesia on 17 August 1945. In contrast to its predecessors, part 11b, which was full of the atrocities committed by the Japanese, was positively received by those from the former East Indies. Some historians found it notable that De Jong voiced sharp criticism of the far-reaching collaboration with the Japanese occupation regime of Sukarno, the leader of the nationalist movement and after the war the first president of independent Indonesia. De Jong particularly condemned his active collaboration in the recruitment of Indonesian forced labour, the so-called *romusha*. One wonders whether De Jong was not judging Sukarno's deeds from an overly Dutch perspective, all the more so because in Indonesia his collaboration has hardly been the subject of public debate. Most Indonesians consider the Japanese occupation only as a prologue to a far more important episode in their history: national independence from the Dutch colonizer. These kinds of considerations, however, did not shake De Jong's own moral views on the collaboration issue, which were shaped by the German occupation of the Netherlands.

The final part dealing with the Dutch East Indies in wartime, part 11c, appeared in 1986 and describes the Dutch contribution to the Allied war efforts in the Pacific and the preparations for the return of the Indies government and its officials. Nevertheless, De Jong's history of the Dutch East Indies had not yet come to a close. The final part of the series as a whole, part 12 (*Epiloog*), published in 1988, dealt with, among other things, the post-war decolonization of the Dutch East Indies. In the draft chapter on this subject (De Jong always had his drafts commented upon by expert 'readers') there is a section discussing the occasional war crimes supposedly committed by Dutch troops. Before then, it had been customary to employ the term 'excesses'. De Jong's passages on the lapses of the Dutch soldiers elicited fierce criticism, chiefly from veterans. A case for criminal libel was even filed, and dismissed. De Jong, however, succumbed to the pressure and replaced the term 'war crimes' by 'excesses'. He also permitted one of the 'readers', Lieutenant General F. van der Veen, to add an appendix setting out his vision of the 'systematic terrorism' by the Indonesian troops and the 'occasional measures of counter-terrorism' on the Dutch side.[3]

The vehement reactions to the Indies volumes make clear just how sensitive an issue judgement of the colonial past was for those from the East Indies in the Netherlands – even forty years later. Many felt that their suffering during the Japanese occupation and the Indonesian struggle for independence had simply been overlooked by their countrymen. For many of them, the Indonesian archipelago, more than the Netherlands, was their motherland, while the colonial state was their homeland. They had been brutally dispossessed: the colonial East Indies as they had known it existed no longer. Their frustrations were aimed chiefly at Japan, the country considered to be the bearer of misfortune. The fierceness of the anti-Japanese sentiments first surfaced in 1971, when the Japanese emperor, Hirohito, visited seven Western European countries, including the Netherlands and Great Britain. Incidents occurred during the visit in both of these countries, as well as in Denmark and in West Germany. However, in no other country were the reactions so passionate as in the Netherlands. In The Hague a stone was hurled through the windshield of Hirohito's car and the Japanese flag set on fire.

Figures explain a great deal. An estimated 300,000 Dutch citizens experienced the Second World War in the East Indies and of them an estimated 42,000 prisoners of war and 100,000 civilian internees were held by the Japanese authorities. The approximately 160,000 Eurasians of mixed Dutch and Indonesian origin who remained outside of the camps also led an exceedingly difficult existence. In no other Western colony in Southeast Asia was the number of Europeans and the number of civilians interned by the Japanese so great. As a point of comparison, in the Malay peninsula 20,000 British civilians and in Indo-China 27,000 French civilians were interned. The

---

[3]   J.T.M. Bank, 'L. de Jong over de oorlog in en de dekolonisatie van Indië', in De Keizer 1995: 140.

number of British prisoners of war is estimated at 50,000. Only in the Dutch East Indies did the number of interned civilians exceed that of the prisoners of war; only there were the interned families completely divided by sex; and in no other European country was the number of war victims returning to their motherland (300,000 individuals) so great in relation to the total population (10 million in 1945, 12 million in 1964). Due to the presence of this relatively extensive and well-organized group from the East Indies, memory of the war in the Pacific may be stronger in the Netherlands than in any other European country.[4]

De Jong's part 11b was well received by those from the former colony because the work lavished attention – disproportionally so perhaps – on the terrible experiences of the prisoners of war and the civilians in the Japanese internment camps. The vicissitudes of those of mixed Dutch and Indonesian origin, most of whom remained outside of the camps, and of the great bulk of Indonesians were somewhat understated. The same may be said of developments in the Outer Islands. De Jong's history of the Japanese occupation of the Dutch East Indies centres on the Europeans and on Java. In the author's defence it should be noted that this is an unavoidable consequence of the nature of the available sources (as well as reflecting certain biases in their acquisition). The simple fact is that far more is known about the camps on Java than about any other aspect of the Japanese occupation.

Some historians have reproached De Jong for not employing the techniques of oral history and failing to delve into the Japanese and Indonesian archives, which makes his work chiefly: 'an extensive compilation of older and recent literature, limited Dutch archival material and numerous ego documents'.[5] This is how De Jong's Indies volumes should be viewed: as a comprehensive synthesis, a survey of the state of affairs in historical research at the time. As such, his work continues to be of inestimable value.

This book

This is a translation of Chapters V through X of De Jong's *Het Koninkrijk der Nederlanden in de Tweede Wereldoorlog. Deel 11b. Nederlands-Indië II* (1985). These chapters make up approximately half of part 11b. Omitted are chapters concerning the general course of the war in the Pacific, the Japanese occupation policies, the role of Sukarno, and the run up to the proclamation of the

---

[4]   Elsbeth Locher-Scholten, 'In Nederland na *de verre oorlog*; Publieke herinneringen aan de Tweede Wereldoorlog in Azië', in Remco Raben (ed.) *Beelden van de Japanse bezetting van Indonesië* (Zwolle/Amsterdam, 1999), pp. 56, 225, note 7.
[5]   Elsbeth Locher-Scholten, in De Jong 1991, 14:839-40.

Republic of Indonesia on 17 August 1945, as there are plenty of publications
in English in which these matters are treated extensively.[6] Until now, however, there has been no good scholarly study in English on the vicissitudes of
the Dutch and Dutch Eurasians during the Japanese occupation of the East
Indies. This publication hopes to fill this lacuna.

Because only a few chapters from De Jong's enormous work are presented here, it was necessary to make minor adjustments to the original text
in order to tie up loose ends. These mainly concerned references to other
sections and chapters, and have been eliminated or when necessary replaced
by an explanation in a footnote. People, institutions and events introduced
elsewhere in De Jong's work and not mentioned in this 'Introduction' are also
clarified in footnotes. Changes, additions and corrections made by De Jong
himself in part 13 of his series have been incorporated here. For the rest, his
text has been left unaltered.

All that remains is to sketch the course of events up to the point where De
Jong's story begins: from the arrival of the Dutch in the Indonesian archipelago to the capitulation of the Dutch East Indies in March 1942. Several
aspects of the Japanese occupation policies with respect to the Indonesian
population will be discussed. Perhaps in the following brief survey of the
pre-war history of the Dutch East Indies, certain affairs will be scrutinized too
closely and others neglected, but it is not the intention of this 'Introduction'
to do justice to every aspect of this subject. In the following survey, only elements considered relevant for a proper understanding of De Jong's account
will be addressed.[7]

[6]   George McTurnan Kahin, *Nationalism and revolution in Indonesia* (Ithaca/New York, 1952);
M.A. Aziz, *Japan's colonialism and Indonesia* (The Hague, 1955); Harry J. Benda, *The crescent and
the rising sun; Indonesian islam under the Japanese occupation 1942-1945* (The Hague, 1958); George
S. Kanahele, *The Japanese occupation of Indonesia; Prelude to independence* (n.p., 1967); B.R.O'G.
Anderson, *Java in a time of revolution; Occupation and resistance 1944-1946* (Ithaca, 1972); Anthony
Reid and Oki Akira (ed.), *The Japanese experience in Indonesia; Selected memoirs of 1942-1945*
(Athens, 1986); Theodore Friend, *The blue-eyed enemy; Japan against the West in Java and Luzon,
1942-1945* (Princeton, 1988); William H. Frederick, *Visions and heat; The making of the Indonesian
revolution* (Athens, 1989); Shigeru Sato, *War, nationalism and peasants; Java under the Japanese occupation* (n.p., 1994). On Sukarno: J.D. Legge, *Sukarno; A political biography* (London, 1972). To be
used with caution is *Soekarno; An autobiography, as told to Cindy Adams* (Indianapolis, 1965).
[7]   This survey is based on De Jong 11a and 11b; J. van Goor, *Indië/Indonesië; Van kolonie tot
natie* (Utrecht, 1987); H.W. van den Doel, *Het rijk van Insulinde; Opkomst en ondergang van een
Nederlandse kolonie* (Amsterdam, 1996); J.J.P. de Jong, *De waaier van fortuin; Van handelscompagnie
tot koloniaal imperium; De Nederlanders in Azië en de Indonesische archipel 1595-1950* (Den Haag,
1998).

The origin of Dutch rule in the Indonesian archipelago

On 2 April 1595, four ships commanded by Cornelis de Houtman and Pieter Dirksz. de Keyser set sail from Amsterdam harbour destined for 'the Indies'. In August 1597, three ships with 87 of the original 249 men returned. Though the first Dutch voyage to the Indonesian archipelago was not a commercial success, this did not prevent others from waging new attempts. The primary motive for undertaking such distant and dangerous journeys was to conduct trade. The Portuguese, who had already established an extensive commercial network in Asia, had demonstrated just how profitable the Asian products were and the Dutch were eager to follow their example. Between 1598 and 1601, at least fourteen Dutch fleets sailed to Asia, sent there by eight different trading companies. As a means of combining the various enterprises, the Verenigde Oost-Indische Compagnie (VOC, Dutch East Indies Company) was founded in 1602.

The VOC was a great success. In a relatively short time, it established an extensive Asian trading network extending from the Cape of Good Hope to Japan. The core of its activities, however, lay in the Indonesian archipelago. The Company was first and foremost a commercial enterprise, but it also had the military capacity necessary to establish and defend its commercial imperium. The Portuguese were routed from the Indonesian archipelago, first from the Moluccas, the source of the profitable trade in cloves, nutmeg and mace, and subsequently from the other islands. In 1619, Governor-General Jan Pieterszoon Coen built a fort called Batavia on West Java, in the indigenous city of Jakarta. This settlement became the Company's Asian headquarters. At the end of the seventeenth century, the VOC controlled the monopolies of many goods important to Europe, and European rivals were successfully kept out of the Indonesian archipelago. In the course of the next two centuries, the Company expanded its territorial authority in the archipelago to the North Javanese coastal cities, West Java, a number of islands in the Moluccas, the island of Madura, and several places on Sumatra and Celebes. The local rulers were too divided to effectively prevent this domination.

In the second half of the eighteenth century, the VOC ran into financial difficulty, chiefly due to fierce competition from the English East India Company (EIC). The war between the Dutch Republic and England from 1780-1784 spelled the coup de grâce for the Company and it was forced to declare bankruptcy in 1796. Its possessions were taken over by the Dutch state and the colony of the Dutch East Indies was born. Establishment of colonial authority, however, did not take place without bloodshed. The traditional Javanese elite attempted to restore its old position in the Java War (1825-1830), during which about 15,000 Dutch soldiers and 200,000 Javanese perished. The Dutch prevailed in the end, but the bloody conflict had depleted their coffers. In The Hague it was deemed time for the colony to earn money again.

In 1830, a highly lucrative system was introduced on Java, the centre of the colonial economy: the Culture System. This system was based on the principal that the colonial government owned all of the land on Java and that it could claim a certain amount of rent from those cultivating it. This rent would be collected in the form of agricultural products suitable for export: indigo, sugar, or coffee. Henceforth, every indigenous village had to use a fifth of its farmland for the cultivation of these products and the Javanese farmers were required to work on these government crops for a maximum of 66 days per year. In the event of a crop failure, nothing had to be handed over. The farmers were compensated for their labour with the so-called 'crop payment'. Profits ended up in the Dutch treasury. In theory, this system appeared to be advantageous to both parties. In practice, the burden on the villagers was seriously increased by the forced labour. On the other hand, the system further opened up the Javanese economy to international trade, stimulated local industry, and advanced the prosperity of certain groups in Javanese society.

For the Dutch state, the Culture System was the goose that laid the golden egg. Profits from the East Indian possessions up to 1870 amounted to a total of 725 million guilders. The income from the system gradually grew from a fifth to almost a third of the national revenues. Of this money, only a small share benefited the Dutch East Indies. Resistance to the Culture System grew steadily in the Netherlands as of the end of the 1840s. It was chiefly the government's unassailable monopoly in the economic life of the colony that met with opposition. The monopoly encouraged abuses of power and nepotism. The liberals, moreover, were convinced that entrepreneurs in the mother country and Indonesian labourers in the colony were entitled to a free market in the Dutch East Indies so that they too could profit from the lucrative export trade: 'free labour', was the slogan.[8] The system's adversaries prevailed and in 1870 it was determined that the government enterprises would gradually disappear. The Dutch East Indies were thrown open to private initiative. Consequently, all manner of new economic activities were developed, including the cultivation of tea and tobacco, and the mining of tin ore. Toward the end of the nineteenth century, oil began to be extracted on Sumatra, and at the beginning of the twentieth rubber was added to the range of colonial products.

Accompanying the economic expansion of Dutch business interests was the territorial expansion of the colonial government. In the nineteenth cen-

---

[8]   Some predicted that 'free labour' would be more lucrative for the western employers than for the Indonesian labourers. They were proved right.

tury, in the archipelago there were almost 300 (semi-) independent indigenous kingdoms. In the course of the century, a cautious and gradual expansion of Dutch influence in the islands beyond Java and Madura, the so-called Outer Islands, took place, chiefly in reaction to the imperialistic escapades of the great powers. Regions claimed by the Netherlands were taken into formal possession. This process of forming a territorial state was completed around 1900, and the borders of present-day Indonesia were set.

The 'rounding off' of the archipelago was sometimes accompanied with brutal acts of war. Infamous was the more than forty-year long military struggle with the sultanate of Aceh (North Sumatra), a region with an estimated half million inhabitants. The first attempt to subjugate the kingdom was undertaken in 1873. The conquest of the sultan's residence and the destruction of the Acehnese villages, however, could not prevent the expedition from becoming mired in unending guerrilla warfare. An effective method for crushing the resistance was only found in 1898. Governor J.B. van Heutsz organized a counter-guerrilla offensive carried out by a small group of Indonesian soldiers under European officers. Large numbers of the enemy were thus eliminated. The most important leaders of the Aceh resistance surrendered in 1903. Others continued the struggle until 1914, with atrocities being committed on both sides. The region remained troubled until the early 1930s. The conflict cost the Dutch the lives of approximately 12,000 European and Indonesian soldiers (the majority died from infectious diseases), while between 60,000 and 70,000 people perished on the Aceh side. Incidentally, about 25,000 Javanese forced labourers deployed by the government also died.

The Ethical Policy

The victory of liberalism with respect to the Culture System did not silence criticism of colonial policy. The gradual abolition of the feudal economic structures and growing integration in a world dominated by European culture had great consequences for the indigenous population in the Indonesian countryside. In the 1880s and 1890s, Java was ravaged by an economic crisis. Because this coincided with an explosive increase in the population, on the whole the Javanese did not become richer, but poorer. All manner of popular protest was heard. The Javanese farmers agitated not only against poverty, but also against the disintegration of traditional Javanese society. In reaction to this unrest, around 1900 the colonial policymakers embraced a new ideology with respect to the responsibility of the Dutch government in the East Indies, the so-called 'Ethical Policy'. Before that, the government had more or less allowed the colony's social development to take its own course, but this aloof stance now made way for the view that the Netherlands needed to be actively involved with the fate of the Indonesian people.

The Ethical Policy, which officially commenced in 1901, had two elements: the development of the city and country to home rule under Dutch guidance and according to a Western model (the idea of guardianship) on the one hand, and a policy aimed at the unification of the entire archipelago under Dutch dominion on the other. Traditional indigenous rulers resisting Dutch authority also rejected Western views concerning freedom, civilization, culture and prosperity, and it was therefore in the interest of the indigenous population to bring these rulers into line, by force if need be; such was the theory. This unshakeable conviction was elevated to systematic policy by Governor-General Van Heutsz (1904-1909), the conqueror of Aceh. At the same time, the Ethical Policy had more elevated goals, such as combating poverty and raising the prosperity of the Indonesian people. The government attempted to improve the standard of living of the Indonesians through migration, education, the development of agriculture and the promotion of industry.

The overpopulation of the most crowded island, Java, greatly added to the poverty of its people. In part thanks to government measures in the area of public health, the population of Java grew enormously in the last decades of the nineteenth century, from more than 16 million in 1870 to 28 million in 1900. In 1905 a start was made with the migration of Javanese from the densely populated regions to South Sumatra. Up to the war, an estimated 125,000 Javanese left permanently for the Outer Islands. This outflow, however, represented little more than a drop in the ocean.

Extending cheap credit helped equally little. The structural poverty of the Javanese farmers was so great that the money was chiefly used for consumer expenditure rather than investment. The expansion of the irrigation systems on Java met with more success. Between 1900 and 1940, many new rice fields came into use and the irrigation of the existing rice fields was improved. Moreover, the government agencies provided agricultural education to the Indonesian farmers and seeds for improved types of rice were introduced. Partly thanks to these measures, by 1939 Java had again become a food-exporting island and it appeared that the large-scale famines were definitively a thing of the past.

Results were achieved as well in education. In 1940, more than 2.3 million Indonesian children were in primary school, more than 9,000 in secondary school, and almost 700 went on to university. Around 1940, an estimated 40% of all Indonesian children aged between six and fourteen-fifteen had been introduced to at least the rudiments of reading and writing. To be sure, 70% of the Indonesian population above the age of ten were still illiterate, but this percentage is comparable to that of other colonies in South and Southeast Asia. At the time of Indonesia's declaration of independence (August 1945), however, the number of well-educated individuals was insufficient to man the civil service at the pre-1942 level.

Drawing up the balance, while advances were made in living standards, chiefly in agriculture, many of the efforts came to naught due to the relentless population growth. For example, between 1900 and 1940, the population of Java grew from 28 to 47 million. Perhaps the government could have done more, but a serious impediment to a more active economic policy continued to be the shortage of manpower and financial resources. As a small country, the Netherlands did not succeed in generating enough investment to initiate enduring, self-sustaining economic development. Moreover, the international economic crisis of 1930 significantly curbed policy efforts. When the economy of the East Indies recovered somewhat around 1937, there was little time left for colonial rule to achieve much of any significance. In the end, the Ethical Policy failed to fulfil the high expectations.

Colonial society

In legal terms the inhabitants of the Dutch East Indies consisted of three groups: Europeans, 'Natives' (Indonesians) and the so-called Foreign Orientals (Chinese, Arabs, Malaysians, British-Indians, and the like). The Europeans (the Dutch being the majority) constituted the upper class. Other rules of law applied to them than to the Indonesians and Foreign Orientals. In the twentieth century, some non-European nationalities were awarded the legal status of Europeans: Japanese, Filipinos, Thais and Egyptians. A select group of Indonesians and Foreign Orientals were also recognized as European upon request. In the Dutch East Indies during the Second World War, approximately 80,000 of the Dutch population came from the Netherlands and over 200,000 had been born in the Indies. In 1940, there were around 68 million Indonesians (approximately 47 million of whom were on Java and Madura), about 1,250,000 Chinese, 50,000 Arabs, and a modest 20,000 Malaysians.

Until 1870 there were never more than a few thousand Europeans, chiefly men, in the Dutch East Indies. Many of them, primarily the soldiers, took a native wife and had children of mixed descent. As of 1892, the offspring of European fathers and Indonesian mothers were granted European nationality on condition that they were recognized by their father. This group, the so-called Eurasians or Indo-Europeans, therefore automatically belonged to the legal category of Europeans.

The Dutch population in the East Indies rose dramatically after 1870, when the government cultivation projects were gradually replaced by private enterprises and the colony began increasingly producing for the inter-

national market. In the period 1870-1940 the Dutch East Indies was an important provider of raw materials and food for Europe and North America. On
the eve of the Second World War, rubber and oil were the most important
export products. More than a third (37%) of world rubber exports came from
the Dutch East Indies. The flourishing export market lured many from the
Netherlands and other European countries to the archipelago. Moreover, the
government grew apace, and thus so did the number of employees from
Europe in public service.

   As mentioned above, no legal distinction was made between the whites
born in Europe and the people of mixed descent recognized as Dutch. Most
of the Dutch Eurasians, however, had to contend with a social disadvantage
– though only in relation to the people from the Netherlands, not in relation
to the majority of Indonesians. Some Eurasians could rise to the highest positions, while others were swallowed up or threatened to be swallowed up
in the poorer Indonesian circles, and in between these two extremes was a
group endeavouring to distinguish itself from the vast mass of Indonesians,
but which was checked in its upward social mobility by the Dutch elite from
Europe. Many Eurasians did get posts with the government and in business,
but mostly in the lower and middle ranks. In business they began at a salary
level half that of recently arrived, sometimes less qualified Dutch employees.

   A clear political differentiation began to take shape within the group of
Dutch Eurasians. By far the majority clung with redoubled efforts to the
Netherlands and its symbols – chiefly the House of Orange – identifying with
Dutch culture more emphatically than the Dutch themselves, and wishing
to be the most faithful servants of the Netherlands in colonial society. Their
party was the Indo-Europeesch Verbond (IEV) established in 1919. Only a
few rejected this allegiance to the Netherlands. Those who believed it was
better to be an independent Indies, free from Dutch intervention, united as
the Indische Partij in 1912.

The colonial government in the period between the wars

The administrative machinery

The general administration of the Dutch East Indies was in the hands of
the highest representative of the Dutch government in the archipelago, the
governor-general, who was appointed for a five-year term of office. The governor-general usually resided in Buitenzorg (Bogor), situated approximately
50 km south of Batavia. He commanded both the Dutch navy in the Indies
and the army.

   The governor-general's most important advisory organ was the Council
of the Dutch East Indies. The Council consisted of a vice-president (the gov-

ernor-general was president of the Council and chaired the most important sessions) and at least four or at the most six members (in the twentieth century this was usually four), who were appointed for a maximum of five years. Most of the members of the Council had previously held senior administrative positions and the Indonesians who were appointed – for the first time in 1927 – usually came from the highest circles of the Indonesian administration.

In discharging his daily tasks, the governor-general was assisted by an official agency established at Buitenzorg, the General Secretariat, which had separate divisions for social and legal, financial and economic, and personnel matters. In 1940 the position of general secretary was held by J.M. Kiveron. In that year, several officials from the General Secretariat were released in order to staff a new bureau: the Cabinet of the governor-general, which prepared all matters of a political and religious nature for the governor-general. The Cabinet's director was P.J.A. Idenburg. The officials of the Cabinet and the General Secretariat constituted the governor-general's extensive staff.

There were eight departments: Justice, Finance, Internal Administration, Education and Religion, Economic Affairs, Transport and Communications, Defence, and the Navy, in addition to which there was also a separate and independent Office of Indonesian Affairs. The Department of Internal Administration was responsible for organizing the complex administrative machinery that was in direct contact with the Indonesian authorities. The Department of Internal Administration consisted solely of Dutch personnel, all of whom had been specially trained. Those taking up service with the Department of Internal Administration began as a junior controller. If they proved suitable, they could rise from the position of controller and controller first class to the higher ranks: that of assistant resident, resident and finally governor.

Governors were charged with the supervision of a province (on Java) or of a governorate (in the Outer Islands). At the time of the Japanese invasion, there were three provinces on Java: West, Central and East Java. The Outer Islands included Sumatra and Borneo, and the so-called Great East – Celebes, the Lesser Sunda Islands, the Moluccas and Dutch New Guinea – each with its own governor. Under the governors were the residents, who were in charge of a residency. Java (including Madura) had 17 residencies, Sumatra ten, Borneo two and the Great East five. Residencies in turn were divided into divisions under assistant residents, and subdivisions under controllers first class. In total, at the time of the Japanese invasion there were almost 800 Internal Administration officials working in the Dutch East Indies, and of them about 500 were stationed 'in the interior', namely outside of Batavia.

The Dutch East Indies had a dualistic administrative system. The Dutch felt it desirable to leave the Indonesian population under the leadership of its own rulers to the greatest extent possible. This explains the existence of an Indonesian administrative system parallel to that of Internal Administration and serving as a buffer between the government and the mass of Indonesians. The heads of the Indonesian administration on Java and Madura were the regents, who were appointed by the governor-general. In March 1942 there were 67 regents. While subordinate to the Dutch residents, they had a more equal position with respect to the assistant residents. If necessary, a regent could disregard the advice of the assistant resident. Purely Indonesian affairs were taken care of by the regents in collaboration with regency councils in part elected from the indigenous population that were instituted in the first half of the 1920s. In the 'self-ruling regions', the principalities (Vorstenlanden) on Java and a few hundred autonomous regions in the Outer Islands, an Indonesian sultan or raja headed the Indonesian administrative machinery. In these areas there was absolutely no effective Dutch supervision on a lower administrative level.

In his administrative duties, a regent was assisted by a *patih*, a kind of chief of staff. One level lower than the regents were the *wedono* (district chiefs).[9] *Patih* and *wedono* were appointed by the governor-general. The assistant *wedono* and the lower Indonesian administrative officials (with the exception of the village headmen) were appointed by the Dutch residents. Usually, however, the regents' suggestions for these appointments were followed. In 1930 there were more than 1,600 *wedono* and assistant *wedono* in all of the Dutch East Indies. The village headmen (*lurah*) were chosen by the villagers, that is by those who owned land. There were tens of thousands of village headmen in the entire archipelago.

The Indonesian administrative machinery was the mainstay of Dutch dominion. In many instances, the attempts of the Indonesian nationalists to free themselves from that dominion were aimed not only against Dutch rule, but also against the Indonesian authorities that were part of that system. Some of the politically aware minority among the Indonesians saw these administrators solely as the instruments of the foreign oppressor.

The KNIL

Maintaining law and order in the colony was one of the government's main tasks. The immediate responsibility for this lay with the police, which came under the Department of Internal Administration. In an emergency, the KNIL could be called upon. The KNIL was primarily a police force that was better equipped for suppressing internal disturbances than for opposing a foreign aggressor. It consisted mainly of Indonesian soldiers. In peacetime, the KNIL numbered about 35,000 men: approximately 10,000 Europeans (most of

---

[9]   They had different names in the Outer Islands.

them Dutch), and about 25,000 Indonesians. In 1937, the Indonesian share consisted of almost 13,000 Javanese, more than 5,000 Manadonese, approximately 4,000 Ambonese, almost 2,000 Sundanese, more than 1,000 Timorese and several hundred others.

Manadonese and Ambonese played a relatively large role in the KNIL. Religion was an important factor in this. On the Moluccas (which included the island of Ambon), Protestant missionary efforts had met with substantial success. This also applied to Minahasa (the northeast tip of Celebes, with Manado as the principal town). The Protestant Ambonese and Manadonese in the KNIL were treated as almost equal to the European lower ranks: for instance, they were better paid than the other Indonesian soldiers. However, this only applied to the rank and file, all Indonesian corporals and NCO's received equal pay. On the Islamic island of Java, however, the Ambonese and Manadonese soldiers were regarded as infidels and some of the Indonesians saw them as helpers of the colonial regime.

The administration of justice

The administration of justice in the Dutch East Indies was a motley collection of differing rules of law dispensed by separate organs. In criminal cases, only one code was applied: Dutch criminal law. Europeans and those granted the same legal status, however, enjoyed greater legal protection than Indonesians and Foreign Orientals. For example, the latter could be taken into preventive custody without trial, while this was not possible with Europeans. In contrast to criminal law, which was the same for everyone, in civil law three differing sources of law were recognized: Dutch private law, *adat* law (the Indonesian customary law, which exhibited important regional differences), and the Koran and its commentaries.

With respect to the Europeans and those granted equal status, also the Foreign Orientals in part, simple civil suits came before the residency courts. The more complicated cases were heard in the Courts of Justice. It was possible to appeal to the High Court at Batavia. All of these courts meted out justice based on Dutch private law.

With respect to the Indonesians, *adat* law was the foundation for civil justice. In cases of matrimonial law, Islamic justice was administered by councils of mullahs. As of 1938, their rulings could be appealed at the Court for Islamic Affairs seated in Batavia. All other civil cases between Indonesians and between Foreign Orientals were heard (depending on their importance) before district courts, regency courts or *landraden*. The chairmen of the *landraden* on Java and in the more developed regions of the Outer Islands were trained lawyers, who could be either Dutch or Indonesian. Elsewhere in the Outer Islands, it was the task of the Dutch controller or assistant resident to serve as chairman – he nevertheless only had an advisory say in passing judgement.

The hesitant beginnings of Indonesian nationalism

As a colonial power, the Netherlands steered a decidedly conservative course in the area of constitutional law. Even during the heyday of the Ethical Policy, colonial policy was above all aimed at preserving the Dutch East Indies. The growing strength of Indonesian nationalism was – sometimes against better judgement – systematically denied. With the exception of a small minority, people simply refused to acknowledge that the times were changing.

The British in India and the Americans in the Philippines, in contrast, were more progressive and – as one could argue in hindsight – also acted with greater wisdom than the Dutch in the East Indies. In British India, as of 1892 members of the Indian National Congress were accepted in the colony's legislative council, and in 1917 the British government (albeit under the pressure of the First World War) consented to British India eventually becoming a self-governing territory within the British empire, with a government responsible to its own parliament.

In the Philippines, a Legislative Assembly was instituted in 1907 consisting only of Filipinos who were elected via a voting system based on an income qualification. In 1916, the American governor-general was presented with an Executive Council, in which Filipinos would constitute the majority. And, in that same year, the American government declared that it would endeavour to make the Philippines independent.

Compared to the concessions made by Great Britain and the United States, the Netherlands pursued a highly conservative policy. Even though it was the objective of the Ethical Policy to prepare the Dutch East Indies for home rule in the long run, the colonial administrators felt that the time was far from ripe to seriously consider its practical application. Unlike the Americans, the Dutch made absolutely no concessions with respect to potential independence, and unlike the British they flatly rejected discussions at an equal level with Indonesian leaders pressing for independence or even autonomy. In colonial circles there was no wish to rush matters and no intention of being put under pressure by – as they saw it – the impatience of a handful of Indonesian hotheads. Politically speaking, at the beginning of the twentieth century Dutch rule in the East Indies displayed dictatorial features: there was an entirely autocratic administration by the Governor-General, repressive control of the press, and political associations and assemblies were prohibited until 1915. These restrictions were the reason why Indonesian nationalism experienced such a hesitant beginning.

The first Indonesian association to make unequivocal social demands known to the government was established in 1908. The initiative for the founding of Boedi Oetomo ('High Endeavour') was taken in Batavia by students at several schools. The members of the organization insisted that the government further the education of the Indonesians, grant permission for the founding of Boedi Oetomo village schools, open shelters for beggars, combat usury more effectively, and establish public libraries. However, Boedi Oetomo was soon divided by a struggle between modernists and traditionalists. The latter won the day and the 'radicals' disappeared from the executive. The organization, which had around 10,000 members at the end of 1909, subsequently developed into a movement rejecting all radicalism and was fairly conservative in social terms. The most notable, virtually revolutionary, significance of Boedi Oetomo lay in the fact that the allegedly passive Indonesians for the first time undertook independent initiatives to arrive at common positions in an organized association.

Another comparable Indonesian organization was Sarekat Islam (Islamic Union), founded in 1912. Originally an anti-Chinese association of Islamic traders, it called for the founding of Islamic commercial enterprises and cooperatives, wished to advance the education of the Indonesians, and disseminate Islam. Sarekat Islam rapidly grew into a broad popular movement which was not only concerned with cultural recovery and mutual economic support, but also made political demands. Membership grew explosively. Between 1912 and 1916 the movement attracted an estimated 700,000 members. This kind of mass movement was unique in the history of the Dutch East Indies. Sarekat Islam mobilized the widespread discontent about the destruction of the old familiar structures and the destabilization of traditional society. The wide support for the organization, however, was short lived. The many streams united by Sarekat Islam differed too greatly to be able to work together for very long. In the 1920s, the union simply withered, on the one hand because of a break with the left wing of the movement, and on the other because of competition with more orthodox Islamic organizations. In the 1930s, membership again grew gradually, from about 20,000 in 1930 to 60,000 at the beginning of the war. Sarekat Islam was the first social movement in Indonesia whose leaders made serious attempts to organize the population of virtually all of Indonesia into a single union. It flew a red and white flag, the traditional colours of the ancient Javanese empire of Majapahit. This flag was important as an independent symbol, clearly distinct from the Dutch red, white and blue of the colonial regime.[10] Even though Sarekat Islam did not call for resistance against Dutch authority, many Europeans nevertheless found it inconceivable and alarming that it was not banned by the government.

A far more radical organization rose along with Sarekat Islam. In 1912 the first clearly anti-government political party was founded, the Indische Partij. Its chairman was the colourful Dutch Eurasian E.F.E. Douwes Dekker, and

10   The red and white flag later became the flag of the Republic of Indonesia.

leadership of the party was in the hands of the triumvirate Douwes Dekker, Tjipto Mangoenkoesoemo and Soewardi Soerjaningrat. The Indische Partij aspired to an independent East Indies that would encompass the entire archipelago and all ethnic groups. This new state would be led by an elite group of Indonesians and Eurasians. Douwes Dekker, also called 'DD', was a charismatic figure who exerted a great attraction on the less prosperous Eurasians. He promised them a better future in a free and sovereign East Indies, which would have no room for colonials from the Netherlands. The Indische Partij had more members among the Eurasians (about 5,500) than among the Indonesians (1,500).

Even though the adherents of the Indische Partij were relatively limited in number, the government did not wait long before banning this radical organization. In the summer of 1913 the three party leaders were detained and exiled to different remote islands in the archipelago. Their request to be allowed to leave the Dutch East Indies was granted and they set sail for the Netherlands. The government hoped that they had learned their lesson. Tjipto was allowed to return as early as 1914, Soewardi in 1918. Douwes Dekker had yet another short-lived and completely unsuccessful adventure as a secret agent in the service of Germany (he ended up in Singapore in a British cell) before returning to the Dutch East Indies in 1918. The incorrigible 'DD' once again threw himself into politics and spent most of 1920 in preventive custody. After his release, he turned his attention to education.

The triumph of Dutch conservatism

In itself, the rise of the Indonesian nationalist movement was not considered a negative development by the colonial regime. Colonial politics were still dominated by the Ethical Policy movement. In the eyes of the 'ethicists', the policy aimed at the uplifting of the Indonesian people bore fruit sooner than expected and the challenge was to accelerate rather than delay development in the direction of home rule – under Dutch leadership, of course. Political reforms were deemed necessary, and the colonial regime needed to be democratized. This led to the foundation of the first central body with a clearly representative character in the Dutch East Indies, the Volksraad (People's Council). The institution of this council was approved by the Dutch parliament in December 1916. The Volksraad had a primarily advisory function. Members were elected or appointed by the governor-general. At the Volksraad's first session in 1918 the majority of the 35 members were Dutch or Eurasian. In 1927, the number of members was raised to 60, including 30 Indonesians and 5 Foreign Orientals (Chinese, Arabs). Owing to this, the Volksraad acquired an Indonesian majority. This did not satisfy the

Indonesian nationalists in the least. The Council still contained far too few Indonesians and had far too few powers to be a fully fledged parliament.

The Ethical Policy found itself in deep water around 1920. Developments in East Indies society were moving too quickly for many of the Dutch. Most of the colonial civil servants looked upon the rise of Indonesian nationalism with misgivings. While Boedi Oetomo and the small Indische Partij elicited no great concern in colonial circles, the mass movement Sarekat Islam did. What would happen if the exceedingly small European minority in the East Indies found itself facing confident and politically articulate Indonesian masses? Suddenly, the colonial government seemed very vulnerable indeed. The lessons of the First World War fuelled apprehensions. It was clear that the Dutch navy and the KNIL were nowhere near adequately equipped for a large-scale war. The East Indies forces trained for police tasks did not have the ghost of a chance against the huge modern armies of the great powers, among whom Japan now had to be included. The fears of the Europeans were further fed by the outbreak of an uprising in Jambi (South Sumatra) in 1916. Dissatisfied with the Indonesian authorities imposed by the government, high taxes, severe forced labour and crop failures, the people in that region had taken up arms. It took more than two months before the KNIL could quell the rebellion, during which an estimated 500 insurgents were killed. Other incidents followed on Java and Celebes in 1918 and 1919. An accusatory finger was pointed at Sarekat Islam.

For most of the Dutch in the East Indies the limit had now been reached. They demanded more resolute action on the part of the government against the Indonesian nationalists. The idea of self-rule for the Indies went too far for the more conservative element among the Dutch. They acquired a powerful ally when the conservative Simon de Graaff became minister for Colonial Affairs in November 1919. To be sure, he reformed the colonial regime, but in a direction disappointing to both Indonesian nationalists and Dutch ethicists. The East Indies received a jumble of councils – municipal councils, regency councils, provincial councils and a Volksraad – which in practice had little authority. Behind this democratic façade, the colonial officials were still in charge. The ethicists tasted final defeat when the conservative D. Fock was appointed governor-general in 1921. Conservative tendencies now had the upper hand in the colonial administration.

As of 1929, governor-generals averse to reforms could count on the unconditional support of the Vaderlandsche Club (VC), which had been founded in that year. This highly conservative Dutch group acquired a great following in a very short period. Only Dutch citizens were allowed to join. Approximately 9,000 joined the VC within its first year, more members than any Dutch political society in the East Indies had ever had. When a new Volksraad was assembled in 1931, the VC instantly won five of the six seats held by elected Dutchmen. The party's reactionary slogans were endorsed by much of the European press. A Dutch East Indies without the Dutch was something the VC could not envisage. Not surprisingly, they had nothing good to say about Indonesian nationalism.

The PKI

The conservative reaction of the Dutch engendered deep distrust on the part of the politically aware Indonesians and reinforced their conviction that if push came to shove, the Netherlands would be unwilling to relinquish final control over the archipelago. The nationalistic movement became radicalized.

Communism initially played a leading role in this development. The Indische Sociaal-Democratische Vereeniging (ISDV), founded by a Dutchman in 1914, was given a new name in 1920, Perserikatan Komunis di India (Communist Association in the East Indies), or simply PKI. The very small party (in 1921 it only had 210 predominantly Indonesian members) joined the Communist International. At the end of 1921, the Sumatran Tan Malaka became chairman of the PKI. Trained in the Netherlands as a teacher, this young man made a great impression on his supporters. However, when he called for a general strike he was arrested and exiled in February 1922. He travelled from the Netherlands to Moscow to take part in the Comintern's fourth congress. In December 1923 the organization sent him to the large port of Canton in South China in order to pass on directives to the PKI and the other communist parties in Southeast Asia.

In 1924 the name of the Communist Association in the East Indies was changed to the Partai Komunis Indonesia. Against the advice of Tan Malaka and the Comintern, it was decided that an uprising against the colonial regime had to be organized. In November 1926 a communist rebellion erupted in West Java, and the same occurred in West Sumatra in January 1927. The revolts were limited in scope and poorly organized, and the authorities had little difficulty in putting them down. However, for the first time, deliberate violence had been utilized to assail the colonial system and this created quite a shock. The government reacted with brutal repression and at least 13,000 people were arrested. This spelled the end of all mass communist activity. After this debacle, Tan Malaka founded a new Indonesian party in Bangkok, the Partai Republik Indonesia, or Pari, which rejected the leadership of the Comintern in principle. Tan Malaka experienced difficult years living in one or another Asian country and constantly struggling to get by. He finally wound up in Singapore in 1937, where he taught English at several Chinese schools.

Hundreds of Indonesian communists were deported to the newly created camp in Upper Digul in New Guinea. The camp was extremely isolated in the interior, 450 km from the south coast. The detainees were plagued by the heat, humidity, malaria, and chiefly homesickness. In 1928 there were more than 810 exiled communists, 15 of whom were accompanied by their wives. Later, non-communist Indonesians were also interned in Upper Digul. In 1930 there were around 1,150 deportees in the camp, accompanied by some 1,000 women and children. Some of the deportees were released as of the beginning of 1931. At the end of 1939 there were 355 prisoners. It is estimated that approximately 1,400 people were accommodated for a longer or shorter period of time in Upper Digul, several dozen of whom perished. The camp was the symbol of the rigid politics of repression to which the government had sought recourse.

The blossoming of the Indonesian national movement

A new generation of Indonesian nationalists emerged around 1927. They were characterized by their emphasis on Indonesian unity, their demand for independence and their unwillingness to work together with the Dutch. They fully understood just how little could be expected from the colonial government. One of the most important of these new nationalist leaders was Sukarno, born in Surabaya in 1901, who had been educated as a civil engineer at the Technical College in Bandung. Two other prominent leaders, Mohammad Hatta born in 1902, and Soetan Sjahrir born in 1909 (both Sumatrans), came from the Perhimpoenan Indonesia, an association of politically active Indonesian students founded in the Netherlands. Its magazine was called *Indonesia Merdeka* (Free Indonesia), in which a call was made to close nationalist ranks. Only a united Indonesia could hope to break the colonizer's hold.

The Partai Nasional Indonesia (PNI) was founded in the East Indies in 1927. The PNI openly pursued Indonesian independence by mobilizing the masses. Sukarno rapidly became its most important member and developed into a charismatic leader in a fairly short time. The PNI tried to reach the masses by organizing large-scale political meetings, founding its own schools, adult education centres and unions, and by supporting new youth organizations of schoolchildren and students. In October 1928, Sukarno was present at a youth congress of Indonesian students in Batavia, where three vows were made: one fatherland had to emerge, namely Indonesia; a single nation had to be created, namely the Indonesian; and one language spoken, namely Indonesian (Malay). To symbolize all of this, at the closing session the red and white flag was raised and the song *Indonesia Raya* (Great Indonesia) composed by the journalist W.R. Soepratman was played. The PNI soon adopted it and *Indonesia Raya* became the battle song of the Indonesian national movement.[11] Seen in retrospect, this was the definitive breakthrough of an Indonesian nationalism based on a single indivisible nation.

Sukarno's great oratorical gifts and the response to his message caused the government to fear possible disturbances. At the end of 1929, Sukarno and three other leaders were arrested and sentenced. Sukarno was given four years in prison, later commuted to two years. The other party leaders were given prison sentences varying from one year and three months to two years. The PNI did not recover from this blow. The party's management dissolved it to prevent any further government reprisals. Immediately thereafter, a new organization was founded by former PNI members, the Partai Indonesia, or Partindo. This led to great uncertainty and division in the ranks of the nationalists. Many condemned the fact that the PNI had been allowed to vanish and that the word 'Nasional' had been dropped. Chiefly Hatta and Sjahrir insisted from the Netherlands that a new PNI be created. And, this took place in December 1931 in the form of the PNI-Baroe (the new PNI). Sjahrir, fresh from the Netherlands, was its first chairman. He was succeeded by Hatta in August 1932.

What was the difference between the Partindo and the PNI-Baroe? Both parties were aiming for an independent Indonesia, but differed as to how this should be accomplished. From the very outset, the Partindo wanted to follow the path of mass agitation, while the PNI-Baroe that of education. Hatta and Sjahrir believed that first a broad, well-educated cadre had to be created before new action could be undertaken. The education had to be socialist in content, for they believed that an independent Indonesia should be a socialist Indonesia. The Partindo, in contrast, wanted to directly mobilize the Indonesian masses, just like the PNI had done previously.

Sukarno was released on 31 December 1931 and welcomed back as a hero by his followers. After fruitless attempts to unite the Partindo and the PNI-Baroe into a single organization, he joined the former party, whose chairman he became in April 1932. Rooted in Javanese culture, Sukarno was a flamboyant demagogue who understood that the power of Islam in the Indonesian archipelago should not be underestimated. Hatta and Sjahrir were more reserved intellectuals who had been educated in the West. They considered this rabble-rouser aspect of Sukarno's person and demeanour a danger. For his part, Sukarno saw Hatta and Sjahrir as intellectuals who did not appear to realize that nothing could be achieved without the support of the masses. Demagogy was necessary in order to communicate with these masses, and Sukarno succeeded in cultivating this contact like no one else of his generation. Moreover, he was able to establish a link between the Western ideology of people like Hatta and Sjahrir on the one hand, and the world view of

---

[11]   This later became the Republic of Indonesia's national anthem.

the more traditional Indonesian masses on the other. These qualities made Sukarno the undisputed leader of the national movement.

The Depression

Like the rest of the world, in 1930-1931 the Dutch East Indies was plunged into a deep economic crisis. As an exporter of raw materials, it was especially hard hit. The cost-cutting measures taken by the government caused widespread unrest. It was not only the Indonesians who suffered; the Europeans too were increasingly threatened by unemployment and a drop in living standards. This was the situation when in September 1931 jonkheer B.C. de Jonge was appointed governor-general of the Dutch East Indies. As an extreme conservative, De Jonge had not the slightest sympathy with the aspirations of the nationalist movement. His 1936 statement was characteristic and legendary: 'I believe that now that we have worked in the Indies for three hundred years, another three hundred years will be needed before the country will perhaps be ripe for a form of autonomy' (De Jong 1984, 11a:359). It seemed to be only a matter of time before the colonial government again took action against Sukarno and the other nationalist leaders.

Cuts in the pay rates of the East Indies navy provoked a mutiny on the cruiser *Zeven Provinciën* in February 1933. The crew, made up of both Europeans and Indonesians, took control of the ship. The mutineers surrendered after a bomb was dropped on it. The mutiny was a social protest in the first place, but most Europeans in the Indies saw it as a political uprising. The government took a hard line. The crew of the *Zeven Provinciën* was punished and there was a purge of all navy personnel. The KNIL seized the opportunity provided by the need for spending cuts to dismiss all those who were not completely trusted.

Governor-General De Jonge was determined to impose his authority. All opposition, whether European or Indonesian, would have to toe the line. The trades unions and the press were kept under strict control. Police surveillance of the Partindo and the PNI-Baroe was stepped up and in practice both these organizations were deprived of the right to hold meetings anywhere in the Dutch East Indies. The fact that in the course of 1933 Sukarno had expressed himself in increasingly radical terms at mass meetings was sufficient reason to rearrest him on 1 August 1933. He was exiled to the island Flores and later transferred to Bengkulu on Sumatra. More arrests followed. In February 1934 five leaders of the PNI-Baroe were also detained. They included Hatta and Sjahrir, who ended up in Upper Digul and later on Banda in the Moluccas. Deprived of their leaders, the Partindo and the PNI-Baroe were in a sorry state. In November 1936 the Partindo decided to dissolve itself.

Most members of the Dutch community in the East Indies applauded these tough measures. The mutiny on the *Zeven Provinciën* had greatly added to the desire among Europeans for strong government. One of the consequences was that from the end of 1933 a far-right party, the Nationaal-Socialistische Beweging (NSB), gained considerable support in the East Indies. The NSB stood for an anti-socialist and authoritarian Netherlands which would have stronger armed forces and be purged of all divisions, liberated from party bickering. The main demand of the East Indies branch of the party was for strong colonial rule. This ensured that by the end of 1935 the NSB had about 4,500 members in the Indies. After this point support for the party crumbled. The leaders of the NSB in the Netherlands were increasingly drawn towards Nazi Germany, and this did not go down well in the colony. Germany was an ally of Japan, and the European community in the Indies was deeply suspicious of Japan's imperial aspirations. The more positive the NSB was about Germany, the more its support in the colony declined. At the end of 1939 there were only 1,708 members and 1,016 sympathizers left.

The Soetardjo petition

Under Governor-General De Jonge the Dutch East Indies increasingly came to resemble a police state. Controls were imposed on the press, political meetings were banned, associations could be prohibited, police powers of supervision were drastically extended. The only places where Indonesians could express their political views without let or hindrance were the Volksraad, and the regency and provincial councils. Given that the members of the Islamic parties and the hard-line nationalists took no part in the Volksraad on grounds of principle, most of its Indonesian members were moderate nationalists or delegates from the various associations of civil servants. It was from among their ranks that the so-called Soetardjo petition emerged in 1936.

It proposed that a conference should be held on the future of the Kingdom. The subject of the discussions would be the granting of self-determination – autonomy, not independence – within ten years. This proposal was phrased in very moderate terms and, of course, it fell far short of what many nationalists wanted, but for some of the Dutch groups in the Volksraad, particularly the Vaderlandsche Club, it was a bridge too far. Nonetheless, the proposal was passed by the Volksraad, but only after the limit of ten years had been dropped. The crucial factor was the backing of the Indo-Europeesch Verbond (IEV) for the petition. This was the party of the Dutch born in the East Indies, a group which had been severely affected by the Depression. The IEV thought that its members might well secure a dominant position in an autonomous East Indies.

In October 1936 the amended Soetardjo petition was submitted to the Dutch government and parliament. There was no great rush to reach a decision, and it was not until November 1938 that the petition was denied by Royal Decree. It was felt in The Hague that enough was being done towards the emancipation of the Dutch East Indies and that matters should not be dealt with too hastily. The Indies was not yet ripe for autonomy, so it was thought. This uncompromising rejection confirmed the Indonesian nationalists in their belief that the Dutch attitude would be obdurate.

The Indonesian nationalist movement changes course

On the surface the policy of repression seemed to be successful. One by one the PKI, PNI, Partindo and PNI-Baroe had disappeared from public view; their leaders were detained or exiled and the small groups of supporters who were left were barely capable of any activity. The nationalists learned their lesson, and it was thought advisable not to provoke the colonial government again. The Indonesian leaders who were still at liberty now expressed themselves in more cautious terms and avoided the word 'independence'. The policy of confronting the authorities was abandoned. The idea of cooperating with the government or taking part in representative bodies such as the Volksraad was no longer rejected out of hand. New organizations were set up to implement this change of course.

December 1935 saw the founding of the Parindra, an acronym for Partai Indonesia Raya (Party of Greater Indonesia). This was a combination of the old Javanese group Boedi Oetomo and several other organizations. The Parindra was a movement of city-dwellers from the upper classes of Indonesian society. Their chief aim was to improve the socioeconomic position of the Indonesians and thus gradually arrive at independence. The number of members remained limited – less than 4,000 in 1937, possibly 10,000 in 1940 – but the party's support was undoubtedly much greater than these figures suggest.

In 1937 a new group, the Gerindo, was formed from the remnants of left-wing parties that had disappeared or been prohibited. The name Gerindo stood for Gerakan Rakjat Indonesia or Indonesian People's Movement. The main difference between the two parties was that the Gerindo was in favour of radical reform of Indonesian society, whereas the Parindra was opposed to this idea. The Gerindo did not openly call for Indonesian independence (that would immediately have led to its being outlawed), but demanded autonomy within the Kingdom of the Netherlands and the setting up of a proper parliament based on general elections. How many members the Gerindo had is uncertain, probably between 5,000 and 10,000. In 1941 the Gerindo repeatedly warned of the threat posed to Indonesia by fascistic Japan.

Both the Parindra and the Gerindo came to be represented in the Volks-raad. Early in 1938 Mohammed Hoesni Thamrin, the leader of the Parindra deputies in the Volksraad, decided that the time had come for broad cooperation between the nationalist parties. In May the new organization was founded: the Gaboengan Politik Indonesia (Indonesian Political Federation) or Gapi, in which virtually all the nationalist parties, including the Parindra and Gerindo, were united. In future these parties would coordinate their political activities in the context of Gapi. The new political federation had one principal aim: the formation of a fully fledged parliament in the Dutch East Indies. It was to be elected from and by the people of Indonesia and the colonial government was to be accountable to it (had this been implemented it would have meant the end of the dominant role of the governor-general). The Gapi adopted the red and white flag and the anthem *Indonesia Raya* as symbols of unity. Indeed, unity within the Indonesian political movement was greater than ever before.

Repression

The new governor-general who took office in 1936, jonkheer A.W.L. Tjarda van Starkenborgh Stachouwer, was as conservative in his views as his prede-cessor De Jonge, and he was not about to even consider administrative or political reforms. The Dutch authorities underestimated the strength of Indonesian nationalism, possibly because they were misled by how relatively easy it was for the government to keep the nationalists under control. In addition, there was a deep gulf between Europeans and Indonesians which was bridged by only a few individuals.

The Dutch moved in their own circles, and social contacts with Indonesians were generally limited and superficial. The only Indonesians with whom they had frequent contact were their servants, who were believed to be loyal and devoted. As a rule, Europeans had no idea of what was going on in Indonesian society. This was why urban Dutch society was barely aware of the rapidly spreading nationalism being inculcated by the indigenous schools, press and literature and by religious and political organizations. Nor were the Europeans interested. The great majority of them in the Dutch East Indies regarded their own culture as superior, and this stood in the way of any interest in or appreciation of Indonesian culture.

There was another factor clouding the Dutch view of reality. The East Indies provided jobs for some 100,000 Dutch citizens and made a substantial contribution to the national income of the mother country. Few could reconcile themselves to the idea that the Netherlands would one day have to give up the colony. The saying 'Indië verloren, rampspoed geboren' (With the Indies gone, calamity is born) reflected the views of many. People looked the other way rather than face the fact that Indonesian society was changing rapidly.

This lack of awareness of the extent of social and political developments in Indonesian society gave rise to a mistaken assumption that the nationalist movement was supported only by the urban elite and that the great majority of poor Indonesians wanted nothing to do with it. The colonial policy-makers concluded accordingly that the Dutch would have to stay in the Indies for a long time to come in order to protect the indigenous rural population from exploitation by its own urban elite.

The stubborn refusal of the colonial government to engage in serious dialogue with the nationalist movement looks very much, certainly in retro-spect, like a case of burying one's head in the sand. Where such a dialogue might have led remains a matter for speculation. But a more favourable atti-tude towards those Indonesian nationalists who were prepared to cooperate would not have been unwise, particularly in view of the increasingly evident threat from Japan.

War

The Netherlands was drawn into the Second World War in May 1940, when German troops invaded. After four days' fighting the Dutch army capit-ulated. The Dutch government fled to London. The Dutch East Indies sud-denly stood alone. Fearing a fifth column, the colonial government decided to intern not only the Germans in the East Indies but also members of the NSB. In total nearly 2,800 'Germans' were detained, including German Jews, Indonesian youths with a German father and about 100 completely harm-less Protestant and Catholic missionaries.[12] The number of NSB members arrested was around 500. On Java they were concentrated at three locations: Fort Van den Bosch at Ngawi (East Java), Ambarawa (Central Java) and the island Onrust (West Java).

After the German invasion of the Netherlands, several Indonesian organizations in Batavia issued manifestos calling on their members to stand behind the colonial government and support the authorities. The Parindra even sent money collected by its youth organizations to a relief fund for the Netherlands. Following the German invasion, and particularly after

[12]   After the outbreak of war with Japan the colonial government decided to transfer the German internees to India. In January 1942, 473 of them embarked on an old steamer, the *Van Imhoff*. The day after she sailed, the ship was bombed by a Japanese aircraft and began to sink. The Dutch crew and guards abandoned ship, leaving the internees behind. Only 65 Germans survived.

the declarations of loyalty from Indonesians which it provoked, some kind
of good will gesture towards the nationalists was expected from the Indies
government. After all, it was 'a time for defending the democratic countries
and the idea of democracy,' according to the Indonesian press (De Jong 1984,
11a:567). No such gesture, however, was forthcoming. The Governor-General
took the view that no fundamental policy changes could be initiated while
the war continued and so let this opportunity pass. The Upper Digul internment camp stayed in place and the nationalist leaders Sukarno, Hatta and
Sjahrir were not released from exile.

The only positive measure taken was the appointment of the Visman
Commission. It was set up by Governor-General Van Starkenborgh in mid-
September 1940 and given the task of 'enquiring into the wishes, movements
and views among the different nationalities, classes and levels as to constitutional development [of the Dutch East Indies] and, in connection with that,
the position of the various groups in the population' (De Jong 1984, 11a:
580). The chairman of the Commission was F.H. Visman, a member of the
Council of the Dutch East Indies. There were six other members: two other
Dutchmen, three Indonesians and one Indonesian- Chinese. The Commission
reached clear conclusions on three points: that all the Indonesians, Chinese
and Arabs it had questioned wished to be fully equal in status with the
Europeans; that the Chinese wished to have this status even if it was not
granted to the Indonesians and Arabs; and that the Indonesians, Chinese and
Arabs complained bitterly about social discrimination.

The Commission also conducted a survey of the constitutional views
of the various Indonesian groups and organizations. This proved to be an
extremely confusing survey: the groups and organizations were not named
(for example, the Gapi was referred to as 'a large combination of Indonesian
groups') (De Jong 1984, 11a:585), and no account was taken of their relative
importance. Moreover, the Commission took the view that the political activists could not be regarded as speaking for the great mass of Indonesians, who
were thought to be indifferent to politics. The Commission underestimated
the influence of the nationalist activists on the masses, and consequently its
report presented too rosy a view of the East Indies' future as part of a 'revital-
ized' Kingdom of the Netherlands. The Commission was convinced that the
unity of the Kingdom would be preserved.

On 9 December 1941, one day after Japan's entry into the Second World
War, the Commission completed its report. No changes in policy were actually
made. The only concession the authorities were prepared to make was that
after the war the Indonesians could make their wishes known to the Queen
and that a conference would be held to discuss modifying the structure of
the Kingdom. It was a classic case of too little too late. The Soetardjo petition
had proposed such a conference in 1936, but the idea had been rejected out

of hand. Now the colonial government was agreeing after all, but this late concession was no longer satisfactory. The Indonesian political movement had changed: it showed greater unity and was more self-confident. The break between the government and the nationalists was now final.[13] The politically aware Indonesians would be satisfied by nothing less than the immediate recognition of their right to self-determination. The Netherlands was not prepared to grant this.

The Dutch East Indies and Japan

In the early 1930s a military elite determined to extend the country's sphere of influence came into power in Japan. However, Japanese expansionism in Asia inevitably led to conflict with China and the Western powers. In 1937 war with China broke out. In the United States especially, this was seen as proof of the aggressive nature of Japanese policy.

After the fall of the mother country, the position of the Dutch East Indies was precarious in the extreme. On its own it was too weak to defend itself successfully against the Japanese; it needed help from allies – Britain, Australia and the United States. For the time being, however, little support could be expected from them. Britain was fighting for survival in Europe and was forced to plunder its defences in Southeast Asia in order to maintain its position in the Middle East. Australia, too, sent all the resources it could muster to the Middle East. In fact, the European colonies in Asia depended for their defence on the military might of the United States, where the influence of isolationism was still strong. For the time being the Americans remained neutral.

A Japanese attack on the Dutch East Indies was a serious possibility. Japan was short of raw materials. Its weak point was oil: the country's own resources could only meet one tenth of its requirements. The official estimate was that a war with the United States, the British Empire and the Netherlands would require 7.9 million tons of oil per year, while in 1941 Japan's reserves amounted to 9.4 million tons. So Japan would be able to wage such a war for a little more than a year. If the war lasted longer, control of the oil wells of the Dutch East Indies (which produced 7.9 million tons in 1939 – exactly the amount thought to be needed!) would be a crucial factor. As well as oil, the East Indies could supply bauxite (the raw material for aluminium), tin and rubber, so the colony was a rich prize.

---

[13] There was a dramatic incident involving the death of one of the government's sharpest critics, Parindra leader M.H. Thamrin. In early January 1941, while Thamrin was ill with malaria, the police searched his house. He was put under house arrest and five days later he died. The Indonesians saw him as a martyr.

Early in February 1940 – when the Netherlands was still neutral –
the Japanese envoy in The Hague put forward a number of far-reaching
demands: trade between Japan and the Dutch East Indies had to be expanded (Japan wanted more oil and bauxite); more Japanese citizens and companies had to be allowed to move to the colony; and the press in the Indies
had to be prevented from writing in an anti-Japanese spirit. On 15 April the
Japanese foreign minister declared that, because Japan had close economic
ties with Southeast Asia, and in particular with the Dutch East Indies, if the
Netherlands should be drawn into the war in Europe, this would create 'an
undesirable situation from the point of view of peace and stability in East
Asia' (De Jong 1984, 11a:523). The American government responded with
a statement to the effect that any change in the position of the Dutch East
Indies, other than by peaceful means, would endanger peace in the entire
Pacific region. This was a very clear warning.

The answer of the Dutch government (now in exile in London) to the
Japanese demands came in early June 1940. The colonial government could
supply more bauxite, though not as much as the Japanese wanted, but
increased oil deliveries could not be promised; for that the Japanese government would have to make agreements with the oil companies in advance.
The other demands were rejected.

The Japanese did not give up. In September 1940 a delegation arrived in
Batavia to continue negotiations. Tokyo raised the stakes: the Japanese made
it clear that the Dutch East Indies would have to form part of a Southeast
Asia dominated by Japan and known euphemistically as the 'Co-Prosperity
Sphere'. Among other things Japan demanded extensive facilities for exploit-
ing minerals (especially oil). The negotiations dragged on for months. The
position of the Dutch East Indies was extremely weak: the mother country
was occupied and no guarantees of help had been given, neither by Britain
nor by the United States. It was feared on all sides, including in Washington,
that the colonial authorities would give in to Japanese pressure, but they did
not. In June 1941 most of the Japanese demands were rejected. Governor-
General Van Starkenborgh feared for a while that there might be a declaration of war by Japan, but to his great relief Tokyo took no action. Diplomatic
relations continued as normal. The leader of the Dutch East Indies delegation, H.J. van Mook, was given the credit for standing up to the Japanese.[14]
He was regarded as a hero, the 'saviour of the nation'.

The Japanese succeeded in French Indo-China where they had failed in the
Dutch East Indies. In July 1941 Japan demanded the right to maintain a large

[14]   Governor-General Van Starkenborgh deserved at least as much credit, but because he had
stayed in the background during the negotiations it seemed as if Van Mook had acted entirely
on his own initiative.

garrison in all of Indo-China and to make use of the existing naval bases and airfields. The Vichy government in France soon agreed. Washington tried to save the situation by holding out a carrot: in return for the evacuation of French Indo-China, all restrictions on American exports to Japan would be lifted. Tokyo hoped that its actions in Indo-China would make the East Indies government more flexible, and refused to deviate from the course it had chosen. Roosevelt then extended the American embargo to cover all exports to Japan and froze all Japanese assets held by American banks. This meant that Japan could no longer get hold of the dollars it needed to pay for oil from the East Indies. But even with dollars, Japan would have got nowhere. In addition to Britain, the Dutch East Indies joined the general embargo too.

Japan was now in a fix. It had to choose between two evils: giving in to America's demands (which meant among other things withdrawing its troops from China) or waging war against the Western powers. At the end of November 1941 it chose war.

It came as no surprise to the authorities in the Dutch East Indies that a Japanese attack was in the offing. There was more than enough evidence, both from their own intelligence service and from the exchange of information with the British and Americans, that something was imminent. The only question was where the first blow would fall. At the end of November the Dutch navy left port and dispersed to prevent the ships being destroyed at anchor. The KNIL and the air force were put on full alert a week before the attack on Pearl Harbor. On 3 or 4 December, KNIL cryptologists deciphered a telegram from the Japanese foreign ministry to the consul general in Batavia. The contents were immediately passed on to the American consul general. On 4 December he signalled to the State Department in Washington:

> War Department at Bandung claims intercepted and decoded following from Ministry Foreign Affairs Tokyo: 'When crisis leading to worst following will be broadcast at end weather reports: (1) east wind rain – war with United States, (2) north wind cloudy – war with Russia, (3) west wind clear – war with Britain including attack on Thailand or Malaya and Dutch Indies. If spoken twice, burn codes and secret papers.'

The American consul general added, 'I attach little or no importance to it and view it with some suspicion. Such reports have been common since 1936' (De Jong 1984, 11a:723).

In the night of 7-8 December 1941, the American fleet at Pearl Harbor was attacked by surprise. On 8 December 1941 the Netherlands declared war on Japan. The same day about 2,000 Japanese all over the Dutch East Indies were arrested as a precautionary measure.[15] The elimination of the

---

[15] At the end of December 1941, 1,400 Japanese men, 300 women and 200 children were sent

main part of the American fleet in Asia and Japanese supremacy in the air made the Allies' position weak from the outset. In the first weeks of war the only Allied successes were achieved by Dutch submarines, which put out of action a Japanese destroyer and twelve transport ships. As a result of these feats, Vice-Admiral C.E.L. Helfrich, the commander of the Dutch East Indies navy, was given the nickname 'ship-a-day Helfrich'.

The armed forces of the Dutch East Indies

The Japanese offensive operations in the Nampo (the south Pacific) were carried out by the Nampo Army Group commanded by General Terauchi. This Group had only ten infantry divisions, supplemented by three brigades. The troops were divided into four armies. The 14th Army had the Philippines as its target; the 25th Army was to overrun Malacca and Singapore before taking North and Central Sumatra; the 15th Army was to invade Burma through Thailand; and the 16th Army was to conquer the Dutch East Indies (except for North and Central Sumatra). The 16th Army, the KNIL's main opponent, had three infantry divisions and a brigade at its disposal.

What forces did the East Indies have with which to oppose the Japanese? At the outbreak of war in the Pacific the strength of the regular KNIL was nearly 1,400 officers and slightly over 40,000 non-commissioned officers and men. Indonesians made up more than two thirds of the army. The senior commanders doubted whether many of the Indonesians, and particularly the Javanese, were capable of fighting a modern war. About half of the KNIL were on Java and Madura; the rest were dispersed over the Outer Islands. The KNIL's weapons were more suited to maintaining law and order and suppressing internal unrest than to defending the country against a foreign power. Most of the troops on the Outer Islands were armed only with a carbine and a machete. Automatic weapons were in desperately short supply there. On Java too there were severe shortages of machine guns, field artillery, mortars, anti-tank weapons and anti-aircraft guns. Some of the few pieces of artillery were completely obsolete.

In addition to the regular KNIL there were small auxiliary corps of Indonesians in the principalities (Vorstenlanden), on Madura and on Bali, but their military value was limited. In December 1941 some 32,000 conscripts (all Dutch or Dutch Eurasian) were mobilized. Again, not too much could be expected from them. There were also two auxiliary corps, the Stadswacht and the Landwacht, which could take over some of the KNIL's policing duties.

---

to Australia. During the voyage a number of them died. In mid-1942 nearly 1,000 of the Japanese sent to Australia were exchanged for allied citizens interned in Japan.

The Stadswacht was a militia set up in the cities in 1940. It was hoped that it could deal with fifth columnists and possibly enemy paratroops. Moreover, this kind of force might be useful if the Indonesians took to large-scale plundering, in which case the police would be glad of reinforcements. The Stadswachten consisted of Europeans and the Chinese and Indonesians considered reliable. The army provided uniforms and instructors. Weapons were a problem, however: the Stadswachten were equipped mainly with shotguns. Thirty-six towns, seventeen of them on Java, were given a Stadswacht. These small, local units had a combined strength of about 28,000 men.

From late 1940 militias were also formed on the plantations. The European planters had often felt threatened when there was unrest in parts of the East Indies, and many plantations had their own militia consisting of Indonesians under European command. On the basis of these plantation militias, Landwachten modelled on the Stadswachten were formed. The shortage of weapons was less acute than in the case of the Stadswachten because the plantation militias were already armed, if only with machetes. Several hundred Landwachten were set up in the East Indies.

The Military Air Force (as the air force of the Dutch East Indies was known) had ninety-five modern and fifty-six older fighters and eighty outdated bombers. However, even the modern fighters made in America were considerably slower than the Japanese aircraft. Moreover, crews were not available for all these aircraft: of the ninety-five modern fighters forty-five could be sent into the air, and only sixty-six of the eighty bombers.

In 1940-1941 the Dutch Navy in the East Indies consisted of three cruisers (the *Java*, the *De Ruyter* and the *Tromp*), seven destroyers, fifteen submarines, one gunboat, six minelayers, eight minesweepers, the old ironclad *Soerabaja* (the renamed *Zeven Provinciën*), two supply ships, two tankers and four mother ships for the flying boats of the Navy Air Force. Most of these vessels were outdated and did not have modern equipment for finding and following the enemy.

In 1936 a single official body was established to coordinate the defence efforts of the Dutch East Indies, the Staatsmobilisatieraad (State Mobilization Council). It came directly under the governor-general and was intended to ensure that increased defence efforts did not disrupt economic life. The Mobilization Council oversaw the supply of raw materials and labour to those sectors of trade and industry that were important for the defence effort. It also concerned itself with improving the infrastructure of the armed forces and with air-raid defences.

One of the Mobilization Council's important tasks was planning the demolition work that would have to be carried out just before the Japanese captured an area and the removal of supplies that must not fall into enemy hands. This was the job of the Removal and Demolition Corps of the KNIL.

In the port of Surabaya, where a great deal had to be demolished, the Corps had nearly 3,000 men. It was assumed that, even if the Japanese succeeded in taking parts of the East Indies, they would be driven out again fairly quickly. So the demolition work was not to be too thorough. It was thought to be sufficient if the factories and installations concerned, including the all-important oil wells, were put out of operation for six months.

In 1941 the Mobilization Council also drew up a document with the long title *Aanwijzingen betreffende de houding, aan te nemen door de bestuursorganen van het Land, de Zelfbesturende Landschappen, Provinciën, Regentschappen, (Stads-) Gemeenten, Waterschappen, Groepsgemeenschappen, locale ressorten en Inlandsche gemeenten en het daarbij in dienst zijnde personeel, alsmede door de bevolking in geval van bezetting van Nederlandsch-Indisch gebied* (Directions as to the attitude to be adopted by the National Administrative Bodies, the Self-Ruling Regions, Provinces, Regencies, (City) Municipalities, Water Boards, Group Communes, local jurisdictions and indigenous municipalities and their personnel and by the population in the event of an occupation of Dutch East Indies territory). In principle all administrative bodies and their personnel were to stay at their post 'in the interests of the population'. If Japan annexed the East Indies, or part of the territory, or installed another government, the administrative officials were to leave their post under protest. They were also to resign or refuse to cooperate 'if it was made impossible for them to fulfil their duties honourably or if they were asked to perform services that were not permitted'. Ten thousand copies of these 'Directions' were printed and distributed among civil servants (De Jong 1984, 11a:671-3).

There was one area, however, which had not received sufficient attention from the Mobilization Council, the military or the government: the formation of an intelligence network that could pass information to the Dutch authorities outside the colony in the event of its being occupied by Japan. It was only at a very late stage, at the end of 1941 and early in 1942, that Ch.O. van der Plas, a member of the Council of the Dutch East Indies, was asked to set up a secret intelligence organization. Van der Plas was seen as the right man for this job because of his extensive contacts in Indonesian circles (he spoke perfect Malay). But he had too little time and too few resources to make adequate preparations. On 6 March 1942, just a few hours before he was evacuated to Australia by plane, Van der Plas gave a powerful transmitter to three Indonesian policemen in Bandung; they were paid 500 guilders each to look after it. Later it fell into Japanese hands unused.

The conquest of the East Indies oil fields

The chief targets of Japanese operations in the Dutch East Indies were the oil installations at Tarakan (an island off northeast Borneo), Balikpapan (southeast Borneo) and Palembang (south Sumatra).

In the night of 10-11 January 1942 6,000 Japanese troops landed on Tarakan. The wells had already been put out of action and the oil tanks set on fire. The demoralized KNIL troops on the island (about 1,300 men) surrendered on the morning of 12 January. The most southerly coastal battery received news of the surrender too late, however, and sank two Japanese minesweepers at the last moment. A week later the 215 men of this battery were thrown into the sea with their hands tied at the spot where the two ships had gone down.

The sabotaging of the Tarakan oil installations was a serious blow to the Japanese. To ensure that this would not happen again, two Dutch officers were sent to Balikpapan with an alarming message: all troops and civilians would be killed if the oil installations there did not fall intact into Japanese hands. The two officers gave their account and reported that the Japanese could arrive at any moment. That same day the oil installations went up in smoke. On 21 January a Japanese invasion fleet sailed from Tarakan bound for Balikpapan. The few Dutch and American ships, aircraft and submarines in the area managed to sink some Japanese ships, but too few to prevent the landing on the night of 23-24 January. The KNIL detachment then withdrew into the interior. Seventy-eight Europeans, civilians and soldiers, were captured by the Japanese. They were all killed.

The next target was Palembang, the source of more than half the oil produced in the East Indies. Here the Japanese tried to prevent sabotage by means of a surprise attack by paratroops. On 14 February 1942 600 paratroops landed at one of the two airfields at Palembang and captured it undamaged. They also landed in and around the two refinery complexes in the town. A Javanese KNIL company drove the Japanese out of one complex, but only partly out of another. When it became clear that Japanese infantry were approaching – they were coming by ship along the Musi River – the KNIL commander in Palembang was ordered to retreat (most of the troops escaped to Java) after destroying the oil installations. This was only partly accomplished because of the general chaos and the presence of the enemy paratroops.

The oil installations were not completely destroyed anywhere. The authorities' plan was to make them unusable for about six months, in the hope that by then the Japanese would have been repulsed. But even this limited goal was not achieved. One of the two big refineries at Palembang was only slightly damaged (repeated Dutch air attacks in the second half of February had little effect) and on Tarakan the Japanese were able to produce oil after a few weeks. After six months full production resumed at Tarakan, as it did at Balikpapan. Palembang was working normally even earlier. The Japanese war machine might have run into trouble earlier on if the oil installations had been put permanently out of action. It remains an open question whether the war would then have ended sooner.

The Battle of the Java Sea

By mid-February 1942 the outlook for the Allies was bleak. They had established a joint supreme command on Java, ABDA Command, made up of Americans, British, Dutch and Australians. The commander-in-chief was the British general Sir Archibald Wavell. His area of command extended from Burma to Darwin in Australia. ABDA Command suffered one defeat after another. Singapore, the most important link in the Allied defensive ring, fell on 15 February, the same day on which the Japanese took Palembang. Celebes and Borneo had been lost earlier and from there Japanese aircraft were within range of Java and the Java Sea. After the fall of Singapore, Wavell concluded that Java could not be saved. Two Australian divisions which were on their way there were sent elsewhere. Java was given up. On 25 February the ABDA headquarters was disbanded, and responsibility for the defence of the Indonesian archipelago again came to rest with the government of the East Indies.

The Japanese made rapid progress in the east of the colony. By the end of January Ambon had been captured, followed by Bali and Timor in the third week of February. At the end of February a strong Japanese squadron, with four aircraft carriers, was operating in the Indian Ocean south of Java. This meant that Java was completely isolated. On 20 February 1942 the transfer of the Dutch East Indies ministries in Batavia to Bandung began. This had been decided on because the authorities realized that the land forces on Java faced an unequal battle and that Batavia on the north coast would be highly vulnerable in the event of a Japanese attack. It was thought that if resistance for any length of time proved possible it could only be in the higher country around Bandung.

General Terauchi, the commander of the Nampo army group, determined that the invasion of Java should take place on 26 February. Two big convoys were approaching from the north, one sailing west of Borneo, the other going round its east coast. In the Java Sea there were still quite strong Allied naval units. Under the command of the Dutchman Rear Admiral Karel Doorman, they undertook a desperate attempt to prevent the Japanese invasion. The plan was to stop the eastern fleet first, and then the western one. The lack of aircraft was a major handicap. Without proper air support the chance of success was naturally small. Nonetheless, the commander of the Dutch navy in the East Indies, Vice Admiral C.E.L. Helfrich, persisted with the plan.

On 27 February Doorman's five cruisers (two Dutch, one British, one American and one Australian) and nine destroyers (four American, three British and two Dutch) encountered a Japanese squadron of four cruisers and thirteen destroyers that was escorting the eastern convoy. The Japanese guns and torpedoes had a greater range than the Allied guns. Doorman's group was virtually destroyed and he went down with his ship, the *De Ruyter*. The remnants sailed back to Java.

The Battle of the Java Sea was a great victory for the Japanese. Only one of their ships, a destroyer, was badly damaged. The Allied losses were catastrophic. The Dutch cruisers *Java* and *De Ruyter* and three Allied destroyers (two British and one Dutch) were sunk. The British cruiser *Exeter* suffered heavy damage and was sent to the bottom two days later. The two undamaged cruisers, the Australian *Perth* and the American *Houston*, tried to escape from Java but were intercepted by the Japanese fleet and also sunk. Robbed of its Allies, the Dutch navy had no choice but to give up the defence of Java. On the orders of the Governor-General, Vice Admiral Helfrich left Java by flying boat on 2 March 1942 to establish a new naval headquarters in Ceylon. The remaining Dutch ships and flying boats were ordered to disperse to Australia or Ceylon.

The conquest of Java

The naval battle had succeeded only in delaying the Japanese invasion of Java by a few days. The landings took place in the night of 28 February and 1 March 1942 at four places on the north coast: Merak, Bantam Bay (Teluk Banten), Eretan Wetan and just east of Rembang. For the defence of Java the KNIL had about 18,000 poorly trained and lightly armed troops. There were also 2,200 Australians (part of the 7th Infantry Division), about 500 American gunners and over 11,000 British soldiers (mainly anti-aircraft units and unarmed RAF ground crew). There was no hope now of successfully defending Java; the aim was to inflict as much damage on the Japanese as possible.

The Japanese forces that landed at Merak and Bantam Bay, numbering about 20,000, encountered little resistance and their advance towards Batavia and Buitenzorg was hindered only by blown-up bridges. But at Leuwiliang, west of Buitenzorg, stiff resistance was put up by Australian troops supported by American gunners and fifteen British light tanks.

At Eretan Wetan, which was 'defended' by eight members of the Dutch East Indies coastguard, a brigade of 5,000 men under Colonel Toshinari Shoji landed. This brigade had the important mission of capturing the strategically vital airfield Kalijati, about eighty kilometres from the landing site. This was done at lightning speed. Their advance on Kalijati was virtually unhindered. As early as the morning of 1 March Japanese troops simply drove onto the airfield and in less than an hour the British and Dutch defenders were over-powered. About 60 British soldiers were immediately executed and later another 20 who were wounded were also killed. Next day the completely intact airfield was being used by Japanese fighters and bombers.

The loss of Kalijati on the first day of fighting was a severe blow for KNIL General Headquarters, which was at Bandung. It played havoc with the defence of West Java, and the recapture of Kalijati now had the highest priority. However, hastily improvized attacks intended to take back the air-field and the landing site at Eretan Wetan from the Shoji brigade all failed. General Headquarters then decided to abandon Batavia and Buitenzorg and to concentrate the defence on the Bandung plateau. On 5 March the first Japanese soldiers entered the undefended Batavia. Two days later the com-mander of the Japanese 16th Army, General Hitoshi Imamura, held a speech in the building of the Council of the Dutch East Indies. According to the Dutch burgomaster, who was present, the gist of what he said was that the Dutch East Indies had ceased to exist, that the territory would be annexed by Japan and that in future it would share in the blessings of the Co-Prosperity Sphere. Imamura evidently thought that the battle was over.

In this he was not mistaken, for in the meantime the KNIL's position on the Bandung plateau had become critical. General J.J. Pesman, the commander of the 'Bandung Group' (the KNIL troops who had been stationed on the pla-teau from the beginning), had had positions prepared in the mountains north of Bandung with the aim of halting the Shoji brigade, which was advancing southwards from Kalijati. On 5 March the first Japanese troops reached the north end of the Ciater Pass, through which ran the road from Kalijati to Bandung. A company of KNIL infantry was in position at the entrance to the pass. Under cover of thick fog the Japanese broke through the position. The KNIL troops retreated to the south end of the pass. Reinforcements were hastily scraped together in Bandung and sent forward, and after a day of fierce fighting (on 6 March) the KNIL managed to stabilize the front line. On that day the Japanese took 72 Dutch prisoners of war. A few hours after being captured they were taken to a clearing in a wood and killed.

New attacks by the Shoji brigade were very likely to result in a break-through towards Lembang and subsequently Bandung. The continual retreats had lowered the morale of the KNIL troops to a minimum. Many of the Indonesian soldiers, and in particular the Javanese, had deserted. The Japanese had control of the air, and the Dutch East Indies air force was as good as eliminated. All available reinforcements were sent to the KNIL positions just north of Lembang in a last attempt to save Bandung. General

Headquarters planned to abandon the plateau as soon as the positions at Lembang were breached. One of the reasons for this decision was the fear of air raids on Bandung while it was crammed with civilian refugees.

On the morning of 7 March the Shoji brigade stormed the KNIL's positions. At the same time the troops were attacked by Japanese bombers and fighters. The line at Lembang was soon at breaking point. At the end of the afternoon (the same afternoon on which General Imamura was holding his victory speech in Batavia), General Pesman sent an officer to the enemy with the offer of a partial surrender of the KNIL, that is, all the troops on the Bandung plateau. Colonel Shoji was ready to accept this but the next day (8 March) the offer was rejected by his superior, General Imamura. The General summoned the two highest authorities in the East Indies, Governor-General Van Starkenborgh and the army commander, Lieutenant General H. ter Poorten, for talks about a general capitulation.

The two sides met the same day at Kalijati airfield. Van Starkenborgh still resisted and then withdrew, leaving the discussions to Ter Poorten. The latter accepted the Japanese demands and undertook to announce the general capitulation in a radio address no later than 8 a.m. the next day. Afterwards he would return to Kalijati with details of the location of the KNIL units and their equipment. And this he did.

Many hundreds of Dutch Eurasian, British, Australian and American soldiers tried to avoid being taken prisoner after the surrender of Java. A group of about 100 Australians and British hid in the mountains south of Sukabumi, near a gold mine. A Swiss geologist, Paul Vogt, who worked for a mining company, helped them to set up a camp there. But one by one the soldiers fell into Japanese hands, the last in September 1942. Vogt was also arrested and given a long prison sentence by a Japanese court. It is likely that all the fugitive soldiers were caught in the course of 1942 and 1943.[16]

The conquest of North and Central Sumatra

After the fall of Java and the surrender of the KNIL, Central and North Sumatra were still in the hands of Dutch East Indies units. The Japanese 25th Army was ready to take these areas. After its troops landed on the coast of North Sumatra, it received substantial support from the local people. The

---

[16] It was said (in the absence of more accurate information) that the Japanese put hundreds of them into bamboo cages and threw them into the sea. According to D. van Velden this story was probably based on the fact that the bodies of dead Australian soldiers were transported in crates (Proposition X in her dissertation *De Japanse interneringskampen voor burgers gedurende de Tweede Wereldoorlog*, Groningen, 1963).

Japanese had gone to some effort to establish fifth columns in the western colonies in Southeast Asia. This was the responsibility of an officer on the Japanese army staff, Major Iwaichi Fujiwara, who set up a small group known as the 'Fujiwara' or 'F organization'. On Malacca and in Singapore it tried to create a movement for the independence of British India. Originally, Major Fujiwara did not plan any operations in the Aceh region of North Sumatra. The fact that his F organization was active there was the result of an initiative by the Acehnese themselves.

In the ports on the west coast of Malacca, directly opposite Aceh, there were a great many Acehnese. A number of them, headed by the influential religious leader Said Abu Bakar, reached an agreement with Fujiwara. Acehnese would cross over to Sumatra to make contact with leaders of the Poesa, an orthodox Islamic association of Aceh ulamas who opposed both the Dutch and the traditional indigenous chiefs. The Poesa leaders were to recruit Acehnese who were ready to inflict damage on the KNIL as soon as the Japanese landed and to help the invaders in any way possible.

Between January and mid-February 1942, groups of Fujiwara agents were taken from Malacca to Sumatra. The local Poesa leaders were immediately prepared to cooperate. The saboteurs went to work in the second half of February, even before the Japanese arrived in North Sumatra. They tore up the railway line from north Aceh to Medan, blocked bridges and roads and cut telephone and telegram lines at many places. In the course of this sabotage a government official and a railway employee were killed. The area commander of Aceh and Sumatra's east coast, Colonel G.F.V. Gosenson, managed to restore order to some extent, but several Aceh chiefs concluded that Dutch rule was bound to collapse and made the best of a bad bargain by joining the secret organization. One of these chiefs, Teukoe Nja Arif, even undertook to lead the resistance.

In the night of 7-8 March the F organization again carried out sabotage operations. Pamphlets were also distributed among the indigenous population which called for resistance against the Dutch and threatened those who supported the colonial authorities with death. The Dutch resident in Aceh ordered the immediate evacuation to Medan of the European families still in the territory. The resident and Colonel Gosenson organized a meeting of the principal chiefs on 11 March. Eight of them demonstrated their loyalty by attending, but the rest stayed away. Gosenson treated those present with a total lack of tact. He accused the chiefs of not opposing the saboteurs vigorously enough and had them arrested. This removed any remaining support for the colonial government in Aceh. The uprising spread rapidly.

The next night Japanese troops landed at four points on the east coast of North and Central Sumatra. The KNIL detachments in Aceh retreated inland in small groups, with the idea of waging guerrilla warfare from the mountains of central Aceh. Nothing came of this plan. Most of Colonel Gosenson's units did not even manage to reach the mountains. Weakened by the desertion of large number of troops and plagued by rebellious Acehnese, they surrendered to their Japanese pursuers. Gosenson realized that there was no point in continuing the struggle. Before surrendering, he decided to consult the territorial commander of Central Sumatra, General R.T. Overakker, whose troops were still resisting the advancing Japanese further to the south, in the Alas Valley. However, their morale was also on the point of collapse. Together Gosenson and Overakker reached the conclusion that surrender was the best option. They carried out this decision on 28 March.

On Sumatra a group of KNIL soldiers managed to avoid capture for nearly a year. After the capitulation of Overakker and Gosenson, Lieutenant H. van Zanten and one European sergeant and over 70 Indonesian soldiers moved to a forest bivouac in the interior of Aceh where they remained in hiding for a long time. At the end of 1942 the Japanese got wind of this group and from then on it gradually crumbled away. On 10 March 1943 Van Zanten himself was caught, as one of the last. Six months later he was executed.

Drawing up the balance

The Japanese suffered only limited losses while capturing the Indonesian archipelago. According to Japanese sources, 845 of their soldiers died in the Dutch East Indies. The losses on the losing side were greater: 1653 naval personnel and 896 KNIL soldiers. The fighting on land did not generally last long and was not especially heavy. This is hardly surprising. The KNIL faced an impossible task: in numbers, weapons, training and morale it was far inferior to the Japanese, who also controlled the sea and the air. 'Many may have felt that the brief duration of the fighting on Java was sadly disappointing', writes De Jong, 'but when one looks in hindsight at the balance of military power and the possibilities, it was only to be expected' (De Jong 1984, 11a:1126).

The Indonesians under Japanese occupation

Pre-war attempts by the Japanese to win over the Indonesian masses and the intelligentsia had only limited success. The number of Indonesians who went to study in Japan was only a fraction of the number who went to the Netherlands. Several nationalists, among them Hatta and Sjahrir, openly opposed Japanese imperialism. Sukarno's attitude was ambivalent. He admitted that Japan could be described as 'a state run by louts' but on the other hand he could understand that it wanted to extend her influence at the expense of that of other powers (De Jong 1984, 11a:568). The great mass of the Indonesian population were not unsympathetic to Japan, but it was only in the north of Sumatra, in Aceh, that the Japanese had managed to build up a secret anti-Dutch organization.

Immediately before and during the Japanese landings on Java, Radio Tokyo broadcast daily news commentaries in Indonesian which always ended with the anthem *Indonesia Raya*. Japanese aircraft also dropped posters featuring the red and white flag of the Indonesian nationalists. Yet there were varying reactions among the Indonesians to the Japanese victory and the defeat of the Dutch. In some places the Japanese were greeted by cheering crowds, at others the local people remained indifferent. There was no question of active resistance to the Japanese by Indonesians. The occasional attempts by Dutch and Australian troops to wage guerrilla warfare were doomed to failure because of the lack of support from the local population.

Many Indonesians viewed the coming of the Japanese as the fulfilment of the so-called Djojobojo prediction, which was said to have been made in the twelfth century by a Javanese king of this name. It stated that as a punishment for their sins the Javanese would long be ruled by foreign peoples, among them a white-skinned race. The last foreign rulers would have yellow skins, but their rule would not last long – according to one version of the prediction as long as the life of a maize plant (three months), according to another as long as the life of a cockerel (about three years). After this last period of oppression a new era of independence, peace and prosperity would dawn.

Immediately after the Japanese troops appeared, Indonesian nationalists spontaneously formed 'Freedom Committees' in various towns on Java and Sumatra. The aim of these committees was to push aside the old indigenous administration, which had been the mainstay of Dutch rule, to form their own administrative bodies and to offer assistance to the Japanese in maintaining law and order. However, they were to be short-lived. The general instructions given to the Japanese forces by the government in Tokyo said that as far as possible the existing administrative bodies and structures should continue to be used. There was a war to be won and this was no time for wild experiments. So the new committees were quickly brushed aside by the Japanese without much trouble.

Tokyo saw Indonesian nationalism primarily as a very useful way of getting the population involved in the Japanese war effort. The new rulers seemed to feel no greater sympathy for the Indonesian masses than their Dutch predecessors. At a few places looting of Chinese and Dutch property occurred, but the Japanese cracked down hard on this. One of the first measures taken by the Japanese military administration was to ban all political activity. Not even the red and white flag or *Indonesia Raya* was allowed. In fact Japan behaved as the new colonial ruler.[17] The political development of the country was made secondary to its economic exploitation. The archipelago was not governed as an entity but divided into three administrative areas. Java and Madura came under the 16th Army, and Sumatra under the 25th Army (which also governed the Malay peninsula); the other islands came under the navy.

The press, radio and cinemas were placed under strict Japanese control. Throughout the war the Indonesian public was subjected to a flood of propaganda directed against the Allies. At the same time the Japanese example was lauded. Certain elements from Japanese society were introduced in the East Indies: the dating system (which was 660 years ahead of the Christian system), the time (one and a half hours ahead of Java time), holidays, the ubiquitous Japanese flag, the compulsory bow to Japanese soldiers, worship of the emperor and – most unpleasantly – frequent administration of corporal punishment. All radios were registered and 'castrated' to make it impossible to listen to Allied broadcasts. Sometimes insulating tape with two wax seals was put on the tuning knob for the short wave, sometimes components inside the radio were cut, sometimes a drop of lead was soldered onto the wavelength control so that it could not be turned further than a certain point. These measures were not one 100% effective: the 'castration' was often done inexpertly and could be reversed even when wax seals had been used.

Japan advocated a new order in Asia, to be known promisingly as the 'Greater East Asia Co-Prosperity Sphere'. Asia had a bright future, provided it accepted Japanese leadership. In the second half of March 1942, the Japanese military administration on Java started a major publicity campaign extolling the new order. The name of the campaign was *Tiga A*, the three A's, which stood for *Asia tjahaja*, *Asia pelindoeng* and *Asia pemimpin* – 'Japan the light of Asia, the protector of Asia and the leader of Asia'. Although these slogans undoubtedly struck a chord to some extent, the AAA campaign never really got off the ground. It was dropped in October 1942. The Japanese authorities came to the conclusion that attempts to mobilize the Indonesian masses would probably be more successful if the nationalist leaders were involved.

The Japanese military administration brought Sukarno, Hatta and Sjahrir back to Java from exile. On the evening of 9 July 1942 the three met in Batavia to decide what course to follow. Sukarno was convinced that Japan, Germany and Italy would win the war and that accordingly the nationalists would have to take into account some form of continuing Japanese supremacy. Thus cooperation with the new rulers was unavoidable. Hatta and Sjahrir, on the

---

[17]   Nevertheless many of the Japanese stationed in Indonesia believed their government's propaganda about 'Asia for Asians'. They certainly felt that they came as liberators.

other hand, believed that, however strong Japan's position appeared to be, the three aggressor nations would be defeated. Nonetheless, like Sukarno, Hatta was ready to cooperate with the occupiers because this would enable him to alleviate the worst effects on the people and to promote the ideal of an independent Indonesia. Sjahrir alone refused categorically to work with the Japanese, and indeed he was the only one of the three, so argued De Jong, to 'come through the occupation with his reputation unsullied' (De Jong 1985, 11b:273). Sukarno went furthest in working with the Japanese and, unlike Hatta, he also lashed out at the United States and Britain in the most virulent terms.

The Japanese could not entirely ignore nationalist sentiment among the Indonesians because – as the Dutch had previously discovered – this could damage attempts to involve the indigenous population as much as possible in the Japanese war effort. So the occupiers set up various organizations that offered scope for expressions of Indonesian nationalism. Nationalist leaders were given some room to manoeuvre within them, more so as the war began to go badly for Japan. At first, however, it was extremely limited. On 5 July 1943 the Japanese military administration on Java announced that Local and Regional Advisory Councils and a Central Advisory Council for all Java would be established. Though this sounded promising, these bodies would only be able to pronounce on matters put before them by the Japanese military administration. The chairman of the Central Advisory Council was Sukarno, and Hatta was one of the members.

Sukarno and Hatta were also allocated important roles in the organization of the successor to the *Tiga A* campaign, the Poetera (Poesat Tenaga Rakjat [oentoek membantoe oesaha perang], 'Centre of the people's power [to help the war effort]').[18] Sukarno was the chairman and Hatta one of the vice chairmen. The chairman was provided with a secretariat paid for by the Japanese and had the power to appoint regional chairmen in all the residencies, although these appointments had to be approved by the Japanese residents. The Poetera had a council with twenty members, among them ten Japanese, which was to meet at least every three months in Jakarta (De Jong 1985, 11b: 282, 285-6). The organization did not come up to Indonesian expectations. Their request for the words 'Indonesia' and 'Indonesians' to be included in the name of the new movement and for it to be allowed to use *Indonesia Raya* and the red and white flag were rejected by the Japanese military administration. The Indonesians at the top of the organization were given the means (money, cars) to move about the country easily and could deliver speeches which made them better known and – so they hoped – strengthened their listeners' sense of national identity, but in essence they were no more than

---

[18]   *Poetera* is also the Indonesian word for 'son'.

propagandists for support for the Japanese war effort, in return for which the Japanese had not so far made a single concession (De Jong 1985, 11b:916).

The Japanese recruited about 25,000 Indonesians as *heiho*, a kind of un-armed auxiliary. In the course of 1943 they also founded a number of para-military organizations for Indonesians with strict discipline and ideological training. In April 1943 the Keibodan and the Seinendan were set up, a sort of auxiliary police force and a youth labour corps respectively. Towards the end of the war two million young Indonesians were estimated to have had deal-ings with these two organizations. In addition, in January 1943 the Japanese army had begun organizing the Peta (Pembela tanah air), an abbreviation for 'Volunteer Army for the Defence of the Fatherland'. This army of Indonesians consisted of 36,000 men in August 1945. Because of the constant nationalist indoctrination, the Peta would later be an important factor in the struggle for Indonesian independence.

During 1944 the attitude of the Japanese to Indonesian nationalism changed slightly. The main reason for this was the series of defeats suf-fered by Japan in the Pacific. These military disasters led to a change of government in Tokyo in February 1944. Hideki Tojo was succeeded as prime minister by Kuniaki Koiso. The new leader was a little more sympathetic to the Indonesian independence movement than his predecessor. Japan's own interests also played an important role. By making some concessions to the nationalists, Koiso hoped to secure an enlarged Indonesian contribu-tion to the war effort. On 7 December 1944 he produced the so-called 'Koiso Declaration', which promised that the East Indies would be made independ-ent 'in the future', without giving a date (De Jong 1985, 11b:981). As a sign of Japanese good will, *Indonesia Raya* might be played again and the red and white flag of Indonesia might be flown alongside the Japanese flag. Ever more Indonesians were appointed to senior administrative posts.

To what extent the Koiso Declaration actually had an impact on the Indonesian masses is hard to establish. On the one hand, Japanese policy had an attraction for many Indonesians that should not be underestimated. On the other, as a consequence of Japan's shocking economic mismanagement, most of them were so caught up in the daily struggle to survive that they had little interest in politics. There is no doubt that the war brought about two significant changes. First, the rapid Japanese advance and the equally rapid Dutch collapse seriously damaged the latter's prestige. It was further under-mined by Japanese propaganda and by the disappearance of the Dutch from public life. Second, the Japanese occupation resulted in the total mobilization and disruption of Indonesian society. Hundreds of thousands lost their lives, but Indonesian groups and individuals also found themselves in utterly new situations, with previously unknown opportunities. Many intellectuals had a chance to develop their potential. In brief, the Japanese occupiers were able to break down the old order completely. They were much less successful, however, in building up a new order.

CHAPTER I

The elimination of 'the Netherlands'

This study is primarily concerned with the relatively small groups formed by the Dutch and the Eurasians, that is those of mixed Dutch and Indonesian origin. These groups each had their own history and there were also social and cultural differences between them. Nonetheless, they had all enjoyed the same legal status under the colonial government: they were all Dutch citizens and as Europeans they were distinct from the Chinese and other 'Foreign Orientals' such as Malays, Arabs and Indians and from the Natives, as they were still officially known.

It had been the Dutch and the Dutch Eurasians who had formed the back-bone of the defence of the Indies and so it was they who were particularly affected by the unexpectedly rapid end of the fighting on Java: from one week to the next they saw the familiar colonial regime replaced by a Japanese one.

It was hard enough to bear the rule of a foreign power, but in addition it was imposed by soldiers who struck many among the Dutch and Dutch Eurasians (reacting emotionally in shocking circumstances) as repulsively ugly. 'Bandy legs,' wrote Rudy Verheem, who was Eurasian, 'lots of bandy legs; a long torso, relatively short legs and nearly always bandy' (Verheem 1979:62). Japanese uniforms were greenish yellow: soldiers and non-commissioned officers usually wore a peaked cap with flaps sewn on at the back and brown shoes with white laces or tennis shoes. Officers all had samurai swords and the hilt often came far above their waist. If they also wore boots, they gave the impression of barely being able to walk. Many of the soldiers wore glasses (this also applied to the Japanese civilians who came with the troops) and the high-ranking officers could be grotesquely fat. 'They smiled incessantly, bowing, over-polite in their contacts with the enemy' (all Europeans qualified as enemies), wrote Verheem, 'mostly cool, the officers coldly formal, the lower ranks icily ruthless, at best gently teasing' (Verheem 1979:63). Their language, often spoken in high falsetto voices, seemed incomprehensible. Orders were bellowed out so loud and so often that a medical student in Bandung told the journalist J.B. Bouwer in May that he had decided to write a thesis on 'The connection between Japanese commands and throat cancer' (Bouwer 1988:76). The Japanese would not have understood the joke, let alone appreciated it.

'These people', again according to Verheem, 'who were for ever smiling, showing their white and gold teeth [the number of gold teeth was striking], froze with spiteful, suspicious looks at the slightest hint of European humour' (Verheem 1979:63). The Japanese wished to be taken deadly seriously at all times. The slightest thing could be taken as an offence to their national honour, and the ways of reacting that had developed in Japan from childhood may perhaps have been intensified by the fact that they found themselves in foreign, far-off and in many ways mysterious territory. To many they seemed like creatures not from another country but from another planet. There was a distance between them and the Dutch and Dutch Eurasians which did not exist in the occupied Netherlands between the Germans and Dutch. The German occupation was seen as a humiliation, the Japanese occupation as an absurdity as well.

This was how it was perceived in March 1942, when Japan had achieved victory over the East Indies, and it was still perceived like this in August 1945, when Japan faced defeat in the Pacific.

First reactions

In Bandung (see Map 1 for all the places mentioned on Java) the first occupation troops appeared on Monday 9 March. They belonged to the brigade led by Colonel Shoji which had captured Kalijati airfield and broken through the defences at Lembang on 7 March. Most were Japanese, with some Korean and Formosan soldiers, many of whom had grown up in primitive circumstances. Those living in the northern, European part of the city were forced to leave their homes taking only a few clothes. The next day, after the Japanese commander and his staff had installed themselves in the largest club, most of the invading troops were assembled at central locations and the inhabitants were allowed to go home. What they found there was complete chaos. It was described by W.H.J. Elias (1946:37), the head of the Financial Department of the General Treasury of the Ministry of Finance:

> Curtains had served as sheets. On the floor and the carpets lie remains of food, empty tins, rice; many household items and pieces of furniture are ruined. In cupboards and in the garden there are piles of excrement. The soldiers tried to wash rice in the toilet. They left the gas burning under empty pans and had never seen electric light; many were evidently peasants who had not encountered the comforts of Western civilization before.[1]

---

[1]   It was the same in Cirebon. 'The soldiers,' observed one Dutch woman, 'moved into houses the like of which they had never seen, slept in cupboards laid on the floor and washed their rice in the WC, amazed that it was flushed away when you pulled a handle' (MacGillavry 1975:36).

It seemed inconceivable that the armed forces of the Netherlands and its allies could have been defeated by troops of this primitive level. The disillusionment was profound. How could the rapid collapse be squared with the optimistic tone and the often optimistic content of the communiqués issued by the Army General Headquarters during the one week of fighting on Java? Many felt they had been deceived, even betrayed. Where were the British, and the Americans? What they heard about failures to supply the Koninklijk Nederlandsch-Indisch Leger (KNIL, Royal Dutch East Indies Army) troops properly and about the chaos that had reigned in many of the operations led to bitter accusations against the army command and all officers in general. The higher their rank, it was said, the greater their failure.

There was not only anxiety about the future but also, for many, great concern about the fate of fathers, sons, other family members and friends who were regular soldiers or reservists. Had they been killed? Or wounded? All lines of communication had been broken: those in Bandung did not know what was happening elsewhere on Java, and those outside the city knew nothing of what was going on inside it. There was scarcely a Dutch or Dutch Eurasian family that was not worried about people who were missing. The Nederlandsch-Indische Radio-Omroep Maatschappij (NIROM, Dutch East Indies Radio Company) still broadcast daily on Japanese orders, and it was immediately used for finding missing people. Up to the middle of April, when you switched on the radio you heard long lists compiled by the Red Cross being read out. They gave people's addresses or the names of those whose address was sought. 'In the absence of news', the announcer then said, 'we will continue with cheerful sounds'. To one Dutch woman living in Central Java they were 'dreadful sounds' (Helfferich-Koch 1981:19).

Some news was broadcast, however: reports from the Japanese press agency Domei and the complete texts of the first ordinances issued by General Hitoshi Imamura, the commander of the 16th Army and head of the Japanese military administration on Java. According to an engineer who was temporarily attached to the headquarters of the State Railways in Bandung, these were read 'in a ludicrous version of Dutch' and the announcers 'made a terrible mess of them by always getting the intonation wrong. We laughed at this, but that was not very sensible of us.'[2]

The Japanese soon began to make use of the NIROM broadcasts for their own purposes in other ways as well: the personnel of the Artillery Construction Workshops and the Pyrotechnics Workshop of the KNIL were told to go back to work and a similar call went out to all who had been employed at the oil installations – these had been sabotaged by the KNIL

---

[2]   L.R. Oldeman, 'Verslag', p. 18 (Netherlands Institute for War Documentation, Indische Collectie (hereafter referred to as: NIOD IC), 81,206 A).

and the Japanese wanted them back in operation as quickly as possible.[3] All Europeans who obeyed these calls were given a white armband with a red ball (and Japanese stamps) which safeguarded them against internment. The same armband was given to the Dutch and Dutch Eurasians among the civil servants who were told they must resume work. We will come back to the question of resuming work later – here it need only be said that the resident of Bandung felt unable to provide any leadership. A lower-ranking official who had served under him in the early 1920s and who visited him in his private office six days after the capitulation found him 'a broken man, dazed with misery. [...] Rarely in those sad days did I see anyone more affected by our inglorious collapse than he whom I had known as a young, forceful administrator.'[4]

In this demoralized atmosphere in Bandung there were those who tried to curry favour with the Japanese. They collected signatures in support of a petition to the Japanese authorities in which, according to the Dutch writer Jacques de Kadt (1978:76), who saw the text, 'the declarations of war on Japan by the Netherlands and the East Indies were condemned, the Japanese goal of a Co-Prosperity Sphere [...] was praised and the duty of the Dutch was declared to be loyal cooperation with the Japanese regime' (the Vichy government in France had instructed the French authorities in Indo-China to cooperate in similar fashion). De Kadt had 'nothing but contempt' for this policy.[5]

It is doubtful whether there were many who put their signature to this document – a more militant mood soon spread among the Dutch and Dutch Eurasians. As part of the AAA campaign, three balloons were hung above Bandung with the words Asia Timoer Raya (Greater East Asia), and posters with the three A's were put up at street corners to drive home the message that Japan was *'Asia tjahaja'* (the Light of Asia), *'Asia pelindung'* (the Protector of Asia) and *'Asia pemimpin'* (the Leader of Asia). The Dutch and Dutch Eurasians, however, read the three A's as abbreviations of *'Amerika Ampir Ada'*: 'America is nearly here' (Elias 1946:44). On 13 March Bouwer noted that

[3]   These oil workers were first assembled in Batavia, the present Jakarta, and then in April 1942 about 300 were taken to Palembang and put to work there.
[4]   R.W. Hofman, 'Verslag', 17 December 1947, p. 59 (ARA, Archief proc. gen. Batavia, 850).
[5]   A condemnation of the Dutch declaration of war was included at this time in a radio broadcast made by a former Japanese consul general in Batavia, Yutaka Ishizawa on Radio Bandung. From November 1940 he had been a member of the Japanese delegation conducting economic negotiations there. The Secretary of the Raad van Indië (Council of the Dutch East Indies), L.F. Jansen, expressed his agreement with this speech in writing. A few weeks later Jansen informed Prof. Hoessein Djajadiningrat, a member of the same Council, that he had offered his services to the Japanese propaganda campaign; when asked where he had last worked, he had said nothing about his post with the Council. Jansen soon came to regret his offer, but was then forced by the Japanese to cooperate. We will return to this matter in Chapter IV ('Prisoners of War') because several prisoners of war also worked in the same department as Jansen.

rumours were circulating that the Soviet Union had declared war on Japan and that the British had landed in western Europe; because of the Djojobojo prediction some were convinced that the Japanese would not stay longer than 100 days in the East Indies. But 'pessimists say the Japanese are here for good. There are thousands of possibilities between these two extremes. I am not going to risk making a guess myself.' (Bouwer 1988:27.)

Throughout Java many among the Dutch and Dutch Eurasians drew encouragement from the fact that the NIROM broadcasts, however meagre the content, ended every evening with the Wilhelmus, the Dutch national anthem: a reminder of the past and a promise for the future. The landlady of the manager of the NIROM, J.P.W. Kusters, asked him if it would not be better to drop the anthem. 'But it's a help to people,' replied Kusters.[6]

One of the consequences of broadcasting the national anthem was that prisoners of war who heard it in their camps near Bandung stood to attention each time (what happened to the prisoners of war in the first year of the occupation will be dealt with in Chapter IV). This attracted the attention of several Japanese guards. The situation was explained to them, and the reaction was not long in coming. On the morning of 19 March Kusters was arrested by Japanese soldiers along with the two technicians who put on the record of the anthem each evening, V. Kudding and N. van der Hoogte. They were taken to the building of the Kempeitai, the Japanese military police, where they were beaten horrifically. Then they were transported to Batavia, where they were condemned to death by the recently established Japanese military court. On 7 April they were beheaded. The Japanese headquarters announced that their 'heinous deed [...] was a violation of international law', as a consequence of which 'a heavy penalty was imposed'.[7] The fact that it was the death penalty was not revealed.

What was the attitude of the Indonesians to the Dutch and the Dutch Eurasians at the beginning?

The general picture that emerges from the (limited) information available is that in the first weeks and months some Indonesians were quite aggressive and that at that time few dared to give any sign of solidarity, but that later in 1942 this changed in that some began to see themselves, like the Dutch and Dutch Eurasians, as victims of the Japanese regime.

In Bandung, according to the railway engineer already quoted, the attitude of the Indonesians who came into or sought contact with the Japanese was 'with the exception of a few outstanding examples, nauseating. They

[6]   Statement, n.d., by H. de Winter-Termaate, p. 1 (NIOD IC, 2,317).
[7]   Statement, n.d., by H. de Winter-Termaate, p. 2 (NIOD IC, 2,317).

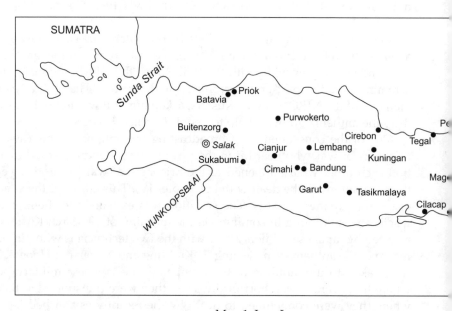

Map 1. Java I

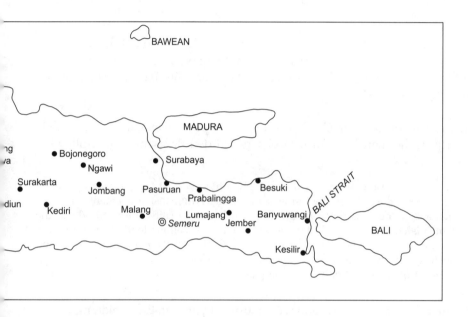

bowed and laughed with the Japs.'[8] But six months later, in September, in the
same Bandung, Bouwer (1988:120) was struck by:

> how friendly the Indonesians [...] now are towards Europeans and Eurasians.
> Conversely, there is a proportionate increase in the resentment of the Japanese.
> *'Nippon nipoe'* (Japan is a swindler) is the catch phrase among the Indonesians.
> Not a day passes without an Indonesian being beaten up somewhere in the city.[9]

In Batavia in the first months of occupation the Dutch and Dutch Eurasians
sometimes had 'hateful remarks' hurled at them on the street such as *'Blanda
tai! Boesoek! Sekarang tida dirèken lagi!'* (Dutch are shit! Bad! Don't count any
more!) and so on.[10]

At the end of October C.D. Ricardo, the deputy manager of the Batavia
branch of the mercantile firm Jacobson-Van den Berg, made the following
note:

> Now that the Indonesians are increasingly convinced that *Indonesia Raya* ['Greater
> Indonesia', the title of the battle song of the nationalist movement, later the
> national anthem] is not a utopia but will become reality, their attitude to the
> Dutch is changing as each day passes and, almost self-evidently I would say, in
> an unfavourable sense. [...] The term *'andjing-Blanda'* [Dutch dog] has acquired
> such charm for the Indonesians that it is used to insult European women as if it
> were a fully accepted part of the language.[11]

A Dutch Eurasian man who made a journey by foot in the Semarang region
in 1942 later wrote:

> The attitude of the population in these parts to the Chinese and above all the
> Europeans was aggressive and hostile. [...] They repeatedly tried through words
> and gestures to provoke a reaction. The European or Chinese who could not con-
> trol his temper would be attacked and beaten up. Even if the situation in these
> parts cannot be regarded as representative, it must be said that throughout Java
> the population displayed an unfriendly attitude, less so in some areas than in

---

[8]   L.R. Oldeman, 'Verslag', p. 20 (NIOD IC, 81,206 A).
[9]   In the early phase of the occupation an official of the gas company in Batavia gave one of
his Indonesian clerks leave to visit his relatives in Buitenzorg. He was away for six weeks and on
his return told 'how on the way he had been pulled off his bicycle by the Japanese and forced to
work on an airstrip. He had done that for a month under strict supervision with more beatings
than food and no payment. In the end he had managed to escape. Hating everything Japanese
from that time on, he made no secret of his views. There were thousands of cases like his.' (Van
der Grift 1946:43.)
[10]   W.F. Grashuis, 'Verslag', 17 December 1946, p. 3 (ARA, Alg. Secr., Eerste zending, XXII, 45,
447).
[11]   C.D. Ricardo, *'Andjing blanda'*, 28 October 1942, p. 1 (NIOD IC, 30,933).

others, and least so in the cities.[12]

This observer had settled with his family in Hollandia on New Guinea in 1939 as a colonist. In May 1940 he had been taken from there to Java because he was a member of the NSB (Nationaal-Socialistische Beweging), a Fascist party in the Netherlands and the Dutch East Indies. After the German invasion of the Netherlands in May 1940, the government in the East Indies decided to intern not only the Germans in its territory but also the NSB members. With great difficulty he succeeded in obtaining permission from the Japanese to return to Hollandia. In September 1942 he reached Makassar on Celebes and after looking for three days found a billet with an Indonesian policeman. 'It must be said,'[13] he added:

> that sadly this was a rare case of an Indonesian taking pity on a European. At best one generally encountered indifference and reserve in their own interests. The Manadonese and a high percentage of the Ambonese were an exception.[14]

In Medan on Sumatra the journalist and writer W.B. Klooster[15] was struck by the sympathetic attitude of the Indonesian print workers at the *Deli Courant*, a daily paper of which he had been the editor. 'They cycle along beside me, my old setters and printers, when I ride through Medan, just for a little way because there are Japanese all over the place, and we nervously exchange a few words of encouragement and trust' (Brandt 1947:76).

In March word spread in Batavia among the Indonesian traders that they would be well advised not to offer their goods at the houses of the Dutch and Dutch Eurasians. It was even said that the Japanese had made this a capital offence. 'It was a month', wrote Ricardo, 'before the truth caught up with this foolish rumour'.[16] There were no punitive measures by the Japanese, but among the Indonesians on Java it was said that it was wiser not to perform personal services for the Dutch and Eurasians any more. Thus in May 1942 at the home of one Dutch housewife in Semarang:

---

[12]   H.C.B., 'Verslag', June 1944, p. 5 (NIOD IC, 60,910).
[13]   H.C.B., 'Verslag', June 1944, p. 7 (NIOD IC, 60,910).
[14]   On the other hand, when the controller of one of the subdivisions of Central Celebes left his post to report to the Japanese he encountered 'not the slightest threat. Some repeatedly gave encouragement and wished me a "speedy return". One of the old faithful chiefs, in the privacy of his garden, put his hand on my hip and his gentle brown eyes looked at me calmly and steadily as he said, "*tida lama, tuan*" – "it won't last long, sir".' (J.M. van Lijf in *Gedenkboek ambtenaren* 1956: 181).
[15]   After the war, under the pseudonym 'Willem Brandt', Klooster wrote an account of his experiences entitled *De gele terreur* (The Yellow Terror).
[16]   C.D. Ricardo, 'Prijsopdrijving mitsgaders de straf', 30 September 1942, p. 1 (NIOD IC, 30,934).

there is a gentle knocking at the door and our dear *kokki* [cook] enters dragging her feet. She sits on the mat in front of my bed and says in tears that she doesn't dare stay any longer. She is *takoet*, afraid, because of all the things they are saying in the *kampong* about the bad Dutch people. And now she feels so *kassian* (sorry) for the *njonja* (madam). So *kokki* is leaving us.

A few days later:

> After dear, loyal *kokki* the *baboe* (nanny) also came in tears to say goodbye: '*Tida brani lagi, ada takoet!* I'm scared, I daren't stay any longer!' They're afraid because of everything being said about the Dutch in the *kampong*. About how stupid and wrong it is to go on working for those who are no longer the boss. After all, Nippon is going to bring about a golden age for the Asian peoples. They probably don't understand half the political propaganda [...] They just realize that it's best to keep well away from the *Belandas* (Hollanders). (Helfferich-Koch 1981:26, 32.)

In Batavia Ricardo noted that in many Dutch or Dutch Eurasian households soon after the beginning of the Japanese occupation the Indonesian servants either frequently went sick or never came back at all. 'It is appalling', he wrote, 'to see how untrustworthy the servants have shown themselves to be just when one had hoped to be able to rely on them'. 'Not hundreds, but thousands' gave notice.[17] Was this a general phenomenon? It is open to doubt. Many Dutch and Dutch Eurasian families had excellent relations with their Indonesian servants, and the latter would sorely miss the income thus earned. In the case of one Eurasian woman on Java, until she was interned in March 1943 the *babu* stayed on, 'although she was beaten up three times for helping a white'.[18] There may have been more such cases.

Two factors were crucial in the changed attitude of many Indonesians: the resentment against the colonial elite which had developed among the more aggressive elements in the population, especially in the cities, and which now forced the less militant to conform accordingly; and the policy and attitude of the new masters, the Japanese, who made it clear from the outset that they regarded the Dutch and Dutch Eurasians as inferior beings. They were finished, claimed the Japanese; their rule was over.

[17]   C.D. Ricardo, 'Onze huisbedienden in oorlogstijd', 8 November 1942, pp. 1, 6 (NIOD IC, 30,932).
[18]   C.A. Wessel, 'Uittreksel uit verslag', 1944, p. 4 (NIOD IC).

The Dutch administration is pushed aside

After leaving Batavia on the night of 21-22 February, the Governor-General of the Dutch East Indies, jonkheer A.W.L. Tjarda van Starkenborgh Stachouwer, moved into a villa in Bandung owned by the Chinese millionaire H.H. Kan, a member of the Volksraad. On 8 March he went from there with the commander of the KNIL, Lieutenant General H. ter Poorten, to Kalijati for a meeting with General Imamura, the commander of the Japanese 16th Army. At this meeting Imamura demanded the general capitulation of the KNIL, which was agreed to by the demoralized Ter Poorten. Back in Bandung at the official residence of the resident, on the 9th, Starkenborgh gave an account of events at Kalijati to several highly-placed officials: the three members of the Council of the Dutch East Indies (Raad van Nederlandsch-Indië) still in Bandung (two had flown to Australia), the president of the Volksraad, J.A. Jonkman, the heads of the departments of general administration and the heads of a number of important services. In the evening he returned to Kan's villa, accompanied by his navy adjutant and his intendant as well as by the head of his private office, P.J.A. Idenburg, one of the senior officials of the General Secretariat, E.O. baron van Boetzelaer, the governor of the province of West Java, B.J.G. Hogewind, and the two members of the Department of East Asian Affairs who had gone with him to Kalijati because they spoke Japanese, H. Hagenaar and A.A.F.P. Hulsewé. Kan's villa was big enough for all eight of them, and each had his own room. On 10 March the Japanese placed a military guard in front of the villa but telephone communication with others in Bandung was still possible. There was a swimming pool and a large garden.

Van Starkenborgh took the view that, now that the general capitulation was a fact, he should no longer exercise his authority. He gave no more instructions and if telephoned and asked for them he refused; he did feel able, however, to give advice in such cases. He also refused to receive visitors because the Japanese would have to give permission for that; he did not want to ask for favours.

At the beginning of April one of the fuses in the villa failed and the result was that a light went on and off for some time. The Japanese sentry thought this was Morse code: consequently, on 6 April Starkenborgh and all those with him were taken to Sukamiskin Prison, just outside Bandung, where they were put in separate cells. The Japanese had meanwhile decided that the Governor-General should be regarded as the commander-in-chief, that is a military officer, and that therefore he should be held in a prisoner-of-war camp. To this end on 16 April he was taken by train with a number of high-ranking officers to Batavia, 'where', he told the Parliamentary Commission of Enquiry into Government Policy during the War in 1948, 'on arrival I saw

quite a large crowd, who also saw me'. After that many among the Dutch and
Dutch Eurasians knew that he had arrived in Batavia: 'word spreads quickly
in the Indies' (*Enquêtecommissie Regeringsbeleid* 1956:26).

Among some of the high-ranking members of the government left in Bandung
after the capitulation there was a degree of irritation with Starkenborgh
because of his, as they saw it, passive stance, even though this had not been
required of him by the Japanese. Meanwhile, he could not leave Kan's villa,
while they could move freely around Bandung. Many of them had moved
into the comfortable bungalow hotel Olcott Park, which was not far from the
city centre; this made it all the easier to keep in touch.

In the absence of the governor-general or the lieutenant governor-general, the vice-president of the Council of the Dutch East Indies was the
highest Dutch authority in the Indies. This office was held by H.J. Spit, an
experienced official whose morale was far from broken. He believed that
under his chairmanship they should turn their thoughts to the future. On
12 March at Olcott Park Hotel he held the first talks with all the authorities
he had been able to reach. All those approached were Dutch; Prof. Hoessein
Djajadiningrat, who was a member of the Council of the Dutch East Indies
and still in Bandung, was not invited. These first talks were followed by
more: in total about forty people appear to have taken part on one or more
occasions, and the number of participants, fifteen at the first meeting, grew
steadily. It is known that among those present once or several times were: G.F.
de Bruijn Kops (member of the Council of the Dutch East Indies), Jonkman,
J.M. Kiveron (head of the General Secretariat), A.S. Block (Attorney General
of the High Court), H.J. Levelt (officer for general affairs in the Volksraad),
three heads of departments – F.A.E. Drossaers (Internal Administration), L.
Götzen (Finance) and C.E. van Haeften (Transport and Water Management)
– W. Hoven (head of General Administration at the Department of Internal
Affairs), J.H. Ritman (head of the Government Information Service), C.C. van
Buttingha Wichers (president of the Javasche Bank), J.C. van Waveren (director and first deputy president of the same institution), C. Hillen, head of
the Post Office, and the three former naval officers and section heads in the
navy department, Captains W.J. de Jong and A.G. Vromans and the administrative field officer J.G. van Kregten. At the suggestion of Vice-Admiral
Helfrich, the commander of the navy, Van Starkenborgh had dismissed them
from military service in the hope that as civilian officials they would be able
to supervise the winding up of naval affairs. Among the others who attended
occasionally were several members of the Standing Committee which acted
as the executive when the Volksraad was not in session (including C.C. van
Helsdingen, chairman of the Christelijk-Sociale Partij, J. Verboom, chairman
of the Vaderlandsche Club, and E.D. Wermuth, a member of the executive of

the Indo-Europeesch Verbond), and several members of the provincial council of West Java. Meetings went on until 25 March, apparently quite regularly,
but it is not certain that they were held on every day between 12 and 25
March. That a great deal was discussed is nevertheless evident.

But what exactly? We have little information about this. It seems likely
that at the first or one of the first gatherings Spit, who had taken the initiative, said that it must be assumed that Japan would be defeated, that Dutch
authority would then have to be restored, that as long as the Japanese occupation lasted civil servants should follow the *Aanwijzingen*[19] or 'Directions
regarding the attitude to be adopted [...] in the event of the occupation of
Dutch East Indies territory' drawn up and circulated by the colonial government in 1941, and that this should be impressed on officials. The general
advice given by Spit was later summed up by Vromans as 'we were to obey
Japanese orders and wait for our chance',[20] and this corresponds with a
Kempeitai report on resistance on Java written in February 1944,[21] according
to which Spit said:

> You should act according to the written instructions and orders of the governor-
> general from now on. Even if you accede to the orders of the Japanese army, you
> should believe completely in the eventual reconquest of Java and the might of
> England and America. Await the opportunity to strike.

The Japanese report continues: 'From now on you should report in detail the
contents of every type of order and any intelligence about the Japanese army
to this office'.

Did Spit really say that? It is possible that he asked to be informed of
all orders issued by the Japanese military administration, and it is also possible that he urged people to report to him on the strength and disposition
of Japanese forces, but the latter request, if he made it, was not so that the
information could be immediately passed on to the Allies (he had no transmitter and the only high-ranking figure who knew that a transmitter had
been left behind in Bandung, Ch.O. van der Plas, a member of the Council
of the Dutch East Indies, was in Australia). It would in fact have been used
for another purpose which was certainly discussed at the Olcott Park Hotel
– the restoration of Dutch rule. There were three important points in this connection: first, how best to help the British and Americans when they landed

---

[19]   The reference is to the document entitled *Aanwijzingen betreffende de houding, aan te nemen
door de bestuursorganen van het Land, de Zelfbesturende Landschappen, Provinciën, Regentschappen,
(Stads-) Gemeenten, Waterschappen, Groepsgemeenschappen, locale ressorten en Inlandsche gemeenten en
het daarbij in dienst zijnde personeel, alsmede door de bevolking in geval van bezetting van Nederlandsch-
Indisch gebied.*

[20]   A.G. Vromans, 'De landvoogdij van Imamoera', 1975, p. 96 (NIOD IC).

[21]   Java Kempeitai HQ, 'Anti-Japanese activities in Java', February 1944, p. 8 (NIOD IC 2, 171).

on Java (at which stage any military information about the Japanese would obviously be valuable); second, how to restore Dutch authority as effectively as possible; and, third, what reforms should then be carried out. It seems that it was this third point which was most discussed, on the basis of both the report of the Visman Commission and the programme for reform drawn up at Van Starkenborgh's request in mid-1941 (but which he personally had not yet approved!). After the war the East Indies was to be an autonomous part of the Kingdom of the Netherlands, and a council of ministers of the Kingdom was to be set up to deal with matters of common interest (foreign policy, defence, economic affairs). It also seems that the participants in these talks were convinced that after the restoration of Dutch authority the East Indies' first need would be for large-scale economic aid.

We do not know to what extent all this was discussed in detail, or what differences of opinion emerged. Various people did tell outsiders about the talks, but only in rather vague terms. As far as is known, nothing was put on paper.

During the deliberations Indonesian hotel staff came into the room from time to time with refreshments, and on 24 or 25 March one of the waiters or another member of the personnel informed the Kempeitai. The result was that on 25 March the Olcott Park Hotel was surrounded by Japanese soldiers and the participants in the talks at that point, who numbered about thirty, were arrested by the Japanese military police, assisted by officers of the PID (Political Information Department),[22] and taken to the Kempeitai office in Bandung, which was now in the former house of a Catholic brotherhood. Those arrested were first held in small groups but the next day they were all brought together in a large hall. Their number increased because people who had taken part in the talks before 25 March but were not present on that particular day were picked up at home or reported of their own accord, as Levelt did. Thus about forty detainees were assembled in the large hall. By day they sat in cane chairs lining the walls, all of them tied up (Spit protested against this). They slept on the stone floor, at first without blankets, but these were provided later. No one was ill-treated, which means that no one was interrogated. 'Many were badly shaken', wrote Vromans in his account of his

---

[22]   Under Dutch rule in the East Indies since the 1920s the police force had included a Politieke Inlichtingendienst (Political Information Department, PID), which acted as an intelligence service. It had kept an eye on Indonesian nationalist groups in particular. The Japanese military administration on Java soon decided to remove all Dutch and Dutch Eurasian personnel from the police force. The Indonesian members of the force were retained, including those who worked in the PID. This department was placed under direct Japanese control and given the task of investigating whether anyone was violating the orders issued by the occupiers. The PID set up offices in every town or place of any significance. The Japanese Kempeitai soon came to be hated because of its cruelty, but this was just as true of the Indonesian PID.

experiences under occupation:

> They read the Bible [they had found the Bibles in the building] and prayed, but others were tougher. It was then that I became fully aware of the collapse of the Indies that had been a paradise for us (even in wartime) – how ingloriously the house of cards had fallen down. Many said at the time that the bureaucrats' Utopia, where the natives could have a good life too, was gone for ever.[23]

After a few days these detainees were also taken to Sukamiskin Prison, where they were put in the section for political opponents of the Dutch regime in 'very good cells'.[24] Other prisoners, Indonesians, who had been jailed for ordinary crimes, could move freely about the prison 'and laughed at us, who were now behind bars'.[25] Vromans admired 'the calm counsel and wise attitude' of Jonkman; 'it is curious that it has been said here [by Jonkman] that the Japanese will certainly leave but that then a Java War will follow in order to restore normal Dutch rule'.[26] Vromans also had some contact with Van Starkenborgh: 'he told us that he found some consolation in the fact that those who subjected him to this treatment were so different from civilized people that they could hardly be held responsible'.[27]

Several of the prisoners, among them Buttingha Wichers, Götzen and Van Haeften, were questioned about the subject of the talks at the Olcott Park Hotel, but the Japanese did not bring them to trial. On 16 April the three naval officers were taken as prisoners to Batavia in the same train as Van Starkenborgh, and Van Haeften was ordered to resume his work in Bandung.[28]

Two of those imprisoned at Sukamiskin, Ritman and Drossaers, were used by the Japanese for their own purposes.

On 4 April Ritman together with C. de Vries, the editor of the Aneta press agency, and Major A. Zimmerman (a former journalist), the head of the Army Information Department, were brought to Batavia by the Kempeitai. The car in which Ritman was travelling skidded near Buitenzorg, the present Bogor. He jumped out and a Japanese soldier struck his leg so hard with the butt of his rifle that it broke. He was not given medical help. The next day in Batavia

[23] A.G. Vromans, 'Verslag ... 1941-1945', February-April 1946, p. 27 (NIOD IC, 53,501).
[24] A.G. Vromans, 'Verslag ... 1941-1945', February-April 1946, p. 28 (NIOD IC, 53,501).
[25] A.G. Vromans, 'Verslag ... 1941-1945', February-April 1946, p. 29 (NIOD IC, 53,501).
[26] A.G. Vromans, 'Verslag ... 1941-1945', February-April 1946, p. 29 (NIOD IC, 53,501).
[27] A.G. Vromans, 'Verslag: "Enige aantekeningen over jhr. van Starkenborgh"', n.d., p. 16 (NIOD IC).
[28] One of the participants in the discussions at the Olcott Park Hotel, C. Hillen, the head of the Post Office, was not immediately arrested. He was interned at the beginning of 1943 and only later treated as a 'conspirator' by the Kempeitai; he was interrogated, tortured and given a prison sentence early in 1945. He died as a consequence of his treatment in early November 1945.

a manager of the Japanese Overseas Broadcasting Service, Metsui, asked the three of them whether they were prepared to help the Japanese. They said they were (their work will be described in Chapter IV) – Ritman was then admitted to hospital, where the nuns working there managed to keep him for three months by claiming that he had an infectious disease.

Drossaers was told that on 29 April, Hirohito's birthday, he would have to make a speech on the radio in Dutch in which he would lavish praise on Japan and the Emperor and condemn the Dutch regime in the Indies since the time of the Dutch East India Company. He refused and was tortured. When he continued to refuse, he was told that the lives of his wife and children were at stake. He said he was prepared to cooperate, bearing in mind, we may assume, that it would be clear to everyone who could follow his speech that he was acting under duress. That was apparent from the tone in which he spoke. 'He was obviously having trouble controlling himself', noted Brouwer (1988:70), 'and was on the verge of bursting into tears'. According to Elias (1946:60), 'many, particularly civil servants, listened to this speech with tears in their eyes and fists clenched'.[29]

In the *Aanwijzingen* the government had said that civil servants should stay at their posts if the Japanese came. During the months of the invasion seventeen out of a total of about fivehundred colonial civil servants had been killed by the Japanese and nine by Indonesians. This had happened mainly on the Outer Islands, especially on Borneo. In practice there was little question of continuing to work on Borneo and the 'Grote Oost' ('Greater East', the islands east of Borneo): here all the Dutch were quickly interned, and this included civil servants and other government employees.[30] On Sumatra and Java, however, most officials were able to continue working for a while, but they faced great difficulties. There were hardly any means of communication with the administrative centres, and where such communication was re-established the colonial civil servants were often forbidden by the Japanese to use it. In some cases they were also forbidden to leave their station, and many others had their car seized. On South Sumatra a controller was told by the Japanese that he should stay at work as normal, but his car had been requisitioned, his telephone was cut off and he was not allowed to leave his home. Civil servants were often stripped of all their police and legal powers, and it was decided that not they but only the Indonesian administrative officials should be in contact with the Indonesian population. There was most

[29]   Drossaers later told his fellow prisoners that when he had finished he added only one word: 'forced'.
[30]   Most of the internees from the Grote Oost were brought together in camps near Makassar (Celebes) in the course of 1942 and 1943.

confusion where Indonesian Freedom Committees tried to take the place of both the Dutch and the Indonesian authorities. 'In addition,' writes C.G. Zijlmans in his account of the East Indies administration in 1940-1942 (which was based on information from over a hundred former colleagues), 'at various localities some of the Indonesian officials and ordinary people adopted a reserved or hostile attitude towards the colonial administration or avoided all contact with it'.[31]

Sometimes colonial civil servants were able to advise Indonesian rulers or offer them moral support if they were being hard pressed by the Freedom Committees. Zijlmans writes:

> Moreover, they were still generally in charge of the purchase, storage and distribution of the necessities of life. Where possible they went on paying salaries and advances from all kinds of sources and funds, and made sure that the various departments were continuing to perform their duties. [...] Those who were largely or entirely relieved from their duties [...] had as their main task to advise the Japanese authorities in a wide range of fields. The questions raised had to do with administration and food supply as well as financial, economic, topographical and ethnological matters. [...] In several cases the Japanese orders were only carried out by the civil servants after some hesitation, because the activities concerned could aid the Japanese war effort. They included supervising the repair of damaged bridges and ferries, protecting them from sabotage, providing equipment and labour and registering goods and equipment used for the transport and billeting of Japanese army units.[32]

One of the first matters the Japanese wanted to have arranged for these units was the setting up of brothels. This led to a serious incident on the afternoon of 14 March in Sukabumi (west of Bandung). In a police station there, in the presence of the controller, H. Jongbloed, a Japanese officer demanded that a Dutch inspector should turn a house into a brothel and assemble locally known prostitutes there. Jongbloed told the Japanese officer that the police could not do that 'because they are not pimps'.[33] A heated discussion followed and Jongbloed was pushed into a car and taken to a hotel where the local Japanese commander had his quarters. He was not there. A Japanese sergeant and a soldier then led Jongbloed away with his hands tied. As they came outside Jongbloed struck the soldier in the face with his tied hands. The soldier fell to the ground with a broken nose. Jongbloed took to his heels but the sergeant caught up with him and struck at his calves with a sword. This

31 C.G. Zijlmans, 'De Indische bestuursdienst 1940-1942', 1982, pp. 21-2 (NIOD IC).
32 C.G. Zijlmans, 'De Indische bestuursdienst 1940-1942', 1982, pp. 22-3 (NIOD IC).
33 Regeringscommissaris tot opsporing van oorlogsmisdadigers, proces-verbaal by W.F.D. van den Bijl, 10 September 1946, p. 3 (NIOD IC).

was followed by a blow to the neck before he finished him off with a revolver shot. The Japanese commander ordered that Jongbloed's body should be left where it was for three days with a sign on it saying in Indonesian: 'This is what happens to those who disobey Nippon'.[34] 'All day', (that is, on 15 March) according to the Dutch wife of an Ambonese soldier, 'the Indonesians paraded [...] past the body. [...] For us Dutch it was a terrible sight; our deepest feelings of compassion went out to the wife of the poor victim.'[35]

The chief of police of Sukabumi, with the support of the assistant resident and the regent, managed to persuade the Japanese commander to give permission in the course of the 15th for Jongbloed's body to be taken away in the evening.

In Sukabumi and elsewhere on Java there were persistent rumours that Jongbloed had refused to select Dutch and Dutch Eurasian women for a brothel for Japanese officers.[36]

In the first days of the Japanese occupation several arrests were made in Batavia. On 7 March the resident, two assistant residents, the burgomaster, the deputy burgomaster and the inspector of municipal finances were taken to prison; on 9 March they were followed by the Dutch police officers as well as the Dutch officers and some of the Dutch members of the Stadswacht or militia. On 10 March it was the turn of the department heads of the town hall and the heads of government departments and services. Some of the Dutch civil servants, particularly those left behind in Batavia when the core of the departments had been moved to Bandung in February as a precaution, remained at liberty and tried to carry on working as best they could. This situation soon ended for the European administrative and legal officers and for the officials and office staff of the Department of East Asian Affairs (whose main task was to advise the government on matters to do with the

---

[34]   M. Leatenua-van Os, 'Verslag', 27 May 1946, p. 3 (NIOD IC, 47,538).

[35]   M. Leatenua-van Os, 'Verslag', 27 May 1946, p. 3 (NIOD IC, 47,538).

[36]   There were a few cases of rape in Bandung on 9 March and the following days, but on the 14th three Japanese soldiers who tried to rape three Dutch girls on the highway were shot dead by one of their officers.

In this connection it should be added that in March or April 1942 in Surabaya a Dutch girl travelling with two Dutch boys got into trouble with some Japanese in the tram. She refused to stand up for a Japanese soldier who got on with other soldiers. Her handbag was knocked out of her hand, scattering the contents all over the tram. 'She stayed in her seat, white with fury. At the next stop', according to the account given by a Dutchman in Batavia, to whom she told the story shortly after it happened, 'two Japanese officers got on the tram. They saw immediately that something was going on and asked what was wrong. The Dutch boys explained in their schoolboy English what had happened. The officers rang the bell to stop the tram, grabbed the soldiers by the scruff of the neck and threw them off, meanwhile cursing and striking them. Then they helped to gather up the contents of the handbag and saluted the girl, saying "Sorry, so sorry" and "Excuse me please" in broken English.' (Van der Grift 1946:37.)

Chinese community, but which also played an important role in countering Japanese espionage in the East Indies). The former were interned on 14 March in Struiswijk Prison (followed on 15 and 16 March by all lecturers and all heads of European educational institutions). The latter were accused of working against the Japanese before the outbreak of war in the Pacific and imprisoned by the Kempeitai in the School of Law which they had commandeered. There the prisoners were interrogated and tortured. To a Dutchman working for the gas company who went into the School of Law ('for my work and to see what it was like'):

> the screams and cries behind the locked door made things plain enough. A Dutchman from East Asian Affairs who had been held by the Japanese for two days without food or drink whispered to me, 'If you know what's good for you, don't come back here'. (Van der Grift 1946:26.)

This was just the beginning.

At the end of March Imamura's staff issued a secret order that the Dutch and Dutch Eurasians should be kept on only in the lower ranks of government service and that all high-ranking public servants, including judges and police officers, and all other prominent figures among the Dutch and Dutch Eurasians must be imprisoned. In the course of April this order resulted in action being taken against these people throughout Java. Their internment was announced in the press on 23 April. The reason given was that, as an intercepted document showed, on 'Thursday 20 March 1942' (20 March in 1942 was in fact a Friday) members of the Removal and Demolition Corps had held discussions in Surabaya. The Japanese had either faked the date of the document or read it incorrectly: the meeting in question had taken place on 20 March 1941.

On Central Java the governor, M.F. Winkler, was taken to the prison in Semarang on 20 April and two days later he was followed by 500 to 600 Dutch and Dutch Eurasian detainees, who had been summoned to attend gatherings at the government offices and the club. Many distrusted this summons 'and of course went with fearful misgivings', wrote a Dutch woman next day in her diary (Boissevain and Van Empel 1981:33). Before they were taken away, those who had obeyed the Japanese summons were addressed by several members of the Fascist NSB who had been interned by the Dutch and released by the Japanese.

Another trick was used in the Kedu residency: here about threehundred people who were due to be arrested were told to report to Magelang (see Map 1) in order to make the acquaintance of the Japanese commander.

On East Java the schoolteachers among the Dutch and Dutch Eurasians were also arrested. On 22 April in Surabaya scores of Japanese soldiers stormed into the Court of Justice building. 'The judges and lawyers', wrote a police inspector present in court, 'were dragged out still in their robes' and ended up with other detainees in the prison in Werfstraat and the temporary prison Bubutan.[37] Of the others arrested, the administrative officers had been summoned to a meeting at the office of the governor, C.C.J. Hartevelt, and the police force had been told they would be taking an oath of loyalty to the Japanese at police headquarters. There was also a group from Jombang (which lies about 65 km west-southwest of Surabaya) who had had a difficult journey:

> Each passing lorry carrying internees was greeted by the local people with coarse insults and it would probably have come to blows had they not been restrained by fear of the Japanese soldiers.[38]

In Malang those detained, whose names were noted by the Japanese, had been told to attend a gathering at the Club; from there they were taken away.

In Surakarta special treatment was given to the governor, K.J.A. Orie, the European officials and high-ranking police officers, the doctor from the Public Health Department, the vet and two missionary doctors: they were ordered to come to a hotel on 25 April at noon. There those present, numbering about seventy, were offered 'an excellent lunch (with port)'. 'Various Japanese commandants (civilian, army, Kempeitai) made speeches'.[39] Afterwards the governor and his assistant residents were taken away by limousine, and the others by bus, to their first internment camp – a hospital where 'the first six weeks [...] were quite tolerable'.[40]

In Yogyakarta too the Japanese showed every respect. Here slightly over 80 people assembled at the house of the governor, L. Adam, on 23 April in response to a summons. They were received with drinks and sandwiches, after which a Japanese officer appeared and informed them that they were all to be interned. They were taken by lorry through the city, 'watched in dismayed silence by the inhabitants' according to one of the controllers,[41] to the prison. There 'the food was awful'[42] and concern grew because they heard that the Japanese had announced in the local press that before being interned some of those arrested had made plans for an uprising. Governor Adam was

---

[37]   F.L.A. Catoire, 'Verslag', 1 February 1947, p. 1 (ARA, Alg. Secr., Eerste zending, XXII, 45, 915).

[38]   A. van Leeuwen, 'Verslag', 7 November 1946, p. 5 (ARA, Alg. Secr., Eerste zending, XXII, 45, 690).

[39]   W.L. Klijn, 'Verslag', 15 April 1947, p. 3 (ARA, Alg. Secr., Eerste zending, XXII, 45, 502).

[40]   W.L. Klijn, 'Verslag', 15 April 1947, p. 3 (ARA, Alg. Secr., Eerste zending, XXII, 45, 502).

[41]   W.S. Schmoutziguer, 'Verslag', n.d., p. 1 (ARA, Alg. Secr., Eerste zending, XXII, 45, 170).

[42]   W.S. Schmoutziguer, 'Verslag', n.d., p. 1 (ARA, Alg. Secr., Eerste zending, XXII, 45, 170).

severely mistreated: the Kempeitai submitted him to the infamous water torture (his mouth and nose were filled with water until he almost suffocated)
and, according to another controller, his arms and face were 'beaten completely black'.[43] 'After each session,' said yet another controller, 'he always
walked [...] back to his cell with his head held high'.[44]

Not all those arrested in April were held for long. The women who had also
been picked up here and there, many Dutch Eurasian detainees and those
who had had a monthly salary of less than 300 guilders were released after a
while, sometimes after only two days. The civil servants among those freed
could not go back to work; they had to consider themselves dismissed. They
were not paid unemployment benefit. Other releases followed: officials from
the Post Office, from the railways and tramways and from the water boards
(the last because of the irrigation works in progress). The occupation authorities had discovered that they could not do without these people's experience
and expertise; they were required to resume work as 'ball boys', so-called
because of their white armband with a red ball on it.

How many people were detained in total is not known exactly, but there
were undoubtedly several thousand, many of whom left their family and
friends behind in anxiety.

As for the police, in April 1942 only the Dutch and Dutch Eurasians among
the higher ranks were arrested and many of the latter were subsequently
released. On 15 May they were dismissed and thus from one day to the next
they had no way of earning a living. Those Dutch Eurasians who had taught
at the Police School at Sukabumi had to go back to work, but two months
later, in mid-July, this came to an end as well.

The vacancies in the police forces were filled by Indonesians and the
Japanese strengthened the forces substantially; for example, they established
a police school in every residency.

It may be assumed that replacing the Dutch and Dutch Eurasian police
officers by Indonesians was no easy matter, but it was even more difficult to
replace the public prosecutors and judges.

On Java (and probably on the Outer Islands too, but we have no information about this) the administration of justice was greatly simplified. At the
end of April 1942 the occupation authorities issued an order stipulating that
all inhabitants, apart from the Japanese, would in future appear in the same
court and that, except for Islamic cases (the mullahs' courts and the Court
for Islamic Affairs were retained) and the Japanese military courts (more on

[43]   W.C. Schoevers, 'Verslag', 7 May 1947, p. 4 (ARA, Alg. Secr., Eerste zending, XXII, 45, 534).
[44]   C.J.S. Becht, 'Verslag', 4 March 1947, p. 3 (ARA, Alg. Secr., Eerste zending, XXII, 45, 525).

this in Chapter II), there would be only four kinds of court. These were, from higher to lower, the *Landraden*, the *Landgerechten*, the Regency Courts and the District Courts. The High Court, the Courts of Justice (there had been three on Java) and the Residency Courts were abolished. By the end of May some of the empty places in the judiciary had been filled by the appointment of sixty Indonesians to the higher courts – no more trained candidates were available. Thus courses to train public prosecutors, judges and clerks of the court were established on Java, but not until May 1943. Over fivehundred candidates applied – fifty were accepted.

The administration of justice was also simplified by the abolition of the right of appeal, which did not normally exist in Japan. This was done by ruling that a single piece of legal evidence, for example a confession (even if extracted under duress), was enough to secure a conviction and that in court only the rules that had previously applied for Indonesians and Foreign Orientals were valid. On Java the law of criminal procedure was thoroughly reformed. In mid-1944 the military administration introduced a new criminal code which made it much easier to hold suspects on remand and opened up the possibility of continuing to detain prisoners who had served their sentence. Obviously, all this was a grave infringement of the citizen's legal rights.

At the same time as the removal of European judges, the authority in whose name justice was administered was changed too. In the territory administered by the Japanese navy (all Indonesia except for Java, Madura and Sumatra), from the beginning all judgements were given 'In the name of the Greater Japanese Empire'. We have no information about Sumatra; on Java either no authority was named or the judgement was given 'In the name of the Commander of the Armed Forces of Greater Japan'. The old formula 'In the name of the Queen', which was used quite widely until late April 1942 (and even a little longer here and there), was prohibited. However, the paper shortage ensured that forms with the old heading continued to be used; it was simply crossed out.

Anti-Dutch campaigns

The Japanese regarded the Emperor's birthday, 29 April, as a specially significant date. They often aimed to have certain tasks completed by then, which could lead to orders being announced on that day. The celebration of the first Emperor's birthday since the start of the occupation appears to have received extra attention. This was also true on the Outer Islands, although only in the case of Java do we have detailed information.

There it was announced on 25 April that for three days – 28, 29 and 30 April – all the inhabitants must display the Japanese flag and that on 29 April they must take part in festive parades everywhere. The same announcement also stated that all symbols of Dutch rule had to be handed in at the offices of the Indonesian administration: Dutch flags, portraits of Queen Wilhelmina and members of the Royal Family, images bearing the words 'Nederland zal herrijzen' (The Netherlands will rise again), V-badges and the buttons with a W on them worn by officials. Furthermore, the names painted on all offices of the colonial administration were to be removed together with any metal or wooden nameplates.

To what extent the Dutch and Dutch Eurasians (and the wives of KNIL soldiers) complied with this order remains unknown. Those who feared betrayal and punishment probably obeyed; others did not. In Bandung, according to Elias, 'hardly anyone' complied: people hid the flag or separated the bands so that they were left with a red, a white and a blue strip. Portraits of the Queen and members of the Royal Family were concealed behind other framed pictures. Among those who held decorations (such awards were always published and, in the case of civil servants, could easily be checked in the annual publication *Regeeringsalmanak voor Nederlandsch-Indië*), according to Elias (1946:51), there were 'many who obeyed the Japanese order'. The decorations were handed in and on 29 April, at least in Bandung (it may have happened elsewhere as well), they were publicly burnt together with the flags and royal portraits. Again according to Elias (1946:61), those who watched the burning 'fortunately included very few of the Dutch population'.

Information on how many of the Dutch and Dutch Eurasians took part in the parades on 29 April is available for some places, but not all. In Magelang a Dutch woman watched with her children through the venetian blinds of her closed house and saw a 'spectacle that invited mockery as well as laughter, combined with a sense of unease because of the enthusiasm of the [indigenous] people'. 'The Dutch women [not all of them, it may be assumed] followed meekly at the back of the parade' (Helfferich-Koch 1981: 26). In Semarang about hundred pupils from a high school had to take part in the parade. 'We march slowly towards the school', wrote a teacher in her diary.

> There's a long wait and when the Nipponese officers are lined up outside one of them comes to tell us that we must turn towards them and then shout *Banzai!* three times. This we do, but the shouts of *Banzai!* come from the other side, not from us! We march on in good order. We file past the sentries and are photographed and filmed, all of us holding flags.[45]

It was the same in Bandung. 'Dutch children from Bandung took part in the

---

[45]   Quoted in I.J. Brugmans (ed.), *Nederlandsch-Indië onder Japanse bezetting; Gegevens en documenten over de jaren 1942-1945* (Franeker, 1960), p. 140 (referred to hereafter as Brugmans).

parade', noted Bouwer, 'but shouted *Bangsat!* (Scoundrel) instead of *Banzai!* when they marched past the Governor [that is, the military commandant] of West Java, who watched from the steps of the resident's house'. It took four hours for the whole parade to pass.

> The children were rewarded with half a currant bun and three biscuits. The cameramen from the Barisan Propaganda [the Japanese propaganda organization] shot hundreds of metres of film. Later these films will of course be shown in the Axis countries and Japan itself as proof of the spontaneous celebration of Hirohito's birthday on Java. In the afternoon the city was full of drunken Japanese. (Bouwer 1988:69-70.)

The following should be added: the controller of one of the subdivisions on Timor, W.E. Palstra, who had raised the Dutch flag alongside the Japanese flag on the Emperor's birthday, was beheaded by the Japanese. In March 1942 the same fate had already befallen a raja in Minahasa who refused to strike the Dutch flag (three of his followers were also killed) and in 1943 the Ambonese Izak Mawa, who had hidden a Dutch flag in his home in Palembang. In the same year the head of the NIROM radio station in Bandung, a certain Anderson, was beheaded for allegedly calling the Emperor a 'bastard' among other things on 29 April (which is why he was arrested more than six months later).[46] Orders corresponding to those issued on Java on 25 April were not announced on the Moluccas until September and November 1942. Subsequently, in June 1943 on the island of Saparua an Ambonese former KNIL soldier, Sahetapi, was beaten to death by the Japanese for refusing to remove a portrait of Queen Wilhelmina from his house. On the Moluccas (and probably in the Minahasa too) there were many cases of portraits of the Queen and Dutch flags being hidden by those who identified particularly strongly with the colonial authority.

Attempts to eradicate the memory of Dutch rule also took other forms. Dutch monuments were removed, among them in Batavia the statue of Jan Pieterszoon Coen and the memorial to Governor-General Van Heutz.[47] The monuments to the Battle of Waterloo and to the first radio link between the Netherlands and the East Indies also disappeared. Dutch street names were changed: in Batavia, for example, Van Heutz Boulevard became Djalan Imamoera (Imamura Road) and Oranje Boulevard became Djalan Raya Sjowa (Great Showa Road).[48] In Bandung, however, where the Japanese resident

---

[46]   Temporaire Krijgsraad (TKR, Temporary Court Martial) Batavia, Judgement in the matter of the Bandung Kempeitai, 19 April 1948, p. 47 (NIOD IC).
[47]   Up to then these monuments had been covered up by wooden planking or reed mats.
[48]   Emperor Hirohito's reign was known as *Showa* or 'Bright peace'.

was relatively moderate, such changes were not made until March 1945.[49]

The bans announced in April 1942 were later extended or supplemented. Early in 1943 it was made illegal to buy or sell articles incorporating the colours red, white and blue or orange, the V-sign, the coat of arms of the Netherlands or a Dutch or English trademark. The use in public of the Dutch or English language was also prohibited (we shall come back to this point); all Dutch or English signs on shops, cafés, restaurants and hotels disappeared in mid-1942 and were replaced by Japanese or Indonesian versions. This process was not completed overnight (early in 1943 several regents drew attention to the Japanese regulations by way of a warning) and was not always easy. In March 1943, for example, a competition was held for the best replacements in Indonesian for the English names of various brands of cigarettes and rolling tobacco.

All these attempts by the Japanese to root out the memory of Dutch rule were ineffective in 1942 if only because they were forced to keep in circulation the postage stamps with the image of Queen Wilhelmina and the silver money with her effigy.[50]

Pressure on the Dutch community

The presence of the Japanese put heavy pressure on the Dutch community from the outset. After only a month of occupation, they felt the effects of measures taken by the Japanese military administration, such as the switch to Tokyo time and to Japanese dating, the requirement to put out the Japanese flag and the obligation to bow to every Japanese sentry. Moreover, from the start Japanese policy was designed to drive home to the Dutch and Dutch Eurasians that the old colonial regime had gone for good. The numerous

---

[49]   Conversely, Japanese monuments were raised at five places on Java where important events had taken place between 1 and 8 March 1942. The officers' quarters at Kalijati airfield where the capitulation talks had been held on 8 and 9 March were restored to their original state in 1943. In Villa Isola near Bandung, which had been the advance headquarters of General Pesman, commander of the Bandung Group, a war museum was opened on 8 December 1943 (the second anniversary of Pearl Harbor). The exhibits included the official uniform of Governor-General Van Starkenborgh and the uniform of the army commander, General Ter Poorten. In 1942 the Japanese had put up posters at many places with a photo of the 'second' capitulation meeting at Kalijati, that of the morning of Monday 9 March 1942. It was at this meeting that Ter Poorten gave the Japanese commander Imamura precise details of the numbers and location of Dutch troops and their weapons (see Introduction, p. 39).

[50]   *Dai Nippon* was printed on the stamps; it was not until March 1943 that new stamps printed in Japan were issued. The silver coins were never withdrawn from circulation, but they disappeared because they were hoarded and because the Japanese tried to gather them in (more on this in Chapter III).

arrests of prominent figures in Batavia in the first ten days of the occupation caused great concern. They were not known about outside Batavia for some time: communications were disrupted, permission to travel was rarely granted, there was no postal service and the press was silent about the first wave of arrests. The same was true of the arrests made later in March in Bandung. Of all the East Indies newspapers on Java, only one was given permission to carry on publishing in Dutch: the *Soerabaiasch Handelsblad* (in May it was printed partly in Dutch and partly in Indonesian, but in mid-June the Dutch section was dropped). Copies of this paper reached other districts on Java only rarely and after some delay. The Dutch and Dutch Eurasians were reliant on the Indonesian press and many of them, especially the former, found it difficult to follow the specific form of Indonesian used in the newspapers. It was different from the *pasar* Malay ('market' or simplified Malay used by the Dutch in their everyday dealings with Indonesians, for example at the market) of which many had some command. Another obstacle was that when the postal service on Java resumed in May, only postcards written in Japanese or Indonesian could be sent.

For the Dutch and Dutch Eurasians there was another important change when, after a few days of uncertainty, all schools were closed. When the Japanese military administration on Java granted permission at the end of April for schools to reopen, the European schools were excluded. So the children had to stay at home. But a solution was soon found. Clandestine education began, despite the objections expressed by some who regarded it as a dangerous provocation of the Japanese. The teachers who made themselves available (generally women, because most of the men were prisoners of war) received small groups of pupils in their own house or that of the parents. Despite all the difficulties (many families had got rid of or burned Dutch teaching materials when the Japanese arrived or soon after), education continued. 'It was quite exciting, because of course it was forbidden', wrote one girl at a clandestine 'primary school' in Surabaya (Vermeer-van Berkum 1980:13). Another wrote:

> We were taught by Miss Jansse, our teacher from the third form. [...] We went to her twice a week, always at a different time so we wouldn't be noticed. We didn't carry a satchel but put our books and exercise books in a shopping bag. We were never caught. (Thomson 1965:19.)

Here and there this clandestine education acquired a clear structure: in Malang, for example (and possibly elsewhere), a clandestine high school developed, and in Surabaya a school which had begun with education only for the first and second class added higher secondary classes later in 1942, a secondary girls' school and a pre-university class. All the normal subjects were taught except for gym and drawing, and there were not enough teachers for history. According to the postwar account of one teacher, 'fear was the reason' why not every history teacher dared to resume giving lessons.[51]

If clandestine schools were also set up in the Outer Islands, Dutch pupils cannot have attended them for long since they were interned after only a few weeks. On Java internment of Dutch women and children did not begin until the end of 1942 – after that the children could only get clandestine education in the camps. The education organized in Surabaya stopped in January 1943; the 'high school' in Malang was disbanded about the same time for fear that the Kempeitai was about to intervene. As for the Dutch Eurasian children, it is reasonable to assume that teachers from this group carried on with clandestine lessons here and there, but no further details are available.

It may also be assumed that in 1942, and later, the teachers who provided European education outside the camps generally received some form of compensation, whether in kind or in money. School fees were requested for the higher classes in Surabaya. According to the teacher's account already quoted:

> We made five guilders per month the norm, but we left it to the parents to decide whether they could afford this amount. The idea was to pay each [teacher] two guilders per month per weekly lesson. So someone giving 30 lessons a week would receive 60 guilders. That was not much compared with salaries in the past […] but it was more than enough to live on.[52]

That meant that each month the teachers received the money they needed to buy food at the *pasar* or markets. Other purchases were impossible. It is worth noting that some of the parents could no longer spare five guilders a month. This indicates the financial difficulties in which many of the Dutch and Dutch Eurasians soon found themselves.

For some of the Dutch and Eurasians these problems did not yet arise in March and April because at the end of February the colonial government decided to pay out two months' salary in addition to the salary for that month – an example that was followed by many European companies. Those who were paid cash could manage for a while, but this did not apply to those who had their salary paid into a bank account or who received a postal order, since in all the areas that came under the Japanese military administration the banks were closed and postal orders could not be cashed.

In April the problems for government employees and pensioners became acute. All payments stopped on 1 April. Dutch departments which still had sufficient cash were not allowed to make any payments. As a consequence

---

51   'Verslag', 6 January 1946, in Brugmans 1960:319.
52   'Verslag', 6 January 1946, in Brugmans 1960:320.

government employees now received nothing at all, nor did the wives of those who had been mobilized in December 1941 (on Java this had happened to about 20,000 men on leave); many of these women had received no money since the mobilization because of various delays in the military administration.[53] Then there were the pensioners. The East Indies had about 86,000 of them living alone or with their families who had to manage on a government pension. Another 40,000, including over 20,000 Indonesians, received a civil pension averaging 1,000 guilders a year, and 46,000 had a military pension – about 30,000 of these were retired KNIL soldiers who were paid slightly less than 600 guilders a year. It was announced at the beginning of April that none of these pensions would be paid in future. This created so much alarm that the Japanese military administration on Java, where the great majority of pensioners lived, announced on 8 April that pensioners need not be concerned. These were empty words: the payment of pensions was not resumed, not even after pensioners were required to register.

On 15 March the Japanese military administration on Java let it be known that from 1 April Japanese pay scales had to be applied and that, consequently, no one would be allowed to receive a monthly salary higher than 500 guilders (at the same time rents were lowered – the lowest by 25% and the highest by 50%). On average the Japanese pay scales represented a cut of over a third; it should also be borne in mind that in March and April there were substantial rises in prices at the *pasar* on Java where the daily shopping had to be done (more often than in the past because some of the street traders now avoided the houses of the Dutch and Eurasians).

These measures meant that virtually all the Dutch and Dutch Eurasian families found themselves in financial difficulties and in many cases in dire need as early as April. Some families were already dependent on various forms of clandestine or open help (we shall come back to this point at the end of this chapter); others tried to cope on their own. Many started small businesses: a controller in Bandung, who simply stayed away from work from 9 March, set up a transport company at the end of that month together with someone who knew about horses. By the time he was interned in early December it had grown to be the largest transport business in the vicinity. 'In my heyday', he wrote after the war, 'I had three hundred [Indonesian] employees and six European assistants'. There were days when 'I was work-

---

[53]   In Surabaya the Japanese civilian governor (who had worked there for a long time) permitted the payment of monthly salaries up to 300 guilders. With his agreement, Dutch civil servants borrowed money from the cash funds of East Java province, above all to pay the wages of the coolies who had been sent to Cilacap in December 1941 and who had returned to Surabaya after the surrender. In Cilacap they had received only a small part of the wages promised. Overtime was not paid for in Surabaya either; this led to fierce protests.

ing with over a hundred rented wagons'.[54]

The assistant resident of Bandung, a Eurasian who was released after being arrested in April, got in touch with a nearby plantation where coffee and quinine were grown and which had a dairy and about 30 cows. He was made the manager and was able to employ two controllers who had been dismissed. Shortly afterwards the Japanese appointed him Head of Disease Prevention at Garut on a salary of 500 guilders a month.[55] He hoped to use this salary in the first place to assist 'the many wives of civil servants who were stranded here in Bandung and had no source of income', but in practice he was able to do little. Instead of 500 guilders he was paid 200 (it was only in August 1943 that this became the official maximum salary for all employees). In Batavia a dismissed police inspector set up a business making rubber shoes that were sold by Indonesian helpers. Others took to the streets themselves. 'Court officials', says Elias (1946:47), 'sell medicines door to door. Civil servants from the Internal Administration peddle charcoal and cornflour.'

No doubt there were many other men who undertook some activity that would produce an income. Many women did the same, taking up sewing or cooking delicacies. 'Many', again according to Elias, 'manage to earn a little by selling home-made *sambal* [hot dishes made from peppers], jams and fondant. Others go round the houses with an entire grocer's shop on their bicycles.' What a transformation! 'In the Indies, where there used to be no European peddlers, we now get ten or twenty women, boys and small children coming into the garden selling things every day' (Elias 1946:73).

Those who could not raise enough money to live on began by selling their possessions, initially surplus clothing or household items. A woman living in Malang who was married to a Dutch Eurasian and had been a teacher at the Commercial School wrote:

> Our little bit of money disappeared like snow in the sun. [...] We began selling clothing; they were good clothes like evening gowns and lovely afternoon dresses that we didn't wear any more. Natives went round the houses buying up everything, cheaply of course, before reselling them at high prices. They earned a living this way; there were no more jobs to be had with Europeans. We were the losers, because we were horribly swindled. The native buyers knew very well, of course, that the women left behind with no husband and no job needed the money.
>
> But you learn through experience. At first we were glad of a few guilders for a whole pile of clothes. Later [...] we became more critical and sent a buyer away if his offer was too low. Sometimes there wasn't a cent in the house; then you watched him go with fear in your heart and you were deeply relieved when he came back and offered a bit more.
>
> [...] In the end this bargaining and haggling became our daily occupation. (Moscou-de Ruyter 1984:30.)

---

[54]   A.F. Holm, 'Verslag', 10 April 1947, p. 1 (ARA, Alg. Secr., Eerste zending, XXII, 45, 194).
[55]   L. Croes, 'Verslag', 1 May 1947, p. 2 (ARA, Alg. Secr., Eerste zending, XXII, 45, 249).

To keep costs down, many women switched from expensive European cuis-
ine to cheaper indigenous food and moved in with each other, which always
saved a substantial amount. But, according to the journalist W.C. Donraadt,
who lived in Surabaya, in his postwar account based partly on diaries, 'the
weak characters couldn't cope; they were ruined or resorted to prostitution
[...]. This exploitation of women was completely open. Brothels sprang up
like mushrooms.'[56] Donraadt pointed out that there were also brothels with
Japanese prostitutes and that 'for many' in the other brothels it was not a new
profession.

In Magelang (Central Java) the situation was similar. A young Dutch
Eurasian soldier who had escaped from captivity in March later wrote:

> The occupation was less than four months old [that takes us to the end of June
> 1942], but most families with the men in camps were already in want.
>   [...] On my evening stroll through the town I became ever more aware of how
> young girls were working in canteens that were only open to Japanese soldiers.
> After closing time they were picked up by military cars and then spent the night
> with some Japanese officer. It was awful and my blood boiled over. (Jalhay 1981:
> 136.)

In Batavia, according to a Dutch Eurasian man who escaped from Java in late
September 1942 and managed to reach Australia, 'the dance halls were packed
with Japanese officers and European women'. Eurasian musicians playing in
a jazz band in a large dance hall located in a street full of brothels told him
that the prostitutes working there were paid ten guilders a day plus ten guilders for every guest they took to their room. In his report he put 'the emphasis
on the fact that the sole cause for this prostitution by European women was
lack of money and hunger'. Nonetheless, the Indonesians found it offensive:
'as a result the prestige of the Europeans has fallen to almost zero'.[57]

It should be added that, if there was 'new prostitution' born of need alongside the existing prostitution before the Japanese invasion, the statements
quoted are no guide to its extent. We are inclined to believe that the 'new
prostitution' was limited, and there are two pieces of evidence for this. First,
in 1943 the Japanese opened a brothel in Batavia where the women came from
one of the camps for women and children, not from the part of the population
who were 'at liberty'. Second, they took girls from several camps on Central
Java and forced them into prostitution – more on this in Chapter V.

As stated, banks throughout the East Indies were closed by the Japanese. On
Java they went further. On the very first day of the occupation of Bandung,

---

[56] W.C. Donraadt, 'Dagboek', uittreksel, n.d., p. 8 (NIOD IC, dagboek 42).
[57] H.J. de Haas, 'Verslag', 19 January 1943, p. 5 (ARA, Alg. Secr., Eerste zending, XXIII, 56-1).

9 March, the managements of the Dutch and other Western banks operating in the Indies, which had moved their headquarters to that city at the end of February at the request of the colonial government, were summoned by the Japanese military commander and forced to sign statements whereby they transferred the assets of their banks to the Japanese army. Early in April it was announced that all these institutions would be liquidated and that their functions would be taken over by three Japanese banks: the Yokohama Specie Bank, the Bank of Taiwan and the Mitsui Bank. These and other banks were to operate in the whole Nampo area (the South Pacific) and would be under the supervision of a new institution founded in Tokyo, the Nampo Kaihatsu Kinko or Treasury for the Exploitation of the Nampo countries. It was this Japanese government bank that took over the role of the Javasche Bank in the East Indies (except for the area administered by the navy, where the Taiwan Bank had this role). It became the note-issuing bank, providing loans to the Japanese military administrations, the Japanese armed forces and Japanese companies in the Indies, supervising the activities of the other Japanese banks and controlling foreign exchange dealings in the Indies and between the Indies and the rest of the Japanese Empire.

The bank moratorium remained in force until 20 October 1942. On that date an order was issued on Java that allowed bank operations to resume but at the same time stipulated that the four Dutch banks (the Javasche Bank, the Nederlandsche Handelmaatschappij, the Nederlandsch-Indische Handelsbank and the Nederlandsch-Indische Escompto-Maatschappij), three Chinese banks and two English banks were to be dissolved and should begin settling their debts and claims. The liquidation of the Javasche Bank did not mean that the notes issued by the bank were of no value; they remained in circulation.

A short time later a similar decision was taken with regard to eight savings and mortgage banks. However, the two financial institutions founded by the colonial government, which had been used almost exclusively by Indonesians – the Algemeene Volkscredietbank and the Gouvernements Pandhuisdienst – were allowed to continue their activities through their numerous local branches.

The Japanese liquidators of the dissolved banks concentrated on recovering the outstanding claims. Of course, nothing could be obtained from those in internment, but the Chinese and Arabs, who could carry on their businesses, came under great pressure to pay off their overdrafts. This was not an unattractive proposition: debts in guilders could be paid with Japanese notes with a nominal value that was far too high (the yen had been worth 44 Dutch cents in international trading before the war, but in October 1942 it was made equivalent to one guilder). In 1944 and 1945 many came to realize that after the war these notes would not be worth the paper they were printed on. So much money flooded into the Nampo bank that in the second half of 1943 a first liquidation payment of 30% could be made to all those who had claims on the banks that had been closed down, for example in the form of bank balances. These payments were made only to Indonesian, Chinese, Arab and other non-hostile natural and legal persons, and taxes owed were deducted. Dutch claimants received nothing; on the contrary, they suffered because part of the valuables they had given to the banks for safe keeping, such as jewellery, gold and silver objects and table silver, was sold at auction at very low prices. 'Fortunately', wrote H.J. Manschot, president of the resurrected Javasche Bank, after the war, 'the liquidators turned out not to have the slightest interest in shares, so that the share holdings of the East Indies, which were entirely concentrated in the War Vault in the Javasche Bank in Bandung, remained intact.'[58]

After the war it was found that the Japanese on Java had confiscated over 52 million guilders in cash from the 17 liquidated banks (they charged over one million guilders for the costs of liquidation), and that the amount of the first liquidation payment had been about the same as the repayments of debts to the banks, so that the balance on the liquidation account at the Nampo bank was not much lower than the amount of cash confiscated, namely just over 51 million guilders. Manschot concluded:

> To the extent that one can speak of a good side to the liquidation of the banks, it should be pointed out that it gave the Japanese an interest in preserving the banks' records and archives. In view of what happened to the files of the shipping, oil and other large companies, this was undoubtedly what saved this valuable material.

The records and archives of the other European companies had been destroyed, lost or left in chaos.

The mere fact that most communications were disrupted meant that the Dutch export and wholesale businesses had little to do in the first phase of the occupation, and they were further hindered by the closure of the banks. At various concerns stocks of goods were seized by Japanese army units – the companies were told that they could submit a bill to the military administration. The Nederlandsch-Indische Vereeniging van Importeurs – Groothandelaren (NIVIG, Dutch East Indies Association of Importers and Wholesalers) made an effort to see that these bills were paid – with little success. A circular issued by the Association in early May (which had to be distributed by messenger since the post office was still not working) warned that:

> We have enquired about the possibility of payment for the goods taken by the army

---

[58]   H.J. Manschot in *Economisch Weekblad voor Nederlandsch-Indië*, 16 March 1946.

authorities. The answer received was that by way of exception invoices from small firms for sums that are not too high will be paid. But in general importers should not count on receiving payment for their deliveries to the Japanese authorities.[59]

About a week after this circular was issued, Dutch importers and wholesalers in Batavia were told to come to the Internatio (Internationale Krediet- en Handelsvereniging Rotterdam) building on 18 May at 3 pm and to bring all the keys to their warehouses. The deputy manager of the trading company Jacobson-Van den Berg, C.D. Ricardo, later recalled:

> Once a great crowd of importers had assembled, standing in a semicircle in front of a table, two Japanese sat down at the table (the importers had to remain standing) and read out a sort of proclamation in Japanese; one of the Japanese gave a translation in very poor English. The gist of it was (insofar as it was intelligible) that these two Japanese announced that they had been appointed Nippon administrators, that they were taking over all goods (which was why all the keys had to be handed in) and that in future they were the boss. Anyone who did not follow their instructions exactly or did something without their knowledge would suffer the severest consequences.[60]

The Dutch import and wholesale businesses had thus lost their stocks. In some cases cash and office furniture was also confiscated, and all were told to cease collecting payments. 'The scant information we have', noted Ricardo in October 1942, 'suggests that the situation at our other branches [Jacobson van den Berg had offices on the Outer Islands] is if possible even more dismal than in Batavia. We have no reports from Medan, Padang or Manado – just a telegram from Medan, from a British associate, saying that our people are in good health.'[61] Cash, goods and claims on third parties were also seized from European small businesses, government concerns and private individuals. The Japanese usually sold the goods. A card index system they maintained reveals that, apart from what had happened to the banks, on Java and Madura alone they had confiscated 12 million guilders in cash, collected 25 million in payments due and sold goods for 94 million; another 12 million was also received for which they could specify no source.

It all amounted to theft on a vast scale.

From the beginning of the eighteenth century to about 1820 large areas of land on Java, mainly in the region south of Batavia, had been sold to private buyers: to the Dutch and other Europeans, and often to wealthy Chinese

---

[59]   Circular, 7 May 1942, quoted in 'Aantekeningen 1942' by C.D. Ricardo, Brugmans 1960:271.
[60]   Circular, 7 May 1942, quoted in 'Aantekeningen 1942' by C.D. Ricardo, Brugmans 1960:271.
[61]   C.D. Ricardo, 'Aantekeningen 1942', p. 24 (NIOD IC, 29,422).

and sometimes to wealthy Indonesians. In 1915 there were nearly 600 of these private estates, with a total population of almost two million. Many of the owners had put the Indonesians who lived and worked on their estates under great pressure. Starting in 1906, the colonial government began buying estates back, and each family farming and living there was granted the hereditary right of possession of a piece of land. By 1940 more than half of the private estates had been liquidated (the owners received a total of 92 million guilders), but the nationalists and the Indonesian press continued to complain about conditions on the remainder; there were frequent calls for the government to expropriate them too. But no funds were available.

The Japanese military administration on Java chose a simple solution: on 1 June 1942 an order was issued by which all private estates, except for those owned by Indonesians, were expropriated without payment or compensation. The new owner was the Japanese army. The army entrusted the management to a Japanese syndicate, which in turn made the previous owners, provided they had not been interned, responsible for the day-to-day running of the estates. Although corvée (unpaid labour which, unlike in the rest of Java, had been retained on the private estates to its full extent) was officially abolished early in 1943, the lot of the Indonesians in these areas did not improve. At the end of July 1942 an Indonesian reported to the Japanese military administration that:

> In most cases the former owners and their staff [the overseers] are still in charge. In theory they are no longer landowners, but in fact they have the same power over the people as before [...]. This enables them to continue their scandalous practices against the people. It is said that this has even got worse. The officials [...] threaten anyone who dares to criticize their abuses by saying 'You're anti-Nippon'. They let it be known that they now represent the Nippon army administration.[62]

Did relations on the private estates improve later? We do not know, nor do we know the total amount of profit generated by the sale of products grown on the estates and handed over to the Japanese syndicate set up by the army.

The whole course of events was a sad blow not only for the former owners of the private estates but also for the farmers and Indonesian nationalists involved: they were disappointed in their expectation that the Japanese would put an end to an abuse – instead, a worse abuse took its place.

In May the military administration on Java came to the conclusion that it would not receive enough money to pay for all the expenditure it planned up to 1 April 1943 (the Japanese financial year began on 1 April). The simplest solution was to print more military bank notes to cover the deficit, but that

---

[62]   Report, end of July 1942, in Brugmans 1960:494.

would lead to inflation. It was therefore decided to add a second levy to the first one already imposed on non-Indonesians living on Java (they had to pay for the identity cards that would be issued to them – more on this below). The extra levy was expected to raise 50 million guilders.

The second levy was announced in mid-July. The Dutch, Eurasians and other Europeans (except for citizens of states allied to Japan) who owned capital of 25,000 guilders or more would have to pay an additional amount of seventytimes the tax assessed on them for 1941 or, if they had earned 3,000 guilders or more a year, half the tax assessed for 1941. All Foreign Orientals would have to pay half as much: thus, thirty-five times the wealth tax assessment or a quarter of the income tax assessment. Payment could be made in rice (this was important for wealthy Chinese who owned a rice-husking plant or a wholesale business). The tax demand had to be paid within two months of receipt – the first demands were delivered at about the same time as the announcement. 'Some of the amounts', noted Bouwer in Bandung on 18 July, 'are as high as 22,000 guilders or more. Of course, there isn't the slightest chance that the Japanese will collect this money.' (Bouwer 1988:107.) Nonetheless, they certainly did their best.

In 1939 (we have no later figures for the various groups) 56% of the Europeans and 21% of the Foreign Orientals had a net income of over 3,000 guilders. It is fair to assume – given the improved economic situation since then – that by 1941 these percentages were higher. The extra levy might then have applied to about 60% of Europeans and 25% of Foreign Orientals. Some of these taxpayers were experiencing difficulties because of the closure of banks, and the Europeans had also been affected by the non-payment of pensions, the salary cuts and the fact that European business and commerce was grinding to a halt. Moreover, most of the European breadwinners were in captivity. The Japanese assumed that many taxpayers (or the wives acting for them) did not have enough cash to pay the extra levy, and so they announced that those in this position could take out a mortgage on their property with a Japanese bank.

In Batavia the Indonesian tax officials, who had kept their jobs, got to work. According to a post-war account,

> they carried out searches, rummaging in cupboards, handbags, purses and so on. When arranging a settlement at the tax office, the European wife left on her own was subjected to rude or humiliating treatment. The standard answers at the tax office were 'Nippon wants it that way' or 'Otherwise Nippon will grab it' or 'Otherwise we shall be forced to bring in the Kempeitai'.[63]

How much was raised through the extra levies is not known. Some people

---

[63]   Klerks, 'Verslag inzake het *relief*-werk te Batavia', n.d., p. 1 (NIOD IC, 52).

were allowed to delay payment, but not beyond 31 December 1942. 'I'm curious to see', noted Bouwer (1988:151) on that day, 'what the Japanese will
do now. According to Indonesian sources [Bouwer was in touch directly or
indirectly with indigenous reporters], less than 2% has come in. The majority of the European taxpayers [nearly all the Dutch and a small number of
the Dutch Eurasians who were not prisoners of war] are now held in the
concentration camps [internment camps]. Consequently, everyone else's tax
administration is in a mess. So no one who is still free is about to pay.'

It seems indeed likely that the Japanese were only able to collect part of the
extra levies. They did, however, obtain most of the fees charged for identity
cards.

Registration

On the Outer Islands registration of non-Indonesians was not made compulsory, but it was on Java. It was announced in the press there on 11
April 1942: Ordinance No. 7 issued by the Japanese commander-in-chief,
Imamura,[64] stipulated that all Europeans and Foreign Orientals aged 17 and
older had to report to the town hall to sign a declaration of obedience to the
Japanese army and receive a registration certificate, known as a *pendaftaran*
(referred to hereafter as an 'identity card' on the analogy of the registration
certificate issued in the occupied Netherlands in 1941). They had to bring a
photo that could be put on the identity card. The declaration of obedience
was in Indonesian and read: 'With a sincere heart I swear complete loyalty
and submit myself entirely to all orders by the Japanese army' (Van Velden
1963:78). Registration appeared to have a positive side: Artcle 4 of Ordinance
No. 7 stated that, 'Those who do not register and do not swear loyalty to the
Japanese army will have no protection of their social position or life'. So if
one did register, there would be this protection, it seemed. This impression
was strengthened by the fact that one had to pay to register: 150 guilders for
each European man, 80 guilders for each European woman, 100 guilders for
each Foreign Oriental man and 50 guilders for each Foreign Oriental woman.
Citizens of states allied to Japan were also obliged to register, but they did
not have to pay for the identity card.[65]
    Once filled in, the identity card contained an awkward abundance of

---

[64]   Text in D. van Velden, *De Japanse interneringskampen voor burgers gedurende de Tweede
Wereldoorlog* (Groningen, 1963), p. 549 (referred to hereafter as Van Velden).
[65]   In May 1943 this obligation was also applied to Indonesian women married to non-
Indonesian men.

information: under A the number of the card in the place where it was issued; under B name, age and sex; under C address; under D 'national origin' (for example, 'Dutch', 'German', 'Chinese', 'Arab'), place of birth and racial classification (we shall return to this point); under E occupation (in the case of married women, husband's occupation); under F length of time spent in the Indies; under G marital status and number of children and their sex. On the right side of the card were the photo, a thumbprint and a space for noting payments towards the registration fee, all one beneath the other.

Our general impression is that most of the Dutch and Eurasians were not unduly concerned about being required to 'swear loyalty', in part because there was no question of actually taking an oath. Many viewed the promise of obedience as in accordance with the general directions of the colonial authorities to continue working under occupation and not undertake acts of violence against the occupiers. Others thought that any means of deceiving the occupiers was permissible. In Batavia the journalist W.C.J. Bastiaans heard that the Reformed minister had said that 'in a time of lies and deception one is allowed to repay the occupier in his own coin'.[66]

In the second half of April the newspapers reported that the registration fee had to be paid before 10 May. For many that was impossible, and it was agreed that it could be paid in up to ten instalments. For this a thumbprint had to be given and two witnesses had to do the same. However, large trading companies (and we assume Chinese businesses) also sometimes paid the fee for their employees. 'Thus in May', says Elias (1946:49), 'one sees a long queue of people wanting to pay in front of the town hall [in this case, in Bandung]. They are crowded together between lattice fences. The slowly shuffling throng is like a flock of sheep in the hands of the shearer.'

How many of the Dutch and Dutch Eurasians on Java (and Madura) had to register is not known exactly: around 100,000 seems a likely figure and most of those would have been women since so many men were prisoners of war. It is possible that the Japanese counted on receiving about 10 million guilders in registration fees from the Dutch and Dutch Eurasians and about 35 million guilders from the Foreign Orientals (Chinese, Arabs, Indians).

How much they actually received is unknown. According to Bouwer, in Bandung in November 1942:

A serious fraud involving registration fees came to light [...]. Indonesian registration 'officials' have channelled large sums into their own pockets. It is not clear how much has been stolen, but an Indonesian police inspector put the figure at 'around 100,000 guilders.' As a matter of fact, I saw for myself during the registration how sloppily the money was handled. No record was kept of the amounts received. There were no cash registers or strongboxes. The money usually disap-

---

[66]   W.C.J. Bastiaans, 'Verslag', n.d., p. 5 (NIOD IC, 80,230 I).

peared into a drawer in a desk or table, or sometimes into a wastepaper basket beside the 'official'. (Bouwer 1988:140.)

Less than a week later he noted:

> It has now emerged that there are a lot of false registration cards in the hands of 'foreigners' which were forged, complete with all the stamps and thumbprints, by various Chinese and Eurasians for the trifling amount of 15 guilders. (Bouwer 1988:141.)

Assuming that Bandung was not an exception in either regard (the corruption or the forging of identity cards), it is clear that not all who were obliged to do so actually registered, and that only part of the money paid in registration fees reached the occupying forces. At the end of August a newspaper in Malang reported that over 15,000 foreigners had registered there and that more than 700,000 guilders had been received, 'whereas', wrote Bouwer, 'allowing for 100 guilders per "foreigner" [rather high as an average in our view], the takings should have been over 1.5 million' (Bouwer 1988:117-8).

As said, the identity card also had to show the racial classification. The Dutch born in the Netherlands, the so-called *totok*, were generally registered as *Belanda-totok* – the same happened in Batavia (and possibly elsewhere, but definitely not everywhere) with the Dutch-born Eurasians, 'even if', according to Bastiaans, 'you were black as coal'.[67] Conversely, in Semarang and Cirebon (and perhaps elsewhere but certainly not everywhere) the rule was that 'if you were born in the Indies', noted a Dutch woman, 'you are *Belanda-Indo*, even if you haven't any Indonesian blood. Everyone is wondering what to do for the best: let it go or try to have it changed.' (Boissevain and Van Empel 1981:42.) This question became more pressing later in 1942 when internment started; we shall come back to this point. Suffice it to say here that determining the racial classification was a highly arbitrary affair: the official at the desk often made a decision which was simply accepted; equally, he could often be misled because it was practically impossible to verify the information given. A full-blooded Dutchman could be registered as *Belanda-Indo* if he claimed to have been born of an Indonesian mother somewhere in the Outer Islands. When asked where he got his blue eyes, it was enough to answer, 'That's a freak of nature'.[68]

From the date of issue (this took several months) one was obliged to carry the identity card everywhere. In Batavia there were frequent checks; according to Bastiaans they were 'rigorous and ill-mannered'. If the card had been left at home or not yet collected, there followed 'heavy-handed punishment

[67] W.C.J. Bastiaans, 'Verslag', n.d., p. 5 (NIOD IC, 80, 230 I).
[68] F. de Rochemont, 15 June 1982.

and detention. All by Indonesians' (that is, the indigenous police). 'Nippon is watching'.[69]

Raids

There were many among the Dutch and Dutch Eurasians who believed on the grounds of Article 4 of the registration ordinance of 11 April that receiving an identity card and above all the solemn promise, confirmed by a thumbprint, to strictly obey the orders of the Japanese army guaranteed that they would be left alone. Nothing was further from the truth: it was precisely during the months in which identity cards were being issued that raids took place on Java in which many Dutch men were arrested.

This began in Batavia on 11 May, that is, a day after the deadline for paying the fees prior to the issuing of identity cards. According to Ricardo, 'almost three quarters of the male European population' had complied with this obligation by then.[70] Not that that made any difference. In the early hours of the 11th, the largest European district was cordoned off by Indonesian police. The same observer noted:

> If you wanted to enter the districts that were closed off, you were curtly advised to go home and stay there. In the districts ripe for plundering, where these had not already been worked over, you could admire the indigenous policemen at their bravest and best. With their *klewang* (sabres) raised menacingly and revolvers drawn, with fiercely gleaming teeth and flashing eyes, they forced their way into the homes of peaceful citizens and demanded to know where the 'men' were.[71]

Their orders were to arrest all Dutch men (but not Eurasians) between the ages of 17 and 60. Those arrested had to pack their bags and were then taken in groups to police headquarters. 'The indigenous population took a keen interest [...]. Layabouts young and old loudly expressed their approval at the arrest of the *Belandas*.'[72]

That morning around 600 Dutch men and youths were picked up. The Japanese thought that was too few and in the afternoon they:

> gave a demonstration of how to round up Europeans. On the streets all men with a white skin were pulled off their bicycles and loaded into lorries. The bikes were given to passing Indonesians to do with them as they pleased. No account was

---

[69] W.C.J. Bastiaans, 'Verslag', n.d., p. 5 (NIOD IC, 80,230 I).
[70] C.D. Ricardo, 'De inpikkerij', 21 October 1942, p. 2 (NIOD IC, 30,931).
[71] C.D. Ricardo, 'De inpikkerij', 21 October 1942, p. 2 (NIOD IC, 30,931).
[72] C.D. Ricardo, 'De inpikkerij', 21 October 1942, p. 2 (NIOD IC, 30,931).

taken of age. Boys of 14 stood next to greybeards long past 80. It was as if a vast comb had been dragged through the European district.[73]

This raid was not based on any general Japanese order. Imamura did not issue such an order until 17 May: with the exception of those who were still at work in their old jobs (the 'ball boys', so-called because of their white arm-bands with a red ball), all Dutch men between the ages of 17 and 60 were to be arrested throughout Java.

As a result of this order, in the last week of May there were big round-ups in Batavia and elsewhere on Java. The men were picked up on the street or taken from their houses. Whole districts were searched and sometimes addresses were obtained from telephone directories. In this way between 11 May and the end of the month about 3,000 Dutch men were detained in Batavia. They were held in the Struiswijk and Bukit Duri prisons and in the camp of the Algemeen Delisch Immigratie Kantoor, the Adek camp, where in the past the indigenous labourers bound for the plantations in Deli (eastern Sumatra) to work as coolies had been assembled.

In June the raids continued, in Batavia too. There, according to Ricardo:

> it became a kind of game to stay out of the hands of the police. When a policeman approached, the men who were still free disappeared through the windows or over the walls into other houses or hid themselves. Others dressed as women, taking care to cover up their hairy calves with stockings and to wear a wig obtained from some coiffeur over their short back and sides. Rouge and lipstick were even used to make the transformation from man into woman as convincing as possible. Yet every day it became more difficult to stay at liberty and those who managed it were condemned to stay in their one room.[74]

Elsewhere on Java, as in Batavia, there were intervals between the waves of arrests, so that at first some Dutch men and youths were still at liberty. In Garut those who were still free were summoned to Bandung in July. The controller of Garut, J. Bakker (who had not been arrested in April because he had a post with the air-raid defences) later described how:

> Each man had to bring a case with the most essential things. I said goodbye to my wife and children and reported to the LOG in Bandung. This was the detention centre for young offenders, which had been turned into an internment camp. Half the men were sent home; the rest were interned. Everyone was baffled. Later I found out that the regent had had to draw up a list of the men who had not yet been detained. Then he had to choose 50% of them who should be immediately interned. A tricky job! Anyway, I went home and everyone thought it was odd.

---

73   C.D. Ricardo, 'De inpikkerij', 21 October 1942, p. 3 (NIOD IC, 30,931).
74   C.D. Ricardo, 'De inpikkerij', 21 October 1942, p. 3 (NIOD IC, 30,931).

And the gossiping that went on! Not one of the sweet European ladies congratulated me. All I encountered was jealousy and slander.[75]

In Surabaya those arrested in July were put in the old prison in Werfstraat. It had large cells which in the past had been intended to hold no more than 19 Javanese – now about 50 Dutch men were packed into each cell. An assistant inspector of the Stoomvaart Maatschappij Nederland shipping line was taken to one such cell with 51 other prisoners. He wrote, 'When we stood before it, after being driven and beaten by the native warders, we looked at each other and said, "No, that is impossible". But we had to, and it turned out to be possible.' (De Roever 1951:362.)

Not all those arrested were detained. Many of those who had earned less than 300 guilders a month (the limit which had also been applied in April) were released and a short time later others were transported to the Kesilir colonization area in the far southeastern corner of Java. What happened there is described below.

Round-ups of men and youths began later in Bandung than elsewhere; they started in August. Here too lorries went round collecting those arrested – if you heard the lorry coming, you tried to hide. In August and September around 3,000 men and youths were arrested. They were interned in a hotel and two schools. Others were still free, but it was a very precarious freedom. On 13 October things went wrong. Elias (1946:127-9) writes:

> The men who had gone to their offices [that is, the 'ball boys'] send notes to those in hiding to warn them to stay off the streets that day. Lorries are already waiting in front of the offices, and unsuspecting passers-by are being loaded on to them.

The raid began in the centre.

> In the afternoon the Japanese man-hunters slowly reached the outskirts, which they systematically combed, leaving the houses stripped. The offices are now closed, so all the men ought to be home about that time.

Throughout the afternoon men and youths were picked up, but some managed to avoid capture.

> As evening falls, another lorry passes. Again the Japanese and the police force their way into houses; they creep through bushes and alleys and sewers. On the roads the half-frozen men are herded together in the pouring rain. It is an intensely sad, miserable and wretched sight: these men packed together like animals, guarded by a few policemen with rifles.

On 13 October they were held in an empty monastery. About 1,000 men and

75 J. Bakker, 'Tien bewogen jaren', 1961, p. 22 (NIOD IC, 63,522).

youths ended up here and they included many Dutch Eurasians.

As mentioned, Dutch Eurasians were not covered by the general arrest warrant of 17 May, but a number of them were picked up in June as part of an operation aimed at some of those who had been in the Removal and Demolition Corps.

We described above how in April the Japanese explained the arrest of prominent Europeans by referring to the minutes of a discussion which supposedly showed that members of the Demolition Corps had met in Surabaya on 20 March 1942. We noted that the Japanese had either faked the date or misread it. At any rate, the Kempeitai concluded that members of the Corps, who had resumed their normal work after the surrender (only the higher officers were regular soldiers), were plotting sabotage. 'Immediately after the occupation', said the Kempeitai report of February 1944 on resistance on Java already cited, 'technicians in almost every area scattered and took up positions in railroads, ships, harbours, shipyards and other key offices; and hatched demolition plans of a highly dangerous nature'.[76]

It took the Kempeitai two months to prepare the arrests of all the lower ranks in the Demolition Corps. Lists of names and addresses had to be drawn up and they had to establish who was already in prison: this proved to be the case with about 700 men – over 100 soldiers in prisoner-of-war camps and nearly 600 government employees who had been arrested in March, April or May. On 8 June the operation aimed at Demolition Corps members still at liberty was launched all over Java. Nearly 500 were arrested, in addition to an unknown number of Indonesians (*wedono*, assistant *wedono* and *desa* heads who had been involved in the sabotage plans).

On 29 June, three weeks after the round-up of Demolition Corps members and while the arrests of Dutch men aged between 17 and 60 were still continuing here and there on Java, the Japanese official gazette, the *Kan Po*, carried an 'announcement for the Dutch' which defended these arrests.[77] It said that the authorities in the Dutch East Indies had arrested the Japanese left in their territory and sent them to Australia for 'bad treatment'. 'They will not escape God's punishment for this act'. The Japanese authorities in the Indies, on the other hand, had initially limited themselves to arresting only those among the Dutch population who were 'considered to be a danger to law and order'. As for the rest of the Dutch inhabitants, it continued:

> we have carefully considered the situation for some time. Yet there are those among them [...] who are confused by rumours and false propaganda from

[76]   Java Kempeitai HQ, 'Anti-Japanese activities in Java', February 1944, p. 2 (NIOD IC 2,165).
[77]   Text in Brugmans 1960:376.

England and America. And it seems that some are making unlawful plans. This is why the military authorities have now decided [...] to designate a certain place for the Dutch men to stay in, with the exception of those who have demonstrated their loyalty and obedience to the Japanese authorities. The Japanese military authorities will continue to leave these men in peace in the future [...]. The military authorities also declare that no measures of any kind will be taken against women and children and, indeed, that consideration is being given to providing protection for them.

'Protection' – how and where? In separate districts, perhaps? The end of the announcement, meant to be reassuring, sounded ominous.

The mood

The blows suffered by the Dutch and Dutch Eurasians in the first months of the occupation came as a shock. In the minds of many they gave rise to a mixture of concern and optimism about a speedy liberation. As the concern deepened, people clutched all the more desperately at shreds of hope. This hope was fed by two sources: the Allied radio broadcasts and the rumours that circulated everywhere.

Until radios were 'castrated'[78] in mid-1942 (not always effectively, as we have seen), anybody who had one could listen to Allied stations in defiance of the Japanese prohibition. Especially important were the broadcasts from Australia, in which Dutch authorities evacuated from the Indies were heard, and those from Radio San Francisco, which broadcast 15 minutes of news in Dutch every evening. Phrases used in these broadcasts that were little more than a general call to hold on were often interpreted as announcements of imminent Allied offensives. Thus at the end of March the commander of the KNIL air force, Major General L.H. van Oyen, ended an address on Radio Melbourne with the words 'I hope to see you again soon' (Bouwer 1988:43). This was generally seen as a promise that the Allies would be landing on Java and elsewhere in the archipelago, not in a few years but in a few months, and perhaps in just a few weeks. This hope was also fed evening after evening by Radio San Francisco, where at this time every news bulletin ended with the words 'Keep your courage up! We'll be coming soon!'[79]

In April, as described, many Dutch and Dutch Eurasian families found themselves in financial difficulties. It was clear to them that the Japanese regarded the Dutch regime as permanently over and that, as shown by the AAA campaign, they were trying to win over the Indonesians to their

---

[78]   See Introduction, p. 43.
[79]   J. Rups, 'Verzetsverslag', n.d., p. 1 (NIOD IC, 2,484).

cause. There were other pointers in this direction: when in April the cinemas reopened, it appeared that the Dutch and Dutch Eurasians could buy only the cheapest tickets (not many wanted to go anyway) and so had to sit in a section where in the past only Indonesians had sat.[80] Then there were the general Japanese regulations. The flag of the victor had to be flown in front of one's house. Not complying would have led to immediate punishment, so people made sure they had a flag flying, but did so with conspicuous nonchalance. 'Mummie', according to a girl in Surabaya, 'used the cheapest material she could find. The result was that at the first rain shower the red of the ball ran into the white. We deliberately left the flag in the rain as long as possible.' (Thomson 1965:17-8.) The wife of a doctor in the same city later described how 'We used red material that was so poor that it ran the first time it got wet in the rain. We laid it on the floor, trod on it and then hung it outside all wrinkled.' (Keizer-Heuzeveldt 1982:14.)

No doubt many more people did the same (we know of no examples of the Japanese taking action on this particular point)[81] and the temptation to do so must have been all the stronger when at the end of April all Dutch flags had to be handed in and were subsequently publicly burnt at various places on 29 April, Hirohito's birthday.

A day later, 30 April, was the 33rd birthday of Princess Juliana, the crown princess. In Bandung Bouwer (1988:70) observed:

> It was noticeable how many ladies were wearing red, white and blue or orange blouses today. A curious group strolled past our pension. From left to right: a young lady in a red dress, a gentleman in a spotless white suit, a young lady in a blue frock and a young lady in an orange blouse. There were also a great many orange parasols in front gardens [...]. On the lawns of many houses various combinations of red, white, blue and orange cushions were laid out to dry. An ice cream bar in Bragaweg had only orange ice cream today. The word most often heard was 'Ozo!', 'Oranje zal overwinnen!' [Orange will triumph!].

It is likely that there were similar scenes elsewhere on Java (we have no information on this point).

At this time it was said in Dutch and Dutch Eurasian circles that Japanese rule would be over in June. The letters of the name of the month ('juni' in Dutch) were said to stand for: Japan Uit Nederlands-Indië (Japan Out of the Dutch East Indies). When the assistant resident of Garut, who had been

[80] A few months later a Japanese propaganda film featuring an Indonesian family with exclusively European servants was shown in the cinemas.
[81] It is known that in 1944 the Dutch administrator of a plantation on Java who had been allowed to stay at his post was executed by the Japanese because he compared the flag to a used sanitary towel. He was reported to the Kempeitai in a postcard signed by five or six Indonesians.

arrested in April, was asked by the Japanese if he knew what 'juni' meant he laughed and explained. When asked where he had learnt this interpretation, he replied that 'every schoolboy' knew it.[82]

In May and June (months in which the Japanese fleet had been kept at bay in the Coral Sea and suffered a heavy defeat at Midway) the optimistic rumours persisted. Even inside Bukit Duri Prison in Batavia it was said that the Allies had landed on Java's south coast and had already advanced from there to Sukabumi. In the prison, according to a senior official of the office of the Adviser on Native Affairs who was held there, the prisoners promptly began 'setting up assault and other teams which were ready to go into action'.[83]

This optimism was encouraged by a message broadcast by Radio San Francisco on 20 June and addressed to 'Lieutenant De Jong'. (This was the KNIL Lieutenant J.A. de Jong who, together with Lieutenant W.H.J.E. van Daalen and a group of KNIL soldiers, had carried on fighting on Central Celebes and had asked the Dutch authorities in Australia for help by means of a radio transmitter from Internal Administration.) He was told not to send any more radio messages, because his location could be traced, and that help would be sent but it would 'take several weeks'. 'Fighting was still continuing somewhere in the Indies!' noted Bouwer.

> All Java (and possibly all the Indies) has heard this message, and people talk of nothing else. Everyone tries to guess who this mysterious 'Lieutenant De Jong' might be, where he is, what he's doing and what help he's asked for. People break their brains over complicated calculations as to how long 'several weeks' will be. Of course, the Japanese heard the message too and are just as much in the dark. They have offered a reward of 25,000 guilders for information leading to the capture of this elusive lieutenant.' (Bouwer 1988:94-5.)

A few days later 'several De Jongs were arrested' in Bandung (Bouwer 1988: 97).

This optimistic mood continued into July. An engineer with the State Railways who had been kept on in his job in Madiun on East Java visited the headquarters in Bandung in that month. 'Everybody there', he later wrote, 'was highly optimistic. Just a few weeks more, a month at most. The rumours were even better than in Madiun, but I had to correct a story that Madiun had been burned down.'[84] Bouwer heard several of these rumours: the island of Wake had been taken by American marines; Prince Bernhard (on whose birthday, 29 June, 'many Europeans' had worn white carnations)[85] had

---

[82]   R.W. Kofman, 'Verslag', 17 December 1946, p. 76 (ARA, Archief proc. gen. Batavia, 850).

[83]   J.M.J. Morsink, 'Verslag', n.d., p. 2 (ARA, Alg. Secr., Eerste zending, XXII, 45, 288).

[84]   L.R. Oldeman, 'Verslag', n.d., p. 20 (NIOD IC, 81,206 A).

[85]   Prince Bernhard, Crown Princess Juliana's husband, always wore a white carnation in his buttonhole.

arrived in Australia with 10,000 Dutch troops; Admiral Helfrich had landed on an island in the Sunda Strait with Dutch armed forces (Bouwer 1988:99-100.) It may be assumed that similar rumours continued to circulate in July and perhaps in August too, when the Americans landed on Guadalcanal.

Queen Wilhelmina's 62nd birthday, on 31 August, was not forgotten. The colours red, white and blue and orange were shown all over Bandung. Bouwer (1988:119) wrote:

> the game of 30 April was repeated. It was now much more dangerous, but even foraging prisoners of war wore orange. At the time signal for 12 o'clock there were no Europeans on the streets. Indoors, by unspoken agreement, a two-minute silence was observed. In the house next door we heard the first and last verses of the Wilhelmus [the Dutch national anthem] being sung to soft piano accompaniment.'

There were similar scenes elsewhere. In one case they ended badly. At a hospital in Paree (about 100 km southwest of Surabaya) the nurses organized a festive meal for which the table was decorated with red, white and blue flowers. An aunt or cousin of one of the nurses who was visiting for the day had typed a menu[86] which was headed by a large W and read as follows:

> Queen Wilhelmina dish
> Orange Nassau soup
>   Toast: Long live the Queen!
> Royally stuffed bird with liberty compote
> Victors with conqueror sauce
>   Toast: To the tremendous things to come!
> Fresh Pacific fruits, Allied selection
> Tricolour with Orange on Top
> Coffee in the hope of a happy outcome.

Some time later a copy of the menu was found at the home of one of the nurses by an Indonesian police chief. He immediately informed the Kempeitai and the result was that all the nurses who had been at the meal were imprisoned for between 10 and 17 months. All were severely mistreated by the Kempeitai.

In September 1942 the optimistic rumours reached a climax. At the beginning of the month it was said that under American pressure the Japanese had handed over Java and that on 7 September the Dutch administration would be officially restored. In Bandung Elias (1946:64) wrote:

---

86   Text in Brugmans 1960:145.

Eyewitnesses have seen the governor-general negotiating with high-ranking Japanese officers in the Preanger Hotel. The end of the war is near [...]. Women are spending their last money on evening gowns to wear at the forthcoming peace ball at Hotel Homann. Those who are still not convinced are ostracized by the Europeans. The manager of the Preanger Hotel says that the governor-general has not been in his hotel. The reply is that of course he has to say that, but people are not fooled.

Elias based this summary on what he remembered, but Bouwer gives a more detailed picture in his diary for Wednesday 16 September:

I have a strange story to relate. How it came into the world I don't know. Nor do I know how it could be so widely believed. I only know that for a few days the whole city was in turmoil. The gist of it was that under American threats Japan had given up Java and that we had only to wait for the arrival of the Allied re-occupation troops. How it all began is not entirely clear to me. It started with the release from the internment camp at the 'Sterre der Zee' monastery of a number of Ambonese and Manadonese who had evidently been interned by mistake. All of a sudden there was a rumour that the American president, Franklin D. Roosevelt, had announced on the radio that Japan had agreed to withdraw from Java (others said: from all of the Indies), that the military commanders were sorting out the details, but that the American troops would land shortly. Without exaggerating, I can state that 90% of the European population initially believed this tale.

Then it got steadily crazier. The East Indies were to be exchanged for New Guinea. Only the Kempeitai and Japanese civil servants would remain to uphold law and order and the formal transfer of the territory, while the army would withdraw. There was a rush on the shops. Women bought new dresses to celebrate the liberation. The takings at the Gerzon fashion shop in one day were 10,000 guilders. People bought up stocks of spirits. Japanese wearing white armbands had already been seen. Last Monday the euphoria of victory was felt everywhere. The mood was one of 'Well, that's all over now'. It reached the prisoner-of-war camps. 'No need to send any more packages', was the message from the camps, 'we'll be home in a couple of days'. Women came from East Java to collect their husbands interned here. Even the Indonesians began to believe it. A dogcart driver told a European passenger, *'Tiga minggoe lagi boleh bilang koed morning sur'* (In three weeks we'll be saying: Good morning, sir). The liberation fleet was on its way. Timor had already been taken. A flying boat carrying American negotiators had arrived at Surabaya.

If you asked what they were going to negotiate, if everything had already been decided at the highest level, people looked at you as if you were not right in the head. The Governor-General had been seen in Bandung. One piece of nonsense was piled on another.

It was difficult to keep a cool head and not be infected. Only today is the euphoria beginning to fade a little, because still nothing has changed. But you have to be careful not to say anything disparaging. (Bouwer 1988:122-3.)

Three days later:

Although a large percentage of people still believe in the 'liberation' story, most are now convinced it was a hoax. Depression has inevitably followed. If this was the aim of the Japanese, they have succeeded. Pessimism has reached new depths. (Bouwer 1988:124.)

Did the Japanese indeed deliberately spread false rumours? There is no evidence of this and we are inclined to doubt it: this kind of psychological warfare was not at all their style. Moreover, there is no need of Japanese manipulations to understand what happened. If something occurred, as in this case in Bandung, that looked odd, such as the release of Indonesian soldiers, the intense yearning for the end of Japanese occupation was enough to make some interpret that event in a general but evidently not yet revealed context. And then the appearance in Hotel Preanger of one European who from a distance bore a slight resemblance to Van Starkenborgh would lead some to give free rein to their imagination.

Indeed, a mood of despondency was bound to follow when such high hopes were dashed, but, quite apart from these rumours that proved unfounded, there was every reason to be depressed on Java in September. The Japanese military administration had announced that, now that virtually all Dutch youths and men aged (as a rule) between seventeen and sixty had been apprehended, all Dutch women, girls and boys aged under seventeen would be moved to closed districts.

Internment

In contrast to what would take place on Java, on the Outer Islands the Dutch and most of the Dutch Eurasians (along with the citizens of the other countries at war with Japan) were interned shortly after the arrival of the Japanese troops.[87] Exceptions were made only for some civil servants, doctors, people working in certain business sectors, and Protestant and Catholic missionaries. From the beginning, a division was made between the men and the 16- or 17-year-old youths on the one hand, and the women and the remaining children on the other.

Internment was a simple matter on Celebes and on several other islands in the Great East, such as Ambon and Dutch Timor, because except for those called up by the armed forces, when the Japanese arrived, most of the Dutch and Dutch Eurasians were already in evacuation camps. At the end of January 1942, when evacuation became impossible due to a lack of ships, the Dutch

---

[87]   This general information is taken from D. van Velden's study, *De Japanse interneringskampen voor burgers gedurende de Tweede Wereldoorlog*.

authorities in the Great East established evacuation camps in remote areas for civilians in the hope they would be spared the ravages of war. These, in fact, became the first internment camps. A few months later, the Dutch and Dutch Eurasians from other islands in the Moluccas as well as New Guinea and the Kai, Aru and Tanimbar Islands (all to the north of Australia), were also detained in the camps on Ambon.

Internment also took place almost immediately on Borneo by order of the Japanese army. When the Japanese navy assumed command of Borneo from the army in July 1942, the army transferred the internees from West Borneo to British Borneo, which remained under military rule. Moreover, many Dutch and Dutch Eurasian women and children from Borneo as well as other islands in the Great East were transferred to Java shortly after the outbreak of the war in the Pacific.

On Sumatra (for the location of all of the places mentioned, see Map 2), the Dutch and Dutch Eurasian citizens from North and East Aceh were trans-ferred to Medan, and those from West Aceh to an isolated rubber plantation. This area was home to many thousands of wives and children of Indonesian KNIL soldiers. They were concentrated in the camp on the upper reaches of the Alas River built by the colonial government in 1940 for the interned Germans who were transferred in large groups (one of which sank with the *Van Imhoff*)[88] to India.

In Medan, the Dutch and Dutch Eurasians were first placed under house arrest with the stipulation that they were not to be seen from the street. 'So that we could no longer use our front room', according to one of them who was only thirteen at the time.

> In order to still take advantage of a section of the back garden and to maintain contact with the neighbours, an improvised fence was erected there. In the after-noon we drank tea and played ping pong behind this fence. (Leffelaar 1959:28.)

This situation lasted for several weeks. On 11 April, however, the Japanese military administration announced that everyone under house arrest had to assemble at various places in Medan bringing along 30 kilos of luggage, food for two days, and cutlery, and then proceed to the square in front of the town hall. The possessions they were unable to take along, furniture and house-hold effects for instance, were to be stored in a single room which could be secured with a lock, the key to which they were allowed to take with them.[89] Large processions wended their way to the square on 13 April. According to Klooster ('Willem Brandt'), the Japanese intended to 'make a big show for the Indonesian population' of this exodus, to no avail, however, for the streets

---

[88]   See Introduction, p. 27 note 12.
[89]   The same regulation was imposed in occupied China and the Philippines.

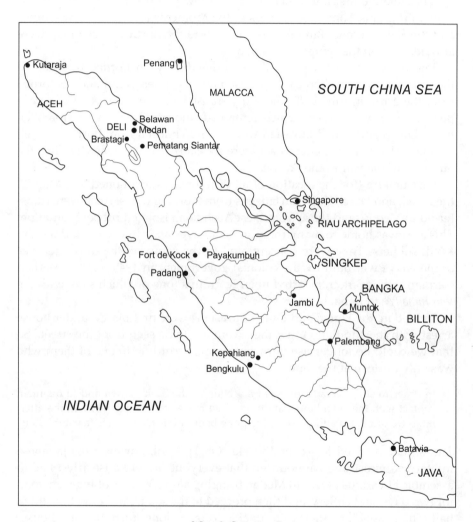

Map 2. Sumatra I

were 'as empty as never before' (Brandt 1947:30-1). The men and older boys were conveyed to Belawan, Deli's shipping port, and confined in the housing area intended for arriving contract coolies, the Unie *kampong* (or district), while the women and children were sent either to a former quarantine station or to the Deli Railway Company's workers' quarters. Several hundred men and their families nonetheless remained in Medan; we shall come back to them later.

In the area of Deli, which had many European enterprises, were four other places, including Brastagi and Pematang Siantar, where internment camps were created in prisons, hospitals and schools.

Padang became the main internment centre for the Dutch and Dutch Eurasians from the west coast of Sumatra. Most of the men and older youths here were initially confined to a prison, while most of the women and the rest of the children were housed in a missionary school complex.

This is more or less what also took place on South Sumatra. The prisons were used for the men and the older youths, and other accommodations (a city district, a barracks, a school) for the women and the remaining children.

According to the information gathered by Van Velden (which is incomplete because figures are not available for all of the camps), in the Great East a total of almost 3,900 Dutch and Dutch Eurasians (and approximately 240 people of other nationalities) were interned, all of whom – except for a group of about 500 on Ambon – either stayed on Celebes or arrived there in the course of 1942. The number of internees on Dutch Borneo was around 500, 300 of whom were transferred to British Borneo, where approximately 260 people of other nationalities (chiefly British) were also interned. On Sumatra around 12,000 Dutch and Dutch Eurasians were interned along with more than 1,200 people of other nationalities, nearly 700 of whom were British. All of these internees instantly lost both their freedom and virtually all of their possessions.

Imamura wanted to follow a different policy on Java. Initially, he wished to leave the Dutch Eurasians alone (because of their partial Indonesian background, he felt that once they had relinquished their allegiance to the Netherlands they would take part in the creation of the 'Greater East Asian Co-Prosperity Sphere'), and to the extent that they were not prisoners of war, he planned to unite the Dutch in their own large colonization area on Java. There, they would provide for themselves though agriculture, primarily the cultivation of rice (for which *sawah* or rice fields had to be laid out).[90] This

---

[90]   There are indications that Imamura also wanted to include the British, Australian and American citizens on Java in the colonization area as well as at a later stage the Ambonese and Manadonese KNIL soldiers and their families.

scheme was to be implemented in Kesilir near Java's southeast tip, where the Indo-Europeesch Verbond (IEV) had received an area of approximately 2,500 hectares on leasehold in the 1930s. The IEV was the party of the Dutch and Dutch Eurasians born in the East Indies. In the 1920s and 30s, it tried to improve the economic prospects of poor Dutch Eurasians by training them as farmers. The union experimented with agricultural colonies in three areas: on South Sumatra, New Guinea and in Kesilir, none of which succeeded. The agricultural colony in Kesilir failed because laying out rice fields and cultivating rice proved too difficult for the Dutch Eurasians who had settled there as tenants. They brought in Javanese who in recompense were allowed to keep one third of the harvest. It may be assumed (there is no additional information) that this project was largely abandoned around 1940.

For his new scheme, Imamura needed the approval of General Terauchi and the military authorities in Tokyo – which he received. General Count Hisaichi Terauchi was commander in chief of the Nampo (South Pacific) army group. He had his headquarters in Singapore from March 1942 to June 1944, and thereafter in Manila. He was appointed field marshal in June 1943. The following announcement subsequently appeared in several Indonesian daily newspapers on Java at the end of June:[91]

> Full-blooded Dutch people must emigrate. They must report as soon as possible pending further instructions. In the name of the commander of the Nippon army, the emigration of full-blooded Dutchmen without work was announced on 25 June. [...] The Nippon army is taking these measures so that those without work may earn a living. However, people still hesitate and hope for joy in their life.[92] Such an attitude in wartime is utterly improper.

In addition, it was noted that several 'full-blooded Dutchmen' who had reported, were refused (presumably because they were not subservient enough) – 'it's their own fault and they will have to live with the consequences.'

In this proclamation, the formulation 'full-blooded Dutchmen must emigrate' (what was probably meant was 'change their place of residence') indicated Imamura's goal. The first stage for achieving this was that only the 'unemployed full-blooded Dutchmen', and of them only those living on East Java who were no younger than seventeen and no older than sixty and in good physical condition, had to leave for Kesilir. This area had a sparse indigenous population, was unhealthy (with many outbreaks of malaria) and had no adequate drinking water – water from the *kali* or rivers would have to be purified.

---

[91]   Text which appeared, also in Dutch, in the Japanese official gazette *Kan Po*, and was included in Van Velden 1963:72.
[92]   That is to say, the ousting of the Japanese.

The Japanese felt it necessary to appoint a Dutch leader to the project. Accordingly, the Japanese military administration of East Java contacted J.G. Wackwitz, who had represented the Handelsvereeniging Amsterdam, the HVA (one of the largest Dutch agricultural companies), in Surabaya, where on 28 June he was presented with the regulation drawn up by the Japanese for 'the new Settlement of the Dutch people' along with a letter of appointment signed by Imamura, which ended as follows:

> What great pleasure it will give us to see our trust in you rewarded by your unceasing efforts to perform this burdensome task. We sincerely hope that you will be successful in saving your people from unemployment. Be always healthy and happy. (Quoted in Van Velden 1963:73.)

Now that the Japanese plan was definite and publicized, Wackwitz was anything but happy with the task he had felt unable to refuse from the very start. According to Van Velden (1963:74), Wackwitz was 'a powerful and sound leader and a good organizer', and the first thing he did was to point out that Kesilir was completely unsuited for an agricultural colony. Upon being told that he was not familiar with this region, he travelled there in a car put at his disposal by the Japanese and, following his return, he restated his objections with even greater force. All that he achieved was that the departure of the staff assembled for the colony (he succeeded in getting several people released from Bubutan Prison in Surabaya where government officials, policemen, teachers, judges and lawyers from the city were confined in April 1942) originally set for 1 July was moved to 5 July. The Japanese agreed to the first colonists arriving on a date later than 6 July; he was allowed to establish a liaison office in Surabaya, and he had freedom of movement to acquire countless necessary goods. He also demanded and received about 1 million quinine tablets from the Japanese instead of the 30,000 initially offered him and which he had refused to take.

Each staff member 'collected', as Wackwitz wrote in his postwar report, 'what he could, and a great deal of help was given by Surabayan institutions, businesses and private individuals'.[93] Tablets and charcoal filters to purify water, medicine, medical instruments, cooking utensils, office supplies and non-perishable foods were gathered.

Wackwitz drove to Kesilir for the second time on 5 July and took stock of the designated colonization area for six days. His conviction that the Japanese were implementing an absurd plan only intensified. In a report in English, he pointed out that the Europeans were not suited for heavy farming in the tropics; that the low-lying plain of Kesilir had a remarkably hot climate; that the rice plants in the fields were rotten; that of the area designated for cultiva-

---

[93] J.G. Wackwitz, 'Rapport inzake de kolonisatie Kesilir', March 1946, p. 4 (NIOD IC, 28,991).

tion, no more than 600 hectares was suitable for planting; that living on this 600 hectares were only 36 poor indigenous families, a figure that could be raised to a maximum of 70 Dutch families; that these 70 families would have no income in the first year; that 70% of the indigenous population of Kesilir suffered from malaria; that there was no clean drinking water; that the closest place to get supplies was 30 kilometres away; that the remaining houses of the colonists of the Indo-Europeesch Verbond were in a ruinous state; that the small dwellings of the indigenous people (these would be evacuated) were totally unsuitable for occupation by Europeans; and that the colonists had to be carefully selected. He concluded 'that Kesilir for colonization by pure Europeans is unsuitable' and colonization could succeed only if better regions on Java were made available. Should the Japanese army wish to carry on with this project, then initially no more than 300 people should be sent to Kesilir.

On his way back to Surabaya, he passed lorries with the first shipment of people who had received notification to leave for Kesilir. He drove to Surabaya, typed up his report on 12 July, handed it over to the Japanese and the next day drove to the sugar testing station in Pasuruan where he received help in amassing essential goods, such as means for purifying water and tins in which food could be cooked (a machine works in Pasuruan made a number of boilers). Upon his return to Kesilir, he found about 700 colonists already there – by mid-August there were about 2,400: close to 1,400 Dutchmen and 1,000 Dutch Eurasians. Some of these people had applied of their own accord following Imamura's announcement, while others had been taken from their homes. The Japanese had conducted raids for three days in Malang. In his diary, a young Dutch man noted on 12 July:

> Every house is being thoroughly searched and the Japanese look under the beds and in closets. Many men fled to the *sawah* [rice fields], but the Javanese betrayed them to the Japanese. [...] For the time being, the men are in the house of a Catholic brotherhood. Old men, boys, members of the NSB, Germans, Dutchmen, Dutch Eurasian, you name it.[94]

The wife of a Dutch Eurasian quoted earlier who had been a teacher at the Commercial College in Malang went to the boarding school where groups of people who had been rounded up were being chased inside from Japanese lorries. She had taken a cart with goods, including a mattress, which she wanted to give her husband. In her memoirs she wrote:

> The streets were teeming with Indonesians [...] jeering at [...] the European women who, laden and burdened, were walking to the house of the Catholic brotherhood [...] It took a great deal of restraint to act as if nothing was going

[94]   Quoted in Brugmans 1960:377-8.

on [...] 'Madam', I heard a hoarse woman's voice whisper next to me, 'what are they doing to our husbands? My husband lay in bed deathly ill with pneumonia [...] He's going to die, really, he's going to die.' [...] 'Oh, shut up', snarled another woman. 'Just look how they're treating that lame man over there! What do they care, they just lug people about. [...] That's my husband.' We looked and saw a lame man being beaten out of the lorry. [...] Today I saw people crying everywhere. (Moscou-de Ruiter 1984:18-20.)

In Surabaya people meant to leave for Kesilir had to report to Bubutan Prison. According to a young Dutchman writing in his diary, 'Men and boys packed up and ready were everywhere. Not a trace of dejection could be detected. English war songs were sung and they called out: "We'll come back soon!"'[95]

Among the approximately 2,400 Dutchmen and Dutch Eurasians arriving in Kesilir from the beginning of July to mid-August were close to forty NSB members (resentful of the Dutch colonial government which had detained them without inquiry in Fort Den Bosch in Ngawi from May 1940 to March 1942), almost all 'betrayers of the Dutch cause' who, according to Wackwitz (1946:47), 'continued to be in league with our enemies'. Among these 2,400 people was another group comprising a few dozen individuals, who, having arrived in Kesilir with all of the optimistic expectations held by the Dutch and Dutch Eurasians at the time ('We'll come back soon!'), assumed that the Allies would be landing shortly on Java's south coast, naturally at Kesilir, and according to Wackwitz (1946:29), 'began forging plans for what to do when the Allies arrived [...] without informing me.'

Though in these early days Kesilir was not officially an internment camp, in fact it was just that: the entire colony, about 2,500 hectares, was enclosed with barbed wire, there were Japanese guards, and the area could not be visited or left without special permission – Kesilir will be discussed again in the chapter on internment camps.

The additional turmoil among the Dutch and Dutch Eurasians on East Java in July and August 1942 resulting from the compulsory departure of so many to Kesilir did not take place on West Java. Little was known about the events on East Java and there was no question of a forced departure for Kesilir, except for here and there on Central Java. Many Dutch and Dutch Eurasian women, incidentally, had plenty of worries, in the first place concerning the men who were prisoners of war or who had been arrested along with the youths aged 16 and older in the months of May through July (or earlier).

And then, on 9 September, appeared Imamura's Ordinance no. 33 (text in Van Velden 1963:550), which created quite a stir among the Dutch women in

---

[95]   Quoted in Brugmans 1960:373.

Batavia and everyone who heard of it elsewhere. Article 1 read as follows:

> Full-blooded Dutch, English, American and Australian women (no Eurasian
> women), living apart from their husbands or providers, and residing in the
> municipality of Batavia, as well as full-blooded Dutch men younger than 17 or
> older than 60, must move to the protected district indicated in the notice below,
> and according to the appended articles. Those falling under this regulation must
> register with the Municipal Department for the Protection of Foreigners by 20
> September 2602 at the latest.

The notice in question made it clear that there would be two protected districts, the Kramat district and the Cideng district. The remaining articles of
Ordinance no. 33 stipulated that people who did not belong to the groups to
be isolated but who were living in these districts had to leave them before 1
October, that the move had to take place in October and that whoever was no
longer living there after this would need a special permit to get in.

The Japanese were in no way being derisive by calling the town hall
department where people had to register 'Protection of Foreigners'. Indeed, as
announced in a notification at the end of June, they wished (and this certainly
applied to Imamura) to protect these white 'foreigners'. Incidentally, this was
required of all Japanese authorities in occupied China and in the Nampo
countries (Southeast Asia) at the end of April 1942 by the instruction circulated by the War Department (text in Van Velden 1963:583) stating that: 'People
in need [that is, 'people having trouble providing for themselves'] must be
subject to internment and surveillance, in groups, in a designated place'.

'All of Batavia was in an uproar', wrote a Dutch woman in her diary after
the appearance of Ordinance no. 33,[96] and this referred not only to those who
would have to move to the closed districts but also to the 'humblest of people
with even less money'[97] who had to leave these districts at a moment's notice
without any arrangements having been made for their relief.

Was there any way of escaping the dictates of this ordinance? It appeared
to afford two possibilities for doing so: first, the ordinance only affected 'full-
blooded Dutch women' and, second, of this group only those 'living apart
from their husbands or providers'.

Advantage was immediately taken of both possibilities. Some women did
their level best to find an employed Dutch or Dutch Eurasian man willing
to live with them as a 'provider' (the Dutch diarist cited above spoke of a
'general man hunt in Batavia'[98] – though a 'provider' would only be recognized if he were a member of the family in question and already living with

---

[96]   C. Lanzing-Fokker, 'Dagboek', 11 September 1942 (NIOD IC, dagboek 140).
[97]   C. Lanzing-Fokker, 'Dagboek', 11 September 1942 (NIOD IC, dagboek 140).
[98]   C. Lanzing-Fokker, 'Dagboek', 13 September 1942 (NIOD IC, dagboek 140).

them. Other women racked their brains trying to figure out whether they had
Indonesian ancestors so that they would not qualify as 'full-blooded Dutch
women'. What rules applied in this case? There was no published information and the first reports to make the rounds were contradictory. 'Batavia', as
the diarist noted on 16 September, 'has become a madhouse. As nothing is
announced with any certainty, decisions are being made only to be reversed
the next hour.'[99] These decisions were also made in haste, for people had to
report at the town hall by 20 September at the latest.

The situation with respect to the issuing of identity cards, the *pendaftaran*,
had been strange in so far that in Batavia, the Dutch Eurasians born in the
Netherlands were registered as Belanda-totok – which was also stated on
their identity cards. Were they then required to move to the closed districts?
Evidently not, for they were Eurasian. These individuals therefore took
the trouble to have the designation 'Belanda-totok' changed to 'Belanda-
Indo'. When such changes indeed proved possible, and one could qualify
as a Belanda-Indo if there was at least one distant Indonesian ancestor (one
Indonesian great-great-great grandmother was sufficient), various pure
Dutch women began to wonder whether there was a way of demonstrat-
ing that they were not pure Dutch. They sought information in the birth
records of the Registry Office, or in the marriage and baptism registers
extending back to the time of the VOC housed in the Algemeen Landsarchief
in Batavia. The state archive employees lent their full support (although a
low-ranking official accepted large sums of money for this) in drawing up
a line of descent, an *asal usul*. Accordingly, a presumably limited number
of pure Dutch women succeeded in becoming registered as Belanda-Indo,
and thus they and their children did not have to move. Some of these
statements of parentage were based on actual facts, while others relied on
made-up information. It should be added that they did not always prevent
internment. After all of the Dutch women and the men above sixty had been
accommodated in separate, closed districts, anyone who looked pure Dutch
ran the risk of being immediately forced to move to one of these districts on
the orders of a Japanese or of an Indonesian policeman. Of two pure Dutch
men, both above the age of sixty, one remained in Batavia in freedom, 'even
though', as one Dutch woman was told, 'he sang the Wilhelmus in the street'
(MacGillavry 1975:49), while the other one was interned, and perished in
the camp where he was detained. Everything was arbitrary, as was the fact
that the British, Australian and American women (including the wife of
Governor-General Van Starkenborgh) mentioned in Ordinance no. 33, who
had already spent some time in Struiswijk Prison in April, were rearrested in
early October, this time with their children, and taken for the second time to

[99]   C. Lanzing-Fokker, 'Dagboek', 16 September 1942 (NIOD IC, dagboek 140).

this same prison.[100]

Most of the people in Batavia who had to move to the Kramat or Cideng districts realized that they could not take all of their possessions with them. As mentioned above, before September many women had already felt compelled to sell off part of their belongings. This began taking place on a larger scale in the second half of September and in the course of October, and many buyers took advantage of the sellers' predicament, acquiring goods such as furniture, carpets, refrigerators, paintings and the like for ridiculously low prices.

In Batavia initially about 2,000 people were transferred to each of the districts mentioned.

Elsewhere on Java, internment – in keeping with Ordinance no. 33 which applied to Batavia – took more time.

In January and February 1942, many women and children had fled to Bandung when it became clear that the Japanese would also land on Java. The coastal regions were considered vulnerable and unsafe, and Bandung, further inland, seemed the safest place on West and Central Java. In October (large round-ups of men took place on 13 October), an announcement was made in Bandung that all full-blooded Dutch women, children and men older than 16 would have to move, were they not already living there, to a residential neighbourhood, the Cihapit district, in November. 'But', Van Velden (1963:84) writes, 'many refused to go. The internment took place in a relatively unorganized fashion and with far greater difficulty than else-where.' It took a few months, until March 1943, before the groups in question had all been transferred to the Cihapit district, about 7,000 people in all.

The other men in Bandung and families with sick people, about 900 indi-viduals all together, were forced into a second neighbourhood in Bandung, the Rama district. At the beginning of December, women and children, in the end numbering close to 6,000, from the rest of West Java and the western part of Central Java moved into a third one, called the Karees district; after first being confined in schools and hotels, they were only allowed to bring some hand luggage with them to Bandung.

In December, dwellings and a barrack in Cimahi (the Baros Camp) became the enforced place of residence for around 1,200 women and children from this area and its surroundings.

Internment also took place in Semarang at the end of 1942. About 8,000 women and children were sent to the Lampersari-Sompok city district,

---

[100]   Elsewhere on Java, the British, Australian and American women and children were separ-ately interned around this same time: in Bandung in a school; in Semarang and Surabaya in a prison; and those from Malang and other places on East Java in a children's sanatorium. The group in Batavia did not stay in Struiswijk, but was transferred to a 'normal' internment camp in 1943.

some of whom had been transferred from elsewhere on Central Java and from Surabaya. Other women and children from Central Java, for example Yogyakarta, all told numbering about 10,500, were either interned in Ambarawa in old barracks which had already been condemned by the Dutch colonial government and an equally unsuitable military hospital (6,000 people) or in the barracks in Banyubiru near Ambarawa (4,500 people). In contrast, about 550 women and children from Surabaya found their way to high-lying, good KNIL barracks, while other women and children from parts of Central Java moved to residential complexes in agricultural enterprises.

On East Java too, some 7,000 women and children were interned in a good city district in Malang at the end of 1942 and beginning of 1943.

The last to lose their freedom in this part of the island were the women and children in Surabaya: in January 1943, the families unable to support themselves who had received aid, and in the period May-September 1943, the remainder. In the end, a total of about 6,000 people were assembled in the Darmo district, which was one of the best in the city.

Older Dutch men from Central and East Java were either sent to Fort Den Bosch (their number is not known), or to a barracks in Malang, which would eventually have about 1,000 inhabitants.[101]

According to Van Velden's information, eventually about 29,000 men (this figure includes those arrested earlier), about 25,000 women and 29,000 children were interned on Java: they included about 80,000 Dutch nationals, 700 British nationals, 100 Americans and about 800 people of other nationalities. However, adding up the numbers we have given in this section produces a total of 52,600. To estimate the total number of Dutch civilians deprived of their liberty through internment, to this figure must be added the approximately 2,400 men and older boys transferred to Kesilir and those caught in raids or otherwise, 18,200 people all together, according to Van Velden. The

[101]   The Dutch staff at the large State Railways Works in Madiun, were told at the office at the end of December that they were dismissed as of 1 January 1943. According to a report by one of them, the engineer quoted earlier, 'moreover, we had to go to the residency office to hear what would happen to us. Well, we were not expecting much good. We went to the office under police escort. [...] We were invited to be seated around a table and the Japanese resident took a seat at the end. He told us that we had worked for the State Railways so well that it had been decided that we would not be considered as enemies and therefore would be interned with our families. We were allowed to choose where we wanted to go': to a hotel, or a bungalow complex. On New Year's eve they said goodbye in the Works. 'Many Indonesian labourers also came to give us courage and express their hopes of seeing us again soon. [...] People I did not even know by name. My Japanese chief also began to cry.' After all was said and done, it was nonetheless internment, but in a hotel where the people had to pay 1.50 guilders per day. 'If we couldn't pay, the men would have to go to the internment camp at Ngawi and the women [...] to Semarang. [...] We calculated that we could keep this up for four months and naturally we accepted. Perhaps the war would be over by then.' (L.R. Oldeman, 'Verslag', pp. 16-7 (NIOD IC, 81,206 A).

total of 52,000 plus 2,400 plus 18,200, or 72,200, is too low given that there is
no data on the number of internees confined in some of the camps; moreover,
for a number of camps only the people confined at the end of 1942 or beginning of 1943 were counted, while more were interned there later. To the extent
that information is available, it appears that at the end of 1942 and beginning
of 1943, only the Dutch – and not the Dutch Eurasian – civilians were interned
as a *group*. The latter eventually did find themselves in a precarious situation,
which is described in Chapter VI.

It should be added that the districts or other locations where the women,
children and older men were sent were 'evacuated and cleaned beforehand',
according to Van Velden (1963:86), and 'were not crowded', at least not in the
beginning.

It is worth noting that in the Indies, the Dutch NSB members were treated no
differently from their fellow countrymen. The Japanese released them from
Fort Den Bosch in Ngawi, after which some attempted to get into their good
graces by wearing a band with the swastika. Only those who could do useful
work for the Japanese were designated 'ball boys'. As for the rest of the NSB
members, the Japanese treated them in the same way as they did the other
Dutchmen.

Back in occupied Holland, did Anton A. Mussert, the leader of the NSB,
try to help his followers? Indeed he did: on 5 March 1942, namely in the
week in which fighting took place on Java, he submitted a request to A.
Seyss-Inquart, head of the German civil government in the Netherlands, and
the representative of the German Ministry of Foreign Affairs, O. Bene, that
Germany press the Japanese government to accord the NSB members in the
Indies a unique position. Seyss-Inquart and Bene passed on this request to
the German Ministry of Foreign Affairs. Nothing happened, and when Bene
took up the matter again later in 1942, German Foreign Minister Joachim von
Ribbentrop, aware of just how sensitive the Japanese were to anything that
bordered on meddling with their business, stated that 'as a matter of principle' he was not inclined to forward Mussert's appeal to Tokyo.[102]

It was almost impossible for Dutch women to avoid internment, particularly
if they had children. Those who went into hiding needed help – which could
only be provided by Dutch Eurasians, themselves already struggling, and,
moreover, all parties justly feared harsh reprisals on the part of the Kempeitai.
In addition, should people who had taken cover venture outside, they would
instantly be noticed. According to Van Velden (1963:440), 'some' (though this
could not have been many) sought a way out by means of a sham or real

---

[102]   Note by the *Auswärtige Amt*, 19 September 1942 (NIOD FO/SD, 500 680).

marriage with a Japanese or other non-European, or by finding 'work in a Japanese restaurant or brothel'. Dutch Eurasian women relied more readily on these measures than Dutch women.

Going into hiding was equally difficult for Dutch men, although, according to Van Velden (1963:438), 'some men succeeded in hiding out to the very end', including J.B. Bouwer, whose diaries have been frequently quoted. A journalist, correspondent for the American news agency United Press and for the American broadcasting company CBS (Columbia Broadcasting System), he was married to a Dutch Eurasian woman who was not interned. When at the end of March 1942, Bouwer heard at his residence in Bandung that he was being sought by the Kempeitai, he changed his name and in July 1942 decided to go into hiding as much as possible. He had a realistic understanding of the war's progress and the strategy the Allies would follow: on 10 August 1942, upon hearing on the radio that the Americans had landed at Guadalcanal, he wrote in his diary that the Allies would reconquer Java only when they had defeated Japan, 'which could well take a few years'. Behind the garden of the house where he lived was a bit of jungle, where he hid whenever danger threatened. His wife stood by his side, exhibiting great courage and ingenuity. She was able to earn some money with which to support herself and her husband, and as of February 1945 also their first child. She was nevertheless arrested on 11 August 1945, four days before the announcement of Japan's capitulation – her imprisonment, however, did not last long.

Who escaped internment for the time being? In the first place Europeans who were not Dutch or British, including citizens of countries allied with Japan, such as Germany and Italy.

About 75 elderly or ill Germans remained behind when the Germans interned in the camp in the Alas Valley on Sumatra were shipped off to India. The Japanese helped them return to their residences and most went to Java. At the time of the arrival of the Japanese, on Java and Sumatra there were still several hundred German women and children (about 500 women and some 400 children had sailed for Japan in 1941), including Dutch Eurasian women who had acquired German nationality by marrying a German. They were not required to pay registration fees on Java. As a result, when they registered, Dutch Eurasian women claimed to be married to a German who was no longer in the Indies. Some of the German men and many of the (real or supposedly) German women encountered serious difficulties – all of the Germans' wealth and property had been seized by the Dutch colonial government in 1940,[103] and the possibilities for making a new life were limited.

---

[103] In May 1942, the head of the Foreign Department of the German Nazi party, the *Auslandsorganisation der NSDAP, Gauleiter* E.W. Bohle, informed Seyss-Inquart that the Germans in the

Only in July 1943, after the German consul general in Mukden (Manchukuo) and the German economic negotiator Helmuth Wohltat had visited Java, was a relief scheme implemented for all disadvantaged Germans. They had to present their papers, and only those whose papers were not in order were interned. The needs of all the others on Java were apparently covered by a budget of 10,000 guilders a month, since this was the amount made available by the Japanese military administration.

This scheme was discontinued in May 1945. Germany had capitulated and the Japanese broke off contact with the Germans, at least on Java. Bouwer (1988:345) concluded in his diary at the end of May as follows:

> Many Germans now try to prove that they are 'actually Swiss by birth'. Swastikas and other pins indicating German nationality have vanished from the streets and the Germans have become very, very small.

To the extent that they were still at liberty, Germans and Italians[104] were interned in hotels by the Japanese, at least in Bandung, a few months later.

The fate of European nationals other than the Dutch, British, Germans and Italians is outlined in the chapter on internment camps. A closer look will now be taken at the Dutch group that was not initially interned comprising individuals who, according to the official announcement at the end of June motivating the arrest of Dutch men and youths seventeen to sixty years old, 'had demonstrated their loyalty and obedience to the Japanese authorities. The Japanese military authorities will continue to leave these men in peace in the future.'

These men had continued to do their normal work under Japanese orders and as a rule had to wear a white armband with a red ball and various Japanese stamps: they were known as 'the ball boys'. Was this reference to a group of people who on average were far from young somewhat derogatory? Perhaps. In any case it emphasized the subservience expected of those involved – a subservience experienced by many deprived of their freedom by the Japanese as coming close to, or in fact being, reprehensible collaboration.

Indies had suffered great losses: he wondered whether the damage could be recovered from the Netherlands. Seyss-Inquart stated his willingness to make available funds from the Netherlands to German women repatriated from the Indies who required assistance. Meetings were held on this matter in the second half of 1942 in Berlin and there it was finally decided to ask for no compensation from the Netherlands, given that such payments would reveal the extent of German economic interests in the Indies – their restoration remained the aim of German policy. Had this become apparent to the Japanese, it would have further reinforced their distrust of Germany!

104   When the Italian government of Field Marshal Badoglio broke with Germany in September 1943, all Italians on Java were interned. However, those willing to swear allegiance to Mussolini, who had established a new government in Northern Italy, were released at the end of 1943.

Two comments should be made here. First, in its *Aanwijzingen*, the colonial government had issued the general instruction to continue working, even under Japanese occupation, as long as it was not clearly in the interest of the Japanese war effort. Second, one should not lose sight of the fact that large and important business sectors in the occupied Netherlands were directly and indirectly active for the sake of the German war effort. 'Ball boys' is here replaced by the less deprecatory term, also used by Van Velden, 'Nippon workers'.[105]

How many Nippon workers were there in the Indies? The exact number is not known, but there were at least several thousand, not several hundred.

What follows is a survey of the situation. In general, no work of any duration was performed in the areas run by the Japanese navy, though this did occur on Sumatra and primarily on Java.

Point 8 in a Japanese instruction for the administration of Sumatra of April 1942 determined that: 'The influence of Dutch citizens will be promptly eliminated on Sumatra [which it was], with the exception of special areas such as that of technicians of agricultural undertakings.' 'Technicians' should be construed as those who could best continue the work on these plantations, namely the managers.

We do not know how many Dutch managers and other Dutchmen were required to continue their work at the agricultural concerns. In Medan, the Nippon workers were lodged in a Catholic boarding school which also afforded shelter for about 150 family members. Elsewhere in Medan about 1,600 wives and children of Nippon workers were interned in two districts. Given the total of 1,750 women and children, there were probably around 400 Nippon workers. In any event, the Japanese military authorities on Sumatra gave a general interpretation of the instruction of April 1942, for the estimated 400 Nippon workers could only partly have been involved in agricultural concerns.

As mentioned above, elsewhere on Sumatra, about 300 employees of oil companies (Dutch and Dutch Eurasians) worked in the oil fields and refineries at Palembang. On Billiton Island, three staff members of the Billiton Company (which extracted tin ore on the island) were employed for a year as of July 1942 to service the water supply and lighting of one of the tin mines and to create saltpans. It was office work. According to a report by one of the company's engineers written at the end of 1946: 'We were in no way to be involved with the tin mining. [...] After a few months we were only allowed

---

[105]   The use of this term is not intended to indicate anything negative about the group in question. Many belonged to it who were aware that by continuing to work they were not burdening the relief funds. Moreover, this continuation seemed important because when liberation was at hand certain posts would still be under their control.

to go back and forth to the office under police escort. We had to wear a badge [the armband]. [...] The 100 guilders per month salary was later reduced to 50 guilders.'[106]

On Java too, Dutchmen were retained in the management of agricultural enterprises. In August 1946, a Dutch sugar planter on East Java remembered:[107]

> Everything continued as though there were no Japanese. Our company was still there, the Japanese were not to be seen and the people behaved as though nothing had ever happened. [...] In the *desa* [rural villages], too, everything was just as before.
>
> In December our hope of doing without the Japanese proved to be an illusion. The first Japanese was taken on in the factory, for the bookkeeping. [...] The following January brought us the second Japanese, namely the administrator,[108] and 14 days later the third, namely the planter. We realized then that we had become a Japanese agricultural concern and that our company was gone. At that point we did feel strongly that we should stop, but our lives were at risk should we leave and moreover it was better for us to remain in order to exert some European influence over the population for as long as possible.

As was also the case in many other places, sugar production at this company was halted later in 1943.

> The entire workshop was taken to the navy base in Surabaya. Lorry and haulage equipment was sent to various airfields. Clearly, they were slowly dismantling the factory. We were interned in September 1943, which we experienced as a relief after months of tension and working without hope.

The Dutch administrator of a coffee and rubber company on East Java, which employed about 3,000 coolies at harvest time and 800 to 1,200 the rest of the year, was interned in May 1943. His wife had to continue his work before she, too, was interned in a district of Malang in August 1943. Later she wrote:

> I was subordinate to a Japanese man about 25 years old who had never even seen a coffee bean and spoke no Malay or French. He 'managed' six large companies. [...] I had no problems with the labour force. I supervised the work as best I could, walked through the factory amidst the hundreds of coolies, and was never bothered.[109]

Like the Dutch employees (how many is not known) with agricultural companies on Java who initially had to continue their work, there were groups

---

106 Text in Brugmans 1960:273-4.
107 Text in Brugmans 1960:277-8.
108 The 'administrator' of an agricultural concern managed it.
109 Text in Brugmans 1960:278-9.

in the cities to which this also applied. Except for doctors, dentists and clergymen, who did not have to move, in general they and their families were accommodated in closed residential complexes, which they had to leave every day to go to work. Similar complexes were created in Batavia, Buitenzorg, Bandung, Yogyakarta, Semarang and Surabaya. About 250 people, including some 60 Nippon workers, came to the complex in Buitenzorg, according to Van Velden's information. There are no figures for the remaining residential complexes – though a young Dutch Eurasian man in Surabaya noted in his diary in March 1943:

> There are still a fair number of Dutch men walking around freely because they work for the Japs. After all, all of the companies are now in Japanese hands! However, factories are regularly [...] 'purged' of enemies. The Dutch then find themselves on the street and can count on being in Werfstraat within a week.[110]

He was referring to the prison on Werfstraat. In July 1943, however, approximately 200 Nippon workers were still free in Surabaya; they were detained in the middle of the month.

Dutch citizens carried on as Nippon workers in various departments, for instance the Tax Department, the Post Office, state and private railroads and tramways, electricity and gas companies, as well as in banking, at oil companies, the Algemeen Landbouw Syndicaat (General Agricultural Syndicate), the Goodyear tyre factory, lumber concerns, the dry dock companies in Surabaya and Tanjungpriok, the State Botanical Garden, a large printer's, and the KNIL workshops in Bandung. Then there were those who had to act as interpreters for Japanese departments, chiefly for the Kempeitai (there were five in Bandung, only one of whom, the Japan expert G.H. de Heer, whose mother was Japanese, was ultimately retained). Some were also involved in the Japanese international radio broadcasts, but because they worked with a few prisoners of war, they will be discussed in greater detail in the chapter devoted to prisoners of war.

The employment of virtually everybody who either could or had to continue their work wearing an armband came to an end in the course of 1943: they were interned along with their families. As far as is known, there were only four exceptions to this: a few interpreters, the radio propagandists, the agriculturalists of the State Botanical Garden, whose research the Japanese deemed important, and finally a group of technicians at the Post Office's Radio Laboratory who came to work for the Japanese Sumitomo concern and who, as was customary at the company's foreign branches, were transferred to Japan with their families in January 1944.[111]

---

[110] Text in Brugmans 1960:378.
[111] The information in this section applies only to Java.

Upon receipt of their identity cards, the Nippon workers and their family members 17 years and older had promised to obey all Japanese orders. Moreover, in 1943 the management of the Saibai Rigyo Kanri Kodan, the Government Plantation Companies (the Japanese corporation which the General Agriculture Syndicate[112] and all agricultural companies now came under), required the Europeans still working in the syndicate or in agriculture to promise in writing that they would turn in to the Kempeitai anyone committing anti-Japanese acts. (The pledge was necessary because the chairman of the General Agriculture Syndicate, F. Kramer, had supported resistance groups.) As far as is known, the only people who refused to do this were a number of the Syndicate's officials, an event which is discussed later.

Finally, it appears that the civil servants among the Nippon workers in the larger places on Java were given Japanese courses taught in Indonesian which, according to Elias (1946:83),

> many pupils do not understand sufficiently. Every evening these civil servants with 10 to 25 years of service in the Indies have to attend a Japanese lesson and if they do not know the words the next day, they are reprimanded. Should this occur more than once, punishment follows in the form of a cut in pay or even dismissal. The diligence and dead seriousness with which some (fortunately not all) attempted to learn the language of the temporary despot! The most revolting thing these 'ball boys' were forced to do is to take singing lessons, where they had to sing the Japanese national anthem at the top of their voices and learn other songs.

This passage bespeaks a certain bitterness. Indeed, many of those who were interned in closed districts came to resent the Nippon workers who facilitated the Japanese war effort and in so doing enjoyed a privileged position.

Assistance

This chapter has outlined the great difficulty many of the Dutch and Dutch Eurasians who were not arrested experienced in providing for their daily needs.[113] Incidentally, the poor among the Chinese and Indonesians, and among the latter primarily the wives and children of the Indonesian KNIL

---

[112]   The Algemeen Landbouw Syndicaat or General Agriculture Syndicate in Batavia promoted the interests of the European mountain estates on Java and also had the task of advising the colonial government and the Internal Administration on Java with respect to industrial processing of agricultural products, with the exception of the sugar industry.
[113]   The general information about assistance is derived from the master's thesis 'Steunverlening aan Nederlanders gedurende de Japanse bezetting in Nederlands-Indië', written in 1971 by G.T. van Aalderen, a student at Nijmegen University, on the basis of the material in the Indische Collectie of the Nederlands Instituut voor Oorlogsdocumentatie (NIOD IC, 74,509).

soldiers, who were traditionally housed in the barracks, also had trouble keeping their heads above water. In parts of the Outer Islands, for example in Aceh, these women and children were moved elsewhere as the Japanese approached (and in Aceh also with a view to the popular uprising against Dutch rule); and on North Sumatra the Japanese transferred them to the internment camps abandoned by the Germans on the upper reaches of the Alas River.[114]

Where they were housed is known only in a limited number of cases (discussed below). In any event, many men were soon able to join their wives after 29 April 1942, Hirohito's birthday, when the Japanese military administration proclaimed that most of the Indonesian KNIL soldiers would be released. This is discussed further in Chapter IV devoted to prisoners of war.

The information on assistance extended to the Dutch and Dutch Eurasians in the Outer Islands is limited to Banjarmasin in South Borneo (see Map 3). This is hardly a coincidence, for the assistance led to an event that must be qualified as 'mass murder', and which was thoroughly reconstructed by the judicial authorities after the war.

In Banjarmasin only the Dutch, and not the Dutch Eurasians, were interned. Many of the latter soon had to go on relief. With the permission of the Japanese authorities, a support scheme for the internees (and the prisoners of war) as well as for people on relief was launched by the Dutch Eurasian A. Santiago ('Santi') Pereira, a civil servant at the Inspectorate of Finances. He established the Santi Pereira Fund, contributions for which he received from those not on relief among the Dutch Eurasians, Chinese and Arabs, and even from a Japanese doctor. The fund was also joined by a small group whose aim was to smuggle money, supplies and medicine into the camps. This group, led by Nurse C.J.M. Reichert, head of the psychiatric hospital, included the local health inspector Raden Soesilo, and an Indian called Abdullah – the latter succeeded in bringing money and goods into the camps on about tenty occasions. Pereira scrupulously administered the money deposited into his fund because it was meant to be reimbursed by the colonial government after the war; he kept a list of the names and addresses of everyone who had contributed money along with the amounts.

All went well for about a year, but in May 1943 the Japanese authorities in Banjarmasin became alarmed by rumours (evidently based on Allied broadcasts) circulating among the public at large relayed to them by their

---

[114]   Some financial aid was given from Medan to the wives and children of the indigenous KNIL soldiers on Sumatra: this assistance was organized by G. Sauberts, an agricultural expert at the testing station of the Algemeene Vereeniging van Rubberplanters ter Oostkust van Sumatra (which had been taken over by the Japanese); he lost his life in 1944 in a ship transport of prisoners of war.

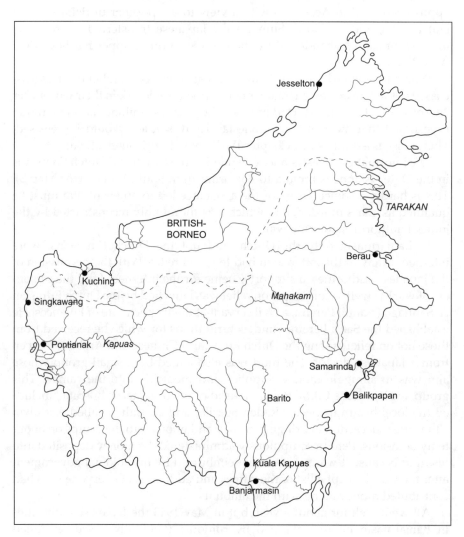

Map 3. Borneo

Indonesian spies. The first arrests took place on 10 May: in the women's camp the Japanese confiscated all the paperwork and singled out a group of women, including the wife of Governor B.J. Haga – they were forced to disrobe before them and dance around naked. This was followed by three waves of arrests in June and August, the one in June being the largest during which Japanese tanks rolled through the streets of Banjarmasin while Japanese bombers flew above the city, all in an effort to intimidate. A total of about 250 people were arrested, including Santi Pereira, Nurse Reichert and Soesilo. Evidence of punishable offences was found: clandestine contact had been maintained with internees, radios were discovered in various places, Dutch flags and pieces of red, white and blue coloured fabric had been hidden, and it also appeared that those who used their radios had passed on messages to third parties. Moreover, some Chinese owned firearms which, they claimed, they only wanted to use to protect themselves from looters: on Borneo, as elsewhere in the archipelago, all firearms had to be turned over to the Indonesian police.

On the basis of these facts, the Japanese authorities in Banjarmasin could have prosecuted the parties in question, but this was not enough. The Japanese police chief, Iwao Sasuga, informed his superiors that he was convinced that in Borneo an anti-Japanese uprising was being secretly planned, which would break out the minute the Allies landed there. Whether this was his honest conviction fuelled by the suspicion so often evident in the actions of the Kempeitai, or whether he was attempting to stage a situation that would enhance his reputation in Japanese circles, is a matter of conjecture. One fact is sure, however; he hounded his subordinates to unearth the so-called evidence of the uprising. And thus, it appeared that an Ambonese midwife had regularly gone from Banjarmasin to Surabaya and returned with provisions and medicine destined for the internees, as well as clandestine letters which, evidently, contained instructions for the revolt. An Indonesian radio mechanic owned a – defective – radio and radio parts: this was the secret transmitter, and a second transmitter was said to be functioning from the telephone office. Moreover, it appeared that a diary had been kept by a woman in the women's camp filled with caricatures of the Japanese, and that Governor Haga's wife had in her possession a letter smuggled into the camp reporting: 'The news is exceptionally good, keep up your courage'. The revolt was thus at hand. It appeared that everyone in the women's camp had agreed to seek shelter in the Chinese school when the Allies turned up: thus, the arrival of the Allies was imminent. Governor Haga, in the men's camp along with ten other officials, allegedly wrote a document about the post-war administrative reform of Borneo, so he too was counting on the landing of the Allies. The head of the Baseler Mission (a Swiss organization with a missionary hospital) in Banjarmasin, the Swiss doctor C.M. Vischer, had passed on an amount of 40,000 guilders to the treasurer (partly the subsidy he had received from Basel in early 1943, and partly colonial government monies entrusted to him by Haga): this was the money financing the revolt. Now the weapons! And these too were 'found', namely the 400 rifles that had been handed over to the *jaksa*, the Indonesian public prosecutor in Kuala Kapuas, about 100 kilometres northwest of Banjarmasin.

In the eyes of a Japanese court of law, in this case a navy court, all of these suspicious events could only serve as proof of an impending uprising if there were also confessions to this effect. These confessions were provided. A large number of detainees were brutally mistreated: they were kicked, beaten with clubs and pistol butts, electrocuted, and subjected to water torture. At Sasuga's trial in 1948, one of the warders stated:

> I heard Soesilo's interrogation behind closed doors. The sound of beating could be heard through the doors. Begging for mercy, Soesilo's voice went on through the screams of: 'Confess or you will die!' Then I was called in and the doctor lying unconscious on the floor was sprinkled with water. He was dragged away. [...] Following another interrogation [...] Soesilo only collapsed once he was back in his cell. On many occasions I saw that prisoners had blue and swollen areas after they had been interrogated.[115]

Each forced confession led to new arrests, even in places as far away as Surabaya, Tarakan and Balikpapan. Five KNIL soldiers were transferred from Balikpapan to Banjarmasin: three officers who were to have functioned as leaders of the so-called uprising, and two NCO's. As mentioned, a total of about 250 arrests were made, including everyone (except for the Japanese doctor) whose name and address was on Pereira's list, because he had 'confessed' that he had been planning the uprising, and not providing assistance. The prison in Banjarmasin and several temporary prisons filled up and remained full even after some 100 detainees were successively released. The Japanese authorities found a simple solution to this problem: in August and September 1943, more than 120 detainees were led in large groups to the airfield in Banjarmasin and beheaded. One day when such a mass execution took place, the Japanese airfield commander told an Indonesian coolie working there: 'Stay here. There is no work today, Dutchmen are going to be slaughtered.'[116]

Twenty-six detainees, including Haga, were called before a navy court. He had a heart attack on the first day of the trial and died while on the way to the

---

[115]   Witness Oesman daeng Koello in the judgement, of the TKR Banjarmasin against Iwao Sasuga, 17 July 1948, p. 14 (NIOD IC).
[116]   Witness Slamat in the judgement, of the TKR Banjarmasin against Iwao Sasuga, 17 July 1948, p. 17 (NIOD IC).

hospital. The 25 remaining detainees were condemned to death and beheaded at the airfield, including Pereira, Soesilo, the ten Dutch officials, Vischer and his wife, the Indonesian radio mechanic, Haga's wife, Nurse Reichert and two other women. With or without the verdict of a court, this case cost the lives of about 150 people, including 33 Chinese, a number of Arabs (among them the leader of the Arab community in Banjarmasin and his two sons) and 12 Ambonese and Manadonese. Those decapitated without a verdict or who succumbed in prison included the Indian Abdullah, the Ambonese midwife who had smuggled letters from Surabaya, the treasurer of the Baseler Mission and his wife, the wife of the Indonesian radio mechanic, the three Indonesians who had worked at the telephone office, the *jaksa* of Kuala Kapuas and the three Dutch officers who had been taken from their camp in Balikpapan.

The death sentences were announced in the *Borneo Shimbun* on 21 December 1943 (the Americans had taken the Gilbert Islands and were getting ready for their jump to the Marshall Islands). It was claimed that a dangerous revolt had been nipped in the bud. 'The strategic plans', it continued:

> that will guarantee our victory in the Greater East Asian war are now complete and the peoples of Greater East Asia must join forces. [...] Therefore rigorous measures must also be taken against those disrupting law and order, and the imposition of the strictest punishment on those found guilty of this serious crime is justified. [...] As the war becomes more fierce, the enemy, who is almost exhausted, will undoubtedly attempt to infiltrate even more deeply into our territory with his cursed spies. The naval authorities sincerely hope [...] that the entire population realizes just how vengeful the enemy is and that it enters the final phase of this decisive war with the spirit necessary for our victory.

Finally, it should be mentioned that on 18 August 1945, that is three days after the announcement of the Japanese capitulation, the Swiss envoy in Tokyo was informed by the Japanese Ministry of Foreign Affairs that Vischer was recognized as the delegate for Borneo of the Comité International de la Croix Rouge. Since 1942, the Comité had been calling for this for more than three years, to no avail, and Vischer had been beheaded almost two years earlier.

The measures described above adversely affected many of the Dutch, Dutch Eurasians and Indonesian former KNIL soldiers and their families on Java. The banks and post-office savings bank were closed, postal money orders were no longer cashed, payment of pensions was discontinued, all salaries were drastically reduced, Dutch businesses were taken over by the Japanese and/or liquidated, Dutch and Dutch Eurasians had to pay relatively high prices for their identity cards and additional taxes were levied on all who in 1941 had earned more than 3,000 guilders annually or had capital worth 25,000 guilders or more.

Many could get by for a time by starting up a small business or selling their possessions, others were helped by their employers. Various businesses (including the Bataafsche Petroleum Maatschappij (BPM), an oil company; the Koninklijke Paketvaart Maatschappij (KPM), a shipping line; the Internatio, a banking and trading company; the Lindeteves Stokvis trading firm; the Nederlandsch-Indische Gas Maatschappij, a gas company; the Factorij van de Nederlandsche Handelmaatschappij, a banking and trading company; and the other Dutch banks) succeeded in concealing part of their cash resources and were in a position to help the employees they had been forced to dismiss.[117] In many instances, they made available the money needed for registration at the end of April and beginning of May. Nevertheless, even before the end of April other help proved necessary on a relatively large scale.

This was provided by the churches and municipal organs, and by private committees sometimes working in conjunction with them, and on East Java by the Red Cross, among others.

In Batavia, the Protestant parish poor relief immediately resumed its normal work on behalf of the Dutch, Dutch Eurasian, Chinese and Indonesian Protestants. It also established its own shop where provisions could be bought for a normal price, which was significant chiefly in March and April, when prices rose dramatically at the markets. It also had a small hospital, a housing and transport department (important because many Dutch and Dutch Eurasians needed cheaper rentals or had begun to share accommodation), and a workshop for bicycles and electrical appliances. Help was also given to Protestant and neutral institutions outside of Batavia, and right up to the Japanese capitulation a total of more than 130,000 guilders was paid out, providing solace to some 6,000 people. The work of the Batavian parish was led by H.H. van Herwerden, and continued by several Dutch Eurasian Protestants when he was suspected of anti-Japanese actions in November 1943 and arrested by the Kempeitai.

In Bandung, the Japanese military administration refused permission for Protestant relief work, which therefore was carried out clandestinely under J.A. Verkuyl, among others, who was swiftly interned. The clandestine relief work also assisted non-Protestants. Its financial resources were chiefly provided by two Jewish diamond dealers from Belgium, the Kinsbergen brothers, who were able to continue selling diamonds and jewellery primarily to the Japanese, and who also took out loans, we assume from wealthy Chinese. Incidentally, it was Chinese rice wholesalers who, whenever they had to transport rice to Bandung by train, passed on one wagon to the par-

---

[117] The BPM was able to withhold 1.2 million guilders, which was entrusted to eight Swiss men; they were able to disburse money until February 1943, when this scheme was discovered and terminated by the Kempeitai.

ish. The rice was then taken to a secret address and distributed to the needy. This operation ran into trouble in 1943 when those in charge following Verkuyl's internment (including K. Posthumus, who had been the headmaster of the Protestant High School in Bandung) were also interned. However, Dutch Eurasians were able to continue the relief work and the soup kitchen remained operative.

In Malang, the Protestant parish performed comparable relief work until August 1943, when a Kempeitai raid temporarily shut it down. When work was resumed under the leadership of a few Dutch Eurasians, they got into trouble with a pro-Indonesian and also pro-Japanese group among the Dutch Eurasians, which will be discussed in greater detail in Chapter VI.

From the beginning of the occupation, the Catholic church also undertook both open and clandestine relief action. Several Catholic social institutions were able to continue their work, and Monsignor Willekens provided powerful support from Batavia.

With respect to the municipal organs, various large cities, including Batavia, had established soup kitchens in the invasion months for people involved with air-raid defence and other war services. These were reinstituted to provide the needy with hot food at minimal prices. In Batavia, this assistance was set up only a few days after the arrival of the Japanese on 5 March. How long it remained operative is unknown.

In addition, in the capital, the Indo-Europeesch Verbond, or IEV, which had given aid to destitute Dutch Eurasians since its establishment, expanded its assistance. It is important to note here that the deputy burgomaster, A.T. Bogaardt, a member of the IEV's executive board, was released by the Japanese shortly after his imprisonment on 7 March so that he could restore the supply of food to the capital, which at that point had broken down. He saw to it that the Stichting Indo-Europeesch Arm-Bestuur, the Sievab, extended help to all disadvantaged Europeans, thus also the Dutch.

As a result of the progressive impoverishment and numerous arrests, by mid-1942 the need for aid was even greater than it had been in March and April. A new plan was devised: at the end of June, a delegation of European inhabitants in Batavia (Dutch and Dutch Eurasians) received permission from the Japanese burgomaster to establish a Gemeentelijk Europeesch Steun-Comité (GESC, Municipal European Assistance Committee), the GESC, headed by the man (the Japanese always wanted a single person to be accountable to them) who had also led the delegation, Frans Kramer.

Kramer was still chairman of the General Agricultural Syndicate in Batavia. He had been a member of the executive of the East Indies Employers Association and of numerous committees active in the area of economic planning, and in late 1940 he had founded the Landwachten, analogous to the already established Stadswachten. He had instituted a Comité van Stadsen Landwachten which had collected large amounts for both semi-military organizations. When Batavia was occupied, the Comité had about 200,000 guilders in cash. Kramer was responsible for making the lion's share simply vanish from the books; it was first concealed in his home in Batavia and later transferred to his country house in the mountains beyond Buitenzorg. He was 47 years old in March 1942, a man full of drive, with many friends and not a few enemies. His friends were also his admirers, regarding him as being cast in the same mould as the able governors-general, while his enemies considered him a busybody driven by objectionable ambition. No one denied that he was a fine organizer.

The GESC established a general board in which the existing Catholic and Protestant relief organizations as well as the (Dutch Eurasian) Sievab were represented, and a managing board consisting of three members: Kramer (chairman), H.J. Manschot, department chief of the Javasche Bank, and the Jewish diamond dealer A. Gutwirth.

Even before the GESC was founded, the municipality of Batavia had decided to disburse basic help to needy Indonesians, Chinese and Arabs in the form of half a litre of rice and five cents a day. In July, this basic help was extended to Dutch and Dutch Eurasians; to qualify they had to fill in a form in Indonesian about their income. The following question in Dutch was included in a section intended for Dutch women: 'Do you presently take part in prostitution?'[118] Information about the number of people receiving municipal relief in Batavia is only available for a period of four weeks: the second week of August 1942, the third and fourth weeks of January 1943 and the first week of February 1943, as well as about one month, namely March 1943. In the second week of August 1942, aid was given to almost 36,000 Indonesians, more than 4,400 Chinese, almost 1,500 Arabs and over 9,000 Europeans, in total representing about a tenth of the population of Batavia (of the Europeans, about a quarter received aid). The Japanese proceeded to introduce a division, determining that the payment of support to Europeans should no longer be done by municipal organs, but by the GESC, with the understanding that it could also provide aid to Indonesians, Chinese and Arabs to the extent that they had been accorded legal status equal to that of Europeans by the colonial government over the years.[119] For those granted this equal standing, the GESC's support proved appealing, for – once it was up and running – this organization offered far greater support than the municipal organs.

[118]   Cited in Klerks, 'Verslag inzake het *relief*-werk te Batavia', n.d., p. 2 (NIOD IC, 52).
[119]   Under the Dutch colonial administration it was possible for some socially successful Indonesians and Foreign Orientals to be legally included in the category of Europeans. Criteria of a social and cultural nature were decisive in this. Between 1881 and 1940 about 16,500 people were made 'equal' to Europeans.

By the end of August various subcommittees were functioning under the GESC's general and managing boards. One relief subcommittee initially only extended money but by the end of August was able to distribute fairly substantial amounts of food, soap and other articles which were purchased from municipal reserve supplies at low prices. A medical subcommittee took over 17 larger and smaller hospitals, set up an outpatient clinic and distributed medicines via its own dispensaries – all medical help was provided free of charge (the idea was that the patients would pay for treatment after the war). A third subcommittee took care of the acquisition of food. A fourth one took responsibility for all transportation. A fifth one arranged for housing, that is to say helping people move to less expensive quarters or joining two families under a single roof. A sixth one took care of packages of clothing, smoking materials, soap, and so on, which were occasionally sent (this was possible up to April 1943) to prisoners of war and male civilian internees.

Of these subcommittees, the one for relief had the most extensive organization: about 30 stations were set up throughout Batavia, each under the leadership of a woman and staffed by a group of female helpers. These aid stations processed requests for support and in cases of proven need took care of giving money and goods. Each aid station had a nurse on duty capable of dispensing first aid and simple medicines and when necessary of arranging for treatment by doctors and specialists.

In September, the GESC was assigned a new task. It had to organize the housing in the Kramat and Cideng districts where the Japanese wanted to isolate the Dutch women, children and elderly men. When these districts were evacuated in the course of October, the GESC had the dwellings cleaned and also managed the distribution of these dwellings, while the subcommittee for transportation took care of the actual moves. The GESC also set up camp shops in both districts for which it regularly supplied goods.

As mentioned above, in the second week of August 1942 more than 9,000 Europeans (we assume these were primarily Dutch Eurasians) received relief. When the Dutch were interned, however, the relief payments for Europeans were made solely to Dutch Eurasians: more than 11,000 people received aid in the last two weeks of January and the first week of February 1943, and about 10,500 in March 1943. Moreover, in this period, the GESC supported approximately 1,500 Indonesians (these may have been primarily Ambonese and Manadonese ex-KNIL soldiers) and almost 400 Chinese. The money necessary for direct aid was partially extended by the municipality at a rate of five cents per person per day. On this basis, in the periods in 1943 just mentioned, the GESC received a municipal subsidy of about 18,000 guilders a month. Naturally, it needed far more to carry out its work: according to the budgets for January and February 1943 (additional information is lacking), more than 15,000 guilders was needed for January and almost 18,000 more for February. These additional disbursements must have been greater in the period prior to the internment of the Dutch, when the work was more extensive, than after.

In addition, one more committee was established in October 1942. The composition of this financial committee is unknown, but in any event it included the three members of the managing board, Kramer, Manschot and Gutwirth. Chiefly through the efforts of Gutwirth, who had numerous business relations, the committee received funding from small firms run by Europeans that had not yet been taken over by the Japanese, and primarily from wealthy Chinese. All of this money was borrowed – it would be repaid after the war at an annual interest rate of 6% and on the gold basis (no one knew what the Indonesian guilder would be worth). Bonds issued by the colonial government were usually signed by Manschot, who was authorized to do this by the president of the Javasche Bank, Van Buttingha Wichers, who had been contacted even though he was interned. The fact of this author-ization was relayed to anyone desiring greater assurance than Manschot's signature. This clandestine borrowing was discovered by the Kempeitai in mid-1943, after which it was no longer possible. According to the Kempeitai report of February 1944 regarding the resistance on Java quoted above, the government had loaned a total of 95,999 guilders.

Clearly, Kramer did not use the almost 200,000 guilders he had with-drawn from the Comité van Stads- en Landwachten and hidden in his country house for the GESC work. He had earmarked that money for other purposes, namely to finance a broad-based underground movement to initi-ate activities on Java that would expedite the arrival of the Allies and assist them after their landing.

As chairman of the General Agriculture Syndicate, Kramer enjoyed a certain freedom of movement – on occasion he could travel to Buitenzorg, Bandung, and Sukabumi, and once to Semarang. Even though it was forbid-den by the Japanese, he sometimes took along money for aid organizations that had originated outside of Batavia, money from the GESC, and from the GESC's cash funds he also contributed to the largest relief organization which had been set up in Semarang. Some GESC employees eventually came to suspect that he also financed all sorts of underground groups: unaware of the almost 200,000 guilders he had stashed away, they assumed he was doing this with GESC monies. The former secretary of the GESC board stated in April 1947:

> The suspicion some of us had was a certainty for Mr Gutwirth. This is why he contrived means of tactfully putting an end to this. After all, should this suspi-cion prove correct, then our aid organization, which was so essential to the Dutch community, would be placed in grave jeopardy. Consequently, we did not at all

approve of Mr Kramer's actions, no matter how well intended and in the interest of the Allied cause.[120]

Tension between Gutwirth and Kramer mounted. Gutwirth wanted Manschot and himself to have the right of veto for all of Kramer's expenditures, but Kramer, who had no need of the GESC's money to support underground groups, refused to accept such supervision. This conflict was still unresolved when Kramer was arrested by the Kempeitai at the end of December 1942.

His underground work is discussed in the following chapter, and the further development of the GESC is examined in Chapter VI. Here we will limit ourselves to the remark that the risks Kramer created for the GESC were not so much related to the allegation that he made monies destined for the GESC available for illegal purposes, but to the fact that he, the chairman of the GESC, was at the same time (and completely independently of this) financing illegal work.

In Bandung, the city council set up three soup kitchens at the end of March 1942: one for Indonesians in need, one for Chinese (it soon became unnecessary and was closed) and one for Europeans. They offered simple meals for five cents per person. Soon several thousand people a day were using the soup kitchens, among them an unknown number of Europeans. These Europeans, and particularly the poor among the Dutch Eurasians, needed more help. In mid-1942 it was decided at the recommendation of the GESC to establish a committee to raise funds to this end. The committee collected in Bandung and its surroundings but also received support from elsewhere: 11,000 guilders from Surabaya and 10,000 from Batavia (from the GESC). The collection and distribution of the funds (30,000 guilders a month was required) and of the goods they managed to obtain was done clandestinely. To be on the safe side, all these activities took place under the cover of the church committee already mentioned, which itself had to operate clandestinely – the assumption was that if the Japanese found out they would object less to a church operation than to general humanitarian work.

Around September 1943 those who had run the church campaign and all those who had organized non-church help were interned. Help, however, continued to be given on a smaller scale.

With respect to Central Java we only have information about Surakarta, Magelang and Semarang.

In Surakarta most of the Dutch women went to live in a school complex

---

[120]   Subcommissie Batavia van het Regeringsbureau ter opsporing van Japanse oorlogsmidaden, proces-verbaal by J.E. Eckenhausen-Tetzner, 6 April 1947, p. 2 (NIOD IC, 28,991).

after their husbands were arrested (in the end it had nearly 700 inhabitants). The Japanese military administration set up a camp for Ambonese, Manadonese and Dutch Eurasians in need: about 1,000 people a day were given some money here, fifteen cents at first, five later. The city council determined later in 1942, however, that Dutch Eurasians who were not in need had to raise money to assist the approximately 1,000 who were. They managed to do this, with the aid of several wealthy Chinese and the Mangkunegoro, the autonomous ruler of Mangkunagaran, which had broken away from the principality of Surakarta in 1757. (From 1916 to July 1944, the ruler was the pro-Dutch Mangku Nagoro VII.) This aid could be given only until December 1942, when the school and the camp were evacuated and the occupants taken to internment camps elsewhere.

From May 1942 until the internment of the Dutch women and children, Magelang had a soup kitchen organized by a Dutch woman, the two Protestant ministers and the Catholic priest. The necessary funds were given by the Dutch community. They began by providing about 300 meals a day but the number soon grew, though by how much is unknown.

In Semarang a woman doctor, M. van Oort-Lau, began providing help in April 1942. At first she was on her own (after a few weeks she was handing out rice to 200-300 needy individuals three times a week), but help soon came from two Dutch people, and some time later she had the cooperation of the three priests. Her own property and the Catholic and Protestant orphanages became distribution points. 'Each week', she wrote in her report in 1947,[121] 'more and more people registered; the maximum was 1,960, exclusively Europeans, mainly Dutch Eurasians, soldiers' wives and children, all with no source of income'. Mrs van Oort also organized a shelter for the homeless 'where in the end between 80 and 100 people lived, supported entirely from my rice fund'.

In October 1942 Kramer came to Semarang, where the Japanese had appointed the former burgomaster district manager of the Europeans. There were serious objections to him, however, because he had been in too much of a hurry to leave Semarang on the first day of the invasion, Sunday 1 March.[122] Kramer said that he could make 2,000 guilders available for Semarang in Batavia, 500 guilders of which had to be used to set up soup kitchens in the internment district of Lampersari. What was to be done with

---

[121]   Brugmans 1960:292-5.
[122]   During the night of Saturday 28 February and in the course of Sunday 1 March 1942, the Japanese landed near Rembang, about 100 kilometres east of Semarang. That same afternoon almost all the government officials, police and paramilitary units left the city in great haste. After this chaotic exodus, houses, shops and commercial premises in Semarang were plundered and set ablaze. The authorities then quickly returned to restore order. Japanese troops did not enter Semarang until 7 March.

the remaining 1,500 guilders? The former burgomaster wanted to use this money for a social service with himself in charge, but at a gathering of prominent members of the Dutch and Eurasian community it was decided that the 1,500 guilders would be put in Mrs van Oort's rice fund. She went to Batavia herself to collect the 2,000 guilders, having been granted a travel permit on the grounds that she had to see a consultant there. In December, with another permit, she was again able to collect 2,000 guilders from the GESC.

Meanwhile she had begun collecting food, cigarettes, money and medicines which were smuggled into a nearby prisoner-of-war camp in an operation run by a Madurese. He relayed a request to supply the prisoners with news about the progress of the war. 'I agreed: we listened ourselves every evening and so about twice a week I typed reports on a slip of paper, a compilation from the bulletins from the BBC, San Francisco and Sydney'. In December she was arrested by the Kempeitai for smuggling these news reports. 'I had to promise never to do it again, and I was released after about an hour's interrogation'. She resumed passing on news and was re-arrested in mid-January 1943. This time she was taken to Batavia and there sentenced to five years in prison by the Japanese military court. This was the end of her relief efforts.

The former burgomaster subsequently set to work with his social service, but with little success. In October 1943 he was arrested on suspicion of espionage and appallingly mistreated by the Kempeitai. Early in 1945 the Japanese military court sentenced him to ten years' imprisonment.

In Surabaya the local military administration agreed in March 1942 that the Housewives' Association should take charge of social assistance. Here it was the same as elsewhere: as soon as one organization, no matter which, was recognized by the Japanese, it could count on help from any number of people who had barely known of its existence before. The Association was able to help no less than 10,000 families. Mainly because of the aid that European companies could still give (in Surabaya, which was governed by the Japanese navy, they were less strictly supervised and less quickly liquidated than elsewhere on Java), the Association was relatively well off (the 11,000 guilders made available for help in Bandung came from it).[123] When it had to cease its work in August 1943, it was in a position to give all the Dutch Eurasians registered with it an amount sufficient to live on for about five months. There had been earlier money payments too, as well as the distribution of goods: rice, flour, oil, soap and other articles, and for young mothers milk and baby food and clothes. Lastly, the Association had succeeded in

---

[123]   Part of these funds had been clandestinely raised by P. Colijn, the agent of the Nederlandsche Handelmaatschappij.

housing evacuees from parts of East Java and the families of Ambonese and Manadonese KNIL soldiers in empty school buildings.

The Dutch East Indies Red Cross was also active in Surabaya. The executive of this organization, located in Bandung, had stopped work in April 1942, hoping that it would be granted permission in Batavia to resume its activities. This did not happen, partly because the official delegate of the Comité International de la Croix Rouge located in Geneva, W. Weidmann, Switzerland's consul general in Batavia, was not prepared to take any risks – he did nothing of any significance for either the prisoners of war or the internees.

The Swiss consul at Surabaya, on the other hand, M.E. Keller, and his Swedish colleague A. Wiesländer protected the local department of the Red Cross, and at their instigation the Japanese naval commander gave permission for the Red Cross to provide all kinds of help to the prisoners of war on East Java. It was also authorized, when the internment camp at Kesilir was established, to collect everything needed there. The same thing happened with the internment locations, among them the Darmo district, in Surabaya. It was important too that up to the end of 1942 the Red Cross's information office managed to secretly collect the names of about 56,000 prisoners of war and internees.[124] Lastly, before it was abolished in May 1943 (Keller had been arrested shortly before),[125] from Surabaya the Red Cross was able to set up departments in ten places on Central and East Java. Of these, the one in Malang, headed by a doctor, J.H. Soesman, was particularly active. With the permission of the Japanese, Soesman was able to turn his Red Cross Committee, which included a Japanese officer, into a Central Assistance Committee that found cheap accommodation for the destitute, set up shelters for the homeless, organized soup kitchens and arranged for medical services. The Committee, which helped 2,000 family members of ex-KNIL soldiers among others, collected about 150,000 guilders, not least from wealthy Chinese, for its work, which it was able to continue until August 1944.

What emerges particularly clearly from the facts set out in this section is the extent to which the East Indies had become fragmented. Under Dutch rule it had been one territory with highly efficient, rapid communications. The postal service reached the most remote corners of the archipelago, and there was a network of post offices and bank branches through which payments could be made.

[124] This work was continued during a period (late August to late November 1942) in which several of the leading officials were imprisoned and tortured by the Kempeitai.
[125] After the abolition, activities continued clandestinely on a smaller scale under the leadership of the Dutch Eurasian J.W. Wiedenhof.

The only inter-island connections that continued to function under the Japanese, apart from the proa trade, were those run by them purely for the use of their military and civilian administration and of their banks and other commercial organizations. Otherwise the Indies was fragmented, with Borneo and the Great East administered almost as a separate state by the Japanese navy and little contact between the military governments on Java and Sumatra. On the Outer Islands, the Dutch and Dutch Eurasians had to help themselves as best they could; there was no assistance from elsewhere.

Java was no longer an entity. In each town, and each district, the Dutch and Dutch Eurasians had to rely on their own resources; groups facing the same problems had to find solutions of their own. There were few cases in which organizations in one region (the GESC in Batavia, the Housewives' Association in Surabaya) were able to help similar bodies in another one.

This fragmentation was reflected in everything known about the relief efforts. A central approach was no longer possible – so what was nonetheless achieved locally and regionally despite all the difficulties was all the more admirable. There is no doubt that their efforts, which cannot be described in full (much of the information has been lost), were a great support to tens of thousands among the Dutch and especially the Dutch Eurasians and the Ambonese and Manadonese ex-KNIL soldiers. As an example of spontaneous social commitment, it was comparable to the campaigns organized in the winter of 1944-1945 when the western Netherlands faced famine. In that case this activity had not been prohibited by the occupying forces, whereas in the Indies it was followed by the Kempeitai with deep suspicion. Indeed, these efforts ran into difficulties everywhere, either because of the intervention of the rightly feared military police or because, on Java at least, assistance for Dutch Eurasians in 1943 and 1944 was taken out of the hands of the bodies they themselves had formed and entrusted nearly everywhere to the small pro-Indonesian and pro-Japanese group we shall come back to in Chapter VI. After that the Eurasians were even more isolated than before.

Isolation

At the beginning of November 1942, at the time when the mass internment of women, children and elderly men started on Java, the Japanese military administration took a measure that substantially increased this isolation. With the exception of Nippon workers and the citizens of neutral states or states allied to Japan, all 'foreigners' had to hand in their radios on 8 November.[126] This rule thus also applied to the Dutch and Dutch Eurasians.

[126] Radios belonging to Chinese or Indonesians who were imprisoned also had to be handed in.

Several of those in Batavia who had moved at an early stage to the Kramat and Cideng districts had brought their radios and others planned to do so. This was now impossible. To be sure, the radios had generally been 'castrated' several months earlier, but many had been able to go on listening to Allied broadcasts. Keeping your radio was risky: it had to be assumed that the post office had records of the radios for which the licence fee had been paid.[127] Only those whose radio was not registered could consider ignoring the Japanese order.

In Malang, according to the later account of one Dutch woman:

> We stood with our radios in long lines in the forecourt of the resident's house, where now the Japanese flag flew. There were lorries in the drive, with native police parading about importantly. Native officials sat at a table and were very curt and aloof when asking their questions (a brilliant imitation of the Japs): 'Nama?' (name), 'Ini radio poenja siapa?' (whose radio is this) and so on.
>   High-ranking Japanese officers were present here and there. If they said something to the 'big-shots' at the tables, the latter instantly turned into obsequious, smiling and bowing 'little-shots' who looked elatedly at the Europeans. They [...] were spoken to by demigods! (Moscou-de Ruyter 1984:58.)

In Bandung, noted Bouwer on 10 November, radios were brought to the town hall 'by the dozen' on the first day for handing them in.

> It's a hard blow for people. Even after the 'treatment', with most receivers you could still listen to the foreign stations. That is what people lived for. It made everything so much easier to bear. Of course news will still reach people, but it's bound to be less reliable. And the Japanese are determined to put a stop to clandestine listening. So anyone who can still listen to a hidden, sealed and mistreated radio or an unregistered receiver will have to be extremely careful about passing on what he hears.
>   [...] The local police, using certain lists, came round yesterday and today to collect radios from people who had not yet obeyed the order. But before that we were able to hear how strong American and British forces have landed in North Africa.[128] [...] It made parting with the radio all the more painful. (Bouwer 1988: 137-8.)

Bouwer's registered radio was seized by the Indonesian police on 11 November (he still had an unregistered one hidden in his garden). 'The

---

[127]   A van arrived at a company on Central Java on 8 November and all the Dutch and Dutch Eurasian employees were told to put their radios in it. One Dutchman hung on to his – 'the next day the heads of the *kampong* came to ask us to hand it in, because otherwise they would be in deep trouble with Nippon'. The radio was surrendered 'since, as just a handful of Europeans, we were to some extent reliant on the good will of the indigenous population' (L. van Empel in Boissevain and Van Empel 1981:50).
[128]   These landings took place on 8 November 1942.

houses were not searched. 3,000 radios are still missing,' he wrote on 14 November (Bouwer 1988:138); he evidently heard the last piece of information from a policeman or another contact.

The fact that on the third or sixth day after the deadline of 8 November so many radios (leaving aside whether or not the figure of 3,000 was correct) in Bandung had not been handed in shows the depth of resistance to this measure. Did the police seize all those receivers at a later date? We do not know, but Bouwer was certainly not the only person with an unregistered radio. Some people were able to assemble a radio from separate components and thus resume listening to Allied broadcasts.[129] But it must be assumed that most of the Dutch and Dutch Eurasians lost their radio, to their deep regret. This link to the free world had been a great support and now they were deprived of it.

A new Japanese measure followed the compulsory handing over of radios belonging to the Dutch and Dutch Eurasians: the broadcasts in Dutch intended for Java were ended. The last broadcast in Dutch on 7 December 1942 (that is, on the eve of the anniversary of Pearl Harbor) included the following announcement:[130]

> Since the military radio station has been on the air, we have provided Dutch listeners with an opportunity to follow day-to-day events in their own language. In this respect the noble and wise policy of the imperial Nippon army cannot be sufficiently praised. This policy is inspired by the high principles of justice. In accordance with these principles, this policy gives an honourable place to the defeated opponent.
>
> How very different is the situation in the Allied countries, where women and children are assembled in concentration camps in godforsaken places, where they are subjected to humiliations and hardships.

This was a reference to the fact that in California over 100,000 American citizens of Japanese origin, the so-called *Nisei*, who were viewed after the outbreak of the war in the Pacific as a highly dangerous fifth column on America's west coast, were detained in March and April 1942 and interned, initially in fairly primitive camps in the Rocky Mountains.

The announcement in the last broadcast in Dutch continued:

> Tomorrow, 8 December, Nippon and the parts of Asia liberated from Western imperialism will celebrate the first anniversary of the founding of the Greater East

---

[129] In March 1943 an ordinance was issued by the Japanese obliging anyone who assembled radio installations or manufactured or supplied components for them to report all such activities to the indigenous authorities by means of forms.

[130] Text in Brugmans 1960:190-1.

Asian order. [...] The enrichment of intellectual and cultural life makes it necessary to use only the official languages on the radio. [...] Nowhere in the world
do political norms or propriety demand that the language of an enemy country
should be spoken on the radio.

   The Dutch should consider that they have had sufficient time and opportunity
to learn enough Indonesian to meet their everyday needs. If, because of nar-
row-mindedness or arrogance, they believe they can manage with just their own
language, they must realize that in the new social order there is no place for such
delusions stemming from a closed chapter in the past.

On 30 November 1942, shortly before the ending of radio broadcasts in
Dutch, the following official announcement appeared in *Asia Raya* and the
other daily papers:[131]

   It is forbidden to use the Dutch or the English language. In connection with
   national security and in order to promote the use of the Japanese and Indonesian
   languages, from today all telephone conversations in English or Dutch will be cut
   off. Therefore everyone will do better not to use English or Dutch any more.

The general advice contained in the last sentence became a command in the
first months of 1943. Dutch and English were also banned in correspondence
and in conversations outside the home, and all the Dutch texts in advertising
signs were to be replaced by Indonesian.[132] Subsequently no Dutch books were
allowed to be reprinted; the only exception was the New Testament in the
Dutch Bible Society translation. In the course of 1943 it was also decreed that a
number of specifically named books in Dutch published by or in conjunction
with the colonial government had to be handed in to the Indonesian police.

   The ban on telephone conversations in Dutch was an impediment for
Dutch Eurasians. Anyone with a secondary education could get around it
by speaking German or French, which were allowed. Telephones could be
monitored, of course, but effective checks on conversations outside the home
were impossible. It is assumed (in the absence of further information) that
Eurasians often spoke Indonesian in their contacts with Indonesians but that
among themselves or with Indonesians they could trust they continued to
use Dutch inside and outside the home.

This section has the heading 'Isolation' and, indeed, less than nine months of
Japanese occupation were enough to achieve the social isolation of the Dutch
and to a large extent the Dutch Eurasians on Java step by step.

   Through the obvious privileging of Indonesians, the Japanese had directly and indirectly driven home the message that they viewed the Dutch and

---

131   Text in C.D. Ricardo, 'Aantekeningen 1942', p. 24 (NIOD IC, 29,422).
132   In Surakarta this order had already been announced in October 1942.

Eurasians as the lowest rank of inhabitants. Some Indonesian servants had given notice; Dutch civil servants and many other leading Dutch citizens had been arrested in April, and they had also disappeared from the police force; only the low-ranking Eurasian government employees had been kept on for the time being; the symbols of Dutch authority had had to be handed in; the last of the Dutch daily papers had disappeared in June and all the Dutch schools remained closed. Furthermore, between May and October 1942, most of the Dutch men and youths aged seventeen and over who were at liberty were caught and imprisoned. On East Java over 2,000 Dutch and Dutch Eurasian men and older youths had been sent to the closed area of Kesilir. Throughout Java the internment of Dutch women, children and elderly men had begun in October.

While they were being subjected to all these measures, most of the Dutch and Eurasians were locally isolated; they knew little of what was happening elsewhere on Java, let alone on the Outer Islands. What they experienced found no expression in the press or on the radio. It had become extremely difficult to correspond with people living elsewhere, and virtually nothing was heard from the prisoners of war or all the others who were being held. They had plenty to worry about. There was fear of the Japanese, fear of a sudden intervention by a power which, though it saw its policy as 'inspired by the high principles of justice', had shown itself to be unpredictable and at times shockingly cruel in its reactions.

The Dutch and Dutch Eurasians faced not only local isolation: fragmented in smaller and larger communities, they were also isolated as ethnic groups. The degree to which most of them were repeatedly taken in by absurdly optimistic rumours was a sign of the pressure they were under, and of their fear about the future. Their position was fundamentally more difficult than that of the population in the occupied mother country.

From the start of the German occupation, many there drew comfort from the knowledge that on the other side of the North Sea, not so far away, another nation was defying Germany. Royal Air Force bombers soon began attacking targets in the Netherlands or crossing Dutch air space by night. Radio broadcasts from London were widely listened to. But, above all, people knew that practically everyone yearned for the day when German power would either collapse or be defeated by the British. On this point, as early as the summer of 1940, there was an encouraging unanimity within the Netherlands.

How different was the situation in the East Indies! The Dutch and Dutch Eurasians together made up no more than about 0.4% of the population, or 4 in every 1,000. They might long for the arrival of Allied liberators, but was that also true of the overwhelming Indonesian majority? In general they had watched passively as the Dutch and Dutch Eurasians were forced into increasing isolation, even delighted in the spectacle occasionally. They had helped the Japanese here and there, and numerous prominent figures from their ranks had demonstratively sided with Japan.

All this meant that by the end of 1942 the Dutch and Dutch Eurasians were no more than a small, hard-pressed minority, perhaps remembering a past they thought of as glorious, and perhaps dreaming of a glorious future, but at present isolated and thrown back on their own resources. Until radios had had to be handed in, many drew hope from the Allied broadcasts, but no Allied planes appeared in the sky. The only power that could bring liberation had withdrawn a long way from the Indies, and far from Java in particular, infinitely far, it seemed.

As a rule, severe obstacles had to be overcome in order to escape from the occupied Netherlands. One had to cross the North Sea, or find a ship bound for Sweden, or make one's way to Switzerland or France with or without the help of underground organizations and then journey on to Spain or Portugal – from Portugal it was possible to reach England. A distinction may be made between those who escaped to England in order to continue the fight against Germany from there and the, chiefly Jewish, refugees. This is not an absolute distinction: there were non-Jews among the refugees and Jews among those who escaped in order to fight. From the summer of 1940 to that of 1944, about 200 of those trying to reach England crossed the North Sea; about 900 reached Sweden; about 1,000 France; and about 400 Switzerland. Out of these last three groups, about 500, 200 and 200 respectively were unable to go any further. Thus a total of about 1,600 reached England. As for the refugees, about 1,400 reached Switzerland, and about 2,200 France, of whom about 1,300 reached Spain and Portugal; from there they went to the East Indies (before the Japanese occupation, of course), the West Indies and to various points in North and South America.

With respect to the East Indies, as far as is known, throughout the entire Japanese occupation no attempt was made by any Indonesian to escape the area controlled by the Japanese from the main islands in the archipelago. At the end of 1943 this was done from the eastern Moluccas by, among others, Indonesian prisoners of war who were forced to work there by the Japanese. Van der Plas, the chairman of the Dutch East Indies Commission for Australia and New Zealand located in Melbourne, sent the following telegram from Washington to Van Mook[133] in London at the beginning of February 1944:

---

[133]   H.J. van Mook was lieutenant governor-general of the Dutch East Indies and minister for Colonial Affairs. He was evacuated to Australia just before the capitulation of the KNIL.

Apart from four Indonesians who have escaped from the eastern Moluccas and come to beg for a Dutch reoccupation of their islands, seven prisoners of war have escaped and brought extremely important military information.[134]

As for the Foreign Orientals (Chinese, Arabs, Indians and others), some Chinese may have tried to reach Nationalist China by means of the trade links they had built up in that part of Asia, but whether this actually happened is not known.

In the case of the Dutch and Dutch Eurasians, it should be borne in mind that on the Outer Islands nearly all of them were soon interned and that on the principal island, Java, the last months of 1942 marked a change: this was when most Dutch men aged between seventeen and sixty, excluding prisoners of war, were arrested, and most Dutch women and children and elderly men disappeared into 'protected districts' and other internment sites. As for the Dutch Eurasians, the majority of whom were not interned, they had little freedom of movement. Many of them looked different to Indonesians, so they were conspicuous. They could not travel freely, but had to obtain a permit (from December 1942 Eurasian women were in principle forbidden to travel). They were only allowed to buy a train ticket if they had a permit and could show their identity card, which, as 'foreigners', they always had to carry with them.

Furthermore, it would be wrong to imagine that society in the Indies had a primitive structure largely lacking the element of control and in which one could thus move freely with little hindrance. The forest is virtually impenetrable and where there is no forest there are swamps, mountains and inhabited areas. The swamps close to and the mountains generally far away from the coasts are inhospitable. In the inhabited areas outside the main cities (of which on Java only Batavia, Semarang and Surabaya are close to or on the coast) there was strict social control. A stranger in a *desa* immediately stood out. He would have to assume that his presence would be instantly reported to the head of the *desa*, the *lurah*, who would not fail to inform the subdistrict head, the assistant *wedono*. *Lurah*, assistant *wedono*, *wedono* and regents knew that the Japanese would be furious if they kept silent about the presence of strangers. It might be true that, given the extent of the island, the Japanese were numerically weak on Java, but they could take action anywhere and were thus potentially present everywhere. In the Philippines, on Malacca and in Burma whole regions were in the hands of anti-Japanese forces, but in the Indies there were no areas like that (disregarding Portuguese Timor in 1942 and a few districts in the hinterland of Dutch New Guinea).

Finally, the Indonesian archipelago consists of islands – Sumatra and Java are separated by oceans from Ceylon and Australia. Anyone planning to

---

[134] Telegram from Van der Plas to Van Mook, 2 February 1944 (ARA, MK, M 105, A 9-B).

escape from Sumatra, Java or another island needed a seaworthy boat which he could rig unnoticed, to which he could bring food and drinking water unnoticed and in which he could leave port unnoticed before venturing unnoticed on to the ocean, with all its dangers.

Eighteen Dutchmen are known to have taken this gamble from the islands east of Borneo.[135] A KNIL lieutenant, F. Hieronymus, escaped from captivity as a prisoner of war on Ambon and sailed via Ceram to Australia in a proa. H. Visser escaped in February 1942 from a prisoner-of-war camp on Ambon and reached Australia in a sailing boat.[136] Four KNIL soldiers – Lieutenant J.C.L. Stoll, Medical Officer H. Neel and Sergeants J. de Maar and F.H. Meyer – sailed from Timor and after finding two others on Flores – Lieutenant H.P. van den Dool and Sergeant C.E. Kroese – reached Australia in early April after a difficult voyage in a schooner. The last was T. Nieuwenhuyzen, who was in charge of the island of Saparua (near Ambon). When told in April 1942 that he should sail to Ambon to be interned there, he managed to escape to Australia. In the words of the *Gedenkboek van de Vereniging van Ambtenaren bij het Binnenlands Bestuur in Nederlands-Indië* (Memorial Book of the Association of Civil Servants of the Internal Administration in the Dutch East Indies):

> He reported to the Dutch authorities in Brisbane. It had been a dangerous voyage across seas controlled by the enemy, but those placed in the provisionally exalted position of the colonial government in exile took a rather different view: he had actually disobeyed orders by deserting his post (*Gedenkboek ambtenaren* 1956:23-4).

At the end of June 1942 an expedition commanded by Lieutenant Hieronymus was sent from Australia to the Kai Islands to raise the Dutch flag there, and Nieuwenhuyzen was sent along as an administrative officer. The expedition was a failure. A strong Japanese detachment landed on the same island and, after being betrayed, Hieronymus and Nieuwenhuyzen were arrested. They were taken to Ambon, tortured and killed: Nieuwenhuyzen was beheaded at the end of August or beginning of September 1942; Hieronymus was bayon-

---

[135]   In addition, an entire KNIL company reached Australia from Bobo (New Guinea) in March 1942.

[136]   Another successful escape from Ambon was made by the commander of the KNIL detachment at Laha airfield, First Lieutenant L.G. Snell. With eight other Dutch soldiers he crossed by proa to Ceram, there fitted out a boat and sailed to the Kai Islands, where he chartered a coaster and by way of Dobo and Merauke reached the Australian coast at the end of March 1942. The eight others were Medical Officer C. Ouwehand, Lieutenant J.F. de Bruyn, Sublieutenant W.F. Kniestedt, Sergeants G. Teljeur and A.G. Hueting, Corporal N.H.M. Donders and Privates T.J.C. Benningshof and T. Luitjes. Hueting was wounded in a shooting accident and had to be left behind on Ceram (where he was executed by the Japanese). Two Australian soldiers were taken from there. In Dobo Snell tried to make contact with Lieutenant F. Hieronymus, and H. Visser was picked up on the way to Merauke. During this part of the voyage a sailing boat carrying Australian soldiers was towed.

eted to death in October 1942.

As far as is known, no one from the Dutch or Dutch Eurasian communities tried to escape from Sumatra or Borneo – there was little time for that anyway because internment began early on.

There were a few escape attempts from Java, but only in 1942. Two succeeded; how many failed is not known. We do know that a group of nine Dutch and Dutch Eurasian men made preparations in June and July to escape to Australia. They were arrested at the end of July in Madura Strait near Probolinggo (see Map 1), almost certainly as the result of betrayal.[137] Early in December two Dutchmen left Banyuwangi on a mission for an underground group (more on this in the next chapter) in a proa provided by a Chinese. On arrival on Sumbawa at the end of December they were arrested by the Japanese and given prison sentences in Makassar. A third attempt also failed – that of the British Flight Lieutenant Gordon Coates, who was in touch with several Dutch underground groups in Buitenzorg and Bandung in mid-1942. The Kempeitai report on resistance on Java of February 1944, which has been quoted several times, says that there had been a total of three failed attempts to escape from Java, which could thus be correct.

Of the two successful escapes, the first was mainly organized by Reserve Lieutenant Cornelis C. van der Star[138] of the KNIL, and the second by a Dutch Eurasian regular NCO, Sergeant-Major H.J. de Haas.

Van der Star, who was 26 in 1942, had taken part in a long voyage across the Pacific on a sailing boat owned by a rich Canadian at the age of seventeen, and so had some experience of ocean sailing. He had his own small boat and had been member of the Yacht Club at Tanjungpriok; he had learned to use a sextant, and with it and a chronometer he could determine his position at sea.

As a reserve lieutenant, he was mobilized in December 1941, but on the grounds of his position with the electricity division of the Dutch East Indies Gas Company in Batavia he was soon able to resume his civilian work. This proved useful after the arrival of the Japanese: he was kept at his post and so had some freedom of movement, and, as a Nippon worker, he was exempt from the waves of arrests in April, May and June.

His decision to escape from Java if possible took firm shape soon after the occupation began. Escape in the direction of Ceylon seemed too risky. He

---

[137]   The leader died in captivity. The eight others and all who had helped were sentenced to 12 years in prison.
[138]   The description of his escape given here is largely based on his own account published in 1946, *Vier maanden onder de Jappen op Java en mijn ontsnapping*, supplemented by the information provided by Frank Visser in his *De Schakel; Een selectie authentieke verhalen van Nederlandse Engelandvaarders* (Baarn, 1976, pp. 66-83), corrected here and there by information from the official reports compiled immediately after the escape of Van der Star and his companions.

thought he would encounter numerous Japanese ships between Sumatra and Ceylon. Moreover, in a sailing boat with no engine on that route he would have to cross an area where there were often calms. If he wanted to have the benefit of the trade winds from the southeast, he would have to sail south or southwest. The Cocos Islands lie southwest of Sunda Strait (see Map 4) – Van der Star did not know that they were still in British hands. He decided to sail to Rodriguez, which he believed to be the nearest British-held island to the southwest.

He needed helpers as well as a boat and supplies. He found the first helper in May in Batavia, when through friends he met Willem Stokhuyzen from Bandung. He was 26 and had first worked for an oil company on Sumatra before becoming a planter on Java. When the Japanese landed, he was working for a building and housing agency in Bandung. A KNIL officer, Captain Frans van der Veen, was in hiding in the house next door to his. He had been in the Netherlands in May 1940, having been sent there by the KNIL. With other KNIL officers he had refused to sign the loyalty declaration that had been presented to all army and navy officers by the Germans in the summer of 1940. He was then imprisoned with others who had refused in Colditz Castle in Saxony. He had managed to escape from there in April 1941 and made his way back to the East Indies by way of Switzerland and Lisbon. When the KNIL capitulated he was in Central Java. But he had not escaped captivity in Germany only to fall into the hands of the Japanese! He travelled, largely on foot, to Bandung in the company of a young Dutch Eurasian. He went into hiding in Bandung in the home of a widow whose husband, a KNIL officer, had been killed on Tarakan. In April 1943 he was 33.

Before meeting Stokhuyzen and Van der Veen, in Batavia Van der Star had found some sea charts, an old sextant, a compass, a chronometer and a sea almanac for 1938. He had also established that his boat had sunk, but in the old harbour at Tanjungpriok he had seen another yacht that looked suitable for an escape. Once he, Stokhuyzen and Van der Veen were sure about the seriousness of each others' intentions and trust had grown between them, the latter two moved to Batavia and preparations for the escape went ahead. One evening in May, disregarding the curfew, they went to take a look at the boat Van der Star had found. It was gone. A short time later they found another, the *Pieternel*, about seven metres long and two metres wide, with a small cabin and a mast but no sails. It lay in a yard owned by a Chinese and turned out to be the property of a Dutch prisoner-of-war. How could they obtain it without arousing suspicion?

Stokhuyzen had a solution. Before meeting Van der Star, he had already decided in Bandung to leave Java if at all possible. While trying to find a boat, he had met a Swede who claimed to own a boat that he had used north of Celebes for pearl diving. Stokhuyzen suggested they should try to get a permit for deep-sea fishing for the boat. This idea appealed to the Swede, but when Stokhuyzen had obtained an official permit from the Japanese military administration in Bandung, the Swede confessed that his boat was in Makassar and thus impossible to reach. When he moved to Batavia, Stokhuyzen took a copy of this permit with him and it proved to be enough to get the *Pieternel* transferred to them.

A lot of work had to be done to get the boat ready for the voyage. A Chinese built a water tank in it that took up half the cabin. Two Makassar sailors (one had been a member of Van der Star's crew) from the marina were hired and paid to carry out the necessary repairs needed. A mainsail was brazenly requisitioned 'on behalf of the Japanese' from the wife of a Dutchman who was in prison, and a jib was found too. The water tank was filled (it held 200 litres); food (chiefly rice and tins of corned beef) was collected with the aid of several Dutch women; a charcoal stove turned up; and a hammock was made, because there was room for only one berth in the cabin. All these preparations took over a month – during which time Stokhuyzen and Van der Veen had to make sure they were not picked up in a raid, like so many others. On 1 July the decision was made: departure on the 6th.

On the afternoon of that day Van der Star used an ox-cart to bring most of the supplies to the *Pieternel*. That evening they took two bicycles and two trishaws, which carried the rest of their baggage, to the boat. They had five revolvers with several hundred rounds – if anything went wrong, they meant to sell their lives dearly. They were not spotted. The two Indonesian sailors helped them to cast off, and they sailed out of the harbour unseen in the dark. They had few charts for the first stretch, across the sea to Sunda Strait, which is full of reefs, but sailing blindly they reached the entrance to the strait by daylight. It was crowded with fishing boats. Stokhuyzen and Van der Veen sat in the cabin, while Van der Star put on an Indonesian fisherman's hat and threw a coloured blanket over his shoulder – they risked it. With some difficulty (the wind blew in the wrong direction for a time), they passed through Sunda Strait; it took them 36 hours. Now for the Indian Ocean!

After a week's sailing, during which they were often becalmed, the *Pieternel* was just north of the Cocos Islands. They pushed on. That same evening they were struck by a fierce hurricane. The mast broke off and fell overboard with the rigging – it all had to be hauled back on board with tremendous effort. The mainsail proved to be in shreds. A blanket was raised on the stump of the mast with the aid of a boathook. Lifted by gigantic waves and then smashed back down again (one wave left more than half a metre of water in the cabin, so that half the rice was soaking wet and had to be thrown away), the *Pieternel* was able to make some progress. The hurricane blew for four days and nights. When it was over, the mast was shortened with a knife (the only tools on board were the knife, a file, a screwdriver, a hammer, some nails and a dozen

Map 4. Journey of C. van der Star c.s.

darning needles). A triangular piece was cut out of the mainsail and fashioned into a new mainsail with enormous difficulty (eight of the twelve needles broke); it had to be repaired regularly. The trade wind pushed the *Pieternel* in the right direction again. To be on the safe side, they made a Dutch flag from pieces of red sports socks, a white shirt and blue shorts.

After four weeks at sea (the three men could hardly stomach rice and corned beef any more), the mainsail collapsed. A piece of it was nailed to the mast and, together with the small jib, this was enough to keep the boat moving.

On 6 August, with some difficulty, the *Pieternel* put into the harbour of Rodriguez. In 31 days it had covered about 5,000 kilometres. The first two British officers to come on board were told 'We're from Java'.

One British cruiser took the three men to Mombasa and another took them to Colombo. There they were the first to be able to give Admiral Helfrich a description of what had happened on Java up to the beginning of July. 'There was not much good news', he wrote later (Helfrich 1950, II:78).

The three men went their different ways. Van der Star was first attached to the Dutch secret service, the Nefis (Netherlands Forces Intelligence Service). In 1944, as a lieutenant in the Dutch Naval Reserve, he was given the command of a torpedo boat. After the war he became first adjutant to Lieutenant Governor-General Van Mook and then president of an aluminium-manufacturing company in California. Stokhuyzen went to England, where he became a reserve second lieutenant. He died in a road accident in Australia early in 1947. Captain Van der Veen stayed in Australia in military service throughout the war. Afterwards he continued his military career, which he ended in 1968, with the rank of lieutenant general, as Chief of the General Staff and chairman of the Dutch Committee of Chiefs of Staff.

At the end of 1942 an account of the escape appeared in *Collier's Weekly* in the United States. Copies of the magazine reached the Japanese legations in neutral states, and so the Japanese authorities on Java found out what had happened. In its February 1944 report on resistance on Java, the Kempeitai wrote, 'There is only one known case of a successful escape from Java'. In fact, there had been two cases and the Japanese were unaware of the second.

The second escape was carried out by five people: three of mixed origin who looked rather dark and could pass for Indonesian if they wore the appropriate clothing, and two Manadonese. The three of mixed origin – Sergeant Major H.J. de Haas[139] of the KNIL, customs officer C.D. Schlette and J.C. Buxton, who had recently earned a little money as a jazz drummer – had Indonesian mothers. De Haas and Schlette had a Dutch father; Buxton's father was of Anglo-American origin, and he was the only one who spoke English. All three spoke Indonesian well. The two Manadonese were a military policeman called Danus and a KNIL cavalryman, Mongan. De Haas, Danus and Mongan were married and had children. De Haas's wife and children lived in Salatiga on Central Java, the other four in Surabaya. Danus and Mongan had been released from captivity by the Japanese on the grounds that they were Indonesians. Schlette had been arrested in April as a Dutch civil servant but released because he earned less than 300 guilders a month. Buxton had stayed out of Japanese hands, possibly because he played drums in a club frequented by Japanese troops.

De Haas had avoided capture as a prisoner of war in March 1942 and made his way across Java in Indonesian dress, first going to see his wife and children. At the end of May he arrived in Salatiga for the second time. There

---

[139] Born in Batavia in 1904, he had enlisted in the KNIL at the age of 17 and had received various decorations.

he declared himself ready to carry letters from Dutch women in a case with a
false bottom to such places as Magelang, Yogyakarta, Bandung and Batavia
for one guilder per letter – with the money he would be able to take trains.
He travelled to these places, and saw hundreds of sick-looking prisoners of
war in and near Bandung who were collecting supplies for the camps. He
learned from them that conditions in the camps were bad, and also heard
vague rumours in Bandung and elsewhere about Dutch and Australian soldiers continuing to fight as guerrillas. He got a clear picture of the difficulties
the Dutch and Dutch Eurasians were having everywhere in keeping their
heads above water. With his own eyes he saw how the Japanese regularly mistreated Indonesians and others. In Bandung he heard from a twenty-year-old
niece how she and over twenty others had been arrested by the Kempeitai
for listening to Allied broadcasts and how they had been punished by having
their eardrums punctured.[140] To his considerable annoyance, he noted that
the Indonesians received preferential treatment from the Japanese, but his
impression was that they were very afraid of the occupying forces. He was
pained to see that many seemed to be under the spell of Japanese propaganda
and, in particular, that the Indonesian police treated the Dutch and Dutch
Eurasians with contempt.[141] He had no contact with educated Indonesians.
As for Sukarno, he heard only that he had invited various prominent figures
to dinner in Semarang and that he and all his guests had been arrested by the
Japanese and detained for some time.

Gradually the idea took shape in his mind that he ought to inform the
authorities in Australia, above all about the continuing guerrilla warfare and
the hardships faced by the Dutch and Dutch Eurasians. This became a firm
decision when in Bandung at the end of June he read the Japanese 'announcement to the Dutch' in a newspaper. It said that all Dutch men were to be
interned and that in the case of Dutch women and children consideration was
being given to 'offering them protection'; he kept this cutting with him. He
then told several individuals in Bandung that he intended to buy a proa and
sail to Australia. Initially he managed to collect 900 guilders: 200 from a minister, 200 from a pharmacist and 500 from the wife of an officer in the Military
Air Force. In Yogyakarta he secured a further 200 from the wife of a Dutch
judge and in Surabaya he got another 100, also from a Dutch woman.

Meanwhile he had begun looking in Surabaya for people who were prepared to risk making an escape with him. He already knew Schlette; how he

---

[140]   If the perforation is not too large, it will grow back together. In other cases perforation can
lead to permanently impaired hearing and infections.
[141]   As for the restoration of Dutch rule, he said on his arrival in Australia, 'First we'll have to
shoot a few million natives.' ('Notes on the interrogation of Sergeant Major De Haas', 25 January
1943, p. 2, (ARA, Alg. Secr., Eerste zending, XXIII, 56-I).

met the two Manadonese and Buxton is not known, but we do know that he included Buxton because he spoke English. He gave the two Manadonese some money for the dependants they were leaving behind. The five men decided not to leave from Surabaya because security was too tight there. They travelled to Banyuwangi (see Map 5), where they heard more about the Kesilir internment camp, which they had already learned something about in Surabaya. In Banyuwangi, De Haas, who acted as the leader of the group, pretended that he was a Sumatran who wanted to sail to Sumbawa with some helpers to buy horses and clothing (the Japanese had commandeered many horses on Java and textiles were in short supply). He was able to charter a fishing proa with its crew from a Balinese haji for 300 guilders. The proa left Banyuwangi at the end of September. When it reached Sumbawa, De Haas persuaded the skipper to go on to Sumba for an additional 200 guilders. At Sumba, he and the others went on shore and the proa sailed back to Java.

On Sumba, of course, the five new arrivals immediately stood out. One day De Haas was informed that he was to be questioned the next morning in the presence of several indigenous headmen. By chance, in the place where the five had found accommodation there was an Indonesian official born on the island of Savu. De Haas had heard that he was a Christian. He visited the official at night and received from him the names of several Ambonese living in Kupang, the principal town of Dutch Timor. De Haas could now say that he wanted to travel on to Kupang to do business with various Ambonese he knew there. The interrogation went off well, and the official and two Christian teachers, also from Savu, were able to find them a new proa. One of the teachers went with them to Savu in order 'to build trust, because the island was very strictly controlled', in the words of notes based on the report written by De Haas after he reached Australia.[142]

On Savu the five men were indeed promptly arrested. The raja had to decide what was to be done with them. According to the notes, he 'was urged by two headmen to hand De Haas over to Kupang', in other words, to the Japanese authorities there.

> A public investigation followed, but De Haas's fluent answers, referring to the so-called contacts in Timor, satisfied the raja, who released him. It turned out, however, that the raja knew about the pretence: on his departure [the raja had lent De Haas his third proa, a rather dilapidated craft] he saw De Haas off, saying in Malay, 'Gentlemen, I do not know your purpose, nor where you are going. I hope only that you will not get me into trouble as a result of this. I wish you a safe journey.'[143]

---

[142]   Notes based on the report of H.J. de Haas, 19 January 1943, p. 4 (ARA, Alg. Secr., Eerste zending, XXIII, 56-I).
[143]   Notes based on the report of H.J. de Haas, 19 January 1943, p. 4 (ARA, Alg. Secr., Eerste zending, XXIII, 56-I).

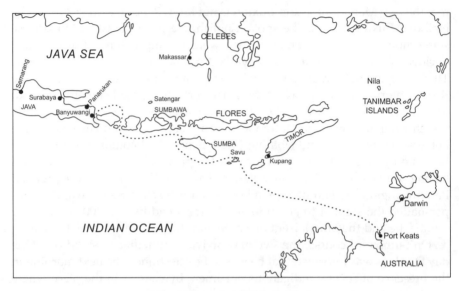

Map 5. Journey of H.J. de Haas

De Haas sailed past Timor and headed for the Australian coast, landing there on 13 December near a mission post. He was told to sail on to Port Keats. From there he and the others were flown to Darwin. Buxton remained in Darwin; De Haas, Schlette and the two Manadonese flew via Brisbane to Melbourne, where they were at first treated with suspicion by the Nefis. Early in February 1943, Rear Admiral F.W. Coster, second in command of Eastern Forces, wrote to Helfrich, the commander located in Ceylon:

> Initially there was some doubt (given the ease with which De Haas travelled in the Indies and left there) as to whether he was genuine or should be regarded as a Japanese agent. This has been investigated as thoroughly as possible, and not only De Haas but his companions have been interrogated on several occasions. They were also questioned by Van der Plas, who informed me that he is now entirely convinced that De Haas is a bona fide escapee.[144]

Nothing is known about the subsequent fate of Schlette, Buxton or the Manadonese Danus and Mongan (except that in January 1945 Mongan took part in a failed reconnaissance in Minahasa). However, we do know what happened to De Haas. He became involved in the training of secret agents by the Nefis until September 1944, when, with the rank of sublieutenant, he was himself sent to Java as an agent. At the end of that month he was taken by

---

[144] Letter from F.W. Coster to Helfrich, 5 February 1943 (ARA, MK, M 180, A 8 I).

flying boat to the small island of Nila (west of the Tanimbar Islands, see Map 5), where the Nefis had set up a base. De Haas's party consisted of eight men: himself, six Ambonese and a Javanese, Sergeant Soeprapto of the KNIL, the son of an assistant *wedono* in a district just west of Surabaya, who was to land on Java with him. There De Haas and Soeprapto were to carry out no less than six missions: they were to assist any underground organizations (the Nefis did not know whether there were any), find hiding places for agents to come after them, find people willing to make contact with the Nefis, collect military intelligence, inform Indonesian officials about the state of the war and, where possible, give help to prisoners of war and internees. They had money, over 50,000 guilders, but no transmitter, and the only addresses they had were the most dangerous – those of their own families. It was an absurd collection of assignments, and they had to be carried out without proper resources (and well into the third year of occupation).

The party sailed by proa from Nila via Sumbawa to the island of Satengar, one of the Paternoster Islands lying north of Sumbawa. From there De Haas, Soeprapto and an Ambonese sergeant reached Panarukan, a harbour on Madura Strait, around 7 November. De Haas and Soeprapto went ashore there. De Haas gave the sergeant orders to return to Satengar, and visit other islands from there to collect military intelligence and then sail back to Panarukan, where he and Soeprapto would come back on board at the end of December or beginning of January. The sergeant sailed to Satengar, and from there to Makassar with an Ambonese soldier; they spent four days on land, and then went back to Satengar, where the other Ambonese had gathered information about Flores. The Ambonese twice set sail for Panarukan and twice a head wind made it impossible to get there. They waited on Satengar until the end of January – no De Haas, no Soeprapto. Following their orders, they then sailed back to Australia.

What had happened to De Haas and Soeprapto? After arriving in Panarukan they got in touch with the regent of that locality, for whom De Haas had a letter from Van der Plas. Others heard about this and one of them, a high-ranking Indonesian official, informed the Kempeitai. About a week after his arrival, De Haas and the regent were arrested and taken to the prison at Jember. The regent was shot at the beginning of 1945, but the Kempeitai did not execute De Haas until August 1945, according to some reports on 15 August, according to others on 25 August, ten days after the Japanese surrender. What happened to Soeprapto is uncertain. Most probably, he also fell into the hands of the Kempeitai soon after De Haas (it is said that he was betrayed by a *desa* head) and died in prison.

Van der Star and his companions, who left Java in early July 1942, were en route for two months before they made contact with the Dutch authorities. It took De Haas, who left Java at the end of September 1942, three months. Naturally, the information they brought was of value,[145] but no more than that. From the end of September 1942 to the Japanese surrender in mid-August 1945, not a single Dutchman or Dutch Eurasian managed to escape from the archipelago. The Dutch intelligence service on Ceylon made attempts to put secret agents on Sumatra but was not successful until mid-1945. It did not attempt to put agents on Java (which in any case belonged to the South-West Pacific Area under MacArthur's command); the Dutch intelligence service in Australia did try, but with very little success, as stated in our account of De Haas and Soeprapto's mission. Not one of the very few agents landed on Java managed to make his way back to Australia.

The end result was that for almost three years the Dutch intelligence services and other authorities received no information at all, at least not from eyewitnesses, about what was taking place on the principal islands in the archipelago.

[145] Shortly before De Haas and his party, which included two Manadonese, a third Manadonese arrived in Australia, H.D. Pitoi. He did not come directly from the Indonesian archipelago but from Guadalcanal. He too was a KNIL soldier. On Java he had been held in a camp by the Japanese together with other Manadonese KNIL troops. In September he and six others had been attached to a Japanese company, which was among the troops landed on Guadalcanal by destroyers in October. The seven Manadonese had to take part in a difficult march through the jungle before reaching the area where they were to fight the Americans. Pitoi decided to defect. He slipped out of his bivouac, past a sleeping Japanese sentry, and after a march of four days (on bare feet and without food) he came near to an American patrol. 'I no Japanese, I Dutch soldier!' he called. He was taken prisoner and sent to New Zealand with a number of Japanese prisoners of war. With some difficulty (he had to write Dutch and Malay, name the days of the week in Dutch, and count up to 40 in Dutch) he managed to convince a New Zealand officer that he was a KNIL soldier. He was also questioned in Wellington by Van der Plas, chairman of the Dutch East Indies Commission for Australia and New Zealand, before being allowed to join the other KNIL troops in Australia.

CHAPTER II

Resistance and clandestine activities

The terms 'resistance' and 'clandestine work' were used interchangeably from the beginning of the German occupation in the Netherlands, and this remained so after the liberation: while one might speak of 'resistance fighters', the other would refer to 'clandestine workers'. This was no less the case in the East Indies, where a Federatie van Ex-Illegale Werkers in Indië (Fiwi, Federation of former clandestine workers in the East Indies), was created and investigations were conducted to determine who was eligible for the Resistance Star of East Asia 1942-1945.

In chronicling the German occupation of the Netherlands, an attempt was made to create greater clarity by distinguishing between the terms 'resistance' and 'clandestine work'.

'Resistance' was defined as any action intended to prevent the German occupiers from realizing their objectives. Four of these objectives were: to transform the Netherlands into a National-Socialist state that would somehow be incorporated in Germany ('subjugation'); to mobilize the Dutch economic potential, including the work force, to the extent that the interests of the German war efforts were a priority ('exploitation'); to deport well over 100,000 Dutch citizens, or residents (the Jews, and subsequently in 1944 the Gypsies) to concentration camps or extermination camps ('deportation'); to prevent support being given to persecuted groups within the Netherlands and first-hand help from the Netherlands being offered to the Allied Forces, for example by means of espionage, sabotage or semi-military actions. Anyone rejecting these objectives offered resistance, that is when done with a view to harming the enemy and not for one's own benefit. For instance, anyone trading on a large scale on the black market or slaughtering pigs clandestinely or helping Jews escape across the border for a large sum was, indeed, breaking the prevailing regulations, but was a profiteer and not a resistance fighter. While approximately 100,000 Dutch citizens are listed in the registers of the German Public Prosecutor's Department, the *Staatsanwaltschaft*, more than 80% were suspected of what could be termed normal or war economy-related criminal offences.

The German occupiers more than amply realized two of their stated objectives: they exploited the Dutch economic potential on a vast scale and they succeeded in deporting more than 100,000 Jews and several hundred Gypsies. On the other hand, their attempts to subjugate the Netherlands failed due to broad popular resistance and they were unable to prevent support from being offered to persecuted groups in the Netherlands (for example, an estimated 25,000 Jews and more than 300,000 labourers were able to go into hiding) and direct assistance from being given to the Allied war efforts.

Touching briefly on the matter of the Jews in hiding, it is clear that three groups offered resistance: the Jews themselves who went into hiding, the families (also roughly estimated at 25,000) with whom they could stay for shorter or longer periods of time, and those referred to as 'the organizers of secret shelter for Jews' (roughly estimated at 1,000), who had assumed the task of finding places where people could hide, escorting them there, and ensuring that they regularly received what they needed in their hiding places (ration cards, in many instances money, frequently also false identity cards) as well as solving the countless problems that could arise in hiding. Only those who organized shelter for the Jews in hiding are here called 'clandestine workers'. This is also based on the assumption that clandestine work was generally performed in an established organizational set-up. The occupied Netherlands boasted various such large bodies, for instance the Landelijke Organisatie voor Hulp aan Onderduikers (National Organization for Assistance to People in Hiding), or LO, established early in 1943. It provided help to, among others, those who refused to work in Germany or were no longer willing to do so, and Jews, and ultimately numbered about 13,000 clandestine workers. And, with respect to the large underground newspapers such as *Vrij Nederland, Het Parool, De Waarheid, Trouw, Je Maintiendrai* (papers that hindered the Germans from realizing any of their goals), many thousands of clandestine workers were actively involved in their production at any given time.

Hence, 'resistance' is a broader term than 'clandestine work' – every clandestine worker offered resistance, but not everyone who offered resistance was a clandestine worker (based on our definition).

Likewise, four objectives can be distinguished in the policy pursued by the Japanese occupiers in the East Indies, comparable to those of Germany in the occupied Netherlands. The Japanese demanded that the population of the East Indies clearly accept Japanese supremacy and commit no acts in conflict with this acceptance; that the East Indies' economic potential be involved in the Japanese war efforts; that the Dutch (and the British, Australians and Americans) be isolated; and that no direct aid would be given to the Allied war efforts in or from the East Indies. Anyone thwarting these objectives was offering resistance, provided one was not driven by acquisitiveness.

Linked to these Japanese objectives were numerous regulations and injunctions. These have been outlined in the case of Java. As for the Outer Islands, for which less information is available, it may be assumed that comparable regulations and injunctions applied.

The regulations are grouped below according to the objectives described and, anticipating what will be discussed in this and other chapters, some general comments are made regarding the behaviour in this matter of the Indonesians, the Chinese and Arabs, the Dutch and the Dutch Eurasians.

The acceptance of Japanese supremacy
There was a regulation requiring that honour be paid to the Japanese emperor and to Japanese officers and sentries and that the Japanese flag be flown on certain occasions. This was generally obeyed, albeit that some Dutch and Dutch Eurasians complied with the stipulation regarding the flag with demonstrative nonchalance, an attitude not without an element of resistance.

There was also a regulation forbidding any political activity in public (establishing political associations, holding political meetings) not approved by the Japanese military administration. On the whole people complied with this regulation, though it should be noted that both within the Dutch and Dutch Eurasian population groups clandestine talks were held on the East Indies' post-war future in which it was assumed that the Japanese would be driven out of the East Indies and to which (as had already been evidenced in Banjarmasin) the suspicious Japanese authorities responded fiercely.

There were bans on listening to the Allied radio broadcasts, on using non-'castrated' radios and on spreading anti-Japanese rumours – all of which were violated on a fairly extensive scale and this was always a form of resistance.

There was a regulation stipulating that Dutch flags and so on, be handed in – whoever did not do so (and many did not comply) was committing an act of resistance.

There was a ban on using Dutch or English in correspondence, on the telephone or in public conversations. This ban was surely frequently transgressed by Dutch Eurasians, and this too can be considered a form of resistance.

It must also be noted that among the Dutch there was absolutely no inner acceptance of Japan's lasting supremacy. The same held true for the great majority of Dutch Eurasians, most of the Chinese and presumably most of the Arabs, as well as a large number of Indonesians, certainly the more educated and politically-aware among them, including Sukarno.

The mobilization of the East Indies' economic potential
A multitude of regulations were meant to ensure that the East Indies would make a maximum economic contribution to Japan and the Japanese military forces in the Nampo. What happened to the East Indies in economic terms is described in the following chapter – suffice it to say here that on the whole

the Japanese acquired what they needed in the way of raw materials and labourers, but that the export to Japan as of the fourth quarter of 1943 was foiled by a factor that had nothing to do with the East Indies, namely the tremendous loss of Japanese ships. The extent of the resistance in the economic sector is unknown, other than that in 1942 on Java several Dutch businesses succeeded in concealing part of their cash reserves. Furthermore, as Japanese pressure mounted, it is assumed that the Chinese, Arabs, and Indonesians (by then most of the Dutch Eurasians and all the Dutch had been detained) would have been inclined to give Japan less than it demanded, but there is no concrete information to this effect.

Though forbidden, sabotage was committed here and there, but to a far lesser extent than was assumed by the suspicious Japanese, who blamed every mishap in production and in transport on sabotage.

The isolation of the Dutch

Before the Dutch on Java were registered and subsequently isolated, all Dutch educational facilities were shut down and the organized relief for needy Dutch and Dutch Eurasians became subject to the general rule that such organizations required the approval of the Japanese military administration. Nevertheless, both education and relief were clandestinely restarted. This, too, included an element of resistance.

On Java there was a regulation in effect that all Dutch and Dutch Eurasians (and until the end of 1943 also all Chinese and Arabs) aged 17 and older had to carry an identity card, a *pendaftaran*, bearing a thumbprint as a sign of loyalty to Japan. Several Dutch and Dutch Eurasians in Batavia refused to pledge their allegiance. They resisted, just as did those who forged *pendaftaran*. At the end of November 1942 in Bandung, Bouwer noted in his diary – as mentioned in the previous chapter – the existence of 'false registration cards [...] which were forged by various Chinese and Eurasians for the trifling amount of 15 guilders'. It should be added that when new registration of non-Indonesians took place on Java in October 1943, the same diarist wrote: 'One suspects that the Japanese are searching for a large number of false registration cards, with false stamps, false names and just about everything that can be falsified. These cards were excellently forged by a small group of Indo-Europeans.' No further details about this group of forgers (were there others elsewhere?) are known.

A regulation applying to all of the East Indies was that Dutch civilians had to enter internment camps and after a while contact with the internees, as described in Chapter V, was prohibited. Some, like Bouwer in Bandung, simply eluded this regulation by going into hiding, others by seeking recognition as a Dutch Eurasian on the basis of either authentic or false information – when false information was involved, this was deception, hence a form of resistance. In Chapter V, furthermore, it is demonstrated that the Japanese ban on establishing contact with interned Dutch civilians was often violated by both Chinese and Indonesians.

The ban on offering direct assistance to the Allied war efforts
The Japanese prohibited all direct assistance to the Allied war efforts: arms, ammunition and the like had to be turned in. In fact, locally on the Outer Islands (on Sumatra, Borneo, Central Celebes, Dutch New Guinea and primarily on Timor) small KNIL units continued to fight and on Java a number of Dutch Eurasians, British, Australian, Ambonese, Manadonese and Timorese soldiers attempted to stay out of Japanese hands. Small groups on Java tried to collect and conceal arms that had been kept by deserters or had escaped confiscation by the Japanese.

Spying was forbidden – on Java and Sumatra, espionage organizations were set up by the Dutch and the Dutch Eurasians as well as by the Chinese. On Java, these groups attempted to convey their intelligence to Japan's adversaries by means of transmitters, but as far as is known only one group, a Chinese one, succeeded in doing this.

A fortiori escape from the archipelago, also to inform Japan's adversaries, was forbidden. Several attempts to escape from the Outer Islands succeeded in 1944. Three attempts to leave Java failed, and two succeeded: that of Van der Star, Stokhuyzen and Van der Veen, and that of De Haas and his men.

In trying to picture in greater detail the clandestine activities that took place during the Japanese occupation,[1] it is useful to recall what happened in Banjarmasin. Prisoners of war and Dutch civilians were interned there and money was collected for their needs with the permission of the Japanese. Furthermore, however, and this was forbidden, goods were smuggled into the camps that were partially (the medicine) clandestinely conveyed from Surabaya by a woman who also maintained a clandestine postal connection. When the Japanese got wind of this they initiated investigations, from which it appeared that not all of the radios had been turned in, that reports from Allied radio broadcasts had been passed on, that some Chinese had held back arms, and that in his internment camp Governor Haga had held discussions with other officials concerning the measures that should be taken on Borneo after the war. The Japanese elected to think of all of this as a complex of related acts, as a dangerous conspiracy – and on this premise they claimed that two secret transmitters had been operative and that in Kuala Kapuas a large stash of arms had been assembled for an uprising.

---

[1]   Most of the general information is derived from the unpublished study by A.G. Vromans and R. de Bruin, 'Het Indisch Verzet' (Nederlands Instituut voor Oorlogsdocumentatie, Amsterdam).

This conspiracy was a total fiction and the bloody repression initiated by the Japanese reflects their suspicion rather than reality. As will become clear, this suspicion also created many victims elsewhere, and not only those who were executed on flimsy charges, but also those who on the basis of real or fictitious clandestine activity fell into the clutches of the Kempeitai or its collaborator, the Indonesian Politieke Inlichtingen Dienst, or PID.

An overview of all of this with respect to the various population groups in the East Indies will be given, divided territorially. The genuine clandestine activities, but also those which, without sufficient grounds in reality, were branded as such by the Japanese will be reviewed. Should the latter be omitted, the image of the activities of the Kempeitai and the PID, of the trials conducted by the Japanese courts of law, and the fate of those sentenced to prison would be highly incomplete. There was a striking difference between the *Sicherheitspolizei und SD* and the organs of German justice on the one hand and the Kempeitai, the PID and the organs of Japanese justice on the other. The former pursued only real activities, the latter both real and fictitious, and in this respect too life was more difficult for the Dutch and Dutch Eurasians in the occupied Indies than for the Dutch in the occupied Netherlands.

By way of introduction, finally, it should be noted that the documentation on the clandestine work performed in the Indies (like that on the resistance) is sparse indeed and in no way can compare with that on the clandestine efforts (and the resistance) in the Netherlands. Virtually no Kempeitai documents have survived; there is only scant information concerning the Indonesian and Chinese clandestine work, and far from everything is known about the clandestine activities that took place in Dutch and Dutch Eurasian circles. Documents dating from this time are almost entirely lacking and reports drawn up after the war are not all equally reliable.

Java

Little clandestine activity was carried out by Indonesians on Java. Brief uprisings were staged on several occasions.[2] On West Java in 1943 and in 1944, local revolts took place in response to the Japanese rice requisitioning (these events are discussed in the following chapter) and in Blitar, on East Java, at the beginning of 1945 a mutiny was mounted by a battalion of the volunteer army created by the Japanese (it was quickly suppressed). These expressions of resistance had nothing to do with any clandestine organizations. Two such organizations were in fact active, albeit in a limited fashion: the Partai Komunis Indonesia (the Indonesian Communist Party) or PKI, and Sjahrir's group.

---

[2]   See Map 1, for all of the places mentioned.

The PKI had been ravaged by division when it revolted against Dutch authority in some parts of Java at the end of 1926 and in Sumatra's West Coast residency at the beginning of 1927. Its liaison man with the Comintern, Tan Malaka, had tried to prevent the uprising and many party departments had remained passive. Tan Malaka then broke with the Comintern and established a new party in Bangkok, the Partai Republik Indonesia (the Indonesian Republican Party), or Pari, which only had a modest following in the East Indies. In 1941 he ended up in Singapore where he taught English at several Chinese schools. Following the mass arrests made by the government in 1926 and 1927, the PKI was virtually put out of business. The majority of the leaders together with the chairman, Sardjono, were confined in Upper Digul, and of the leading figures only Moesso and Alimin remained at liberty, for they were in Moscow at the time. Moesso was able to reach Surabaya in 1935 and began rebuilding the PKI, but had to leave the Indies again in 1936, returning to Moscow. From there, in 1940, Alimin reached the areas in North China controlled by the Chinese communists.

When the Japanese landed on Java, there was a small number of communists, some of whom were in prison. They remained incarcerated until Imamura granted amnesty to all Indonesian political prisoners on 29 April, in honour of Hirohito's birthday. The chairman of the clandestine PKI was Pamoedji, a communist from Surabaya. In the course of 1942, Amir Sjarifoeddin began working with the PKI. He was one of the founders of the Gerindo, and within this organization an advocate for the creation of a popular front. He had become a civil servant in the department of economic affairs in 1940, converted to Christianity in 1941 and, at the end of February 1942, been paid a large sum of money (how much is unknown, but one assumes it was tens of thousands of guilders) upon the initiative of Van der Plas to launch a broad clandestine campaign during the Japanese occupation. What did Sjarifoeddin do with this money? All that is known is that in the week when fighting took place on Java, he visited Sukabumi and gave several thousand guilders to Hatta and Sjahrir for them to live on. He probably attempted initially to build up an intelligence network on Java. In 1935-1936, Moesso had been active chiefly on East Java, which is where Sjarifoeddin found most of his helpers, some of whom were members of the PKI, and others of the Gerindo's left wing. At first, this all remained hidden from the Japanese. In December 1942 Sjarifoeddin became one of the members of a committee established by the Japanese in preparation for the 'new people's organization', the founding of which was announced in *Asia Raya* (Great Asia, a daily newspaper published in Batavia as of the end of April 1942) on 7 December and by Sukarno in a public speech in Batavia on 8 December. The PID discovered what Sjarifoeddin was up to in the course of January 1943; the Kempeitai was informed and Sjarifoeddin and 53 other Indonesians – mainly ex-members of the PKI, Gerindo and Parindra – were arrested at the end of January. Most were sentenced to long prison terms by the Japanese military court more than a year later, at the end of February 1944. Sjarifoeddin as well as the four leading figures of the PKI in Surabaya (including Pamoedji) and two leading figures of the Gerindo were condemned to death. Four of these seven death sentences were actually carried out, those of the communists, but not those of Sjarifoeddin and of the two Gerindo leaders. Sukarno and Hatta had succeeded in getting Lieutenant General Kumakishi Harada, commander-in-chief of the 16th Army and head of the military administration on Java and Madura from November 1942 to the end of April 1945, to commute three of the death sentences to life imprisonment; the three condemned men were confined in the prison in Malang.

A group of PKI members remained active on Java. In 1964, one of their leaders confessed to George S. Kanahele (an American historian from Hawaii and author of *The Japanese occupation of Indonesia; Prelude to independence*) that they had done 'a bit of sabotage', such as blowing up trains (Kanahele 1967: 308). Kanahele, however, believed that the PKI's activities consisted chiefly of disseminating anti-Japanese propaganda verbally and in the form of pamphlets as well as producing a clandestine newspaper, *Menara Merah* (The red beacon), with a circulation in the thousands. It is not certain who was active in or heading the PKI operations as of mid-1943. Possibly, the leader or leaders had some contact with Moscow. In 1944 W. Haccou, former police chief in Semarang and head of the PID there, was informed in the prison in Ambarawa by members of the PKI incarcerated there since 1927 that Alimin had clandestinely visited the Indies twice, and on behalf of the Comintern directed the PKI to collaborate with other groups (the clandestine Communist Party in the Netherlands received similar instructions) rather than focus on the creation of a communist Indonesia after the war.[3]

Also after the arrests at the end of January 1943, more communists were apprehended on Java. According to the oft-cited Kempeitai report, up to February 1944 a total of almost 700 people were arrested who were either members of the PKI or affiliated with it. It is worth remembering that the Kempeitai interpreted the concept 'communist' very broadly; for instance they also considered Hatta and Sukarno to be communists.

Quite possibly, there were also Pari members among the almost 700 detainees. It should be added that in July 1944 Tan Malaka succeeded in reaching Java, which he had left more than 20 years earlier, from Singapore.[4] Calling himself 'Hoessein', he went to live in a *desa* not far from Jakarta. He first worked in a shoe factory and later as a clerk in the administration of

3   What Haccou heard was most likely just a rumour.
4   This is based on what is described by H.A. Poeze in his book published in 1976, *Tan Malaka. Strijder voor Indonesië's vrijheid. Levensloop van 1897 to 1945*.

a coal mine in Banten, where he tried hard to improve the lot of the indigenous workers employed there. He also wrote several manuscripts in which he pleaded for the foundation of a Southeast Asian Federation after the war, but for the rest remained out of the political limelight. Only at the beginning of 1945, when the Japanese imperium was about to collapse, did he go to Jakarta, where under his real name he would immediately gain influence on several youth organizations.

What was Sjahrir doing?

Some time after his discussion with Sukarno and Hatta in Batavia on the evening of 9 July 1942 (see pp 43-4), Sjahrir conveyed his intentions to Jacques de Kadt,[5] who reported his words as follows in 1978:

> He was in touch with Hatta and wanted to continue that [and not with Sukarno who, after all, was convinced that the Japanese would be victorious], but he himself would go into hiding and build up a clandestine organization to take action against the Japanese, where possible, primarily by drawing attention to social and economic grievances. But he felt that the most important thing was to build up the cadre for the period after the Japanese occupation. (De Kadt 1978:84.)

From Sukabumi, the abode forced on him by the Dutch colonial government, Sjahrir had been able to establish a few contacts with former members of the PNI Baroe he and Hatta had led. He attempted to expand these. In his own words:

> Traveling in overcrowded trains to East Java, I found the sentiment still strongly pro-Japanese. I nowhere tried to make immediate contact with my old party workers. Instead, I tried to survey the situation carefully, because pro-Japanese sentiments among formerly reliable nationalists made the work extraordinarily dangerous. [...] In Central- and East-Java it happened more than once that I could not afford to make any contact whatever because the old contacts had become unreliable. But we managed to form an organization, even though it was hurt by the arrests.

(Details of these arrests are not known – it is entirely possible that the Kempeitai counted the detainees among the 700 'communists' mentioned above.)

---

[5]   De Kadt was a Dutch socialist with great sympathy for Indonesian nationalism. De Kadt and Sjahrir had met when Sjahrir was studying in the Netherlands. At the time, the two saw each other regularly. After the German invasion of the Netherlands, De Kadt fled to England and arrived in the East Indies in August 1940. Some time after the meeting of Sukarno, Hatta and Sjahrir in July 1942, Sjahrir visited his old friend De Kadt in Bandung and told him what they had discussed.

From my sister, who approved of my decision not to have anything to do with the Japanese, I received an offer to tend her orange garden, her rice fields and her house in Cipanas in the mountains.[6] I thought it a perfect place for my plans.

[...] Several of our members fixed the house up as our working headquarters. We brought the equipment needed for a radio listening post, and throughout the occupation this listening service continued in operation. [...] One of the goals I sought as soon as we became active was contact with other resistance organizations. I realized that we needed the active guidance of a military expert and also of groups having connections in the secret police and the civil administration. Contacts were needed among the Eurasians[7] and the Chinese as well. The point was not only to prevent each group from impeding the others' work, but to provide for co-operation among them where possible, as for example through the exchange of reports. Another thing we were particularly interested in was obtaining information concerning weapons: if and where the Netherlands Indies Army had left or hidden weapons, and how we could lay our hands on them.

[...] In general it appeared that the colonial government had made very inadequate preparation for underground-action.

[...] Our hope that the Chinese might be a reserve support for us was only partially realized. However, we did later get some weapons through the Chinese.

[...] I also found that in Batavia there were still a few small groups that tried to do such resistance work as they could. A Frenchman and a Ceylonese were involved.[8] The Ceylonese occupied an important position from our point of view – he was a translator of Allied news in the Japanese radio monitoring service.[9] We managed to keep in touch with these people and also with an Indonesian major who had been connected with the nationalist movement.[10] The major was closely watched by the Japanese police, but he was still active among the Eurasians, the Ambonese, the former military people, and later also among our students.

Officially I was almost always in the mountains in Cipanas. The nationalists who were working with the Japanese politically were naturally somewhat unfriendly toward me.

At the end of 1942 and the beginning of 1943 Sjahrir also received a permanent abode in Batavia:

I received an offer from a Dutch lady who was soon to be interned, to rent her house in Batavia inexpensively, and I made use of the opportunity to set up a station there. During the last year, in fact, I was in Batavia more than in Cipanas. (Sjahrir 1949:240-8.)

---

6   Cipanas is located southeast of Buitenzorg (Bogor). See Map 1.
7   The Dutch Eurasians.
8   The name of the Frenchman is not known, while the Ceylonese was a nationalist, Tambu, who had first fled from Ceylon to Singapore and then from there to Batavia.
9   In Chapter IV it will appear that Tambu provided far more important services to the Japanese.
10   Major Santoso, one of the Javanese KNIL officers.

From this relatively scanty account we infer that Sjahrir generally succeeded in assembling a core group of likeminded individuals in the cities on Java, that he regularly received information on the course of the war through Allied radio broadcasts, and that he acquired 'some weapons' from the Chinese – he did not allow these weapons to be used. It is assumed that he also transmitted news reports and other information, not only to trustworthy people on Java, but also on Bali and Sumatra, where, according to Kanahele, 'some liaison' was maintained. He did not publish his own clandestine pamphlets or newspaper. Kanahele (1967:157) wrote:

> [His] network merely served to exchange information about the war, conditions in various parts of Java or other islands, Indonesian politics, both present and future, and the like. Although a few members of the organization were arrested by the police, the system continued intact until the end of the war.

All this time, Sjahrir – who wanted no further contact with Sukarno – remained in touch with Hatta, who was able to warn him on several occasions when the Kempeitai were going to make general arrests. No specific action was taken against Sjahrir's group. According to Kanahele (1967:159):

> In fact, Japanese reports show that apart from the communists, Menadonese and Ambonese [the two latter groups will be discussed below] the military could find no anti-Japanese movement or underground organization among Indonesians that was important enough to be suppressed or even recorded. [...] If the Japanese feared any group, it was not the Indonesian but rather the Chinese underground which seemed to be the best organized, financed and led.

The Japanese did not trust any of the Chinese minorities in the conquered Nampo countries: they knew that no matter how integrated these minorities were in society – as in the Indies – they were affiliated to a certain extent with the regime of Chiang Kai-shek. The Japanese attempted to break these ties: the Chinese, too, had to set their shoulders to the work of rebuilding the 'Greater East Asia Co-Prosperity Sphere'.

From the very start, the Japanese propaganda among the Chinese community – which had been taken over by a small group that had declared its solidarity with Nanking China, was accompanied by coercion. At the end of April 1942, more than 140 leading figures in Chinese circles were locked up and then joined by about another thousand before the end of the first year of the occupation. Almost 600 people from both groups combined were still incarcerated in March 1943 (figures for later years are not known), and the Japanese had by then confiscated property worth close to 15 million guilders. For a variety of reasons, the Chinese were stimulated to outwardly conform to Japanese authority, chiefly to protect what they had built up economically in the course of generations. For the majority though, inner solidarity with the Japanese was an entirely different question.

When Wavell's headquarters, Abda Command, was set up on Java in January 1942, Chiang Kai-shek added a military mission led by a Chinese general. To maintain contact he had a transmitter with him that exchanged coded telegrams with a second Chinese transmitter in Singapore. The general's fate following the collapse of military resistance on Java is unknown – though an officer on his staff, Colonel Lin Pin Fai, went underground under the name of Lin Chan taking with him the transmitter and the four technicians who had serviced it. Colonel Lin went to Batavia, where he undertook a multitude of clandestine activities: he established an intelligence group which gathered information that was passed on via a transmitter to Singapore and from there to Chungking, and he encouraged groups of Chinese to gather weapons, probably less for use against the Japanese than to defend themselves when in the further course of the war plundering and wholesale massacre aimed at Chinese merchants would be instigated, as had also occurred with the coming of the Japanese. Furthermore, an organization for dispensing medical assistance was established. Later in 1942, Colonel Lin felt very threatened in Batavia: he knew that there were Chinese who wished to get in the good graces of the Japanese by betraying him. He therefore moved his headquarters and his transmitter to Purwokerto on Central Java. To no avail. In November the Kempeitai was informed of his whereabouts by a Chinese, and the police struck on the 28th: Lin's headquarters were raided, the transmitter discovered, and he was arrested along with the four technicians and another 17 Chinese. Of the 22 detainees, 6 were killed or tortured to death, and 16 condemned to long prison sentences by the Japanese military court 6 months later.

The February 1944 Kempeitai report about the resistance on Java mentions Lin's activities. It also notes that in Batavia in August 1942, a group of Chinese were discovered who had put into circulation more than 100,000 guilders in counterfeit Japanese ten-guilder notes (this group was also betrayed by a Chinese, leading to an additional 20 Chinese being sentenced, some to death) and claims that this affair was politically motivated: the goal being the disruption of Java's economy. However, it is not in the least certain that Colonel Lin's group, which presumably received sufficient financial support from wealthy Chinese, ever had anything to do with the case of the counterfeited notes.

The Kempeitai report makes no mention of Chinese clandestine activities for the year 1943, and later Kempeitai reports other than that of February 1944 are lacking. Did no other clandestine Chinese organizations remain in existence on Java? It seems unlikely, but nothing further about this is known.

No clandestine news magazines originated in the Dutch and Dutch Eurasian circles on Java. Because of fundamentally different circumstances, what could be called the 'clandestine press' (which played a very significant role in the occupied Netherlands) remained limited to a few clandestine newsletters, actually more news pamphlets, namely typed, or at best mimeo-graphed, surveys of the news from Allied broadcasts. As far as is known, these surveys only had a set title in Bandung, *Red-white-blue* (they were compiled by an escaped prisoner of war, Theo Jans): elsewhere, they were disseminated without a title. In Batavia this was done by an assistant at the Aneta press agency, A.L. van Hoorn, who had been forced to resume his work on behalf of the Japanese and translate the reports on the Allied broadcasts – he was able to pass on copies of these reports to former colleagues until his arrest in early July 1942.

In mid-1942, W.F. Grashuis, a police inspector fired by the Japanese who had not registered himself, began typing up reports from the Allied broadcasts, which were passed on to one of the prisoner-of-war camps in Batavia. Through this work, Grashuis came into contact with a group attempting to gather weapons. When the Kempeitai tried to track down that group in 1943, he also ran into difficulty. It was, as he wrote in 1946, 'an extremely nervous time'.[11] Despite this, he was able to continue transmitting reports from Allied sources well into 1944 – he was arrested at the end of September because he could not produce a *pendaftaran*, or identity card.

There were more people like this. Whoever still had access to Allied broadcasts passed on the reports, most likely verbally for reasons of safety and lack of technical means.

This is how a group of 14 Dutch women ran into trouble in Batavia in mid-1942. They were primarily the wives of prominent men who were either confined on Java or were elsewhere, including the spouses of Lieutenant Governor-General Van Mook and of the director of Van Starkenborgh's cabinet, Idenburg. As of May 1942, they were all arrested in turn (they had received reports from the above-mentioned Van Hoorn) and subsequently subjected to the tortures of the Kempeitai. The sentences were not severe: two to three months' imprisonment.

It was mentioned above that on Java a fairly large number of Dutch and Dutch Eurasians (most of the former until 1943) had to stay at their post as Nippon workers. Presumably a number of them tried to slow down the pace at which they were working. There is only one clear example of such a go-slow: Dutch Eurasians and Manadonese working on East Java for a company making diesel engines for coasters deliberately worked as slowly as possible. One of the Manadonese was arrested by the Kempeitai at the end of 1943: he

---

[11]   W.F. Grashuis, 'Verslag', 17 December 1946, p. 3 (ARA, Alg. Secr., Eerste zending XXII, 45, 447).

confessed to the go-slow and said that one of the Nippon workers, a Dutch Eurasian, had concealed some weapons. He was arrested in turn and denied the charge. However, under serious threats his wife disclosed the location of the concealed weapons. Five more arrests were made. The director of the company, a Dutch Eurasian, perished in captivity, the Nippon worker and the Manadonese were executed, and the rest sentenced to eight years in prison.

The Japanese were effectively sabotaged by seven Nippon workers who continued working at the KNIL's Pyrotechnics Workshop in Bandung until July 1943. This group was led by the head of the metal-working shop, E.C.L. Verwoord. Primarily by misinforming the Japanese, they succeeded in preventing several important machines from being shipped off to Japan; putting out of service other machines that could be used for producing cartridges of the calibre used by the Japanese army; and destroying vast amounts of perfectly good ammunition. The group furthermore continued to work as slowly as possible on the tasks imposed on them by the Japanese. According to a post-war report, however, there was one Japanese:

> who saw through Mr Verwoord; he was a trained technician from a good background. [...] He was, however, a soldier and did not dare inform his commander. He was often drunk, upon which occasion he referred to Mr Verwoord as 'Inchiki', [...] [which] means something like 'deceiver'.[12]

On Java, hundreds but less than a thousand KNIL soldiers as well as the British, Australian and American soldiers stationed there were able to avoid captivity. These were not the Javanese and Sundanese KNIL soldiers – the Sundanese are the indigenous inhabitants of West Java and speak a different language than the Javanese – who had deserted during the week of fighting on Java and returned to their homes, but those who kept their weapons (light arms only, of course) and began roaming around, many quite likely intending to inflict as much damage as possible on the occupier. Among them were Dutch Eurasians, and primarily Ambonese, Manadonese and Timorese soldiers. We are in the dark regarding their activities on Central and East Java, but there are indications that they all (at least all who continued their clandestine existence) fell into Japanese hands in 1942 or 1943. As far as is known, there were no survivors.

With respect to West Java, a group of Australian sappers retreated into the mountains south of Sukabumi in March 1942 (see Map 1), to be joined by a small number of British officers, including an intelligence officer, Lieutenant Colonel Laurens van der Post. These men remained at liberty only briefly: Van der Post and about 20 others were captured on 20 April, and of those

---

[12]   F.E. Eyken, 'Rapport aan de Knil-Commissie van Gedragingen', 6 August 1946, p. 82 (NIOD IC, 32,244).

remaining the last three became prisoners of war on 2 August.

Some of those who had tried to continue fighting following the KNIL's capitulation on Java, including Van der Post, were locked up in the existing camps, but all of the others were killed by the occupier, the majority by drowning. As was established after the war, ships left the harbours of Priok, Cirebon, Tegal and Surabaya for this purpose; in other words, groups of soldiers who had escaped the Japanese were discovered not only on West Java, but on Central and East Java as well.

On West Java, in addition to the group south of Sukabumi, there was a similar one on the slopes of Salak Mountain south of Buitenzorg (about 50 Australians, the last of whom were arrested in January 1943). On Central Java there was a group in the mountains at Gombong (Ambonese soldiers under the command of Lieutenant Siahaja – they were tracked down in February 1943, and Siahaja was beheaded). On East Java there were three groups: one at Kediri (Australian soldiers and a few Dutch Eurasian youths, all of whom were eliminated at an unknown point in time); one on the slopes of a volcano north of Malang; and one on the slopes of Semeru Mountain southeast of Prabalingga. The latter two groups consisted of Ambonese and Manadonese KNIL soldiers and young Dutch Eurasians. When these groups were eliminated is not known and there is no clear picture of their possible engagements with the Japanese or of their other clandestine activities.

Along with the Javanese and Sundanese KNIL soldiers, some Ambonese, Manadonese and Timorese KNIL soldiers were also released from captivity at the end of April and in May 1942: they thus entered into Indonesian society, where they had to try and earn a livelihood for themselves and possibly also their wives and children. They received very little assistance. The Dutch were soon rounded up; most of the Dutch Eurasians had troubles of their own, and in the eyes of many Javanese these KNIL soldiers, quite a number of whom were Christians, were identified with the Dutch regime that had proved powerless to resist the Japanese and against which resentment was growing in general as well as being stimulated by Japanese propaganda. Some of these Ambonese, Manadonese and Timorese soldiers joined Japanese units out of need or were pressurized to do so, but most refused to serve the occupier. The Ambonese and Timorese were supported by the civilians living on Java who came from the Moluccas and Timor. The situation was somewhat different for the Manadonese civilians: a number fell under the sway of the Indonesian leader G.S.I.I. Ratoe Langie from Manado, one of the nationalists who had thrown in his lot with Japan.

In Batavia it was chiefly the Ambonese who, here and elsewhere living together in groups, remained true to the Dutch cause. In mid-1942, several released Ambonese soldiers joined a secret organization aimed at helping the Allies upon their landing on Java and combating possible indigenous looters. Were it to come to that, members of the secret organization had to be able to recognize one another. For this purpose they were required to carry a red handkerchief and this identifying mark lent its name to the organization, Sapoetangan Merah (The red handkerchief). They were probably attempting to gather military intelligence and weapons, though there is no information to this effect. They do not appear to have been discovered by the Kempeitai, at least they were not prosecuted.

There was a prosecution in the case of a similar organization of Ambonese and Timorese created in various places in Central Java in mid-1942 that referred to itself with the letter V, for Victory. This organization gave every member, including a number of Dutch Eurasians, a red insignia with a black V in the middle. Groups originated in Semarang, Ambarawa, Magelang, Purworejo and Yogyakarta.[13] Locally, these groups consisted of subgroups of 15 men, each group led by a commander, the idea being that when the Allies landed they would overpower the police, take their weapons in order to occupy militarily strategic points, and hinder the movements of Japanese troops by blowing up bridges, among other things.

Initially these V groups maintained regular contact. This was done by a retired sublieutenant of the KNIL, the Dutch Eurasian Korff, upon the orders of the police chief in Semarang, the above-mentioned W. Haccou, who had become well acquainted with several Ambonese and Timorese living in Semarang. Haccou was arrested by the Kempeitai in September 1942, Korff two weeks later. The V groups nevertheless carried on though without much contact. But it was difficult. They had been helped financially by Haccou; now they received some money from the most prominent organizer of the relief work in Semarang, M. Van Oort-Lau (she possibly used part of the money she in turn had received from Kramer in Batavia), but it was not enough. Moreover, and graver still, at the end of November all persons on Java who came from the Outer Islands were required to register separately, and as they subsequently had to carry a separate identity card, the freedom of movement of the members of the V groups was seriously limited.

In January 1943, all of these groups, with the exception of the one in Semarang, were rounded up. Their fate is known only with respect to the group from Magelang: 49 Ambonese and Timorese were all sentenced to death and executed. Moreover, when on 1 February 1943 all of the Timorese in Semarang had to report for registration and the men were asked whether they wanted to work for the Japanese, some of the local V group members refused. They were all arrested. Most were released in March but the leader of the

[13] On East Java there was a V group in Malang. It was rounded up in July 1942, betrayed by a brother of one of the members.

Timorese subgroup, Johannes Ndoen, who had assumed full responsibility, was sent to Batavia along with six other Timorese. These six were sentenced to 15 years' imprisonment. Like the leader of the V group in Ambarawa, KNIL Sergeant J. Frans, Ndoen was condemned to death: both were beheaded.

This rounding up of the V groups may have led to the arrest in Batavia of the leaders of the local Ambonese community in mid-August 1943. The chairman of the Sarekat Ambon (the Ambonese Union siding with the Indonesian nationalists), J. Kajadoe, died while under arrest by the PID in Buitenzorg: all of the remaining prominent figures suspected of collaborating with a resistance group, 'De Toorts' (The Torch, about which nothing further is known), were released.

Let us return for a moment to the guerrilla groups – a term here used for lack of a better one. Many did indeed intend to conduct guerrilla warfare (while others only wanted to remain at liberty in order to join the Allied Forces, whose landing was thought to be imminent in 1942, as quickly as possible), but it would appear that they had little opportunity to do so. No wonder! They had few weapons and no chance on Java to acquire more: all weapons were in the hands of the Japanese and of the collaborating Indonesian police and paramilitary organizations. The guerrilla groups had trouble enough just staying at liberty, and this in relatively inhospitable regions with little food and little cover, prolonging their existence under what one imagines were exceedingly difficult conditions (no report of this has been preserved) and far removed from one another (the distance between Sukabumi and Semeru was more than 700 kilometres as the crow flies). How different the situation would have been had these groups received support from the indigenous communities, as was the case with their counterparts on the Philippines and on Malacca! This was certainly not so on Java. The fact that the groups had retreated to the mountains, often to the slopes of volcanoes, was no coincidence: there they were far removed from the *desa* where each *lurah*, or chief, could reveal their presence to the Japanese via his superiors. They could only count on the small minorities (the Dutch, Dutch Eurasians, Ambonese, Timorese, and here and there also the Manadonese), which were also being subjected to increasing Japanese pressure.

It was mainly Dutch and Dutch Eurasians who in the first months of the Japanese occupation realized that Dutch and other Allied soldiers were to be found in certain places in the mountains, and a part of the clandestine work described below, also consisted of extending support to these soldiers. None of those who risked this foresaw that three full years would pass before the Allies would approach Java, on the contrary. In the atmosphere of tense optimism in which, as was underlined above, many Dutch and Dutch Eurasians lived at least until October 1942, it was believed that powerful Allied Forces would imminently deliver the guerrilla groups from their isolation. Many felt compelled to inform the Allies of the location of these groups and various attempts were made to establish direct communication with Australia from home-made transmitters on Java. Not a single one succeeded.

Five attempts on Java are known (there may have been more) to send reports by radiotelegraphy to Australia, and to establish regular two-way contact.

The first was made in June 1942 by a group in Buitenzorg which received information from Batavia that had been assembled by a Chinese who had formerly worked for the KNIL's Military Intelligence. These reports were passed on to a Dutchman employed at the Goodyear factory, C. Bakhuys. He handed them over to an Armenian who was to give them to the guerrilla group south of Sukabumi, whom Bakhuys knew to have a transmitter at its disposal. Whether the Armenian ever found the sorely diminished guerrilla group is not known – what is certain is that no one succeeded in contacting Ceylon with this – Van der Post's – transmitter.

The second attempt was also made by a group in Buitenzorg led by a deputy head of department of the General Secretariat, the reserve First Lieutenant L.J. Welter, a son of C.J.I.M. Welter who had several times been Minister for Colonial Affairs. Welter was in contact with the guerrilla group on the slopes of Salak Mountain. In July and August 1942, he had parts gathered from which a transmitter was assembled at an estate on the Bandung plateau. It was ready or almost ready when Welter was arrested by the Kempeitai in early September. In so far as is known, the transmitter was never used.

The third attempt was made in Batavia. Shortly after the capitulation in 1942, a transmitter was built for the director of the Aneta press agency, H.A. Colijn, who had been dismissed by the Japanese. He wanted to pass on information to the Allies not included in the Japanese-controlled radio broadcasts. According to an assistant, Charlotte Hoogenkamp: 'Transmissions [uncoded, naturally] were made every evening at 7.35 pm, and repeated at 10.45 pm. After the reports were transmitted, reception was attempted and at least once the reply "Thanks message Batavia" was received.'[14] The sender is unknown. Colijn was interned in June 1942 and detained by the Kempeitai shortly thereafter: he died in prison.

The fourth attempt took place in Bandung, where in the first months of the occupation a transmitter was built by an official of the Bureau Radio Omroep (Radio Broadcasting Agency) of the Post Office, B. van der Heyden. Around July 1942, he was asked by the head of the agency, C.W.L. Schell, to report to the head of the Post Office, C. Hillen. The latter knew that the chief of his technical department, C.J. Warners, had left for Australia intending to

[14]   Quoted in A. Zimmerman, 'Verslag werkzaamheden', October 1945, p. 8 (NIOD IC, 80,772).

organize a monitoring service there: Hillen and Warners had agreed a code as well as the call sign PKP. Van der Heyden was willing to allow the radio traffic to take place on his transmitter and, according to his post-war report, he received a total of four coded telegrams from Hillen via intermediaries, 'each of which was transmitted every other day for a couple of weeks'. Transmissions were made up to November 1942 and following a break (the PID and the Kempeitai had raided Van der Heyden's home in November but found nothing), again in February-March 1943. In the latter month, Van der Heyden disassembled the transmitter because one of the middlemen had been arrested – his wife threw all of the parts into the river when the Kempeitai appeared on their doorstep for the second time. According to Van der Heyden's report, reactions to these transmissions were received only in late February 1943, and moreover not from Australia but from Ceylon. The telegram received in morse code read as follows: 'PKP DE CICEF YR CODE MSG DEST NETH LEG MBN RCD OK', or: 'PKP. De' (From) 'Commander-in-chief Eastern Fleet. Your code-message destination Netherlands Legation Melbourne received okay.'[15] The Dutch authorities in Melbourne may have responded to this telegram (no evidence to this effect has been found), but by then the transmitter-receiver had presumably been destroyed.

Finally, the fifth attempt. This was also undertaken in Bandung, namely by a clandestine group founded by a Dutch Eurasian in mid-1942, O.R. Werd-müller von Elgg. In his post-war report he wrote that he wanted to establish a secret transmitter both in Bandung and in the mountains; that the transmitter in Bandung could, indeed, transmit (he makes no mention of receiving telegrams) until the transmission team was arrested in July 1943; and that the transmitter in the mountains got no further than the stage in which an engineer 'was constructing an appliance to produce electric energy by means of a generator, powered by riding a bicycle'.[16]

From the remaining records of the Nederlands-Indische Commissie voor Australië en Nieuw-Zeeland (Dutch East Indies Commission for Australia and New Zealand, later the Dutch East Indies government) and of the Netherlands Forces Intelligence Service, or Nefis, it appears that there never was regular contact with secret transmitters constructed on Java.

With respect to the Dutch and the Dutch Eurasians in Batavia, mention must first be made of the clandestine work of Frans Kramer, chairman of the Gemeentelijk Europeesch Steuncomité (GESC, Municipal European Assistance Committee) which will be discussed below.

---

[15]   B. van der Heyden, 'Verslag', n.d., p. 1 (NIOD IC, 30,621).
[16]   O.R. Werdmüller von Elgg, 'Verslag', 7 August 1946, p. 1 (ARA, Alg. Secr., Eerste zending, XXII, 45, 516).

Furthermore, two clandestine groups are known. The first was led by a reserve KNIL captain who had escaped being captured, A.L.J. Wernink. He said that he was acting with the approval of General W. Schilling (who favoured conducting guerrilla warfare on West Java but for lack of support had to abandon this plan virtually immediately). Wernink recruited several young Dutch and Dutch Eurasian men along with a few Ambonese and Manadonese ex-soldiers and civilians. Working together with the Welter group in Batavia (see below), he tried to provide support to the Australian soldiers on the slopes of Salak Mountain and gathered a great deal of intelligence. They were soon plagued by arrests: the first three in early May and then six Dutch and Dutch Eurasian youths along with an unknown number of adults were taken by the Kempeitai – the nine youths received prison sentences, and two of them died while in custody. When these young men were eliminated, Wernink found support via a Chinese clergyman from a Chinese clandestine organization: in Batavia he helped two Australians and a Dutch officer go underground. Nothing more is known about his group and what it did, and it appears to have been in decline when Wernink was arrested in Buitenzorg in June 1943. He was only executed one and half years later, in December 1944.

All that we know about the second clandestine group established in mid-1942 by Frans de Preter is that it consisted of young Dutch Eurasians, including members who were only 13 years old. They worked together with young Ambonese. None of its activities are known. The group was broken up by the Kempeitai in September 1943: De Preter was subsequently sentenced to death and six others to imprisonment. Five perished in captivity, and De Preter was executed in August 1944.

With respect to Buitenzorg, it was mentioned above that L.J. Welter was in contact with the Australians on the slopes of Salak Mountain and that he tried to build a transmitter. At the time of the capitulation, he was commander of the Buitenzorg Stadswacht. Unlike the situation in Batavia, the Japanese did not arrest the members of the Stadswacht in Buitenzorg. Welter devised a plan to seize the weapons of his Stadswacht that had initially been stored in the General Secretariat. Whether he succeeded is not known, but with the help of others he did amass a modest number of weapons which he concealed in his house (the Kempeitai found 3 machine guns, 2 automatic pistols, 10 rifles, 17 ordinary pistols and 33 hand grenades at his house and the homes of other members of his group). He followed the Allied radio broadcasts (anyone working clandestinely must have done the same) and gathered information on the Japanese military and administrative machine. According to a post-war report of his work, he did this 'with the intention of creating an organization throughout Java which, in the event of the reconquest of Java by the Allies, would attack the enemy from behind as well as protect the European women and children'.[17]

After establishing contact with the Australians on Salak Mountain (it is not known how), he collected provisions and medicine for them. He received medicine from a Danish doctor, Olaf Munck, and when several Australians in Buitenzorg went into hiding, the doctor prevented the secret addresses from being searched by posting notices that an infectious disease had broken out in the houses concerned.[18] Welter came into contact with one more Allied officer: the British flight lieutenant Gordon Coates. He had registered as a Dutchman, 'Pieter Cornelis Koets', in Sukabumi, where he established a group that maintained contact with British prisoners of war confined there. When the Kempeitai got wind of this group, Coates left for Buitenzorg. The rounding up of all white men there in July spurred Coates and Welter to shift the centre of their activities to Bandung, where no raids were being conducted at the time and where there was a link with a clandestine group established by Captain R.G. de Lange of the General Staff (more about him below).[19] Welter relinquished leadership of the clandestine work in Buitenzorg to three other Dutchmen, C. Bakhuys (mentioned above in connection with his attempts to pass on reports to Van der Post's transmitter via an Armenian),[20] H. Drielsma, and a certain De Rooy. According to the above-quoted report, in Bandung, Welter:

> Carried on in the usual way, attempted to recruit as many decent people as possible, coordinated the incoming messages and worked on the preparations for Coates's departure. Provided with the most comprehensive intelligence and introductions to our government officials in Australia, he was to attempt to reach that country. For this goal, Mr Welter wrote an extensive report containing economic, political and military information concerning the situation on Java.[21]

17   Fiwi, 'Rapport omtrent het verzetswerk van mr L.J. Welter', n.d., p. 1 (NIOD IC, 503).
18   Welter was also in contact with a Dutch office assistant in Batavia, Hanny Hilgers, who had helped two Allied soldiers go into hiding at her mother's: her fiancé, a British lieutenant in the Royal Engineers, John L. Appleby, and a soldier with a British-Dutch background, L.H. Powell. These two wanted to leave Java by boat, but were unable to find one. When their position in Java became dangerous, Hanny Hilgers found them a secret address in early 1943 in a private mental hospital in Buitenzorg and when it was announced that this institution was closing down, a third hiding place with a Dutch Eurasian, P.M. Mulder, who was already accommodating a KNIL sergeant in his house, W. Bechtholt. Hanny Hilgers was betrayed at the beginning of August 1943 and arrested together with her sister. This was followed one week later by a raid on Mulder. His people in hiding had a few hand grenades which they wanted to use against the Kempeitai, but they did not work. Appleby, Powell, Bechtholt and Hanny Hilgers were summarily beheaded three weeks after the raid, Hanny Hilgers as the last.
19   Welter's wife initially stayed behind in Buitenzorg. She moved into another house, taking two revolvers and a few hand grenades in the dirty nappies. Only later did she and the children move to Bandung.
20   It seems plausible that Bakhuys did this in consultation with Welter.
21   Fiwi, 'Rapport omtrent het verzetswerk van mr L.J. Welter', n.d., p. 2 (NIOD IC, 503).

Welter was arrested in Buitenzorg, in early September (the transmitter he wanted to have built was almost finished). Though he was detained for four weeks and subjected to brutal interrogations, he continued to deny everything he was accused of, and was confined in a civilian internment camp in early October. Disguised as an Indonesian, Coates first attempted to find a boat on Java's south coast and when this failed he set off for the north coast. He succeeded in sailing from Cirebon in November, but was nevertheless discovered by the Japanese navy while still on the Java Sea. All of the documents he had with him (the most recent communication mentioned was dated 18 October) fell into Japanese hands – they are reproduced in two chapters taking up more than 100 pages in Japanese in the Kempeitai report drawn up in 1944. The summary made by American Intelligence consists of 28 (large) pages[22] and distinguishes the information gathered in Bandung (exclusively or primarily by De Lange's group) and that gathered by Wernink's and Welter's groups. The following additional details can be given.

All three groups succeeded in gathering an impressive amount of intelligence concerning the strength and the disposition of Japanese troops on Java, the airfields and the number and types of Japanese aircraft stationed there, and the most important harbours. The groups were able to form a clear picture of the Japanese command structure and knew the location of the Japanese headquarters. Moreover, Wernink's and Welter's groups gathered similar information about the Japanese forces on Sumatra, Borneo and Celebes. The latter two groups also mentioned the transfer of Japanese troops from Java eastwards (they thought to New Guinea); the establishment of a reconnaissance network in the waters of the archipelago deploying 50 native proas; and the departure of the technicians of the oil companies to Palembang. The groups had become aware that the Japanese on Sumatra were being helped by F groups, that General Overakker had surrendered on North Sumatra (they did not know that the general had done this together with Colonel Gosenson), that Lieutenant Van Zanten had avoided the capitulation on North Sumatra and that Lieutenant De Jong had to cease his resistance activities on Central Celebes in early August. They also wanted to relay reports to Australia about what was taking place in the Indonesian world: namely, that in Padang Sukarno was in charge of an Indonesian People's Committee; that on Java, Hatta and Soekardjo Wirjopranoto provided services to the Japanese; that the AAA movement was a Japanese set up ('the AAA movement supports the Indonesians and the Japanese support the AAA movement'); and that the Indonesian nationalists were unhappy with the Japanese decision to reserve all of the high administrative positions for themselves. The groups furthermore reported many irregularities: Islamic extremists subjected 1,000

---

22   pp. 65-93 (NIOD IC).

men on Java and 500 on Sumatra to forced circumcision; on Java 2,000 ('90% Chinese') and on Sumatra 500 ('mostly Chinese') women were raped by Indonesians; and in Batavia, where 200,000 Indonesians were unemployed, 50,000 of whom received relief, 300 robberies were committed daily. Finally, above all the groups wanted to warn the Dutch East Indies authorities in Australia that the Dutch and Dutch Eurasians were desperate: all the Dutch men and boys 17 and older had been arrested, 'the Japanese army intends to starve the whites to death', 'Java is in a state of virtual lawlessness – I beg you to make public all of the information I sent you in previous telegrams' (these telegrams are unknown; in any event, they were never received).

How people in Bandung and Wernink's and Welter's groups succeeded in assembling so much information not only on Java but also on the Outer Islands in such a relatively short period of time is not known, other than that, according to the Kempeitai report, messages from Sumatra were conveyed by a KNIL lieutenant, E.V.F. Toers Bijns, who had escaped to Java at the end of March 1942.

From the documents, it became clear to the Japanese that there were people in Bandung who had maintained contact with free Australian soldiers. Efforts to track them down were intensified – Bakhuys, Drielsma and De Rooy were arrested in early December on the basis of 'overwhelming evidence', according to the Fiwi report, having been betrayed by a member of their group;[23] Olaf Munck was arrested as well, betrayed by a nurse. The Kempeitai discovered that Welter had played a central role until early September in the clandestine work in which the four detainees had been involved. He was transferred to Buitenzorg in January 1943 (the month in which the last Australians on Salak Mountain were captured) by the Kempeitai, yet again grievously abused and subsequently detained in Batavia pending trial before the Japanese military court. According to the Fiwi report:

> After the first interrogations it was clear to him that he had little chance of staying alive. Yet even with this knowledge he was a model of enormous moral courage for his fellow prisoners. To the very end he exhibited great dignity, courage and unfailing confidence in the Allies; even the Japanese commented on this to other prisoners.[24]

Welter, Bakhuys, Drielsma and De Rooy were beheaded in Batavia in May 1943,[25] and the same fate befell Olaf Munck, whose arms were still paralysed as a result of the abuse he had been subjected to by the Kempeitai. Coates had

---

[23] Fiwi, 'Rapport omtrent het verzetswerk van mr L.J. Welter', n.d., p. 2 (NIOD IC, 503).
[24] Fiwi, 'Rapport omtrent het verzetswerk van mr L.J. Welter', n.d., pp. 2-3 (NIOD IC, 503).
[25] Welter's wife who had smuggled several arms from Buitenzorg to Bandung in July and August 1942, was arrested by the Kempeitai in July 1943 and held for two months.

been executed earlier, in March. Lieutenant Toers Bijns also fell into Japanese hands (when is unknown) and was beheaded along with Captain Wernink, thus in December of 1944.

The General Staff captain, R.G. de Lange, mentioned above, was involved in the organization of the KNIL troop trains and had to resume his work at the main office of the State Railways in Bandung as a Nippon worker after the capitulation. He was soon active clandestinely, coordinating a relief operation for the benefit of the families of KNIL soldiers, extending aid to Allied soldiers who had retreated to the mountains near Bandung, and encouraging young Dutch and Dutch Eurasian men to train themselves as soldiers in order to support the Allied Forces which, he assumed, would land on Java's south coast, probably near Wijnkoopsbaai (see Map 1). Via the railway network, De Lange established connections with like-minded individuals in Buitenzorg (Welter), Batavia (Kramer), Semarang, Surabaya and Malang. In Sukabumi he came into contact with three people: Coates, Captain John Douglas, a British army officer who like Coates had evaded captivity, and the chief inspector of police in Sukabumi, S.J. de Vries, who, after being fired by the Japanese in May 1942, worked for the auxiliary police of the regency of Sukabumi up to August. At De Lange's request, De Vries sent a reserve officer of the Dutch navy to Wijnkoopsbaai 'to intercept possible contact from the sea'[26] – De Lange evidently did not expect this to take too long.

During later house searches some letters dating from early July 1942 fell into the hands of the Kempeitai which, even if not by Captain de Lange (this is entirely possible), nevertheless afford a clear picture of the attempts to track down weapons. The letter of Thursday, 2 July, as included in the Kempeitai report on the resistance on Java, reads as follows:[27]

> Intelligence has been received stating that a large number of rifles are hidden under the roof of the warehouse in Tanara tea plantation.[28] Manager Van der Meer is in charge of the plantation. It is considered that he possesses full knowledge of this matter but he might refuse to give any information. There is no trace of these weapons being sent elsewhere from this place. The place remains as it was because the Japanese garrison unit took the key of the warehouse which was in custody. However, it is expected that authentic intelligence regarding the warehouse will be obtained by next week, and will be in the hands of the Dutch garrison unit.
>
> It is expected that large numbers of automatic rifles will be obtained. The exact name of the place cannot be stated. The person who has the full knowledge of

[26]   S.J. de Vries, 'Verslag', n.d., p. 2 (ARA, Alg. Secr., Eerste zending, XXII, 45, 73).
[27]   Java Kempeitai HQ, 'Anti-Japanese activities in Java', February 1944, pp. 71-2 (NIOD IC, 61,326 III).
[28]   The names are translated from the Japanese – in actuality they could have been different. In fact, the guns in question were not stored in the attic of the warehouse at the plantation, but in the sealed house of an employee.

the matter is the son, Sgt. Maler, Maj. Maler, and Probation Officer Hildegard, but they were formerly in Jatinegara, and I think they are in Cimahi at present.

If someone is to send reliable persons to Mrs Gouw of Nassaulaan No. 73 area on 3 July, he will have to give the following passwords: 'I have come to buy thread for knitting zurosu' [swimming trunks] (Ik kom breikatoen voor een zwembroek kopen). I think this lady will make sure whether the previously mentioned persons are in the Cimahi internment camp or not. Mrs. Gouw possesses the roster of the probation officers in Cimahi internment camp.

The person called Van Berkel desires to enter the Dutch guerrilla squadron together with the others. A plan is being made to find the weapons in the northern part of the lake.

There is complete mine equipment with detonating caps end seven searchlights in the warehouse of Cimiruwan and Kina factory [the Cimiruwan quinine factory].

There are no Japanese forces in Ciheran, Banjaran, Dayeuhkolot, Ciparan and Santosa.[29]

According to very reliable intelligence, there were nine cans of gasoline and several firearms hidden at a certain place in Telaga Petenggang. It is said that they are in safe custody at the present.

Yesterday there was intelligence stating that next week, one platoon of the guerrilla unit will creep into the mountains in the vicinity of Telaga Petenggang. Berkel and I are thinking about communicating with this platoon.

According to rumours, Erujinnarumono[30] (of Helmersstraat, address unknown) was a former supervisor of the airfield and produced authentic intelligence heard from Japanese officers while being employed by them. Owing to this, all of the Dutchmen in the city will be detained. The day after tomorrow Erujin will also escape into the mountains from the city.

Last Monday, the minister Reddingius came from Batavia. According to my representative who gathered information from him, many Dutchmen were captured in Batavia. He himself was also interned in the camp. In this camp, from which he escaped, he was able to look into the namelist of persons who were imprisoned near Bandung.

The above mentioned must be submitted immediately as it is confidential. My representative has informed me that Erujin is a hard man to convince.[31]

This letter bears witness to a frantic searching for arms and great readiness to fight. Indeed, there was so much optimism within De Lange's group that they exercised little caution with respect to what they were attempting to achieve in and from Bandung. In the previous chapter it was mentioned that a state railways engineer, L.R. Oldeman, left his station in Madiun to visit the headquarters of the railways in Bandung in July: 'everyone there was very optimistic'. Oldeman later wrote:

---

[29] Small places south of Bandung partly in the mountains.
[30] Japanese transcription of an unknown name.
[31] What may be meant is someone who does not rely on empty words.

At headquarters I was asked to participate in a resistance operation. It was suggested that as a reserve officer I could not decline. This conversation was held in the midst of the surrounding Indonesian personnel. I thought it so amateurishly set up, however, that I refused to go along.[32]

M.A. de Jonge, who had headed a military hospital in Bandung and subsequently gone to Batavia was back in Bandung in the same month of July. She was stopped on the street by one of her former nurses, who according to De Jonge in her post-war report:[33]

asked me if I wanted to work for the underground. [...] The aims were approximately as follows: to collect money and medicine and take them to the military groups that were still in the mountains; set up first aid stations throughout the city; contact the prisoner-of-war camps; [establish] radio contact with foreign countries; gather arms and ammunition; conceal cars and petrol supplies; provide shelter to resistance people on the run; and anything else that could occur in this connection.

M.A. de Jonge became a member of the 'underground'.

When I had just joined the organization, there were six groups each of which was still intact, perhaps there were even more. I did not have a radio in the beginning, but heard everywhere that the news was so good that we had to make all of the preparations to protect the [Dutch and Dutch Eurasian] civilian population upon the return of the Allies.

One of these 'six groups' may have been the so-called Java Legion. It consisted of Dutch and Dutch Eurasian boy scouts assembled as of May 1942 at an estate in the Preanger mountains by a scoutmaster, W. van der Vorst, who styled himself 'Lieutenant', where they were trained by Dutch Eurasian, Ambonese, Manadonese and Timorese former KNIL soldiers. A few of these scouts showed off with their weapons and target practice was held which could be heard far and wide. The Kempeitai was alerted and the estate was raided at the end of July. Two were killed. Van der Vorst was arrested along with about 160 youths, some of whom were caught after fleeing. Van der Vorst was executed in Batavia in April 1943; the boys were shown clemency by the Japanese, who had received an appeal signed by many Dutch and Dutch Eurasian women. After spending some time in Sukamiskin Prison they were transferred to a civilian internment camp in Cimahi.

The Java Legion incident caused the Kempeitai in Bandung to redouble their efforts. Captain De Lange was arrested in mid-August 1942, probably because his name was divulged by one of the detained members of the Java Legion. De

32   L.R. Oldeman, 'Verslag Japanse tijd', n.d., p. 24 (NIOD IC, 81,206 A).
33   Text in Brugmans 1960:439-41.

Lange's organization disintegrated and group after group was rounded up in the following months. Welter's arrest in early September may also have result-ed from the initial arrests of people in De Lange's organization. Naturally, all of these arrests engendered great tension among those still at large.[34] The last person still functioning to some extent as a central figure, Captain Douglas, fell into the hands of the Kempeitai at the end of November.

Various detainees died while being interrogated; others received either the death penalty or lengthy prison sentences. Captain De Lange was con-demned to death and the same sentence was meted out to Captain Douglas and 'Lieutenant' Van der Vorst. According to a fellow prisoner after the war:

On 10 April 1943, Captain De Lange was sentenced to death. At about two o'clock in the afternoon he was brought into my cell wearing handcuffs. He looked wan and tired. [...] He was ordered to sit facing the window. 'This is not justice' were his first words. An [indigenous] guard was placed before the window to prevent him from saying anything more to us. When the guard asked the prisoner what he thought of the fact that he was sentenced to death, he answered: 'Fine'.

On 12 April he was taken to the place of execution. When De Lange asked the guard to loosen his handcuffs because his wrists were hurting, the guard answered: 'That's the way it should be'. Eating, drinking, he had to do everything wearing handcuffs. He was not allowed to lie down. He did receive permission to write a letter to his wife and on the morning of the 12th a lock of his hair was cut and put into the envelope. Later he also had to place his thumbprint on some papers.

At two o'clock he came to take leave of us with a brief handshake and the words: 'Never give up, chaps!' Van der Vorst and John Douglas were executed

---

[34]   A few notes in English have been preserved which were written by one of the members of De Lange's organization, J.G. Koeleman (he was arrested at the end of November 1942), and bur-ied by him at his house in Bandung. They were dug up after the war. In mid-September he wrote that he had spoken with a certain 'Smith' (presumably this was Captain John Douglas, an officer of Australian Intelligence). 'He said that he had warned various people that the Kempeitai was on their trail', and he named Welter and a few other 'bloody fools. According to Smith there do not exist guerrilla troops of ours' (indeed, at the time the last soldiers in the mountains south of Sukabumi had already been caught). At the beginning of October, Koeleman wrote: 'Smith says there are no military groups in the mountains, so that no money is required for them. He says he now wishes to work for the camps only' (the prisoner-of-war camps) 'as conditions are very bad there.' 'Smith' believed that clandestine work should be limited to assistance to the prisoners of war, the registering and maintenance of private automobiles, preparing a Red Cross organization and the gathering of information on people who had assisted the Japanese, 'to have it at hand when the time comes to deliver it to the authorities that will deal with the Fifth Column activities here.' ('Reports and notes from mr. J.G. Koeleman', NIOD IC, 518.)
Are these notes reliable? Probably, but it should be mentioned that the Dutchman G.H. de Heer who had been an interpreter for the Kempeitai-Bandung and as such had been able to speak with many prisoners, in June 1946 stated 'that Captain De Lange had told him that he considered Koeleman a dreamer'. De Heer also said 'that the relationship between Douglas and Coates was bad, that Coates was willing to spill the beans in order to save his own skin'. (proces-verbaal, by G.H. de Heer, 18 June 1946, cited in TKR-Batavia, Judgement in the case of the Bandung Kempeitai, 19 April 1948, p. 39, NIOD IC, 27,468).

together with him. While walking past our window, John Douglas said: 'Keep fit, keep smiling'. The conduct of these three was exemplary.

Later we were informed about their execution by the highest Indonesian police official, who revealed the following to us. A small green car took those sentenced to death to a graveyard in Ancol. They had to dig their own grave (one grave for all three) and then kneel before it blindfolded and with bound hands. At a signal from the commander they were beheaded. Their bodies were kicked into the grave. The soldiers then filled the grave.[35]

That De Lange had not acted on his own initiative was beyond doubt for the suspicious Kempeitai. Some time after his arrest, they subjected the former director of transport and public works, Van Haeften, to gruelling interrogations. Consequently, in the Kempeitai report of February 1944 it was recorded that sometime between 10 and 20 February, General Ter Poorten is believed to have said to Van Haeften: 'We plan to leave spies in the service of the Japanese, and I am now selecting competent officers'. This is why De Lange would have attempted to seek employment at the office that arranged the troop trains for the Japanese army. According to the report, 'In the light of this fact it would appear that Lt. Gen. Ter Poorten has many of his officers on special missions working in this way. It was the plan of Capt. De Lange's subversive group in Bandung that the "Java Army" [presumably this refers to the Java Legion] should revolt when the counterattack of the Allied Army comes.'[36]

Three clandestine groups have now been mentioned which attempted to gather as much intelligence as possible, collect weapons, and provide support to the Australian soldiers still at large: Captain Wernink's group (Batavia), Welter's (Buitenzorg, later Bandung), and Captain De Lange's (Bandung). These groups received money for their activities from Frans Kramer who, as reported in the previous chapter, had been able to hold back almost 200,000 guilders as chairman of the Comité voor Stads- en Landwachten. He made 60,000 guilders available to De Lange's group – how much he supplied to Wernink's and Welter's groups is not known.

Kramer saw this financial support as part of a larger plan. Like so many others, he too was convinced that the Allied landing on Java was imminent and considered it essential for a Dutch colonial government to begin functioning immediately thereafter. But where would the governor-general and the department heads be found? To be on the safe side, he deemed it desirable that a new, temporary government come into effect immediately and there are indications that he had assigned himself a leading role. He was

[35]   W.F. Wijting, 'Verklaring', n.d., p. 9 (IMTFE, Exhibit 1,748 A).
[36]   Java Kempeitai HQ, 'Anti-Japanese activities in Java', February 1944, p. 10 (NIOD IC, 2,162-2,189).

widely considered to be suitable for an appointment as governor-general and had no particular regard for Van Mook and the others who had been sent to Australia in good time. He probably felt that as the money provider he was the central figure in the clandestine activities on West Java, and that he would therefore logically remain the central figure in the initial phase after the liberation.

Matters did not quite work out this way, however.

At the beginning of December 1942, as mentioned above, Bakhuys, Drielsma, De Rooy and Olaf Munck were arrested in Buitenzorg. Others were also detained – a massive wave of arrests was in progress in which the Kempeitai considered every Dutch person suspect. On his way by train from Sukabumi to Batavia, Kramer was removed from his compartment and taken to the Kempeitai office. After being interrogated he was released and allowed to continue on to Batavia. Evidently, at that time the Kempeitai was unaware of his clandestine activities, but in the course of December new suspicions against him were raised and he was arrested for the second time, together with some others, in Buitenzorg on Boxing Day. The same day, various prominent figures associated with the the GESC, including Bogaardt and Manschot who together with Kramer sat on GESC's managing board, were also detained. Manschot was interned and Bogaardt was released some time later – he was able to continue the work of the GESC (this is discussed at greater length in Chapter VI). But Kramer was arrested and the Kempeitai discovered (we do not know who divulged this) that he had funded various groups. His house in Batavia was searched in early March 1943. No money was found (Kramer had had someone transfer the money to his country house), and because of this he was subjected to even more excruciating interrogations. He never came to trial, for he died in captivity on 21 July 1943.

Once the Japanese were certain of Kramer's involvement in clandestine work, they decided to ensure that the Nippon workers of the General Agriculture Syndicate (of which Kramer had been the chairman) would cause them no further trouble. In May 1943 the Japanese presented the workers with a new declaration of loyalty which differed from the usual one in that the signatory agreed to report to the Kempeitai everything he or she heard about anti-Japanese activities committed by third parties. About 15 male and 2 female Nippon workers considered this addition an insurmountable obstacle to signing the declaration. They addressed a joint petition to the Japanese authorities saying they were willing to faithfully follow all of the Japanese orders but that they could not in good conscience act as informers. As a result, they were arrested by the Kempeitai: in July the 14 men (the name of one was mixed up with that of his sister who was interned in the Cideng camp), in August the 2 women, and the third one from the Cideng camp. All 17 were summarily beheaded.[37]

After De Lange's group was rounded up, an entirely separate, new clandestine group emerged with comparable goals in Bandung: providing assistance to families in need, gathering military intelligence, assembling arms, ammunition and medicine. The group was founded by a planter mentioned above in connection with his attempts to establish radio contact with Australia, O.R. Werdmüller von Elgg. At the end of 1942 all of this clandestine work became more difficult. The Dutch women were interned and, according to M.A. de Jonge in her report, 'with the women many hiding places and almost all of the first-aid posts vanished, usually along with the equipment' (Brugmans 1960:440). Werdmüller, nevertheless, is believed to have expanded his work beyond Bandung, entrusting the leadership of these activities to a retired KNIL lieutenant colonel, the Dutch Eurasian J. van Ardenne.

In his post-war report, Werdmüller claims that he brought together weapons and ammunition for about 30 men, that Van Ardenne had posted a group of five men at the Puncak Pass (southeast of Buitenzorg), that he sent messages to Australia from his country house, and that a second transmitter had been under construction. He writes:

> As a result of the intensively pursued Japanese propaganda, a fierce hate of the whites on the part of the Indonesians was already evident. In those days it was clear that there was more to fear from the Indonesian side than from the side of the occupier. In short, betrayal by the Indonesian side was widespread.[38]

He attributes his arrest and that of many of his colleagues in July 1943 to betrayal by Indonesians. Van Ardenne was taken about a year later. Whether there were deaths as a result of this affair is not known. In his report, Werdmüller suggests that the Kempeitai could not clarify the matter 'due to obstinate denial by the [...] people who had been arrested'.[39]

In Sukabumi, to the west of Bandung, a clandestine group was formed in May 1942 by a KNIL soldier, Ch. Briët, who was released from captivity after promising to refrain from anti-Japanese activity. He established contact with (otherwise unknown) clandestine groups in Bandung, Buitenzorg and Batavia, but his group was rounded up a mere four weeks later. Briët had

---

[37] In Surabaya as well, two employees of the Koffiefonds refused to sign the declaration of loyalty demanded by the Japanese – they were not tried for this.
[38] O.R. Werdmüller von Elgg, 'Verslag', 7 August 1946, p. 1 (ARA, Alg. Secr., Eerste zending, XXII, 45, 516).
[39] O.R. Werdmüller von Elgg, 'Verslag', 7 August 1946, p. 2 (ARA, Alg. Secr., Eerste zending, XXII, 45, 516).

drawn up a list with the names and addresses of people he had involved in his work and of others he still wished to appeal to. His foster son, a young Indonesian, turned the list over to the Kempeitai, and everyone whose name was on it (including those who still knew nothing) was arrested.

Nothing else is known of the fate of Briët and his group.

Thus far, we have outlined all of the available information concerning clandestine activities undertaken by the Dutch and Dutch Eurasians on West Java. However, the other parts of Java should not be neglected, and so what follows is an account of what took place on Central and East Java.

With respect to Central Java, a number of Dutch Eurasians had joined the V groups consisting largely of indigenous ex-KNIL soldiers, most of which were eliminated by the Kempeitai in January 1943.

There are indications that the governors of Central Java and East Java, Winkler and Hartevelt respectively, interned in Ngawi, maintained some contact with these V groups: they viewed them as a force responsible for maintaining order which would have to function immediately upon the restitution of Dutch rule. In Ngawi, both governors considered what the first measures should be when this took place. Governor Hartevelt spoke of this with only a few people, but Governor Winkler discussed it widely with the higher and lower administrative officials from Central Java interned along with him in Fort Van den Bosch. In the course of 1943 all of the higher officials, including Winkler and Hartevelt, were transferred to Sukamiskin Prison at Bandung. While searching Fort Van den Bosch a short time later, the Kempeitai uncovered some documents that had been drafted within the context of Winkler's plans. It also realized that Governor Hartevelt had been able to visit several places on East Java in March and early April 1942, and discovered during the preliminary investigation for the trial against Sjarifoeddin that Hartevelt had made available 20,000 guilders' worth of bank cheques to an indigenous police official in order to set up an espionage group. The result was that the two governors were taken from Sukamiskin and transferred to Central Java and to Surabaya respectively. The same fate also befell several Dutch residents and senior police officials. Moreover, the internment camp at Ngawi, now considered dangerous, was dismantled – all of the internees were held in a camp near Bandung.

Governor Winkler received a 20-year prison sentence. He died in Sukamiskin Prison and with him perished seven or eight others (not only administrative officials). Governor Hartevelt died in captivity in Surabaya.

In March or April 1942, a clandestine group calling itself the Freedom Fighting Command was founded in Surabaya by a student at the nautical college,

Willy Tan. Its members were recruited among those who had been involved in air raid defence before the Japanese invasion. Its intention was to make the preparations necessary to help the Allies upon their return and to gather military intelligence and weapons. Evidently, this did not work out. Most of the approximately 150 members disassociated themselves from the organization in May 1942. In June there were only 25 left; in July the Kempeitai arrested them together with Tan. Two were executed by the Japanese, the fate of the others is unknown.

A second organization to assist the Allies arose among the prisoners of war in various camps in Surabaya who, via rumours, believed that the Americans had landed on the south coast of Java, and had already got as far as Malang. Clandestine written contact was established between several of these camps and there was communication with a KNIL officer who had evaded imprisonment. Lieutenant H. Groothuizen, a Dutch Eurasian, had escaped from a camp in Bandung and made his way to Surabaya wearing indigenous clothing.

Groothuizen's group endeavoured to smuggle weapons into a few prisoner-of-war camps. And, indeed, some weapons were concealed in one of the camps. A clandestine letter alluding to this fell into the hands of the Kempeitai in July. One of the camps was subsequently raided, and ten officers and ten soldiers were taken by the Kempeitai. The soldiers returned to the camp shortly thereafter; the officers were transferred to Batavia and there sentenced to death by the Japanese military court. Groothuizen was arrested by the Kempeitai along with a Chinese doctor who had helped him in early March 1943 – both survived the prison sentence to which they had been condemned.

A second KNIL officer was also active in Surabaya. This was another Dutch Eurasian who had succeeded in escaping imprisonment, the artillery captain W.A. Meelhuysen, who had been seconded to an airfield near Surabaya. By passing as a Javanese, he had been able to find work at a cattle breeding farm. He set up a clandestine group calling itself 'Corsica' in which important roles came to be played by a certain Ferdinandus, by the agent of the Nederlandsche Handelmaatschappij in Surabaya, P. Colijn, and by the Manadonese Pangemanan and Runtuwene. 'Corsica' established contact with a group of Ambonese in Surabaya and with a few groups on East Java, among others in Malang, which tried to supply assistance to the soldiers in the mountains.

Meelhuysen also attempted to gather military intelligence and weapons, with some success in the case of the latter, and his group was eager to assist the Allies to the greatest extent possible when they landed on Central Java. A reliable link to the Allies was considered essential. To this end Meelhuysen decided to help M. Hamelink, who had been an executive at the Javasche Bank in Batavia, and J. van Lier, a company lawyer for the Koninklijke Paketvaartmaatschappij (KPM) shipping line, escape to Australia. Hamelink was able to obtain a proa through the head of a Chinese coffee company using money made available by Colijn. Meelhuysen decided at the last minute to stay in Surabaya; only Hamelink and Van Lier embarked in Banyuwangi in early December. They had with them a report written by Hamelink, who had been able to travel around Java extensively by virtue of a post given him by Van Haeften, the director of Transport and Public Works. He argued that the Dutch government should grant the Indonesians the right to self-determination, which he saw as the only way of preserving what Dutch enterprises had built up in the archipelago. His hope was that Van Mook would adopt this vision. The report was microfilmed and the microfilm was wrapped in lead. As mentioned above, Hamelink and Van Lier did not get any further than Sumbawa, where they fell into Japanese hands and were transferred to Makassar. They managed to get rid of all of their documents before being arrested and were thus not tried as spies. After their trial, which according to Hamelink was fair, the Japanese navy court condemned them to ten years in prison for an illegal attempt to leave the Indies.[40]

In the meantime, Meelhuysen's organization was experiencing serious difficulties because one of its members had begun spying on behalf of the Kempeitai. Moreover, the Japanese military police was spurred to redouble its efforts for in early December 1942 the first two Nefis parties from Australia had landed on Java's south coast – they were arrested by indigenous officials and delivered to the Kempeitai. The Kempeitai struck in Surabaya in mid-December: first some members of 'Corsica' were arrested, and later a house was raided in which Meelhuysen and Ferdinandus, among others, had been staying (the address was evidently given away). Both managed to escape, but Pangemanan and Runtuwene were seized, and the same day the Ambonese with whom Meelhuysen had been in contact were arrested by the PID elsewhere in Surabaya.

Now on the run, Meelhuysen found a new place to hide. To no avail – the Kempeitai caught him there on 22 December. As the key figure of 'Corsica' he was unwilling to endanger the lives of the others under torture by the Kempeitai, and committed suicide the day after his incarceration.

Colijn was arrested in early January 1943. More arrests followed later that month, and at the end of February the Kempeitai found out where Ferdinandus, who had assumed leadership of 'Corsica' after Meelhuysen's

---

[40]   It is possible that in their documents there was also a new code, created by the head of the post office, C. Hillen, in Bandung, and given by him to a young Dutch Eurasian, F.S. van Davelaer. Hillen's intention was that the Dutch secret service in Australia would use this new code for radio traffic with him. Van Davelaer reached Surabaya in November and was able to find Meelhuysen. After the latter's arrest, he remained active with his own clandestine group; it was rounded up in the beginning of May 1943. Van Davelaer was later interned in one of the camps in Bandung. What happened to the rest of the members of his group is not known.

elimination, was hiding. A wild shoot-out ensued, and he was taken prisoner. This was followed by the rounding up of the medical relief group established by Meelhuysen, which was headed by the Chinese doctor who had also worked with Groothuizen.

In the context of all of their activities against 'Corsica', the Kempeitai and the PID had arrested a total of about 200 people. How many perished in captivity is unknown. Most were sentenced to long prison terms; four were condemned to death and beheaded – Ferdinandus, Colijn, Pangemanan and Runtuwene.

In March or April 1942, Colijn had received information about the talks that Spit, the vice-president of the Council of the Dutch East Indies, had held with numerous Dutch officials in the Olcott Park Hotel in Bandung following the capitulation. He also had copies of the Visman Commission report and of the scheme for a possible post-war reform of the administration of the Dutch East Indies drawn up by a few high officials upon Van Starkenborgh's request. According to the Japanese, a new version of this scheme was drafted (perhaps in connection with the discussions in the Olcott Park Hotel) by Van Haeften in collaboration with others. The Kempeitai found all of these documents in Colijn's home or in the Factory office in Surabaya in October 1943. Japanese translations of these were added to the February 1944 Kempeitai report about the resistance on Java.

A copy of this latter report was found in Hollandia (Dutch New Guinea) after MacArthur's troops landed (22 April 1944). The appendices were then translated into Dutch and presented to Van der Plas and Van Mook, among others.

As noted above, Meelhuysen's group maintained contact from Surabaya with a few other groups on East Java trying to assist soldiers ensconced in the mountains. One group was formed by the administrator of a coffee plantation in the vicinity of Malang, Trouerbach. A second one was created by a retired KNIL lieutenant colonel, the Dutch Eurasian J.K.H. van Steyn van Hensbroek. A third one also arose in Malang under the Dutch Eurasian A.G. Koops Dekker. Finally, in Java's farthest eastern corner there was a group of military policemen, presumably led by a Sundanese sergeant, Saäka.

Trouerbach's group included several Dutch Eurasian youths as well as the indigenous members of the Landwacht of Trouerbach's plantation. A number of these Dutch-Eurasian youths were also members of Meelhuysen's organization, some of whom were arrested in Surabaya at the beginning of 1943. According to a clandestine worker, J. Rups, in a report on the resistance in East Java, 'while being tortured [they] told all that they knew'.[41]

---

[41]   J. Rups, 'Verzetsverslag voor de Fiwi', n.d., p. 2 (NIOD IC, 2,484).

The Kempeitai moved Trouerbach at the beginning of March; while being transported to Malang in the sidecar of a motorcycle he threw himself into a ravine and died. Obviously, the Japanese could not obtain any information from him. Whether any other members of his group were subsequently arrested is not known.

Van Steyn van Hensbroek's group, consisting of Dutch Eurasians and a German, two Austrians, a South African and a few Ambonese, collected weapons and uniforms. The Kempeitai discovered some of these in the possession of the South African, who subsequently made a full confession. The entire group was arrested and all of the members were sentenced to death and decapitated, except for the South African, who had already died in the prison at Ambarawa, and Van Steyn van Hensbroek, who perished in a prison in Batavia.

Koops Dekker's group began by helping the families of ex-KNIL soldiers find housing. This group comprised Ambonese and other Indonesian ex-KNIL soldiers as well as a few Dutch Eurasians. The first to be detained, as early as July of 1942, was the architect J.C.C. Lang. Though he was accused of having concealed weapons, the Kempeitai was unable to pin him down. Lang was transferred to the Kesilir internment camp where he joined the group which, unbeknown to the camp leader Wackwitz, was readying itself for the arrival of the Allied Forces. There is no clear picture of the later clandestine activities of Koops Dekker's group. According to Koops Dekker, it was able to carry on. However, given the vigilance of the Kempeitai and PID and the rather fierce anti-Dutch sentiments on East Java, its activities could not have been spectacular. What was exceptional was that for a few months as of May-June 1943, Koops Dekker was apparently in touch with a Nefis party that had landed in a bay on the southern coast of East Java in early May. This party had a transmitter and after the war Koops Dekker claimed that contact was maintained with Australia until mid-1944 by means of which bombing raids could be requested. The Nefis information contradicts these claims, making it practically certain that the transmitter, from which only a single message was received in Australia, fell into Japanese hands around September 1943. The Japanese tried to set up a *Spiel*, or radio game with it. Nothing more was heard from it in Australia after 24 December 1943.

Finally, there was the group of military police presumably led by Saäka. Though without weapons, it did have the tools to commit sabotage, for example crowbars. Rups called the group, which he may have personally visited, 'the proudest that I met during my underground period. [...] Their best feat was to derail a Japanese military train on a bridge, causing it to fall into the abyss and killing many Japanese.' The group also caused several lorries with Japanese troops to crash and caught a Japanese patrol by surprise.[42]

[42]   J. Rups, 'Verzetsverslag voor de Fiwi', n.d., p. 2 (NIOD IC, 2,484).

Arrests within this group were made in the course of 1944. Rups, himself sentenced to ten years' imprisonment, saw Saäka and two of his Timorese helpers enter the sick bay of Sukamiskin Prison around September 1944. 'These brave lads were transferred several months later to the prison in Ambarawa and I never heard from them again'.[43]

Noted above was the Kempeitai's discovery that Hartevelt, the governor of East Java, had passed on 20,000 guilders in bank cheques to finance anti-Japanese activities shortly before the Japanese landings on Java. This can only have heightened the Kempeitai's suspicion of everything that transpired on East Java in financial terms and which seemed to fall into the category of clandestine manipulations. The suspicion was focused on a group of administrators of agricultural enterprises in the Banyuwangi residency who were initially kept on as Nippon workers but shifted to the camp in Kesilir in the last months of 1942.

These administrators encountered difficulties in the week when fighting was taking place on Java in that they had lost contact with their directors in Batavia or Bandung: they did not have enough cash to pay their coolies. The Assistant Resident of Banyuwangi, A.C.M. Jansen, succeeded in convincing the agent of the Nederlandsche Handelmaatschappij in Jember to place a sum of 50,000 guilders at their disposal. Some administrators had collected the monies reserved for them before the KNIL's general capitulation, others did so thereafter. Moreover, in April 1942 they had consulted with one another at one of the plantations and decided to reinstitute the Landwachten consisting of indigenous people – which had disbanded upon the arrival of the Japanese – in order to protect their plantations from pillaging. This required funds, and a joint account had been set up into which money was deposited.

While the administrators in question were interned in Kesilir they conferred, and some of them may have pointed out the desirability of having Landwachten at their disposal when the Allied Forces landed on Java. The contents of this meeting reached a small group of Dutch Eurasians in Kesilir who had sided with the Japanese, several members of which informed the Kempeitai. In the meantime, the Kempeitai had discovered that Trouerbach had involved the Landwacht of his plantation at Malang in his clandestine activities, and took the matter very seriously indeed: clearly a conspiracy was being plotted with the knowledge of the assistant resident of Banyuwangi! He and a few lower-ranking officials were taken from their internment camp in Ngawi and the administrators in question were fetched from Kesilir – all were locked up in Jember. Moreover, all of the Indonesians in the Landwachten in Banyuwangi were hauled in. A total of about 500 people

43   J. Rups, 'Verzetsverslag voor de Fiwi', n.d., p. 2 (NIOD IC, 2,484).

were arrested, including approximately 40 Dutch and Dutch Eurasians. All of the detainees were soon released with the exception of about 60, who were punished by the Kempeitai without the mediation of any kind of judicial body. At the end of May, 30 administrators and assistant resident Jansen were shot in a wood south of Jember.

Three weeks later, in mid-June, a second group taken from the camp at Kesilir was murdered.

This was the group that had deliberated on what would have to be done were an Allied invasion to take place, and bits and pieces of their plans had also reached the ears of the pro-Japanese Dutch Eurasians imprisoned in Kesilir. Again, one or more of them informed the Kempeitai which, again, took action. Sixty-three internees from Kesilir, primarily from the Malang residency, including the architect Lang who had been an assistant of Koops Dekker, were likewise shot in a wood near Jember in mid-June 1943.

Subsequently the Kempeitai found weapons at a plantation in the Besuki residency used by the plantation's Landwacht. The arrests began in September 1943 – there were 23. This time the former resident of Besuki, A.C. Tobi was transferred to Jember. The military court in Batavia sentenced him and the other detainees to long prison terms in December 1944.

The Kempeitai's suspicion not only cost the lives of dozens of internees from Kesilir and the assistant resident of Banyuwangi, but also led to the persecution of other groups of Dutch and Dutch Eurasians (Nippon workers) as well as of other groups of Indonesians who, on the basis of flimsy evidence, were accused of sabotage or of making preparations for sabotage or other forbidden activities.

In summarizing the known instances in which action was taken against more than one individual at the same time, mention must first be made of the Zoutregie (the government agency that operated the state monopoly on salt) on Madura and of the Madoera Stoomtram Maatschappij (Madura Steam Trolley Company).

During the formation of a freight train on Madura in August 1942, a wagon containing KNIL munitions that had been standing in the yard since early 1942 was mistakenly hooked up. The Japanese found the munitions when the freight reached its destination. The Kempeitai's conclusion: a revolt was being planned. Together with several Madurese and Chinese, all of the Dutch and Dutch Eurasian officials of the Zoutregie (Salt monopoly) on Madura and of the Madoera Stoomtram Maatschappij were arrested and confined in the prison on the island. They were joined by the resident, J.E.V.A. Slors, earlier interned in Ngawi. The interrogations, which took several lives, yielded the desired 'confessions'. Several of those arrested were condemned, but more than 60 (Dutch and Dutch Eurasians and several Indonesians and

Chinese) who were not tried were transferred to Java in February 1944 and shot in a wood to the west of Surabaya. Resident Slors perished in prison.

At the end of 1942 a train derailed near Cirebon. The Kempeitai's conclusion: sabotage. The identity of those accused of perpetrating this attack and the punishments meted out are unknown, but the preparations for it were blamed on 31 Dutch and Dutch Eurasian officials of the State Railways who worked in Buitenzorg and lived there in a district set up for Nippon workers and their families. Of these 31 individuals, several of whom died while in detention in Buitenzorg (some had been sentenced to death, and others to imprisonment), only six were alive at the end of the war.

A similar case, also at the end of 1942, occurred on East Java. Two derailments at the State Railways were caused by the fact that experienced Dutch Eurasian personnel had been replaced by poorly trained Indonesian personnel. This led to the arrest of a group of Dutch and Dutch Eurasian officials at the Surabaya office of the State Railways, all of whom were sentenced to death by the military court in Batavia and decapitated on the basis of 'confessions' by a few of them.

Then, again at the end of 1942, some – completely unnoticed – dynamite left behind by the KNIL was found at a railway yard in Purwokerto (Central Java). The Kempeitai's conclusion: preparations for sabotage were being made. A number of Dutch Eurasian lower-ranking officials of the State Railways were arrested on the spot; higher officials, including the former head of the department of Transport and Trade, J.P. Adèr, were transferred from Sukamiskin Prison in Bandung to Purwokerto. There, Adèr was accused of having made – on the orders of his superiors – preparations for sabotage relying on plans evidently already devised before the war. What, then, had been cooked up by the leaders of the colonial government? There are indications that Adèr made several statements about the meeting in the Olcott Park Hotel in Bandung initiated by Spit in March 1942. The Kempeitai's conclusion: a conspiracy. Spit and six participants in the talks at the hotel, De Bruijn Kops, Enthoven, Götzen, Hillen, Hoven and Jonkman, were taken from their places of detention to Purwokerto, where they were subjected to harsh interrogations. During one of these, Spit referred to the work of the Visman Commission which, according to him, could not possibly be suspected by the Kempeitai as Professor Supomo, who collaborated with the Japanese military administration, had participated in it. The Kempeitai was not reassured: Professor W.F. Wertheim, a member of the Visman Commission in 1941, was also incarcerated in Purwokerto.[44] The Kempeitai saw Spit as the central figure in the conspiracy, but his denials, stated with utter calm and consistency,

---

[44]   This group of prisoners was treated well by the prison personnel, which comprised Indonesians and Dutch Eurasians.

were so convincing that in the course of 1944 he and most of the others were transferred in groups back to 'normal' internment camps. This was a rather exceptional occurrence – presumably due to intervention on the part of the Japanese military administration – because the Kempeitai, as will become evident, remained convinced that they were, indeed, conspirators.

The verdicts reached in the case of the dynamite found in Purwokerto are unknown.

Many more Dutch Eurasians were arrested on Java in the course of 1943 and 1944; they had been kept on at their posts at the State Railways or the private railway companies. The Kempeitai perceived every industrial accident as being the result of sabotage. Railway officials were accused of this in Batavia, Semarang, Purwokerto (a second case!), Yogyakarta and Surakarta. Details are available only with regard to the incident in Semarang. Six detainees were sentenced to death and beheaded. Among them was J.J.E. Teeuwen, head clerk at Dutch East Indies Railways, who had been on the board of the Vereeniging Insulinde (an organization of Dutch Eurasians with purely social objectives established in 1907) and a member of the Volksraad in the beginning of the 1920s. Fourteen others were given life imprisonment. The assumption that the sentences in the remaining cases were equally harsh seems justified. It should be noted that various detainees perished before they were tried and that others, who had received prison sentences, also died while in detention. In April 1944 this fate had already befallen 13 employees at the State Railways.

Furthermore, in October 1943 a number of officials at an electricity company on Central Java which had a technical malfunction were arrested and sentenced to life imprisonment a year later.[45]

Yet, there is more to come.

Surabaya was first bombed by Australian aircraft in the night of 21 to 22 July 1943. The attack came as an utter surprise to the Japanese. They were convinced that light signals had been given in the city to guide Allied aircraft to particular targets – approximately 200 people, mostly former employees of the air raid defence service, were arrested by the Kempeitai: Dutch Eurasians, Chinese, Ambonese and Madurese. At the end of November, in Bandung Bouwer learned that of them, two Dutch Eurasians and five Ambonese had already been shot – details of the other punishments are unknown. On this

[45]   In this connection it is worth mentioning that the distrust of the Kempeitai sometimes also extended to Indonesians. For example, in May 1944, when a fire broke out in a storage area for sugarcane near Kediri (East Java), 30 workers at this enterprise, primarily Indonesians, were arrested, 27 of whom were sentenced to death. Moreover, in October 1944, two Indonesian physicians (one was a professor as well) and an Indonesian employee of the Public Health Service were arrested, accused of having deliberately distributed contaminated serum. Of the three, one was sentenced to death and decapitated, and two perished in prison.

occasion, too, employees of the telephone company in Surabaya were arrested, several of whom were shot – they were accused of having sabotaged the
telephone lines which had gone dead for a while during the air raid.[46]

Can a thread be detected in the actions of the Japanese on Java against
the actual resistance and clandestine activities as well as against those
the Kempeitai wished to perceive as such? If so, then it would be that the
Kempeitai was driven by extreme suspicion and that the Japanese military
court (this point is discussed later in this chapter) failed to discern the worth-
lessness of the numerous so-called confessions secured by the Kempeitai.

Is suspicion the correct word? Did the Kempeitai perhaps act against its
better judgement, motivated either by avarice (its victims' possessions were
confiscated), or the desire to ingratiate itself with its superiors? There are
indications to this effect; nevertheless they do not negate the conclusion that
an element of excessive suspicion was almost always present, certainly in
the Kempeitai's initial, immediate reactions. This was how officials of the
military police in Japan had constantly ferreted out comments by and behaviour on the part of individuals who refused to 'follow the imperial path'. It
must also be borne in mind that (and this applies to all Japanese administrations in the Nampo) it was not the educated, relatively shrewd and balanced
figures from the Japanese government machinery who were sent south, but
(and especially in the lower ranks) the less educated who, fearful of making
fools of themselves and incurring shame (a terrifying thought to the Japanese
at the time), tended all the more to take excessive action. This was further
underscored by the fact that they, who knew little more of the world than
Japan and perhaps Manchuria and occupied China, suddenly found themselves in faraway foreign countries dealing with unfamiliar languages and
feeling the need to constantly be on guard.

This tendency is illustrated by the following example. A Japanese patrol
headed by a captain made several appearances at a tea plantation on Central
Sumatra where three Dutchmen, including a physician, were required to
keep on working (their families also remained with them). The plantation
administrator later wrote:

> Accompanying him was a bungling interpreter who often had to supplement his
> mastery of the Malaysian language by means of a Malay-Japanese dictionary. All
> of our particulars had [...] to be written down on a dubious notepad. A minor

---

[46]   After a subsequent air raid on Surabaya, on 17 April 1944, the Kempeitai was convinced
that the Allied aircraft had been led to the city by means of rockets fired in various places on
East Java by Indonesian administrative officials. This resulted in the execution at the beginning
of 1945 of 51 Indonesians, including 27 officials. On this occasion, eight sons from a single family
were shot. Ten of the arrested officials perished during interrogation.

incident took place when he was about to record the details of Doctor Hagens and his family. The coincidence that the three families present comprised a husband, wife and three children had already aroused his suspicions somewhat: why three each? However, it became even more difficult when I told him that Doctor Hagens was born on Curaçao. He had never heard of it. Holland was located near *Djerman* (Germany), but that a piece of Holland was in the West Indies, no, that was inconceivable. He was not to be talked out of the familiar distrust. In an attempt to clear up matters I sought recourse to a school atlas. Curaçao and what belongs to it was but a small dot on the map. Then he saw at the top of the map: 'America'. He leapt up wildly – America-ke? America-ke? Doctor Hagens, a hated American, was still walking around free?

Try then what you may to make such an excited, distrustful Japanese change his mind.[47]

That same distrust, the same wariness, is most clearly conveyed in the February 1944 Kempeitai report about the resistance on Java. In it the Dutch were described as armed opponents of the Japanese regime – and, indeed, they longed for the arrival of the Allied Forces, but far from everyone participated in clandestine activities. The Dutch Eurasians were judged somewhat differently in so far that it was believed that the pro-Japanese group which had emerged with Japanese support in the course of 1943 was becoming representative for everyone (which was by no means the case, as will become clear in Chapter VI). According to the Kempeitai report:

Next to the Dutch, the Eurasians are the most dangerous. Their speech and actions indicate that they do not differ from the Dutch in their anti-Japanese ideas. It is necessary to supervise rigidly those insubordinate groups which do not understand the true intentions of our benign military administration. However, in view of the recent tendency of the people to cooperate more and more with the Japanese, it is necessary to exercise strict guidance and to bring the people enlightenment. It is likewise necessary to eliminate with one stroke all pro-Allied feeling.[48]

Next to be scrutinized were the Ambonese and Manadonese:

The Ambonese are not inferior to the Eurasians. They are anti-Japanese and pro-Allied Socialists. They have persisted in their anti-Japanese sentiments. The basis of their thinking has not been the same as that of the Javanese and like peoples. This is because of their thorough Christian indoctrination and because of the favours they received from the Netherlands. It also indicates their evil nature and their similarity to the Eurasians.

[47]   J. Balt, 'Onder het juk van *Dai Nippon*', n.d., p. 11 (NIOD IC, 81,321).
[48]   Java Kempeitai HQ, 'Anti-Japanese activities in Java', February 1944, p. 24 (NIOD IC 2,162-2,189).

The Manadonese are slightly more pro-Japanese than the Ambonese, but it is always necessary to keep them under careful observation.[49]

With regard to the citizens of neutral countries, a special section was devoted to the Swiss – it should be pointed out here that Paul Vogt, who had supported the guerrilla fighters to the south of Sukabumi, was Swiss; that eight Swiss had distributed the money that the BPM had concealed; and that the International Red Cross was represented in Batavia and Surabaya by the consul general and the consul of Switzerland respectively. With this in mind, the Kempeitai report states:

> Among the other races, the neutral Swiss must be carefully watched for the following reasons:
> Many of them are members of underground groups (intelligence).
> As members of a neutral nation, they protected a great number of the enemy's vanquished soldiers. [...]
> They furnished anti-Japanese information to the International Red Cross.
> In this manner they have carried out anti-Japanese acts just as much as have enemy nationals.[50]

It was as though the Kempeitai cherished a sinister predilection for making utterly random connections. In the Kempeitai report, reference is made to the work of the Visman Commission, which had done nothing more than draw up – with certain limitations – an inventory of the political aspirations in the Indies that had been expressed to it. The two parts of the report had been published in December 1941 and January 1942 respectively, and could have been purchased by anyone who wanted it. The Kempeitai made of this that Van Starkenborgh had drawn up a plan for the post-war administration of the Indies and secretly distributed copies of it to all of the higher administrative organs. One reads in the Kempeitai report:

> The sabotage groups which were responsible for the direction and execution of this operation were the Wernink group in Jakarta, the Welter group in Bogor, the De Lange group in Bandung, the Meelhuysen group in Surabaya, the Steyn group in Malang (led by [a] Col.), also the GESC Benevolent Society in Jakarta and Bandung, the Factorij Bank Benevolent Society group in Surabaya. For chain of command see appendix 3.[51]

[49] Java Kempeitai HQ, 'Anti-Japanese activities in Java', February 1944, p. 24 (NIOD IC 2,162-2,189).
[50] Java Kempeitai HQ, 'Anti-Japanese activities in Java', February 1944, pp. 24-5 (NIOD IC 2,162-2,189).
[51] Java Kempeitai HQ, 'Anti-Japanese activities in Java', February 1944, p. 17 (NIOD IC 2,162-2,189).

And, in that appendix it would appear – on the basis of dense cross-referencing – that there was a massive conspiracy.

The suspicion manifest in all of the available information regarding the Kempeitai makes it impossible to ascertain the true meaning of some of the statistics in the report. That is to say: if the report states that so many clandestine workers or perpetrators of acts of resistance were arrested in 1942, 1943 and the first two months of 1944, that number will be correct but affords absolutely no certainty that all those concerned had, indeed, been clandestine workers or had committed acts of resistance.

In these statistics, which cover Indonesians and Chinese as well as Dutch, Dutch Eurasians, Ambonese, Manadonese, and so on and in which the Japanese arrests are called 'incidents', three periods may be distinguished: March 1942 through August 1943; September 1943 to 8 January 1944 (during which a special campaign was launched against the 'clandestine activities' on Java); and 9 January 1944 until the end of February 1944. Statistics are given only for the first period and, presumably, for the second and third periods combined. Arrested during the first period were: 484 'members of destroyed units of the Dutch army'; 1,730 'members of subversive underground groups (in the course of 20 incidents)'; 84 'spies, sent out by the enemy and by Chungking';[52] 313 'communists (in the course of 5 incidents)'; 799 'defeated soldiers'; 243 'rumour-mongers'; 1,089 'enemy Chinese'; 17 members of a group 'which disrupted currency by forging Army notes and putting them in circulation' (as we have seen, they were Chinese); 50 'unauthorized listeners to enemy propaganda broadcasts'; 69 'railway saboteurs (in 2 incidents)'; 41 'agitators for national independence (in 1 incident)' (the arrest of Sjarifoeddin and others in January 1943); 'and others', meaning that more individuals were arrested than conveyed by the statistics reported totalling 4,919. The report concludes: 'Satisfactory results were achieved from the standpoint of the enforcement of public order'.[53]

Why, then, was a special campaign instituted on Java in September 1943? In October 1945 a high-ranking Kempeitai official declared that it was prompted by the fact that a large conspiracy masterminded by the territorial commander of Central Sumatra, Major General R.T. Overakker, was discovered on Sumatra in mid-1943, and that this discovery had led to investigations for which Kempeitai officials were temporarily brought in from Java. Evidently their conclusion was that if there was a far-ranging conspiracy on

---

[52] 'Chungking' was not designated as an 'enemy' because China had declared war on Japan, but Japan had not declared war on China.
[53] Java Kempeitai HQ, 'Anti-Japanese activties in Java', February 1944, p. 5 (NIOD IC 2,162-2,189).

Sumatra, there had to be one on Java as well. Whatever the case may be, with regard to this special action the report says only that it ended on 8 January 1944. 'Thereafter' (but we assume that what is meant is from September 1943 until the end of February 1944), '1,468 members of subversive underground (spying) groups were arrested in 42 incidents and 378 communists in 3 incidents' (among the 1,468, according to the report, were 172 Dutch, 665 Dutch Eurasians, 218 Ambonese, 96 Manadonese, 62 Timorese, 136 Chinese, 79 Indonesians[54] and 40 others). 'Aside from the 147 members of the Dutch Freemasons' Association, the 350 Jews and the 174 enemy alien missionaries who were arrested or detained [remanded in internment camps], 126 people guilty of signalling by beacon were arrested in the Surabaya sector'.[55]

Furthermore, the report states that of the 1,468 'members of subversive underground (spying) groups' arrested after the first period, two were subjected to a drumhead court-martial, 507 to the Japanese military court in Batavia and 210 to an Indonesian court; that the cases of 130 detainees were still under investigation; 'that 17 are being used by us against their former accomplices'; and that 301 were interned and another 301 were released.[56]

Finally, the report announces that 'for relief purposes' a total of 3,196,000 guilders had been collected on Java, 'of which 292,206 guilders was raised by ringleaders of resistance groups (they appropriated 23,500 for their own use).'[57] That first amount of almost 3.2 million guilders included monies that the Gemeentelijk Europeesch Steuncomité (which was recognized by the Japanese) had issued in Batavia and the almost 300,000 guilders 'raised by leaders of clandestine groups' that, presumably, included part of the almost 200,000 guilders held back by Frans Kramer.

There is no Kempeitai information from March 1944 onward.

Sumatra

With regard to Sumatra (for all of the places mentioned see Map 2), in September 1942 a fanatic Acehnese ulama resisted Japanese authority by entrenching himself in the mosque in his village. The Japanese torched the

---

[54]   There is a curious contradiction between the 378 arrested communists and the 79 arrested Indonesians – after all, the PKI almost entirely consisted of Indonesians (there may have been a few Chinese members). This contradiction could indicate that the Kempeitai labelled many individuals as such who were not communist in the slightest.

[55]   Java Kempeitai HQ, 'Anti-Japanese activities in Java', February 1944, p. 6 (NIOD IC 2,162-2,189).

[56]   Java Kempeitai HQ, 'Anti-Japanese activities in Java', February 1944, p. 23 (NIOD IC 2,162-2,189).

[57]   Java Kempeitai HQ, 'Anti-Japanese activities in Java', February 1944, p. 21 (NIOD IC 2,162-2,189).

village and the mosque at the beginning of November. In the fighting that ensued, 18 Japanese were killed and more than 120 Acehnese perished. Furthermore a local revolt broke out in Aceh in May 1945.

No other information about actual resistance on the part of Indonesians on Sumatra is known other than that concerning a few individuals who became active in organizations led by Dutchmen (discussed below), and parts of Japanese auxiliary corps.

A little more is known about the Chinese resistance. A Chinese organization that collected money and goods to benefit Chiang Kai-shek had already existed in the Medan region before the war. In mid-1942 it was transformed into a clandestine group by a Chinese student, an envoy of the government in Chungking who had managed to make the crossing from Singapore to Sumatra, and called the Chinese Verzetsbond (Chinese Resistance Union). Leadership of this group was entrusted to an officer of Chiang Kai-shek's army and a Chinese literator, though how and when they arrived on Sumatra is not known. This union maintained contact with General Overakker's resistance organization, which had been formed in a KNIL prisoner-of-war camp at Belawan, not far from Medan, and distributed a clandestine news bulletin. In February 1943 the union was rounded up and its leaders were sentenced to death and beheaded.

A second clandestine Chinese organization also in the Medan region, the Anti-Fascist League, was the work of Chinese communists from Malacca. This League circulated anti-Japanese propaganda and collected money to support the Chinese communist guerrilla fighters on Malacca. The Kempeitai tracked it down at the end of 1943: numerous arrests followed and the leaders were tried.

Whether there was any anti-Japanese activity on the part of the Chinese on Sumatra in 1944 and 1945 is not known.

The resistance organization of KNIL prisoners of war mentioned above was formed in the camp at Belawan in April 1942; namely, the Unie *kampong*, a housing district for incoming contract coolies, part of which was in use as an internment site for civilians. The camp housed all of the soldiers who had been captured on North Sumatra and in the residency of Sumatra's East Coast, including the territorial commander of Central Sumatra, General Overakker, and the territorial commander of Aceh and Sumatra's East Coast, Colonel G.F.V. Gosenson, both of whom had surrendered their weapons at the end of March when they were high up in the Alas Valley. Spurred on by General van Oyen's radio announcement (it had been heard in the Unie *kampong* that in an Australian broadcast at the end of March, Van Oyen had stated : 'We will soon return'), Overakker and Gosenson set up a resistance campaign, presumably around mid-May. In the camp, Overakker announced to Klooster, the interned editor-in-chief of the (discontinued) *Deli Courant*, who reported this later, that :

> there are plans to establish a secret organization to prepare for the arrival of the Allied Forces, which may not be far off. Reserve Captain Ten Velde will assume leadership should the general be removed (which he assumes will be the case). Passing over regular officers and those older or higher in rank, Ten Velde receives written authorization to act as territorial commander of the East Coast. One assumes that when an Allied attack occurs, the Japanese will retreat into the mountains to defend their positions. In the lowlands, with Medan at its centre, a kind of vacuum will then emerge. This would then be the opportunity for the appropriate men to take over at the appropriate moment and make rapid preparations to facilitate the Allied Forces' task. Before it comes to this, the secret organization must do everything in its power to collect military intelligence for the Allied Forces, to have as many weapons manufactured as possible, to maintain contact with the Allied Forces, to undermine the Japanese in any way possible, and to recruit men from the reliable section of the population who will stand behind us at the ultimate moment, who will help protect the women's camps, and lend support as guides or brothers in arms to the Allied Forces. Another organization should also be set up now to ensure the immediate perfect functioning of police and transport, of monetary transactions and food distribution. Furthermore, with the aid of engineers preparations should be made to be able to repair as quickly as possible any bridges the Japanese might damage. (Brandt 1947:44-5.)

Why General Overakker suspected at the time that he would be transferred from Sumatra is unknown – perhaps he caught wind of the fact that the Japanese were intending to move all high-ranking army and navy officers held captive in the Nampo to a single place closer to Japan, but it could also be that the transport on 18 May of the first group of prisoners of war from the Unie *kampong* to Burma led him to suspect that he would experience the same fate. Whatever the case may be, on 18 May he signed an order to Reserve Captain K. ten Velde and Reserve Captain C. Woudenberg. He had selected them not only because they had made a combative impression but also because as Nippon workers (Ten Velde had been the director of the Belgian administration office of the Société Internationale de Plantation et de Finance, and Woudenberg a hydraulic engineer) they had the necessary freedom of movement. The order stated:

> Pending my arrival or that of other military authorities, I have herewith determined that Reserve Captains K. ten Velde and Woudenberg in joint consultation are charged with authority, as laid down in martial law, in the residencies of Sumatra's East Coast and Tapanuli, as soon as Dutch rule has been restored in these residencies due to changed circumstances.[58]

---

[58]   Vromans and De Bruin, 'Het Indisch Verzet' (Nederlands Instituut voor Oorlogsdocumentatie, Amsterdam, vol. 3, p. 50).

Copies of this order were made and given to those persons outside the camps, all Nippon workers, who were to prepare for the restoration of Dutch authority. Some of these Nippon workers, such as Woudenberg, were employed by Public Works in Medan, others; such as Ten Velde, were assigned to the Agricultural Testing Station there. One of the latter, G. Saubert (already mentioned in Chapter I as the organizer of relief for the families of Indonesian KNIL soldiers), specifically sought contact with the Ambonese, Manadonese and Timorese who in the meantime had been released by the Japanese. He received money from affluent Chinese via the Chinese Resistance Union, making it possible for the former KNIL soldiers and their families to keep their heads above water; several of these soldiers began collecting intelligence.

Ten Velde deemed it crucial to find a reliable person who could pave the way for the restoration of the police machinery. He did not feel that the chief of police in Medan, P.H.J.M. Maseland, was a suitable candidate because he had cooperated with the Japanese authorities from the start and had rendered them invaluable services. Instead, Ten Velde chose P.A.J. de Bruyn, who had been the head of the PID on Sumatra's East Coast.

Overakker and Gosenson were removed from the Unie *kampong* in July 1942, and first taken to Singapore and later to Formosa.

Around the time of their departure or shortly thereafter, Klooster was able to speak with De Bruyn in a hospital in Medan. The latter reported:

> The organization is growing. People are working hard: results can already be seen; weapons, bladed weapons, are being made at the various enterprises; there are Chinese able to get hold of machine guns and revolvers and put them in safekeeping. Contact has already been made with an Allied submarine.[59] Great support is given by the Ambonese, mostly former soldiers [...], filled with a deep hatred for anything related to Nippon. (Brandt 1947:62.)

Klooster became a courier for the clandestine organization. He wrote,

> [The money] came from everywhere [...]: from Chinese, Indonesians, from Hollanders who had stashed away a sizeable sum. At one point I had 50,000 in good Dutch East Indies money in the false bottom of my cabin trunk, and this was only a small share of the cash at our disposal, because the risks, naturally, were spread. (Brandt 1947:83.)

Klooster was also one of the people who began gathering military intelligence via couriers. The intelligence amassed in the second half of 1942 was extensive:

---

[59]   De Bruyn had apparently heard this, but the information was incorrect.

We knew exactly how many troops were entering Sumatra and how many were leaving, we were fully aware of all movements of any significance. [...] We knew where new military roads throughout all of North Sumatra were being built and where new railways were being laid. We knew the locations of the oil and petrol. We had contact with weapon smugglers; these were primarily Chinese. [...] Captain Kees ten Velde[60] [...] was also in touch with the former Ambonese soldiers at the plantations, and with the Chinese who were prepared, if necessary, to later take on some Japanese. Extremely important work was also carried out by the assistant resident [Otto] Treffers in organizing resistance among the reliable Indonesian population and combating Japanese propaganda [Treffers will be discussed below].

Not much could happen in those days on the East Coast or even in Aceh that we did not know about. The correspondence with Aceh was conducted by an Indo-European woman who travelled several times between Medan and Kutaradja disguised as an Indonesian. (Brandt 1947:87-8.)

Just as on Java, the Ambonese, Manadonese and Timorese ex-soldiers affiliated with the secret organization set up by Overakker and Gosenson formed so-called V-groups (the V of Victory). The members of these groups used their own identifying marks; a red handkerchief (a sign also used in Batavia) or a white feather. The leader of these groups was a former KNIL sergeant major, the Dutch Eurasian A.W. Ledoux.

Things, however, went very wrong in March 1943: Ledoux was arrested by the Kempeitai. Subsequently, all of the Indonesian ex-KNIL soldiers in possession of a red handkerchief or a white feather were detained. These manhunts lasted several months, and in May a second former KNIL sergeant major fell into Japanese hands. The fate of most of the men arrested is unknown, but it is certain that 35 people were tried (Ledoux, a Chinese, a Sundanese, 2 Timorese, 4 Manadonese, 19 Ambonese and 7 Sumatrans) and 10 received life sentences (a Javanese, a Timorese, a Manadonese and 7 Ambonese).

The Kempeitai learned of Overakker and Gorenson's secret organization through the confessions of the second ex-sergeant major. In August 1943 both men were returned from Formosa to Sumatra where, in the meantime, Captains Ten Velde and Woudenberg had been arrested (the Kempeitai got hold of Overakker's order of 18 May 1942) along with Police Chief De Bruyn and nine KNIL officers, including the territorial commander of Sumatra's West Coast, Lieutenant J.H.M. Blogg. Of all of these men, Blogg was the only one to survive the war; the others perished in captivity, or, as the result of various trials, in which the likes of Police Chief Maseland testified against them,[61] were sentenced to death and executed. Overakker and Gosenson's

---

[60]   Captain Ten Velde's first name was not Kees but Klaas.
[61]   Accused of treason and criminal collaboration, Maseland was sentenced to death by the High Military Court in Batavia in October 1949. In connection with the then imminently expected transfer of sovereignty to the Republic of Indonesia, his sentence was not carried out.

death sentences were only carried out in January 1945. During the trial of the leaders of his organization, Overakker earned the admiration of the Japanese by constantly assuming full responsibility, but that plea was not accepted.

Moving on to Treffers, it was noted above that in the course of 1942, Treffers, the assistant resident in Medan, as described by Klooster, was busily 'organizing resistance among the reliable Indonesian population and combating Japanese propaganda'. The most important of his Indonesian staff was an administrative assistant from Aceh, Rachmat, who was convinced that Japan would be defeated. Treffers also saw to it that military intelligence was gathered and like Overakker and Gosenson he, too, was going to make preparations for the restoration of Dutch rule. He was in touch with Chinese who claimed to be in contact with Chungking by means of couriers.

As mentioned above, the V-groups on Sumatra's East Coast were rounded up in March 1943 and the arrests of the assistants selected by Overakker began in May. Though this must have been known to Treffers and Rachmat, they nevertheless continued to pursue their clandestine activities. Presumably, word had also reached them that a party from the Dutch secret service in Ceylon had briefly set foot on the west coast of Aceh in December 1942, because this had resulted in the ever-suspicious Japanese arresting numerous people, including the headman of the district concerned and the Dutch administrative official to whose residency it had belonged, and knowledge of these arrests circulated throughout Aceh.[62] If this assumption is correct, it explains why Treffers and Rachmat were counting on the arrival of new parties and began going to extra lengths to obtain military intelligence. Whatever the case may be, in June 1944 the Kempeitai discovered that one of Rachmat's assistants had a thermos bottle in which were hidden notes with military intelligence. Rachmat was arrested, as was his wife, who had made about 2000 orange armbands to be worn after the Allied Forces had landed. The Japanese interrogator told Rachmat's wife that he already knew everything; not realizing that she was being tricked, her subsequent confession led to new arrests.

At about the same time as Rachmat, a second Indonesian assistant of Treffers was rounded up. Teuku Amiroeddin (*teuku* is an aristocratic title in Aceh), a son of the sultan of Deli, regularly passed on messages to Treffers he had picked up on a concealed radio, and was betrayed by his indigenous personnel. Treffers himself was then removed from the internment camp in

---

[62]   On North Sumatra in mid-1943, moreover, the Kempeitai arrested approximately 200 individuals, primarily Ambonese, Manadonese and Dutch Eurasians for conducting clandestine correspondences with internees. A few of them were tried and about 100 were given long prison sentences. Most of the latter perished in prison.

which he had earlier been incarcerated. Counting Treffers, the Kempeitai rounded up a total of almost 30 members of his group, about 20 of whom were Indonesians.[63] In deference to the sultan of Deli, Amiroeddin did not receive the death sentence, but instead was condemned to 10 years' imprisonment. On the other hand, Treffers and Rachmat, together with five others, including three local Acehnese chiefs, were shot in August 1944 not far from Medan.

In 1942, a clandestine organization to assist the Allied landings was set up in Padang on Sumatra's West Coast. The initiative was taken by Police Chief W. van Dijk who before being interned at the beginning of April had been able to call in the help of several KNIL soldiers: Dutch Eurasians (including a former non-commissioned officer, a certain Van der Torren), Ambonese and Manadonese. At the end of June, Van Dijk was taken from his internment camp together with the chairman of the *Landraad* in Padang, D. Duursma, to work as a coolie on the grounds of the Japanese officers' club. Here Van Dijk came into contact with an Ambonese ex-KNIL sergeant, Pattinama, who kept him abreast of the clandestine work that had been accomplished and who even managed to get him a revolver. Duursma, who had created the impression that he was pro-Japanese, was kept out of all of this. In November 1942, he informed the Kempeitai that Van Dijk was conducting clandestine correspondence with Pattinama. Later it could not be proven that Duursma had known about the clandestine work begun by Van Dijk and continued under Van der Torren. In any event his denunciation led to the arrest of Van Dijk, Pattinama, Van der Torren and all of the members of their group.

They were tried in Singapore. In April 1943, some were sentenced to long terms in prison; others, including Van Dijk, Van der Torren and Pattinama, were executed.

Finally, with respect to Sumatra, it can be noted that on the basis of a statement by an Indonesian PID official, 50 to 60 Ambonese, Manadonese and Dutch Eurasians believed to have held clandestine meetings were arrested in the Palembang region in July 1943. At the same time elsewhere on South Sumatra, two groups together totalling 340 Ambonese, Manadonese, and Timorese were detained and imprisoned on Bangka (these groups are discussed below). All Dutch and Dutch Eurasians who held posts as Nippon workers at the coal mines on West Sumatra, together with several Ambonese and Chinese working there, were held on suspicion of sabotage (three engineers succumbed in prison, two Ambonese were bayoneted). At the end of August 1943, the resident of Bengkulu, C.E. Maier, was taken from his internment camp and accused of spreading rumours and of committing sabotage,

---

[63]   More arrests followed, both in Aceh and on Pulau We, the island lying off it, where the port of Sabang is located.

following which in September all of the Internal Administration officials of his residency were arrested on the same charge (Maier and five others, including the resident of the Lampong districts, G.W. Meindersma, and the secretary of the Palembang residency, W.F. Lublink Weddik, were executed, and one committed suicide in his cell). On that occasion the European former police officials of the Bengkulu residency were also detained together with groups of Manadonese, and Malaysian and Chinese coolies, which resulted in three Manadonese being executed and approximately 60 others receiving prison sentences, which they had to serve in Kepahiang Prison, about 40 kilometres northeast of Bengkulu. As a consequence of all of these arrests, in mid-September 1943 the Japanese military administration ordered all Nippon workers to be incarcerated in internment camps. At the same time, many Ambonese and Manadonese were also interned or arrested (in the largest raid, on 20 September, approximately 3,000 people were rounded up throughout Sumatra, 150 of whom received the death sentence), and in Palembang the Indonesian nationalist leader A.K. Gani, who had become the chairman of the Gerindo on Java in 1937 but faded into the background in 1941, was also arrested.

Borneo

As for South Borneo, the Haga case has already been mentioned. It relied largely on false accusations in which the Kempeitai perceived clandestine actions as a dangerous conspiracy. Further, all that is known about this region is that in July 1943 several prominent Chinese and Indonesians who had converted to Christianity were arrested for listening to Allied radio broadcasts and that in September the Japanese took action against fanatic Muslims who had established a small independent state in a certain district.

About East Borneo it is known that inland a few Dyak tribes attacked Japanese patrols on occasion. In the first months of 1945 approximately 60 Indonesians who worked on a Japanese estate in Balikpapan (see Map 3) were arrested on charges of wanting to help the Allied Forces (all of them were murdered when MacArthur's naval units began putting Balikpapan under fire in mid-June). In and near Samarinda and near Berau 150 Indonesians, including several women and children, were arrested on the same charges and all were likewise slaughtered.

West Borneo was hit even harder. That the Japanese made mass arrests there may be related to the fact that in 1943 they had taken action on British North Borneo on two occasions. In July 1943 the Japanese discovered that Australian prisoners of war operating from their camp had set up a secret organization of Chinese and Indonesians to provide support to the Allied landing troops (1 Australian, 4 Chinese and 7 Indonesians were tried and executed; 19 Australians and a few dozen Chinese and Indonesians received prison sentences). A subsequent incident in this region was a Chinese uprising in Jesselton (Kota Kinabalu) in October 1943 which cost the lives of about 40 Japanese. As a means of intimidation, the Japanese air force bombed a number of villages in the vicinity of Jesselton and hundreds of arrests were made in the place itself. Many of those detained perished in prison, while others (on one occasion almost 200 people) were killed without any form of legal proceedings.

In September 1943 in Pontianak, shortly after the discovery of the plot on British North Borneo, several Indonesian administrative officials, Chinese merchants and Indonesian physicians were arrested on charges of having established a clandestine organization whose objective was to prepare for the restoration of the Dutch administration. The Japanese military police subjected the detainees to the usual inhuman interrogations and not surprisingly the contents of the so-called confessions became increasingly absurd. For example, a few physicians confessed that there was a plan to serve all Japanese officers poisoned food during a dinner, and several Chinese confessed that they were in contact with Chinese communists in China and Malacca – the arrests thus proliferated constantly. All economically and/or intellectually prominent Chinese were rounded up, as were 12 sultans of West Borneo and other high-ranking Indonesian administrative officials. Among them were Chinese who were arrested solely for having Dutch East Indies bank bills in their possession. Ultimately, about 1,400 suspects were imprisoned. A few dozen were tried in May 1944 (the sultan of Pontianak had by then died in detention) by a special Japanese military court which held session in Balikpapan, and most were subsequently executed. Of the other detainees, more than 1,000 were either shot or decapitated without any form of legal process at a small airfield near Pontianak. According to C. van Heekeren in his book *Rode zon boven Borneo* (Red sun over Borneo):

> transportation there was by lorry, and the victims had to wear a bag or a basket over their heads, so that the people could not see who they were. The unparalleled terror robbed the people of the Western District of their natural leaders. (Van Heekeren 1968:162.)

The terror was continued in August 1944 in Singkawang, not far from Pontianak: approximately 130 Chinese were arrested, all but ten of whom were killed with or without a trial. In March 1946 one of the Japanese police officials declared:

> Many of these people were innocent. [...] Most of them were rich and men of consequence and therefore it was better to kill them. Their money and valuables were

confiscated. [...] According to me, they were arrested because of their wealth, not because they had committed any kind of criminal offence.[64]

The Japanese naval authorities also took action against several Dayak tribes on West Borneo. They had neglected to provide the Dayaks with sufficient salt and tobacco and when a generally respected Dayak head accused of anti-Japanese activity was subsequently executed, several tribes carried out attacks on Japanese patrols in 1945. Five Dayaks were apprehended by the Japanese and beheaded on 22 August, seven days after Japan announced its capitulation.

The Great East

In January 1942, Lieutenant Colonel A.L. Gortmans had been sent from Java to Celebes to instruct the KNIL in guerrilla warfare. At the end of March 1942, he surrendered on Central Celebes after discharging from the army the approximately 400 indigenous soldiers he had intended to train as guerrillas. He ordered a number of them to get ready for the coming of the Allies; some then began to pass on news from the Allied radio stations to prisoners of war and internees in the camps. Dutch Eurasians were also involved in this work. The first arrests took place around March 1943. A few weeks later Colonel Gortmans was taken from his camp to the prison in Makassar. On 23 July 1943, this port was attacked for the first time by Allied bombers based in Australia, and the Japanese police made new arrests in the belief that espionage lay behind the bombing. In total ten death sentences were subsequently imposed. Like General Overakker on Sumatra, Colonel Gortmans tried to save the others who had been arrested by taking all the responsibility himself; he was shot on 6 April 1944. The Japanese court martial gave him an opportunity to ask for clemency, but he refused. As he was about to be executed he called out to M. Hamelink, who was in the same prison, 'Never ask for mercy from these Japanese swine, Hamelink! All the best! God save the queen!'

    In the rest of 1944 and 1945, as far as is known, four people were sentenced to death on Celebes for acts of resistance. Among them was an ex-KNIL corporal who had cut telephone wires. In June 1945 in Manado, where Controller H.J. Stelma had died in prison, the Assistant Resident H.J. Hoekstra, and one of the controllers seconded to him, H.J.G. d'Ancona, were beheaded – for what reason is not known.

---

[64]   TKR-Pontianak, examining magistrate, Interrogation of Shuichi Hayashi, 16 March 1946, pp. 1-2 (IMTFE, Exhibit 1,698).

There was also resistance on Ambon, where a large part of the population had traditionally identified closely with the colonial government. In 1981 the Inspraakorgaan Welzijn Molukkers (Consultative Body on the Welfare of Moluccans) gave the following general picture to the East Indies Resistance Commission set up by the minister of Cultural Affairs, Recreation and Social Work:[65]

> Several village headmen on the Moluccas were killed or severely mistreated by the occupying forces [...] because they did not obey (or did not immediately obey) orders to cooperate in providing labourers and/or young women.[66]
>
> In the raids carried out by the Japanese many were arrested and subsequently executed solely because they possessed material regarded as indicating support for Dutch rule (the Dutch flag, portraits of members of the Royal Family, etc.).[67]

The same Consultative Body also mentions a group which rebelled against Japanese rule. It was led by a retired KNIL sergeant, 'Uncle' Thijs de Fretes. There were others too, for after the Japanese conquest of Ambon and Ceram several groups of armed ex-KNIL soldiers took to roaming about these islands. The Japanese had to go to some trouble to find and eliminate them in 1942 and early 1943. The De Fretes group was still active then, but the retired sergeant gave himself up when the Japanese let it be known that if he did not they would kill the several hundred Ambonese named De Fretes. He abandoned his guerrilla campaign in August 1943 and was beheaded.

This was not the end of resistance on the Moluccas. On Ceram in September 1943 a group was captured after being betrayed by an Ambonese corporal. It consisted of an Ambonese sergeant named Litamahoepoeti, ten Ambonese soldiers and two Ambonese women (they were all executed). On the other islands, too, arrests continued. On Saparua a group was rounded up which had made preparations as early as April 1942 to assist the Allies on their arrival. In 1944 and 1945 on Ambon and elsewhere in the South Moluccas a total of 99 people were sentenced by the Japanese, 39 of them to death. They were usually charged with preparing to help the Allies, giving aid to prisoners of war or resisting Japanese measures locally or individually.

---

[65] Commissie Indisch Verzet, *Rapport*, 1981, Appendix D9, p. 2.
[66] The latter were required for the Japanese brothels.
[67] At the end of March 1945, Van der Plas wrote to the Minister of Overseas Territories that in Australia he was 'constantly' receiving reports 'which bear witness to the extraordinary courage and loyalty of the Indonesians. One of the most striking cases is that of the administrative assistant Manupatty, who refused to work for the Japanese "because", as he wrote to them, "I have taken an oath of loyalty to my queen and so cannot work for a foreign emperor". Though tortured in the presence of his wife, his 18-year-old son and his daughters, he would not yield. He was then beheaded. The Japanese officer asked Manupatty's son, "Will you cooperate or do you want to be beheaded?" The boy replied, "Take my head" and was executed.' (Letter from Van der Plas to J.I.J.M. Schmutzer, 24 March 1945 (ARA, Alg. Secr., Eerste zending, XXIII, 53-I).)

There were many former KNIL soldiers among those condemned to death.

In addition, in April 1944 on Ambon, 44 inhabitants of the Kai Islands (see Map 6), including 21 Ambonese (and among them three clergymen), were found guilty and sentenced, 42 of them to death. On one of the Kai Islands, a month later two women were shot and 37 men were beheaded; they were charged with preparing a guerrilla campaign and had been betrayed by one of the islanders. In one place on New Guinea, an Ambonese official, his family and the local priest were killed by the Japanese because of their attachment to the House of Orange. In Fakfak and Babo on the same island (see Map 6) about 150 members of the indigenous administration and police force were killed. 'Of the 30 gurus [lay preachers] of the Moluccan Protestant Church', according to a 1947 report, '29 were murdered, and we could cite many more such cases. Most of them were Ambonese who demonstrated their loyalty to the House of Orange.'[68]

Kempeitai

Having completed this survey of the resistance activities in the Dutch East Indies (the question of their significance is addressed at the end of this chapter), let us look more closely at the structure and operating methods of the Japanese body that combated resistance and underground work and has already been frequently mentioned: the Kempeitai or Japanese military police. In the areas governed by the Japanese navy (Borneo and the islands east of it) this body was known as the Tokkeitai, but the difference was negligible.

In most states the only function of the military police was to maintain order within the armed forces. However, in an occupied country such as the Netherlands, the German *Feldgendarmerie* often acted as an auxiliary force of the German police. There resistance was dealt with by police organizations, the *Sicherheitspolizei und SD*, which often brought in the *Ordnungspolizei*, and by the military counterespionage body, *Abwehr III*. In Japan maintaining order within the armed forces had become a secondary task for the Kempeitai; its primary responsibility was to find and eliminate all groups and individuals who refused 'to follow the imperial path'.

On Java and elsewhere in the Indies the Japanese armed forces had their own intelligence service, the Beppan. Assisted by numerous agents who were paid 40 to 80 guilders a month, it collected information of all kinds; its officers wore civilian dress. It did not make arrests[69] – that was the task of the Kempeitai and the Indonesian Politieke Inlichtingen Dienst or PID which it

---

[68]   N.A. van Wijk, 'Verslag', 19 December 1947, p. 6 (NIOD IC, 3,602).
[69]   Later the Japanese navy on Java had its own intelligence service which did make arrests.

Map 6. MacArthur's operation area: the South-West Pacific Area.
Dark grey: area under Japanese control, mid-1942.

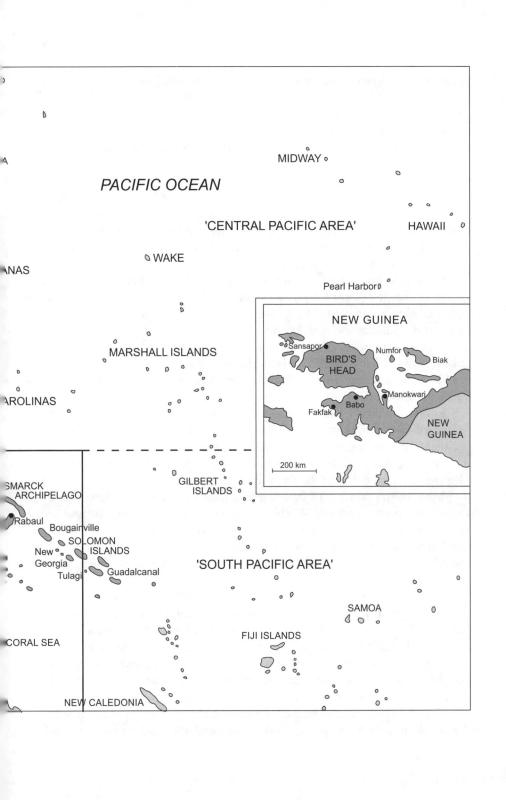

PACIFIC OCEAN

MIDWAY ○

'CENTRAL PACIFIC AREA'

HAWAII

○ WAKE

Pearl Harbor ○

○ANAS

MARSHALL ISLANDS

○AROLINAS

NEW GUINEA

Sansapor ●
Numfor
Biak

BIRD'S
HEAD

Manokwari

Fakfak
Babo

NEW
GUINEA

200 km

GILBERT
ISLANDS

BISMARCK
ARCHIPELAGO

● Rabaul
Bougainville
SOLOMON
New ○ ISLANDS
Georgia
Tulagi
Guadalcanal

'SOUTH PACIFIC AREA'

SAMOA

FIJI ISLANDS

CORAL SEA

NEW CALEDONIA

controlled. There are indications that in the course of 1945 the Kempeitai on Java transferred some of its tasks to the Department of Public Security (the new name given to the Police Department in October 1944) and to a new military intelligence service which came under Singapore. However, the evidence is not entirely clear and in any case the Kempeitai continued to function on Java until Japan's surrender.

The Kempeitai had a department for maintaining order in the Japanese armed forces and a second, more important, department that dealt with 'general matters'. This second department was responsible for counterespionage, hunting down anti-Japanese elements, arresting those suspected of clandestine activities and monitoring all political activity. It had sections for these tasks and for the different groups in the population (Indonesians, Chinese, Arabs, Indians, citizens of enemy states and of neutral states). Other sections were in charge of Post Office censorship and locating secret transmitters. If found, transmitters and the captured codes were used to try to set up a *Spiel* or Radio Game, as the *Abwehr* and *SD* had done in the Netherlands.

The headquarters of the Kempeitai on Java was located, as mentioned above, in the School of Law building in Batavia (women prisoners were held in the adjacent former French consulate, and men sometimes in the police station opposite). In Bandung the Kempeitai used the former house of a Catholic brotherhood, in Semarang and Surabaya the building of the Court of Justice, in Surakarta a hotel, and in Malang the Protestant secondary school (we have no information about other places).

On Java and Sumatra the head of the Kempeitai was a major general; on Borneo (and probably in the Great East) he was a colonel.

Initially, the number of Japanese Kempeitai personnel on Java was quite small, but by the end of 1942 the figure had grown to about 500 and in the end to nearly 700, made up of a few dozen officers and for the rest NCO's and other ranks. They all wore on their left arm a white band with the word 'Kempei' in red. Indonesians were also recruited, but how many is not known. Most of the first 500 Japanese had served in Manchukuo, and they were very surprised to find themselves on Java; they had expected to be deployed in the areas to be conquered in the Soviet Union, and some of them had accordingly learned Russian. After the war a Japanese civilian attached to the Kempeitai headquarters in Batavia described the personnel as 'mostly coming from peasant backgrounds [this applied equally to most of the ordinary Japanese soldiers]: irrational, ultrapatriotic and one-track-minded' (Kanahele 1967: 273).

The last characteristic was all the more dangerous because the Kempeitai detachments, each consisting of one officer and a few dozen lower ranks (the largest, with a strength of 52, was in Batavia) were allowed to operate with considerable autonomy. There was absolutely no direction from Tokyo and the heads of the Kempeitai were strongly inclined to protect their subordinates. Those heads were also the presidents of the military courts, so that the military police and the military administration of justice were in fact one and the same. Assuming, that is, that a case actually came before a court. On Java there was a period, from July 1943 to March 1944, when it was decided not to burden the military court with new cases: during those months the Kempeitai officers could pass sentences, including death sentences, which had to be approved only by the head of the Kempeitai and by one of the staff officers of General Harada, commander-in-chief of the 16th Army. On Sumatra military justice was similarly suspended from August 1943 to March 1944. On both islands the rule during these periods was that death sentences (nearly 300 on Java, an unknown number on Sumatra) had to be carried out in secret.

The Kempeitai had many helpers. As stated, it added Indonesians to its ranks; it employed interpreters (Japanese civilians, Chinese, Indonesians, and a few Dutch people); and it made use of traitors on a large scale, some of them as cell spies. It found traitors among all groups in the population of the archipelago, and in the case of the Indonesians they included both the humble and the highly placed.

Besides regular traitors, there were incidental informers who were paid per service rendered. Thus, at the end of March 1943, it was announced on Java that any Indonesian who betrayed a Dutch person in hiding would receive the very high reward of 500 guilders. In contrast, those who came to give information about an intercepted letter or an overheard telephone conversation or radio broadcast were often fobbed off with only one guilder. In our view this indicates not that the Kempeitai was uninterested in this information, but that there were many who came to offer it.

How many traitors were there? In February 1946, G.H. de Heer, an interpreter for the Kempeitai in Bandung from May 1942 to August 1945, was able to give the Nefis the names of 19 Dutch Eurasians who had committed treachery occasionally or regularly, and he added that 'many Indonesians' and 'a few Chinese' had done the same.[70] In a study written in 1985 F. de Rochemont estimated that the Kempeitai's informants were 80% Indonesian, 10% Chinese and 10% European (including Eurasians).[71] Among the Eurasians there were a few NSB members (they were embittered by their internment in Ngawi). As for the Indonesians, it was rumoured in Surakarta, 'to the great alarm of the inhabitants', that there were a thousand Javanese

---

[70]   Nefis, Interrogation of G.H. de Heer, 3 February 1946, p. 1 (NIOD IC, 16,268).
[71]   F. de Rochemont, 'De Kenpeitai op Java', 1985, p. 43 (NIOD IC).

spies there 'who received ten cents a day for reporting someone'.[72] It should be added that some of the Japanese semi-military organizations formed on Java must also be regarded as sources of information for the Kempeitai.

The services performed by the Indonesian PID for the Kempeitai were invaluable. The PID was part of the police force, which was expanded throughout the East Indies. At the end of the 1930s all the forces together had about 30,000 officers, but by August 1945 on Java alone there were 27,000 (with almost 10,000 rifles and 16,000 pistols). How many of these officers belonged to the PID is not known. Only in the case of Bandung and Surabaya do we have estimates: 90 and 160 respectively.

The PID was under strict Japanese control. On Java the police department, later the department of public security, was headed by Japanese and the main sections of the PID were each led by two people, one Japanese and one Indonesian. There were sections for the affairs of Indonesians, of Chinese and of foreigners – on Java the last of these was in charge of the internment camps until March 1944, when the Japanese army took over. In May 1944 this division according to population group was replaced by one based on function: in addition to sections dealing with travel permits and the censorship of printed matter, a research section was established. In Batavia it had about 35 detectives, 'the majority' according to one of them after the war, 'were ex-PID detectives' (meaning the PID under Dutch rule). The work of this section consisted:

> largely of investigations into listening to foreign radio stations, whether radios were sealed, the spreading of rumours, finding *mata mata moessoeh* ['the eyes of the enemy', that is, spies] and possession of prohibited objects, for example flags, sometimes weapons. [...] Another important task was gauging the public mood, especially when the Japs had introduced a new measure.[73]

The PID had its own offices and most of them included a primitive cell complex. When interrogating prisoners, the PID often displayed a cruelty matching that of the Kempeitai. After the war, when Dutch and Dutch Eurasians compared their experiences, they generally took the view that the PID had been even worse than the Kempeitai. Thus when we describe the interrogation methods of the Kempeitai (about which information is available because numerous Kempeitai officers, unlike PID officers, were tried after the war), as a rule it may be assumed that the PID acted at least as badly. Indeed, our impression is that the Kempeitai often had its customary torture carried out by Indonesian helpers – members of the Kempeitai were not officially allowed to use physical force. Moreover, in Japanese procedural law the con-

---

[72]   C.A. Wessel, 'Uittreksel uit verslag', 1947, p. 3 (NIOD IC, dagboek 83).
[73]   TKR-Batavia, proces-verbaal by E.S. Pohan, 9 February 1946, p. 4 (NIOD IC, 18,916).

fession was the crucial piece of evidence. The pretence thus had to be maintained that it had not been obtained under duress, at least not on the part of Kempeitai officers. In fact, they frequently ignored the regulations and applied torture themselves, but of course it was easier to have Indonesians do it instead. In that way the letter of the regulations was observed.

The regulations were also taken into account in that efforts were made to avoid causing physical injury that would be visible in a trial, and prisoners who were in danger of dying in a Kempeitai building were often hastily transferred to a hospital. There they suffered what could be termed 'a natural death'.

What happened to those arrested by the Kempeitai? According to Elias (1946: 118), basing himself on numerous statements:

> When they entered they were thrown into a small cell, often a pigsty, where [...] they were given almost nothing to eat or drink. The rice ration was minimal and was put in front of the trough, sometimes supplemented by a dead cockroach or other vermin. The vegetables consisted of a little water with a few pieces of unripe papaya in it. Talking was forbidden.
> [...] By day they had to squat and were not allowed to lean against a wall. They were also not allowed to sleep during the day. Of course there were no mattresses, but sometimes there was a mat on the stone floor, a haven for bedbugs and other insects. There was usually nowhere to relieve oneself. As a result, the conditions soon led to outbreaks of diarrhoea, dysentery and other diseases.

There were cases in which the bodies of prisoners who died suddenly in crowded cells were left lying there for more than 24 hours; in the tropical heat they soon began to decompose.

As described, the resident of Besuki (East Java), Dr Tobi, was moved to Jember after an arms cache had been found on a plantation. In December 1943 he was taken to a school that had been turned into a Kempeitai prison. He was entered in the register. According to his account:[74]

> Then the entrance to Cell I opens. 'We'll break their morale', says 'the bend-bend man'. The front of the cell consists of heavy iron bars with a low door that forces you to bend over to go through it. That's how you enter the cell. That's how it is with every Kempei. No doubt we'll get used to it. We've had to take off our shoes and socks and hand over our belts. Each of us is allocated a place on the floor where we have to sit with our legs crossed. The house rules are made emphatically clear to us: sit, no lying, no leaning, no talking, on pain of *dipoekoel* (a beating).
> [...] Food at one o'clock, one of the three meals a day. A mess tin of rice with some *sajoer* (vegetable sauce). Eaten with fingers – my spoon is in the rucksack I had to leave at registration. Oh well, this is quite tasty, even if there's no nutrition in it. It comes with a mug of tea. Same thing again at 6 pm and for breakfast.

[74] Text in Brugmans 1960:239-43.

> The evening is long, we sit endlessly waiting for the word that will allow us to lie down. It comes at 10.30 pm, after blankets have been distributed.

After a while Dr Tobi was moved to the annexe of a European residence in which cells had been constructed. He remained there for five months.

> The cell is three by three metres. Part of it, about a square metre, is taken up by the lavatory and water tank; the cell is already occupied by eight Chinese, Madurese and Ambonese. They line the walls, leaning against them – that was not allowed by the previous Kempeitai but is here because it's so full you cannot avoid it.
> [...] Every day people are brought in for questioning: Chinese traders, *desa* headmen, hadjis, simpletons and beggars. Many sit and shake their head. Indeed, we are all stunned as we suddenly become aware that we have been driven into a pen like animals for nothing and left to sit there. [...] The Chinese sit quietly, they don't involve themselves with anyone, it's too dangerous. You never know what the guard might do, if he notices.

Some time later:

> We now have some idea of what the cells hold: a total of 83 men. All of them, and those yet to come, are accused of giving money to the enemy, or passing on information or sabotage.

And the truth of this accusation had to be confessed.

A few examples of what took place during Kempeitai interrogations follow. Kramer's secretary was picked up in August 1943 (he had died in prison a month earlier) by Yoshida, the head of the Kempeitai in Buitenzorg. According to the statement she made in April 1947:

> On the first day I was interrogated almost continuously by Yoshida alone in his room from about eight in the morning to about two at night. For all that time I was not allowed to eat or drink anything. Yoshida questioned me in poor English. [...] I was treated like an animal. For most of the day and evening I was forced to kneel. My knees were pressed against the stone floor and he would not let me lie down. [...] Yoshida constantly beat me hard with a split bamboo cane about 1.6 metres long and 5 cm thick. He beat me for long periods wherever he could hit me. This treatment was extremely painful and almost unbearable. I remember that once that day I lost consciousness from exhaustion. By way of a change, he tortured me with a bodkin under my fingernails. He also terrified me by bringing a red-hot needle close to my eyes.
> On the second day I was again interrogated by Yoshida from early morning to late at night and subjected to the same brutal treatment. The matters I was chiefly questioned about were the expenditure by the GESC assistance organization, the actions of Mr Kramer, for what purposes he used the funds [...] and who his contacts were. In addition Yoshida asked what seemed to me nonsensical questions. It was apparent from the interrogation that Gutwirth was suspected of economic espionage and/or being in the service of a foreign power.

[...] In the course of five days I was mistreated by Yoshida for an estimated 50 hours. On the last two days he exchanged the bamboo cane for a cosh or truncheon. He hit me all over my body and repeatedly kicked me with his boot. He also struck me in the face with his open hand or clenched fist. The second time I lost consciousness was when I was hit on the back of the head with some object. [...] The whole left side of my body was black with contusions, and my right leg was bruised and severely swollen.[75]

A woman pastor from Bandung who was suspected of hiding arms was first mistreated by the PID, by Indonesians and Japanese, for four weeks in April 1944, and then held for six months (from late May to late September) in a cell in the Kempeitai building. Her account reads as follows:

In the cell was a *baleh-baleh* (bench) with planks lying on it. The planks lay on top of each other rather than fitting together, so that there were sharp edges and you couldn't lie comfortably. There was no bolster, mattress or blanket. I was allowed to go to the lavatory twice a day, and all requests to go there at other times were refused. I had no comb, soap, towel, clothes, nothing. In all those months I never took off my clothes and all my requests to be allowed to bathe and receive clean clothes were resolutely rejected. By day I was not allowed to lie on the *baleh-baleh* and some of the guards were strict about that. I had to walk or stand, even when I could barely do so because of the beatings.

I was interrogated by two Japanese twice a week on average. Several [...] other policemen were present. During these interrogations I was not allowed to sit; however long they went on, I had to stay standing.

During all these interrogations I was beaten by hand, with knotted ropes soaked in water or with sticks, so badly sometimes that I collapsed unconscious. In the second month of my stay with the Kempei, while I was unconscious they cut off the two plaits I wore. I only discovered that when I came round later in the cell.

Because I could only continue to deny all the accusations, in the fourth week they began the so-called water test. I was tied to a table and a tube was thrust into my mouth through which water poured into me until the Japs decided it was enough. By then my stomach was swollen with water and the Japs started pounding on it with their fists. The pain was unbearable. I can hardly describe how terrible that torture was. In the ninth and fourteenth weeks it was repeated. All together each session took about an hour.

In the sixth week all my fingernails were pulled out during an interrogation. After that I was dragged back to the cell, because I couldn't walk. I took off my petticoat, tore it into strips and bandaged my fingers as best I could. The next morning the Indonesian who was on guard outside my door saw the bandages and immediately tore them off. This happened again twice later.

During the tenth week I was hung up. This took place as follows: my arms were tied together behind my back around a tree, and a rope went round my feet and the tree. Other ropes went round my waist and my neck, with a cloth in between. Then the stool on which I stood while being tied up was removed, so that I was left hang-

75   Regeringsbureau tot opsporing van Japanse oorlogsmisdaden, proces-verbaal by J.E. Eckenhausen-Tetzner, 6 April 1947, p. 3 (NIOD IC, 28,991).

ing from the tree. This lasted for about two and a half hours. Afterwards I was tired to death, and all my limbs were paralyzed, so that they had to carry me to my cell.

In the fifth month I was electrocuted. What happened was as follows: I had to stand alternately on a wet bag and an electrical plate. At the same time electrical appliances were pressed against various parts of my body, giving me the feeling that red-hot needles were being pushed into me. After this treatment, which lasted for about an hour, I again had to be carried back to my cell.

These were all the tortures I underwent. In addition, there were recurring daily torments such as being allowed out into the fresh air only once a week, and then not being permitted to walk in the shade, and sleeping in a cell with the light on all night, surrounded by rats and cockroaches which ate my clothes. But the worst of all was that I could never wash myself, for I was never given any water.[76]

This woman was released after six months; she had made no confession and she suspected later that the Kempeitai had counted it in her favour that, using money raised by selling her jewellery, she had unselfishly supported the families of Indonesian KNIL soldiers.

During this period the Bandung Kempeitai detained the Dutch Eurasian wife of an Ambonese man: it was said that a bicycle shop she owned had been damaged (that counted as sabotage) and that she was involved in clandestine work. The court judgement against members of the Bandung Kempeitai states that in the course of one of the many interrogations she underwent her two interrogators put her:

in a barrel of water and then [...] sat on the lid, so that the witness nearly drowned. Next she was undressed and tied to a bench before being raped by both men. She was then put on a table which was suddenly pulled out from under her, so that in falling she broke her wrist. When she did not get up quickly enough, her tormentors jumped on her right foot until it was dislocated.[77]

This woman was also held for six months.

In general the treatment of male prisoners was as bad, if not worse. Captain Wernink, who was mentioned above, was the head of an underground group in Batavia; according to a fellow prisoner, he was tortured 47 times and beaten unconscious 14 times. The same prisoner, Professor E. de Vries, former head of the Faculty of Agriculture at Buitenzorg, described how a Manadonese sergeant, a regular soldier, was:

tied to a kind of cross with his arms and legs stretched sideways as far as possible for a week. [...] The planks were moveable, so that the arms and legs could

[76]   Regeringsbureau tot opsporing van Japanse oorlogsmisdaden, proces-verbaal by J.M. Schaap-Bolk, 11 February 1946 (NIOD IC, 204).
[77]   TKR-Batavia, Judgement in the case of the Bandung Kempeitai, 19 April 1948, pp. 55-6 (NIOD IC, 27,468).

be pulled as far apart as possible. The man was given no food during these seven days, only water. For the first four days he was not allowed to sleep, and was continually beaten, kicked and questioned. [...] I heard all this from the man himself, who was in the cell next to mine.[78]

In March 1943, a doctor in the prison at Medan was able to see from his cell window how a Dutch Eurasian, one Portier, aged about 40, was tortured in the courtyard by the Kempeitai. The doctor made the following statement (in English) in February 1946:

Portier was entirely stripped and his wrists were tied on his back with the end of a long rope. Then he was put with his back to a pole, of about 3 m. long. The other end of the rope was thrown over the upper part of the pole, and this was drawn up with a few sharp jerks at the wrists and at the arms, until the victim was suspended with his feet hardly reaching the ground. The long end of the rope was tightly fastened to the pole. While [...] Portier stayed in this attitude, something was read aloud and some questions were put to him. I could not understand what was spoken, because I reckon my cell having been at a 35 or 40 m. distance of the pole. While Mr. Portier was suspended in this way, the brutes punched him and beat him in the face. As if this torture did not suffice, they put the end of another pole between the pole and the lower parts of Mr. Portier's legs. Then they began to wriggle with the other end in this way, that one of the Japanese who was busy ill treating Mr. Portier, walked round the pole, so that the body was turned round till it was almost impossible to continue. They kept their victim in this attitude until he lost consciousness. Then the two Japanese put their victim on the ground until he came to his senses and then they began to torture him anew.

This happened certainly four times but they thought it not enough. Mr. Portier, still being suspended in this way, was drawn up a little higher. Some paper was heaped up under his feet over which some liquid was poured. Then the paper was put to fire. It burned excellently with a black smoke so that I suppose the paper had been drenched with kerosene. The roaring and the groaning of the tortured man was terrible to hear. After some time he lost consciousness again because of the pain and the smoke. To my utmost surprise, Mr. Portier was next day able to walk, though very difficultly.

In the cell next to mine was an Ambonese sergeant named Parinoessa. He asked me to help him with his wounds at scrotum and penis. During the airing I have seen these wounds. The scrotum was scalded with an irregular open wound of about 5 cm in diameter, while also at the lower part of the penis was a scalding with an open wound. The wounds were slightly inflamed. He told me, if I remember rightly, that these wounds had been caused by a burning candle while he was suspended to the pole.

[...] An Indonesian, a former servant [...] had also been illtreated terribly.

I have seen for myself that the man was suspended at the wrists in the way as I just mentioned. Then his legs were wrapped in rags which were drenched in

[78]   Ministry of Justice, The Hague, proces-verbaal by E. de Vries, 18 June 1946, quoted in Brugmans 1960:218.

a combustible liquid, probably gasoline, because of the big flames coming from the fire when the rags were being burnt. The Indonesian groaned and yelled with pain, too horrible to hear.[79]

These few examples would seem more than sufficient. To these should be added the list of tortures committed by the Bandung Kempeitai according to the judgement of the Temporary Court Martial in Batavia in April 1948. It said that they had:

tortured [prisoners] by conducting the interrogations in an inhuman fashion which involved:
   frequent and protracted beating by hand and fist until they bled, and with all sorts of sticks, bars, truncheons, sheathed swords, twisted electric cable, coshes and whips;
   throwing them to the floor by judo holds;
   pressing burning cigarettes against their body;
   applying the water treatment, which consisted of pouring excessive amounts of water into the mouth by means of a rubber hose connected to the mains or a funnel and a bucket, and then stamping or dancing on the stomach;
   applying electric current to the most sensitive parts of the body, while previously or at the same time pouring water on all or part of the body;
   causing wounds to the body with electric current;
   hanging them on a pole between two chairs with their hands and feet tied together behind their back and the pole pushed between their back and their limbs;
   hanging them up by their hands tied behind their back;
   raping women prisoners while they were tied up;
   deliberately dropping them from a height;
   dancing and jumping in heavy boots on various parts of the body;
   inserting needles under nails;
   putting hexagonal pencils between the fingers and then clenching the fingers while at the same time turning the pencils;
   making them kneel on the sharp edges of two triangular beams placed at the level of the knees and the transition from shoe to foot; at the same time a plank was placed over the calves and weights put on the ends, or members of the Kempei and/or their accomplices stood or danced on it;
   making them stand for days in the sun, or elsewhere, without food or drink;
   hanging them up by the legs, with their head down;
   pricking their hands with an iron rod;
   deliberately withholding food, water, medicines and medical treatment;
   confining them for days in packed cells where they could not stretch their limbs;
   this systematic terror, abuse and torture [...] caused the deaths of prisoners or severe physical and mental suffering.[80]

[79] Medan Public Prosecutor, proces-verbaal by H. Koperberg, 3 January 1946, pp. 1-2 (NIOD IC, 393).
[80] TKR Batavia, Judgement in the case of the Bandung Kempeitai, 19 April 1948, pp. 3-4 (NIOD IC, 27,468).

There is no reason to think that this list is in any way unrepresentative: this is how the Kempeitai behaved not only in Bandung, but elsewhere on Java and on the Outer Islands,[81] and the PID generally proved to be a worthy pupil of its Japanese master.

One example. In 1945 in Malang the former teacher who has already been quoted several times was called on – because she had a little medical knowledge and some medicines – to help several girls (probably Dutch Eurasians) released by the PID. She later wrote:

> My arrival was greeted with rejoicing, but also with some embarrassment. The girls were extremely shy about being examined, but they had to agree in the end. They had scabies in and around the genitals. When I'd treated them and stayed to talk a little, the stories began to come out. Without exception they had been 'hung up': with their wrists tied behind their back, they were hoisted up backwards. Some had torn tendons under their arms next to their breasts. They were hung in that position for a quarter of an hour, while being questioned. Then they were dropped to the floor with a thud. If they stayed lying on the floor because of the terrible pain, they were kicked and hung up again. Others were forced to run round a table naked until they were out of breath and then burnt with cigarettes: the nipples and genitals, especially round the vagina, were the favourite places.
>
> The native brutes sat on the naked, squatting girls with their penis on their heads. Hands and the soles of feet were roasted while they were interrogated. And what was it all about? Nonsense, trivia. It was pure sadism, just to see deadly fear and watch the effects of different tortures. (Moscou-de Ruyter 1984:183-4.)

No wonder that both the Kempeitai and the PID soon became feared organizations. Those who fell into the clutches of the PID perhaps had the advantage, being Dutch or Dutch Eurasian, of themselves speaking Indonesian in many cases, while the members of the PID, certainly those who had been in the service under the colonial government, spoke or at least understood Dutch. With the Kempeitai, on the other hand, one entered the foreign, almost sinister world of the Japanese. Not a word of what they said to each other was intelligible. Their names, when they were known, were as hard to remember as their language was incomprehensible. In every Kempeitai building the Dutch and Dutch Eurasian prisoners gave their captors names that seemed to fit them, such as 'Bent Nose', 'Horse Jaw', 'Gold Tooth', 'The

---

[81]   It should be noted in this connection that it was the Kempeitai who murdered an entire leper colony on Halmaheira in the northern Moluccas in March 1945. Because MacArthur's forces were approaching, several *kampong* on the island had to be evacuated and the Japanese army shied away from this job in the case of the leper *kampong*. There were about 40 lepers, half of them women and children. In September 1947 the Kempeitai officer involved stated at his trial that he had felt sorry for the victims. 'I also thought it was dirty work', he said, 'to have to behead these people. There could have been a real risk of infection.' (TKR-Morotai, proces-verbaal, 12 September 1947 in Brugmans 1960:252.)

Tiger', 'The Whip', 'The Little Brute'.

How many died during their detention by the Kempeitai or the PID is not known, but, given what we have described in this chapter, it must have been hundreds rather than dozens.[82]

Trials / Prisons

Except during the period when the Kempeitai did not transfer any cases to the military court, on Java those whose cases were considered to be 'completed' were taken to the cells in the Kempeitai building in Batavia (the men) or to those in the former French consulate there (the women). On Sumatra they were usually put in the prison in Fort de Kock. Java and Sumatra each had only one military court and in Batavia this was also in the French consulate building.

There it could take weeks, or indeed many months (sometimes as long as eight months), before a case was finally dealt with, even though the suspects were already in Batavia. This waiting period was terrible, not only because of the uncertainty as to the sentence, but because of the conditions in which prisoners were kept. According to the woman doctor in Semarang who was caught passing on radio reports to prisoners of war early in 1943:

> The food was the worst you can imagine; after six weeks I had hunger oedema, as did half the other prisoners. There were about 100 of them. All day long you had to sit on the floor, in the dark shadows of thickly barred *gudang* rooms [storage spaces], with your knees drawn up. Leaning or talking was strictly forbidden. [...] Every minute the patrolling Kempei soldier [...] passed your window. Washing once a day, *lekas-lekas* [quick-quick] in full view of Kempei troops. At 7.30 pm the night bell, at which you instantly collapsed on the floor. No mat (but a wooden floor [...]), no pillow, no extra clothes, blinding light (danger of escape) and your ears filled with the buzzing of mosquitoes.[83]

A Dutch Eurasian man who was confined in the consulate building at the end of September 1944 spent three weeks in a cell measuring four by five metres

---

[82]   According to a Dutch official, at the beginning of November 1945 in Batavia the central committee of the RAPWI (Recovery of Allied Prisoners of War and Internees) had 'the list of people who had died while "in arrest". This list contains 234 names. There is also a list with 88 names of people who died during interrogation.' (Report dated 6 November 1945, Brugmans 1960:172.) We assume that 'in arrest' means 'while imprisoned'. In any case many more than 88 people died 'during interrogation'. In November 1945 the authorities in Batavia still had no clear picture of what had happened on Java, let alone the Outer Islands, and we also suspect that the figure of 88 relates only to the Dutch and Dutch Eurasians.

[83]   M. van Oort-Lau, 'Verslag', p. 4 (NIOD IC).

with five others. Describing his ordeal at the end of 1946, he wrote:

> Each day you spent about 12 hours in the same position staring at a completely white wall, without being allowed to look left or right. Talking was absolutely forbidden. Any slight infringement of this rule was punished with the samurai sword in a metal scabbard: the victim was hit with it, preferably on the head, until he bled. The cells were closely guarded by Japanese NCOs who secretly spied on their victims. [...] Drinking water was limited to two tea cups a day, at 12 pm and 5 pm. This waiting until their case was heard meant daily suffering for every prisoner.[84]

What passed for justice in the Japanese military court had little or nothing to do with justice by normal standards. The court consisted of three officers – the president, as stated above, was the head of the department that had collected the incriminating evidence, the Kempeitai. The prosecutor was an officer too, as was the defending counsel, who also usually read out and explained the indictment drawn up by the Kempeitai. There was no appeal. Insofar as those charged could follow it (the only languages allowed were Japanese and Indonesian), the so-called trial struck them as a sham. The evidence often consisted solely of confessions obviously obtained under duress, which were nonetheless persuasive in the eyes of the military judges. One such piece of evidence was regarded as sufficient – if a suspect continued to deny the charge, he could be convicted on the grounds of a confession by one of his co-suspects. Indeed, in the absence of any confessions, sentence could be passed purely on the grounds of a statement from the Kempeitai. In Bengkulu, where at the end of October 1943 all the Dutch members of the former Internal Administration of the residency appeared before a special Japanese military court, the officer who was both prosecutor and defender spent most of the time asleep. In very many cases the verdict had been decided before the court even met. The reaction of Captain de Lange on hearing the death sentence passed on him is understandable; his first words to his fellow prisoners were 'This isn't justice!'

There is no detailed description of any of the numerous cases heard by the Japanese military courts in the archipelago, and so one can only speculate as to the attitude shown by those who appeared before them. Only in the case of Batavia is it known how many death sentences the court passed – 493. Most of the victims were beheaded at Ancol, on the northeast side of Batavia.

By no means was the death sentence imposed in all cases, as we indicated above. How many were given prison sentences is not known. Our general

---

[84]   P.F. Böckel, 'Verslag', 11 December 1946, p. 2 (ARA, Alg. Secr., Eerste zending, XXII, p. 45, 134).

impression is that these were usually long: life or 10 to 15 years. In retrospect it is clear that this often amounted to a death sentence, because conditions in the prisons were appalling. The Japanese exercised barely any supervision over the prisons. The general scarcity of food that was becoming increasingly evident (more on this in the following chapter) meant that only minimum rations were provided. There was a great deal of corruption among the poorly paid Indonesian prison warders, and many of them took pleasure in treating the Dutch and Dutch Eurasian prisoners especially badly (on Java in 1944 and 1945 these included many youths, discussed in Chapter VI). In quite a few jails Indonesian criminals had established positions of power over all the other inmates.

In and near Batavia there were four prisons: Bukit Duri, Glodok, Struiswijk and Cipinang. In 1942 the first three were in use as internment centres for some of the men rounded up in Batavia, and in 1944 Struiswijk was also used as a prisoner-of-war camp for officers. We shall come back to them in Chapters IV and V. Cipinang became a prison for those sentenced by the courts.

Cipinang was an old jail. How many real and supposed clandestine workers were held there is not known. There are only three descriptions of conditions inside: one by the Jesuit priest C. Teppema, who spent 18 months there, and two by prisoners who were each there for about a year – the Semarang chief of police, W. Haccou, and the editor of the underground newspaper *Rood-wit-blauw* (Red, white and blue), T. Jans.

In September 1942 Teppema found himself there with five other prisoners in 'a fairly spacious cell'. He later wrote:

> Life was quite hard, but still much better than at the court martial. Never saying Mass, except at Easter and Christmas; the whole day spent weaving mats. Food: rice with hard vegetables, never meat. [...] A terribly monotonous and dispiriting life. As time passed, the amount of food was reduced; hunger began to gnaw, and all we did was weave mats. Our warders were Indonesians; a few were troublesome, most indifferent; the odd one gave us cigarettes.[85]

Jans and Haccou were put into Cipinang about six months after Father Teppema. There were then, wrote Haccou, 'about 600 prisoners' (by which he means only the political prisoners): about 300 Dutch and Dutch Eurasians, about 200 Chinese, 100 Ambonese, 8 Javanese and 2 or 3 Manadonese ('in my view these figures are a clear reflection of the involvement and loyalty of the different ethnic groups').[86] The cells were more crowded than at the start of Teppema's detention: each one now held 13 to 18 prisoners.

---

[85]   C. Teppema, Letter, 20 September 1945, in St. Canisius College, *Ons College-Jaarboek 1944-1945* (1946), p. 85.
[86]   W. Haccou, 'Verslag', n.d., p. 19 (NIOD IC, 2,190).

'We were badly treated', according to Jans, 'and humiliated, and the food was insufficient. As political prisoners we were under the command of [...] trusties who were criminals (murderers and thieves). There were regular beatings, both by the *mantri* [overseers] and by the [...] trusties. Cases of hunger oedema were frequent.'[87]

In March 1944 these three and the other Dutch and Dutch Eurasian prisoners were transferred to Sukamiskin Prison near Bandung.

Sukamiskin was still partly in use as an internment centre. Father Teppema wrote:

The accommodation was good: small but clean cells. At 8 a.m. you were taken out of your cell and went to your place of work. I ended up at a large printer's, where the work was very boring but light; if you talked quietly, it was allowed. The great drawback of Sukamiskin, however, was [...] that there was far too little food, ridiculously little. We were starving: many became ill, their legs swelled up with water [hunger oedema] and they died. [...] It was also cold there; Bandung has a cold climate.

[...] There were 500 Europeans in Sukamiskin and half of them died of hunger.[88]

'Conditions in the hospital', wrote Haccou, 'were such that admission generally meant a swift death.'[89]

Word of the hunger suffered in Sukamiskin reached the outside world because the Dutch Eurasians among the political prisoners were allowed to have visitors on the first and third Sunday of each month. On Sunday 16 April 1944 in Bandung, Bouwer noted:

Today the first stream of visitors set out for Sukamiskin. We had heard that several of our friends were now in Sukamiskin. [...] Many ladies went to surprise random prisoners [...] with a package. Registration cards [that is, identity cards] were not checked and everything went smoothly. They were allowed into the rooms in groups of 20, and there were only two Indonesian policemen on guard. The conversation was in Dutch. The prisoners were not permitted to take food back to their cells, and so they had to gulp down everything in the course of the ten-minute visit. The stories about how the starving prisoners devoured the food are too terrible to pass on. In ten minutes some of them gobbled down eight eggs or ten bananas or two whole loaves of rye bread (made of maize and very tasty). They washed it down with a whole bottle of orange juice or milk.

For the most part people were unrecognizable: dressed in rags, grey-haired,

---

[87]   T. Jans, 'Verslag', 1 October 1946, p. 26 (NIOD IC, 2,806).
[88]   C. Teppema, Letter, 20 September 1945, in St. Canisius College, *Ons College-Jaarboek 1944-1945* (1946), p. 85.
[89]   W. Haccou, 'Verslag', n.d., p. 23 (NIOD IC, 2,190).

thin, with their bones showing. [...] There is a severe shortage of calcium among the prisoners, which leads to various horrible skin diseases and impaired vision. They do prison work from seven in the morning to seven in the evening. Contact with the outside world is possible, but extremely dangerous. All of them begged for medicines. (Bouwer 1988:250-1.)

In March 1947, an ex-prisoner who had been able to consult the Sukamiskin death registers reported that from August 1944 to August 1945 1,246 prisoners had died: 207 Europeans, 30 Ambonese, 37 Chinese and 972 Indonesians – the last group consisted of criminals.

There was also a prison in Bandung, Banceuy. It was a filthy building where the prisoners had to work and where they suffered hunger. There was a primitive sick bay where criminal prisoners appropriated the food meant for the patients. A Swiss employee of the BPM who spent eight months in Banceuy in 1944-1945 noted that during that time the prison doctor did not make a single appearance in the sick bay, and he always avoided touching the patients. Some prisoners were able to have food and medicines smuggled in by bribed warders; you could even order a meal from a Chinese restaurant through the head jailer.[90]

The prison in Cirebon generally held about 3,000 Indonesian criminals. In 1944 they were joined by about 40 Europeans charged with aiding clandestine activities; they included whole families – husband, wife and children. Here too there was very little food. According to the wife of a Dutch Eurasian:[91]

Less than once a month a small piece of sugar, not a grain more, and nothing that tasted salty. Never fruit, never real vegetables, never a shred of meat. Never anything, except 150 grams of rice a day with a bowl of leaves you could press together until they fitted on a spoon. And twice a day a fish the length of your little finger. (MacGillavry 1975:112.)

During the wet monsoon, life in the cells was even more difficult than during the dry season:

There is a wooden lid over the hole in the ground that is our toilet, at the front of the cell. But the sewers cannot cope with the amount of water: stinking fluid runs across the floor, the wooden lid lifts and floats round on a rising tide amid the excrement of countless numbers. Then, with the wave of filth a horrible underworld of shining insects comes up. They all come out, they swim, scrabble, creep over each other in the slowly rising maelstrom. They climb up our walls by the hundred, an army of centipedes and cockroaches, beetles and scorpions, more monstrous than Hieronymus Bosch could paint, for it moves. We watch

[90]   R. Flachs, 'Report', n.d., p. 5 (IMTFE, Exhibit 1,752 A).
[91]   She, with her child, was in the same prison as her husband – she was not allowed to see him until he had died because of his treatment.

with a fixed stare, nauseous in growing fear, our back ice cold, 'have a look at my back'. We are coated with damp by the stifling air. This horror is not to be borne. (MacGillavry 1975:129.)

After the war this author discovered that out of about 3,000 prisoners five sixths had died; 'the natives were no better off than we were' (MacGillavry 1975:132).

In January 1945 about 300 Dutch and Dutch Eurasian prisoners were transferred from Sukamiskin Prison to the old prison at Ambarawa, south of Semarang. According to a Dutch civil servant:

We were shackled together in fives for the journey. It is hard to describe what that meant. [...] Our arrival at the jail [...] will always be etched in my memory as a nightmare. We were hardly inside before we had to squat in rows, after which we were mercilessly kicked and beaten by several guards (evidently by way of introduction). After that we had to [...] strip naked and put on other prison clothes while being struck and cursed. We were given something to eat but we were all too frightened and shaky to get it down. Then we were taken to our cells.

This was the start of a horrific period, which was to last until the liberation.

[...] In Ambarawa it was not a case of being poorly treated, but of being continuously *mis*treated. Day in, day out prisoners were kicked and beaten by warders and trusties. [...] Nearly all these trusties were criminals who had been given life sentences under the Dutch East Indies government, and so most of them were filled with hatred for the Dutch.

[...] The number of sick rose each day. At a certain point, of the 300 prisoners from Sukamiskin only 70 were still on their feet (just about); the rest had died or were in hospital.[92]

The inmates of this prison had to weave; it was heavy work and 'the food was extremely bad and insufficient'.[93] 'According to our figures', wrote Haccou, who was transferred from Sukamiskin, 'in one year 2,600 of the 3,000 prisoners in Ambarawa died'.[94] Of the 300 who were moved there from Sukamiskin, about 140 survived, mainly because Dutch Eurasian women who had not been interned managed to smuggle money or food into the prison for some of the inmates more or less regularly. With that money it was possible to get a larger part of the amount of rice provided for all the prisoners. According to a civil servant transferred from Sukamiskin who did not benefit from this aid, the effect was that 'our suffering was made worse, since shared hunger would have been easier to bear. My weight fell from 90 to 35 kg.'[95]

[92] A.F. Holm, 'Verslag', 10 April 1947, p. 6 (ARA. Alg. Secr., Eerste zending, XX, 45, 199).
[93] A.F. Holm, 'Verslag', 10 April 1947, p. 6 (ARA. Alg. Secr., Eerste zending, XX, 45, 201).
[94] W. Haccou, 'Verslag', n.d., p. 27 (NIOD IC, 2,190).
[95] P.F. Böckel, 'Verslag', 11 December 1946, p. 2 (ARA, Alg. Secr., Eerste zending, XXII, 45, 134).

After the war it was established on the basis of Japanese statistics that in the prisons on Java and Madura where figures had been collected (they were available for only one in three prisons), nearly all deaths occurred in 1944 and 1945: 26% in 1944, 72% in 1945. In these prisons, almost 70% of the prisoners for whom the dates of sentencing and of death were known died within six months of being sentenced. At the Cipinang Prison about 4% of the over 4,000 prisoners died between 1 May 1943 and 1 May 1944, and over 51% between 1 May 1944 and 1 May 1945.

In the prisons on Sumatra and Bangka for which figures are available, the death rate among the prisoners was higher than in a prison like Cipinang, namely 70% or even higher in some cases.

In the small jail at Payakumbuh on Sumatra's west coast (see Map 2) there were about 130 inmates in 1943, including about 40 Dutch and Dutch Eurasian prisoners, and 113 of these 130 died. The Japanese who was in charge of the jail was 'not so bad' according to one of the prisoners later, but he was powerless against the corruption of the Indonesian personnel. The Indonesian responsible for distributing rations 'stole most of our food and said to us: "Everybody, including the prison workers, knows what is going on but everybody gets his share of the proceeds."'[96]

The prison at Pematang Siantar on the east coast of Sumatra was headed by a Japanese who, according to a prisoner serving life, 'did not care a bit about us'. This prisoner thought that between November 1943 and August 1945 about 60% of the prisoners died and that, except for three of them, the Indonesian warders had shown themselves to be 'cruel beasts'.[97]

In the prison at Kepahiang, where among others the civil servants from the Bengkulu residency who had been convicted of conspiracy were held, conditions were 'exceedingly terrible' according to one of them. Of the total of 60 prisoners transported from Bengkulu, 40 died.[98]

Three Swiss who were confined in the prison at Palembang from December 1943 to December 1944 saw on arrival, as one of them later described:

> all around us starving prisoners, covered with sores, and many typhoid and dysentery cases, and men at the point of death. Once a day we received a cup of hot water to satisfy our thirst, and four spoons of rice at 10 a.m. and 3 p.m. During the whole time I was in prison at Palembang we received no more.

---

[96]   No. 4 War Crimes Investigation Team (Palembang), proces-verbaal, by F.E.A. Frietman, 23 March 1946, p. 1 (NIOD IC, 18,547).
[97]   No. 4 War Crimes Investigation Team (Palembang), proces-verbaal, by W. Greene, n.d., p. 1 (NIOD IC, 451).
[98]   No. 4 War Crimes Investigation Team (Palembang), proces-verbaal, by W. Hartsteen, 25 February 1946, pp. 2-3 (NIOD IC, 66).

They were, however, allowed to have rice sent in from outside.

> In this prison we witnessed the most horrible scenes. Every day between four and seven men died. [...] Those prisoners who were culpable of the slightest infringement of the rigid orders were beaten terribly and afterwards confined for seven, fifteen or even thirty days without food or water. They were chained and left to lie in their own filth. A bestial smell came from the cells of these dying martyrs.
>
> The corruption amongst the Indonesian guard personnel and the cooks was disgusting. [...] The Japanese Hariki was responsible for this jail. [...] He made no effort to improve conditions. When asked to increase the rations in order to reduce the number of deaths, he replied cynically: 'The more deaths the better'.
>
> We were released from the jail on 12 December 1944 and were told that the Emperor of Japan had granted us mercy. Later I heard from Mr Gani that all our fellow inmates at the time of our release died before they were released.[99]

Finally, it should be added that in July 1943 on South Sumatra a large number of Ambonese, Manadonese and Timorese were arrested on suspicion of setting up an anti-Japanese organization. The fate of the two groups referred to above is known. In January 1944, 169 detainees were put in a prison on the island of Bangka. When the group was released at the end of December 1944, only 18 were still alive. 'We were never maltreated or beaten', stated one of the survivors[100] – in other words, here the high death rate was the result of starvation and the lack of medical care. In the case of the second group, consisting of 171 prisoners who were put in a second jail on Bangka, seven survived.

Conclusion

This chapter began with a description of the four objectives that the Japanese wanted to achieve in the East Indies. There was fairly general resistance to them in that the concept of a *lasting* Japanese supremacy was rejected by the Dutch and Dutch Eurasians, and in our view this attitude was shared by politically aware Indonesians. We have no clear picture of the extent of resistance to the unbridled exploitation of the country's economic resources. There were Indonesians, Chinese and Dutch Eurasians who tried to give some help, although this was prohibited, to the Dutch detainees held in internment camps. On the other hand, Indonesians took almost no part in the organized clandestine work; their only clandestine organizations were the Sjahrir

---

[99]   No. 4 War Crimes Investigation Team (Palembang), proces-verbaal, by A.V.A. Coulin, 5 April 1946, p. 1 (NIOD IC, 424).
[100]   No. 4 War Crimes Investigation Team (Palembang), proces-verbaal, by O.E. Kayadoe, n.d. (NIOD IC, 18,831).

group and the PKI, both on Java. In this respect we regard the Ambonese, Manadonese and Timorese as separate ethnic groups, from which many people, above all the Christian Ambonese, and especially former KNIL soldiers, participated in clandestine work.

There were also Chinese clandestine activities, but unfortunately no further details are available.

Is the fact that most of our information relates to clandestine work by the Dutch and Dutch Eurasians purely the result of the one-sided nature of the sources? There can be no doubt that they are one-sided: we have been able to give details about the activities of, for example, the Wernink group in Batavia, the Welter group in Buitenzorg/Bandung, the De Lange group in Bandung and the Meelhuysen group in Surabaya which are missing from our accounts of the work of Chinese clandestine groups (or that of the Sjahrir group and the PKI). The statistics show that, indeed, most clandestine activity was carried out by the Dutch and Dutch Eurasians, often in conjunction with Ambonese, Manadonese and Timorese. In 1943-1944 in Cipinang, Haccou encountered about 600 political prisoners: about 300 Dutch and Dutch Eurasians, about 200 Chinese, 100 Ambonese, 2 or 3 Manadonese and 8 Javanese. He wrote, 'in my view these figures are a clear reflection of the involvement and loyalty [to the Netherlands] of the different ethnic groups'. More important, of course, are the figures found in the Kempeitai report on resistance on Java. There the Kempeitai made a total of 1,468 arrests between September 1943 and February 1944: 172 of those arrested were Dutch (most of them were probably Nippon workers), 665 Dutch Eurasian, 218 Ambonese, 96 Manadonese, 62 Timorese, 136 Chinese, 79 Indonesian and 40 'others'. It must be remembered that not all of them were arrested for actual clandestine activity; in many cases they were only suspected of it. Still, this factor applied equally to all these groups and thus does not affect the relative proportions.

These figures show that on Java between September 1943 and February 1944 nearly four times as many Dutch Eurasians as other Dutch subjects were arrested by the Kempeitai. Whether this ratio was the same between March 1942 and August 1943 is not known; the total number of arrests then was 4,919 (plus arrests of 'others'), but this figure is not broken down by ethnic group in the Kempeitai report. It seems reasonable to assume that, compared with the period from September 1943 to February 1944, the Dutch played a greater role in clandestine work in the first six months of the occupation in particular – after those six months, except for the Nippon workers, nearly all Dutch male civilians had lost their freedom and towards the end of 1942 nearly all Dutch women (many of whom had supported clandestine activity as best they could) were in internment camps too.

Documentation of clandestine work is never complete: in the East Indies as elsewhere there was no doubt clandestine activity that has left no trace in

the sources. It is significant, however, that as a rule the clandestine organizations that were the subject of post-war reports are the same as those found
in the Kempeitai records; in other words, we do not believe that there were
large organizations that have remained completely unknown. As to the Dutch
and Dutch Eurasians and the Ambonese, Manadonese and Timorese who
cooperated with them, their organized clandestine activities were more evident in the first year of occupation than later – our impression is that in the
later years the proportion of people arrested by the Kempeitai for suspected
rather than actual clandestine work was greater.

In the first year there was a clear emphasis on activities comparable
with those of the Ordedienst in the Netherlands: they were aimed at restor-
ing Dutch rule. On Java this applied to the groups in Batavia, Buitenzorg,
Bandung and Surabaya already mentioned and also on East Java to the
Trouerbach group, the Van Steyn van Hensbroek group, the Koops Dekker
group (the only one able to assist a Nefis party) and to the group of indigenous ex-KNIL soldiers thought to have been led by Saäka. On Sumatra,
the groups were those of General Overakker and of Treffers in the vicinity of
Medan and the Van Dijk group near Padang. All these groups believed that
it would not be long before the Allies reappeared in the archipelago. They
wanted to help the Allies and collected arms and military intelligence to this
end. They also looked forward to the speedy restoration of Dutch rule, and
preparations were also made for this. As we have seen, Kramer, the financier
of clandestine work on West Java, went as far as contemplating and perhaps
even preparing for the formation of an interim government.

In contrast to what proved possible in Burma, on Malacca and on the
Philippines, all this clandestine work in the East Indies had little effect.
Weapons could be found only with the greatest difficulty (Captain de Lange's
letter of 2 July 1942 quoted above gives a telling account of such attempts).
More successful, both on Java and Sumatra, was the gathering of intelligence
about the Japanese administrative and military machine. Without hesitation it
can be stated that the reports Flight Lieutenant Coates was carrying when he
fell into the hands of the Japanese in the Java Sea in November 1942 provide
striking evidence of successful espionage. However, despite the enormous
efforts made by some, no permanent channel of communication with Australia
or Ceylon was established, and so none of this espionage had any effect.

Was all this effort pointless then? Not in our view. Those who initiated
this work could not have foreseen in 1942, given their limited knowledge
of the course of the war and their understandable optimism (fuelled by the
radio broadcasts from Australia and the United States), that it would be 1945
before the Allies approached the main islands of the archipelago. They did
what they could in an effort to inflict damage on the Japanese occupier. In
this way they tried to serve both the Allied and the Dutch cause. In this aspir-

ation, the resistance in the Indies deserves as much respect as that in the mother country.

Moreover, it is our belief that the clandestine activities in the East Indies were carried out under substantially greater difficulties than in the Netherlands. There the *Sicherheitspolizei und SD* and the *Abwehr* were formidable opponents, but those in the underground could melt into society and find support. In the East Indies things were different: Indonesian society was a hindrance, not a help, and the Dutch and Dutch Eurasians engaged in clandestine activities, who almost all stood out by their appearance, must have been aware that, with a few exceptions, they could not expect the Indonesian masses to actively sympathize with their actions; rather, they had to reckon with the general passivity of the masses and with the anti-Dutch and pro-Japanese sentiments of many. An additional factor in the Netherlands was that, after a very modest start in 1940-1942, from 1943 the underground received vitally important support from England in certain areas, particularly in the last winter of the occupation; the underground in the Indies received no support whatsoever from outside.

How many of the Dutch and Dutch Eurasians in the East Indies took part in actual clandestine work? This is a difficult question to answer. No attempt was made immediately after the war, in either the Netherlands or the Indies, to keep a record of those active in the underground. The Dutch government had a great many other matters to worry about and relatively few (we shall return to this point) of those involved had survived. A large amount of information was collected to incriminate the Kempeitai officers who had fought against the underground, but in the preparation of their trials the emphasis was on the tortures they had inflicted and no attempt was made to give a picture of what the victims had done prior to their arrest. It was October 1948 before the Resistance Star of East Asia 1942-1945 was established on the recommendation of the Minister of Overseas Territories, and March 1949 before a Resistance Star of East Asia 1942-1945 Commission was appointed in Batavia with the task of determining who was eligible for the decoration. Two months later, in May 1949, the Commission held its first meeting and it subsequently met in the Indies 25 times, the last time in April 1950, four months after Indonesia became independent. In making its decisions it relied on research carried out at its request by the Decorations Committee of the office of the Army Commander – this Committee was dissolved on 1 May 1950.

The work was moved to the Netherlands, where in September 1950 the minister for Union Affairs (that is, matters to do with the Netherlands-Indonesian Union founded at the time of Independence) and Overseas Territories re-established the Resistance Star 1942-1945 Commission. In July 1953, when the Union no longer existed, it came under the minister

for Foreign Affairs. By the time the Commission completed its work later in
1953, it had examined about 1,000 cases to see if people were eligible for the
Resistance Star – it was awarded in 471 of these cases. It must be added, however, that the Commission, as it said in its Final Report, 'had not been able to
reach everyone who might have been eligible for the Resistance Star'.[101]

The Resistance Star was not awarded only to those who had taken part
in the clandestine activities described here; the term 'resistance' was more
broadly interpreted. When the decoration was introduced, it was stipulated
that it could be awarded:

> to those who in the years 1942-1945 in areas occupied by Japan or in Japanese
> territory in East Asia through their strength of mind, character and public spirit
> have given outstanding service to the Dutch subjects who fell into enemy hands
> as prisoners of war or internees or by other means, or to the resistance against the
> enemy.

Those engaged in clandestine work were covered by the words 'the resistance against the enemy'. The others were those who had given aid to prisoners or internees from inside or outside the camps – this was illegal, if it took
place from outside, but was not generally done in an organized clandestine
context.

In 1979-1980 an East Indies Resistance Commission appointed by the
Minister of Cultural Affairs, Recreation and Social Work looked into the
matter and established that in the case of only 333 of the 471 decorations
awarded were the grounds for the award present at the Chancery of the
Netherlands Orders of Knighthood. Of these 333 decorations 204 were
awarded for 'resistance against the enemy'. After examining the grounds,
the East Indies Resistance Commission concluded that not all the 204 cases
involved clandestine work in the sense intended in the Wet Buitengewoon
Pensioen (Special Pensions Act, which made financial provision for members of the resistance and their next of kin and for seamen) applying in the
Netherlands. For example, smuggling food for prisoners had been regarded
as 'resistance against the enemy'. The Commission took the view that only
127 cases involved resistance within the meaning of the Special Pensions
Act (in 71 of these the Resistance Star had been awarded posthumously). To
these the Commission was able to add another 19 cases involving 'resistance
against the enemy' according to the records of the Pelita Foundation.[102]

So, were there only 146 people engaged in clandestine activities? No. The

---

[101] Commissie Verzetsster Oost-Azië 1942-1945, *Eindverslag* (1953), p. 12.
[102] This foundation was established in the East Indies in November 1947 by the Dutch
authorities to alleviate the suffering of war victims. After Independence it was moved to the
Netherlands, where it is still active.

East Indies Resistance Commission was only able to find the grounds for awards in about 70% of cases, but (more importantly) there is, in our view, a striking difference between the relatively low figure of 146 (to which should possibly be added 30% of 127, or 38) and the Japanese figures cited earlier in this chapter. The Japanese military court in Batavia sentenced 439 people to death, many of them Dutch or Dutch Eurasian, and between September 1943 and February 1944 alone the Kempeitai arrested 836 Dutch or Dutch Eurasian suspects, that is, nearly 57% of all arrests in that period. If that percentage was just as high in the period from March 1942 to August 1943, when over 4,900 people were arrested by the Kempeitai, then more than 2,700 would have to be added to the figure of 836. On the other hand, the Kempeitai made no distinction between actual and suspected clandestine activities, and there were many among the over 3,500 Dutch and Dutch Eurasians arrested on Java who were accused, as Nippon workers, of illegal acts, such as sabotage, but had not done anything of the kind.

There are two other uncertain factors: there are no Japanese records about arrests made from 1 March 1944, and no figures at all for the Outer Islands.

We dare go no further than to say that, taking into account the soldiers who tried to evade capture by the Japanese, in the East Indies several thousand Dutch and Dutch Eurasians led a clandestine existence or took part in true clandestine work. They were joined by fairly substantial numbers of Ambonese, Manadonese and Timorese, often discharged or retired soldiers, but we shall not venture to estimate how many.

Several thousand – in other words, a great many, were not covered by the investigation carried out soon after the war by the Resistance Star of East Asia 1942-1945 Commission. This is understandable: these had been years of great confusion; some of those engaged in clandestine work were opposed to decorations; many of them had been executed or murdered, by drowning in some cases, and few of those who had been given prison sentences had survived.

This last factor deserves some emphasis. A well-founded estimate suggests that of all those who had to serve a prison sentence imposed by the Japanese around two thirds died. Thus it was not only because of the different setting in which they operated that those active in the underground in the East Indies faced greater difficulties than their counterparts in the Netherlands, but also because of other factors. In the Netherlands only a minority of those involved in clandestine activity fell into the hands of the Germans – in the Indies virtually all of them were arrested. The methods of torture employed by the *Sicherheitspolizei und SD* were admittedly as horrific as those of the Kempeitai and PID, but they led to only a few deaths in the Netherlands, whereas in the Indies many of the victims died. In the Netherlands those in the underground often received support from the Dutch prison staff before or after their sentencing – such support was not generally given by the Indonesian personnel in the Indies, on the contrary. There was no hunger in the Dutch prisons. Conditions were worse in the prisons and detention centres in Germany, where, of the estimated 7,500 Dutch prisoners (a minority of them involved in clandestine activity) serving a sentence, between 350 and 400 died. Finally, of the over 10,000 Dutch inmates of concentration camps in Germany (we are not referring to the deported Jews and Gypsies), about 4,000 died. Losses among the prisoners of the Kempeitai were proportionally much higher. In retrospect, thus, the conclusion must be that those in the underground in the East Indies ran even greater risks than their counterparts in the Netherlands.

It is regrettable that, when writing about the fate of the underground workers, we have only been able to portray their suffering in their own words to a limited extent. Detailed descriptions are rare in the sources. In fact, we have had to appeal to the readers' imagination, telling them about courageous men and women who, usually after a brief period of clandestine activity, saw all their dreams go up in smoke on being arrested by the Kempeitai or PID; who were then tortured by Japanese or Indonesians with sadistic refinement; and who, if they survived, were next subjected to the farce of a Japanese trial. If a death sentence was passed, they often had to dig their own grave before being beheaded. If they received a prison sentence, they generally found themselves in filthy cells, hot and close in the tropical heat, dripping with damp in the wet monsoon, when an army of creeping vermin appeared – cells where every scratch festered, where there was no medical care, and where one felt one's strength dwindling day by day because only starvation rations were provided.

In Cipinang Prison, as noted above, from 1 May 1943 to 1 May 1944 4% of all prisoners died, and from 1 May 1944 to 1 May 1945 over 51%. Presumably, in other jails on Java, too, most of the prisoners who died did so in the latter period, roughly the last year of occupation. At that time the famine in the prisons was such that, while the end of the horrors was coming into sight, the life of every prisoner was threatened.

Was this deliberate? Did the Japanese authorities intend to create such desperate conditions? It is possible. At all events they did nothing to alleviate the suffering and were thus responsible for its effects, but we should not lose sight of the fact that there was a severe shortage of food in many areas in the East Indies and particularly on Java in that last year of the occupation – several million people died of hunger outside the prisons.

CHAPTER III

Starvation in the Indies

In order to describe what happened to the economy of the East Indies in the three and a half years of Japanese occupation, we must start from the situation encountered by the Japanese in 1942. There was what one might call a dual economy: the indigenous, which was traditional in character, and the European, which was modern. These two were not strictly separated, for the European economy had come to influence the indigenous one in numerous ways. Modern industries extracting minerals, above all the oil industry, provided work for tens of thousands of Indonesians, and there were even more jobs on the large plantations producing sugar, tea, coffee, rubber, tobacco, fibres and palm oil. Many hundreds of thousands, perhaps even a million Indonesians, were able to support themselves by working for the big Western concerns. There were others, also numbering over a million, who earned extra money by working in the harvest season, for example on the sugar, tea and coffee plantations. Furthermore, hundreds of thousands themselves produced crops for the world market. The cultivation of coconut trees for copra had developed on the Outer Islands and was almost exclusively the preserve of Indonesians. Apart from the Java coffee produced chiefly by Western companies, coffee was cultivated on the Outer Islands on almost entirely indigenous plantations. Rubber, the principal export of the Indies in terms of value, was produced half on European and half on indigenous estates. The basis for this dual economy consisted of a modern infrastructure that had been built up in the first four decades of the twentieth century by or with the aid of the colonial government. In fact, that government had undertaken many tasks that had benefited the traditional indigenous economy: major irrigation schemes had been carried out, erosion prevented and epidemics combated; agricultural education had been improved and an extensive system for cheap loans established.

The economy as a whole had two weak points. First, there were few industrial enterprises; this was because general Dutch policy was to promote industrialization in the mother country. Moreover, there were no large reserves of iron ore in the East Indies, and the coal mined there was of poor quality, particularly on Java. In 1939 what industrial companies there were employed only about 30,000 Indonesians (compared with about two million working in 'cottage industries': batik workers, tin- and coppersmiths, carpenters and so on). Second, Java was overpopulated. Because of better medical care, the number of people living on this most populous island had grown more rapidly than employment, especially in the twentieth century. In the 1930s the Dutch authorities began promoting emigration from Java to the Outer Islands, specifically to Sumatra, Borneo and Celebes. By the end of 1940 there were 200,000 migrants on the Outer Islands, and a further 65,000 were due to leave in 1941 (this was prevented by the outbreak of war). This was a substantial number, but in the same year of 1941 the population of Java was expected to increase by at least 650,000, in other words ten times as many.

The millions of Indonesians on Java needed rice above all for their daily food. It has been estimated that the indigenous farmers on Java normally sold 42% of their rice on the indigenous markets, the *pasar*, and 20% to the husking plants (which were largely owned by Chinese). They kept the remaining 38% – for planting new fields, for feeding their own families and for paying the harvesters, who normally received 15-20% of the crop in payment. Government departments carefully monitored whether enough rice had been planted, and if there was a danger of a shortage rice was imported. There had indeed been shortages in 1937, 1938 and 1939, but in 1940 Java had been able to export a small amount of rice to the Outer Islands. The rice production in that year (the estimate for 1941 is not known) was over eight million tons, or about 150 kilos per head of the population. It should, however, be noted that the government proceeded from the assumption that on Java, if serious malnutrition and famine were to be avoided, at least 120 kilos per year per head of population was needed.

Unlike India under British rule, the Dutch East Indies had experienced malnutrition but not disastrous starvation. The Dutch authorities were constantly aware of this danger, as the result of a failed harvest, and could intervene if necessary. On the Outer Islands there were areas that usually had a rice surplus, and it could also be bought on the world market.[1] In other words, the fact that there was freedom of movement between the islands in the archipelago and that the East Indies was integrated in the world economy meant that potentially critical problems could be resolved.

The Japanese occupation changed the situation described in four ways. First, the East Indies was taken out of the Western economy and made part of the territory under Japanese control, which was subject to an Allied blockade. Second, the Indies no longer formed an administrative entity. Third, the

---

[1]   Burma, Thailand and French Indo-China generally had rice surpluses.

management of government departments and commercial companies was entrusted to Japanese who did not have the expertise required. Fourth, the Japanese were concerned solely with their own interests; Indonesian interests were of no account at all.

The first of these changes meant that there was a much smaller market for the crops produced by the sugar, tobacco, coffee, tea and rubber plantations. Parts of their land were used to grow food or raw materials required by the Japanese. Most of the sugar refineries on Java (further discussed below) closed down, and on Sumatra the tapping of rubber was halted in June 1943[2] and the amount of land used for cultivating tobacco was reduced by three quarters. All in all, the effect was that substantial numbers of the indigenous population lost the main or extra income provided by the cultivation of these products. Had the Japanese Empire been a well-organized entity, part of the export trade might have continued, but a shortage of ships was already becoming apparent within its territory in late 1942 and early 1943.

Within the archipelago the indigenous proa trade continued. It flourished in the first year of occupation when the Japanese had great difficulty in reopening the modern harbours, which had been severely damaged, for large seagoing vessels. At that time they made frequent use of proas for their own inter-island traffic, although these boats could not carry large loads. When the harbours were made accessible once more in the course of 1943, the shortage of seagoing ships on the Japanese side had become more acute. From the autumn of 1943, by which time American submarines were finally equipped with properly working torpedoes, this shortage was desperate. The Japanese could only compensate for the loss of mass imports from abroad to a small extent, and consequently numerous goods were in short supply. The textile industry, which depended on cotton imports, ground to a halt, and many other products apart from textiles became scarce.

In 1943 the shortage of shipping capacity led to a fundamental change in Japanese economic policy throughout the Nampo region. The Japanese government had first decided that industrialization should not be encouraged there (the idea was that the Nampo countries would obtain their manufactured goods from Japan), but now it determined that these countries must meet their own needs for these goods and for everything else. Subsequently, attempts were made to establish or expand local industries both in the two islands governed by the Japanese army (Java and Sumatra) and in the area governed by the navy (Borneo and the Great East).[3] On Borneo two Japanese

---

[2] By then such large quantities of rubber had accumulated on Java that trials were carried out in which roads were given a top layer consisting of a mixture of rubber and resin.

[3] As part of these efforts, on Java in mid-1943 all goods needed for existing or new businesses were registered: machinery, nails, wire, drive belts, and so on. The owners had to provide details

companies set up small steel works, planning to use the steel for shell cases. Only one factory was completed, and steel production could not begin because of a range of technical problems. Then from 1943 the construction of wooden ships, which had begun on Java in 1942, was undertaken on the Outer Islands too. It was not a success. There were not enough engines for the ships (some of them proved to be incapable of withstanding the elements) and the companies trying to manufacture engines were largely dependent on the import of machines and machine parts from Japan, and these arrived too late or not at all. Moreover, in the course of building new local factories it was found that there was a shortage of cement and other materials as well as of trucks to deliver them. Lastly, at many places it became clear that the Japanese had chosen poor locations. When all these defects became evident in 1944, new plans were drawn up, but they could not be put into action because, with the approach of MacArthur's forces, all the available shipping capacity was reserved for military purposes.

The second change, the breaking up of the administrative unity of the Indies, meant that instead of one government in charge of the situation there were three, each giving priority to its own interests. In certain respects Java and the Outer Islands had made up for each other's shortcomings: for instance, Java had supplied sugar and salt to the Outer Islands, while the latter (Sumatra and Borneo) had sent coal to Java. Furthermore, for Sumatra in particular, the links with Malacca and Singapore were important. The Japanese would not release any seagoing ships for use in inter-island trade that was part of the indigenous economy. The effects soon became apparent. There was a severe shortage of sugar and salt on the Outer Islands. On Java, where 700 tons of coal a year had previously been imported (chiefly for the gasworks and railways), a huge effort had to be made to expand the mines in the south of Banten. The production target was 300,000 tons a year. It is not known whether this was achieved, but the locomotives pulling the few trains left increasingly ran on wood rather than coal.

On Java the break-up of administrative unity went still further as regards the economy. In 1942 the Japanese military authorities there, unaware that in the war in the Pacific the tide had turned as early as June, did not foresee any danger, but in the second half of 1943 they began to consider the possibility of Allied landings sooner or later. Imamura's successor, General Harada, had only a small force and knew that Tokyo could make no more divisions available. He therefore assumed that his defence against the Allies would

---

within 15 days or be punished by having their capital seized. There was so much resistance that the deadline had to be extended to 40 days. After that, the Indonesian police were told to check that everything had been properly reported. It is not known what useful goods were unearthed by this campaign, but there was a flourishing black market in them.

have to consist of local campaigns: the fighting would be fragmented. With this in mind, on 1 October 1943 he ordered that supplies must be stored in every residency on Java (here and there in tunnels dug by Indonesian labourers) and that each residency must be self-supporting. As a consequence, and in order to further this aim, imports and exports between residencies were forbidden. Java (including Madura) was thus divided into 17 self-sufficient areas. It was an absurd measure. One of the main drawbacks was that residencies which produced large amounts of rice were unable to export it to those with a shortage. Of course, this ban on imports and exports could not be effectively enforced, and smuggling on a huge scale soon developed. Extra high prices were asked for the smuggled goods.

The effects of the third change, in which the management of government departments and commercial businesses was entrusted to Japanese who lacked the required expertise, were felt in many fields. The three Japanese administrations (the 16th Army on Java and Madura, the 25th Army on Sumatra, and the Navy on Borneo and the Great East) were authoritarian. Regarding themselves as bearers of the highest civilization on earth, the Japanese felt no need to consult non-Japanese experts (most of whom were either in jail or dismissed from their post) or to take part in considered discussion. They decreed, that is to say, they announced targets without ascertaining whether they could be achieved. Those given assignments had to ensure that they were carried out; if not, then they had failed, not the Japanese management that had set the impossible target. In addition, all the cooperative organizations and monitoring bodies that had gradually been established in the East Indies under Dutch rule were dissolved and replaced by Japanese corporations, known as *kumiai*, which often failed to get a grip on the situation.

The fourth change, as mentioned, was that Japanese policy took no account of Indonesian interests. Indeed, the Nampo region had to help Japan win the war. The 'Principles for the administration of the occupied areas in the Nampo' – which were approved by the highest Japanese government body, the Liaison Conference between cabinet ministers and the military leadership, on 20 November 1941, that is, before it had been decided to go to war – put it as follows: 'If the acquisition of resources vital to the national defence and the aim of making the troops self-sufficient adversely affect the standard of living of the indigenous people, this must be accepted'. It was thus foreseen that there would be an adverse effect, and this was regarded as acceptable in principle. In late 1941 they could not predict how severe this effect would be, but it had already been decided that the military administration in charge of the East Indies would not be overly concerned about it. All that mattered was how far they could go without causing numerous, widespread revolts. After the war the head of the supply department of the

16th Army (Java) said that if he had to draw up plans, '[I] had only to know how much exploitation the native population could endure' (Quoted in Nakamura 1970:7).

As Sukarno, Hatta and Sjahrir had foreseen, on the basis of this policy the Indonesians were mercilessly exploited by the Japanese. It may be true that the latter did their best (of necessity) to increase the production of food, and of simple manufactured goods here and there, but when commandeering what was required 'to make the troops self-sufficient' they took no account of the needs of the local population. A large part of the rice harvest in particular was always requisitioned (the figures are given below), and in this case the concept of 'making the troops self-sufficient' was interpreted to mean that Java must provide rice not only for the Japanese soldiers stationed there (perhaps 25,000 counting both army and navy at the end of 1942) and the civilians (over 23,000 in the government alone) but also for Japanese soldiers and civilians in other parts of the Nampo.

These four factors brought about a substantial decrease in production in the Indies. In Volume II of his *Sociologisch-economische geschiedenis van Indonesië* published in 1975, Professor D.H. Burger gives figures for this decline (they are probably estimates in part) for the whole archipelago (Burger 1975, II:160-1). Compared with the years 1937-1941, during and as a result of the Japanese occupation the production of rice fell by 32%, of maize by 66%, of cassava by 56%, of *bataten* (sweet potatoes) by 27%, of peanuts by 64%, and of soya beans by 60%. He goes on to say:

> Commercial agriculture came to a virtual halt. Tree crops were severely affected by years of neglect, although rubber was an exception because the trees benefited from not being tapped. Of all the cash crops grown by the local population, 75% of the pepper was lost on South Sumatra and 99% on Bangka. [...] Of the kapok trees planted, 30% were felled and the rest deteriorated. On South Celebes half of the coffee was lost through neglect.
>
> The Western agricultural concerns were practically all closed down. The culti-vation of annual crops, such as sugar, was almost entirely halted. [...] Many com-mercial plantings of perennial crops were lost because they were cut down by the local people so that the land could be used for growing food. The worst affected were the tea and coffee plantings, of which 30% and 25% were lost respectively. In the case of oil palm and rubber plantings, 14% and 10% were felled respectively. Only the cultivation of quinine remained intact.

The Japanese needed quinine to combat malaria among their troops and civilians.

> Livestock decreased by about one half during the war years. [...] The fishing fleet declined by 30%. There was also a severe shortage of fishing gear.

Finally, Burger notes that much of the forest on Java was destroyed; in the five years between 1942 and 1947 more trees were lost than had been planted in the previous 45 years. This deforestation led to erosion, which in turn adversely affected agriculture. Incidentally, the works the colonial government had put in hand to improve agriculture came to a halt under Japanese rule.

These are striking figures, and perhaps the most striking of all is Burger's figure for the decrease in rice production: a drop in the production of the main food crop by nearly a third. Let there be no mistake: this did not mean that a little more than two thirds was now available for the population, because the amount commandeered by the Japanese came out of that two thirds.

Especially on overcrowded Java,[4] the food supply of the Indonesians had also been somewhat uncertain in the years 1937 to 1941. This applied less to the *desa* inhabitants than to those for whom no land was available and who had found usually primitive accommodation in the urban *kampong*. As stated, there was no famine in the pre-war years on Java, but many Indonesians were undernourished, especially in populous areas, and so they were particularly vulnerable to the catastrophic fall in food production.

This decline in production does not tell the whole story. In all the belligerent countries, except in the United States, the war meant that fewer goods could be made available to consumers. Everywhere attempts were made to allocate the available goods fairly. One of the difficulties was that, with the drop in civilian production, government spent so much on the armed forces, which had to be equipped, paid and maintained, and on other tasks regarded as vital that the total amount of money in circulation rose. In each belligerent country thus, the public and business had at their disposal formidable amounts of money, but no goods on which to spend it – this was known as 'floating purchasing power'. It was thought to be the task of government to prevent this 'floating purchasing power' from having a disruptive effect on society. If it was to ensure that scarce goods were fairly divided between all citizens, the government had to begin by limiting floating purchasing power by promoting savings, raising taxes and negotiating large, possibly compulsory, loans. At the same time it would have to control prices strictly and set up a system of rationing based on accurate registers of the population so that everyone could buy fixed amounts of food, fuel and textiles in exchange for coupons.

To achieve this, an extensive, trained and honest body of administrators was required that could regulate and oversee every sector of economic life (production, transport and distribution). There was no administrative machine of that scope in the East Indies and the Japanese did not create one.

[4]　The migration of Javanese to southern Sumatra resumed in May 1943: over 100 families moved there at that time. Whether other groups left later is not known.

This would have been very difficult in any case, given that the great majority of Indonesians could neither read nor write.

The assessments imposed on the Chinese in the East Indies (50 million guilders on Sumatra in 1942), which were mentioned above, together with the additional amounts they gave to the Japanese under pressure (how much is not known), may be seen as one of the ways in which floating purchasing power was 'driven down'.[5] However, a great deal more purchasing power remained in the form of coins, paper currency, banknotes and balances with banks, finance companies and post office savings accounts. There are no further details about the size of these balances (they were not very large). As for the coins (Dutch East Indies half cent, one cent, five cent, ten cent, twenty-five cent, fifty cent, guilder and two and a half guilder pieces), it is known only that many soon began saving them and that the Japanese went to some effort to collect them with the intention of shipping them to Japan so that they could be melted down for their copper, nickel and silver. This yielded between 20 and 25 million guilders' worth in the case of silver coins and an unknown amount from bronze coins.[6]

At the time of the surrender of the Dutch East Indies, the amount of money in circulation was 610 million guilders,[7] which included about 100 million in paper currency and about 400 million in banknotes issued by the Javasche Bank. At that point this bank had a reserve of about 3 million in paper currency and 83.5 million in banknotes. Unlike the bank's gold, these reserves had not been sent abroad (it was not envisaged that the fighting on Java would be over so quickly), and the Japanese put them into circulation. In addition, the Japanese authorities issued their own paper currency and banknotes.[8] They could have insisted that notes issued by the Javasche Bank be exchanged for Japanese notes, but they did not do so. The Javasche Bank notes soon began to disappear from circulation, suggesting that those who did not have to spend all their money to support themselves (this applied to a relatively large number of Chinese) had greater faith in the continuing value of Dutch East Indies money than in that of Japanese money. In March 1944 on the black market in Bandung it was possible to exchange Dutch East Indies

---

5   At the end of 1942 an assessment of 200,000 guilders was imposed on the Indian traders on Java – they paid 100,000 guilders. There is no information about the assessments imposed on the Arabs and the Indian traders on the Outer Islands.
6   These figures and those given below are taken from an article on the financial system during the Japanese occupation by H.J. Manschot published in the *Economisch Weekblad voor Nederlandsch-Indië* on 2 March 1946.
7   Not in Dutch but in Dutch East Indies guilders, because soon after the occupation of the Netherlands the colonial government had cut the link between the East Indies and the Dutch guilder.
8   These 'banknotes' were actually notes issued by the Japanese government rather than a bank.

silver coins for twice their value in Japanese paper currency, and in May 1945 a banknote for 1000 Dutch East Indies guilders was worth the equivalent of 1600 guilders in Japanese banknotes. In Medan (we have no information from elsewhere) from March 1945 Dutch East Indies banknotes could be exchanged on the black market for twice their value in Japanese notes.[9]

The Japanese armies brought their own notes, invasion money, which came in denominations of 1, 5, 10 and 50 cents and 1, 5 and 10 guilders. The quality of these notes was poor: many were unnumbered and bore no signature or watermark (no wonder that some Chinese succeeded, as mentioned above, in forging them). The 5- and 10-cent notes were printed on Java from October 1943, and the 50-cent, 1-, 5- and 10-guilder notes from September 1944. At this time the Japanese also began to issue 50- and 100-guilder notes, all numbered.

The total value of Japanese notes put into circulation is known only in the case of Java: 1,569 million guilders. Manschot thought that an estimate of 1,600 million in the case of Sumatra would be approximately correct. His rough estimate was that in addition about 330 million guilders in Japanese notes were issued on Borneo and the Great East (governed by the navy). Thus the total amount of Japanese money in circulation in the East Indies came to about 3,500 million guilders. By the end of the occupation, therefore, over 4 billion in Dutch and Japanese paper currency and banknotes were in circulation, nearly seven times the amount in March 1942. At the same time production had probably, based on Burger's figures, been reduced to roughly three fifths of what it had been. The inevitable consequence was that an extensive black market was created, particularly in rice, on which prices constantly rose (some examples will be given). This black market had a disruptive effect on society. The minority who had enough money could supplement their rations with food purchased on the black market, while the majority suffered hunger to such a degree that on Java alone over two million Indonesians died.

Whatever the problems facing East Indies society, the Japanese still went to enormous lengths to ensure that the Indies would produce the raw materials needed by their war economy and armed forces.

Japan succeeded in importing much of the bauxite it needed for its aluminium (and thus aircraft) industry from the Indies. During the occupation the large bauxite company on one of the islands in the Riau archipelago produced nearly 1.4 million tons of ore, of which 275,000 and 600,000 tons were shipped to Japan in 1942 and 1943 respectively; this represented 70% of all

---

[9]   It should be remembered, however, that in October 1942 the Japanese had made the guilder the equivalent of their currency, the yen, which had been worth 44 cents before the war.

Japanese imports of bauxite in this period. In 1944 imports fell to 300,000 tons and in 1945 to 25,000 tons. It is telling that the last ship that managed to reach Japan from the East Indies carried bauxite. The figures lead to the conclusion that nearly 200,000 tons of bauxite did *not* reach Japan.

Figures are also available for oil imports. From Japan 4,600 technicians were sent to the oil fields in the Indies to work with Indonesians and groups of Nippon workers to repair the damage to the drilling rigs and refineries and restart production. In 1941 7.9 million tons of oil and oil products were produced. From April 1942 to March 1943 the Japanese produced nearly 4 million tons (of which 40% reached Japan), from April 1943 to March 1944 over 7 million tons (of which 30% reached Japan) and from April 1944 to March 1945 5.5 million tons (of which nothing reached Japan). It is not known how much in total was shipped to Japan. At all events part of the fuel oil and of the petrol remained in the Nampo to meet the needs of the Japanese administration and armed forces, especially the large naval squadron operating from Singapore from September 1943. As for petrol, the chief product was aviation fuel. The Japanese navy needed more oil products than the army, and since the army and the navy were each in charge of their own oil fields and given that those in the army territory, especially on Sumatra, were the largest, there was a danger that the navy would not get enough. 'Fortunately', according to J.B. Cohen (1949:140), 'it held one trump: it controlled the tankers and the sea lanes. "But for this", one admiral declared, "the Army would undoubtedly have left the Navy without oil."'

The Japanese totally ignored the interests of the civilian population: paraffin, needed for cooking and lighting, became scarce; petrol was only available for traffic allowed by the Japanese; and from the outset there was a serious shortage of lubricating oil, which was a problem for the few machines still working. It was above all to provide a supply of lubricating oil that the Japanese military administration on Java gave orders in 1942 for all grounds and wasteland to be planted with castor seeds. The job of planting the seeds on wasteland was given to schoolchildren: each school was allocated its own piece of land and the one which produced the most seeds won a prize. How much caster oil this campaign yielded is unknown.

The Japanese also obtained nickel and manganese ores (both needed to harden steel) in the East Indies. As early as 1942 Japan had a serious shortage of nickel: large amounts of nickel ore were sent from Celebes to Japan in 1942 and above all in 1943, when the figure was nearly 50,000 tons. In 1944, however, only about 7,000 tons reached Japan. At that time the Japanese were building two large smelting plants on Celebes which were designed to produce 8,000 tons of nickel per year. However, when they were completed in May 1943, they could not be put into operation because of a lack of coke and various catalysts. In August 1943 they were destroyed in an Allied air raid.

Manganese ore was shipped from Java to Japan, but it is not known in what quantities.

There is no information about how the Japanese treated the Indonesian workers who were involved in extracting, processing and transporting these raw materials. All that is known is that a Nippon worker who was an overseer at a gold mine in the Bengkulu residency for two years, from March 1943 to March 1945, observed that the coolies had to do heavy labour for eight hours a day, were poorly housed, could not buy enough food with the wages they earned (50 cents a day) and were often ill-treated by the Japanese. 'Many coolies', he stated in March 1946, 'suffered from TB but were still forced to work, so that many died'.[10] It seems reasonable to assume that the same or similar conditions prevailed elsewhere.

So far an attempt has been made to give a general picture of the economic and social decline that became apparent in the East Indies under Japanese occupation. In the case of the comparable decline in the occupied Netherlands (where real national income fell by about a half and there was five times as much money in circulation by the end of the occupation as at the beginning) a mass of information is available, but there is far less detailed evidence about the East Indies. There is almost no information about the areas governed by the Japanese navy or Sumatra. A little more is known about Java, in particular about the fate of the several million Indonesians who were deployed as labourers on Java or elsewhere (the *romusha*), but still much less than we were able to garner about the occupied Netherlands. We are painfully aware of these gaps in the sources, but they must not prevent us from recounting what is known.

Borneo and the Great East

Borneo and the Great East (Celebes, the Lesser Sunda Islands, the Moluccas and Dutch New Guinea), which were governed by the Japanese navy, had a rice deficit of about 55,000 tons a year before the Japanese occupation. The colonial government responded by arranging for rice to be imported, chiefly from Thailand and French Indo-China and, if possible, from Java. The Japanese navy made an effort to promote the planting of rice and other crops: many families on Ambon were forced to move to Ceram, where the forest had to be cleared to provide new farming land. The shortage of rice persisted. Figures are available only for the month of May 1944 (Benda, Irikura and

10   No. 4 War Crimes Investigation Team, proces-verbaal by J.T. Sagenschneider, 11 March 1946, p. 1 (NIOD IC, 390).

The collapse of a colonial society

Kishi 1965:278): at that point the Japanese calculated that 43,300 tons of rice were needed for the civilians on Borneo and the Great East (23,900 tons on Borneo, 8,400 tons in the inhabited areas on Celebes, 11,000 tons for the rest of the Great East) and 75,600 tons for the Japanese troops, making 118,900 tons in total. The Japanese authorities planned to obtain most of this amount in the form of compulsory supplies, totalling 107,000 tons, from the rice growers. This left a shortfall of 11,900 tons and it was thought that it would, in fact, be greater, because it could not be assumed that all the rice growers would provide the whole amount required of them. Thus it was decided to import rice from Java: 2,900 tons a month. It is not known whether these imports actually took place. The most significant point about these figures in my view is that of the 107,000 tons of rice which were not kept by the growers or sold in the agricultural areas concerned, 75,600 tons, or 70%, were destined for the Japanese troops, and it seems reasonable to assume that they got enough rice.

This is a snapshot of one month. The situation was probably slightly better before, but still more difficult later because the harvest failed in 1944 and all shipping was restricted. Notwithstanding this, information came to light in 1982[11] that in Minahasa (northeast Celebes) there was no problem as regards food ('everything grows here'), but that 'hundreds died of malaria and dysentery because of a shortage of medicines'.[12] Medicines were never sent from Japan for the civilian population, neither to Celebes nor to the other islands of the archipelago.

In the case of Celebes it is also known that the rationing of articles which had become scarce but had been imported by the Japanese administration in small quantities (for instance, textiles, sugar and salt) was a travesty. The intention was that the *desa* headmen should share them out fairly; in reality, a Dutch civil servant reported in November 1945,[13] they were 'divided among family members and friends or sold on the black market. [...] The ordinary man got his ration coupons but no goods'. Also on Celebes, namely in Makassar, a European noted in his diary in May 1945 that, apart from some very expensive foodstuffs, 'hardly anything could be obtained for money, only for *barang* (goods)'. This applied 'particularly to clothing'[14] – which had thus become an important means of barter.

In the case of Borneo there are the tax receipts: 2.4 million guilders in 1942, 3 million in 1943, 8.9 million in 1944, 2.3 million in 1945 (up to August) – a striking decrease indicating how poorly the Japanese administration was

[11] Letter from M.A. Walsen, 3 March 1982.
[12] We conclude from the number of deaths that our correspondent may have been a little too optimistic.
[13] Text of his report in Brugmans 1960:158-9.
[14] H.J.B.J. Lubbers, 'Dagboek', 27 May 1945 (NIOD IC).

functioning. Outside the main centres of population, where appropriate, certain taxes (on, for example, hunting or felling trees) were collected by the *desa* headman or traditional chief, who received 90 guilders a month for this and was allowed to keep 4% of the revenue raised.

Lastly, there is a description of the state of affairs encountered when on New Guinea Hollandia (Jayapura) and its surroundings were liberated. Early in June 1944 the paymaster of the Dutch East Indies administrative team deployed there reported:

> The Papuas in the vicinity here have lost a large part of the produce from their gardens. [...] The Japanese paid 20 cents a day as the coolie wage at first and 25 cents later. Some said this was without food (Hollandia), others said it included food. [...] People gave me an indication of the prices paid by the Japs: 2 guilders for a pig and 15 cents for a chicken. They shot first and paid afterwards. There are indeed very few pigs in the *kampong,* and chickens are rare.
>
> The goods offered by the Japanese consisted of white silk and artificial silk fabrics of poor quality, toilet articles and knick-knacks; small hardware was completely absent. These goods were offered for sale immediately after the coolies' wages had been paid out, while in the bigger places Chinese *toko* were still open. They evidently had some old stock left, because they bought none of the goods introduced by the Japanese.[15]

Sumatra

As for socioeconomic conditions on Sumatra, the only information relates to the reduction of the tobacco-growing acreage, black market prices in Medan, the situation in Aceh and the treatment of Javanese coolies in and near Sabang, which is on the island of We off the north coast of Aceh.

As for the amount of land devoted to growing tobacco, in the Medan area this was reduced from 200,000 to 40,000 hectares. Rice was grown on 160,000 hectares, but the yield was only enough to provide a ration of 15 kilos per person per month for 6 months for 350,000 coolies and their families who had lost their source of income.

In September 1945 a report was drawn up on the black market prices in Medan.[16] It reveals that the price of a tin of rice (16 kilos) rose from 1.60 guilders before the arrival of the Japanese to 35 guilders in the course of 1943, then 150 guilders in March 1945 and 400 guilders in August 1945. The price of salt went from a few cents per kilo to 25 guilders, that of sugar from 12

---

[15]   Letter from W.C. Heybroek to the Dutch East Indies Commander in Melbourne, 5 June 1944, pp. 1-3 (ARA, MK, M 102, NI, 1-4).
[16]   TKR-Medan, Judge Advocate, proces-verbaal Sadimin, 12 August 1946, p. 2 (NIOD IC, 19,463).

cents per kilo to 35 guilders in March 1945 and 70 guilders in August, that of pork from 80 cents per kilo to 35 guilders in March 1945 and 70 guilders in August, that of a yard of cotton from 80 cents to 150 guilders in March 1945 and 300 guilders in August, that of a cotton shirt from 5 guilders to 700 guilders in March 1945 and 1000 guilders in August. These price increases showed three things: there was a severe shortage; there was a great deal of money in circulation; and the systems of rationing and price control had broken down completely.

No doubt there were price rises elsewhere on Sumatra, but no details are available. As far as this island is concerned, thanks to Anthony Reid's *The blood of the people; Revolution and the end of traditional rule in northern Sumatra*, published in 1979, we are best informed about developments in Aceh. This was the region where the indigenous population gave the most support to the invading Japanese forces and where the nationalists were most deeply disappointed.

Aceh had been a rice-exporting area before the arrival of the Japanese: in 1941 it exported about 36,000 tons. Here as elsewhere, the Japanese made the mistake of setting the official price of rice so low that most farmers resisted supplying the amounts required of them.[17] The Japanese demanded for their own use 17,000 tons of rice in 1943, 22,000 tons in 1944 and 33,000 tons in 1945 – that was between 10 and 15% of the estimated crop. Nonetheless, these amounts proved too high. A great deal of land was seized by the Japanese and ever more men and youths were set to work building airfields and coastal defences. Thus in 1943 less than 7,000 of the 17,000 tons demanded were supplied. The low official price meant that a lot of rice was sold on the black market and so ended up in the hands of the well-off. In May 1944 one of the Acehnese headmen, Teuku Panglima Polem, estimated that nearly two thirds of the population of Aceh was not getting enough rice: they included not only the inhabitants of the larger towns and the fishermen but also farmers who had sold their rice before the harvest because they needed money or who had had to give half of the crop to their landowner as rent. When there had been a shortage of rice in Aceh (and elsewhere in the East Indies) in 1918-1919, the Dutch government had ensured that those in need could buy imported rice at low prices with borrowed money. The Japanese did nothing: no rice was imported, loans were not given and the price of rice on the black market was so high that only the wealthy could pay it.

As for putting men and youths to work, in 1944 and 1945, according to Reid (1979:125-6), 'the Japanese imposed a scale of forced labour on the

---

[17]   In November 1942 a group of Bataks living near Toba Lake refused to pay the Japanese tax in kind: one tin (16 kilos) of rice per family per month. Two Bataks were shot dead and their raja was imprisoned.

Acehnese before which the hated *herendiensten* [corvée] of the *Kompenie* [the VOC] paled into insignificance'. All men and youths aged between 16 and 45 had to labour for two weeks every month when called upon by the indigenous rulers. Those who did not turn up were given a prison sentence of 20 years. According to Panglima Polem, the indigenous rulers were caught 'between the frying pan and the fire. If they took pity on the people, they were hit by the Japanese; if they carried out Japanese orders, the people were oppressed. Their work was fraught with hatred.' (Quoted in Reid 1979:126.)

We assume that the Acehnese men and youths who were called up for all kinds of work were treated harshly by the Japanese, but no details are available. Given that they returned to their homes every two weeks, the Japanese may have been more restrained.

There was little sign of restraint in the treatment of a number of Javanese youths aged between 16 and 26 who were living on Sumatra's east coast. In May 1942 they were picked up in raids and made to work as coolies in and near the port of Sabang or were persuaded to work by the promise of three meals a day, 2 guilders a day in wages and free accommodation, clothing and medicines. The result was that in 1942 several hundred Javanese arrived in Sabang and in 1943 several thousand. They were housed in sheds where they had to sleep on the floor. 'Once a year', said one of them, 'I was given a thin jute sack to use as clothing and once rubber shorts'. The food rations were meagre and those who were too ill to work got nothing to eat and no wages. The wages were 60 cents a day in 1942-1943, 70 cents in 1944 and 80 cents in 1945. There were two rest days each month.

> While working we were often beaten by the Japanese. [...] I was punished three times for missing a day's work. The punishment consisted of being shut up in a zinc pen measuring two by two metres. The pen stood in the burning sun. [...] I was twice put in it for three days and once for two days, during which time I was not given anything to eat or drink. [...] After being let out I was given 20 strokes of the cane on my backside by the Japanese guards and had to start work again straight away.
>
> [...] The camp had a sick bay. [...] There almost all wounds became infected because of the unhygienic conditions and inadequate medical care. I saw many coolies with large, deep, jet-black wounds that stank horribly; white fluid dripped from these wounds. Many coolies died of them.
>
> A great many coolies had high fever, badly swollen legs and bellies [hunger oedema] and diarrhoea.
>
> In 1944 and 1945 between two and ten coolies died every day.[18]

A second Javanese estimated that of the Javanese put to work in and around Sabang 'more than half and perhaps as many as 75% died. All the coolies

---

[18]   TKR-Medan, Judge Advocate, proces-verbaal Lias, 12 August 1946, pp. 1-2 (NIOD IC, 17,252).

looked like skeletons and had big ulcers, and there were more sick than healthy people.'[19]

This description of the treatment of the Javanese coolies on Sabang who had been picked up in raids or recruited by false promises provides an apt intro-duction to what should be said about a much larger group of Javanese, most of whom ended up by another route in a situation where they had to labour for the Japanese. They were forced to do so by their own indigenous rulers on the basis of Japanese orders, exactly as had happened to many in Aceh. The difference was that the Acehnese were allowed to go home every two weeks, whereas the Javanese, the *romusha*, were taken away for a long time, many of them far from Java.

The 'romusha'

Romusha is a Japanese word meaning roughly 'work soldier' and the recruit-ment of these 'work soldiers' on Java was simply a continuation of what the Japanese had done elsewhere in Asia. In Korea, Manchuria and occupied China they had formed large groups of indigenous labourers who were put to work under military supervision. Some of these labourers were forced to do the work; others had been recruited with promises of good pay and fair treatment. The work was to be seen as an honour, according to the Japanese: the glory of the Japanese army must also shine on the 'work soldiers'. In the propaganda in Indonesian on Java they were called *pradjurit ekonomie*, 'eco-nomic soldiers'.

At first there was none of this propaganda on Java. Bridges lay under water, roads were blocked, airfields had been damaged – all this had to be repaired as quickly as possible. Sometimes the Japanese soldiers demanded that the indigenous rulers provide sufficient manpower; sometimes they organized raids. In Chapter I the example was given of an Indonesian clerk who was cycling from Batavia to Buitenzorg in March 1942 when he was pulled off his bicycle and forced to help repair an airfield: 'he had done that for a month under strict supervision with more beatings than food and no payment. In the end he had managed to escape. [...] There were thousands of cases like his.'

The Japanese army continued to make such raids: if labour was needed for work on Java or elsewhere, *desa* were surrounded and all the men and youths taken away under armed guard. This happened especially often in 1942 and the first half of 1943. In the first months of 1943 some of those

---

[19]   TKR-Medan, Judge Advocate, proces-verbaal Sadimin, 12 August 1946, p. 2 (NIOD IC, 17,255).

seized were sent to Sumatra to work on the Pekanbaru Railway, which was to join up with the existing line to Padang (see Map 7). Once this link was made, the Japanese would be able to send reinforcements from Singapore to the west coast of Sumatra without any need for their troopships to venture into the dangerous Indian Ocean. Early in 1943 the first *romusha* were set to work on Sumatra's east coast building a railway embankment in the swamps, where malaria was prevalent. In March 1943 Japanese troops surrounded a group of 14- and 15-year-old boys as they left school in Yogyakarta. They were taken to the station and sent to Batavia with many others in locked goods wagons. The journey took a day and they were given nothing to eat or drink. In Batavia there turned out to be about 8,000 *romusha*. They sailed for Singapore in two ships; one was torpedoed and 4,000 *romusha* drowned. The surviving 4,000 arrived in Pakanbaru at the beginning of April 1943. A KNIL prisoner of war (one of many who were added to the *romusha*) later heard the following account from one of the schoolboys from Yogyakarta:

> Immediately on arrival the Japanese showed their perverted enjoyment of power in front of the *romusha*. Eight of them were picked out and told to lift a section of rail. They couldn't do it. The Japanese reduced the number of men, two at a time, until four were left. Of course they couldn't lift it either. [...] The four men were beheaded on the spot with a samurai sword. The Japanese commander told the assembled *romusha*, 'This is what awaits lazy *romusha*'.
> Then the hard life on the railway began: little food, no clothing, no pay and no medical care. They had to build the barracks for their own housing. Until these were ready, they lived in the open air. [...] Clothing was not issued, nor were mosquito nets. [...] Most of them died of malnutrition, dysentery, malaria and tropical ulcers. (Quoted in Neumann and Van Witsen 1982:22.)

In total about 22,000 *romusha* worked on the Pekanbaru Railway; most came from Java, some from the Outer Islands, a few from French Indo-China. By August 1945 about 5,000 were still alive, though many of these died after the Japanese surrender as a result of their forced labour.

How many Indonesians had to toil as 'work soldiers' during the Japanese occupation is not known exactly: in 1951 the Indonesian government put the official estimate at 4,100,000. Most of these, it appears, worked for only a relatively brief period and were not sent away from the island where they lived; the Japanese did not have enough ships for that. On Java the great majority was set to work close to their home, presumably for a short time or brief periods. There were two groups who had to work for a longer time: the *romusha* who were moved away from their homes to other parts of Java, and those who, like the group sent to work on the Pekanbaru Railway, were shipped overseas.

It is also uncertain how many *romusha* fell into Japanese hands in raids,

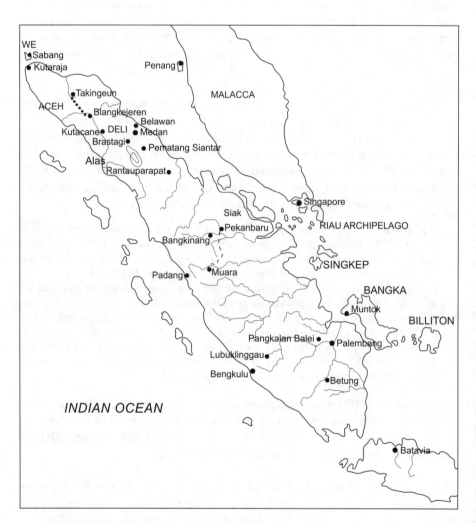

Map 7. Sumatra II

how many volunteered of their own accord because they saw no other way of earning a living, and how many were forced to take part by the indigenous rulers. It is likely that the number of volunteers fell in 1942-1943, when it became known here and there on Java that the Japanese were treating the *romusha* badly. Moreover, from the end of 1943 the Japanese systematically involved the indigenous officials (the regents, the district and subdistrict headmen and the *desa* headmen). The background to this is known. In early October 1943 in Singapore a conference took place of the heads of the labour deployment departments of the headquarters of the various armies in the Nampo area, and there it was agreed that Java was to be the great reservoir from which all those armies would draw the manpower they needed. Subsequently the Japanese 16th Army set up a central labour department on Java as part of the Department of Interior Affairs. It ensured that the Central Advisory Council, which had been established in the meantime under the chairmanship of Sukarno, considered the question of how 'the practical cooperation of the indigenous population in the Greater East Asian War' could be strengthened. The Advisory Council, whose members were aware of how arbitrarily the *romusha* were chosen by the indigenous officials or seized by the Japanese, suggested that a Community of Labour should be founded, that all male inhabitants aged between 16 and 40 and all unmarried female inhabitants aged between 16 and 25 should be registered, that training centres for workers should be set up in each of the 17 residencies, and that all government departments, schools, companies and organizations for Indonesians, Chinese, Arabs and Dutch Eurasians should be told to form groups of at least 50 people who were eligible to become *romusha*. These groups could then be called on if a work force was needed.

These recommendations were accepted by the Japanese military administration: the Community of Labour was founded, registration took place, each residency got a training centre for workers and instructions went out to form groups of at least 50 potential *romusha*. The system was that each residency was told how many *romusha* it had to supply. The residents passed this order on to the administrators of the urban municipalities and to the regents; the latter informed the district and subdistrict headmen (the *wedono* and assistant *wedono*), and they, where necessary, informed the *desa* headmen. This was accompanied by a huge propaganda campaign: in all towns and at big companies meetings had to be held; groups of activists had to travel round every regency; on the 1st, 10th and 20th of every month the radio broadcast a programme about labour deployment from 9 to 10 pm that was heard everywhere over the public loudspeakers (the 'singing towers'). Festivities had to be organized to mark the departure of 'work soldiers' and a sign had to be put on the doors of the houses of those deployed beyond Java. 'The populace are to be told', said the guidelines concerned,[20] 'that the occupants of the house on which this sign is seen will be given the best possible treatment'.

Now for the reality. The selection of *romusha* was just as arbitrary under the new system. The indigenous rulers received premiums according to the numbers who actually turned up at the assembly points. Some of them took the easy way out by designating all the vagrants in their area (to these were added anyone considered troublesome, and sometimes convicts from certain prisons). Others let it be known that those who did not turn up would receive no ration coupons in future. Being chosen did not always mean having to leave. Those who objected and had enough money (as was the case with many Chinese) could bribe the indigenous officials or, if that was not possible, find a poor Javanese who would take their place for a certain sum. On their departure, the *romusha* had to walk to assembly points where they were badly treated and then packed into trains with the windows covered which took them to where they had to work, or to the ports. Afterwards nothing more was heard from them, and the government care for the families left behind was so limited that private Indonesian committees were set up to provide additional help. Hatta, in particular, took the initiative in this. One of the problems was that not a single official body had recorded the names and addresses of the *romusha*.

Calling up workers through the indigenous rulers had produced results the Japanese found highly satisfactory. According to their reports, the first major campaign, which began in November 1943 and ended in March 1944, yielded three times as many *romusha* as they needed. It is not clear whether they meant that this high number gathered at the assembly points or whether this was the total of the numbers reported in writing. It is certain that in the first campaign the Japanese were able to ship 30% more *romusha* from Java than envisaged in their own plans (which were perhaps deliberately aimed too high).

There is no information about the second campaign, which began in April 1944.

As noted, we assume that the great majority of *romusha* stayed on Java. As for how they were deployed there, we know that they had to help extend existing airfields and build new ones and dig tunnels for the Japanese army's reserve supplies. In Banten the coal mines had to be expanded and in connection with this new roads and rail links had to be constructed. In November 1944 there were about 100,000 *romusha* here who were better off than their fellow victims elsewhere in that they were issued with textiles and medicines in that month. However, more than 100,000 *romusha* had been taken to Banten, because whoever got the chance stopped working and secretly

[20]   Text in Brugmans 1960:196-7.

went home. For the *romusha* working in the mines this was difficult. They numbered 20,000 at first and 15,000 later. Tan Malaka, who was put to work in the administration of one mine, saw what happened to them at first hand. According to his biographer H.A. Poeze (1976:517, 519):

> The workers died in scores because of a lack of food and medical care. They looked along the road for a place to die. They were often put in mass graves at the side of the road, which flooded in the wet monsoon. [...] Each month, out of a total of 15,000 workers 400 to 500 died.

At the time of the Japanese surrender there were only about 10,000 *romusha* left at the mines in Banten.

The incidence of death among the various groups of *romusha* taken from Java was proportionally greater. Unfortunately there are only a few reports about the fate of those concerned, but they all point in the same direction.

In 1943, a 57-year-old *mandur*, or supervisor, left Semarang. In August 1946, he stated:[21]

> I had to appear before the assistant *wedono*. The Japanese in attendance there told me that I had to work on Celebes for three months. I would receive high wages, good food and decent clothing. A hundred of us left and I was put in charge. They were all simple *desa* people. [...] From Central Java we were [...] taken to East Java, where we had to do coolie work. The coolies received 50 cents a day and I got 75 cents, even though I had been promised 1 guilder. We worked there for two months and in that time 9,000 coolies were [...] brought together. Subsequently I was sent with 1,500 men to Raha on the island of Muna, southeast of Celebes. I had 50 men under me. We made the passage in a wooden Japanese boat into which the 1,500 men were crammed. [...] After ten days we reached Makassar, where we were given one day of rest. Following that we resumed our journey to Raha. No one died on the way.
>
> Once in Raha, we were immediately put to work. We had to unload and clean the boat. This took a week. We worked until 10 at night. [...] We received no pay and food was provided only once a day. When we were done with the boat, we had to lay out an airfield. Here too the coolies were paid 50 cents a day and I received 75 cents. From our monthly wages 3 guilders were deducted for food, 5 guilders had to be saved and 5 guilders were withheld to be transferred to Java.[22] Our frozen credit was never paid out.
>
> [...] We only had one free day a month. Those who were ill were treated decently: there was a hospital with a Japanese doctor for the serious cases. [...] If something went wrong with work, the *mandur* had to step forward. A harsh scolding was followed by a fierce beating. We were mostly hit with a stick on the head.
>
> In the space of a year 500 coolies died on Muna, most as the result of a shortage

[21] The text of his report dated 16 August 1946 in Brugmans 1960:505-6.
[22] Such monies were paid out after some time, but the scale on which this took place is unknown.

of food [...]. I complained twice about the food to a Japanese [...]. Both times the only result was a severe beating.

We were not allowed to write letters and also received none.

On Ambon in mid-1944 a group of Dutch prisoners of war was housed in barracks that had formerly accommodated *romusha* from Java. According to one of the prisoners of war in his report:

What the Indonesians from Java who were press-ganged and coerced suffered here is indescribable. And the few survivors still crawling around, completely emaciated, wasted by dysentery, and sapped by malaria, these wretches covered with large ghastly sores, were indictments against the Japanese never to be forgotten. (Quoted in Veenstra et al. 1982:279.)

Other *romusha*, about 30, were the first with whom officers of the Dutch administrative apparatus on Dutch New Guinea could speak at the end of April 1944. They were unemployed people from the area of Malang and Surabaya who had come into contact with recruiters around September 1943. These were Javanese and Chinese who had offered them work for 80 cents to 1 guilder a day and given them a 10 guilder advance. When 350 men had been assembled they were taken by train to Batavia under military escort; about 25 of them escaped on the way. According to the summary of the accounts given by the 30 *romusha*:

Those who remained marched under Japanese guard to Priok, where they boarded a boat. [...]. Even though no one wanted to go to Batavia, until then their treatment had been fairly good. Treatment on board was far less good, bad food, among other things. The boat took them via Balikpapan to Palau, and from there to Hollandia. Subsequently they were transferred to Aitape.[23] There they had to work on the airfield and the roads. They [...] suffered greatly. No salary, daily nothing more [to eat] than a handful of rice with some dried vegetables. Eighty-six perished from malnutrition, stomach illness or malaria. [...] Those who were ill got no food. Those who did not work hard enough were beaten with a heavy club. Seven were beaten to death [...] in this manner.[24] In general they had no clothes; what they had brought with them from Java had already worn out long ago. Initially there were also Papuas at work, but they ran away.[25]

No complete survey exists of the places where the *romusha* from Java were taken to. A Japanese statement possibly dating from the end of September

[23] In Australian New Guinea.
[24] In Singapore there were instances of *romusha* being punished by being buried alive or wrapped in a mat that was set afire.
[25] Letter from the Nica New Guinea to the Dutch East Indies authorities in Melbourne, 26 April 1944, (ARA, MK, M 102, NI, 1-4).

1945 covering the period June 1943-July 1945 (the transfers began before
June 1943!)[26] says that 200 were sent to French Indo-China, 56,400 to the
Great East, 48,700 to Dutch Borneo and 31,700 to British Borneo, 120,000 to
Sumatra, 31,000 to Singapore and Malacca,[27] and 6,100 to Thailand. Adding
up to 294,100,[28] this total is too low: *romusha* were also shipped to Japan and
Hong Kong[29] and the approximately 4,000 *romusha* encountered in Thailand
following Japan's surrender are assumed to have been the survivors of
groups totalling at least 10,000 Javanese. This estimate was made by a Dutch
officer in Bangkok in September 1945, and he cautioned that detailed information from some of the smaller of these groups suggests that those sent
to work on the Burma Railway experienced 'a death rate of 80 and 90%'.[30]
Burdened with exceptionally heavy work, suffering from a shortage of food
and deprived of all medical care, they were moreover treated by the Japanese
in the harshest fashion. One of the KNIL officers forced to work on the Burma
Railway later remembered:

> Some of us managed to engage in conversation with the Javanese, but they were
> always terrified that the Japs would notice. What they then recounted was alarm-
> ing. The Japs had absolutely no compassion. Sometimes the Japanese put whoever
> was feverish (malaria) in the *kali* [river] for the entire day with only their head above
> water, supposedly to cool off. Sometimes others who were too weak to work were
> chased up a tree, whose branches hung above the flowing *kali*. When they could no
> longer hold on, they fell into the *kali* and were carried away by the current.[31]

How many were driven to death elsewhere and in other ways? The answer
is not known. What is certain is that of the about 120,000 *romusha* transported
to Sumatra not even 23,000 remained alive; of the 31,000 sent to Singapore
and Malacca about 10,000; and of the 31,700 deployed to British Borneo only
about 2,500. Moreover, a large group sent to Dutch Borneo to build the northern trajectory of the Banjarmasin-Samarinda road right through the jungle
had no survivors. After the war, the generally accepted estimate was that of
all of the *romusha* forced to leave Java (and this was considerably, perhaps
even very substantially more than the number of 294,100 given for the period
June 1943-July 1945), only about 77,000 returned.[32]

---

[26]   Text in NIOD IC, 5,709.
[27]   On Java, the Japanese also recruited young women who were told that they would be
nurses in Singapore – in reality they were forced to work in brothels there.
[28]   Letter by J.S. Krom, 21 September 1945 (NIOD IC, 5,228).
[29]   Moreover, Bali had to provide about 7,000 *romusha* (of whom about 6,000 perished) and
Lombok about 4,000 (how many of them died is unknown).
[30]   J.S. Krom, 'Rapport', 21 September 1945, p. 4 (NIOD IC, 5,228).
[31]   J. van Baarsel, 'Onder de Jappen', p. 67 (NIOD IC, 81,359).
[32]   Only a few hundred returned before the end of the war, namely in July and in the first half
of August 1945. They were demonstratively welcomed back. About 300, for instance, coming to
shore on 31 August in Semarang (it is not known where they came from), were welcomed by

As mentioned above, the *romusha* were not allowed to send messages to their families or, to the extent that they were illiterate, have them sent; however, most of them were deployed on Java and not all for protracted periods. Those who returned home had little good to report, which could only have aggravated concern with respect to the fate of those from whom nothing had been heard. Resentment also grew against the Japanese who, insofar as they had made promises, broke them, and had acted with shocking brutality during the roundups. Unavoidably, this resentment was also partly directed at the Indonesian administrators who, even had they given no evidence of corruption or arbitrariness, had actually helped the Japanese labour efforts and had thus lost much of their traditional prestige. Many began to harbour a similar rancour against the propagandists who started travelling around as of November 1943 – how long this continued is not known.

One of the most important propagandists was Sukarno. He gave numerous speeches in which he called upon his supporters to enlist as 'work soldiers', praising those who had already done so. Moreover, on 3 September 1944 he himself put on a show as a *romusha*.

Early that morning a large crowd gathered in Jakarta to accompany Sukarno and about 500 other volunteers (Indonesians, Chinese, Arabs, Dutch Eurasians and a number of Japanese civilians) on their trek to the station where a train stood ready to take them all to Bogor (Buitenzorg). According to a news report:[33]

> At exactly ten o'clock, the group marched off [...] to the inspiring music of an Ambonese flute orchestra.[34] Along the entire route they were cheered by the people of Jakarta. Cheers like 'Long live brother Sukarno!', 'Long live the corps of volunteer work soldiers!' were rife.
> Mr Sukarno was dressed in shorts and a plain shirt. He wore a woven hat.
> [...] Upon reaching their destination, the troop marched [...] smartly in ranks to the Public Works office, where they rested while listening to various speeches.

These were welcome speeches. Sukarno then expressed his gratitude.

> He proposed not shaving for a week to prove that one had worked without stopping. He then explained the meaning of this group, after which the head of the *Romusha* Department presented a box of sweets, a gift from the head of the Propaganda Department to Mr Sukarno to be distributed among the volunteer *romusha*. After

---

the resident, received a sum of money and some clothing. Radio Jakarta reported 'that many Japanese and Indonesian officials' were present at this occasion. Allusion was made to the many who did not return: 'Many speeches were made in which it was said that no independence could be achieved without sacrifice and bloodshed' (Nigis, Monitoring Report no. 1485, NIOD IC, L 69).

[33]   Text in Brugmans 1960:506-7.
[34]   Traditionally only part of the Ambonese sided with the Dutch.

this the men went to work. [...] One had to drag stones and sand from the river, the other swung a hammer reducing the stones to gravel, etc. [...] Mr Sukarno made himself useful together with the resident by working on a pile of stones.

At the end, there was a pleasant evening presented by the cabaret company of the Cultural Centre in Jakarta, which had come along with the volunteer *romusha*.

Sukarno's performance was filmed and photographs appeared in the news-papers. Similar photographs appeared in 1945 when, together with the head of the Japanese military administration, he paid a visit to the mines in Banten, where in his own words he had seen 'pitiable skeletons [performing] slave labour.' The second series of photographs prompted a group of five students to visit him, demanding that he justify his cooperation with the *romusha* campaign. He repeated his answer in 1964: 'If I have to sacrifice thousands to save millions, then that is what I shall do. As the leader of this country I cannot permit myself the luxury of sensitivity.'

All that needs to be said about this defence is that the *romusha* programme destroyed hundreds of thousands and not thousands.

Java's failed war economy

If the chief task of those responsible for a war economy is to fairly divide the scarce consumer goods among the citizenry, it must be stated for the record that the Japanese military administration of Java failed in discharging its duties.

To begin with, the administration was unable to get sufficient grip on the business community. In the course of 1942 and 1943 business was organized in a corporative fashion, that is to say that a multitude of new corporations were founded, the *kumiai*, each covering a specific branch of industry. Each *kumiai* came under a central office essentially run by the Japanese; some had advisory councils including not only Japanese but also Chinese and Indonesian members, but management was not required to follow any of their recommendations. Many businesses had remained Chinese property, while the European ones had been taken over by the Japanese. Usually representatives of the large Japanese family concerns wielded great influence on the new boards as well as the management of the offices. In Japan, these concerns continued to aim for the greatest possible profit – and they did the same on Java, as did the Chinese who dominated commerce there and who had built up a substantial part of the industrial sector. No study has ever been made of any of the *kumiai* or of the effect of the corporate system in its entirety. However, as early as 1942 but chiefly in 1943, the conviction gained ground in Indonesian nationalist circles that no matter how often the

Japanese talked about making 'mutual sacrifices' for the sake of winning the war and building up the 'Greater East Asian Co-Prosperity Sphere', the sacrifices that, in fact, ensued from the war and the occupation, were exceedingly unfairly apportioned.

The nationalists' arguments led the military administration on Java to establish a 'Preparatory committee on the organization of a new economic order for the people of Java'; 32 Japanese, 28 Indonesians, 2 Chinese, and one Dutch Eurasian were nominated as members – the military administration had thus made sure that the Japanese were in the majority. There is no information about the deliberations of the subcommittees into which this body had been divided. All that remains are the reports submitted by the subcommittees in July and September 1944 which, apparently, were considered the final result of their work (Benda, Irikura and Kishi 1965:115-27).

These reports contained countless recommendations, each of which may be seen as an indication of what had gone wrong in the eyes of the members of the subcommittees.

The first two recommendations were as follows:

> To make the Chinese, Arab and native capitalists as well as others with economic capabilities cast aside the concept of individualistic economics with its pursuit of private profit and to instill in them the concept of 'public interests first'.
> To look to arousing a true understanding of the world situation among the general populace and to eliminate economic crimes such as hoarding, withholding goods from sale, and black-market transactions.

The reports also advised: monitoring all wages; stabilising the cost of living by preventing price increases; reducing unemployment; paying out parts of wages in the form of goods; appointing Indonesians as the heads of labour affairs at all of the plantations; improving the medical care of the employed workers; separately registering all technically trained individuals; preventing educated employees from seeking new posts; training new educated employees; charging qualified natives in the areas in question with the management of the confiscated Western plantations; expanding the agricultural cooperatives so that there would be at least one in every *desa*; charging these cooperatives with the buying, storage, transportation and sale of the agricultural products and providing advances to the farmers as well as the allocation of foodstuffs and tools to the *desa* inhabitants; establishing industrial and trade cooperatives, the latter chiefly in cities, to improve the operation of the rationing system; and finally, creating a Central Industrial Fund in Jakarta and an Industrial Fund in each regency.

This long list of recommendations (none elaborated, none provided with an explanation indicating how they could best be implemented in the intractable social circumstances) was simultaneously a long list of complaints.

What happened thereafter? The Japanese military administration established a National Economic Office, which presumably (further details are not known) took stock of all or some of the recommendations. Subsequently, a 'Committee for the Creation of a New Economic Order for the Population of Java' was founded in April 1945.

This 'New Economic Order' had yet to materialize when Japan surrendered four months later.

The end result of the previous three and a half years of occupation was that much of what had been built up by the European businesses had vanished without sufficient compensation for society and that in the non-European sector of this society the play of economic forces, which the Japanese failed to get a grip on, destroyed several million Indonesians.

A significant role in what the European businesses had established on Java was played by the large agricultural concerns, the plantations. In June 1942 five kinds of crops, cinchona, rubber, sugar, tea and coffee were placed under the supervision of a Japanese Control Office for Plantations. The European administrators were to provide statements about the business inventory, the stock on hand and the production figures for 1939, 1940 and 1941. The companies that had established the plantations in question were liquidated by the Japanese military administration and all of their cooperative organizations terminated. Later, the military administration indicated to what extent certain planting could be continued. In June 1943, the monitoring was expanded to all sisal, kapok and cacao plantations. To the extent that they were still making a profit, it went to the Control Office, in other words the military administration. This did not please the entrepreneurs in Japan and in 1944 they succeeded in principle in having the office's work taken over by Japanese firms. And, this was indeed done in the case of the sugar plantations as of May 1944 – it is not known whether this change was implemented with respect to other crops.

As mentioned above, of these crops, cinchona was protected by the Japanese and an attempt was made to promote the cultivation of sisal (important for making rope and sacks) and of cacao.

The remaining crops suffered greatly. On Java and Sumatra together more than one tenth of the rubber acreage owned by the estates was dug up. The percentage was far greater with the tea and coffee plantations on Java: 52% and 28% respectively. The production of tea dropped from 40,200 tons in 1940 to 1,700 tons (in the season 1944-1945), and that of coffee from 38,000 tons (from July 1942 through March 1943) to less than 10,000 tons in 1945. The decrease in production was thus substantially greater than the reduction of the acreage, or put differently: the plantations yielded far less per hectare. This was due to insufficient fertilization and incompetent management. On the tea plantations many factories were damaged, and others transformed for the production of rope and sacks.

Sugar cultivation was dealt an even greater blow. Of the 85 sugar refineries on Java, only 13 were still operative in 1945. Some were completely demolished, others were refitted to make distilled butyl alcohol from sugar cane, which the Japanese hoped to use for the production of aviation fuel. Sugar production, 1.3 million tons in 1942, decreased to 680,000 tons in 1943, 500,000 tons in 1944 and 84,000 tons in 1945, or about 1.7 kilo of sugar per head of the population per year should all of the sugar produced have been distributed.[35] This was not the case. Figures (unfortunately incomplete) suggest that in the years 1942-1945 the Japanese requisitioned about one sixth of the total sugar harvest for their armed forces in the Nampo region. By the end of the occupation on Java, sugar had become an extremely scarce commodity.[36]

It would have been logical for the Japanese to have planted rice in the *sawah* no longer being used for the cultivation of sugar cane, but they did not. On some, though, they allowed the planting of castor oil seeds and even maize. In his memoirs, one European planter wrote:

> You did not know what their plans were, or perhaps they didn't even know them themselves. If their head office said: 'You should see if you can plant maize', then they wanted to plant maize everywhere, even in wet *sawah*. At first I was strongly opposed to this, but then I allowed it, to the great hilarity of the inhabitants. (Brugmans 1960:278.)

Maize won't grow in wet soil.

With respect to the butyl alcohol: when the experimental production – for which five sugar refineries were stripped of their installations and seven others rendered unserviceable – became operational, it turned out that there were no tankers to transport it to Japan.

The Japanese had some success promoting the cultivation of sisal, *rami* (hemp) and other fibrous plants. However, the planting of cotton, which given the shortage of textiles was potentially so important for the entire population, failed: the climate on Java was not suitable and the plants were ravaged by insects. In the Banyumas residency the trial cultivation was 'clearly unsatisfactory', according to the regent Gandasubrata later (1953:11-2), 'but the Japanese authorities [...] reported to [...] Djakarta that the results [...] were

---

[35]   It is likely that that the population cultivated a great deal of sugar cane, from which the unrefined brown sugar did not come on the market.

[36]   In August 1944, sugar distribution had been instituted all over Java: the ration consisted of 1 kilo per person per month. It is assumed that this ration was no longer made available in the course of 1945.

very good.' Even had sufficient cotton been produced, the special oil needed by the spinning mills was lacking. None of this prevented the military administration from including the statement that it had 'thoroughly considered the issue of cotton cultivation' in an official announcement in September 1943,[37] which promised that on delivering their harvest cotton growers would receive coupons with which they could buy a maximum of three sarongs in special stores 'for a far lower price than was being asked on the market.'

Mention was made in Chapter I of the fact that the Japanese requisitioned the stocks of all of the European trading enterprises. This was not the end of it. In August 1943 all of the clothing stores were ordered to close and in February 1944 the same was required of the remaining small businesses. The stock was divided among Japanese shops where Japanese officials and Japanese citizens could make their purchases.

By then the military administration had already ordered the dismantling of iron fences and bridge railings on Java, as well as of tram and train rails on certain routes. The rails were used either for new connections on Java, such as those necessary for transporting coal from Banten, or transferred to other regions in the Nampo where new lines were being laid. In March 1944 the military administration stipulated that everyone had to turn in a share of their iron, steel, and copper implements; should the amount fall short, house searches and seizures would follow. How much was surrendered is unknown. Were the results disappointing? This could be deduced from the fact that, at least in Bandung, house searches were conducted virtually immediately following the first announcement.

A new announcement appeared on 20 December 1944, now from the residents: within a month everyone had to relinquish silver, gold and platinum objects as well as diamonds and other precious stones. The military administration also indicated how much had to be 'voluntarily' produced in the various city municipalities and residencies by the Indonesians, the Chinese, the Arabs and the Dutch Eurasians. The valuable objects would be paid for, that is at the official prices, which were but a fraction of what they would fetch on the black market.[38] According to the Japanese, the yield would be used for the armament of the 'suicide commandos' that were to be created on Java to combat the Allied landing forces, and in their propaganda the Japanese made it clear that they counted on the collection to be a great success. Naturally, it was generally assumed that should the amounts be insufficient, house

[37]   Text in Brugmans 1960:511.
[38]   This is deduced from the fact that the Japanese paid 22 guilders for 1 gram of 22 carat gold (in 1940-41, the price had been 2 guilders), while just a short time later, in March 1945, the same gram fetched 80 guilders on the black market in Medan (and in August 190 guilders).

searches and perhaps also punitive measures would follow. Nonetheless, many were disinclined to part with objects that had been handed down over generations, which had great sentimental value, and which in uncertain times were still considered as an important reserve, and trade them in for Japanese paper currency. On 12 January 1945, Bouwer in Bandung noted:

> The surrendering of gold and precious metals for remuneration is just as great a racket as 'foreign registration' was years ago [in 1942]. Amounts under 150 guilders are paid out with feigned largesse by the Japanese banks charged with collection, appraisal and compensation, but if you are crazy enough to bring something worth more, a 1,000 guilders, for instance, the Tax Office is called and asked to check whether you are in arrears with your Additional War Tax [imposed in 1942], your Personnel or Income Tax, or your Property Tax. If this is the case [...], then to start with the total amount of your arrears is deducted from the amount to be paid out [...] and if you think that you will at least get the rest in cash, you are sadly mistaken. Instead, a current account is opened at the Yokohama Specie Bank in your name, where the rest of the money is deposited and from which you can withdraw 45 guilders a month to live on.
>
> [...] Many valuables thus vanish under the ground and for the time being the Indo-European community appears disinclined to go along with the collection. (Bouwer 1988:314-5.)

Five days later, on 17 January:

> Of the 100 carats' worth of precious stones that the Indo community had to hand over, not even 15 have come in. [...] The large cities are all in arrears. Batavia delivered only 22% of what the Japanese had demanded, Malang 15%, Surabaya 14%. The island of Madura brought in the most, namely 227%, followed by the Central Javanese principalities with 113%. The residency Pati has already reached its quota. [...] The Chinese community in Bandung must bring in 2,000 carats. (Bouwer 1988:315-6.)

23 January:

> The Indos have also finally capitulated to the Japanese threats of terror should not enough precious stones be surrendered. The deadline for turning them in has been extended to the end of the month. With a heavy heart, [my] mother-in-law took two small stones, together 0.34 carats, to a bank and received 85 guilders in Japanese bank notes.[39] Moreover, it also seems like a promotion week for the Bijenkorf [a department store in Amsterdam]: on turning in 1 carat one receives a coupon with which to buy fabric for a gown for the official price in the Tjioda department store. (Bouwer 1988:317.)

---

[39]   As appears from the daily notes of the chairman of the Eurasian Committee in Bandung, they had turned in 19 carats of diamonds on 15 January and 166 carats on 21 January, and another 335 carats had come in on 5 February. So great was the fear!

At the end of this operation, the Japanese military administration announced that twice the estimate (or rather the assessment) of gold had been received, namely 30 million guilders' worth, and that with respect to precious stones parts of East and Central Java had brought in many times more than the estimate: Besuki almost 15 times, Madura 10 and the principalities Kedu and Kediri 5 times. Conversely, only 60% of the estimate was reached in the Batavia residency and only 40% in the municipality of Batavia.

It was just mentioned that when precious stones were handed over in Bandung, 1 carat qualified the bearer for a coupon with which fabric for a gown could be purchased at a department store, and previously that in September 1943 it was announced that upon delivering their harvest the cotton growers would receive coupons entitling them to a maximum of three sarongs. These were symptoms of the shortage of textiles, which will be discussed below. It should be underscored here that the Japanese measures issued from one of the guidelines established in Tokyo at the beginning of the war, namely that in allocating scarce commodities priority had to be given to those serving the Japanese war effort.

Presumably (further information is lacking), this guideline was also followed with respect to other goods, which means therefore that they did not enter into general distribution.

What then did enter into general distribution? There are no surveys of this, and should there be, they would say little. The announcements in question were typically Japanese: they should be viewed as goals, but whether they were reached is another question. When in early April 1945 a rationing scheme for meat was first announced (everyone would receive 50 grams of water buffalo meat every 14 days for 5 cents), Bouwer wrote in Bandung: 'Meat has appeared for the first time in the new ration book, valid for an entire year, which we just received, which does not mean that we will also get it'. On the basis of his experience of more than three years of occupation he added: 'We never receive most of the articles mentioned in the ration book' (Bouwer 1988:330).

To start with, the Japanese authorities failed to get sufficient grip either on the producers of foodstuffs and other consumer goods such as textiles or on the dealers, including the wholesalers. Both the producers and the traders withheld goods – repeated warnings that drastic measures would be taken against those who did not report what they had only shows how ineffective the control was. Many Japanese *kumiai*, or corporations, employed controllers, namely poorly paid Indonesians. Given that everyone attempted to supplement their food rations and that the price of food on the black market continually rose, the temptation was great among the controllers to close their eyes in return for money or goods. Incidentally, on Java, traditionally it was not considered improper for someone in a position of power to exploit it within certain boundaries (this was not to be abused) for their own sake, and that of their family and friends. Also lacking was a proper rationing department. To the extent that officials of this department were paid, they received but a petty amount, but payment was not a general occurrence. When, at the end of 1943 and beginning of 1944, the Japanese introduced the *tonarigumi* system (the grouping of all of the inhabitants in small neighbourhoods) on Java, they entrusted rationing to the neighbourhood chiefs, the *kumicho*, which shows that no general rationing system had existed previously. As of 1944, the goods for rationing thus came via the district chiefs of the *tonarigumi* system, the *azacho* (in the *desa* these were mostly the *desa* headmen), to the neighbourhood chiefs – many surely first took care of their own needs and those of their families and friends (this appears to have been the rule on Celebes).

There was also no effective price control. In the first weeks of the occupation prices on the markets rose because supply stagnated – they began to drop after the supply was re-established. Particularly the wholesalers understood that the scarcity of goods would only become greater, and accordingly they either withheld their stocks or sold them above the official price. In September 1942, the Kempeitai arrested several Chinese and Arab wholesalers, publicized their names, and let it be known that henceforth they would act even more harshly since pushing up prices was to be considered 'a silent rebellion against Japanese authority'.[40] After that, price control was delegated to the Indonesian police and the auxiliary police, the *Keibodan*, created in early 1943. According to an Indonesian from an area near Rembang,[41] in September 1944 this control:

> often takes the form of theft. The small dealers, however, remain calm because the loss incurred through confiscation is amply compensated for by successful smuggling transactions. The tough action by the police and the *Keibodan* thus yields no results, but does give rise to theft by members of the police or of the *Keibodan* itself. For the amount and the weight of the goods confiscated are not standard and no records are kept.

Repeated prohibitions against selling goods or buying them for prices higher than those specified by the military administration (this specification took effect as of 1 October 1943 per residency when, as mentioned above, they had become closed economic entities as it were) had no effect. Reporting to the military administration at the end of November 1942, an Indonesian nationalist said the following about the sale of cigarettes:

[40]   Summary *Kan Po*, p. 54.
[41]   Text in Brugmans 1960:498-9.

It is forbidden to ask for more than is indicated on the revenue band, but the retailer already has to pay a higher price clandestinely to the wholesaler, from which it follows that the price for the consumer is much higher still. To be sure, cigarettes are also sold for the official price, but the number of shops doing so is insufficient –

(other shops thus sold them only for the high prices).

> The consequence is that those wanting to buy a 12-cent pack of cigarettes have to stand in line two or three times, which often leads to fights because of the jostling.
> This is exactly what happens with the trade in other goods, but that is not so visible as with the cigarettes.[42]

The Japanese themselves contributed to the illegal price rises in that they delegated the purchasing of the large stocks they needed themselves to Chinese buyers. These buyers paid cash (most dealers were wary of bank transfers to a current account at a Japanese bank) and knew that only one thing mattered to their Japanese clients: that the goods paid for were delivered. Although the clients had paper currency in abundance, they did not pay rapidly – whoever delivered something to the Japanese had to wait a long time for their money. The buyers took this into account: they imposed a substantial surcharge on the already excessively high prices they paid themselves.

The Japanese also contributed in one other way to rising prices. After the Japanization of banking, manufacturers and wholesalers (mostly Chinese and Arabs) received no more credit. On the contrary, as mentioned in Chapter I, they had to repay their bank debts. It was thus crucial for every one of these manufacturers and wholesalers to radically increase the amount of cash at their disposal (in order to then exchange the Japanese money either for banknotes of the Javasche Bank or for goods bought on the black market). How could they do this other than by raising the prices of their goods?

Holding on to cash became a general phenomenon: virtually no one on Java saved anymore.[43] When the Post Office Savings Bank was reopened in

---

[42] Text in Brugmans 1960:486.
[43] Compulsory saving was introduced in the regions controlled by the navy. On Borneo it was determined that the inhabitants who could be assumed to be able to save (that is save at the branches of the Algemeene Volkskredietbank, the number of which was increased), would be excluded from rice and salt allocation should they stop saving. On Celebes it was determined that no one could have more than 500 guilders in cash at home and an amount was saved from the salaries of civil servants. It should be remembered that the *romusha* deployed on Muna who were entitled to about 15 guilders a month in wages, had 5 guilders a month withheld as savings. On Java, no one was allowed to have more than 100 guilders at home. Naturally, any effective control of this regulation was impossible.

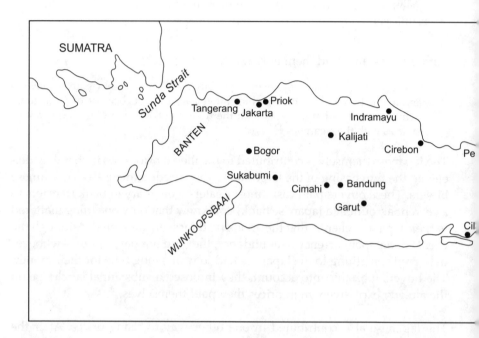

Map 8. Java II

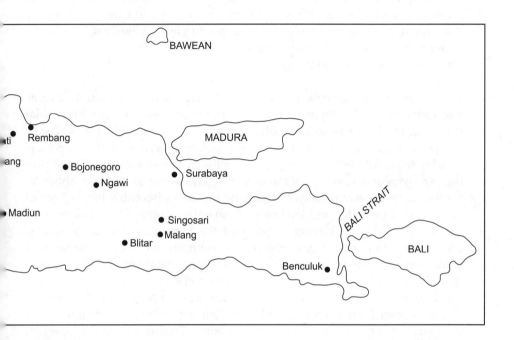

May 1942, the military administration expected that many would deposit their money there. The target was announced in July 1944: a total of 120 million guilders had to have been deposited by May 1945. Only a little more than 10 million guilders had come in by July 1944 (later figures are not known): 7.4 million guilders were deposited by Indonesians, 1.7 million guilders by Japanese, Germans and Italians, and 950,000 guilders by 55,000 Chinese, whose average savings were only 17.30 guilders.

The circumstances described so far in this chapter: the isolation of Java as part of the blockaded Japanese sphere of influence; Java's far-reaching isolation from the Outer Islands; its division (as of 1 October 1943) into 17 self-sufficient areas; the incompetence of the Japanese occupiers; their doctrine that Japanese interests came first; the ineffectiveness of their corporations; the deployment of several million men and boys as in effect forced labourers for longer or shorter periods of time; the massive discontinuation of planting that had provided millions of *desa* inhabitants with additional income; the requisitioning or buying of parts of the harvest and of trade stocks; the forced selling of valuable objects; the pumping of colossal amounts of banknotes into the economy; the defective price controls and the equally defective rationing system – all of these circumstances (and these are but the most important) aggravated the poverty on Java. To be fair, Java's economy had also been fragile under Dutch rule, but the colonial government had prevented emergency situations from arising. Leaving aside the question of whether the Japanese even had the power to prevent this, they certainly did not feel the need to do so. Should the harvest fail, famine would be the inevitable result.

And this famine was soon forthcoming.

In order to afford a picture of the shocking impoverishment that ravaged Java, a description of the rice supply must first be given.

Impoverishment and famine on Java

The beginning of the Japanese occupation was accompanied by local shortages of rice.[44] Transportation only got going with difficulty (and would never approach the efficiency that had characterized it before the arrival of the Japanese).[45] Moreover, contrary to the colonial government's

---

[44]   When we refer to Java as a whole, Madura is included. For the places mentioned, see Map 8.
[45]   Increasingly fewer trains were running on Java, thus those in operation were generally overcrowded: passengers repeatedly rode on the roofs of the carriages. In this connection it should be mentioned that the private railways on Java were fused with the State Railways, that

instructions the Removal and Demolition Corps destroyed the machines of numerous rice-husking plants on the north coast of Central Java. With the support of Dutch civil servants, the Japanese military administration was able to counterbalance the shortages here and there by putting up for sale large supplies of rice that had been stored by the colonial government. The harvests had been good. In the years 1937-1941 they averaged 8.5 million tons: of unhusked rice (*padi*), that is, which yielded more than 6 million tons of husked and polished rice (*beras*)[46] – per head of the population (but there were many young children who needed less rice than older children and adults), which amounted to about 300 grams of rice per day. Rice was the primary though certainly not the only food available: also important for the indigenous population were in the first place maize, tuberous plants such as cassava and *bataten* (sweet potatoes), and fruit. The maize harvest in the years 1937-1941 averaged 2.1 million tons, the cassava harvest 8.3 million tons, and the *bataten* harvest 1.3 million tons. Finally, it was significant that the very starchy cassava and *bataten* could be supplemented with fish, which is rich in protein.

The Japanese military administration considered the rice harvest to be too limited. Part of it would be needed to feed Japanese soldiers throughout the Nampo region, and it was hoped that large quantities of rice could be exported to Japan. Plans were made to double the rice harvest on Java within three years and experts from Japan were involved to this end. They recommended the introduction of Japanese production methods: the fertilization of the *sawah* had to be altered and the seedlings, the *bibit*, planted in a different fashion. Though these changes had caused the rice harvest in Japan to increase, according to Regent Gandasubrata: 'the Japanese did not remember the difference of climate, soil condition and way of life of the people of Indonesia' (Gandasubrata 1953:10) – indigenous growers strongly resisted the introduction of change in a centuries-old cultivation. The Japanese experiment was a failure in many respects.

The years 1942-1943 displayed a slight decrease in the *padi* harvest: 8.3 million tons were harvested in 1942, and 8.1 million tons in 1943. Not that this harvest was made fully available to Java's inhabitants! As early as 1942 a share was requisitioned by the Japanese army, though the exact amount is not known.

How did the Japanese get hold of the husked rice, or *beras*, that they wanted in 1942 and for most of 1943?

Beras was delivered to them by the rice-husking plants, the majority of

---

in the rural areas hardly any buses were running anymore and that in March 1945 a horse-drawn tram was instituted in Surabaya.

[46]   White rice is obtained when *beras* (red rice) is polished, that is the coat is removed.

which by far were owned by Chinese. In 1941 the Dutch colonial government had grouped these plants into three associations of rice-huskers, Rijst-Verkoop-Centrales, or Rice Selling Federations: one for West Java, one for Central Java and one for East Java. The executives of these three federations were recognized in April 1942 by the Japanese military administration and they were designated as the only institutions that could buy and transport rice (*padi*). At the same time a corporation, a *kumiai*, was set up, the Association of Wholesalers in rice, charged with selling husked rice (*beras*) to the Japanese army and to the rice retailers, who were mostly dealers with a stall, a *warung*, as their outlet.

In August 1942, at the time of the re-establishment of the Departments of General Administration, an Office of Food Supply was established under the Department of Economic Affairs and charged with the regulation of all rice-related matters – the Association of Wholesalers in rice was given a purely executive function.

The fall in the harvest and the Japanese requisitioning already caused a shortage of *beras* in 1942 and 1943. This is clear from the increase in the prices on the black market. In 1938 a kilo of average *beras* cost around 3½ cents on the *pasar*. *Beras* of the best quality was more expensive, going for 10 cents a kilo in Batavia in 1939. Initially, the Japanese were confronted with price rises ensuing from supply problems (the price of a kilo of *beras* rose to 24 cents on the *pasar* in Batavia), but they combated this, which was also related to the general lowering of wages they had introduced. In April 1942 the maximum price on East Java (there is no information for Central and West Java) was set at 3.6 cents per kilo. This meant that the farmers received far less for their *padi*. Understanding that the low *padi* prices would only reinforce the farmers' inclination to withhold *padi* from the buyers of the Association of Wholesalers in rice, in early 1943 the Japanese Office of Food Supply realized that the purchase price of *padi* had to be raised: at the end of March 1943 it was set at 3¼ to 3.6 cents per kilo (depending on the quality) throughout Java.

Even though the farmers received more money, this could not prevent the price of *beras* from rising on the black market: in June a kilo of white rice sold for 1 guilder on the black market in Batavia and for 1.20 guilders in Cirebon.

This development contributed to a fundamental change in Japanese policy, which was also connected to the fact that Java was divided into 17 self-sufficient regions (the 17 residencies) as of 1 October 1943. The purchase price of *padi* was raised to 4 or 4½ cents per kilo, the entire Indonesian administrative apparatus – from the regents to the *desa* headmen – was mobilized to ensure that every farmer would deliver enough *padi*, and a system for the distribution of *beras* was created.

A few comments on this are in order. The first is that the institution of the 17 self-sufficient regions meant that the residencies that yielded relatively large amounts of *padi* were less easily able to transport *padi* or *beras* to residencies where less *padi* grew – transportation, moreover, was complicated because there were fewer goods wagons and lorries. The second is that the increase in the purchase price of *padi* proved ineffective because the farmers could buy virtually nothing of value for the money they received. The third is that with the rationing of *beras* priority was given to the urban municipalities and other large places, while no account was taken of the needs of the populations in smaller ones. Worse still, the amounts demanded of the farmers were not based on the harvest from the period March-September 1944, but rather on the one that was just over, March-September 1943. In determining the amounts to be delivered by each residency the Japanese set unrealistically high harvest figures. As usual, the buyers had purchased and paid for the *padi* in the field – the requisitioning was imposed in a period when most of the farmers had already delivered the *padi* to the buyers (who often experienced great difficulty in getting it transported from where it was stored); these farmers were left only with the *padi* they needed to feed their families and for the planting in 1944. Farmers with but a small *sawah* had virtually nothing left over after giving the requisitioned amount of *padi* to the *desa* headman. Though warned about the situation, the Japanese determined that these farmers could more than stay alive by planting enough maize, cassava and *bataten*.

Rationing in the cities only slowly became operational. As an Indonesian reported to the Japanese administration at the end of 1943 with respect to the situation in Jakarta:[47]

> Every afternoon thousands and thousands of people stand before various *warung*. Brawls have become a daily occurrence, especially to get a litre or a litre and a half of rice. The same is also seen in other cities. Reports are coming in from various quarters that so and so was unable to get rice for so many days. The number of days varies from five to two.

This observer also mentioned that indigenous administrators had forced farmers to sell a share of the scant 100 or 200 kilos of *padi* they had retained for their own use. 'In addition to the fact that people basically have nothing left to live on, one wonders how seeds for the next planting can be acquired'.

In January 1944, Achmed Soebardjo, a prominent journalist, risked travelling around Java without permission to do so from the Japanese to investigate the problems caused by the forced deliveries in 60 *desa*. He concluded that the farmers had had to turn in 10% to 30% more of the *padi* harvested in 1943 and that no account whatsoever had been taken of the differences in yield of the various *sawah*. Furthermore, he noted that the rationing system did

---

[47]   Text in Brugmans 1960:489.

not work properly, that the rations in many small places were minimal, that the Chinese buyers acting as the agents of the Office of Food Supply were putting large amounts of rice on the black market and that the majority of the population was unable to pay the prices being asked there.

The rice rations (there is little information on this) varied greatly from place to place. In Bandung the ration of 200 grams per person per day instituted at the end of October 1943 was reduced to 160 grams in mid-December. In February 1944, the daily ration in Yogyakarta was 75 grams; in March in Jakarta it was 115 grams, later in that first year 200 grams, and as of 1 October 160 grams – and it is not even clear if all of the official rations (at the beginning of 1944 they were portioned out by the *tonarigumi*) were always available.

Three things are known: that drought resulted in the *padi* harvest dwindling by 1.2 million tons in 1944 compared to 1943 (from 8.1 to 6.9 million tons); that the Japanese requisitioned more than two and a half times as much rice for their own use on Central Java in the harvest year 1944-1945 as in the harvest year 1943-1944; and that the prices on the black market were continually rising. On the black market in Yogyakarta one had to pay 1.55 guilders for a kilo of rice in February 1944; in Surabaya 1.90 guilders in August; in Pati (Central Java) 70 cents in September; in Bandung 60 cents in January 1944, 95 cents in August (in Bandung Bouwer (1988:280) noted, 'the sellers ask their own and not the official prices. They will not part with their wares for less than their own prices and destroy them if necessary. And nobody does anything to stop this'), 2 guilders in October, and 3 guilders in December; and in Jakarta 1.70 guilders in February 1944, 85 cents in June, 1.80 guilders in October, and 3.60 guilders in November.

At that time, the Dutch Eurasian writer Beb Vuyk living in Sukabumi sent an indigenous assistant, Simin, every month with money and food to her mother-in-law in Jakarta. In her notes she wrote:

> Lately we have only been able to send cooked rice, the transportation of raw rice is forbidden. Those who are caught are forced by the Japanese to eat up the smuggled goods. At the station, Simin saw a man and a woman forced with a bayonet to their stomachs to swallow handfuls of raw rice. They weren't real smugglers, just people from outside bringing a few litres of rice to their hungry families in the city.
>
> [...] The daily worry of finding food is so great that we rarely think about the future. Food is a problem even here in the mountains, although our house lies between the rice paddies and mama owns a *sawah*. One fifth of the yield has to be handed over, the assessment is done before it is harvestable. This assessment is always too high, so that we sometimes lose more than one third of the harvest. Two years ago I complained to the subdistrict chief. 'Don't think that I am treating you unjustly, madam' he said, and then, first looking behind with a gesture that has now become familiar: 'Officially I have to confiscate one fifth of the assessed yield, and in addition I also have the official, though secret, order to make such high assessments that no more than [...] half remains'. (Vuyk 1962:256.)

This random indication (relating to the end of 1942) underscores the extent to which actual events could deviate from the officially proclaimed regulations.

In 1944 West Java experienced several serious disturbances which were closely linked to the compulsory rice deliveries.

In January 1944 in a district near Tasikmalaya (located approximately 35 kilometres southeast of Garut, see Map 8) general resentment had grown which a fanatic *kiai* (an Islamic leader), Djenal Moestapa, head of a *pesantren* (an Islamic seminary), fanned. He preached that Allah demanded the expulsion of the Japanese and to this end he armed his disciples with bamboo spears, saying that these would prove stronger than the weapons of the Japanese and that anyone coming to blows with this enemy would be invincible. A small group of Kempeitai soldiers began an investigation on 18 February and took in Moestapa for interrogation, which was coupled with the usual maltreatment. A fight ensued in which a Kempeitai officer was killed. Moestapa was freed and the Kempeitai group had to clear out. However, two weeks later, on 1 March, this group returned substantially reinforced. They were confronted with many hundreds, according to some even many thousands, of Indonesians, a lot of whom were armed with stones, bamboo spears and knives. Fierce fights broke out which reportedly cost the lives of five indigenous policemen, more than 50 Japanese and more than 100 rebels. Around 400 rebels were arrested by the Kempeitai, and 82 were sentenced to death by the military court in Jakarta; taking account of the sentiments of the Muslims, the Japanese spared Moestapa's life, declaring him to be of unsound mind.

In May, June and August 1944, similar disturbances occurred in the Indramayu regency, part of the Cirebon residency. In these incidents too Islamic leaders were prominent. The disturbances were severest in August: the regent and the *wedono* of the district in question who had come to inspect the delivery of *padi* had to flee, forcing the Japanese to send strong troop detachments to the regency; it is not known how many victims there were on that occasion.

After quashing the latter uprising, the Japanese military administration agreed to have an adviser working for it in Jakarta, the Indonesian *Raden* (a Javanese title of nobility) Prawoto Soemodilogo, investigate whether Islamic fanaticism or other factors lay at the root of what had transpired in the Indramayu regency. The report he submitted to the Japanese military administration at the end of October 1944[48] basically said that the views of a few haji had found a response only because a true crisis situation had emerged in the district concerned. In 1943 the district had already been forced to hand over such a large portion of the rice harvest that some had had to resort to eating the leaves of banana trees and numerous children and old people had died of starvation. It had been determined in this district (this regulation was also in force elsewhere) that for every 500 kilo of *padi* that a farmer delivered he would receive a maximum of five items of clothing. The wealthy farmers had received all five, several of which they then sold illegally, while the poor farmers had been given none because they could not reach the target of 500 kilos. Moreover, this clothing had been allocated via the indigenous administrative officials, who had helped themselves, their family, their clerks and the police first. Resentment was thus already running high but reached boiling point when for the harvest of 1944 it was determined that, while other regencies in the Cirebon residency only had to deliver 350 to 400 kilos per hectare, the farmers of Indramayu had to turn in 1500 kilos per hectare. Some of them had already sold their harvest to buyers and had had to purchase their *padi* on the black market for 20 cents per kilo, for which they received 4½ cents upon handing it in. And just why had Indramayu been subjected to such a high assessment? The farmers were convinced that the civil servants of the Internal Administration had been bribed by the owners of the rice-husking plants and the wholesalers – Chinese who, moreover, had allegedly given bribes to railway personnel. There was also resentment because the *romusha* from Indramayu, most of whom had signed a three-month labour contract, had yet to return after more than a year. This had led to a meeting of farmers who decided not to submit their *padi*; according to Prawoto's report they had said that, 'were they to be shot by the police, their fate would be better than if they were to starve to death'.

In 1942 the Japanese military administration had appointed Indonesian advisers to the departments of general administration. Naturally, these advisers maintained contact with one another, but when they agreed that a particular Japanese measure was having an adverse effect, their concern fell on deaf ears: as a group they had no status. In general, the Japanese were not particularly interested in recommendations and had absolutely no need of advice dispensed by individuals or institutions not specifically ordered to do so.

When in September 1944 Prime Minister Koiso announced that the 'East Indies' would be granted 'independence', the Japanese military administration on Java realized that Indonesians had to be prepared for this 'independence'. Consequently the departmental advisers received permission to form their own council – the Board of Advisers – alongside the Central Advisory Council established in 1943. The Central Advisory Council could have been perceived as a first step towards a parliament; the Board of Advisers could be seen as a first step towards a cabinet. Sukarno became the chairman of the new board and the 14 members (some departments had more than one adviser) included

48   A copy is in ARA, Alg. Secr., Eerste zending, XXV, 19.

Ki Hadjar Dewantoro (in the 1920s the initiator of the founding of independent Indonesian schools), Oto Iskandardinata, Abikoesno Tjokrosoejoso (chairman of the Partai Sarekat Islam Indonesia), Hatta, Professor *Raden* Soepomo (of the Law School in Batavia), *Raden* Prawoto Soemodilogo and *Raden* Soekardjo Wirjopranoto (chairman of the Parindra).

The board first convened (without the presence of the Japanese!) on 16 December 1944[49] to deliberate on the first question that the Japanese military administration had posed with a request for advice, namely how *padi* deliveries could be better organized. All of the advisers knew that serious abuses had been committed in this area – was it wise to point this out to the Japanese? Sukarno reassured them, saying: 'without a single objection even the most secret matters relating to the *padi* deliveries can be included in your response.' One of the members then pointed out that the Central Advisory Council had already received information regarding this matter from one of the chief officials of the Department of Economic Affairs: the military administration had demanded 'approximately 23% of the *padi* harvest'. This, he contended, was not an inordinate amount; nevertheless shortages had arisen everywhere, in fact, there had even been famine. The ensuing discussion led to the idea of assigning several board members to conduct an investigation in the various regions of Java. An investigation into what? Only into *padi* deliveries? One of the advisers, Raden Mas Ario Woerjaningrat commented:

> At present, society is dissatisfied, not only with the sale of *padi* but also with the distribution of *beras*.
> SUKARNO: The question posed concerns *padi* deliveries to the government. As to why the population is not satisfied, there are a thousand and one reasons. You can list them all.
> WOERJANINGRAT: Chairman, can you answer the question of what percentage of the crop should be sold to the army?
> SUKARNO: I don't know.

Six members of the board were assigned to carry out an investigation – Sukarno took it upon himself to organize the travel passes. Iskandardinata became the chairman and Prawoto one of the members of this investigative committee. The six divided the various residencies among themselves and the Board of Advisers decided that they would not only gather information on *padi* deliveries but also on food provision in general, the rationing system, the official and the illegal prices of *padi* and *beras*,[50] the consequences of clos-

---

[49]   The minutes of the meetings of the Board of Advisers were translated into Dutch by R. de Bruin; the report of the first meeting is in NIOD IC, 36,580.
[50]   When on 27 December the second meeting of the Board of Advisers took place, Hatta said that according to an investigation he conducted, in October 1944 the average asking price for

ing off the residencies and the misappropriations.

　　After almost three weeks the members of this committee convened again in Jakarta. They drafted their report, which was read out loud by Iskandar-dinata at the fourth meeting of the Board of Advisers on 8 January 1945.[51] They concluded that there had been a crop failure in 1944; that the population in the various residencies believed that the *padi* delivered was being shipped out of the residency concerned, 'indeed, out of Java even'; that 'the sense of solidarity' had not yet got through to 'the rich farmers, the wealthy in gen-eral and influential individuals', and that there was insufficient supervision of the *padi* 'during its passage, especially from the buyers to its arrival at the government'. All of this was explained in detail and it was pointed out that the *padi* delivered remained far too long in the storage areas due to a short-age of transportation ('so that the *padi* has often gone bad, in fact sometimes it has even germinated') and that in the residencies of Bogor and Banten new delivery standards had been implemented. In the Bogor residency, 90% of the harvest of the *sawah*, which were the property of people living in the cities, had to be turned over, and for the cultivation of one's own land a sliding scale applied, beginning with the owners of *sawah* smaller than one hectare who had to hand over 40% of the harvest, and ending with the owners of *sawah* measuring five hectares or more who had to deliver 75% of their crop. In contrast, a uniform scale was applied in the Banten residency; every farmer had to cede two thirds of his harvest. These figures were substantially higher than the 23% mentioned by the Department of Economic Affairs!

　　With regard to rationing, the investigative committee discerned great differences: in Jakarta the daily rice ration was 180 grams, in Kediri 150, in Garut 120, but in Pekalongan 230, and outside such cities 'the rice dis-tribution generally [remained] limited to civil servants' while 'the common people' received virtually nothing. In a *desa* in the Bandung regency it was 32 grams per day per person, in a district in the residency of Bogor 30 grams per day per dwelling and in a district in the residency of Bojonegoro 20 grams per day per family.

　　Black market prices differed per residency depending on the *padi* yield. In the Besuki residency the price for one kilo of *beras* was 20 cents, in the cities it was nowhere less than 1.50 guilders, and in Bogor and in the vicinity of Jakarta even 4 guilders.

　　When Iskandardinata had finished reading, Prawoto described what he had noted in the Pekalongan residency:

---

beras on the black market had been eight and a half times higher than the official price (10 cents per kilo), and in December eleven and a quarter times higher.
[51]　　The minutes of the fourth, fifth and sixth meeting are in NIOD IC, 36,626.

The farmer brings the *padi* on a long pole to the home of the *desa* headman. [...] From there the farmer carries his *padi* to the storage area. [...] If the *padi* being transported to storage is wet, a deduction is calculated based on weight, sometimes up to 30%. Cheating takes place with the weighing of the *padi*, with the weights, up to 20%. Furthermore, the rice-husking plant can also exact a deduction based on weight due to poorer quality, up to 10%. In this way, the deduction can amount to 60%. [...] In places where the *kumiai* is represented a contribution of two cents per kilo can be demanded from the farmers.

Prawota's finding was that the farmers in Pekalongan had received only 1.88 guilders on average for 100 kilos of *padi*, which should have brought them 4 guilders. Moreover, that substantially lesser amount was not paid out immediately; the husking plant had to do this and even deducted a percentage corresponding with the part of the harvest that had been stolen from the storage area (this was not guarded) or had diminished in weight due to shrinkage.

One regency in the Pekalongan residency, Prawoto continued, had delivered more than 16,000 tons of rice, while the rice-husking plant had only paid for 11,000 tons, 'thus 5,000 tons have disappeared. This is only one regency! How will it look when an investigation is conducted in an entire residency or throughout all of Java?' Clearly supervision fell short. No wonder! 'The control boards include the owners of the husking plants' (Hatta: 'Self-regulation!') 'Dogs don't bite each other.'

The member of the investigative committee who had visited the Pati regency announced that there not 23% but 57% of the harvest assessment had had to be handed over. The assessment was over 300,000 tons and approximately 170,000 tons had to be submitted. However, the actual harvest only totalled 130,000 tons. 'It was reported to me that the farmers were obliged to hand over the entire yield from their *sawah*; in fact, some had to give more than the entire yield from their *sawah* and just how they went about this was their problem'. This created so much turmoil that the 170,000 tons demanded was reduced to 70,000 tons. On the other hand, from the Kedu residency only 60,000 tons had been demanded of a *padi* harvest yielding 460,000 tons.

Iskandardinata summarized the situation: 'The farmers feel that they plant *padi*, but receive no food. This is the atmosphere in which the population is living.' For the benefit of the war, he said, sacrifices had to be made, but they were most unequally divided:

> In Banten and Preanger there are many village chiefs who own *sawah*, but quite a few of them do not participate in the *padi* deliveries. They have so arranged it that others are obliged to deliver *padi*. Especially in the Banten residency the religious scholars have a strong position and usually these ulamas are wealthy. A village head dare not dictate how much *padi* they should deliver. [...] From house searches it appeared that much *padi* is hoarded, indeed that even people who work for the Propaganda Service stash *padi* in the basements under their houses.

[...] The small farmers generally do comply with their delivery obligation because they are afraid.

Woerjaningrat subsequently wondered whether a residency that yielded much *padi* could help other residencies. 'That comes under the competence of the central government,' Iskandardinanta responded, 'and we know nothing about that'.

How much did the Japanese army actually receive? Woerjaningrat thought: 'in every residency 20%' (not of the total *padi* harvest but of what was turned in). 'No', retorted Iskandardinata: 'it differs: in Banten 25%, in Preanger 15% and in Bogor 20%', but he was the only one who could produce figures: the five other members of the investigative committee had not inquired into the matter (presumably they *dared* not ask).

The situation was grim all around. How could it be improved?

Soekardjo Wirjopranoto suggested that the Board of Advisers propose to the Japanese military administration the setting up of 'an efficient system', 'both for the collecting of *padi* and for the rationing of *beras* among the population'. He contended that eight to nine million tons of *padi* were produced annually (actually in 1944 the figure was only 6.9 million tons), and that supervision of rationing had to begin with the rice-husking plants. Abikoesno countered that everything relating to rice ought to be supervised by a directorate and he had arrived at that proposal based on, he said:

> the circumstances in which the population now lives, in which our people, so to speak, no longer have an existence, especially as regards food; they have absolutely no protection anymore and do not know to whom to turn in their grief, when the *desa* headmen are as corrupt as the Internal Administration above them.

Was a directorate the solution? A vote was taken: only three advisers voted in favour.

Another proposal was submitted, namely by Iskandardinata: *padi* had to be considered a commodity that was not allowed to be traded. But why only *padi*, one of the advisers asked: other foodstuffs such as maize and cassava were equally important!

Dewantoro warned against excessive government control, whereby ever more goods would be withheld. He argued in favour of :

> addressing the pessimism prevailing among the people. In the past cow's milk could be bought, even if it was very expensive. Ever since *padi* has been administered by the government, milk has disappeared. This is the case with other goods as well that are administered by the *kumiai*. They disappear from the normal market, but are still available on the black market.

Iskandardinata withdrew his proposal.

Hatta had another one: for every *desa* a calculation needed to be made of how much *padi* had to be kept, and what remained had to be transferred to the government, not to the rice merchants and the rice-husking plants. 'It is logical', he said, 'that there is no free market'.

Again a vote was taken: seven were in favour, seven against. Sukarno abstained.

The third proposal: the rice-husking plants should be placed under the supervision of a body comprising not only Japanese and Chinese but also 'representatives of other population groups, for example, Indonesians.' Prawoto added to the proposal: the Japanese military administration should take control of the rice-husking plants. Didn't they already come under the Japanese corporation? Yes, but the Chinese owners did as they pleased. Soekardjo Wirjopranoto noted:

> Their buyers go to the villages feeling that they are protected by the Japanese. They are haughty and rude. They lay down what the local population has to pro- duce. They say: 'On such and such a day you must bring *padi* to such and such a place, because the representatives of the rice-husking plant want to come then and buy the *padi*,' and they do this in the name of Nippon.

All of the advisers agreed that the owners of the rice-husking plants were no good. What was to be done? Did these husking plants have to be purchased or simply nationalized? The Board of Advisers finally reached a consensus: they ought to be nationalized.

Likewise, another proposal was accepted unanimously: the price of *padi* had to be increased.

Both proposals, together with the report of the investigative committee and a full account of the discussions (these had lasted three days: 8 and 13 January and 6 February 1945), were submitted to the Japanese military administration at the beginning of March.

That administration implemented only the simplest change: the *padi* price was increased from 4 or 4½ cents per kilo to 15 cents,[52] a fairly ineffectual measure since the farmers could purchase nothing with the extra money they received.

For the rest nothing changed.

The year 1945 witnessed yet another severe decrease of the *padi* harvest: from 6.9 to 5.6 million tons. There was thus even less *beras* to distribute. On the black market in Jakarta in February rice cost 6.50 guilders per kilo, in Bandung at the end of March 4 guilders, at the end of April 2.25 guilders,

[52]   This triggered an increase of the official price of *beras*. In this regard it is only known that in July in the Preanger regencies this was 18 cents per kilo.

and two weeks later 3.50 guilders, and the price of 'the other articles', Bouwer noted, had then also risen 'proportionally'. On 16 July (later in May and in June the price of *beras* had slightly decreased) he wrote:

> Everything is going wrong again with the rice rationing. Today in some districts only a part of the daily ration has been handed out, supplemented with *ketan* (sticky rice)[53], *jagung* (maize), *ubi* (sweet potato) or *gaplek* (dried starchy tubers [cassava]), foodstuffs to be distributed on a regular basis from now on. The military authority is experiencing serious difficulties with requisitioning rice, which has produced far less than it had anticipated. Many farmers have stopped producing, so long as they are obliged to hand over their rice for 12 cents per litre[54] to the government, while on the black market they can really get as much as they like for it, provided they can transport it themselves. Now that this is impossible, they grow just enough to sustain themselves and their families. Farmers still willing to grow more, withhold [...] a large amount to sell on the black market. Whatever still comes in to the government collecting offices cannot (and this is the third impediment) be distributed throughout the districts due to a lack of transport. Bandung's storehouse is in Cirebon, where (it is said) fairly substantial supplies are waiting to be transported. The Japanese have even laid on army lorries for this and for the time being they are relieving the shortage by distributing the foods mentioned. Meanwhile the rice supply is a mess. Black market dealers instantly took advantage of this situation. The price of rice rose today to 2.60 guilders per litre.[55]
>
> 17 July. A year ago terror would have been used; now it's done with bribery. This evening the *Tjahaja*[56] will be publishing an official announcement that farmers delivering the set amounts of rice at the registration offices within the month will be given a sarong and two metres of fabric. Every *lurah* (*desa* headman) in the region where the set quantity is submitted in time will profit in the same manner. (Bouwer 1988:360-1.)

As it turned out, this measure had already been applied in the Indramayu regency in 1944, the result being that farmers who owned only small *sawah* were not eligible to receive clothing.

Was this measure effective? Bouwer's description suggests that the Japanese, at least in the Bandung residency, were steadily losing their grip on the indigenous administrators, who in turn were losing their grip on the farmers. There is every reason to believe that this was a general phenomenon. An indication of this is the fact that the representative of the Japanese military administration who outlined the situation on Java to Rear-Admiral Sir Wilfred R. Patterson on 24 September on board the British cruiser

---

[53] Sometimes of poor quality.
[54] Fifteen cents per kilo.
[55] Per kilo 3.25 guilders. In Jakarta at the time the black market price fluctuated between 3.75 guilders and 6.25 guilders per kilo.
[56] An Indonesian daily newspaper in Bandung.

Cumberland said that the *padi* harvest was estimated at 4½ million tons, that of that amount he hoped to collect 700,000 tons for distribution and 200,000 tons for the Japanese armed forces, that the farmers could keep one fifth of the harvest (900,000 tons), and that he assumed that the remaining 2.7 million tons would most certainly not end up in normal distribution channels but would be hoarded or sold on the black market.

While, as has been emphasized, rice was indeed the primary staple, it was not the only one, and in that connection maize, cassava, *bataten* (sweet potatoes), fruit and fish have been mentioned. With respect to the well-to-do, meat and dairy products may be included.

There is little information about these supplementary foodstuffs other than the annual production figures of the most important ones (maize, cassava and *bataten*).

Only the *bataten* harvest approximately maintained the pre-war level of 1.3 million tons throughout the Japanese occupation.

The maize harvest decreased steadily: from 2.2 million tons in 1942 (an average of 2.1 million in the period 1937-1941) to 1.6 million in 1943, 1.2 million in 1944, 0.9 million in 1945 – in other words, in comparison to the years 1937-1941 a decrease of four sevenths.

Equally catastrophic was the decline of the cassava harvest: from 8.7 million tons in 1942 (an average of 8.2 million in the years 1937-1941) to 7.5 million in 1943, 5.3 million in 1944 and 3.1 million in 1945 – in other words, in comparison to the years 1937-1941 a decrease of more than three fifths.

These falls were compounded by those of the *padi* harvest, which decreased by one third compared to the years 1937-1941.

Data for fish and meat are available only with regard to the black market prices: a pound of meat that had cost 24 cents in 1942-1943, cost 1.20 guilders on East Java in 1944 and a piece of steamed fish 12 cents instead of 3 cents. Furthermore, a coconut that had cost 2 cents before the war fetched 2 guilders in Semarang in July 1945 and the price of a bottle of peanut oil which had been 12 cents before the war had risen to 3.50 guilders in Jakarta by February 1945.

As for dairy products, we only know that in Bandung in April 1944 Bouwer (1988:252) recorded: 'For a quarter ounce of butter people are queuing up at 3:30 at night in front of the Bandung Milk Centre. [...] We haven't laid eyes on cheese in years.'

Duck eggs were rationed in July of 1944 in Bandung for the official price of 7 cents – they promptly cost 20 cents on the *pasar* ('and the *pasar* police, the so-called price monitors', Bouwer (1988:272-3) noted, 'do nothing about this'). A year later the price of a duck egg was 90 cents; 'a chicken varied, depending on age and "fat content" between 9 and 20 guilders a piece' (Bouwer 1988:359).

Most people by far were unable to pay these high prices. The same applied to the products of the larger and smaller industries. The shortage of textiles became particularly dire. What was available on Java in 1942 in the way of cotton fabrics at the weaving mills and wholesalers, was confiscated by the Japanese army. 'Textiles are nowhere to be found', a Dutch Eurasian later remarked on the situation at the end of 1942.

> In the past months we have had to sell quite a lot of white bedding because we desperately needed the money to live on. White sheets command a good price since the Indonesians [...] can no longer make white fabrics. Their dead absolutely have to be buried wrapped in white cloth, you know. This is why they will go to great lengths to obtain such material. (Jalhay 1981:210-1.)

As mentioned above, the Japanese had cotton planted. The yield was disappointing. Here and there new spinning mills were set up and manual spinning machines from Japan were handed out, yet this failed to alleviate the shortage of textiles. The scant amount that became available was parcelled out as of 1943 on the orders of the Japanese, but this rationing, which was very uneven (it applied in one district and not in another), remained limited to the farmers who had delivered enough rice. In 1944 clothing was made of substitute materials including jute, rubber, and even tree bark. Attempts to make clothing from the leaves of the banana palm failed.

Obviously the prices for textiles on the black market constantly rose. In 1945 a cotton cloth, the asking price of which before the war had been 75 cents, cost 25 to 30 guilders.

There were shortages of everything that was machine-made and the quality of what was produced was usually very poor. In Bandung in July 1944 Bouwer (1988:272) wrote:

> Toothpaste manufactured here dries out after two days and cannot be squeezed from the (paper) tube. A pencil made here is half lost due to repeated sharpening, and at most you can write your name with it three times before having to throw it away. [...] Toothbrushes, shaving brushes and brooms 'shed' after having been used only once.

Paper too became scarce. This was already the case in the first year of the occupation. The Japanese military administration then proceeded to circulate administrative KNIL and navy documents as wrapping paper. Lieutenant Vromans, who had been head of supplies in the navy department, later wrote that while he was confined in a prisoner-of-war camp in Batavia from April 1942 to January 1943, 'someone kept coming to him to announce: "Colonel, here's another piece of paper with your name on it"; this was wrapped around an ounce of rice or meat or the like'.[57] Various editions of the New Testament

---

[57]   A.G. Vromans, 'Notities bij het achtste verslag van de Enquêtecommissie', n.d., p. 114.

that were stored as unbound flat sheets at the Dutch Bible Association in Bandung were also used by the Japanese as wrapping paper. Due to a shortage of fat, good soap could no longer be manufactured. In Bandung in May 1944, a piece of this inferior soap cost 85 cents to 1 guilder in the store. The price of a piece of pre-war soap ranged from 20 to 125 guilders on the black market at the time.

Cigarettes were rationed in May 1944: one pack per week per family for 30 cents. In Bandung rationing began on 15 May – a year later one had to pay 2.50 guilders or more for the most popular brands. Loose tobacco was cheaper and one could roll cigarettes with it, but good cigarette paper was also 'very scarce', according to Bouwer (1988:342).

Comparable price increases also occurred on the black market in the occupied Netherlands and reached excessive levels in the west of the country during the so-called hunger winter in 1944-1945, when all goods had become very scarce and many people in the urban areas were in dire need primarily due to a shortage of fuel and food. Earlier, however, the black market in the occupied Netherlands had been a marginal phenomenon; bolstered by strict price controls and a swift administration of economic justice, rationing had functioned well there. On Java, in contrast, price control had been a shot in the dark from the onset and the police and the courts never succeeded in getting a grip on the black market, and, at least this is my impression, they hardly even tried to. Consequently, the cost of living rose, fueled also by the increase of money in circulation.

In 1946 the Central Office for Statistics, which was then functioning again in Batavia, gave some idea of this increase, though solely with respect to the expenditures of non-interned Dutch Eurasians – this is discussed in further detail in Chapter VI. Comparable statistics regarding the expenditures of Indonesians are lacking. Incidentally, this data would be of value only if statistics of their income development were also available, and these too are absent.[58] We do know, as indicated above, that the prices of textiles had risen so steeply that only a very few could buy them, and basic foods such as rice also became increasingly expensive on the free, that is to say, black, market. One should bear in mind, though, that rice was also offered at official, low prices. However, the amounts were ampler in urban centres and other populated places than in the rural districts. It is useful to recall the findings

[58]   That the incomes were too low was acknowledged in August 1943 by the Japanese military administration on Java, when it ordered everyone working for the government (a privileged group!) on the occasion of the Muslim New Year to be paid a half month's salary extra. Whether it was also paid out in 1944 is not known.

of the investigative committee that was set up in December 1944: while in Jakarta the daily rice ration was 180 grams (and in Garut 120, in Kediri 150, in Pekalongan 230), outside of the cities rice rations were 'in general limited to civil servants', and the 'common folk' received virtually nothing. In a *desa* in the Bandung regency the ration was 32 grams per day per person; in a district in the Bogor residency 30 grams per day per house; and in a district in the Bojonegoro residency 20 grams per day per family. The Indonesian population on Java suffered immeasurably during the last two years of the Japanese occupation, and presumably more in rural areas (except the farmers themselves) than in urban ones. The Japanese requisitions, the failed harvests of 1943 and 1944, the inflation, the feeble structure of the governmental machine and the all pervasive corruption gave rise to a society in which the weak succumbed in large numbers.

Medical care for the population drastically deteriorated. The Dutch physicians, dentists and pharmacists were interned in the course of 1943 and numerous hospitals had been requisitioned by the Japanese.[59] Perhaps even worse was that there was hardly any medicine anymore. In 1942 the Japanese had seized large supplies and, as noted above, nothing was imported from Japan. In January 1944 Bouwer (1988:232) recorded in Bandung that many fake medicines were being sold:

> The most fantastic swindling occurs in this area. Empty tubes of Cibasol tablets[60] are sold for 15 guilders, as long as they bear the brand name Cibasol. The tubes are then filled with calcium tablets and sold for 80 guilders per tube of 20 tablets. [...] Most patented medicines are also [...] fakes.

More than three months later he wrote:

> Presently, the scarcity of medicine in the city is such that patients who, for example, need to enter a hospital for an operation have to bring their own ether, cotton, gauze and other medicine, otherwise they will not be admitted. If a patient cannot supply ether, he is operated on without anaesthetic [...]. Family or acquaintances also have to take care of feeding the hospitalized patient. Operation wounds are sutured with Brook's thread[61] and the surgeons in the city [...] are presently appealing to the public to hand in thread of said brand for this purpose. (Bouwer 1988:249-50.)

The shortage of soap was felt not just in the hospitals but throughout society. In September 1944 in the Pati residency (northeast of Semarang), according to

---

[59]   In October 1944, Indonesian physicians, dentists and pharmacists were allowed to continue their work only if they would also treat the Japanese armed forces.
[60]   These were tablets containing a sulpha preparation for the treatment of infections and fever.
[61]   This was regular sewing thread.

a report by an Indonesian,[62] it emerged 'that a large part of the population is suffering from scabies. Malaria too is rampant.' This residency was relatively poor. Presumably, the same illnesses also occurred elsewhere but to a lesser extent, although it is a plausible assumption that as quinine became scarce and expensive (evidently as a consequence of large Japanese requisitions), malaria claimed more lives during the years of occupation than before the war.

Nevertheless, the greatest ravages were wrought by hunger. A Dutch Eurasian woman later recalled the situation in Batavia in 1944:[63]

> The misery outside was a sight not to be borne. Beggars draped in burlap sacks or entirely naked with the most hideous wounds were lying by the side of the road. Their faces [were] like a full moon and their stomachs incredibly swollen. Downtown I saw several bodies being loaded onto a garbage truck; with his booted foot a Jap kicked many other poor wretches who, if they showed a sign of life, were allowed to remain lying there. [...] Poverty, poverty and misery everywhere! No medicine and no clothing, no food. My God, I thought, how long must this go on?

On Central Java in September 1944, an Indonesian[64] 'repeatedly [saw] people walking around with no clothes at all or in rags'.

Writing about December 1944, the author Beb Vuyk (1962:255) recounted:

> The beggar who had been lying under the tree in front of the bakery for weeks is dead. Every day beggars die; their bodies remain along the side of the road and are removed once a day by the garbage truck. [...] 'He died in the afternoon and lay there until the following afternoon', the baker's wife told me. [...] His place has already been taken by a woman with a child. She lies on a piece of old matting, another strip of it bound around her waist, around her enormous swollen belly. Her arms and legs are sticks and her face bloated from oedema, so that her eyes appear to be deeply sunken. The child is a skeleton clawing like an animal at the empty flaps of skin that are her breasts. A rash covers its entire head. I place a couple of *pisangs* [bananas] next to her. She snatches them from under my hand and begins to eat them peel and all. When I'm standing in the bakery, I see her feeding her child with bits she has chewed.

In his Bandung hiding place in June 1945, Bouwer heard from:

> people who frequently go to the city, [...] that daily one sees the corpses of Indonesians who have died from starvation lying in the streets. Not a day passes that bodies are not found under viaducts, in air-raid shelters and in unfinished dwellings.[65]

[62] Text in Brugmans 1960:498
[63] Text from her report in Brugmans 1960:601.
[64] Text from his report in Brugmans 1960:496.
[65] J.B. Bouwer, 'Dagboek', 8 June 1945, p. 340 (NIOD IC).

How many casualties were there throughout all of Java?

According to Regent Gandasubrata (1953:11), in the Banyumas regency 'at the peak of the shortage' (presumably at the beginning of 1944) out of a population totalling 740,000, 32,000 were suffering from starvation: thus more than 4%. But that figure says nothing about the number of starving people in this one regency during the occupation as a whole. Reliable birth and mortality figures are known only for the Batavia residency for the period from January 1943 to June 1945. Before the Japanese occupation one and half times more people were born than died in this residency; however, in the first six months of 1945 almost twice as many people died than were born. Figures for all of the residencies on Java and Madura are known only for the years 1943 and 1944. While extrapolating the figures for Batavia, in May 1946 a statistician concluded in the *Economisch Weekblad voor Nederlandsch-Indië*[66] that 'without taking into account [...] the Javanese forced labourers, who were removed by the Japanese', on Java and Madura in 1943 there had been a death surplus of 120,000 people, in 1944 of 813,000, and in 1945 of approximately 1,500,000 – constituting a total of about 2,250,000, to which should still be added the *romusha* who died outside of Java (at least 200,000).

Approximately 2,500,000 deaths would appear to be a realistic estimate. That figure should be set against a total population numbering close to 50 million.[67]

No wonder the comparison between the circumstances people had known under Dutch rule and those which arose under Japanese rule was soon seen as most unfavourable to the Japanese. In 1942 the Japanese got a grip on the vast majority of nationalists and groups of Indonesian youths allowed themselves then (and later) to be won over by Japanese slogans, but 'the ordinary, older *kampung* population remained virtually impervious to this', according to a Nippon worker who in 1942 travelled to Batavia's city *kampung* 'many times [...] in order to gauge the mood of the population. [...] The primary complaints were those related to a lack of food and clothing.'[68] And this as early as 1942! In April 1943 the Japanese military administration in Bandung noticed that the city's inhabitants exhibited a distinct lack of enthusiasm during the celebration of Hirohito's birthday.[69] In the same place six months later, in October 1943, Bouwer was visited by an Indonesian friend who worked in

---

[66]   Volume XII, no. 8 (4 May 1946), p. 43.

[67]   Of those who were cared for in psychiatric institutions it would appear that the great majority died: they received even less food than those in prison. In one institution in Pekalongan (Central Java) of the 4,000 patients only 900 survived.

[68]   O. Peltzer, 'De Japanse bezetting tot 16 december 1944', 30 August, 1946, p. 3 (NIOD IC).

[69]   The Japanese military administration in Bandung, Monthly report for April 1943, p. 1 (ARA, Alg. Secr., Eerste zending, XXVI, 17).

the translation department of the headquarters of the State Railways:

> He immediately relayed some important news regarding the openly expressed dissatisfaction among virtually all of the Indonesian personnel at the government offices. [...] Many Indonesians, who at the beginning of the Japanese occupation had shouted: 'Never again under the Dutch!', now ask: 'When will this end? When is the Dutch government returning?' The primary reasons for this are: poor payment, poor treatment (beating and more beating) [...] and constantly having to honour any Japanese peasant who is now 'department head'. Every time a Japanese enters the room, the entire personnel jumps up and has to bow. This happens 20 to 30 times a day. (Bouwer 1988:215-6.)

Bouwer (1988:241-2) wrote in March 1944:

> I have [...] a good indication of the dissatisfaction of the population. The Japanese have taught the Indonesians various anti-Allied songs. The timetables of all of the Indonesian schools begin every morning with an hour-long rehearsal of these songs. [...] One [...] has the following refrain: *Hancurkanlah! Musuh kita! Itulah Inggris dan Amerika!* ('Destroy our enemies England and America!'). The people have changed it to *Hancurkanlah! Bola merah! Datang lekas, Amerika!* or 'Destroy the red ball! Come soon, America!'

Finally, at the end of 1944 a Nippon worker then still active as a technical expert in the harbour of Cilacap[70] heard from 'someone who kept me informed about the mood in his *kampung*, [...] that people there spoke openly about the arrival of the Americans and when the Dutch would be back here again'. Yet: 'In general, the teachers were anti-Dutch'.

We dare to put forward the thesis that, just as in the occupied Netherlands where the Germans were held fully responsible for the shortages, in the Indies as a whole and especially on Java resentment against the Japanese grew among the masses due to the staggering poverty that had begun to manifest itself under *their* rule. When Indonesians spoke of the desire for a speedy return to 'normal living conditions', *'jaman normal'*, they meant the Dutch period.

At a rough estimate, one out of twenty inhabitants of Java died during the Japanese occupation. It should be borne in mind that more than half of the political prisoners who were confined in prisons on Java lost their lives. The chance of survival for those who remained at liberty was substantially greater.

This conclusion serves as an appropriate transition to the two chapters which describe the fate of the two large groups who were robbed of their freedom: the prisoners of war and the internees.

---

[70] Report, 25 January 1946 in Brugmans 1960:327-9.

CHAPTER IV

Prisoners of war

Let us begin by giving a few figures – not without some hesitation because several are unverifiable. In 1978, more than 30 years after the war, a precise comparison between the information available in the archives of the Dutch Navy and of the KNIL was made by Major H.L. Zwitzer, who was attached to the War History Section (now Military History Section) of the Staff of the Commander of Land Forces.[1] He concluded that of the European troops in the Dutch East Indies a total of 42,233 became prisoners of war: 3,847 Dutch naval personnel, 36,869 KNIL soldiers and 1,517 members of KNIL auxiliary corps.[2] In captivity 648 of the naval personnel died (16.8%) as well as 7,552 KNIL soldiers and members of associated formations (19.6%). Thus, out of the total of 42,233 European prisoners of war, 8,200 died (19.4%). Roughly speaking, one in five of the European prisoners lost their lives. Moreover, many of the survivors (how many is unknown) suffered permanent physical or mental damage as a result of the terrible suffering they endured as prisoners.

We are thus on firm ground as regards the figures for European troops, but as soon as we venture further we find ourselves in a morass of uncertainty: there are no accurate figures for the indigenous naval personnel or the indigenous KNIL soldiers. While this was only a small group in the case of the seaborne navy, that did not apply to the KNIL, which consisted of a total of about 65,000 troops (of whom some 800 were killed) in the months of the Japanese invasion, including 23,000 indigenous soldiers from different ethnic backgrounds. In 1937 the KNIL included nearly 13,000 Javanese, nearly 2,000 Sundanese, over 5,000 Manadonese, about 4,000 Ambonese and over 1,000 Timorese, making 25,000 indigenous troops in all. The total number was thus slightly lower at the time of the Japanese invasion, and it is not known what proportion belonged to the different ethnic groups at that point. It was certainly not the case that over 23,000 indigenous soldiers fell into Japanese hands. Both on the Outer Islands and on Java many of them deserted after the

---

[1] His figures may be found in *Mededelingen van de Sectie Krijgsgeschiedenis*, Vol. I, no. 1 (1978).
[2] Stadswachten: 816, Landwachten: 122, Removal and Demolition Corps: 307, Reserve Corps: 272.

Japanese landed: how many were taken prisoner is unknown. The Javanese and Sundanese among those captured were soon released, but initially the Japanese held on to most of the Manadonese, Ambonese and Timorese. It should be noted that the Japanese quite soon made a distinction between the European (Dutch and Dutch Eurasian) and the indigenous prisoners of war. In Bandung they also distinguished between the Dutch and the Eurasians among them. We shall now leave aside the subject of the indigenous prisoners in the rest of this introduction and return to them later in this chapter.

Most of the Dutch and Dutch Eurasian prisoners of war did not stay on the islands where they had been during the invasion months. Those on Borneo did, but most prisoners on the other islands were moved elsewhere. On all Borneo, including British Borneo, the Japanese took about 4,500 prisoners according to their own figures,[3] and of them 2,067 (KNIL, British and Indian troops) were transferred to British Borneo in 1942. This was because British Borneo came under the Japanese army, and the Japanese navy had undertaken to hand over all its prisoners to the army. In fact, including on Borneo, the navy only partly kept to this agreement, continuing to hold about 700 KNIL prisoners of war in its sector of the island.

On Celebes in July 1942, apart from the indigenous prisoners, there were rougly 2,700 soldiers in captivity: about 800 from the KNIL, 885 British troops and 185 Americans (survivors of the Battle of the Java Sea) together with 830 seamen of the Dutch navy (survivors of the same battle and navy men who had been on board two ships which had left Cilacap bound for Australia but had been intercepted by the Japanese). Before July 1942, namely in April, a number of officers and other survivors from the cruisers which had been sunk by the Japanese navy, in total about 500 men, were sent to Japan to be interrogated again. They were treated reasonably, and it is worth noting that Japanese naval officers sometimes showed a measure of respect for Allied naval personnel that was entirely lacking in the attitude of the Japanese to Allied soldiers.[4] Finally, as regards Celebes, it should be added that some

---

[3]   It was not until 1982 that these figures were published by the Japanese S. Adachi in No. 45 of *Studies of Cultural and Social Sciences*, published by the National Defense Academy in Yokohama. The subtitle of Adachi's study is 'A brief history of Japanese practices on treatment of Allied war victims during the Second World War' and the telling formulation in the title is 'Unprepared regrettable events' ('unprepared' no doubt means 'unintentional'). The tenor of this study is that the intentions of the Japanese authorities were beyond reproach, but that in practice everything went wrong. Some responsibility for the latter failure is accepted. Adachi (1982:324) writes: 'Practices of maltreatment of enemy personnel by Japan had left [a] considerable scar in the Japanese mind'.
[4]   In this connection it is worth recording that the 32 survivors of the Dutch submarine O 20, which was sunk by a Japanese destroyer on 19 December 1941 off the coast of Malacca, were taken to Saigon by a second destroyer and interrogated. In January 1942 they were transferred to Hong Kong, where they arrived on 22 December. A few days later two officers, A.M. Idema and

of the prisoners of war left behind there were moved to Java in 1943, 1944 and 1945. According to Japanese figures, 1,411 prisoners of war were still on Celebes in April 1945.

On Sumatra about 4,500 Dutch and Dutch Eurasian and about 1,200 British and Australian troops were taken prisoner. Of them around 1,500 Dutch and Dutch Eurasian and about 500 British prisoners were sent to Burma in May 1942 to work first with Australian prisoners on building airfields and later with large numbers of *romusha* on the northern section of the railway that was to link Thailand and Burma, the Burma Railway. The prisoners who had remained behind on Sumatra were subsequently used for two tasks: the construction of a road in Aceh which provided a through route from the east to the west coast and the construction of the Pekanbaru Railway, which served the same function. The railway was completed on the day on which the surrender of Japan was announced, 15 August 1945.

The Japanese had taken the most prisoners, about 70,800, on Java, among them about 900 Americans, 2,800 Australians, 10,600 British and 56,500 seamen from the Dutch navy and soldiers from the KNIL (including indigenous troops). As mentioned above, most of the indigenous prisoners were soon released. In October 1942 nearly 700 (almost all Dutch Eurasians) of the remaining prisoners and in September 1943 another 3,400 were taken to Japan to work in mines, factories and docks there. From October 1942 onwards most of the Americans and Australians and about 16,500 Dutch and Dutch Eurasian prisoners were transferred to Burma and Thailand to work on the Burma Railway. Around 45% of all the non-indigenous prisoners taken by the Japanese in the Nampo area[5] were set to work on this project. When the railway was finished (in October 1943) some of the surviving pris-

---

R.J. Hordijk, together with a Canadian naval officer, succeeded in getting out of the camp at night through a sewer. They emerged above ground just behind the Japanese headquarters. Helped by Chinese, they stayed hidden for several days at various places, and it was also Chinese who found a rowing boat for them. With this and a second boat (the first capsized when they reached the Hong Kong mainland), they reached the Chinese coast on the 11th day of their escape. Money was collected for them in a poor village and they were shown an area where there were guerrillas of the Chinese Nationalist Army. They were taken there by proa and a second proa brought them to the headquarters of one of Chang Kai-shek's generals. The three escapees were joined by four British officers who had also got away from Hong Kong and a family from Manila. After a journey by foot and train they reached a town where they received their first telegram from the Dutch embassy in Chungking (they had been able to inform the embassy of their escape by telegram from another town). On 10 April they flew to Calcutta and eight days later were able to report themselves all present and correct to Admiral Helfrich in Colombo (Ceylon), or more accurately (according to Frank Visser in his account of this escape in *De Schakel; De geschiedenis van de Engelandvaarders* (1976:253)): 'present after some delay'.
5   They numbered 142,766: 50,016 British, 42,233 Dutch and Dutch Eurasians, 26,943 Americans (most of them prisoners of war taken on the Philippines), 21,762 Australians, 1,691 Canadians (captured on Hong Kong) and 121 New Zealanders.

oners were kept on to carry out maintenance or stayed in Thailand for other reasons; a second group was sent back to Singapore and put to work there; a third group was taken to French Indo-China to build airfields; and a fourth group, which included numerous Dutch prisoners (and only a few Dutch Eurasians), was sent to Japan. In the end more than a quarter, that is 27%, of all non-indigenous prisoners of war were made to work in Japan.

Four other groups of prisoners from Java were deployed elsewhere. In April 1943 3,540 Dutch and Dutch Eurasian and 2,760 British prisoners were shipped to Flores and the Moluccas to build airfields. Most of the survivors of these groups were brought back to Java in 1944. In November 1943 around 2,000 prisoners, half Dutch and Dutch Eurasian, half British, were taken to South Sumatra to build airfields in the Palembang district. Starting in the beginning of May, a total of about 5,500 prisoners (mainly Dutch and Dutch Eurasians combined with British, Australians, Ambonese, Manadonese and a few Americans) were taken in three groups to Central Sumatra to work on the Pekanbaru Railway. Lastly, in September 1944 around 750 prisoners were transported to Singapore to help excavate a dry dock; smaller groups were sent later for various other types of work.

During the months of the invasion the Japanese also took prisoners on Ambon and Timor: on Ambon about 250 Dutch and Dutch Eurasian and 800 Australian troops, and on Timor about 1,000 Dutch and Dutch Eurasian and 1,000 Australian troops. In October 1942 nearly all the Dutch and Dutch Eurasians and about 260 Australians were taken from Ambon to Hainan and put to work there. The remaining Australians stayed on Ambon and no group of prisoners of war received worse treatment: four-fifths of them died. Of the prisoners on Timor, the Australians were sent to New Britain, while the Dutch and Dutch Eurasians were added either to the groups on Java or to those on Celebes.

Is this survey complete? Not yet. It should be added that 572 Dutch and Dutch Eurasian merchant mariners who had been interned as civilians on Java in a camp near Bandung were suddenly given the status of prisoners of war in July 1944. They were put to work in Batavia. About half of this group, principally the masters and other officers, were added in September 1944 to the approximately 750 other prisoners of war who were sent to Singapore, as mentioned above. The other half, that is, the younger officers, were put to work on the Pekanbaru Railway.

In the above description the number of deaths among these groups of Dutch and Dutch Eurasian prisoners during work on the various projects has not been given: where figures are available they will be given later in this chapter. It should be pointed out that of the total of 8,200 who died, many drowned while being transported by sea; according to the Japanese figures, almost 11,000 Allied prisoners of war died in this way.

Only the bare figures have been given in this introductory survey. Behind them lies a world of suffering and it is this world that we shall try to portray, often following the overview completed by E. van Witsen in 1971 after years of research,[6] and above all by using the accounts of the prisoners themselves. It will become apparent that the Japanese completely disregarded the norms for humane behaviour that applied in the Western world as well as most of the regulations governing the treatment of prisoners of war that were derived from the Geneva Convention of 1929.

Japan and its prisoners of war

In the course of their eventful history, the Japanese had never taken prisoners in their campaigns against each other. Their norms required that a warrior must fight to the death: if he failed in that he was usually killed by the victor. If that was not the case, that is, if after being held as a prisoner of war he was able to return home, then he would be put to death there because this was seen as the only way in which he could expunge the disgrace he had brought on his family, other relatives and forefathers.

Japan was well aware, after ending two and a half centuries of isolation in 1854, that other countries had different views regarding prisoners of war. Indeed, it made special efforts from then on to show that its treatment of prisoners was exemplary. This first became apparent with the Chinese troops captured in the Sino-Japanese War of 1894-1895. In the Russo-Japanese War of 1904-1905 nearly 80,000 Russian soldiers were taken prisoner: the Japanese gave them more food and better clothing than their own troops had. The Russians were allowed to receive money and goods, and those who had wives living in Siberia were able to lead a normal family life in the prisoner-of-war camps. It was the same in the First World War: in the Germany territory in China and on the Caroline, Mariana and Marshall Islands, which were then German colonies, Japan took several thousand German prisoners, who were held in particularly agreeable camps in Japanese holiday resorts where not a hair on their head was touched.

In the second half of the 1920s international talks were held in Geneva to draw up rules laying down the precise rights and duties of prisoners of war and of the powers holding them, in accordance with what had become normal practice in most countries in the nineteenth and twentieth centuries.

---

[6]   A photocopy of his study 'Over krijgsgevangenen in Japanse handen' (On prisoners of war in Japanese hands), numbering nearly 700 pages, is in the collections of the Nederlands Instituut voor Oorlogsdocumentatie. An earlier version was published in 1971 under the title *Krijgsgevangenen in de Pacific-oorlog, 1941-1945* (Prisoners of war in the Pacific War, 1941-1945).

The principal provisions of the 'Convention on the treatment of prisoners of war' that resulted were as follows.

The Convention stipulated that prisoners of war should always be humanely treated and protected. Reprisals against them were prohibited. They had to be housed in buildings or barracks that guaranteed hygienic conditions and proper sanitation. Their rations had to be equivalent to those of the depot troops of the power holding them prisoner. That power must also provide them with adequate clothing, linen and footwear. Prisoners were also to be given opportunities for physical exercise and spending time in the open air. Medical inspections were to be held at least once a month. Healthy prisoners, with the exception of officers, could be given work to do; in the case of non-commissioned officers this could only be guard duties unless they explicitly asked to do paid work, that is, economically productive work. However, Article 31 of the Convention contained an important restriction with respect to work carried out by NCOs and other ranks:

> Labour furnished by prisoners of war shall have no direct relation with war operations. It is especially prohibited to use prisoners for manufacturing and transporting arms or munitions of any kind or for transporting material intended for combatant units.

Prisoners were also supposed to be able to send a fixed number of letters and postcards that were subject to censorship. They could receive letters, postcards, parcels, money and books, but the power holding them had the right to examine this post.

Prisoners could be punished. Cruel and collective punishments for acts committed by a few individuals were forbidden, but military or judicial punishments were permissible, the latter for example in cases where a prisoner of war had committed a crime while in captivity. An attempt to escape was not a crime, but it could be punished, for example by a period in detention of up to 30 days (a military penalty) or by a regime of stricter security. In the case of escaped prisoners no punishments other than military penalties were allowed.

The rules to be observed by each power that was a signatory to the Convention were thus strict (only the most important have been described here). What if such a power broke these rules? The Convention included provisions dealing with such cases. Prisoners had the right to complain to the camp commandant; they also had the right to complain to the representatives of the so-called Protecting Powers. These representatives were empowered to visit every place where prisoners were being held, and the prisoners there were to be allowed to talk to them in person.

What if the prisoners' complaints were justified? On this point the Convention said nothing. It was clear, however, what should then happen:

the Protecting Powers would call for improvements and inform the power whose interests they were looking after.

The International Red Cross in Geneva also had an important role in this situation. It was to be the body through which the belligerents gave each other information about the prisoners, through which messages from and to prisoners could be exchanged by the belligerents, and through which prisoners could be sent help in the form of food parcels and clothing.

The Convention was signed by the Japanese delegation in Geneva. It was not, however, accepted by the Japanese government, and so not submitted to parliament for approval or ratified. The Japanese armed forces opposed acceptance, their principal argument being that in a war far fewer Japanese soldiers (they had been taught that they must never surrender) than soldiers on the other side would be taken prisoner, so that in applying the Convention Japan would take on much greater obligations than its opponents. But other factors also played a role: irritation in Japanese ruling circles at being constantly opposed by the United States in particular, and the growing acceptance of the idea that the Japanese were the noblest people on earth and thus above such things as international agreements. Added to this, from 1937, was a coarsening that resulted from the war with China, in which from the outset Japanese soldiers robbed and murdered civilians on a large scale – prisoners of war were also killed. All these developments meant that the Japanese troops (whose official regulations said: 'Do not live to bear the shame of being taken prisoner'[7]) who entered into the Second World War at the end of 1941 generally (there were exceptions) felt a deep contempt for the Allied soldiers who fell into their hands: they had not fought to the death and so deserved no better than to be treated like slaves. It should also be noted, however, that the Japanese lower ranks were not treated a great deal better by their officers: they were beaten, they were given meagre rations and scant attention was paid to their medical care. Nonetheless, this did not prevent them in turn from feeling themselves elevated far above all Allied prisoners.

Naturally, Japan's enemies were aware that it had not accepted the Geneva Convention and they were already concerned about this in December 1941. British and Canadian troops had been taken prisoner in Hong Kong, as had British troops on British North Borneo and American troops on Guam and

---

[7]   American and British troops took very few Japanese prisoners during the war: as opposed to approximately 140,000 Allied prisoners held by the Japanese, in October 1944 the Allies had only about 6,000 Japanese prisoners. Some of these Japanese prisoners refused to give their names; they wanted to spare their families the shame of knowing that a family member was a prisoner. Other Japanese did give their names, which were passed on to Tokyo together with their personal messages through the International Red Cross. The Japanese authorities did nothing with this information; the families were not informed.

Wake. The American government contacted the Japanese authorities through the Swiss envoy in Tokyo and urged them to declare that they would act in accordance with the provisions of the Convention. After consulting the Supreme Headquarters (of the Japanese army and navy), the Japanese government gave this undertaking at the end of January 1942 to the governments of the United States, Great Britain and the British dominions. Shortly afterwards it added that this undertaking also applied to the Netherlands[8] and that it covered interned civilians as well.

This was no more than a gesture in the direction of the internationally agreed rules: had the Japanese government intended to observe those rules, it would have had to inform the navy and army staffs about the provisions of the Convention in good time and make sure that they were complied with. Neither step was taken: the staffs were given no information and the Supreme Headquarters would tolerate no interference from ministries. The result was that in the first months of the war in the Pacific it was the staffs of the armies deployed in the Nampo which decided what should be done with prisoners of war. There were great differences: on Java General Imamura initially allowed prisoners a measure of freedom; in Singapore and on Malacca they were immediately put to work; and on Luzon in April 1942 a large number of the defenders of the Bataan peninsula had to make a forced march and a train journey to their first camp during which about 8,000 of them died.

At the end of April 1942, Tojo, the Prime Minister and Minister of War, chaired a meeting of all section heads of the War Department that was mainly devoted to the question how the non-indigenous prisoners of war were to be treated (it had already been decided to release the indigenous prisoners). Lieutenant General Mikio Murakami, the head of the recently established Prisoners of War Bureau, which came under the War Department, urged that Japan should observe the Geneva Convention in accordance with the undertakings it had given. Tojo rejected this argument. He claimed that the Greater East Asian War was intended to liberate Asia and was therefore unique in character; it must be used to impress upon the indigenous peoples the superiority of Japan. Not only must the prisoners of war, officers and men, be made to work, but this must be humiliating work carried out in front of the indigenous people.[9] An instruction on these lines was issued at the beginning of May, and at the end of June and beginning of July Tojo emphasized its importance in discussions he had with the officers in charge of supervising prisoner-of-war camps in Japan, Korea and Formosa, and in the conquered territories in the Nampo. They were also informed that any prisoner guilty

8   The Netherlands had not been mentioned at first because Japan had not declared war on it.
9   KNIL prisoners of war had to clean the streets of Batavia. Similar orders were given elsewhere.

of insubordination or an attempt to escape must be put to death – this policy had already been adopted in the Nampo on the officers' own initiative.

A new conference was held in Tokyo early in August 1942, now under the chairmanship of General Murakami, who had ordered no less than 50 camp commandants to attend. He pressed for prisoners of war to be decently treated, in part to protect Japan's reputation abroad. He said that it had been decided to separate the different nationalities among the prisoners and to give them a clear status: they were to be thought of as Japanese soldiers of the lowest rank. As such, they would receive pay and their officers would be allowed to wear their badges of rank again, which had been taken from them in many cases. In return they would have to work hard and make a solemn declaration of obedience. On 15 August instructions to this effect were issued; regulations were then drafted in which everything was set out in detail – it was August 1943 before these regulations came into force.

Meanwhile Tokyo had become aware in the last months of 1942 that a great number of prisoners of war in the Nampo region had died. In December 1942 General Murakami issued an order to all army command-ants that the prisoners of war must be better treated. This order did not have the slightest effect in the Nampo. Murakami's Bureau was only influential in Japan, Korea, Manchuria, Formosa and occupied China; it had no control at all over what happened in the Nampo region. According to the Supreme Headquarters, that was a war zone: no outsiders were allowed to enter it (this also applied to representatives of the Protecting Powers and to rep-resentatives of the International Red Cross) and the highest commandants there were not to be pestered.

In turn, the highest commandants felt no need to give Tokyo timely inform-ation. Each commandant of a prisoner-of-war camp had to draw up a report once a month, and they tended to spend quite some time on this. On Java these reports went to the headquarters of the 16th Army. Headquarters forwarded them to Singapore. There they were gathered together once every six months for the benefit of General Terauchi's headquarters and he then sent them to Tokyo. A whole year might easily pass between the writing of the reports and their arrival at General Murakami's Bureau. However, lists with names of prisoners were passed on more quickly, a point we shall come back to.

There are two final points to be made about the policy laid down by Tokyo. The first is that the rice ration of 420 grams per day (640 grams for heavy work) stipulated for prisoners of war was lowered in July 1944 to 390 grams (610 grams for heavy work), whereby it should be said that no prisoner ever received the rice ration officially laid down. The second point is that in the last six months of the war on several occasions the War Department ordered that at no price should prisoners be allowed to fall into Allied hands alive. In Japan and elsewhere these commands led to the digging of long trenches, and the prisoners themselves had the impression that they were intended for their bodies. After Japan's surrender, an order from the War Department was found which said that, as soon as the Americans landed in Japan, the prisoners of war working in the mines were to be driven into a mine shaft and killed. On Java, according to an anti-Japanese Korean who worked in the prisoners of war department of the Japanese headquarters, there was a plan as early as October 1944 to provoke the prisoners and high-ranking internees into rioting if Allied landings were imminent and to use this as an excuse to slaughter them. If the provocations had no effect, they were to be taken from the camps in groups and killed far away from the cities.[10] Because of Japan's surrender, these and other similar orders were not carried out at most places, but they were at some. On Wake and on one of the southern islands in the Philippines several hundred American prisoners of war were killed in the final days of the war. On North Borneo over 2,700 British and Australian prisoners who were building an airfield were driven into the jungle: six managed to escape, all the others died or were killed.

In the case of the Nampo region, the regulations and orders issued by Tokyo have only limited significance: there the prisoners of war (and Japan's own soldiers) were made to work in circumstances in which, as long as the target set, for example completing the Burma Railway, was reached, the number of lives sacrificed had absolutely no importance ('We are faced here', wrote Van Witsen, 'with a sort of ant heap mentality among the Japanese, who are able to see the individual only as a part of the whole'[11]). The regulations and orders were carried out only to the extent that they were seen to serve the war effort. In fact, in some cases orders and rules were issued before they were announced by Tokyo.

Before turning to the actual treatment of the prisoners of war in the East Indies, it is worth looking more closely at a few aspects of Japanese policy which made the fate of the prisoners harder to bear and which have already been referred to in general. They are that in the Nampo region Japan made it impossible for representatives of the Protecting Powers to monitor conditions; it obstructed the work of the representatives of the International Red Cross; it allowed very few aid consignments to be delivered; and, in the absence of international supervision, most of these were appropriated by Japanese troops.

In only one respect did the Japanese authorities make any effort: they did

[10]   Report by Li Uck-Kwam to the Allied War Crimes Investigation Committee, 23 April 1946 (NIOD IC, 1,347).
[11]   E. van Witsen, 'Over krijgsgevangenen in Japanse handen', p. 213.

pass on the names of prisoners of war in telegrams to the International Red Cross, beginning in May 1942. The Dutch government in London received 363 lists with a total of 46,177 names – more names, in other words, than there were Dutch and Dutch Eurasian prisoners (who numbered 42,233). This discrepancy is not hard to explain: in the case of prisoners whose names had been given from, say, Java to the Prisoners of War Bureau in Tokyo, their names were again passed on when they arrived in Singapore or at the Burma Railway. The Bureau simply ignored the fact that the same people were involved. Many of the names (as strange-sounding for the Japanese as Japanese names were to non-Japanese) were incorrectly given; moreover, the Bureau often confined itself to passing on the surname, and the Japanese sometimes treated a prefix like 'van' as the surname.

Incomplete information was given about the locations of the prisoners, with the result that at the end of the war the governments concerned did not know exactly where their prisoners were or what numbers were involved. They had not known this during the war either, which made it all the more difficult to send relief supplies.

Because of Japanese obstruction, only four consignments arrived; they were all intended for both prisoners of war and internees (the receipt of parcels by those interned in the East Indies will be dealt with in the next chapter).[12] Three consignments were taken by Japanese ships that had carried Allied citizens who were going to be exchanged: two ships bound for Lourenço Marques, one in July and one in September 1942, and one to Goa in October 1943. The first ship from Lourenço Marques carried about 20,000 food parcels each weighing five kilos as gifts from the American, Canadian and South African Red Cross as well as other relief supplies. Half of these parcels were shipped to Singapore and half to Japan. It was only a small consignment. The second consignment, which was carried by the second ship from Lourenço Marques, was larger: it contained 140,000 food parcels which were gifts from the British, South African and Australian Red Cross. Thanks to the efforts of the Dutch authorities in London, 40% of these parcels were intended for the prisoners in the East Indies; the rest were to be distributed elsewhere in the Nampo region. This never happened: the Japanese sent part of the 60% to Hong Kong, part to Manila, and part to Japan. Finally, the ship that went to Goa collected 140,000 food parcels that were gifts of the American and Canadian Red Cross; half went to Manila and half to Japan.

All in all, it was precious little: on behalf of the other Allied governments too, the Americans continued to press Japan to allow larger consignments at regular intervals. After a long delay, the Japanese government agreed. A fund was set up into which the American, British and Dutch governments

---

[12]   This information is taken from Van Velden (1963:169).

each paid a million dollars, and relief supplies for the prisoners were taken by American ships (under the Russian flag!) carrying military supplies to Vladivostok. The Soviet Union refused to allow Japanese ships into Vladivostok, and so the consignments meant for the prisoners were transported to a smaller port nearby, Nakhodka. From there in November 1944, 2,000 tons of relief supplies (including an estimated 200,000 food parcels) were shipped to Japan. The Americans and their allies wanted the supplies to go to the Nampo – this was because in September 1944 the Allied governments had first found out about the horrors the prisoners there had faced since 1942. In that month two Japanese ships were sunk off Hainan; they were taking over 2,000 British and Australian prisoners of war who had worked on the Burma Railway to Japan. American submarines had been able to rescue more than 140 of the prisoners. The plan of sending the 2,000 tons of supplies to the Nampo was not carried out. The Japanese shipped about 150 tons to Korea, and the delegates of the International Red Cross in Tokyo agreed that about 850 tons could be sent to the prisoners in Japan and China. The remaining 1,000 tons were picked up, but not until March 1945, by a Japanese ship, the *Awa Maru*, which had been given a safe-conduct by the American government. This meant that she had to indicate that she was a Red Cross ship, follow an agreed route and show lights at night. The *Awa Maru* offloaded the relief supplies in Bangkok, Singapore and Priok – about 49,000 food parcels in the last of these ports. While returning to Japan the ship was torpedoed by an American submarine at night off Formosa. The submarine commander had not recognized the *Awa Maru* (he said that the ship he attacked was not on the agreed route and not lit) and was court-martialled. The American government, leaving aside the question whether the ship had stuck to the rules, paid compensation to Japan. The outcome was that the Japanese, whose propaganda liked to contrast their nobility with American perfidy, distributed the *Awa Maru* consignment with remarkable speed (Emperor Hirohito had urged that the prisoners should not suffer because of the loss of the ship), on Java within six weeks of its arrival. In the case of the supplies brought by the first and second Japanese ships from Lourenço Marques, distribution in the East Indies had taken over a year. The prisoners received only a small part of what was brought in those three consignments, two from Lourenço Marques and one from Nakhodka: not much more than a tenth from the first two consignments and a sixth from the fourth. In both cases the Japanese appropriated everything else, including all the medicines.

It seems that in Japan the goods from Lourenço Marques were correctly distributed at first; at least in one camp, but not until March 1943, a lieutenant reported that 'per man nearly one parcel was distributed, and through the kitchen there was also quite a reasonable amount of sugar for each man and dried fruit and cocoa'.[13] On the other hand, when the consignment from the ship from Goa was distributed he observed that 'quantities of Red Cross parcels were carried into private homes' and 'several persons belonging to the Japanese camp staff and guards appeared [...] in Red Cross clothes and Red Cross footwear'.[14] In another camp when the parcels brought from Goa were distributed, according to a KNIL soldier, 'the Japs' latest stunt [...] was that those who had received Red Cross shoes had to parade wearing them. Then we had to exchange them for worn-out Japanese shoes!'[15]

On Formosa, where the Japanese had gathered together the highest Allied authorities from the Nampo region in a separate camp (the so-called Special Party, to which we shall return), the first Red Cross parcels (from the two ships from Lourenço Marques) were distributed in April 1943. According to Major General P. Scholten, 'the Japanese immediately reduced the rations they provided. That did not dampen our delight.' (Scholten 1971:128.) In May and July 1944 the group received part of the supplies shipped from Goa, first the American, then the Canadian parcels. 'From the American parcels', according to Scholten (1971:184):

we received sugar [...] vitamin tablets, stock cubes and raisins. We found [...] a tin of sliced ham, milk, corned beef, prunes, meat, coffee, butter, soap, cigarettes, chocolate bars, cheese, sugar and a tin opener. [...] A Canadian parcel for six men contained a pound of butter, a bar of chocolate, sugar, salt, a piece of soap, a tin of salmon, a tin of sardines, prunes, raisins, tea, cheese and dry wheat cake. To us a blessing!

The first food parcels (brought by the second ship from Lourenço Marques) from the relief supplies sent for the prisoners on the Burma Railway were not distributed until May 1944, together with some medicines and medical instruments. But in the camps on the railway, writes Van Witsen, 'only 5% at most of the Red Cross goods sent there reached the prisoners'.[16]

In August 1944 on North Sumatra the prisoners toiling on the road in Aceh were given 'one single person parcel between four men [these goods had been unloaded in Singapore in 1942!], at which time we made the sad discovery that most of the cigarettes had been stolen by our hosts' (Van Heekeren 1964:81). The prisoners taken from Java to Palembang received their first Red Cross parcels in September 1944, a reserve officer candidate reported to us in 1984, 'most of the contents had been stolen'.[17] On the Pekanbaru Railway

[13]   J.M. van Well Groeneveld, 'Rapport', 26 October 1945, p. 3 (NIOD IC, 1,219).
[14]   J.M. van Well Groeneveld, 'Rapport', 26 October 1945, p. 4 (NIOD IC, 1,219).
[15]   J.F. van West de Veer, 'Landstormsoldaat 1941-1945', p. 107 (NIOD IC, 81,314).
[16]   E. van Witsen, 'Over krijgsgevangenen in Japanse handen', p. 360.
[17]   Letter from F.B. Nijon, 6 November 1984 (NIOD IC).

parcels were distributed once – one parcel for four men. After the liberation the Japanese commandant was found to have a store full of parcels.

On Java in May 1944 the prisoners were given one four-person parcel for 15 men (parcels from the second ship from Lourenço Marques), and in June 1945 (at least in most camps) one four-person parcel between four men (parcels from the *Awa Maru*). As for the first consignment, Bouwer (1988:265) in Bandung noted:

> The Japanese took whatever they fancied from the parcels. [...] In general [...] the Japanese camp guards stood smoking the cigarettes intended for the prisoners. Some of the clothing sent was given by the Japanese to the Germans – the crews of Axis ships and submarines for whom [...] a rest centre has been set up near Sukabumi.

The second consignment included khaki uniforms, but according to one of the prisoners from Cimahi:

> there were not enough for everyone in the camp. Only the camp commandant [the senior officer] and the barrack heads got a uniform. It was inevitable that the distribution of the food parcels led to fierce quarrels and fistfights. The party was soon over. Three days later there was almost nothing left to show that we had eaten real butter and tinned cheese. The only visible traces were on the black market. (Jalhay 1981:357.)

The black market was the one that had developed inside the camp.

The prisoners of war in the areas administered by the Japanese navy received no Red Cross parcels at all – they simply did not exist in the eyes of the Japanese army authorities, who were responsible for distributing them.

What were the representatives of the Protecting Powers and those of the International Red Cross on the spot able to do for the prisoners of war?

Pitifully little. Sweden acted as the Protecting Power for the Netherlands (in occupied China this task was performed by Switzerland), and the International Red Cross had Swiss delegates in Japan and in all the areas occupied by Japan. But both the Swedish diplomats and the Red Cross delegates, who were all regarded by the Japanese authorities as spies or potential spies, were extremely restricted in their movements, and in the whole Nampo region, to the extent that it was occupied by Japan, no interference with the prisoners of war was allowed. Only in Thailand and in French Indo-China (in the latter up to March 1945) did the Swedes and the Swiss have slightly more opportunities to give aid.

In Japan the Prisoners of War Bureau refused to cooperate normally with the Red Cross delegate. Everything he wanted to raise had to be put in writing – answers (when there were any) took months. In the end he knew the

location of 102 camps in Japan, Korea, Manchuria and Formosa where prisoners of war and internees were being held, but he and his fellow delegates had
been able to visit only 42 of them and they had never been allowed to speak
to a single prisoner in private, nor had the Swedes. In one of the camps in
Japan in November 1943 the KNIL captain who acted as senior officer was
able to talk to the Swedish consul for a quarter of an hour, 'but', he wrote
later, 'only in the presence of the Japanese authorities and a Japanese interpreter'.[18] In a second camp, according to the lieutenant quoted above, the
same consul 'did not see the real conditions, because furniture, medicines
and so on were brought in from outside for the occasion, and then taken
away again after the visit'.[19]

Similar deception was practised by the Japanese on Formosa. General
Scholten described the first visit of the delegate of the International Red
Cross in Japan, F. Paravicini, on 30 May 1943:

> The day before we found 14 kilos of pork, and in our soup there were some
> sweet potatoes. On the morning of the 30th we were given two and a half *pisang*
> (bananas). For the very first time! According to the Convention, every camp was
> supposed to have a canteen. So one was promptly set up. [...] All sorts of wonder-
> ful things were displayed in a glass case. They [...] disappeared immediately after
> the inspection. All the sick [...] were discharged. But none of us got a chance to tell
> Paravicini that he was being tricked. (Scholten 1971:134.)

When the Special Party received a visit on 22 September 1943 from the Swiss
consul in Kobe and from a member of the Swedish legation in Japan, N.E.
Ericson, a spokesman for the prisoners was able to list a series of complaints
and then hurriedly call out 'Affamé' (Starving) to Ericson as he walked
around the camp. 'When he left, as all the Dutch prisoners gathered round
him [Ericson] and the Japanese prevented us from saying any more, he said,
"You must not forget that the war won't last for ever." Then he winked his left
eye. This was greatly appreciated.' (Scholten 1971:155.)

The members of the Special Party were dissatisfied about a visit in early
June 1944 by Paravicini's successor, the Swiss Max Pestalozzi:

> It was obvious that he [...] could exercise absolutely no influence in Tokyo. Nor
> could he do anything about the forced labour, as he took pains to emphasize. After
> the discussion he walked past the hospital, past the pigsties and the generals' bar-
> rack and straight out the gate. (Scholten 1971:178-9.)

In the East Indies the delegates of the International Red Cross were unable
to achieve anything for the prisoners of war (it was mentioned above that

---

[18]   P.J.C. Meys, 'Rapport', 25 September 1945, p. 5 (NIOD IC, 1,085).
[19]   J.M. van Well Groeneveld, 'Rapport', 26 October 1945, p. 7 (NIOD IC, 1,219).

the delegate for Borneo was only recognized when he had already been executed), nor were they more successful in Singapore, on Malacca or in Burma
(where the Japanese had refused to even admit a delegate). From Bangkok,
however, some help was given to the prisoners who were working or had
worked on the Burma Railway, if they could be reached in Thailand, by the
Swiss consul, who was also a delegate of the International Red Cross, and his
Swedish counterpart. In the last months of 1943 the Swiss consul began to
buy food, soap, cigarettes and medicines on the free market with money that
he had received from the British Red Cross via Geneva. He sent these goods,
worth some 32,000 guilders, together with about 8,000 guilders in cash, which
was meant to be pocket money, to the British prisoners on the Burma Railway.
At the end of December a second consignment about the same size was sent.
A report passed on by Bern to London, and also to the Dutch government
there, in February 1944 stated: 'Owing to numerous deaths among prisoners
due to lack of appropriate medical supplies the Swiss consul has been obliged
to make purchases on the black market at very high prices'.[20]

In March 1944 the Swiss consul reported that the Japanese refused to recognize the Red Cross in Thailand: in future the Japanese rather than the prisoners would sign for the relief supplies he would still be allowed to assemble
as a private individual. What guarantee was there that these supplies would
reach the prisoners? None. Nevertheless, the British government decided to
continue transferring funds to Bangkok and the Dutch government did likewise. In May 1944 the Swiss consul handed over a third consignment to the
Japanese and his counterpart in Saigon did the same for the benefit of a camp
with 1,500 Allied prisoners of war (including 800 from the KNIL), of whom
nearly half were sick. In July the Swiss consul in Bangkok arranged a fourth
consignment; his Swedish colleague was responsible for two consignments
worth about 32,000 guilders. In October came the fifth consignment from the
Swiss consul, of which goods worth 43,000 guilders were intended for the
Dutch prisoners; however, at that time the consul strongly suspected that the
Japanese were holding back goods. Nonetheless, the aid was continued until
the end of the war. From London the Dutch Red Cross made available about
120,000 guilders for this purpose – how much of the goods bought with this
money actually reached the Dutch prisoners is an open question. Red Cross
parcels were handed out in some camps in Burma on several occasions, in
January, May, June and December 1944. But it is not known whether they
came from the first ship from Lourenço Marques or whether they resulted
from the efforts of the Swiss and Swedish consuls in Bangkok.

---

[20]   Text in memorandum from the Foreign Office to the Netherlands Department of Foreign
Affairs, 17 February 1944 (ARA, MK, M59, VII 20 B).

The deception carried out by Japanese camp commandants in Japan and Formosa has been described. Is this not clear evidence that they were well aware of how prisoners of war ought to be treated in the eyes of Japan's opponents?

A similar, if anything even more repellent, form of deception was practised when, with the permission of the authorities in Tokyo, the Japanese made films in June 1943 on Java and Formosa and in 1944 in Singapore. They were intended to suggest that Japan's prisoners of war had lacked for nothing.

Copies of the footage shot on Java were to be dropped by parachute over Australia (this plan was not carried out). The title of the film was *Australia Calling*: Dutch, British and Australian prisoners of war and the wives and children of Dutch prisoners of war were forced to take part. Several Australian officers and other ranks were first ordered to act in various scenes. They refused. Then they were given no food. They still refused. The Japanese then announced that if they persisted the senior officer, a Wing Commander in the Royal Australian Air Force, would be executed and the entire camp would receive no food. The Australians gave in. In the scenes subsequently filmed Australians were seen as cooks preparing meals in the kitchen of the Hotel des Indes in Batavia; others swam in a modern pool, played tennis and cricket, and enjoyed a round of golf at a luxury hotel in the mountains near Sukabumi. There were also shots of Australians being nursed in a modern hospital (one was on the operating table) and of KNIL prisoners embracing their girlfriends or wives and children. Other prisoners were handed envelopes, from two of which emerged banknotes (the others contained crumpled paper), and were then given beer, according to the commentary (two of the glasses contained beer, the others tea). A scene was also shot in a clothing shop in Bandung: two Dutch girls with elaborate perms played shop assistants, and several Australian soldiers, who were first seen walking through the streets, bought clothes for their supposed girlfriends. Finally, in a field next to the sick bay of the Australians' camp a memorial ceremony attended by some 500 prisoners was filmed. Standing in front of an impressive-looking cross, the general in charge of all prisoner-of-war camps on Java, Major General Masatoshi Saito, held a speech. The cross was made of cardboard and the barbed wire round the field was camouflaged by branches.[21]

In the Special Party's camp on Formosa, also in June 1943, footage was shot in which a Japanese soldier notorious for his brutal behaviour was shown smiling with his arms around the shoulders of two American officers (the adjutants of the commander on Luzon, General Wainwright). According

---

21   In June 1943 misleading films were also shot in Cimahi and in a hotel at Garut, but they have not been preserved.

to General Scholten:

> A group of American colonels were washing mess kits and clothes with a piece
> of soap that they had to hold up during the filming; afterwards they had to hand
> it in. [...] We took the opportunity provided by a basketball game with screaming
> spectators to roar out 'hungry, bastard, son of a bitch' and more on similar lines.
>   The canteen was also filmed, with a price list invented for the occasion. 'Items
> for sale to-day' was the heading. Some Americans were chosen to stage a pur-
> chase. Next day everything was removed. (Scholten 1971:172.)

Finally Singapore. There the musicians in the British camp orchestra were
forced to give a radio concert for which they were smartly dressed; afterwards they were allowed to dine at the most luxurious hotel in town in the
company of women and young girls who had been drummed up by the
Japanese and given fine gowns to wear. When filming was finished, the
musicians disappeared once more behind the walls of the prisoner-of-war
complex and the gowns had to be returned.

As noted above, at the beginning of August 1942 a meeting was held in Tokyo
under the chairmanship of General Murakami at which it was decided that
in future prisoners of war would have a clear status, namely that of Japanese
soldiers of the lowest rank. 'As such,' we wrote, 'they would receive pay and
their officers would be allowed to wear their badges of rank again, which
had been taken from them in many cases. In return they would have to work
hard and make a solemn declaration of obedience.'
  These three points – the badges of rank, the declarations of obedience and
the pay – will now be considered.
  As to the badges of rank, detailed information is available only in the
case of West Java, and it may be that it was only there, in the East Indies,
that officers and non-commissioned officers had to hand in their badges of
rank. Another Japanese measure, cropping the hair of all prisoners of war,
was originally only implemented on West Java. At all events, on 9 May 1942
the order came that badges of rank must be removed and handed in. Protests
were useless. This measure created enormous confusion: all visible distinc-
tions of rank among the tens of thousands of prisoners disappeared. This
remained the case until the instructions agreed on 15 August 1942 were issued
by Tokyo. At the end of August the senior officers were able to announce that
badges of rank would be returned. In one of the camps at Cimahi this was
made known in the form of a message from Emperor Hirohito stating that,
according to the report by one officer:

> it had pleased him in his great benevolence not to regard us as rebels any longer
> [...] but as true prisoners of war. We were allowed to wear our badges of rank
> again. [...] This announcement provoked various comments, such as 'the bastards

are beginning to get windy', 'the swine realize that they haven't won the war yet and now they're scared they'll be called to account later' and so on.[22]

The order to hand in badges of rank had led to protests, but these were all the louder when the prisoners were ordered to make a solemn declaration of obedience, one by one. It was not only that by making such a declaration they gave up their rights under the Convention (including the right to escape); in addition, the Japanese text of the declaration often referred to 'swearing loyalty', and swearing loyalty to a foreign power was initially regarded as unacceptable by many of those involved, and particularly many officers. On West Java, literally translated, the declaration read: 'I, the undersigned, solemnly swear loyalty and obedience to all orders of the Japanese army'. However, the accompanying text in Indonesian (there was no Dutch or English version) read as follows in translation: 'I, the undersigned, solemnly declare loyalty and respect to the Japanese army'. The difference between 'swear' and 'solemnly declare' seemed to suggest that the Japanese authorities did not interpret 'swearing loyalty' in the same way as others might; nonetheless, the Japanese text was the official version. Elsewhere the prisoners were sometimes presented with a different text – in Singapore, for example, one version (in English) used at the end of August read: 'I, the undersigned, hereby solemnly swear on my honour that I will not, under any circumstances, attempt escape'. This also gave rise to problems, because in the case of British and Australian troops their regulations stated that it was their duty to try to escape if they were made prisoners of war. All the prisoners concentrated in Singapore – over 13,000 British and 2,000 Australian troops – refused to sign the declaration. Here they were asked rather than ordered to sign. They were then all assembled in an open field where there were only two water taps, and were given nothing to eat. The higher-ranking British and Australian officers made it clear to the Japanese that there could be no question of acceding to their request – the situation would be different, however, if the Japanese issued an order, because then the prisoners could say that they had signed under duress. The order came and the men signed.

On Sumatra (which, like Singapore, came under Japan's 25th Army) the prisoners of war were also required to give a written undertaking that they would not escape. All that is known about the reactions is that most of the KNIL prisoners held near Medan initially refused. A woman interned near Medan observed in mid-September 1942 how:

> the Japs locked up all the officers and let them starve for a couple of days. All they were given was a little soup and warm water to drink. In the end they couldn't

---

22   J. van Baarsel, 'Onder de Jappen', p. 32 (NIOD IC, 81,359).

hold out any longer and were forced to sign. But it was under duress and so didn't mean much. (Van Eijk-van Velzen 1983:38.)

On Java at the beginning of July all prisoners of war held in the barracks of the 10th Battalion in Batavia were required to make a declaration which included the words 'swear loyalty'. The highest-ranking British, Australian and American officers, Air Vice Marshall P.C. Maltby, Brigadier A.S. Blackburn and Colonel A.G. Searle respectively, refused and told their subordinates to do the same. Among the KNIL soldiers, according to Captain Vromans (who had been transferred in April from the Sukamiskin Prison in Bandung to Batavia together with General Ter Poorten and other high-ranking officers and Governor-General Van Starkenborgh):

> the general view from the outset was that they should refuse to sign. An alternative wording was rejected out of hand [by the Japanese]. We were more closely confined. No contact other than with armed guards, who began a reign of terror: the slightest offence led to a beating. Bad food [...], bad quarters, a ban on anything resembling relaxation. It got steadily worse, especially the minor ill-treatment. To prevent worse and bearing in mind that what one signs under duress in captivity means nothing [...], in the end everyone signed, including the Governor-General and the Army Commander.[23]

The British and American prisoners also signed (that is, put their thumbprint on the document), and the Australians followed suit a little later.

In the prisoner-of-war camps at Cimahi the inmates were required to sign a declaration at the end of July. The senior officer ('camp commander') in the largest camp, Major J.W.S.A. Hoedt, issued a circular stating that he would sign.[24] He went on:

> Everyone is free to make his own choice. [...] The consequences for those who do *not* sign cannot be foreseen. I can guarantee those who *do* sign [...] that they will never be called to account for this in the future, nor will they be looked down upon or have fingers pointed at them.

Almost all the prisoners followed Major De Hoedt's example. The name of only one of those who refused is known: Reserve Major J.G. Gout. He was confined within the camp for nearly two months, and it must be assumed that the same happened to others who refused.

In one of the two camps in Cilacap, where the commandant had announced that those who refused would be locked up until they placed their thumbprint, something went wrong: one of the prisoners filled the state-

[23]   A.G. Vromans, 'Verslag 1941-1945', p. 31.
[24]   Text in Brugmans 1960:340-1.

ment in wrongly and then threw the papers into a waste basket. According to another prisoner shortly after the war:

> This led to the following reprisal: we all had to fall in immediately. We had insult-ed the Japanese emperor. [...] We were to be severely punished. We had to face east,[25] then kneel and bow our head to the ground, while they shouted out a short Japanese prayer. This bow had to be repeated constantly and heaven help those who didn't bow deeply enough! They were struck with a piece of wood or the butt of a rifle until they were in the right position. This game went on for about two hours, to the great amusement of the Japanese guards. (Van Hees et al., n.d.:197.)

In the camps on East Java the declarations were only presented later, with a slightly different text (in English). The heading was 'Written oath' and it read: 'The undersigned has solemnly sworn henceforth the absolute obedi-ence to all orders of Dai Nippon Government'. This went further than the version used on West Java because it was described as an 'oath' and referred to obedience to the Japanese government. The highest-ranking Dutch officers discussed the oath and came to the conclusion that everyone was free to sign or not to sign, but that they themselves would sign: they would be acting, they said, under duress. Everyone signed. 'We shall not go into the question,' noted one medical officer in his journal, 'of how this affects the oath we swore to our sovereign in the past'.[26]

Declarations were also signed in the prisoner-of-war camps in Surabaya and Yogyakarta, only after 'fierce debate'[27] in the case of the latter. More or less the same declarations had to be signed again when prisoners were moved to another camp in 1943, 1944 or 1945. Some prisoners put their thumbprint under six declarations all together.

In the view of the Japanese, after they had made their declaration of obedi-ence the prisoners of war were entitled to receive pay. In the case of the lower ranks this only applied if they worked: a soldier was paid 10 cents per work-ing day, and a corporal or a sergeant 15 cents.[28] Depending on their rank, officers received more, ranging from 550 guilders a month for generals and admirals to 71 guilders a month for second lieutenants. From these amounts 60 guilders were deducted for food and accommodation and only part, vary-ing between 30 and 10 guilders, was paid out in cash; the rest was put in a savings account with a Japanese bank. The families of captured officers living on Java were allowed to withdraw 15 guilders per month per family member

---

25 Presumably in the direction of the imperial palace in Tokyo, thus to the north-northeast.
26 R. Springer, 'Dagboek', 26 October 1941, p. 10 (NIOD IC, 81,346).
27 E. van Witsen, 'Over krijgsgevangenen in Japanse handen', p. 249.
28 These amounts were sometimes higher elsewhere: 25 and 40 cents respectively.

from this savings account. It is not known whether this scheme was generally applied and in any case it would only have made a difference for very few;[29] it was ended in November 1943.

The end result of all these differences was that officers in the camps on Java had between 10 and 30 guilders a month, while ordinary soldiers got at most 3 guilders and corporals and sergeants 4.50. Officers were forbidden to give financial support to lower ranks, but many ignored this: in most camps assistance was organized, so that the amounts received by the lower ranks were larger. Nonetheless, there remained a substantial difference between officers and men: the money one had was important for buying additional food, and so in the camp conditions the officers were better off than the other ranks.

To what extent the Japanese kept to this financial arrangement beyond Java is not known in all cases – the suspicion must be that they may not have done so during certain periods.

Before looking in more detail at the fate of the Dutch and Dutch Eurasians among the prisoners of war, we shall consider the group that was supposed to be released on the grounds that the 'Greater East Asian War' was a war of liberation: the indigenous KNIL soldiers.

The indigenous KNIL soldiers

As stated, it is not known exactly how many indigenous KNIL soldiers were captured. It may be assumed that during the week of fighting on Java and in the days after the general surrender of the KNIL several thousand Javanese and Sundanese troops made their escape. This was easier for them than for the Ambonese, Manadonese and Timorese, since they could melt into the millions living on Java without standing out; as a rule, Ambonese, Manadonese and Timorese have a slightly different appearance. Many of them had a wife and children on Java (the same was true on the Outer Islands), but no other relatives. Their families were housed in places where soldiers seeking to disappear could not show themselves: in and around the garrison towns. Another factor was that many of the Javanese and Sumatrans felt a certain animosity towards the Ambonese in particular, who were known as outstandingly loyal KNIL soldiers and were mostly Christians in an Islamic environment. In the earliest phase of the Japanese occupation, when Indonesian nationalists laid down the law in many places, this animosity gave rise to a good deal of ten-

---

[29]   For a family of three 45 guilders could be withdrawn, but such an amount would only have been available from the savings accounts of officers with the rank of captain or higher.

sion: on Java there were cases of Ambonese disguising themselves as Arabs for protection.

The Japanese military authorities wanted to press all indigenous former KNIL soldiers to serve as auxiliaries, *heiho*, but they made a distinction in that they kept the Ambonese and Manadonese, who were Christian, in captivity while releasing most of the other indigenous troops.

The first step was the separation of all indigenous soldiers, officers and lower ranks, from the Dutch and Dutch Eurasians by assembling them in special camps and (at least on Java) ordering the indigenous administrators to ensure that indigenous soldiers who had deserted gave themselves up as prisoners of war. In the camp at Magelang (the only one for which information is available), according to J.C. Hamel, who had gone there voluntarily as a minister, this order was obeyed by 'hundreds of Javanese. [...] *Wedono* had rounded them up, for fear of being accused by the Japs of hiding people who had something to do with the Dutch.' (Hamel 1948:35.) On the occasion of Hirohito's birthday, on 29 April, it was announced that all indigenous KNIL soldiers, except for the officers and the Ambonese and Manadonese, would be released on condition that, according to the notice on Java,[30] 'they swore loyalty to the Japanese government, and as soon as enough information had been obtained as to their position in society'. The Japanese had other plans for the officers: on Java, at least, in accordance with the Japanese desire to place the indigenous population above the Europeans, several of them were asked to act as the senior officer in prisoner-of-war camps for Dutch and Dutch Eurasians. They refused and were punished by a spell in prison. 'They emerge,' said Van Witsen,[31] 'as broken men'.[32]

As for the Javanese, Sundanese and Timorese rank and file, it is not known exactly how many of them signed the declaration and were released. On Java (no figures are available for the Outer Islands) at the end of May 1942 the number was about 6,000, but it may be that in the case of others not enough 'information about their position in society' had been obtained at that point. At all events there is no doubt that other Javanese and Manadonese were not released until after May 1942; for example the indigenous members of the KNIL's Volunteer Drivers Corps were held until 10 May 1943.

Many of the released Javanese, Sundanese and Timorese were recruited as *heiho*, as were Ambonese and, in larger numbers it seems, Manadonese. On Java the recruiting of Manadonese as *heiho* began as early as April 1942. A first group of about 800 KNIL soldiers was involved. Some of them refused

---

[30]   Text in Brugmans 1960:169.
[31]   E. van Witsen, 'Over krijgsgevangenen in Japanse handen', p. 158.
[32]   Some indigenous officers were held together with the Dutch and Dutch Eurasian prisoners until the end.

and were badly beaten, after which their own officers urged them to give up their resistance, which they did. Later in 1942 and early 1943 numerous Manadonese former KNIL soldiers became *heiho* – it may be assumed that a significant factor was the awareness that they had little hope of supporting themselves and their families in civilian society (their wives and children had had to move out of the barracks at a moment's notice).

The Ambonese former KNIL soldiers were also put under great pressure to become *heiho*. A number of them were released from the camps in the course of 1942 – it should be remembered that, as described in Chapter II, many Ambonese former KNIL soldiers joined resistance groups, some as early as mid-1942. The Japanese became aware of this and, as also mentioned in Chapter II, it led to their starting a separate register of all the indigenous inhabitants who came from the Outer Islands. Nonetheless, at that time several thousand Ambonese were still in captivity, including around a thousand in Batavia. This latter group was ordered to be present under military guard at the large demonstration held on the first anniversary of Pearl Harbor, 8 December 1942, on the former Koningsplein, at which Sukarno was one of the speakers. Did the Japanese hope that these Ambonese would now be prepared to take part in constructing the 'Greater East Asian Co-Prosperity Sphere'? Far from it: when later in December they were required to sign a declaration of obedience to the Japanese army, they refused. The group was then put in Glodok Prison, where their number grew to about 2,000. They were subjected to propaganda (including films about Japanese victories) and to brutal beatings by Javanese guards assisted by Javanese *heiho*. In these circumstances about half continued to refuse (they were again put in a separate prisoner-of-war camp and pressured to become *heiho*). Around 1,000 were taken to a camp in Bandung to be trained as *heiho* and 500 of them (we assume that the other 500 had again refused) were transported in March 1943 to a camp in Surabaya where there were a number of other Ambonese prisoners of war. In April a group of Ambonese from Batavia already dressed in the *heiho* uniform arrived in the camp. On 14 April 1943 the Ambonese who were still not wearing this uniform were told by a Japanese colonel that the Emperor had agreed that they could leave the camp; first they had to sign an undertaking that they would report for duty as *heiho* at the first call. The interpreter added that it would be enough if only the senior officer in the group actually signed. He did so and a few days later the Ambonese who were still not in Japanese uniform were issued with their *heiho* outfit. A protest by some Ambonese was rejected. A few weeks later the groups assembled in Surabaya were divided into two: some left by sea as *heiho*; the rest were taken to a prisoner-of-war camp in Bandung where they were informed that they too were *heiho*. According to an Ambonese sergeant:[33]

---

[33]   Text in Brugmans 1960:522-3.

We weren't having that, we just wanted to stay as prisoners of war. They made us do all sorts of things, marching and suchlike. But we didn't give in. On the contrary, in front of everybody, especially in front of the internment camps in Bandung, we sang Dutch songs in the streets.

Later in 1943 around 1,000 Ambonese and Manadonese prisoners of war were brought together in Surabaya and again they were put under great pressure to become *heiho*. On one occasion some broke out of the camp – they were caught and taken away (their fate is unknown). Most of these prisoners were sent east as *heiho*. Some of those who refused were taken back to the former barracks of the 10th Battalion in Batavia, which had been turned into a prisoner-of-war camp, and brutally ill-treated by the camp commandant, Kenichi Sonei. In October 1944, together with a large number of European prisoners of war, they were put on board a Japanese ship, the *Junyo Maru*, which was to take them to Padang, from where they were to work on the Pekanbaru Railway. The *Junyo Maru* was torpedoed (we shall come back to the loss of the ship later) and most of these Ambonese and Manadonese drowned.

Some of the Manadonese and Ambonese taken away from Java as *heiho* managed to defect to the Americans. As mentioned in Chapter I, the Manadonese H.D. Pitoi succeeded in this at the end of 1942 on Guadalcanal, and in August 1943 on the Philippines ten Manadonese *heiho* led by a former KNIL NCO, Adolf Lembong, joined up with a guerrilla group under an American officer. From a group of Ambonese *heiho* taken to the Tanimbar Islands 47 escaped, of whom only 22 reached Australia (20 drowned and 5 were caught and executed by the Japanese).

Van Witsen estimates that of the indigenous KNIL soldiers captured on Java about 15,000 became *heiho* (how many Javanese, Sundanese, Ambonese, Manadonese and Timorese were among them is not known) and that nearly half of them died.

It is likely that in the areas governed by the Japanese navy – Borneo and the Great East – pressure was also put on indigenous KNIL troops to become *heiho*, but little is known about this. In Manado in March 1942 about 25 Manadonese, including several former soldiers, who had refused to enter into Japanese service were executed.

On Sumatra, which was governed by the Japanese 25th Army, the indigenous KNIL soldiers were separated from the European soldiers and put in separate camps, although sometimes together with the Dutch Eurasian KNIL troops. In several of these camps the indigenous prisoners were required to become *heiho*; those who refused were shot in front of the whole group. How many were shot and how many taken away as *heiho* is not known.

Prisoner-of-war camps – general

Each prisoner-of-war camp was under the command of a Japanese officer and some of these commandants made a favourable impression on the prisoners. The so-called Nieuwe Kamp (New Camp) in Cilacap (which we shall return to below) was first commanded by a brute. Because he was tall and thin he was known as 'Alva', after the Spanish governor of the Netherlands in the sixteenth century. But the second commandant, known as 'Opa' or 'Grandad', treated the prisoners more than fairly. While road-building in Aceh, C. van Heekeren met a Japanese officer in one of the camps 'who looked very decent and was entirely correct': 'he did not have a single good word for certain leading figures in the Japanese army. He spoke English. [...] He was very moved by our plight and did as much as he could to alleviate it.' (Van Heekeren 1964:89.) In Medan the prisoners encountered a Japanese lieutenant who later became the commandant of the largest prisoner-of-war complex in Singapore and behaved absolutely correctly there: he was incorruptible and always defended the prisoners' interests. Another group of KNIL prisoners working on the Burma Railway had to do with a Japanese lieutenant from whom, according to Major J. van Baarsel:

> they had no trouble whatsoever. He wasn't at all the warlord or windbag type like so many Japs. He showed no sign of the Japanese military spirit. [...] He was seldom seen and if, on rare occasions, he took a walk through the camp, he did not wait to be saluted but nodded shyly and sometimes saluted first.[34]

On the other hand: 'He was no use to us', because he just brushed off complaints about the behaviour of the Japanese NCO with whom the prisoners had to deal every day.[35]

This was a general phenomenon: in many camps the prisoners saw very little of the Japanese officers and had to deal mainly with NCOs or privates.[36] Among the latter there was often one who wanted to be a model of loyalty to the emperor, and who drew strength from brutal behaviour and thus set a standard from which the officers who sympathized with the prisoners' suffering dared not deviate. Even Japanese officers who did their best to 'follow the imperial way' sometimes acted in a manner suggesting they wanted to show a certain chivalrousness, indeed win the approval of the officially despised whites. How else to explain, wrote Van Witsen:

[34]   J. van Baarsel, 'Onder de Jappen', p. 65 (NIOD IC, 81,359).
[35]   J. van Baarsel, 'Onder de Jappen', p. 66 (NIOD IC, 81,359).
[36]   According to Japanese figures, the camps were manned by 2,637 troops in 1942 (including 135 officers) and by 6,798 troops in 1945 (including 423 officers).

Why prisoners were asked about their families with genuine interest, why a Japanese officer invited prisoners to take tea in his house and introduced them to his wife after they had 'voluntarily' trimmed his hibiscus hedge, why another officer personally took a patient in need of an operation [...] to a Japanese hospital in the middle of the night, [...] why so many Japanese asked for English lessons.

Van Witsen also draws attention to the 'near fraternization' (purely from the Japanese side!) during 'festivities' in the camp on Japan's 'great days' and 'finally on the truly sincere honours paid to deceased prisoners'.[37]

The behaviour of many Japanese was noticeably forced. The prisoners on an island in the Moluccas who had to build an airstrip were supervised by a Japanese NCO, 'Bamboo Mori', 'a fat, heavy man with a bull's neck and the gait of a gorilla' (according to a KNIL captain who had to deal with him as an interpreter).[38] Mori prided himself on the name the prisoners had given him.

His temper, as with every true Japanese, was soon roused and at such moments he was very brutal and meted out harsh punishments. The Jap lieutenants [...] had [...] no say when he was around. Where Mori was, only Mori ruled and no one else. His own guards, Koreans, feared him.[39]

Mori drove sick prisoners back to work by beating them with a bamboo stick, and under his regime in six months one in six prisoners died. One of the medical officers, R. Springer, noted, however:

I've been struck by how if you get a chance to speak to the Japanese alone their attitude changes, and this is true even of Mori. It sometimes seems as if their behaviour towards the prisoners is artificial, and designed to make an impression on their own people.[40]

There were sadists among the Japanese, as among every people, but the fate of the prisoners was adversely affected by the fact that not only the sadists but most of the other Japanese whom they encountered regarded them as worthless creatures, and that those who thought differently conformed to the prevailing norm[41] for fear of being seen as weak. Consequently, the prison-

---

[37]   E. van Witsen, 'Over krijgsgevangenen in Japanse handen', pp. 593-4.
[38]   G.P.C. le Clerq, cited in E. van Witsen, 'Over krijgsgevangenen in Japanse handen', p. 614.
[39]   G.P.C. le Clerq, cited in E. van Witsen, 'Over krijgsgevangenen in Japanse handen', p. 614.
[40]   R. Springer, 'Dagboek', p. 103 (NIOD IC, 81,346).
[41]   Just as most prisoners could not understand the norms of the Japanese, so many of the latter were baffled by the norms of non-Japanese. Wim Kan observed a telling example of this in Bandung: 'A Dutch captain who managed to appropriate a tin of sardines while foraging did this so clumsily that he was caught red-handed by a Japanese major. The latter handed him his sword and invited him, absolutely seriously, to commit harakiri, since "he had lost face"! When the captain refused and explained that he had not lost face because of stealing a single tin of sardines, the major picked up three more tins and pressed them into his hands, saying, "In that case, take a few more!", and that was the end of the matter.' (Wim Kan and Corry Vonk 1963:29.)

ers were severely punished for the slightest infringement (throwing away a cigarette butt, shouting Japanese slogans too loudly or not loudly enough, bowing too deeply or not deeply enough). This was often accompanied by the kind of tortures favoured by the Kempeitai: being struck in the face, beaten with wooden poles, pieces of bamboo, iron bars, rifle butts or belts, kicked and knocked to the floor. They had to sit on the floor with their hands above their heads for hours, or stand to attention, or hold up a heavy object, or sit with a rod between their knees on which the Japanese stood. There were endless variants and combinations of these and other punishments, which often resulted from the fact that the prisoner had not understood the Japanese with his foreign language.[42] The roll calls could be terrible because, according to Rob Nieuwenhuys (1979:78):

> Most of the Japanese soldiers could not count further than 20. So then they started all over again from 1 to 20. That worked all right, but as soon as they had to multiply things went wrong. [...] They could not do mental arithmetic, because they had always been taught to use an abacus.[43]

Major problems could arise when low-ranking Japanese soldiers had to make sure that none of the many thousands of prisoners in a camp was missing.

Indicative of the distance between the prisoners and the Japanese ruling over them were the names by which the guards were known. Three have already been mentioned: 'Alva', 'Opa' and 'Bamboo Mori'. The same thing happened in the internment camps. In fact, on Java, after the prisoners from some of the largest camps had been sent to Burma, Thailand, Flores, the Moluccas and Sumatra, their places were taken by internees, who then encountered the same Japanese commandants and officials.

Some of these Japanese were given names based on their appearance: 'Gold Tooth', 'Four Eyes', 'Spectacled Cobra', 'Soup Eye', 'Fat Neck', 'Dog Eye', 'Monkey Face', 'Brownie the Bear', 'The Elephant', 'The Flatfoot'. Other names

---

Perhaps the end of this story should be viewed as an attempt by the Japanese major, who as it were sanctioned the captain's actions, to 'save face' for him.

[42]   Those who acted as interpreters (prisoners with some knowledge of Japanese) could not always solve the problem, especially if they did not understand the type of Japanese in which they were addressed. In a train full of prisoners on the way from Singapore to Bangkok, according to one prisoner, 'at a certain point the Japanese seemed to get all excited, and the interpreter finally concluded that at the next station the officers would be served coffee ice cream. Later it turned out that the Japs had given orders to prevent anyone in the train from giving the V-sign to the local people! (A.H. Douwes, 'Persoonlijke herinneringen', p. 35 (NIOD IC, 81,315).)

[43]   At that time the Japanese learned little arithmetic in school, and mental arithmetic was not taught at all. Once on the Burma Railway a group of prisoners was told to dig out half a cubic metre of earth per day – according to the Japanese guard that was a half of a half of a half metre. Naturally, no one argued.

referred to their behaviour: 'Jan the Bludgeon, 'The Boxer', 'The Mad Dog', 'The Tiger', 'The Sneak', 'The Devil', 'The Murderer'.[44]

The Korean guards were given similar names: 'Fat Piggy', 'Baby Face', 'Pineapple', 'Donald Duck', 'Gary Cooper', 'Blue Glasses', 'Shrew', 'Butterball', 'Club Foot' as well as 'Mean Bastard', 'The Podgy Sadist', 'The Bloodhound' (in the camp in question there were two: 'Bloodhound I' and 'Bloodhound II'), 'The Shin Kicker', 'The Sadist', 'The Hard Hitter'. Insofar as they referred to their general behaviour, the names given to the Koreans were no friendlier than those given to the Japanese. In fact, as a rule the prisoners suffered more at the hands of the Koreans than at the hands of the Japanese. There were two reasons for this: first, in their day-to-day existence the prisoners had more to do with the Koreans than with the Japanese, who rarely appeared in the camps; second, many Koreans tended to be more 'Japanese' in their behaviour than the Japanese themselves.

The first groups of Koreans ('small, filthy, yellow, bandy-legged, monkey-like creatures') (Binnerts 1947:29) appeared in the camps in August 1942. About 2,000 of them had been recruited in Korea for a period of two years. They had been promised honourable civilian jobs in the East Indies, but to their disappointment and anger they were employed exclusively as camp guards. After their two years were up they were not allowed to leave. They knew they were despised by the Japanese – the kicks they received from them they happily passed on to the prisoners. Van Heekeren was in a prisoner-of-war camp in Medan in 1942 and from there in March 1944 he was put to work with the other members of the Aceh Party on building the road already mentioned in North Sumatra. He later wrote:

> We had seen these lads arrive in Glugur: then they were shy, modest, slightly scared boys, who did not know how to behave and were rather frightened by all these big white men. Unfortunately this soon changed: nothing corrupts a simple person as quickly as power over his fellow beings. By the time the Aceh Party left, they had already become intolerable, cruel, sly and cowardly fellows, sentimental in their homesickness, sadistic out of bitterness at the system that had dumped them somewhere on an island they had probably never heard of, charged with one of the least honourable tasks in the Japanese army. (Van Heekeren 1964:18.)

---

[44]   In August 1943, when he had been on Flores for several months, one prisoner, C. Binnerts, was talking to another when the conversation again came round to 'why the Japs leave us indifferent, while we hate the Germans'. 'I believe', he noted, 'that the answer lies in two factors. First, the Indies is not our homeland: [Binnerts and the other prisoner were *totok*]: we may talk grandly about solidarity with the peoples of the East Indies, but most of us are and will remain foreigners [of course, this was not true of the Dutch Eurasians, and many a *totok* also took a different view]. Second, the difference between the Japs, and in particular the Koreans we mostly deal with in the camps, and us is so great that we are barely able to see them as human. A monkey with a rifle is a dangerous thing, but you can't hate it, nor even despise it.' (Binnerts 1947:58.)

In the last phase of the war a change became evident in the Koreans' general attitude: they realized that their Japanese masters were losing and as a result they started chumming up with the prisoners here and there. Some made it clear that, should the occasion arise, they were ready to join forces with the prisoners against the Japanese. Previously they had been the ones who carried out the punishments, sometimes supervised by a Japanese who felt himself far superior, after which the Japanese could add a finishing touch. On one occasion Van Heekeren and others had bought some rice to supplement their meagre rations on the way back to one of the Aceh Party camps; they became the victims of the Korean guards and the Japanese NCO placed above them, 'the Master Sadist'.

> On reaching the camp we found the Koreans waiting for us: everyone was searched and together with nine others (many more had bought rice, but they had thrown it away when they saw in the distance that we were being searched) I was in for it.
>
> On the way to their barracks every few metres there stood a Korean armed with a thick cane; you worked your way past them and got a beating from each one. In front of the barracks stood the Master Sadist. Beside him were three big blocks of wood about the same weight; the heaviest would have been 50 kilos. After first being thrashed, while standing to attention, you had to pick up the block he pointed out and hold it above your head with your arms fully stretched. He then positioned himself in front of you, while a colleague stood behind you, and you were told you had to stand like that for 15 minutes. Naturally, your exhausted body couldn't keep that up and after a few minutes your arms were no longer at full stretch. That was the moment they were waiting for: they leapt into action and struck your wrists with the cane; if your legs bent, they hit the back of your knees. However hard you tried, you couldn't keep it up and the block sank lower and lower and the blows of the cane came faster and faster.
>
> After a quarter of an hour, you could rest, that is, join the others standing to attention. The next one then got his go and that was how the Japanese worked in three series with the blocks of wood. There were always three men demonstrating their strength. At a certain point it was your turn again and the torture started once more.
>
> Behind me an Indo was tackled, a big, strong fellow. There was crying, screaming and wailing [...] and there, surrounded by the mountains, in the deadly quiet camp, you gritted your teeth and tried not to make a sound when the blows rained down on your head, your neck, your shoulders, back, arms, legs, wrists, elbows and the backs of your knees. They struck so hard that the Jap was foaming at the mouth, and you felt the bumps on your head and everywhere, so hard that the blood from the long welts came through your clothes. One man fainted in front of me; after kicking him a couple of times, the Jap let the doctor drag him away unconscious.
>
> After the second round came the third: again you stood beneath the block, again your arms sank, again your knees couldn't hold out.
>
> And under the blows you again collapsed; you were on one knee and the block was on the other. You had no strength or spirit left, and the Jap, in a last attempt to

get you on your feet, struck even harder with the cane. Then there came a moment when you let the block fall; you were exhausted and simply couldn't keep it up. 'Keep hitting, Jap, it doesn't hurt any more!' Then it suddenly stopped: you got a last kick and you had to stand to attention again. With a struggle, you managed to get up, but as soon as you tried to take a step, you lay flat on your face again. You scrabbled to your feet once more, because you didn't want to lose consciousness – you refused to give them that pleasure – just as you kept your mouth shut under the blows. Then at last we were dismissed; you had yourself bandaged and treated and then lay on your bed. Everything hurt and you knew that soon there would be more. Because Baby Face, the 20-year-old commandant, was not in the camp today, but when he returned all hell would break loose.

At seven it was time: you had to line up again, but now you were better prepared, having put on your entire wardrobe to provide some protection for your searing wounds and welts. Then Baby Face came into action. He contrived to make himself more and more furious and worked his way along the whole line. From the corner of your eye you saw him knocking them to the ground one by one, and you calculated how you would fall, for you got a last kick and it was important to protect your vulnerable parts. And when he stood before you, breathing heavily, foaming at the mouth, his features contorted, you were so nauseated by it all that you didn't feel the blows to your face and were barely aware of being kicked as you lay on the ground.

Then the punishment was over: your crime of being hungry and trying to stay alive was paid for.

You had lost your rice, but that wasn't so important, and the wounds would heal; the worst thing of all was the moral hangover. For weeks afterwards you limped, you were stiff, everything hurt, and for months you suffered the mental after-effects. Inside you felt empty and numb, and you never again lost the sense of revulsion, of horror at what had happened. (Van Heekeren 1964:104-6.)

Just one description, but hundreds if not thousands received the same brutal treatment for trivial infringements.

The so-called camp inspections and collective punishments became notorious. As regards the inspections, the Japanese, who were already suspicious by nature (and extra suspicious because they could not follow the normal conversations between the prisoners), felt the need to check continually whether the prisoners had any goods they were not supposed to have, such as paper, a pencil or books that were not approved. Each of these inspections became a huge raiding party. The writing materials and books that did not have a Japanese stamp were seized, as were watches, gold rings and everything regarded by the camp commandant as not essential for a prisoner – a second pair of shoes, a change of clothing. During these inspections the prisoners generally had to assemble on the parade ground – only afterwards could they find out which of their few (and thus very valuable) belongings had been taken this time.

Collective punishments were applied when it was not known who had committed a particular offence. This happened repeatedly. Only one example need be given here. It took place in early April 1942 in one of the barrack complexes in Bandung where about 10,000 prisoners of war were then being held. A note had been thrown over the barbed wire – who had done it? The Japanese commandant ordered all prisoners to assemble on the parade ground. They were asked who the guilty person was. No one came forward. A prisoner described what followed:

> We had to stand to attention while Japs walked down the lines hitting and jabbing with rifle butts if we were not standing stiffly enough. We were given no food, the sun went down, we stood there through the long night and everyone wondered how long this would go on or, like me (I had always said I couldn't keep standing for an hour), when he would faint. That happened on all sides and then the Japs hit hard with a rifle butt to see if the man was faking. Sometimes it was real and sometimes it wasn't, and then he was sent back to his place in the line.
>
> The sun came up: no food, nothing to drink and it got hotter and hotter.
>
> When we had been standing for 24 hours, we thought it would be a good time to end it. Not a chance. Only after 26 hours, when still no one had come forward, were we dismissed.[45]

Other collective punishments were that drinking water was rationed, or that rations were withheld, or that the sick had to attend roll call, or that all prisoners had to kneel on sharp stones, or work longer, or that everyone was beaten – no one knew what to expect in this kind of situation.

It was this same unpredictability on the part of the Japanese that made the post of senior officer highly dangerous and hence unattractive. The rule was that in a prisoner-of-war camp this post was held by the highest or one of the highest in rank. Initially this was a flag officer or general, but when all flag officers and generals were taken away to Formosa as members of the Special Party,[46] an officer of lower rank had to take on this role. This was not an obligation. If none of the lieutenant colonels or naval commanders present wanted to do the job, or if it was generally felt among the prisoners that the officers of that rank were not suitable, then it was taken on by a lower-ranking officer. He had a difficult position. In relation to the Japanese he was responsible for everything done in the camp. He received the Japanese orders, he had to see that they were carried out. If he did not do that effectively, he would be in trouble with the Japanese; if he did it too promptly, he

---

[45]   J.F. van West de Veer, 'Landstormsoldaat 1941-1945', p. 59 (NIOD IC, 81,314).
[46]   At that time flag officers in the navy were those with the rank of rear admiral or higher, and in the army those with the rank of major general or higher. However, the Special Party included naval officers with the rank of captain and army officers with the rank of colonel.

would be in trouble with his fellow prisoners, who would see him as being overzealous. He did not have to work himself – which often caused envy. There was little reason for this, because when punishments were meted out the senior officer was often the first victim. Indeed, if there were problems between a Japanese or Korean and one of the prisoners, it was his job to take the matter up with the camp commandant or his adjutant or the commander of the guards, and all too often the result was that he got the blows that had been intended for the prisoner. Many Japanese took pleasure in humiliating enemy officers in front of their lower ranks.

The senior officer thus had to be a tough character, but toughness alone was not enough. Tact, calm and cheerfulness were just as essential, and high morale above all. The senior officer had to radiate confidence in an Allied victory to all the prisoners, while taking care to conceal this confidence when dealing with the Japanese and Koreans.

His post was also difficult because he had to mete out punishments when the occasion arose. The prisoners were soldiers and they were required to observe normal military discipline. If they did not do so, or if they committed other offences (theft from fellow prisoners, for example), they had to be punished. There were senior officers who decided what the punishment would be without consultation; others sought the advice of experienced lawyers, certainly in complex cases. Most (there were exceptions) refrained from imposing corporal punishment and limited themselves to making the offenders do extra work or denying them certain privileges. On occasion, for instance in the event of food being stolen, the name of the thief and his punishment would be made known by camp order. It was assumed that this would act as a deterrent. This was not always the case. There were forces – originating from the prisoners themselves, from the unpredictability of the Japanese and above all from hunger – that promoted anarchy rather than normal discipline, which proved to be difficult to maintain. On Java Lieutenant Colonel A. Doup was senior officer in two prisoner-of-war camps in Bandung in 1942-1943 and in Struiswijk Prison in Batavia, which served as a camp for officers, in 1944. Shortly after the end of the war he wrote in his report:

> As to the military attitude of the prisoners-of-war in general [...] I cannot be enthusiastic. Many had an inclination (even professional officers) to execute commands properly when given by a Jap and not when given by their own commander, for fear of a beating. In many respects the younger ones gave a better example. In general the head-officers kept apart from the subaltern officers, only a single one volunteered for fatigue, many of them were too stiff in their ideas.[47]

Doup gave a telling example of this. In the Struiswijk Prison a new head of

---

47   A. Doup, 'Report', 1 October 1945, pp. 15-6 (NIOD IC, 1,054).

the garden team had to be appointed. This team worked in the open air and was often picked on by the Koreans. Doup asked whether one of the regular captains would be prepared to act as head. No one came forward. Doup was on the point of simply ordering a regular lieutenant to take the job on, when a reserve naval commander volunteered. It was Doup's general impression that, if it was difficult to exercise authority over the lower ranks, this was much more difficult in the case of officers, since the regulars among them frequently 'pulled rank'. Among the reserve officers there were many who had held important positions in civilian society and had no great respect for regular officers.

Whatever their differences, the prisoners of war all suffered from the isolation in which they found themselves. At the beginning, particularly on Java (we shall come back to this point), some communication was possible between the prisoners and their families and relatives, but after a few months the camps were closed off from the outside world, and contact was possible only by letter (or smuggled letter). Virtually all the Dutch and Dutch Eurasian prisoners had families or relatives living in the occupied Indies or in the occupied Netherlands. Through the mediation of the International Red Cross, it became possible in 1942 to send letters from the occupied Netherlands to the East Indies via Japan.[48] The second Japanese exchange ship that sailed to Lourenço Marques collected 18 sacks of post for Tokyo there in September 1942.[49] In Tokyo, with the help of some captured officers, camp addresses were put on the letters (each camp was given an initial and a number) and they were censored by the Japanese. They were then sent on to the camps in the Nampo, though not until May 1943. In many of those camps they remained for months with the commandant and it is doubtful whether all were given to the prisoners. In the camp at Palembang several prisoners received letters from the occupied Netherlands in mid-February 1944, but nearly five months later more letters from the same consignment were handed out. In the camps on the Pekanbaru Railway some prisoners received letters between May 1944 and August 1945 which had been en route for about a year. Here, piles of mailbags that the commandant had held back were found in his store after the war. In January 1945 finally (no further information is available), a prisoner in Japan received a letter from his parents in Haarlem that had been written in December 1943.

Attempts were also made through the International Red Cross to make it possible for telegrams to be sent between the prisoners of war and the intern-

[48]   The International Red Cross had been able to pass on the names of prisoners of war to the occupied Netherlands through the Dutch Red Cross in The Hague.
[49]   Later consignments went via Iran and the Soviet Union.

ees on the one hand and their relatives in the occupied Netherlands and the Allied countries on the other. The idea was that one telegram and one reply could be sent per prisoner per year. In 1945 Geneva passed on over 60,000 telegrams, but only about 2,000 replies were received from Tokyo.

This brings us to the letters between the prisoners and their families in the Indies. Internees were not allowed to send letters to prisoners of war, and so most of the Dutch internees were unable to communicate with their captured family members. The Dutch Eurasians, insofar as they were not interned, could do so. They had to submit a request to their aid organizations, which would then obtain the number of the camp concerned from the Japanese Prisoners of War Bureau, which was part of the military administration. They could then write a postcard consisting of at most 25 words (the text had to be in Japanese, Malay or English). These postcards were given to the Japanese Bureau. Far from all the cards reached their destination because the Bureau had often not been informed of transfers of prisoners outside the East Indies. In addition, many Japanese thought it unnecessary to carry out the work of censoring, posting, selecting and distributing letters and postcards for the sake of prisoners of war. When the work was done, it was at a snail's pace. In one camp in Japan,[50] where there were hundreds of KNIL prisoners, in January 1945 five married men received postcards from their wives on Java that were more than a year old. Two months later a second consignment of post from Java contained postcards written in January 1943; they had thus taken over two years to reach the addressee.[51]

The delivery of postcards to Singapore also took a long time. One bag with nearly 9,000 postcards written on Java between late 1943 and mid-1944 did not arrive in Singapore until March 1945. It took months before at least some of the cards from this and several later consignments were distributed to the prisoners.

The prisoners in turn were allowed to write to their families rarely if at all. Sometimes the content was laid down in advance. In mid-1942 the Australian and American prisoners of war on Java were told to write letters home saying that they had been frequently assaulted by British prisoners and that they had no doubts about Japanese victory. Most prisoners refused: one

---

[50]   According to Japanese figures, the Prisoners of War Bureau in Tokyo received more than four million letters and postcards addressed to prisoners, or an average of 28 per man. According to the same source, the Bureau dealt with over 850,000 letters and cards written by prisoners. Only a tiny fraction of this post reached the addressee.

[51]   In 1943 and the following years, the Japanese radio on Java included letters written by American and Australian prisoners in its broadcasts, and in 1944 it became possible for Dutch Eurasian women to have a radio letter read out. The texts had to be typed out in the place where they were received. In the prisoner-of-war camp in Singapore the first of these 'radio letters' were not handed out until May 1945. There were 102 of them, but only 39 addressees were present. In June another 554 radio letters arrived; 252 of them could be delivered.

who cooperated ended his letter with the words 'Tell it to the marines!'[52] In November 1942 the British prisoners on Java were given similar instructions, as were the Americans, for the second time. They were all to write a letter whose 'Essentials' had been set out by the Japanese in written guidelines:

1. Point out Britain's (America's) ignorance about the real ability and characteristic of Nipponese.
2. Express your aversion about the war, as: 'How I long for my native land! I wish to return to my sweet home as quickly as possible.'
3. Kindly treated by Nippon authority according to international agreement.[53]

Many prisoners had no objection to sending these letters: they took it for granted that the British and American authorities who would receive them in the first instance would be sufficiently warned by the identical contents (the Japanese had not thought of this), and that their families would welcome any sign of life.

The prisoners on the Burma Railway were also told exactly what to say to their families. In 1943 and 1944 they were given printed cards to which they could add only a few words of their own. At the end of 1944 on one occasion they were allowed to write a completely free message of 25 words at most. Did many of these cards reach their destination? It is doubtful. In Malang early in 1944 a Dutch woman was 'overjoyed', she wrote later:

> by a postcard with printed lines in Japanese and below them the Malay translation followed by a few words [probably censored] from my son. He had been gone for fourteen months and now came the first news from Thailand. [...] The card was more than six months old but that didn't matter. I was mad with joy. I was allowed to write back, though no more than 25 words, in Malay, English or Japanese. My son wrote, 'I am working for pay' and 'Health is excellent!'
> Many women got cards from their husbands, fiancés or sons, but later they found out that the poor chaps had been dead for months before the card brought them such happiness. (Moscou-de Ruyter 1984:139-40.)

We have described how few parcels the prisoners received, how harsh the regime of the Japanese soldiers and Korean guards was, and how the prisoners heard almost nothing from their families and were not allowed to send them news. In fact, once they arrived in areas like the Moluccas, Flores, Aceh, Central Sumatra (the Pekanbaru Railway), Palembang or on the Burma Railway, they also generally heard next to nothing about the one factor that they all realized would determine their fate: the course of the war.[54]

---

[52]   R. Springer, 'Dagboek', p. 20 (NIOD IC, 81,346).
[53]   R. Springer, 'Dagboek', p. 17 (NIOD IC, 81,346).
[54]   The prisoners in most of the camps on Java and Sumatra, in Singapore and Japan did hear

All in all, especially if they had been moved from the islands with which they were familiar, they had the feeling that they had ended up in wretched places where no one knew of their existence – neither their families nor their government. Their suffering was made considerably worse by this sense of abandonment.

They had been used to a fairly comfortable life – now, particularly if they had been moved away from Java and Sumatra, they found themselves in camps where they quickly became dirty and were plagued by vermin such as fleas, head and body lice and bedbugs. These were everywhere, in the barracks and the sleeping mats, and there was no defence. When they had to work, it was generally very hard indeed. Great physical demands were thus made of them, and yet their rations were far too little. There is not much information about this, but it all points in the same direction. KNIL soldiers had been entitled to a daily ration of over 3,800 calories. The rations of the prisoners in Singapore averaged 2,600 calories in 1942, 1943 and 1944, but fell to 1,600 calories during 1945, which was far too little for men doing heavy labour. In one of the camps on Java the calorific value of the daily ration in March 1943 was 2,200; in Japan it was 2,100 in the winter of 1943-1944 and 2,400 in the winter of 1944-1945, again far too little for heavy work. Elsewhere the calorific value of the rations was often even lower.

Not only was the calorific value too low, but there was also no balance between carbohydrates, proteins and fats: the prisoners were given far too little animal protein and, above all, vitamins. This had an adverse effect on the nerves, particularly those extending to the body's extremities. The result was numerous complaints about the eyes (the retina was affected), the fingertips, the soles of the feet and the skin, especially the skin of the scrotum, which became inflamed all over. The prisoners' sight became poorer, they suddenly lost control of their hands and feet, their pulse raced alarmingly, they suffered loss of memory. Nearly all of them also had one or more attacks of malaria – quinine was rarely if ever made available.[55] Dysentery was also common, and on the Burma Railway there was cholera as well. Once a camp was infected, it was extremely difficult to get the infection under control. The doctor N. Beets, himself a former prisoner, wrote:

---

news about the war. Malay or Japanese newspapers sometimes came into the camps, and ingenious technicians usually managed to build a clandestine radio on which they could hear Allied broadcasts. On the other hand, in one of the camps in northern Aceh it was weeks before Van Heekeren saw a copy of an Indonesian daily that lay in shreds in the bottom of a basket. At that point he was the only one in his camp who could read the type of Indonesian used in the press (there had been two others, but they had been moved to another camp shortly before). 'It was typical', he remarks, 'of the colonial society that out of 150 men there was only one who could read the language of the country!' (Van Heekeren 1964:71-2.)

[55]   It should be remembered that 90% of the pre-war cinchona production had come from Java and that its cultivation was not restricted during the Japanese occupation.

The ingenuity of the doctors and nursing staff and kitchen workers and the knowledge of the jungle-boys, who knew what was edible, saved lives. [In particular
the Dutch Eurasians among the KNIL prisoners had a good knowledge of the
nutritional value and medicinal properties of certain plants.] The sacrifices made
by old and young friends and mates, their care of mortally ill comrades, worked
wonders. Patients often lost the will to live, but it was restored by the stubborn
insistence of comrades. (Beets 1981:243.)

In many camps attempts were made in every possible way to compensate
for the lack of animal proteins and vitamins: men ate dogs, cats and rats. 'A
cat is a delicacy, a rat is delicious' (Min 1979:194). 'A piece of dog [...] remarkably tender and tasty' (De Vries 1980:383). Snakes and field mice were eaten;
snails were added to the soup; the fat maggots from the latrines were dried
and fried; all edible plants were regarded as vegetables. But none of this
prevented numerous prisoners from suffering starvation; they wasted away
or became bloated, and died. Medical officers and nurses made enormous
efforts (it was a great advantage for the prisoners that, in violation of the
Geneva Convention, doctors and nurses were also kept in captivity). Many
of them continually put pressure on the Japanese, especially to make more
medicine available, but this rarely had any effect. According to Beets, 'One
came up against a curious ideology of illness among the Japanese. [This ideology applied equally to their own sick soldiers.] The perfect remedy for illness
was: stop being lazy and work harder. Sick prisoners deserved to be punished
for their arrogant rebellion against the Japanese Empire.' (Beets 1981:248.)
This punishment was not long in coming.

In the first year of occupation in the East Indies hardly any prisoners of
war died of natural causes: most of the deaths came later, mainly in the areas
where prisoners were made to work. Of the Dutch and Dutch Eurasians
among them, including those who died on the troopships, 19.4% died; of the
British nearly 25%; of the Americans 33%; and of the Australians 34%. It may
be concluded from this that it was more difficult for the British, Americans and
Australians than for the Dutch and Dutch Eurasians to adapt to the problems
of life as a prisoner of war, and we also suspect that the relatively low death
rate among the Dutch and Dutch Eurasians was largely because of the latter's
ability to adapt to tropical conditions in which they felt entirely at home.

It was very important to have good leadership in a camp. Not everyone
was persuaded that all senior officers and other camp officials were up to
their task. According to a reserve lieutenant of the KNIL, A.J.A.C. Nooteboom,
writing after the war:

There were camp leaders who did not scruple to help themselves to good food,
while the camp as a whole suffered hunger and many of the sick were in a bad way.
The shameless egotism of some leaders was incomprehensible. [...] Some camp commanders hardly ever left their room. Of course, these were only a few cases, but what

happened more often was that the laziness of the camp leaders led to uncontrolled abuses. Thieves stole from the kitchen in a way that would seem incredible later; at times very little was left of a sense of comradeship. Men stole from each other.[56]

No other general condemnations such as this one, which relates to Java, are known and it may present too negative a view.

Even the best camp leadership could not change the general conditions in which they found themselves, and in which concern about the immediate future and fear of what the Japanese might do with their prisoners at the end of the war seemed all too justified. Many a prisoner felt the impulse to resist, but how? By escaping? Very few attempts succeeded (we shall come back to this point). There were no other meaningful forms of resistance. 'Fear', writes Rob Nieuwenhuys, 'was always stronger than resistance. All you could do was endure, however difficult it was.' (Nieuwenhuys 1979:80.)

To the extent that information is available, we shall look briefly at how the various groups of prisoners endured in this way: the original groups in the Great East, on Borneo and on Sumatra, the groups on Java before they were moved, the Special Party, the later groups in Singapore and on the Burma Railway, on Flores and on the Moluccas, in Aceh, on the Pekanbaru Railway and at Palembang, the group that remained on Java, and finally the group in Japan. Their fate will be broadly outlined, and a special section will be devoted to what became one of the worst ordeals: the troopships.

Outer Islands

This section is concerned solely with those who were taken prisoner in the Outer Islands and remained there, thus not with those who were moved away, for example to the Burma Railway. Nor are we concerned here with the prisoners who were moved from Java to the Outer Islands, for example to the Moluccas and Flores and, on Sumatra, to the Pekanbaru Railway and to Palembang for the building of airfields. One exception to this rule will be made: the relatively small group sent from Ambon to Hainan.

Generally speaking, very little information is available.

On Ambon the Japanese military administration set up three camps close together: one for male internees, one for female internees (and their children), and one for prisoners of war. About 2,000 Ambonese were put in the prisoner-of-war camp (they were released on 29 April 1942) together with some 800

---

[56]   A.J.A.C. Nooteboom, 'Vier oorlogsjaren op Java', pp. xv-3 (NIOD IC, 80,991).

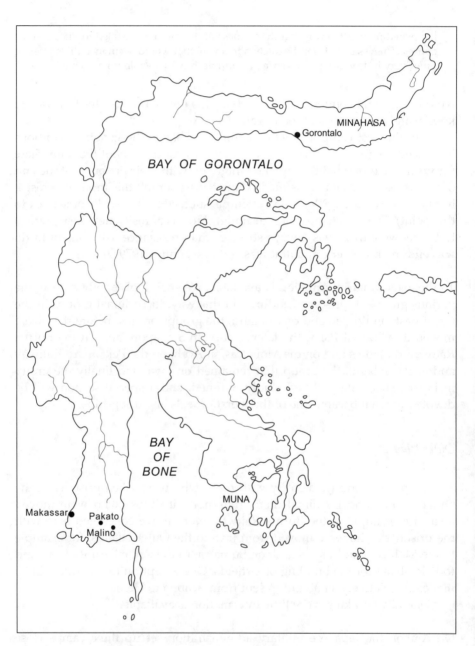

Map 9. Celebes

Australians, 14 Americans and over 250 Dutch and Dutch Eurasians, among them 21 navy men. The camp regime was strict; nevertheless, in July 1942 more than 30 prisoners were caught smuggling notes to the women's camp. They were so severely beaten by a group of Japanese marines on the orders of the camp commandant that three of them died. The Australian senior officer said later, 'Everyone was filled with horror and fear as it was our first experience of the Japanese way of enforcing discipline' (quoted in Wigmore 1957:605).

In October the Dutch and Dutch Eurasians (except for six) and nearly 270 Australians were transferred to a prisoner-of-war camp on Hainan.[57] Conditions on Ambon subsequently deteriorated. To begin with, the Japanese established an ammunition depot close to the three camps; it was bombed by the Allies in February 1943 and August 1944. The first attack caused deaths and injuries in the camps. In addition, from the end of 1942 the prisoners were forced to do heavy labour, while their rations were steadily reduced. Many became ill and there was no medicine. Of the over 530 Australians who were not moved to Hainan, more than 400 died on Ambon. There is no information about the fate of the six European and fourteen American prisoners who stayed on Ambon.

In the northeast of Celebes, namely Minahasa (see Map 9), most of the indigenous soldiers were released in groups, but the Dutch and Dutch Eurasians continued to be held in the prison in Manado. According to a report, conditions there were:

> extremely poor; the space in the cells was so confined that no one could stretch out. For the first two weeks there was barely enough drinking water. [...] The cesspool was full after a few days and the stench in the prison became unbearable.[58]

The prisoners were given little more than rice to eat and it was deliberately burnt, because at the time of the Japanese invasion the Demolition Corps in Manado had set fire to a rice store. The report already cited says:

> The disciplinary measures were bestial. [...] Canes one and a half metres long and four to five centimetres thick were beaten to a pulp on human bodies; it would have seemed incredible if one had not seen it repeatedly with one's own eyes.[59]

---

[57] This group of prisoners was housed in a filthy camp on Hainan at the start of a railway to one of the iron mines. After only a few weeks six KNIL soldiers escaped: they were not helped by the indigenous population and returned to the camp, where they were executed. At the end of 1944 an escape attempt by two KNIL sergeants major, A. Hansma and J. Roelofs, was successful: with the help of Chinese, they were able to join a Chinese guerrilla unit. Of the 4,000 Chinese who had turned to guerrilla warfare in 1938 after the Japanese landed, about 1,200 were then still together. How many prisoners of war died on Hainan is not known exactly – probably a third of the Dutch and Dutch Eurasian group.
[58] 'Gegevens omtrent gevangenen in de Minahassa', 1946, p. 1 (NIOD IC, 62,255).
[59] 'Gegevens omtrent gevangenen in de Minahassa', 1946, p. 1 (NIOD IC, 62,255).

The Japanese claimed that these measures were intended as punishments because they had not yet captured the KNIL commander in Minahasa, Major B.F. Schillmöller. When he was caught and taken to Manado at the beginning of April,[60] the treatment of the prisoners of war improved: they were moved to a former KNIL barracks and some of them stayed there until the end of the war.

There were many more prisoners on Southwest Celebes: in the end, as stated above, over 2,700, consisting of nearly 900 British, 185 Americans, about 830 Dutch navy men and about 800 KNIL soldiers, all Dutch or Dutch Eurasian.[61] Here too the indigenous KNIL soldiers were given an opportunity to leave the camp. It was first located in the infantry barracks and the former Training School for Native Seamen in Makassar,[62] and later, from July 1944, in an indigenous *kampong* which was not far from Makassar in the middle of an area plagued by malaria and other diseases. A small group of prisoners was privileged: 25 linguists who assisted several Japanese with their study of *adat* law on Celebes. The other prisoners had a hard time. On only meagre rations they had to do heavy, sometimes humiliating work: road sweeping, breaking stones, unloading coal, and later building gun emplacements and ammunition stores. They were punished frequently and harshly. Sometimes prisoners, including officers, were forced to assault each other; sometimes the Japanese themselves did the beating. The 'record holder' was an American soldier who in October 1942 withstood 238 blows with a cane without collapsing.

A number of prisoners were killed by the Japanese in Makassar for attempting to escape: three KNIL soldiers and ten Americans[63] in July 1942; and two KNIL soldiers and a navy man in September. All were beheaded.

Afterwards 325 prisoners of war died in Makassar, or about 12% of the original 2,700. However, of this large group, as mentioned, about 500 navy men

---

[60]   There he was asked if he had ordered the demolition operations at Manado when the Japanese landed; he denied it. Several members of the Demolition Corps were subsequently beheaded. One shipping man was told by a Japanese interpreter: 'They were at once dead, the Japanese sword is very sharp'. J. van Duggenaar, 'Oorlogs- en andere herinneringen', n.d., p. 6 (NIOD IC, 81,038).
[61]   They included KNIL soldiers who had been captured on Timor, although most KNIL prisoners on Timor were taken to Java.
[62]   Some of the prisoners – about 150 British and Americans, a few hundred Dutch navy men, several hundred indigenous KNIL soldiers and 23 Dutch and Dutch Eurasian KNIL soldiers, among them the commander of Southwest Celebes, Colonel M. Vooren – were first held in Makassar in the prison, where they were received by the indigenous warders with kicks and punches. They were treated especially badly there. When all these groups of prisoners were allowed to move to the infantry barracks in early April 1942 (Colonel Vooren had gone to some effort to arrange this), the Dutch and Dutch Eurasians arrived 'singing patriotic songs' in the words of one of them (Report in Brugmans 1960:344-5). Colonel Vooren was later moved to Java, where he remained.
[63]   Plus two indigenous persons, presumably for giving assistance.

were moved to Japan in October 1942 and other prisoners were sent to Java in 1943, 1944 and July 1945, so that the death rate among those who remained in Makassar from beginning to end must have been substantially higher.

After the release of the indigenous troops, about 1,100 KNIL prisoners of war were left on Dutch Borneo: about 400 in Pontianak (see Map 3), who were later transferred to British Borneo, and 700 elsewhere on Borneo, of whom the largest group, some 500, was in Balikpapan. Smaller numbers were held in camps on Tarakan, in Samarinda and in Banjarmasin.

KNIL prisoners were put to death for attempting to escape on Dutch Borneo too. Three escaped in mid-June 1942 from their camp at Pontianak (located in the mission house). In the evening the senior officer reported to the Japanese that they were missing. A search was immediately organized, and it was the son of the sultan of Pontianak who with a group of indigenous people found the prisoners about 20 km away.[64] They were handed over to the Japanese. Their execution took place on the banks of the Kapuas before numerous indigenous inhabitants summoned by the beating of the gong and all the KNIL officers. When they had lined up, one of them recalled in March 1946:[65]

> The three soldiers were brought into the camp. Their hands were chained behind them, their backs had been beaten till they broke. [...] They were blindfolded and I could see clearly from their tottering gait that they had already suffered terribly. [...] After a few moments they were each given a mug of water. Then they were taken to the river and I saw how one of them probably said a prayer, because his lips were moving and his face was lifted upwards.
> [...] The bodies [...] were kicked into the river after the beheading.

The group from Pontianak was subsequently moved to Kuching on British Borneo.

Otherwise all that is known about the prisoners of war on Borneo is that they had to work hard building roads and airfields, that their situation was particularly difficult on Tarakan, and that of the group at Balikpapan, which was moved to a Japanese bivouac in the interior shortly before MacArthur's troops landed in 1945, a large number (about 250 of the 400 still alive) managed to escape in the chaos of the final phase.

On Sumatra (for all the places mentioned, see Map 7) in total about 4,500 Dutch and Dutch Eurasian soldiers and 1,200 British and a small number of Australian troops were taken prisoner by the Japanese. Most of the British

---

[64] It should be remembered that the sultan himself died in Japanese detention at the beginning of 1944.
[65] Text in Brugmans 1960:235-6.

soldiers were originally in Padang: they had deserted from the island of Singapore (after continually misbehaving they were disarmed on the orders of the Dutch authorities and confined to the barracks); later they were joined by troops who had been ordered to leave Singapore. The Australian cruiser *Hobart*, the two old cruisers *Danae* and *Dragon* and the two old British destroyers, which had been given permission by Helfrich on 27 February to leave East Indian waters, picked up the deserters in Padang – about 800 British and Indian troops – but left behind 1,200 British and an unknown number of Indian troops. The British were later moved to the Medan district.[66]

There were two camps there: the Unie *kampong* at Belawan mentioned in Chapter II, which had formerly been used to accommodate newly arrived contract coolies, and Glugur camp, which had been used as the first location for contract coolies who had proved recalcitrant while being shipped to Deli – Glugur had much in common with a prison.

Starting from these two camps in Belawan, the lower ranks among the prisoners of war had to do various kinds of work, as described by Van Heekeren (1964:5):

> loading and unloading ships in Belawan-Deli, laying out beds at the agricultural testing station, planting elephant grass at a former tobacco estate, sorting scrap metal, oil drums, and loading and unloading oil, building shelters for the Japanese motor pool and a great deal of other work.

In May 1942 some 2,000 prisoners of war were moved from Belawan to Burma. They included approximately 1,500 Dutch and Dutch Eurasians, among whom there were few graduates. This was because in principle the Japanese military administration wanted graduates to stay in their posts as Nippon workers. Little came of this policy. When in the course of 1943 the Kempeitai built up a picture of the secret organization established by General Overakker and Colonel Gosenson, it was decided, as stated in Chapter II, to intern all Nippon workers and large numbers of Ambonese and Manadonese (among whom there were many ex-KNIL soldiers who had been released).

Few prisoners of war were left in the Belawan area by May 1942. Of them, over 300 Dutch and Dutch Eurasians and just under 200 British and Australians were taken to Aceh in early March 1944 as the so-called Aceh Party under the supervision of one Japanese lieutenant and 22 Korean guards. There they were to build one of three roads (one was never finished) straight through the mountains between Blangkejeren and Takingeun which would make possible a new through route between the east and west coast.

[66] A small number of British and Australian prisoners endured the Japanese occupation largely in two camps in Palembang (one was in a school). In March 1944 this group was put in one camp and subsequently made to work on the construction of new airfields near Palembang.

The prisoners in the Aceh Party were taken in buses towards Blangkejeren, but had to walk the last 120 km. The first part of the route had already been built by many thousands of *romusha*, partly Acehnese and partly Bataks. The prisoners had to widen and improve the road, by installing culverts for drainage among other things, according to the directions of Japanese engineers, who inflicted frequent beatings. When all this was finished after four months of hard work (they had one day off each month), there was also a derelict bridge that had to be strengthened. The prisoners were housed in primitive camps abandoned by the *romusha*. Several of them lay high in the mountains – it was cold there and the mud in the camp rose above the ankle because of the amount of rain. Far too little food was provided, but in various camps the prisoners managed to get extra food, either by trading with the indigenous population or by finding food in the surroundings. 'The Eurasian lads', writes Van Heekeren (1964:101), 'had a huge advantage because they knew of all kinds of sources of food that a *totok* would never think of'. They found edible plants, got hold of honeycombs, and grilled the larvae of bees, ants and woodworms. Field mice and rats were also eaten. Once a big python was killed, 'from which a delicious soup was made', and a nurse managed to catch a bear which was added to 'the general pot' (Van Heekeren 1964:102-3).

The prisoners suffered greatly from swarms of mosquitoes and small flies and gnats. Nearly all of them caught malaria, and a few score developed hunger oedema. Quite soon after work started, however, nearly 50 ill prisoners were allowed to return to the camp in Belawan, and this was one reason why only three of the Aceh Party died on the spot.

When the job was done, the prisoners, many of whom had no footwear left, had to walk back to Kutacane, partly in night marches. This was a special ordeal for those who could no longer see in the dark because of a vitamin deficiency. 'Men held on to each other, and tied more or less white rags to their back'. One prisoner,

> who had real cat's eyes, led a whole group of night-blind men by sticking a firefly to his calf.
>
> On this journey the Koreans behaved extremely brutally and harshly. If prisoners could not keep up, they threw their knapsack into the ravine, which under the circumstances was a disaster for the person concerned. But there are also reports of guards who helped one or two prisoners. (Van Heekeren 1964:121-2.)

In July and August 1944 groups were formed from the prisoners who had not left Belawan and set to work on the eastern part of the Pekanbaru Railway. A similar fate awaited the men of the Aceh Party: at the end of October 1944 they were moved to Padang, from where they were taken to the western part of the same railway – they are discussed below.

Curiously, on North Sumatra the Dutch Eurasian prisoners of war were not sent to 'European' camps, but found themselves together with the indigenous prisoners in a camp high in the Alas Valley that was part of a complex built in 1940 to hold 'German' internees.[67] The complex also included two internment camps, one for men and one for women and children. The prisoners of war were put to work: they had to till *sawah* and cut wood. In May 1943, however, they were informed that they ought to become *heiho*, Japanese auxiliaries; it was clear that a refusal could have grave consequences. Almost all the indigenous prisoners gave in to the Japanese demand, but among the Dutch Eurasians (the families of some of them were in the women's camp) there was resistance. The senior officer and 57 other prisoners thought that the Japanese demand should be complied with; 52 prisoners took a different view. At a meeting organized by a reservist, H. Wolff, who had been a teacher in Padang in civilian life, they decided to draw up a document asking the Japanese to release them from military service: they were prepared, they said, to do any other kind of work.

After this request was presented, all those who had refused (accompanied in nine cases by their wife and children) were taken to Kutacane, lower down in the Alas Valley. There four of them – Wolff and Sergeants M.J. Croes, K. Stoltz and H.F. Voss – were summarily shot. Of the remaining 48, 5 finally ended up in Medan and 43 were put in prison south of Kutacane; none of them survived.

Java: the first period

On Java (for all of the places mentioned, see Map 8) the prisoners of war were initially assembled at locations not far from where the various surrenders had been arranged (the KNIL's on 9 March 1942, followed by that of the British, Australian and American soldiers a few days later). Thereafter they were concentrated in four areas: Batavia, Bandung-Cimahi, Surabaya and Malang, where the British, Australians and Americans were separated from the KNIL soldiers, with a division being made among the latter between the indigenous troops on the one hand and the Dutch and Dutch Eurasians on the other hand. On Java in 1942 and later these Dutch and Dutch Eurasians ended up in several dozen complexes: KNIL barracks (as many as four in Batavia alone and ten in the region of Bandung-Cimahi), military and emergency hospitals, coolie camps, harbour sheds (in Batavia and Surabaya), schools, prisons (two in Batavia), a reformatory (the Landsopvoedingsgesticht in Bandung) and a large exposition site (the 'Jaarmarktkamp' in Surabaya).

---

[67]   See Introduction, p. 27.

In the beginning there was little order in the camps. During the week of fighting units had got mixed up and in the camps it was not always possible to establish who belonged to what unit and whether, with the exception of those who had perished or were wounded, all were present. No one knew exactly who in the navy had got away. Moreover, several thousand had been able to avoid imprisonment and ignored all of the radio announcements calling for ex-soldiers to report to the camps.[68] In the first days the camps were not closed and even when a Japanese stood guard at the entrance, contact with the outside world was still possible. Indeed, in Buitenzorg, Bandung, Yogyakarta and Surabaya relatives were permitted to visit daily and when these visits were subsequently forbidden they could still drop off letters and parcels. Most camps were only closed towards the end of March or mid-April, when a double barbed wire enclosure was placed around them in between which was a two-metre high wall of plaited bamboo.[69] Moreover, in mid-April the Post Office was ordered to stop processing all mail to or from prisoners of war, which it complied with when it resumed operations in May.

Before the camps were closed, outsiders had been able to gain an idea of them. According to Elias in Bandung:

> The impression is one of deep desolation. In front of the main entrance barricaded with barbed wire are vendors selling fruit [...] and all sorts of Indonesian refreshments. Scattered everywhere on the ground are peel, paper and other debris. The soldiers are queued up beyond this, expecting a visitor or hoping to receive one. They look for friends and acquaintances who come for others, and are eager to speak with them about their chances of a speedy release. In these first weeks they are almost all already poorly clothed, without a shirt let alone a collar, wearing slippers or shoes without laces. These chewing, spitting and chattering groups amble around aimlessly. The buildings are dilapidated, unpainted and squalid. (Elias 1946:69.)

In the beginning the mood in the camps was one of irritability. Later, according to Lieutenant Colonel H. Poulus, the senior officer in one of the largest camps in Bandung where initially about 12,000 prisoners of war were crowded together:[70]

> The NCO's and other ranks were decidedly hostile to the officers; among the subalterns in general a hostile disposition predominated vis à vis the field officers and on the whole the Army Commander and his staff were held responsible for

---

[68]   The KNIL had approximately 41,800 European soldiers; assuming that there were about 600 Europeans among the almost 900 who died, approximately 41,200 remain. Of them, 36,900 were taken prisoner. Thus, 4,300 were able to evade this. Of this group the Dutch ended up in civilian internment camps.

[69]   Building these barricades was consistently the first task assigned to the prisoners of war.

[70]   Poulus became senior officer in the camp after Colonel C.G. Toorop was transferred to Batavia – Toorop became a member of the Special Party.

the debacle that had occurred. Maintaining discipline was [...] virtually impossible. This was compounded by the fact that many appealed to the proclamation of the commander-in-chief which had led to much confusion and misunderstanding [...], namely that the Royal Dutch East Indian Army had ceased to exist as a unit.[71] Accordingly, it was concluded that the army no longer existed and consequently the standards with respect to military relations, ranks, discipline etc. were no longer in effect.[72]

In a few camps fights broke out between officers and the lower ranks. This was prohibited by the Japanese, who let it be known that disobeying officers would be considered a crime against the Japanese government and would be severely punished. What kinds of punishment the Japanese government had in mind was not known – various prisoners of war found it hard to accept military discipline again. Escapes were not rare – almost 100 prisoners of war had escaped from the camps in Bandung in mid-April. Escaping was emphatically forbidden as well. Did this help? Only partially – some brooded on it while others did not hesitate to crawl under the camp enclosure the moment it turned dark to spend the night with their wives, returning before dawn.

In April 1942 General Imamura was visited by no less than six authorities from Tokyo: three advisers who remained on Java, and three high-ranking officers, namely the head of the Japanese army staff, the head of the division of military administrations of the War Department, and the head of the personnel division of the same department. All six relayed complaints from Tokyo that Imamura's policy was too mild. Did this result in or contribute to a tougher approach to the prisoners of war? Possibly. Whatever the case may be, on 21 April three KNIL soldiers who had escaped from the camp and had been caught in Cirebon were executed together with two indigenous KNIL soldiers in one of the camps near Bandung. On 22 April the same punishment was meted out to six soldiers in two other camps near Bandung: in one to a low-ranking navy man and two KNIL soldiers who were caught some distance from the camp; in the other to three KNIL soldiers who, as they had done more frequently, had left the camp the previous evening – two Dutchmen and a Dutch Eurasian, the 57-year-old adjutant-NCO Louis August Marks.

The three who had been caught in Cirebon (had they hoped to find a ship there?), were informed early in the morning of 21 April together with two indigenous KNIL soldiers (the reason for the execution of the latter two is unknown) that they would be shot. Later Major van Baarsel recollected:

The two natives were seemingly unmoved by the words of the interpreter. Quite understandably, the three Eurasian boys were desperate. [...] I heard from a few

[71]   This proclamation had been sent out on 8 March and had conveyed that units of the KNIL, where possible, were to take the initiative to become guerrillas.
[72]   H. Poulus, 'Verslag', 22 July 1946, p. 1 (NIOD IC, 2,031).

soldiers, Eurasian lads, who had climbed a tree in the camp and so had been able to see the execution, that the Japanese dragged the five to the graves. There they were lined up with their backs to the graves. [...] His bayonet levelled, a Jap positioned himself in front of each of them. On a signal these Japs stormed forward while belting out a wild Japanese war cry and plunged their bayonets into the stomachs of those five poor lads so that they fell back into the pit. Then, standing at the edge of the pit, the Japanese fired upon their victims. Immediately thereafter other Japanese soldiers filled the graves and placed flowers on them.[73]

On the morning of 22 April, the naval man and the two KNIL soldiers, the seaman H. Karssen and the gunners A. Hielkema and J.W. Mercus, were bound to three poles stuck in the ground near the gate of the camp in question. The senior officer, Lieutenant Colonel Poulus, his camp commanders and the head of the medical service were summoned by the Japanese camp commandant, Captain Kawakatsu, and told via the interpreter that they had to attend the execution of the three escapees. Poulus later recalled:

> No further details were announced. [...] After consulting the interpreter, who was reputed to be an acclaimed expert on Japan, I became convinced that this was a piece of play-acting taken to the extreme with the express purpose of intimidating the prisoners of war. [...] Nevertheless, I wanted to make an attempt to request a reprieve for those involved, but I was given no chance to bring up the matter.

The three escaped soldiers were untied from the poles and were then bound to the barbed wire enclosure with their arms behind them. Poulus and the other KNIL officers had to stand a short distance away from them.

> After the prisoners had been blindfolded, the interpreter was instructed to ask them if there was anything they wished to say. All three made use of this opportunity and their last statements were recorded by the interpreter. Karssen's request that his blindfold be removed was granted by the Japanese. Next, the execution squad took up its position opposite the prisoners aiming their bayonets at them, and on the signal of the commanding Japanese officer began to perform a kind of warrior dance while uttering bestial cries. At that moment seaman Karssen [...] who saw what was about to happen, called out: 'Long live the Queen, hurrah!', to which the other two [...] responded with 'Hurrah!' [...] The dancing and screaming Japs at once brutally stabbed and slaughtered them with their bayonets. When during this gruesome performance several of the Dutch commanders in attendance turned their heads away, Captain Kawakatsu screamed out an order that they continue watching; the medical officer fainted. The man in the middle (next to Karssen) [...] was not yet dead. A Japanese lieutenant stepped towards him, laughingly drew his pistol from its holster with an indifferent gesture and shot him in the head the way one might finish off a rabid dog.[74]

---

73   J. van Baarsel, 'Onder de Jappen', p. 18 (NIOD IC, 81,359).
74   H. Poulus, 'Verslag', 22 July 1946, p. 4 (NIOD IC, 2,031).

The execution was witnessed not only by the selected KNIL officers but by others as well. 'We could not believe what we had seen', a conscript wrote later: 'We were all in shock. We walked around the camp in a daze.'[75]

Together with a fourth soldier, the three KNIL soldiers who were executed in the other camp on 22 April had tried to leave the camp for the night the previous evening. They were caught by a Japanese guard – one of the four shot at the guard with a pistol he had managed to conceal, missing him – and escaped. His three comrades were apprehended. They were immediately bound to poles and battered the entire night. On the morning of the 22nd, according to the account of a fellow prisoner:

> They were brought to the Dutch camp commander, who had to tell them that they would be executed at noon. [...] After being prepared for their deaths by the priest and the minister, they were blindfolded and bound to the barbed wire.
>
> The entire camp was forced to watch. Forty heavily armed Japs closed off the terrain; then two Japs with fixed bayonets were positioned next to each victim. At the last moment the Jap commander asked if they had a last wish; Marks requested that he be allowed to die without the blindfold, this was granted. At a signal from the Japanese officer the executioners leaped towards their victims [...] while uttering savage shrieks. Marks called out: 'Long live the Queen!' The two others followed his example. (Van Hees et al., n.d.:196-7.)

They were stabbed three times with bayonets. Marks was still alive. His last act was to spit in the face of the Japanese commandant who had drawn his pistol to shoot him.

More such executions were carried out and what is known about them will also be recorded here.

In Cimahi nine soldiers who had left their camp for a night were executed on 5 May: five Manadonese, two Ambonese and two Dutchmen. They were beaten, paraded around the camp and subsequently lined up before a wall: the seven indigenous soldiers were bound together, as were the two Dutchmen. Two Japanese soldiers had to first shoot the seven indigenous men. The first two shots ricocheted, the second pair of shots injured one of the indigenous men in the knee. Falling down, he pulled the other six with him. The group was tugged up and fired upon again. Most of the shots were not fatal, so that the men wound up lying on the ground, most of them unconscious. After the two Dutchmen had been subsequently led away from the camp and executed, several Japanese officers returned and finished off the seven indigenous men with revolver shots. One of the two Ambonese was still alive after taking 12 shots – a Dutch medical officer had to point out to the Japanese where the man's heart was located. The two commanding Japanese officers 'got drunk after the execution', according to a Dutch captain who had served as one of the two interpreters, 'in order to forget all of this misery, as they explained to us, the interpreters'.[76] The Japanese camp commandant (who is reported to have gone to the Japanese headquarters in Bandung to plead for a pardon) lay a wreath on the graves the next morning.

In May, two young Dutch Eurasian soldiers who had heard that their mother was seriously ill escaped from the camp in Sukabumi.[77] The Japanese camp commandant there announced that ten prisoners of war would be shot if they were not able to track down the two escapees. To this end, help was offered by a Dutch chief inspector of police, a man who had already done the Japanese so many favours that he was allowed to keep his post when the other Dutch police officials were dismissed. A police commissioner heard 'that he extracted the youths' whereabouts from the father of one of them'.[78] In the presence of all of the officers one of the two soldiers was bayoneted and the other decapitated after the sword used for this purpose was sharpened in his sight.

In Yogyakarta on 23 May three prisoners of war were bayoneted for having left the camp (according to a report, 'one of them crawled out of the pit again and was jabbed back in with the bayonet; the grave was then filled' (quoted in Van Witsen 1971:31)). Three prisoners of war were executed in Batavia, two in Garut, three in Surabaya, four in Singosari and six in Malang, all on unknown dates.

Thus, on Java a total of 43 KNIL soldiers were executed by the Japanese for leaving the camp. These executions made a deep impression on the prisoners. In March and April many had believed that it would not be all that bad; some had even thought that the Japanese might release them, others that the Allies would soon land on Java.[79] Reality had now dealt an almost crushing blow to all that optimism. The prisoners of war realized that for the time being they would remain prisoners, that they had no rights and that the Japanese could act with ruthless cruelty.

In the camps in Bandung (and presumably also in the other camps on West

---

[76] NWCIT Singapore, proces-verbaal by G.P.C. le Clercq, 8 February 1946, p. 2 (NIOD IC, 174).

[77] On the other hand, another prisoner of war in Sukabumi had heard that they planned to flee to Australia.

[78] M.C. Misero, 'Verslag', 18 November 1946, p. 1 (ARA, Alg. Secr., Eerste zending, XXII, 45, 113).

[79] At the beginning of April a rumour circulated in one of the camps that President Roosevelt had promised Princess Juliana that Java would be liberated on her birthday (30 April). On 16 April one of the prisoners of war there made the following note: 'The wildest rumours are doing the rounds. There is talk of three American landings on Java. Someone thought he heard cannon roar. Some believe this to be true. Others are more cautious. After all, no news of this has been heard on the radio, no matter what station you listen to. Radio operators assert, however, that they truly received this news by wire.' (F.B. Nijon, 'Aantekeningen', 16 April 1942 (NIOD IC).)

Java) it was announced at the beginning of May that all badges of rank had to be handed in: this was a move favouring anarchy. In his report, Lieutenant Colonel Poulus noted:

> In those days it became painfully clear that only relatively few men had inner discipline and self-control to such a degree that [...] they could be relied upon fully. With extreme caution and the application of methods other than those used under normal circumstances, an attempt had to be made to create some sort of order in this chaos and bring about a situation in which at least the most elementary standards [...] would once again be respected. That this was ultimately achieved is in part thanks to the (unfortunately relatively few) well-intentioned, inherently disciplined officers, NCO's and other ranks who through their personal example [...] stood by me in this thankless and difficult task.[80]

In the large camp where Poulus was senior officer, conflicts initially emerged because one group of soldiers had more money, that is to say a larger kitty, at its disposal than another, and could use it to supplement the low rations with whatever the groups of foragers – who were allowed to leave the camp on some days with the permission of the Japanese – were able to buy in Bandung. Each group cooked for itself. Poulus demanded that all of the soldiers' kitties be merged into a single camp fund. However, not all of them were handed over and 'attempts to bolster the camp fund with voluntary contributions from prisoners of war and loans on the basis of I.O.U.s met with little success'.[81] It took some time before he was able to get a grip on the situation; a central kitchen unit was set up, and the Japanese camp commandant gave his approval for the foodstuffs needed to supplement the rations to be provided by regular suppliers. Another factor in the restoration of discipline was that Poulus, after the execution of Karssen, Hielkema and Mercus and after he had personally guaranteed the prevention of future escapes,[82] had received permission from Captain Kawakatsu to establish a camp police. It sent out patrols to catch escaping prisoners of war (these patrols were especially vigilant around the stations) and helped maintain order. This camp police, incidentally, had been 'selected and organized such [...] that it could serve as a storm troop in the event of the Allied Forces' arrival [...] (which, naively, was still thought to be imminent) when a collective attempt to break out would be considered appropriate and responsible'.[83]

---

[80] H. Poulus, 'Verslag', 22 July 1946, pp. 1-2 (NIOD IC, 2,031).
[81] H. Poulus, 'Verslag', 22 July 1946, p. 2 (NIOD IC, 2,031).
[82] After Karssen, Hielkema and Mercus, three other prisoners of war had escaped and had also been apprehended. By making a personal guarantee, Poulus was able to negotiate a sentence of only a few weeks in prison for those three.
[83] H. Poulus, 'Verslag', 22 July 1946, pp. 4-5 (NIOD IC, 2,031).

In part already in April but especially in May 1942, overcoming their lethargy, numerous prisoners of war attempted to do something useful again. Officers formed small groups to deliberate on a new organization of the KNIL. Those who were religious sought support from one another (every evening, J.C. Hamel taught catechism in one of the camps in Surabaya to which he had been transferred from Magelang).[84] Musical companies were formed; cabarets were organized,[85] and in particular lectures were given. In Lieutenant Colonel Poulus's camp a kind of literary faculty was created on the initiative of a man from the province of Limburg (in the southern part of the Netherlands), who had been a Dutch language teacher. According to the writer Rob Nieuwenhuys (1979:57):

> He appointed himself vice-chancellor [...] and dressed up the formal opening very nicely. He gave it something of a carnavalesque feel by introducing a beadle with tinkling bells, who declaimed Latin sentences while making an entrance in stately strides, followed by a procession of professors wearing paper hats, the vice-chancellor at the head.

In June the large camps in Bandung were partially cleared out: approximately 4,800 Dutch prisoners of war were transferred from the largest one to Cilacap and a small group of technicians (with regard to the latter, the Japanese wanted to determine where they could be deployed as Nippon workers) and all Dutch Eurasian prisoners of war, together numbering about 5,000, vanished to Cimahi.[86] Moreover, almost all prisoners of war from the smaller camps in Bandung (some of the officers remained behind) went to Cimahi, and this they did on foot. Later, an officer, who had first been detained in the Landsopvoedingsgesticht (National Reformatory, LOG), recounted:

> The news spread quickly and all the women [...] came flocking to see their husbands just once more. However, the accompanying Japanese flogged them from the streets with cane whips. My wife, who tried to give me some money, was whipped before my eyes. I marched on, because resistance would have meant execution and death.

---

[84]   He established a church council with church council members of various denominations. 'All in all', he wrote 'it was a blossoming congregation': 'the congregation of Jesus Christ in captivity' (Hamel 1948:57).

[85]   In the largest camp in Bandung on 6 June 1942, 50 cabaret performances had already been given of three programmes: 'Geen zorgen voor morgen' (No worries about tomorrow); 'Lol' ('Laat ons lachen') (Let's laugh); and 'Pap' ('Pret achter prikkeldraad') (Fun behind barbed wire). Jazz bands performed, and a Hawaiian Band with one Hula dancer ('We're just dying of laughter'). (F.B. Nijon, 'Dagaantekeningen', 3 June 1942.)

[86]   Among the Dutch who went to Cilacap was a group of Dutch Eurasians who in no way looked 'Indonesian'.

In our group was Wim Kan, and the only woman who managed to keep a constant eye on us during the eight kilometre march was Corry Vonk.[87]

Of the approximately 4,800 men who departed for Cilacap, about 1,200 ended up in a half built, completely empty encampment near the sea, the so-called Nieuwe Kamp (New Camp), and 3,600 initially crammed into a small military barracks intended for 300 men. Only some of the prisoners were put to work; as for the others, their 'primary activity' according to Rob Nieuwenhuys (1979:60) became 'avoiding the Japanese patrols that marched around the camp like bullies all day long with their fixed bayonets. [...] They always found a reason to hit, such as an overly penetrating glance or a suspicious twist to the mouth or sometimes just the height of a prisoner.' Consequently, in the camp Japanese soldiers were always chasing after prisoners who tried to hide. As punishment, the Japanese commandant, a 21-year-old lieutenant, 'Browny the Bear', would order nightly roll calls, 'sometimes three times a night [...], preferably when it was raining'. (Nieuwenhuys 1979:60.)

Even worse than 'Browny the Bear' was the commandant of the Nieuwe Kamp, also a young Japanese lieutenant, Takita, otherwise known as 'Alva' (Alva was the Spanish general who ruthlessly suppressed a Protestant rebellion in the Netherlands in 1567). It was he who forced all of the prisoners to bow while kneeling for two hours when one of them threw his incorrectly filled in declaration of obedience in the wastepaper basket. When they arrived at the camp, Takita told Lieutenant Colonel Poulus (in a phase when it had not yet been officially decided in Tokyo that the prisoners of war were soldiers of the lowest rank, that is to say more or less conscripted in the Japanese army) 'that we had to fully understand that we were not prisoners of war but insurgents and rebels and that we would be treated accordingly'.[88] Indeed, the prisoners of war received very little to eat. Outside the camp they had to do heavy clearing work in the destroyed harbour of Cilacap (this was accompanied by a lot of flogging), and in the camp, among other tasks, a hill with 'thousands of cubic metres of soil' had to be levelled 'almost entirely with bare hands' and 'in a similar manner' heavy coconut palm trees had to be uprooted. Furthermore 'all the grass and overgrowth in the camp had to be cleared by hand'.[89]

Under his personal supervision (as 'general director', Poulus writes) Takita had his guards treat the prisoners with excessive harshness:

---

[87]   Letter from H.J.A. Hendrikx, n.d. (end of September 1982). Wim Kan and Corry Vonk (a married couple) were famous cabaret entertainers.
[88]   H. Poulus, 'Verslag', 22 July 1946, p. 6 (NIOD IC, 2,031).
[89]   H. Poulus, 'Verslag', 22 July 1946, p. 9 (NIOD IC, 2,031).

The least transgression (for example, an unbuttoned uniform button, a slightly bent wrist while greeting, not instantly understanding an order given in Japanese, moving the eyeballs when looking at a Jap, not holding one's hands completely straight when standing at attention and countless other comparable trifles) could lead to one's being viciously struck with a fist, a bamboo stick, a piece of iron, the butt of a gun or a bayonet, causing severe harm to many. Favourite activities included kicking open shins and using jujitsu holds, especially in the immediate vicinity of the barbed wire barricade, so that the victim fell into the wire and seriously hurt himself.[90]

Furthermore, collective punishments were the order of the day:

This usually began with a general roll call, often in the middle of the night, when at the blast of a horn the entire camp had to trot to the parade ground and fall in within a few minutes. There the camp had to stand at attention for hours (once even for 12 hours on end)[91] without eating or drinking, under the supervision of several guards who seized such opportunities to flog the men indiscriminately to their heart's content. The programme of harassments and torments on such occasions was richly varied. Prisoners who had not instantly stood motionless or, exhausted, had tried to sit down for a moment were arranged in groups opposite each other and had to hit each other in the face as hard as they could. There was no point in trying to spare one another because the guards would simply intervene and demonstrate just how hard the blows had to be long enough to make matters worse. Others had to hold heavy benches or beams out before them and were beaten and kicked when they allowed these objects to slump. Then there were others who were given a spoonful of finely ground hot *lombok*[92] and had to stand for a long time with this in their mouths. Yet others had to kneel and sharp stones, or other objects were placed in the hollows of their knees.[93]

In effect the way in which the prisoners of war were drilled was also a form of punishment:

The Japanese commands had to be learned in a single day and every afternoon [the prisoners] were drilled in the Japanese manner for hours on end in the burning sun. That hitting was rife throughout these sessions hardly needs mentioning.

---

[90]   H. Poulus, 'Verslag', 22 July 1946, p. 8 (NIOD IC, 2,031).
[91]   According to Nieuwenhuys, that roll call, which occurred on 25 August, lasted 15 hours: from 2 o'clock at night to 5 o'clock the next afternoon. Takita had personally apprehended a prisoner who had bought salt and sugar from a merchant outside the camp. The smuggler and the merchant, Nieuwenhuys reports, were 'first tortured and then beaten half to death' after which the roll call started, both for the healthy and the sick. 'Whoever collapsed, was drenched with water and had to get back in line. You urinated in your place, while standing at attention. The dysentery patients had a particularly hard time of it. [...] I made a curious discovery: a person can sleep standing, even without falling over.' (Nieuwenhuys 1979:85-6.)
[92]   The hot pepper from which *sambal* (a spicy red sauce) is made. On this occasion the mess officer had put enough sugar in the *sambal* that the prisoners could stand it.
[93]   H. Poulus, 'Verslag', 22 July 1946, pp. 8-9 (NIOD IC, 2,031).

Furthermore, day in, day out [the prisoners] had to practice uttering Japanese cries (commands) as loudly and bestially as possible, for which the entire troop had to congregate on the general parade ground where they had to yell in a deafening din for hours on end under the watchful eye of Lieutenant Takita, who observed this spectacle from an elevation and dealt personally with those who did not howl loud enough.

A favourite opportunity for administering mental and physical torture was the camp watch comprised of prisoners of war instituted by Lieutenant Takita himself. This was a 24-hour watch whose guardroom was in the immediate vicinity of the Japanese sentries. Upon the changing of the guard, it had to post sentries at various points in the camp inside of the barbed wire enclosure. Lieutenant Takita would come creeping into the camp at the most unexpected moments, often in the middle of the night, and usually began by punishing the camp guard who, according to him, upon his arrival (which took place as inconspicuously as possible) had not yelled out *Kèrè!* (Bow!) swiftly or loudly enough. In addition to being subjected to severe corporal punishment, the entire watch was also usually made to scream *Kèrè!* for hours on end, sometimes the entire night, until totally hoarse and semi-comatose, they would lean on one another, at which point they were somewhat revived with a bucket of water to allow the game to start all over again. The effect of this torture is illustrated by the fact that following such a watch, young pilots who just shortly before had demonstrated great courage and fearlessness in the sky would collapse on their berths utterly shattered and burst into nervous fits of crying.[94]

Despite this and other types of torture, morale at the Nieuwe Kamp remained good – and this was still the case when the 3,600 prisoners of war initially accommodated in the small engineers' barracks were moved to the Nieuwe Kamp in mid-August 1942. They had been able to build a few clandestine radios with parts found in the harbour complex. According to Lieutenant Colonel Poulus, 'a very extensive clandestine correspondence with family and friends had been set up throughout Java [with the help of Ambonese and via secret hiding places specially installed at the harbour] even with relatively fixed collection times. In this respect it is worth noting that the Japanese general, Saito [commander of all of the prisoners of war on Java], during his visit to the camp unknowingly brought the post from Batavia [...] under the seat of his car, and similarly upon his departure took with him the post from the camp. The birthdays of Her Majesty the Queen [31 August] and of members of the Royal Family [29 June, Prince Bernhard; 5 August, Princess Irene] were celebrated in a spontaneous and appropriate manner.'[95]

General Saito's visit took place on 27 August, two days after the roll call lasting 15 hours. Was it Saito's opinion, now that Tokyo had granted the prisoners of war military status, that Lieutenant Takita was no longer

94   H. Poulus, 'Verslag', 22 July 1946, p. 9 (NIOD IC, 2,031).
95   H. Poulus, 'Verslag', 22 July 1946, p. 11 (NIOD IC, 2,031).

suitable for the position of commandant or did he believe that Takita had acted too heavy-handedly? We do not know. The fact is Takita was replaced on that very 27th of August by another lieutenant, Shono ('Grandpa'), who instituted a radically different policy. Treatment of the prisoners improved substantially, in addition to which officers were soon paid part of their salary and NCOs and other ranks fatigue money. That money could be used to purchase fruit, tobacco and other goods outside the camp – incidentally, the rations were increased. Moreover, Shono allowed the men to swim in the sea and agreed to the erection of a primitive open-air theatre in the camp, which was expanded considerably. Numerous performances took place there and many lectures were held.[96] Permission was also granted to set up businesses such as a market garden, an agricultural enterprise, a rabbit farm, a tannery, a coconut oil business and a snake farm (with the poet-biologist Leo Vroman as snake tender). What remained was the overcrowding of the now improved barracks. However, at the beginning of 1943 the prisoners of war began to be transferred to Bandung and Cimahi – the Nieuwe Kamp emptied and one and half weeks later it was completely vacated.[97]

A total of 18 prisoners died in the two prisoner-of-war camps in Cilacap, 'the majority', according to Poulus, 'of old ailments',[98] and 15 of them during 'Alva's' reign of terror.

Not only in Cilacap but elsewhere on Java as well, the Japanese put prisoners

[96] In one of those lectures a former banker, A. Frankfurther, then a conscripted soldier, outlined the changes that would occur after the war in the political relations in the Indies. According to a fellow prisoner, J.H.W. Veenstra, he also discussed, 'foreign literature on colonial issues'. Lieutenant Colonel Poulus forbade him to speak; later this ban was modified in that Frankfurther was not allowed to speak to professional soldiers. Veenstra felt that the former banker 'exhibited his level-headedness somewhat provocatively in circles holding views highly limited by their colonial blinkers' (Veenstra 1947:77).
Worthy of mention is that Frankfurther took the initiative to set up a camp bank where the fatigue money was deposited as well as the monies that the Japanese paid out to the officers, and the military funds that a professional soldier of lower rank had with him. Everyone received his own account in which deposits and withdrawals were made; the camp bank thus operated 'as a kind of giro office', Frankfurther (1961:145) noted later. It was via this camp bank that supplementary food was bought and fairly divided. Frankfurther's plan, Veenstra wrote later, was to work 'a miracle of justice [...] in a camp where corruption, cheating and the most disagreeable consequences of the law of supply and demand were the order of the day. And, indeed, it was a miracle that after extensive deliberations the camp leadership accepted it.' (Veenstra: 'Een communistisch bankier', article in the festive newspaper on the occasion of the silver wedding anniversary of Mr and Mrs Frankfurther, 17 March 1956.)
[97] Before the great removal, around September 1942 all those who had worked on the sugar plantations had been transferred to the overcrowded 'Jaarmarktkamp' in Surabaya. Apparently, the Japanese were planning to deploy them as Nippon workers. In this camp the group was held in a hastily constructed sub-camp consisting of a kind of animal cages. En route to Flores six months later, Veenstra saw that this group was still in these cages.
[98] H. Poulus, 'Verslag', 22 July 1946, p. 12 (NIOD IC, 2,031).

of war to work – work sometimes meant to be humiliating. Several technicians became Nippon workers and were initially allowed to live outside the
camp, though an end was soon made to this privilege. From the camps in
Surabaya numerous prisoners were deployed to clear and rebuild the devas-
tated harbour. Here a small group called in by the Japanese to handle their
news coverage, and in particular their radio propaganda, will receive special
attention. Two members of this group were already mentioned in Chapter I:
the head of the Government Information Service, J.H. Ritman, and the head
of the Army Information Service, Major A. Zimmerman. It was noted that
after having been brought by car from Bandung to Batavia, on 5 April they
stated their willingness to assist the Japanese propaganda staff.[99] The nature
of this work was not entirely clear to them at the time – and, incidentally,
Ritman was first admitted to a hospital.

It took a while for the Japanese to figure how best to use Zimmerman,
Ritman and other workers from the European community, namely for listening to and transcribing Allied radio broadcasts and authoring propaganda
to be broadcast to Australia and the United States. For these purposes they
created two services under the supervision of the Japanese Metsui, who
had worked in Hollywood for some time and had subsequently become
an advertising agent for American movies in Japan: a monitoring and a
propaganda service. Everyone put to work on this came to live in Batavia
with their families (in itself a great advantage) in separate districts, one on
Billiton Road (the monitoring service) and the other on Tanah Abang Road
(the propaganda service) – both were closed off and could only be left with
the permission of the Japanese. As for how many people were ultimately put
to work, their number is only known for the monitoring service: four radio
operators, four stenographers (two Europeans who had formerly been stenographers for the Volksraad, and two Indonesians), four other technical and
administrative assistants and two editors charged with compiling summaries
of the recorded and transcribed texts.

Both services also employed Indonesians: housekeepers and two stenographers, one of whom, Mochtar Lubis, later became a journalist. After the
war he wrote:

> We Indonesians were allowed to leave if we wanted to, but were strictly forbidden
> to tell the outside world anything about the news we had heard from the Allied
> radio stations. The penalty for breaking this promise was death!
> [...] Life in the camp was not too bad. We received sufficient rice rations, butter
> or margarine, soap, and once in a while luxury items such as fragrant soap, per-
> fume, eau-de-cologne, cigarettes etc., all articles that were both very scarce outside
> the camp and expensive. (Lubis 1975:537-8.)

[99]   In Chapter I mention was also made of Aneta's editor-in-chief, C. de Vries, about whom no
further details are known.

Just *how* scarce and *how* expensive these items were was described in the previous chapter.

Not all of those put to work in or from this 'radio camp' (as I wish to designate the two complexes), a camp for the privileged, remained there until the end of the occupation. The director of 'Radio Holland', W. Stefert, for example, and several of his co-workers, under whose direction the station used by the Japanese for their foreign broadcasts had been improved and for which a new studio had been built, were interned upon completion of their work.[100]

A 'camp for the privileged' is the phrase used above. And those who worked there were, indeed, privileged: in so far as they were married, they were with their families, they were not treated too badly, they were aware of all the news from the Allied stations and through their contacts with Japanese and Indonesians they heard far more than the Dutch and Dutch Eurasian civilians confined in 'regular' internment camps and the prisoners of war. After the war some of them (including Mol) claimed to have taken on the assigned activities solely to conduct espionage. They undoubtedly received information and gained impressions that would have been useful to the Dutch, American and British authorities, had they had the opportunity to pass any of it on, other than the details the personnel at the propaganda service succeeded in smuggling into their radio texts.

One of the editors of the listening service was L.F. Jansen, secretary of the Council of the Dutch East Indies. As mentioned in Chapter I, he offered his assistance to the Japanese shortly after the capitulation in Bandung. He had a reasonably good understanding of Japanese and together with others (including the former member of the Council of the Dutch East Indies, J.H.B. Kuneman)[101] was put to work as an interpreter. However, in April, when all of the prominent figures in the European community were rounded up, he was interned in Struiswijk Prison in Batavia. There he was pressed (because of his knowledge of Japanese he was perceived by the Japanese as a valuable aide) to collaborate on Japanese propaganda, to which he had initially agreed. This time, however, he refused, whereupon he was flogged and even threatened with execution: he acquiesced. Put to work in the 'radio district', he continued with the diary that he had begun earlier.[102]

A highly cultivated man[103] who maintained a critical stance towards the

[100]   The same happened to J.C. Mol, director of the film company Multifilm, who for two and a half years was the technical head of the Japanese firm that produced films.
[101]   He was later interned and died in the camp.
[102]   This diary (preserved only from May 1942) was published in 1988 under the title *In deze halve gevangenis* ('In this semi-prison'). It should be added here that J.K. Brocades Zaalberg, who shortly after the war came into the possession of this diary, offered us additional information about this Japanese 'radio camp'.
[103]   The writer E. du Perron, who at the end of the 1930s had contact on Java with various Dutch

Dutch colonial government,[104] Jansen was aware that by working in the 'radio camp', he ('a spectator who likes comfort, not dying') (Jansen 1988:45) was serving the Japanese cause. This also applied to the others who had been put to work there, a group Ritman joined in July 1942 following his recovery – after retracting his original promise, he also gave in to Japanese torture. Ritman, however, found himself in a situation in which he lent the Japanese considerably more important help than Jansen: he became an assistant in the propaganda service. And not without feelings of guilt! At the end of July 1942, Jansen noted 'The fact of the matter is that we'd all much rather stay out of prison. [...] We are disgusted with ourselves (Ritman has admitted this too) and are concerned about future consequences.' (Jansen 1988:24.)

Now as to Zimmerman.

According to his October 1945 report, a few days after his first meeting in Batavia, Zimmerman was again transferred to Bandung. There he met with Captain De Lange, who told him that he had succeeded in making contact with the Australian guerrillas to the south of Sukabumi who had a transmitter at their disposal. At the end of May, Zimmerman had to again report in Batavia, where at the office of the NIROM he was informed by a Japanese that he was guilty of anti-Japanese propaganda. He was detained in Struiswijk Prison for a week. According to his report, he was given a choice between a death sentence and working on the Japanese propaganda broadcasts, in which case he and his family would be accommodated in the 'radio camp'. He opted for the latter choice and was then allowed to collect his wife and children in Bandung. There, according to his report, he once again consulted with Captain De Lange, who purportedly promised that a clandestine group in Batavia (Captain Wernink's?) would contact him.

As a member of the Japanese propaganda service, Zimmerman, like Ritman, wrote foreign affairs commentaries (at the time this was also being done by an Australian prisoner of war discussed below) but, taking advantage of the relative freedom still enjoyed by the internees in the 'radio camp' at that time, he was also able to establish a small espionage group (the existing group in Batavia never contacted him) with the aid of a Chinese who had worked for the KNIL intelligence service. He had the information thus obtained delivered to a clandestine worker of Welter's group in Buitenzorg, whose address he had presumably been given by Captain de Lange. Later in 1942 he learned that both De Lange's and Welter's groups had been rounded

---

and Dutch Eurasians who believed that the Dutch policy was short-sighted, described Jansen at the end of 1937 in a letter to Menno ter Braak as 'the most intelligent and decent of all of them', 'your *honnête homme*'. (Letter, 29 November 1937, in M. ter Braak and E. du Perron 1967:208.)

[104] However, he doubted that the Indonesians themselves would succeed in giving decent shape to their society: 'It will take at least 25 more years of Western *leadership*', he observed in June 1943 (Jansen 1988:246).

up – the Kempeitai got wind of his assistance to Welter's group and he was arrested together with a female assistant at the beginning of February 1943. He broke down under severe torture and confessed to having received messages. He never came to trial. Why not? We are unable to answer this question – perhaps there was some tug of war between the Kempeitai and the Japanese propaganda service which considered him a useful worker (later he told Jansen that the Japanese considered him 'too unimportant') (Jansen 1988: 236). Whatever the case may be, he was imprisoned in Struiswijk Prison for several months. However, in May 1943 he stated his willingness to resume work at the 'radio camp'– to fellow prisoners he indicated that he just wanted to resume his espionage activities. He did not succeed. With his family he ended up in the closed Tanah Abang camp, 'so that any further direct espionage activities became extremely difficult',[105] he wrote in his report. 'Impossible' would seem to be a more apt description.

More men were deployed for the radio work. In May 1943 the Japanese appealed to several Dutch journalists, former members of the Batavia Stadswacht, interned at Struiswijk. Two of them simply refused; two said they wanted a trial period of a week (after which they had themselves locked up in Struiswijk again) and two others, J.A.M.J.G. van Leeuwen and C.A. de Vries, declared themselves willing to cooperate. Later, an officer of the Batavia Stadswacht, Captain K. Hoonstra, likewise interned in Struiswijk,[106] reported that 'their conduct was strongly condemned'.[107]

The Japanese had earlier successfully recruited a third Dutch journalist, A. Cohen, a former editor of the Aneta press agency, as well as several British and Australian officers bearing great resentment against the Dutch, who, they said, had made a mess of Java's defence. One of these embittered men was the Australian lieutenant Arthur Finlayson Douglas Rodie (he was already working for the propaganda service in mid-1942[108]) who, according

[105] A. Zimmerman, 'Verslag werkzaamheden', October 1945, p. 12 (NIOD IC, 80,772).
[106] K. Hoonstra, 'Verslag', 1 July 1946, p. 5 (ARA, Alg. Secr., Eerste zending, XXII, 45, 386).
[107] Elias (1946:83) mentions that the former editor-in-chief of the *Nieuws van den Dag voor Nederlandsch-Indië*, W.J. Belonje, 'refused to the end', to help the Japanese, saying: 'You can murder me, but I will not work with you!'
[108] The Japanese did their utmost to elicit interest in their radio broadcasts in Australia – at the end of 1942 they went so far as to grant a few high-ranking Allied officers, then still locked up in the former barracks of the 10th Battalion in Batavia, the opportunity of conveying in their texts their trust in the future. Major General G.A. Ilgen, previously the commander of the KNIL 'division' that had defended East Java, said in a speech broadcast to Australia on 21 December 1942: 'We will not lose courage', and ended with 'Long live the Queen!' and a day later a few British and Australian high-ranking officers stated in their speeches that they were certain of victory. Evidently allowing these statements was the price the Japanese had had to pay for their cooperation. Later they also tried to persuade the wives of prominent Dutchmen to address Australia via the radio. Van Starckenborgh's spouse refused to do so – although a letter she wrote at the beginning of May 1943 was broadcast in which she presented an unadorned account of

to Zimmerman in his report, 'allowed himself to be swept away by his hate of the nation which, according to him, was responsible for the fact that he had become a prisoner of war'. He 'wrote scathing commentaries on the Dutch, the Dutch royal family, Dutch colonial rule, etc. etc.'[109] This contradicts what Zimmerman wrote in the same report: 'On the whole, the texts of the broadcasts were completely sabotaged, initially only by Rodie and me'.[110]

What would this 'sabotage' have consisted of? Ritman, Zimmerman, Van Leeuwen, De Vries, Cohen, Rodie and others (including two more prisoners of war: a British lieutenant, a certain Lambert, and a second Australian lieutenant, a certain Nichol or Nichols) had to regularly write texts both in Dutch and in English that were read by announcers (a Dutch-Eurasian and an Australian woman).[111] They assumed that attempts would be made to pick up and transcribe these texts in Australia and the United States. According to their post-war statements, the 'saboteurs' did their best to incorporate as much information as possible that would be of value to the Allies. According to Zimmerman, in their texts Cohen and Lambert, for example, incorporated:

> details about the locations of new training centres for *heiho* – Sukarno's address was disclosed in this manner – while special efforts were made to convey economic news that could contain very valuable clues about the country's general situation.[112]

No significant act of 'sabotage' can be discovered in this, all the more so because the Japanese censored everything that was broadcast.

Nor can it be considered 'sabotage' that in the last year of the war – when everyone knew that the Japanese defeat was imminent (and when sound information would have been particularly useful to the Allies) – the group working for the propaganda service began doing its best, according to Zimmerman, to make the scripts 'so long and boring [...] that no sensible person would listen to them. Sentences of 15 to 20 lines were not uncommon.'[113] Rather, it is a refutation of all the claims on this point.

Even less can 'sabotage' be detected in the fact that during that last year in their texts Lieutenants Rodie and Lambert stressed the need for the allies of the Netherlands to fully understand that the Indonesians would not stand for the reinstatement of Dutch rule. In the later words of a Dutch Eurasian who

---

her confinement in Struiswijk Prison in Batavia and the prison of Tangerang, and subsequently in the internment camp in Cideng. The spouses of Van Mook and Helfrich as well as the latter's daughter personally read out similar letters at the end of July 1943.

[109]   A. Zimmerman, 'Verslag werkzaamheden', October 1945, p. 15 (NIOD IC, 80,772).

[110]   A. Zimmerman, 'Verslag werkzaamheden', October 1945, p. 13 (NIOD IC, 80,772).

[111]   Furthermore, in 1943 and 1944 Ritman, Zimmerman and Rodie edited a Japanese newspaper, *Voice of Nippon*, intended for the internment camps on Java.

[112]   A. Zimmerman, 'Verslag werkzaamheden', October 1945, p. 16 (NIOD IC, 80,772).

[113]   A. Zimmerman, 'Verslag werkzaamheden', October 1945, p. 18 (NIOD IC, 80,772).

also was involved in the radio work, 'the fact that Lambert managed to get the stuff out was clever in itself, because it was forbidden to broadcast local news unless approved by the Nips. [...] Lambert gradually succeeded in getting a script over once a week which exclusively dealt with this matter.'[114] We see no reason why the Japanese would have objected to this kind of text.

In other words: the defence presented later by those who cooperated on the Japanese radio broadcasts for a few years is not convincing in the least. What happened to Rodie, Lambert and Nichols is unknown. After the war, several of the Dutchmen involved were convicted in Batavia for collaboration.

This was not the case with Ritman and Jansen.

Ritman's situation was different in that after some time he had no longer submitted any useful texts (he too had made summaries of the reports of the listening service for the propagandists who remained at work) and he had assisted the Ceylonese Tambu (responsible for propaganda broadcasts to British India) who, as mentioned in Chapter II, was able to pass on Allied radio reports to Sjahrir. Ritman took great risks with the latter activity. His case had not yet come up when in May 1947 Lieutenant Governor-General Van Mook granted a general amnesty to all those who were guilty of collaboration as Nippon workers, except for the most serious cases, and Ritman was not counted among them.

Jansen, who had secretly left the 'radio camp' several times (he was small in stature and would crawl out under the fencing at night wearing local garb), tried in March 1945 to establish contact with the Indonesian leader Hadji Agoes Salim from within the camp.[115] He did this by means of an indigenous messenger. The messenger was arrested and confessed. Jansen was subsequently removed from the 'radio camp' and so severely mistreated while in custody that he died several days after Japan capitulated.

Finally, it seems important to point out that the propaganda broadcast by the Japanese radio had little effect in so far that especially in 1942 and 1943 but also in 1944 Radio Jakarta was barely audible in Australia, let alone the United States.

Let us return to the prisoners of war who did not rank among the privileged.

It was noted above that in June a group of Dutch Eurasian prisoners of war (and a mixed group of technicians) were transferred from Bandung to Cimahi. Arriving at the largest camp, they saw cages built in the open air

114   M.J. de Knecht, 'Rapport', n.d., p. 5 (NIOD IC, 18,955).
115   Salim, in the 1910s a leader of the Sareket Islam, had sunk into political isolation when the Japanese conquered Java. He was briefly imprisoned by the Kempeitai in Batavia in May 1942. After his release he is known to have begun trading and it is assumed that he also earned some money subsequently in the same way.

for prisoners of war who had had contact with the outside world; they were put inside them and deprived of food and drink for days. They heard that about 25 women who had tried to get through to the camp just prior to their arrival had also been subjected to this punishment after first being flogged. According to F.B. Nijon, a reserve officer candidate who was transferred from Bandung to Cimahi:

> The conduct of the camp community was chaotic. [...] Authority and discipline were lacking. A number of high-ranking officers abstained from assuming command. Contact with the Japanese commandant [...] was difficult and the Japanese were thorough in their thrashings. These were the circumstances under which Major J.W.G.A. Hoedt, supported by several officers [...], had assumed command.[116] He established a camp police, in which I had the honour of serving. Given the abominable circumstances, Major Hoedt took firm action. He had no choice. [...] In the case of serious offences he did not shrink from physically punishing the perpetrators. This was done with the whip. However, he did allow them to choose between a flogging or a fight with a volunteer. [...] A remarkable senior officer, this Major Hoedt.[117]

Remarkable, indeed. And courageous. When four young prisoners of war were apprehended trying to establish contact outside the camp in March 1943 and sentenced to death, he was able to secure a reprieve for them on two conditions: a petition for a pardon had to be submitted on behalf of all of the prisoners and he had to personally guarantee that this would not occur again. Which he did (as Lieutenant Colonel Poulus had done before him in Bandung). In retrospect, it is difficult to evaluate the policy of this exceptionally harsh major – however, it is beyond dispute that, even though there was little solidarity in the largest camp at Cimahi, as its leader he was able to contain the chaos there.

Major Hoedt had some luck in so far that in September in Cimahi and elsewhere it was announced that the detainees had officially become prisoners of war, that the officers were allowed to wear their badges of rank again and that, as of 1 October, those officers would receive a part of their salary and the other ranks fatigue money. A share of these payments in Cimahi and elsewhere ended up in the camp kitty – as noted with respect to the Nieuwe Kamp at Cilacap, with the permission of the Japanese these monies were used primarily to purchase supplements to the meagre rations outside of the camp. Furthermore, in the largest camp in Cimahi, individual soldiers (who 'as the initiators, filled their pockets', as a former prisoner of war informed us in 1985)[118] established camp businesses, even more so than at Cilacap.

---

[116]   That is to say: he had become the senior officer.
[117]   Letter from F.B. Nijon, 6 November 1984.
[118]   Letter from J.H.W. Veenstra, May 1985.

Camp *toko*, 'factories' for the production of jam, peanut butter, tobacco, roasted coffee, Norit tablets, *sambal*, oil, medicine and soap sprang up, as did a gardening team, a 'Dutch restaurant', a cobbler, and a distribution centre. All of this industriousness, after all, provided regular work for more than 600 prisoners of war who (they were excluded from the fatigues for which the Japanese on Java paid soldiers 10 cents per day and the NCO's 15 cents per day) as a rule received a weekly wage: first 43 cents, later 70 cents. A profit was made despite these wages: up to 1 May 1943 (later figures are missing) approximately 40,000 guilders, 32,000 of which was spent via the camp kitty to augment the rations and care for the sick.

What was the mood in the camps? There is very little information on this subject. However, those with wives and children on Java surely suffered greatly from their separation: only highly risky clandestine contact was possible; as noted above, normal contact by letter was not allowed and visits were prohibited. As far as is known only one exception was made, namely in the camps in Surabaya on 8 July 1942 (at this time the 8th of every month was celebrated in memory of Pearl Harbor). J.C. Hamel (who had been taken from Magelang to Surabaya) recalled:

> Very early in the morning, through the slits in the bamboo enclosure we could already see the women assembled in the street in long rows, each hauling enormous quantities of a wide range of goods. From time to time a Japanese soldier would slap or kick one of them if he thought they were breaking the tight formation of the queue. Those hundreds of women stood there for many long hours, filled with tension yet in good spirits.
> [...] When the gate was opened, they first had to pass the guards who inspected everything and all too often filched items. (Hamel 1948:65.)

Some had come in vain because far from every woman knew in which camp in Surabaya her husband or son was incarcerated.[119]

Furthermore, it is plausible that, as was the case in the first period of imprisonment, in mid-1942 the prisoners of war were often influenced by optimistic rumours. For instance, it was mentioned in Chapter II that a rumour that the Americans had already penetrated up to Malang had circulated in the camps in Surabaya. On 1 August, Major Hoedt issued a special camp order in Cimahi warning against the spreading of such rumours; in it

---

[119]   In this connection it is worth noting that in September in Surabaya one of the camps, housed in a school, was discontinued. The prisoners had to walk to the so-called 'Jaarmarktkamp' carrying their baggage. On this occasion Hamel saw a prisoner before departure gulp down a tin of butter and burst into tears when he proved unable to carry one of his three suitcases ('it is hard to believe that such people truly exist'). He was also struck by people's willingness to help one another. He wrote that 'this solidarity was strongest among the navy lads' (Hamel 1948: 68-9).

he reported that a European – at that moment locked up in the so-called cage – had been sentenced to death for telling an Indonesian (who had betrayed him) that the Americans had landed on Java.

Such rumours must also have circulated in September when, as evidenced in Chapter I, on Java the hopeful expectations of the Dutch and the Dutch Eurasian civilians reached fever pitch. If this was the case, the prisoners of war must have been particularly apprehensive about being removed from Java and not knowing where they would find themselves when the Japanese were driven from the island.

This transfer was effected nevertheless. It began in mid-September and the first to be sent away (to the Burma Railway) were British, Australian and American prisoners of war, all from the former barracks of the 10th Battalion in Batavia. Their place was filled by prisoners of war brought in from camps elsewhere on Java – so many that several of them were put in Glodok Prison.

Of the first four groups of Dutch and Dutch Eurasians that left, all in October, three went to Burma and one to Japan. For the group destined for Japan, Major Hoedt in Cimahi was ordered to select about 700 prisoners of war with some technical knowledge.[120] As it happened, there were far more than 700 men in the camp who were technically skilled. So how did the Major make his choice? In September 1945, according to Captain P.J.C. Meys,[121] who became the senior officer in one of the three camps in which those selected were placed, they were almost all Dutch Eurasians:

> From reports I received from a Dutch officer in the Cimahi camp, it would appear that in this selection procedure [...] the worst elements were singled out [...] for transport. [...] The majority of this contingent of prisoners of war comprised individuals from the city and from the lower echelons of Indonesian society. Incited and informed by troublemakers [...] this group of prisoners of war was virtually a military gang. [...] All authority other than that of the Japanese was denied. This attitude was also often noticeable among the more educated. [...] A large number of these Dutch Eurasians [...] were opposed to the full-blooded Europeans and saw nothing but good [...] in a collaboration with and an enduring domination by Japan.[122]

That 'a large number' of the Dutch Eurasian lower ranks taken away from Cimahi (in addition to about 600 of them, close to 100 British, Australians and Americans were also selected) had begun to adopt a rather pro-Japanese

---

[120]   At the end of July 1942, Tokyo had requested that 5,000 prisoners of war with some technical knowledge be sent to Japan.
[121]   Meys, together with 16 other officers from the camp for officers in Bandung, was added to this transport.
[122]   P.J.C. Meys, 'Rapport betr. gedragingen Nederlandse militairen in krijgsgevangenschap', 16 September 1945, p. 1 (NIOD IC, 1099).

stance[123] was not known to their families and relatives in Batavia. Naturally, the latter did their utmost to catch sight of the prisoners of war who arrived there by train before being transferred to the Unie *kampong* in Tanjungpriok to await transportation by ship. The first to arrive in Batavia were the officers from Bandung. 'Less than an hour later', according to C.D. Ricardo at the end of October 1942, 'all of the Batavian women' (that is to say, the wives of the prisoners of war) 'knew what was going on and an organized siege was laid on the stations in and just outside of Batavia, while the railway crossings enjoyed a great deal more attention than usual from the ladies'.[124]

This remained so even with the following trains: those with the 700 prisoners of war from Cimahi and others with prisoners from other camps, even from as far as East Java, whom the Japanese were going to put to work on the Burma Railway.

Most of the trains were going so fast that contact was not possible, but there were also some, according to Ricardo, 'from which resounding cheers emanated when the crowds of women gathered along the tracks were spotted [...] and frequently a message was shouted out, which then was promptly relayed a few hours later to whomever it was addressed'.[125] Those women were sometimes bothered by the accompanying Japanese soldiers, who now and then threw rocks at them, and often also by 'the jeering of the gang of Indonesian idlers who [...] safely expressed their cowardly derision of the now defenceless men'.[126] Contact with the men following their arrival in Tanjungpriok proved extremely difficult. On 25 October Ricardo noted, 'Whether prisoners were indeed shipped away and, if so, how many, is unknown'.[127]

This uncertainty was to remain. The first troopships with Dutch and Dutch Eurasians sailed on 3, 7 and 15 October (that of 15 October with approximately 700 prisoners of war, including the cabaret artist Wim Kan); the troopship to Japan departed on 16 October. These four transports, together with the previous one of British, Australian and American prisoners of war, were the first in a long series in which by far the greatest majority of prisoners of war were taken from Java to locations unknown to all of their families who were left behind.

---

[123] This did not remain so. In Japan, according to Captain Meys, 'the mentality of the group changed entirely' and 'fairly rapidly'. (P.J.C. Meys, 'Rapport betr. gedragingen Nederlandse militairen in krijgsgevangenschap', 16 September 1945, p. 1 (NIOD IC, 1,099).)

[124] C.D. Ricardo, 'Gesol met krijgsgevangenen', 25 October 1942, p. 1 (NIOD IC, 30,930).

[125] C.D. Ricardo, 'Gesol met krijgsgevangenen', 25 October 1942, p. 2 (NIOD IC, 30,930).

[126] C.D. Ricardo, 'Gesol met krijgsgevangenen', 25 October 1942, p. 2 (NIOD IC, 30,930).

[127] C.D. Ricardo, 'Gesol met krijgsgevangenen', 25 October 1942, p. 2 (NIOD IC, 30,930).

The Special Party

Why the Japanese assembled the highest-ranking American, British, Dutch and Australian officers they had taken prisoner in the Nampo region (navy officers with the rank of captain or higher, army and air force officers with the rank of colonel or higher) in a separate group, the 'Special Party', is a question that cannot be answered on the basis of Japanese documents. In previous wars, however, it was not unusual for prisoners holding a position of unusual significance to receive special treatment. It is possible that in 1942, with a view to the peace negotiations they anticipated holding with the United States and Great Britain, the Japanese thought the Special Party would afford them a trump card. Also in this Special Party were the highest ranking civil authorities in the Nampo region who had fallen into their hands, such as the American governor of Guam, the British governor of Hong Kong and the British high commissioner of Malacca, as well as several lower-ranking soldiers: adjutants and batmen of the high-ranking officers. The group was ultimately assembled on Formosa and confined in a separate camp. As regards the highest Dutch authorities, as mentioned above, General Overakker and Colonel Gosenson, as well as the governor of Sumatra, A.I. Spits[128] and an officer of the general staff, General Major H.J.D. de Fremery,[129] were transferred there from Sumatra. From Java at the end of December 1942 came first Governor-General Van Starkenborgh, army commander Ter Poorten, 46 other high-ranking officers and 24 adjutants and batmen. In September 1943 came a second group of four officers (including the defender of Tarakan, Lieutenant Colonel S. de Waal) and 28 batmen – very few of whom had been included in the first group, about which the members of the Special Party on Formosa had lodged a complaint. Ultimately, the Special Party was to number more than 400, including 108 Dutch: 52 high-ranking officials and 56 adjutants and batmen.

After his second visit to Kalijati, where the details of the general capitulation of the KNIL had been laid down by the Japanese, on 9 March 1942 General Ter Poorten was interned in his house in Bandung. There, the Japanese soldiers broke open all the locks of all the cabinets and generally wreaked havoc. Another seven generals were subsequently interned in his house. On

---

[128]   The reader is reminded that the governor of Borneo, B.J. Haga, was arrested by the Kempeitai at the beginning of 1943, and that he died on the first day of his trial. Upon the arrival of the Japanese in Makassar, the governor of the area known as the Great East was on Java, where he had gone with the permission of Van Starkenborgh due to his fragile health. His departure bitterly disappointed the Dutch and Dutch Eurasians who had remained behind in Makassar.
[129]   De Fremery was able to embark on the *Poelau Bras* in Wijnkoopsbaai on Java on 6 March 1942. When this ship was sunk the next day, he was among the 72 passengers who were able to save themselves – the Japanese took him as a prisoner of war to Palembang.

16 April, he and those seven were ordered to go to the station, where they encountered a large number of other high-ranking military officers who had first been confined in a clubhouse and a school. There were also men from Sukamiskin Prison, namely Van Starkenborgh and those with whom he had initially been housed in the villa of the Chinese Volksraad member Kan: Idenburg (director of his cabinet), Kiveron (head of the general secretariat), baron Van Boetzelaer (head of the town clerk's office), Hogewind (governor of West Java) and finally Hagenaar and Hulsewé (the two interpreters for the Japanese). Upon their arrival in Batavia, Idenburg, Kiveron, Van Boetzelaer, Hogewind and Hagenaar were transferred to Struiswijk Prison, while all of the officers and Van Starkenborgh together with Hulsewé were taken to the barracks of the 10th Battalion. In the old, dilapidated complex where big black rats sometimes scurried around at night and which was infested with bedbugs and cockroaches day and night, Van Starkenborgh and Ter Poorten were each assigned a small room where they would live for more than eight months; the rooms were furnished with nothing more than a bed and a filthy mattress.

The high authorities in the camp had a few privileges. For example, they were allowed to be treated in the camp by a Dutch dentist. Van Starkenborgh was treated in June and the wife (residing in Batavia) of his intendant (also taken prisoner and transferred to Batavia) learned sometime later from the same dentist that Van Starkenborgh was worried about his spouse having enough money (he knew that many Dutch and Dutch Eurasians had landed in serious financial difficulties) and had requested him to expressly ask her 'not to become involved in any intrigue, no matter how minor'.[130]

Also in June Van Starkenborgh was instructed by the Japanese, according to them, to write down as 'truthfully' and 'as comprehensively as possible' the course of the relations between the Dutch East Indies and Japan from 1939 as well as his 'insights into the war in Greater East Asia and the Second World War'. He made a copy of his lengthy pencil-written report in the third person, which he was able to save.[131] He had come to perceive the Japanese as incalculable and therefore could not foresee how they would react were he to convey to them in black and white that they would lose the war. On the other hand, if they asked him to record his insights 'truthfully', he felt obliged to do so regardless of any personal consequences.

His report was crystal clear: he informed the Japanese that he did not doubt their defeat for a second. He wrote:

> There is such a prevalence of people and resources of all sorts on the side of the Allied Forces that they must have the capacity to utterly exhaust Germany

[130] C. Lanzing-Fokker, 'Dagboek', 17 June 1942 (NIOD IC, dagboek 140).
[131] Text in *Jhr. mr. dr. A.W.L. Tjarda van Starkenborgh Stachouwer; Bijdrage tot een kenschets, verzameld door mr. D.U. Stikker* (1978), p. 25.

and Italy and still be able to deploy very substantial armed forces against Japan that will increase in the course of time. [...] That the British Empire, America or China would be prepared to end the war before their forces have become fully operative and that peace would be made on the basis of the German conquests in Europe and the Japanese successes in East Asia does not strike the undersigned as likely. Accordingly, he continues to expect that the wish, natural to any faithful patriot, will be fulfilled, and that at the end of this terrible world catastrophe a free Netherlands will re-emerge, and again be constitutionally united with the Indies.

This report, in the words of the former minister of Foreign Affairs D.U. Stikker in 1978, drawn up 'with great moral courage' and 'conveying the objective facts [...] as though he were writing it for his minister in The Hague' (Tjarda van Starkenborgh 1978:11), was translated into Japanese, after which Van Starkenborgh heard nothing further about it.

He and the naval captain Vromans were the two wealthiest prisoners in the camp, each with several thousand guilders on them. Van Starkenborgh gave what he had to Vromans, who administered a support fund for less fortunate prisoners of war. Initially Van Starkenborgh had little contact with the other prisoners (he, Ter Poorten and other high-ranking officers were sequestered in a different part of the camp), though later he was given greater freedom of movement within the camp. In keeping with this equal treatment, he, too, had to participate in a long punishment roll call. 'The untrained non-military figure Van Starkenborgh', Vromans later wrote, 'stood by calmly, exhibiting his displeasure lightly without resisting needlessly [it is worthwhile recalling that when all of the prisoners were presented with the declaration of obedience he advised them to sign it and did so himself] and was all in all exemplary'.[132]

General Saito visited the 10th Battalion barracks on 6 December to announce that the prisoners would be moved 'elsewhere'. He was accompanied by Japanese journalists who asked Van Starkenborgh who he thought was going to win the war. His response was as prompt as it was short: 'The Allies'. Ten days later, again with Japanese journalists, one of the top figures in the Japanese military administration, Colonel Yoshito Nakayama, made his appearance. According to General Scholten:

The colonel asked if the GG [Governor-General] believed he had acted correctly by declaring war on Japan. He answered without hesitation that under the same circumstances he would do so again.[133] Nakayama then had the interpreter ask: 'Aren't you sorry that you declared war on us? Had you just acted as your colleague did in French Indo-China, you would still [...] be able to govern the Dutch East Indies'.

[132] A.G. Vromans, 'Enige aantekeningen over jhr. van Starkenborgh', p. 18 (NIOD IC).
[133] If Nakayama indeed posed this question, we assume that Van Starkenborgh, as a stickler for accuracy, first pointed out that it was not he, but the Dutch government that had – with his assent – declared war on Japan.

He replied: 'I would never have chosen, as French Indo-China did, to become a Japanese satellite. Had I to make the same decision again, I would choose the same path. You ask me whether I am sorry. My answer is: no!' (Scholten 1971:90.)

Nakayama was so impressed by Van Starkenborgh's resolve that he promised to convey his answer to his wife, which he actually did, along with a floral tribute.[134]

Van Starkenborgh had made a point of avoiding contact with the Japanese commander-in-chief on Java; however, when he heard that he and other highly placed individuals as well as large numbers of other prisoners of war were to be removed from Java, he made an exception to that rule, and wrote the commander-in-chief.[135] After the war he recalled:

In the letter I summarized some measures known to me in a general sense, such as the mass dismissal of European civil servants, the withholding of their pensions, the deprivation of the right to dispose over one's bank accounts and savings, restriction of freedom etc., whereby the European population especially was destined to end up in dire straits. I also said that until now I had kept silent about measures taken against me personally because I had no hope that I could deter the Japanese authorities from imposing them, but that on the point of being deported and knowing that this was happening to many European soldiers, I could not resist indicating that, when the fortunes of war turned, in the Dutch East Indies too, I and others who would be expected to establish order would not be able to do so due to our absence, which would lead to the most disastrous consequences for a large part of the population.[136]

Written in Dutch, Van Starkenborgh's letter was translated into Japanese and a few days later he heard from prisoners of war doing administrative work in Japanese offices that it had 'elicited a great deal of hilarity' on the part of the Japanese.[137]

On 28 December, he and the other members of the Special Party originating from Java (the first group from Java), were given some warm clothing (Dutch and Dutch Eurasian women had been able to arrange this) and driven to Tanjungpriok. 'Everything [is] dead', naval captain J.G. van Kregten wrote in

---

[134]   At the time, Mrs Van Starkenborgh was interned in a prison together with her daughter, a group of British women and children and a small group of wives and children of other prominent Dutch figures. All of these women and children were placed in 'normal' internment camps at the beginning of 1943, where Mrs Van Starkenborgh refused any form of privileged treatment.

[135]   This was Harada, but Van Starkenborgh probably directed his letter to Imamura because his replacement was only announced some time in 1943.

[136]   Van Starkenborgh, 'Enige aantekeningen', n.d., p. 17 (NIOD IC, Stukken van de GG, bundel 4).

[137]   Van Starkenborgh, 'Enige aantekeningen', n.d., p. 17 (NIOD IC, Stukken van de GG, bundel 4).

his diary, 'not a European in sight, it in no way resembled the former prosperity'.[138] General Saito stood on the quay and presented Van Starkenborgh with a gift: a cardboard box with a couple of fans,[139] two boxes with a substance to ward off mosquitoes and a box of 25 cheap cigars. Saito also extended his apologies for the fact that he could not provide Van Starkenborgh with suitable accommodation. Indeed, the ship that was to transport the governor-general and the others to Singapore was old and dirty. Van Starkenborgh and his fellow prisoners were crammed together with Japanese soldiers in one of the holds. Again according to Van Kregten:

> Sweat dripped from our bodies in no time, morale below zero. [...] Like us, Japanese soldiers lie about and apparently are not dissatisfied. No hostile mood, on the contrary, attempts to fraternize. Also eat the same. Three times rice: in the morning with turtle soup, in the afternoon with some kind of soupy side-dish.
> The toilets defy description. [...] The stench strong and extremely disgusting. Indeed, the entire ship filthy from top to bottom. We wash with our own sweat. In the mornings one mug. [...] Without exception we are terribly dirty and stink. Nails are pitch black. We wipe our hands on our short hair.
> [...] The GG adapts himself admirably to this life. (Brugmans. 1960:348.)

The party arrived in Singapore after three days, and three days later it was transferred to the large prisoner-of-war camp Changi. Already in the camp were KNIL prisoners of war who had arrived from Java. On the afternoon of Sunday, 3 January, Van Starkenborgh attended a soccer match between British and Dutch prisoners of war. A member of the Semarang Stadswacht recalled:[140]

> He received a proper official reception, his presence announced with a fanfare. Everyone came to attention. The Wilhelmus [the Dutch national anthem] resounded over the terrain. The Dutch and English teams marched onto the field with their flags; we had lumps in our throats. [...] We won the match 3-1.
> At 12.30 the GG was in the church, where J.C. Hamel preached on James 4:14: 'You who do not know what tomorrow shall bring. What is your life?'[141] It was a good sermon and a moving service; Psalm 134:3 was sung for the GG.[142]

After the service Hamel spoke with him; 'with his calm words, his dignified bearing, he urged us all to look to the future with courage.' (Hamel 1948:95.)

---

138 J.G. van Kregten, 'Dagboek' in Brugmans 1960:347-8.
139 Japanese samurai always brought along a few fans on their journeys.
140 A.H. Douwes, 'Persoonlijke herinneringen', p. 21 (NIOD IC, 81,315).
141 James 4:14 reads: 'Whereas ye know not what shall be on the morrow. For what is your life? It is even a vapour that appeareth for a little time and then vanisheth away.'
142 'Lift up your hands in the sanctuary: and praise the Lord. / The Lord that made heaven and earth: give thee blessing out of Sion.'

The next day, Van Starkenborgh embarked on a series of visits to the barracks of the KNIL prisoners of war. The Stadswacht member wrote:

> I saw him from very close by; he looks fine and cheerful and not aged, only his bald head [...] was grim, prison like;[143] we heard nothing but praise for the GG from the high-ranking officers. Before his departure from Java he had submitted a written protest to the highest Japanese authority [...] and having barely arrived here, he also protested against the inferior food and sleeping arrangements for the prisoners of war. [...] He recounted that in Sukamiskin Prison he too had slept on the stone floor, but that eventually you get used to it; the worst of it, he said, is the bad food.[144]

On 10 January the group in the Special Party that came from Java set sail on a modern, fast ship to Japan,[145] from where, after having suffered bitter cold in an empty concrete building, they were moved again with a good ship to Formosa.

Joining other groups belonging to the Special Party, this group was first housed in a former American missionary post, where they were given little to eat and on several occasions harshly treated by the Japanese guards. Van Starkenborgh and Ter Poorten were also among those who were sporadically maltreated for trifles. Van Starkenborgh was 'always correct', wrote Scholten (1971:129-30), 'friendly and easy to get along with, the finest man I have ever met'. He worked as a goat keeper; others had to do heavier work. The 78 most prominent Special Party members, including Van Starkenborgh and Ter Poorten, subsequently spent a month in a better camp where they received their first Red Cross parcels and which, as mentioned above, was visited by a delegate of the International Red Cross in Japan. Thereafter Van Starkenborgh, Ter Poorten and 16 other particularly prominent figures, such as Governor Spits, Lieutenant General T. Bakker (who had been chairman of the Mobilization Council[146] in the East Indies) and retired Major General of the Military Medical Service J. Van Rees, were moved to their third camp on Formosa. Here everyone, according to Ter Poorten, 'was given a small room with an armchair, plus a batman. Things can change.'[147] On the other hand, the second camp where the other members of the Special Party ended up was bad: there were more and more protests against the heavy and humiliating work,

---

[143]   All of the prisoners of war in the camp of the 10th Battalion had just recently had their heads shaved. Van Starkenborgh had protested against this.
[144]   A.H. Douwes, 'Persoonlijke herinneringen', pp. 21-2 (NIOD IC, 81,315).
[145]   Hulsewé stayed behind in Singapore and later was able to offer important services as an interpreter to the camp command.
[146]   A government body established in 1936 charged with coordinating the defence efforts of the Dutch East Indies. See Introduction, p. 33.
[147]   Ter Poorten, quoted in Dubois 1946:284.

for example emptying out the latrines of the Japanese, which only resulted in a period of severe disciplinary action and long nightly roll calls. Fortunately, the men had plenty to read: the impounded library of an Englishman in Shanghai had been placed at the disposal of the Special Party. On the whole, though, it was a stultifying existence. One of the Dutch generals wrote:

> Life without women, without joy, the life of a dog in a kennel, even worse: that of a plant in a pot. A life without one's own will. Having to carry out what one is ordered to do. [...] A man's world. Hideous men, whom we have to look at when we bathe outside the barracks. How is it possible that women love naked men and lie in their arms! (Quoted in Scholten 1971:174.)

In October 1944, when Nimitz was established on the Mariana Islands and MacArthur had penetrated into the Philippines, the Japanese began anticipating an Allied landing on Formosa: they decided to transfer some of the Special Party via Japan and Korea to Manchuria, and the rest to Japan. This was done in three groups: the group of 18 (flown to Japan), that of the remaining older members of the Special Party which was sent to Manchuria in October 1944, and the somewhat smaller one of younger men which was taken to Japan in January and February 1945.

The Dutch prisoners of war sent to Manchuria were first assembled in an old Russian railway troops barrack in a camp approximately 300 kilometres north of Mukden. From there the group of 18 was transported about 200 kilometres further to Sian. Prior to Van Starkenborgh's departure, the high-ranking officers of the navy and of the KNIL came to bid him farewell in groups of four – in his, according to Vromans, 'desolately empty and bare room, without a view, with only one chair and an iron bed, nothing more'.[148] Scholten wrote that Van Starkenborgh 'sat on the only chair [...]; the visitors seated themselves on the bed. We spoke, among other things, about the future and the liberation of the East Indies. Van Starkenborgh said: "First restore law and order, then talk and assure the population that they will eventually [estimated by him to be in 30 years] gain independence when they are ripe for it".' (Scholten 1971:209-10.)

All of Manchuria experienced bitter cold in the winter of 1944-1945: it was 40 degrees Celsius below zero. But the defeat of Japan was coming closer! The prison regime was relaxed, the abuse came to a halt and the members of the Special Party received sufficient Red Cross parcels (from the Japanese ship that had sailed to Nakhodka). Except for the group in Sian, in May 1945 the members of the Special Party who had been transported to Manchuria were concentrated in a camp in Mukden already housing about 800 ordinary American and British prisoners of war, along with a few Dutch ones. Their

---

[148]   A.G. Vromans, 'Enige aantekeningen over jhr. Van Starkenborgh', p. 20.

arrival attracted attention: '66 generals and 140 colonels', according to one of the Dutchmen, 'not exactly something you encounter every day'.[149] From the camp in Mukden the prisoners had to work in factories, and they again suffered from starvation.

Transports by ship

The members of the Special Party coming from Java were fortunate in that the first leg of their journey to Formosa (the Priok-Singapore transport) on board a filthy, crammed and slow ship only took a few days and that the second and third parts (the Singapore-Japan and Japan-Formosa transports) were in a modern vessel. Moreover, these transports took place in a phase when American submarines had only ineffective torpedoes, and the other Allied naval and air forces operated far away from the seas in which most Japanese ships sailed. This would change later. The Japanese began to experience such a shortage of shipping capacity that both their own troops and the prisoners of war had to cope with ever less space. As of September 1943 American submarines hit numerous ships carrying prisoners of war with their improved torpedoes; and the other Allied naval forces as well as the air forces could also operate in and above the waters of the Nampo.

The Allied staffs were familiar with the routes of the Japanese convoys[150] they knew exactly where certain Japanese troopships were supposed to be located at noon on each day of their voyage, but they were not aware that these ships sometimes carried thousands of Allied prisoners of war. It is important to recall here that, in general, the Allied governments were almost completely in the dark with regard to the circumstances in which the Allied prisoners of war were transported and in which they had to toil in the Nampo region, where the Japanese prohibited any form of inspection by foreigners. They only gained some idea of this in September 1944 when several prisoners of war who had worked on the Burma Railway were rescued from the sea near Formosa.

As a result most of the troopships became a veritable nightmare for the prisoners of war (there were also less terrible transports) and many men – according to Japanese figures almost 11,000 – drowned. That virtually everyone on these troopships was racked with fear goes without saying. The prisoners of war realized all too well that their ship could become the target of

---

[149] J.D. Backer, 'Dagboek', 21 May 1945, p. 5, (NIOD IC, dagboek 239). Published in 1995 under the title *Buigend riet*.
[150] This was possible because at the beginning of 1943 the code the Japanese army used for all of its transportation and troopships had been broken.

an Allied attack – many were aware of the rumours, moreover, that Japanese ships had been sunk. That they would face grave danger were their ship to be hit by a torpedo or a bomb was clear to them. Moreover, they had to endure this fear in circumstances that in and of themselves were almost unbearable. They were crammed together in the filthy holds of usually slow ships – holds in which it was sometimes impossible to even stand up straight, that were poorly lit and hardly ventilated and which could become unbearably hot and humid (cases of suffocation are known to have occurred). They were hungry and even worse, thirsty; they soiled themselves and there were few possibilities for relieving themselves; many were seasick at times; and if dysentery broke out on board, infection spread rapidly, a stench permeated the holds and deaths were not uncommon. It should be remembered that in 1942 when the Japanese ships did not yet travel in convoy, a sea journey to Japan (there were at least 40 ship transports of prisoners of war to Japan, including at least 28 from Singapore) usually only took ten days, but in 1943 it could take three to four weeks, and in 1944, when the Japanese ships stayed close to the coast of French Indo-China and China, two to three months. The senior officers on board the troopships made repeated efforts to secure better treatment for their co-prisoners. They were unsuccessful. The Japanese officers had little consideration for lower-ranking Japanese soldiers, let alone the prisoners of war. Captain Meys, who left from Priok on 16 October 1942 on a troopship carrying almost 700 men to Japan, embarked on a Japanese ship in Singapore on 27 October together with those 700 men and about 700 other prisoners of war. These approximately 1,400 men were quartered in steerage and on bauxite in the two rear holds. A dysentery epidemic broke out a week after their departure. The ship put in at Saigon. There and at a second port, Meys requested the Japanese officer in charge of the transport to have the most seriously ill patients admitted to hospitals – 'the response to the reasoning that the patients would otherwise die was "I am sorry, but let them die"'.[151]

On this one troopship there were more than 30 deaths among the prisoners of war coming from Java. Meys and his men arrived in Japan after a month at sea. A few weeks later another ship arrived, on board which 80 of the approximately 1,000 prisoners of war had succumbed, while more than 200 died on shore. This spurred the military authorities in Tokyo to issue the following order: 'Measures should be taken to prevent too great a percentage of the prisoners of war from dying during transport; more than 15% cannot be justified' (Leffelaar and Van Witsen 1982:98).

A few troopships are discussed below when the experiences of specific groups of prisoners of war are described, yet other transports also must be mentioned

---

[151]   P.J.C. Meys, 'Rapport', 26 September 1945, p. 3 (NIOD IC, 1,095).

here, in the first place those taking KNIL prisoners of war to Burma.

The troopship about which most is known departed from Priok on 15 October 1942 with about 1,700 prisoners, including Wim Kan. This group was beaten by stick-wielding Japanese into stinking holds. Wim Kan wrote, 'The temperature here is well over 100 degrees and people are constantly fainting' (Kan and Vonk 1963:35). By the time the ship reached Singapore there were already more than 100 dysentery patients (60 severe cases were allowed to disembark) and, moreover, a German measles epidemic had done the rounds. From Singapore a zigzag course was followed to Penang, where the ship lay at anchor for nine days.[152] According to a Dutch naval officer:

> Life in the sweltering holds of this stationary, sun-scorched ship during these [...] seemingly endless days is a hell beyond description. Only three quarters of a litre of drinking water per 24 hours is given, while every drop of moisture seeps out from our bodies. The thick scabs of the German measles covering us tear and burst open. Because our own body odour is unbearable and we cannot walk away from it, some of us (myself included) have ourselves sprayed down with sea water on deck, notwithstanding the torture of the salt water stinging our open wounds. (Quoted in Bezemer 1967:154.)

Rangoon was only reached three weeks after leaving Priok. Kan noted: 'More than half of the prisoners of war have dysentery' (Kan and Vonk 1963:37). There were eight fatalities. Prior to being put to work the survivors were incarcerated in the prison at Rangoon, where they remained for two and a half months. By the time they were mobilized to the Burma Railway, of the approximately 1,630 prisoners of war who had departed from Singapore, about 225 had died: almost one in seven.

A second transport to Burma of about 1,000 prisoners of war, all Dutch and Dutch Eurasian, took place in a ship which after having passed Penang took a direct hit on the open sea from a British bomber and immediately listed. 'Following the first explosions' (initially there had been a few near misses), according to the senior officer of this transport, 'pandemonium broke out. I tried to calm the prisoners and advised them to put on their life jackets [almost everybody had been issued one]. The Japanese guards went out of their minds. They tried to climb up by beating prisoners of war from the [very steep and narrow] stairs and by striking and kicking left and right.'[153] The ship sank about 20 minutes later. Most of the KNIL prisoners were rescued by

---

[152] A sailor tried to escape on the roadstead of Penang: he slid down the anchor chain into the water and was caught. He was subsequently beaten severely by 11 Japanese soldiers, after which he had to stand at attention for three days at the front of the boat. He died in Rangoon.

[153] Regeringsbureau Opsporing van Oorlogsmisdadigers, proces-verbaal by R.C. Soetbrood Piccardt, 20 September 1946, p. 4 (NIOD IC, 738).

another Japanese ship carrying prisoners of war in the vicinity, but about 30 men could not be accounted for and 11 died before that second ship put into Moulmein. The sick and wounded were not allowed to be admitted to the mission hospital based there – all of the rescued men were imprisoned, some who had lost everything in the disaster wearing nothing more than underpants and 'when they wanted to clean them, they had to wait in the nude'.[154]

The two transports with the most Dutch casualties both took place in September 1944: the *Junyo Maru* which, on its way from Priok to Padang (from where the prisoners were to be put to work on the Pekanbaru Railway), was sunk by a British submarine off the coast of Sumatra on 18 September; and the *Hokuku Maru* which, en route to Japan, was attacked by American bombers near Manila on 21 and 23 September.

When it left Priok on 16 September, the *Junyo Maru* carried approximately 4,200 *romusha*, including boys aged 12 and 13, and around 2,300 prisoners of war. These were almost 500 Ambonese and Manadonese (KNIL soldiers, including several retirees, all of whom had refused to become *heiho*) and more than 1,800 other troops: a small number of British, Australians and Americans but the great majority Dutch and Dutch Eurasians, including not only KNIL soldiers, navy men and a few members of the Batavia Stadswacht,[155] but also Dutch merchant mariners designated by the Japanese as prisoners of war. Most of these Dutchmen and Dutch Eurasians were from the camp of the 10th Battalion in Batavia where the Japanese – fearing that upon arrival on Sumatra resistance groups would be formed – also added elderly men, sick people and invalids to the transport. A Dutch prisoner of war, F.F.E. von Fuchs, later recalled that on the way to Priok one saw 'elderly and infirm men stumbling along in ranks, the ill were carried on stretchers'.[156]

For its crew and more than 6,500 passengers the ship had no proper rescue equipment: two old sloops hung in the davits and rafts made of wooden frameworks were on the deck, but none of the *romusha* or prisoners of war had a life jacket – the Japanese on the other hand all wore one. A Japanese aircraft accompanied the ship to keep Allied submarines at bay.

Two days after the ship set sail, that is 18 September, the plane disappeared in the late afternoon. Off Bengkulu, about 20 kilometres from the coast, just before 5.30 pm (Japanese time! It turned dark only after 7.30 pm) the *Junyo*

---

[154]   Regeringsbureau Opsporing van Oorlogsmisdadigers, proces-verbaal by R.C. Soetbrood Piccardt, 20 September 1946, p. 4 (NIOD IC, 738).

[155]   They were from the largest civilian internment camp at Bandung. They had not reported to the internment camp in Cimahi on the insistence of one of them, Professor Wertheim, who warned that the Japanese did not honour the Geneva Convention in their treatment of prisoners of war.

[156]   F.F.E. von Fuchs, 'De torpedoramp van de *Joenio Maroe*', p. 4 (NIOD IC, 15,871).

Maru was hit by two torpedoes, one causing numerous casualties in one of the holds.[157] The ship sank slowly and then began to tilt. Panic broke out , 'first in the hold', according to Fuchs, 'where men hit each other with pieces of wood and iron in order to be the first upstairs, later also on deck'.[158] Soon there was not a Japanese in sight: they had lowered the two sloops in which some of the crew and guards were able to secure a place – other Japanese, who had thrown the life rafts into the sea, had jumped in after them and tried to climb onto them. Only a few of the *romusha* could swim; those who had been able to exit the holds clamped onto anything that afforded a grip on the ever-more slanting deck. When the ship sank about 15 minutes after being torpedoed, they, together with everyone still in the holds including the wounded, were sucked down into the deep.[159] In the sea countless drowning men tried to clamber onto the rafts floating about or board the sloops. No one approaching the sloops stood the slightest chance, however: 'every non-Japanese person who was drowning [...] was pushed away with sword and axe, the headstrong ones had their fingers and hands chopped off or their skull split'.[160] The same occurred on several of the rafts. In April 1946 a Dutchman, H.M. Angenent stated (in English):

> When I was floating around, I noticed a raft on which there were three European prisoners-of-war and three Amboynese. Some moments afterwards I saw three Japanese guards boarding the raft, assisted by the men on it. The Japanese then threw the three Europeans overboard [...] and when they tried to climb on the raft again, the Japanese chopped off these poor men's hands. One of them was hit with the axe on his skull.[161]

Of the two small naval vessels that had escorted the *Junyo Maru* – a gunboat and a corvette (ships built in Surabaya in 1941 that were sunk when the Japanese arrived, and then raised by them) – the corvette took on board a few of the drowning people on the 18th and went on to Padang, but did not return to the site of the disaster. Also on the 18th, the gunboat picked up about 50 drowning people, none of whom were Japanese, and headed for the coast, where those who had been rescued had to swim the last 500 metres.

---

[157]   The general information for what follows is taken from a 1984 publication compiled by E. Melis and commissioned by Stichting Herdenking *Junyo Maru*-Sumatra: *Eresaluut boven massagraf*.

[158]   F.F.E. von Fuchs, 'De torpedoramp van de *Joenio Maroe*', p. 16 (NIOD IC, 15,871)

[159]   Special mention should be made of chaplain Xaverius Vloet who refused to leave, considering it his duty to give general absolution to anyone desiring it. A.F.J. Pieron, a KNIL army chaplain, also remained on board until the very last.

[160]   F.F.E. von Fuchs, 'De torpedoramp van de *Joenio Maroe*', p. 17 (NIOD IC, 15,871).

[161]   No. 4 War Crimes Investigation Team, Verklaring by H.M. Angenent, 1 April 1946 (NIOD IC, 355).

Resuming its efforts, on the 19th this ship concentrated on the Japanese, first of all those in the sloops. Numerous rafts with men seated and hanging on to them were still drifting around, but one after the other was forced to let go due to exhaustion or cramps. The gunboat headed for the rafts with Japanese on board (some of them had little flags with which to wave), but also picked up approximately 300 other people who were drowning: too many for the slender vessel, or so the commandant thought. Some of those who had been rescued who were in bad shape were thrown back into the sea. The rest were all taken to shore. The following day, the 20th, the gunboat again returned to the disaster scene and rescued close to 250 men: about 150 prisoners of war and 100 *romusha*. Still, the ship's commander announced that the only people who could stay on board were those who would not die before arriving in Padang – thus, it seemed safest to stay awake. However, according to Fuchs, who was among those rescued:

> the men were so exhausted that even when they fell asleep, it was impossible to wake them up. And then they were done for, because the commandant did not want any 'corpses' and whoever could not be prodded awake was declared 'dead' and thrown over the railing.

This happened to 23 rescued men: 18 *romusha* and 5 prisoners of war.

In total, only about 200 of the approximately 4,200 *romusha* made it to shore; 219 of the almost 500 Ambonese and Manadonese, and 460 of the more than 1,800 other prisoners of war. The demise of the *Junyo Maru* thus took about 5,600 lives and was the greatest ship disaster ever.

Let us turn to the *Hokuku Maru*.

In Singapore on 27 June 1944, this rusty ship took on board almost 1,300 British and Dutch prisoners of war: survivors from the work camps of the Burma Railway who had been taken back to Singapore and now had to be transferred to Japan. For the time being the ship lay at anchor: the engines were out of order. Dysentery broke out in the holds. It was scorching hot. During the day the prisoners were allowed to spend a half hour on deck in groups of 20; thus each man was given this opportunity only once every three days. The *Hokuku Maru* finally set sail three weeks later. After ten days the ship was no further than Miri on British North Borneo: as the crow flies a distance of 1,200 kilometres. Again the engines were defective, and again there was a wait in a broiling hot roadstead. There were days during which ten prisoners of war succumbed. When, after a three-week delay, the ship sailed on and reached Manila, 100 had died. It lay idle for a week off Manila. When it left on 19 September as part of a convoy of about 35 ships, mostly tankers, accompanied by Japanese torpedo destroyers and corvettes, 115 prisoners had died.

The departure of the convoy was known to American Intelligence.

On 21 September, the accompanying warships and the vessels in the convoy were attacked by around 75 dive bombers from the fleet commanded by Vice-Admiral William F. Halsey, the American naval commander of the South Pacific Area. With the exception of two torpedo destroyers, these aircraft managed to sink the entire escort and then concentrated on the Japanese tankers and freight ships. The *Hokuku Maru* had two near misses and took two direct hits. According to a Dutch prisoner of war:

> Everyone was screaming and running wildly about, there was panic in the holds. The ill cried out for help and the healthy fought over life jackets. Then we were machine-gunned, various lads were hit and crawled deeper into the hold. [...] After two minutes the ship sank into the deep with the majority of our boys still on it. We swam to the rafts drifting about here and there and held on to them. We were repeatedly machine-gunned in the water. [...] Many were hit. [...] We tried to shout 'don't shoot' and wave, but nothing helped. The pilots mistook us for Japs because we were equally tanned by the sun. (Quoted in Leffelaar and Van Witsen 1982:308.)

The sinking of the *Hokuku Maru* cost the lives of almost 800 prisoners of war – about 380 reached the shore, where the Japanese first confined them in an existing prisoner-of-war camp on Luzon and subsequently in the prison in Manila, while 12 others (9 British, 3 Dutch) went unnoticed by the Japanese coast guard and joined a Philippine guerrilla group.

But there is more.

On 13 December, seven days before MacArthur was to land on Luzon, the approximately 380 prisoners of war incarcerated in Manila, together with 1,200 American prisoners of war, were loaded onto a modern Japanese ship with strong defences, the *Oryohu Maru*, which was also going to transport a few hundred Japanese civilians and wounded soldiers to Japan. Just days after its departure, this ship was fired upon for four hours by American navy aircraft and again the day thereafter. A KNIL sergeant major recalled:[162]

> The defensive fire of the heavily armed ship was intense. After about a quarter of an hour the stern took a direct hit. [...] Several hundred men packed together like sardines in the loading shafts in this section lost their lives. When a few near hysterical men attempted to escape from the hatch by the only ladder and by anything that led out, the Japanese guards began shooting down through the suffocating gun smoke. Many lost their lives because of this.

Some time later the prisoners of war were brought to shore. Out of nearly 1,600, close to 900 had died.

The number of Dutch troops who died during the transports with the

---

[162]   Text of his report of 29 June 1946 in Brugmans 1960:350-1.

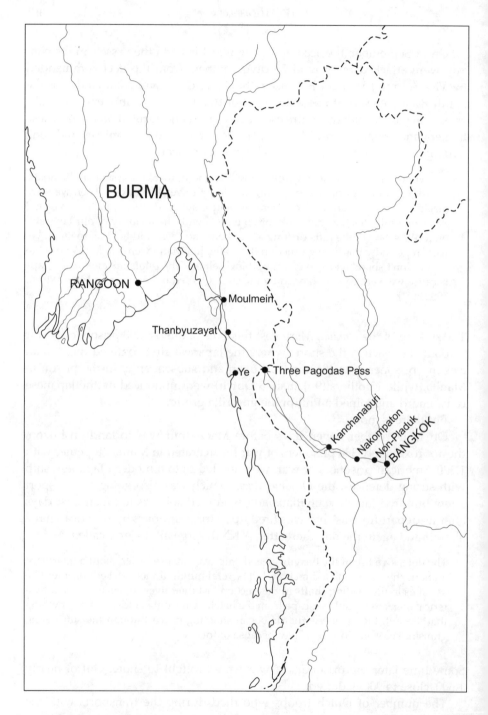

Map 10. Burma railway

Hokuku Maru and the *Oryohu Maru* is unknown. In conclusion, it should be stated that the total number of Dutch and Dutch Eurasian prisoners of war who lost their lives as a consequence of the ship transports is estimated at about 4,000: 900 more than perished on the infamous Burma Railway.

The Burma Railway

For its march to Burma, which began in December 1941, the Japanese 15th Army used an age-old path crossing the mountain ranges that separate Burma from Thailand.[163] Perhaps the Japanese officers had already latched on to the idea of building a railway along this route. However, at the time, in the opinion of those who determined Japanese strategy, it was not perceived as absolutely necessary: they were confident that they could supply their 15th Army in Burma via the ports of Rangoon and Moulmein (see Map 10) and assumed that this would present no problem once the British Eastern Fleet was driven out of the Indian Ocean. This succeeded only partially: indeed, after the sortie of the Japanese battle fleet to Ceylon, Admiral Somerville was forced to move his heavy units to Bombay and Mombasa (on the east coast of Africa), but the British base on Ceylon was not given up and British submarines and bombers continued to take action against Japanese ships travelling from Singapore to Rangoon and Moulmein. The first decision then made by the Japanese commanders in the Nampo was to build airfields at three locations in the far south of Burma, so that the Japanese air force could protect the ships sailing to and from Rangoon and Moulmein. For the sake of the construction of these airfields, in May 1942 about 3,000 Australian prisoners of war on board two ships departed from Singapore. In Belawan, on the northeast coast of Sumatra, they were joined by a third ship with another 2,000 prisoners of war: approximately 1,500 Dutch and Dutch Eurasian and about 500 British troops.

On 25 May, the 1,500 Dutch and Dutch Eurasians reached a coastal area near Tavoy that was a natural harbour, and disembarked three days later. They were then herded along with beatings for four hours to, as the Dutch army chaplain C. Mak noted in his diary, 'a kind of cattle pen filled with the dreck of dysentery patients' (quoted in Leffelaar and Van Witsen 1982: 92). Two days later they had to march to Tavoy: a distance of 33 kilometres. 'Cloudy sky, downpours in the afternoon; wretched, but endured through prayer. The sick beaten, the exhausted maltreated. [...] Deathly tired. [...] No food. [...] For everyone a difficult evening, soaked to the bone. [...] Rumours!' (Quoted in Leffelaar and Van Witsen 1982:93.) On 1 June the first group

---

[163] Most of the general information incorporated into this section is derived from the work by Leffelaar and Van Witsen, *Werkers aan de Birma-spoorweg* (1982).

that had to build the airfield at Tavoy took off. Some Australians worked
there too; eight of them had escaped but were turned in to the Japanese by
Burmese in return for money, and shot. 'Everywhere illness, frailty,' Mak
noted on 9 June. 'Not enough rice, no sugar, no salt'. Hunger oedema made
its appearance – 26 June:

> People are dying completely unexpectedly. Again a new phenomenon, where
> does it come from? Swollen feet, bloated faces, wounds that don't heal. [...] The
> clock of your stomach is running hours ahead of that of the kitchen. (Quoted in
> Leffelaar and Van Witsen 1982:93.)

Some time later, when the airfield at Tavoy had been completed, these prisoners of war were led north to Thanbyuzayat (circa 60 kilometres south of
Moulmein), a place along the railway from Ye to Rangoon, which was to be
the end of the new line that would connect the railway network of Thailand
with that of Burma. Though that new line would mostly be laid on Thai territory, it is nevertheless referred to here as 'the Burma Railway'.

Before the prisoners of war from Thanbyuzayat were put to work, they
first had to listen to a speech given by the commandant of the prisoner-of-
war camps in Burma, a Japanese colonel who, according to a KNIL corporal,
began by saying: 'I am very sorry you are prisoners of war'.

> He called us rebels and the dregs of society, for we had continued to fight on
> Sumatra while our main force on Java had capitulated. After speaking at length
> he ended his speech with the flagrant lie that: 'The most brilliant civilization in
> the world is the Imperial Japanese Army'. (N. Claessen quoted in Leffelaar and
> Van Witsen 1982:106.)

Construction of the Burma Railway had already been contemplated before
the Second World War by a British and a French company, both of which
had even drawn up plans. On 20 June 1942 the Supreme Headquarters in
Tokyo decided to implement the French plan – anticipating this decision,
General Terauchi gave the order to recruit the necessary indigenous manpower, *romusha*, to which substantial numbers of prisoners of war would be
added. Work began on the Thai side on 24 June: in Non-Pladuk (see Map 10)
a group of British and Australian prisoners of war conveyed by train from
Singapore began erecting the workshops and warehouses needed for the
Burma Railway after its completion. Definitive orders to commence work
were received from Tokyo in August, along with a deadline of 14 months: the
new railway had to be finished in October 1943.

It was to be 415 kilometres long: the highest point, the so-called Three
Pagodas Pass on the border of Burma and Thailand was about 300 metres.
The rails, with a gauge of 100 centimetres (the normal gauge is 142½ centi-
metres) would be laid as a single track with about 50 passing places and was

meant to have a capacity of 3,000 tons a day in both directions. Shunting yards and warehouses to store, for example, wood to fuel the locomotives had to be built at these passing places. On both Thai and Burmese territory the first part of the line ran through an inhabited region but in between was a virtually uninhabited mountain region. That area was heavily forested with dense, almost impenetrable tropical forests extending to the very crests of the hills and mountains. On both sides of the Three Pagodas Pass a centuries-old path curved along the valley of a swiftly flowing yellow-brown river (in Thailand the River Kwai) – the railway would be built next to that path.

This was a large-scale operation. Four million cubic metres of earth had to be moved and no less than three million cubic metres of rock removed. Moreover, several hundred railway bridges had to be built with a total length of 14 kilometres. Two of these bridges would be made of iron (they would be brought in from the Nampo area, one from Java), the others of wood.

In June 1942 Burmese and Thai *romusha* were deployed to make a start on the line. They worked so hard and mistreated so often by the officers and other ranks of the Japanese railway troops, in total about 10,000 soldiers, that most of them threw it up after only a short while. Many, mainly Thais, returned to their native homes but others, chiefly the Burmese, fearing that they would be handed over to the Japanese by the local administrators, took to the jungle and formed gangs of robbers who targeted the possessions of both the Japanese and the prisoners of war. This mass desertion on the part of the Burmese and Thai *romusha* spurred the Japanese to recruit *romusha* elsewhere, chiefly on Java and on Malacca (there alone about 60,000 Tamils), all together possibly between 180,000 and 200,000 replacements. It must be emphatically stated that no matter how much the approximately 61,000 prisoners of war put to work on the Burma Railway suffered, these *romusha* suffered even more. About one in five of the prisoners of war died, while eight, or perhaps nine, in ten *romusha* died – from the hard labour, scanty food and lack of medical attention, which led to an excessive number of deaths through cholera. Every two metres of the Burma Railway cost one human life.

Laying down the track required that, once the profuse undergrowth was removed and enough trees cut down and dragged away (this was often done with elephants), certain parts of the line had to be hacked or dug out and then levelled while for others a narrow railway embankment had to be thrown up. The Japanese had no tractors or machines for chopping, digging, sawing and sinking piles: all of the labour had to be done manually. Nor did they make available serviceable tools. With worn-out pickaxes, cliffs had to be hewn to a depth of eight metres, for the removal or bringing in of soil there were only wicker baskets, and digging had to be done with primitive shovels with blades made of pieces of petrol barrels and enamelled advertising signs that the Japanese had found in Burma, Thailand and elsewhere.

In addition, all of this labour had to be performed in an unfavourable climate. In Burma and Thailand the southwest monsoon blows from April until September. Coming from the Indian Ocean, it brings tropical rains with it: sometimes it rains three days at a stretch and two metres of rain can fall in the space of a single month.[164] The rivers become wild torrents, the ground turns into a deep quagmire and the atmosphere is like that in a hot house. From November to March the wind blows in from the highlands of Central Asia: the scorching sun beats down during the day and the nights are cold (6 degrees Celsius above 0 is normal). There is little wind in the two turns, but then the heat is inordinately oppressive.

Reasonable shelter for the masses of people sent to the railway was not deemed necessary by the Japanese. These masses moved up (in Burma to the south, in Thailand to the north) as the track was laid. Here and there they were housed in primitive tents or in barracks they first had to build themselves (large complexes arose wherever the majority of the labourers worked for any length of time: the base camps), but elsewhere the prisoners of war and the *romusha* had to sleep in the open, thus in the mud during the wet monsoon and on the hard, dusty ground during the dry season.

Their nutrition was sadly wanting. Tokyo had laid down, and General Terauchi had passed this on, that each man be given 550 to 750 grams of rice and 50 to 100 grams of meat a day, which amounted to maybe a maximum of 1,700 calories a day. These prescribed rations, however, were very rarely available: at every point the food supplies passed before reaching their destination, the weights were tampered with and dehydration took place. As a result, the workers generally received only 75 to 85% of the official rice ration and many never saw the rapidly spoiling meat. According to reports by British, Dutch and other officers (the Japanese destroyed all of their own reports immediately after their surrender), the daily rations actually received by the prisoners of war consisted of a maximum of 800 grams to a minimum of 300 grams of rice; a maximum of 550 grams to a minimum of 450 grams of vegetables (primarily sweet potatoes); a maximum of 70 grams to a minimum of 40 grams of meat (including bone); a maximum of 25 grams to a minimum of 15 grams of sugar; a maximum of 25 grams to a minimum of 15 grams of oil; 2½ grams of tea; and 20 grams of salt. How often less than the minimum was received is not known. It is estimated that the maximum rations would yield more than 2,000 calories per day, the minimum about 1,100. The maximum rations were already too low for the heavy labour to be done (this required a diet with at the least a calorific value of 3,500) and this applied a fortiori to the minimum rations. Particularly acute were the shortages of fat, protein and vitamins which seriously affected the KNIL prisoners, chiefly

[164]   In the Netherlands the annual average is 70 centimetres.

the Dutch. Making use of the fact that the camps were not closed, the Dutch Eurasians adapted better. A Dutch prisoner noted in early 1943:

> The Eurasian lads (and there are quite a few in these camps) face what we consider hardship with far greater ease than we do. It's as though they are all used to jungle life: they can all cook, know what can be eaten; they find roots and bulbs, leaves etc., in the forest, which they cook and process into something. While diving in the river they instantly find oysters on the bottom – these were already cooked and eaten the first evening.[165]

Inevitably, numerous prisoners began suffering from starvation and from avitaminosis which, as mentioned above, affects sight.

In addition to the fact that they received too little to eat, the prisoners of war were also poorly dressed and shod. Upon their departure from Java and Sumatra they were only allowed to bring along one knapsack (the officers were allowed a suitcase as well) – most had no more than two uniforms with them. This clothing soon wore out and the Japanese only provided loincloths. The army shoes were not up to the working conditions – the leather and canvas simply rotted in the mud. The rubber shoes that were sometimes distributed by the Japanese had an equally short life. As a result, many soon wore wooden clogs or even went barefoot; wounds swiftly followed which became infected, and then developed into dangerous tropical ulcers.

Before the prisoners of war had reached the beginning of the railway line either in Burma or in Thailand they had already endured many an ordeal. Those faced by the group coming from Belawan that first had to build an airfield in the south of Burma were sketched above. The groups from Java were conveyed to Singapore in filthy, overcrowded and suffocating holds. They were detained in the large prisoner-of-war camp at Changi Prison which contained mostly British prisoners, and subsequently transported in closed freight wagons to Thailand.

Work had to be done from Changi Camp, but not by the prisoners of war destined for the Burma Railway who thus received no fatigue money, making it impossible for them to buy any additional food. Changi had an extensive black market but the prices were too steep for the Java arrivals, with the exception of those who had been able to bring along tobacco, a pound of which fetched quite a lot of money.

Let us follow J.C. Hamel on his transport to Thailand, for which he was crammed into a freight wagon in Singapore on 16 January 1943:

> Formerly all manner of raw material was transported in these wagons: flour, cement, fertilizer, and since then no one had taken the trouble to clean them. Now

---

[165]   A.H. Douwes, 'Persoonlijke herinneringen', p. 30 (NIOD IC, 81,315).

26 to 28 men were packed into each wagon with their sweaty bodies and soaked clothing. If everyone pulled up their knees one could just barely sit. Two buckets were issued per wagon, for the time being with an unknown purpose.

[...] In the daytime the wagons were unbearably hot. The sun beat down relentlessly on the iron [...] and sweat poured from our bodies. We sat cheek by jowl, wearing as little as possible. After sunset, however, it soon cooled down and at night it was actually cold.

[...] We stopped two times a day [at a station]; then it was possible to use some kind of improvised toilet along the track, but the number of these establishments was sadly wanting, so that people [...] simply sat along the rails. [...] Every station was now ravaged by an enormous plague of flies – these were the flies that [...] spread dysentery because it was precisely at these stations that food was distributed.

When the train arrived, the rice and the *sayur* (vegetable soup) stood ready in baskets and pots covered with swarms of flies. A few men from each wagon were then permitted to receive the food for their group in the buckets handed out in Singapore. A cold sweat broke out on those who upon their departure had not understood their purpose and had used them during the night. (Hamel 1948: 101-3.)

After a five-day train ride the prisoners of war had to get out at the beginning of the Burma Railway. In early 1943 more than 100 kilometres of rails had been laid from the south which were already used by the narrow gauge train, and the old forest path had been widened into an unpaved road used by trucks. However, neither the train nor the trucks were deployed by the Japanese to convey the prisoners of war to the spots where they were first to be put to work: they had to walk from camp to camp, frequently at night. The KNIL soldiers from Singapore covered a distance of about 200 kilometres before reaching a large base camp.

In April 1943 (the start of the rainy season), a group of KNIL prisoners of war was assembled in Non-Pladuk for a 225-kilometre march to their work camp. The following is taken from a report by one of the prisoners (in Leffelaar and Van Witsen 1982:116-24):

19 April. We fall in at two o'clock in the morning after having consumed a meal. Heavily laden we begin the jungle march. [...] Japanese sentries walk in front and in back of the groups to keep them together. They have fixed bayonets. We walk for 45 minutes and then rest for 10. The initially paved road later turns into a gravelled one.

A distance of 25 kilometres was covered – and the same again the next day.

20 April. After a 25-kilometre march we arrive at Kanchanaburi, [...] a very old Siamese city, and are accommodated in an overfull camp.

21 April. After breakfast we first treat our feet. In the afternoon we all have to go to the Japanese hospital and get injections against cholera, typhoid and dysentery

as well as another smallpox vaccination, losing four hours of our valuable break.

When we arrive back at camp, tired and hot from the waiting and walking we are given something to eat and after that have to pack up everything because at ten o'clock at night we have to fall in all ready to cover the next stage.

22 April. Last night's more than 25-kilometre march has taken its toll on all of us. Just outside of Kanchanaburi we abandoned the paved road and walked all night through wild, barren vegetation. Over narrow and rough sandy roads and often gravel roads broken up by cars. The latter were particularly painful for our already seriously injured feet.

At ten o'clock in the evening we again have to fall in for departure. It's just dry then. Heavy rain clouds float past the moon and the forest is dripping from the rain, it's dark and wet; the roads are a sea of mud in which we often sink up to our ankles. It is slippery and moreover the mud sucks powerfully so that walking is unbelievably laborious and doubly painful. After a few hours many are already so tired that they just lie in the mud after slipping and haven't the heart to stand up.

At nine thirty the next morning we arrive at a new camp utterly exhausted. It's not really a camp with quarters, just a few pig and goat pens.

We leave tonight at ten.

24 April. Deathly tired and totally drained we arrive at nine thirty the next morning at the next camp: Tarsao (131 kilometres). Already during the third 40-minute haul last night, H. (one of the friends in the group with whom we are doing the entire march) began exhibiting clear signs of exhaustion: he vomited and threw off his knapsack, lay down on the side of the path and burst into tears. By talking to him we managed to get him to his feet. However, he was in no condition to lug his knapsack, which we then took turns carrying. During the fourth haul he could go no further and fell out together with L., who exhibited the same symptoms. (H. and L. later died.) We are also dog-tired.

25 April (Easter Sunday). [...] Along with me, another seven patients, almost all with bloody stools [...] were carried to the [Japanese] doctor and his assistant. Treatment is awful and humiliating. We are just Europeans and then prisoners of war to boot. They laugh at us and take the greatest delight in our suffering. Several of us lay down on the ground as we could no longer stand. We were kicked and trampled and sent away without being examined. My wounds were roughly treated; it hurts a lot but I got some salve and a bandage on them. And that's worth a great deal. Only we have to walk further tonight.

26 April (Easter Monday). At seven thirty this morning we arrived at this camp (the name of which I did not hear), we walked last night in groups of 200, a Jap in front and in back of each group.

[...] The nights are dark and so walking through the forest is difficult. We repeatedly bump our already so tender feet against the roots of trees running across the path. Many have night blindness due to vitamin deficiency, a number of the sick fall out, they are just able to reach an English camp and remain behind there.

It is quiet in the primeval jungle through which we walk the entire night. Bird life here is not so lively. It is also colder and swathed in mist. In the forest the *wau-wau*, a species of gibbon, scream. They live in groups and call to one another with doleful howls. We hear them everywhere and all the time; it makes us down and dejected. It is a cry of misery completely in keeping with the sad and sombre misty desolation of the Siamese jungle. We pass the day sleeping and boiling water. At eight in the evening we push on. Upon leaving the camp I begin to get the trots.

April 27. After a terrible night march through very hilly terrain we arrived at Rintin (181 kilometres) at nine thirty this morning. The treatment by the Japanese here is again very rough, if not downright bestial.

Our condition deteriorates rapidly. There are those who relieve themselves 50 times a day and continually have diarrhoea. We are out of medicine and none is provided by the Japs.

Tonight we stay in Rintin and sleep in a place carved out of the jungle.

29 April. [...] When we wake up we have to fall in rapidly because it's the birthday of the *Tenno Heika*, the emperor of Japan. On the road we are lined up in ranks of five: the Japanese commandant gives a speech which nobody understands, after that we have to call out *'banzai'*. But, because this does not meet the approval of the Japanese the first time, as all enthusiasm is lacking, it has to be repeated. This is still not good enough. They begin hitting us with bamboo sticks and finally a resounding *'banzai'* penetrates the silence of the jungle. We then return to our sleeping places. That evening our troop sets off again, but I stay behind at Rintin along with 11 others because we can't walk.

That night there is severe lightning. Nothing can withstand the torrential downpours. The water streams over the ground which cannot absorb the deluge; we are soaking wet. A large empty tent is pitched a bit further from us, but we are not allowed to use it. The sick have no more value for the Japs; they can't work. So why take care of them?

1 May. They also let us lie the next day. It's wet. The forest is dripping from the rain. During the day we look for a sunny spot and so find some warmth. At night it rains again. Our condition is rapidly deteriorating. I dare not sketch a picture of how we look, it defies all description.

2 May. [...] In the morning we are told that there is a car. We are loaded in, but our hope of being taken to a hospital again proves to be vain. We are taken to the next jungle camp, Brankasi (208 kilometres). In the *alang-alang* [a type of grass with long, narrow plumes] wilderness with some wild bushes and a few tall primeval trees a small area has been burned clear. We are set down there in the shade of a tall tree. We total 12. Ten empty Japanese tents stand but a short distance away, but we are not allowed to use them. No food is given us. I try to get to the kitchen. To our great good fortune a Dutchman is there. He helps us, gives us some rice and some weak vegetable broth in a bucket; he can't spare any more.

3 May. An English party arrives the next morning. I ask if there is a doctor present who can help us. The doctor can do nothing; there is no medicine. That morning trucks loaded with bales of rice pass by. We can ride with them. With difficulty we drag ourselves to the road and clamber up on to the trucks, which have to set off immediately. One of us is not fast enough, or is he already too weak?

We drive on, the country is very hilly and the road takes us past tall limestone mountains and through deep ravines. We arrive at Takanun (218 kilometres) around one and rejoin our own party. We thank God that we are back with them and our own doctors.

It seems that we all have arrived at Takanun 14 days too early. Only a very limited number of barracks and tents are available to us. The sick are accommodated in them.

When we arrive there is still a fairly large number of British and Australian troops. They have been here since October last year. Their health leaves much to be desired. Stomach complaints and malaria have sent many of them to their graves. Their clothing is threadbare, and many have only rags. They are covered with lice, which they rapidly transfer to us. It's wet and cold.

The monsoon rains are expected at the end of May.

The author of this report was fortunate: he was able to make part of the journey by truck, a rare occurrence. Many prisoners of war in no condition to reach their final destination stayed behind in one of the camps, where they overnighted, but as they were not part of the official camp manpower they were usually not entitled to rations. On the long nocturnal marches where it seemed as though their feet were gripped by the suction of the mud, carrying their baggage proved too difficult for many and it was sometimes just cast aside or sold to Thais, no matter how low a price was offered.[166] If prisoners of war remained behind on their night march there was a very real chance that they would be ambushed and robbed by bandits. As a rule only the strong were able to keep up the pace set by the Japanese, and that tempo was many times faster than appears in the report just quoted. There was a group of 600 prisoners which had to cover about 30 kilometres a night in six marches. The group lost virtually all of its luggage and of the 600, 230 remained behind, while of the 370 who reached the large base camp exhausted, only 200 were in any condition to go to work.

Relatively few remained in such a base camp: most of the prisoners of war were housed in work camps, where at first only tents and later barracks (actually bamboo huts) were erected. These were long structures with sleeping places on the sides, at right angles to a centre aisle. There were also better barracks, but these were always reserved for the Japanese railway troops and the Korean guards. Only one thing mattered to the Japanese and the Koreans, namely that the railway be finished on time. And so the utmost was required of the *romusha* and the prisoners of war.

They had to toil from dawn to dusk and when there was enough moonlight also until two o'clock in the morning – in Burma they once worked for a solid 33 hours. Labour did not begin immediately on the work days: an average of one to four kilometres had to be walked from each of the 50 work camps just to reach the place where the actual construction was carried out. Those who were to dig had to shift at first two, later three cubic metres of soil a day. Special treatment was given only to the approximately 400 men who laid the rails and drove home the spikes: the strongest were selected for this task and assuming that about four kilometres of rail had to be laid per day, the Japanese gave them additional food. The members of the 'spike crew' also sometimes had a break when the next section of the tracks was still unfin-

---

[166] On the Burma Railway, prisoners of war also sold the gold fillings in their teeth.

ished. Here the weakened prisoners of war had to level the ground or throw up an embankment or hack away at rocks or, sometimes stumbling through mud up to their knees, drag the sleepers or the heavy beams necessary for the construction of the bridges. This was done amidst swarms of flies, with feverish bodies, half empty stomachs, often with cuts on the feet threatening to turn into tropical ulcers, to the bellowing of the Japanese (and this applied equally to the Koreans) and the daily floggings. And every morning in all of the camps, according to Leffelaar and Van Witsen (1982:150), one saw the:

> same horrible scene [...] to chase the men to work at the first light of dawn. The men emerged from their overcrowded huts or leaking shelters in the pouring rain. Even the strongest seemed to be exhausted. [...] They were dressed in rags or just a loincloth, most were barefoot and their feet were injured or swollen. Joining them were the 50 or 60 patients from the hospital barrack, leaning on canes or crouching in the mud. [...] They had to appear at the roll call to make up the number. Sometimes all, and at other times only some, of these patients were nevertheless sent out to work and they left the camp leaning on their canes and half dragged by their comrades.

Were these patients unable to work any further, the railway troops' and guards' initial impulse was to consider them saboteurs: soldiers of the lowest rank who refused 'to follow the imperial way'. If verbal and physical abuse proved ineffective the miscreants received permission to remain lying only until their group stumbled back to camp: resting in the mud lashed by torrential downpours, or on the hard ground in clouds of dust. In many camps it was the rule that the sick received no rations – the Japanese camp commandants repeatedly heard from their superiors that in general it mattered not in the least whether the sick died.

Hunger oedema and avitaminosis were not the only conditions afflicting the prisoners of war: the list includes dysentery, tropical ulcers, malaria, and for a while a cholera epidemic. In April 1943 two out of five prisoners of war were in no condition to work. The first paragraph of a special order issued at the end of that month by one of the department heads of the Japanese administration of the prisoner-of-war camps in Burma read as follows: 'I am pleased that construction of the railway is progressing entirely as expected as a result of the continued efforts of all of the prisoners'. And the last: 'I regret that at this time 40% of all of the prisoners of war are ill. All of the camps must strive to lower the number of patients as quickly as possible to increase the percentage of those who are at work.'[167] This directive was typically Japanese: a goal was set,

---

[167]　Order from the head of the third department of the administration of the prisoner-of-war camps in Burma, 26 April 1943 (NIOD IC, 363).

but the means for attaining it (more and better food, improved medical care, that is primarily more medicine) were not indicated, let alone made available.

When the minister J.C. Hamel arrived at Camp Rintin (mentioned earlier in the long march cited above) in February 1943, he visited the tents housing the patients. 'The conditions I encountered here', he later wrote:

> defy all description. [...] Ill prisoners literally lay rotting.[168] They had virtually no clothing. Many were also without blankets, their bodies covered only by gunny sacks; others lay on the hard ground. [...] The men lacked everything: there were no lamps, no urinals, no bedpans, no bandages, no medicine. Long, deep trenches covered with bamboo sticks served as latrines.

This sick bay was condemned.

> One afternoon we were summoned before the Japanese: we were informed that orders from above had been received to move the hospital elsewhere, about a half kilometre further away; the old spot was too infected. We cheered the decision, but our joy turned into utter astonishment when it appeared that the move had to take place immediately, with no delay. Japanese soldiers accompanied us, unfastened the tent ropes and with the greatest equanimity allowed the tents to fall on the patients still lying there.

With help from the prisoners of war still working who, 'dead tired' after their day's work 'stumbled back in the camp', the move was a fact by 11 o'clock. 'All of the patients were then transferred. A few were nearing their end as a result of all of the tossing and dragging about.' (Hamel 1948:128-9, 131, 134.)

The Dutch minister got a clear picture of the medical officers' achievements in Rintin. He wrote:

> I have gained great respect for most of them: they were able to work miracles with nothing. The calm certainty with which they went around the tents, taking temperatures, a patient's pulse, was heartening. Occasionally they spoke a few words, prescribed some strong tea or charcoal, and even though they knew better than anyone else that this medical care was nothing but a charade, they created an atmosphere of confidence, you felt in good hands with them. Unfortunately, not all were worthy of this regard. Some shamefully betrayed their duty, perhaps their courage failed them. (Hamel 1948:130.)

While two out of five prisoners were ill in Burma in April 1943, this percentage was far higher by mid-1943. Permission to transfer the critically ill to a base hospital was received in July, but only when the Japanese camp commandant agreed. Permanent hospital camps were built in two places in Thailand only in early 1944 (the railway was finished then, but a substantial number of the

---

[168]   As a consequence of the gangrene that developed from tropical ulcers.

prisoners of war had to remain behind for maintenance) and a few months later a large hospital in Bangkok was put into use on the orders of Tokyo.

Of the almost 62,000 prisoners of war working on the Burma Railway during or shortly after its construction more than 11,000 died, including 3,100 of the roughly 18,000 Dutch and Dutch Eurasians. Their losses, more than one in six, were lower than those of the Americans, Australians, and British. In terms of percentages, the sacrifices made by the last groups of prisoners of war sent to the Burma Railway were the greatest. These comprised almost 3,300 prisoners of war, including about 500 Dutch and Dutch Eurasians, who were transported from Singapore to Thailand at the beginning of May 1943 when the Japanese feared that construction would not be completed on time. Included in these groups were many of the British and Australians in Changi Camp who had been declared unfit to work on the railway in 1942. Moreover, the groups deployed to Three Pagodas Pass had to make the longest marches. In these groups more than one in three of the British troops and more than one in four of the Australians perished, in contrast to only one in sixteen of the Dutch and Dutch Eurasians.

The group of Dutch and Dutch Eurasians from Belawan worked on the Burma Railway for more than a year – this was a few months less than the groups from Java. Many of the prisoners of war lost all awareness of time. 'Time ceased to have any significance', an Australian soldier later wrote:

> No one knew what day of the week nor what week of the month nor even what month of the year it was. [...] If one were to survive, it was essential not to acknowledge the horror that lay all around, still more not to perceive the effect it had upon oneself. It was not wise even to look in a mirror. Life accordingly evolved into a blur of continuous work, people dying, guards bellowing, heavy loads to be carried, fever which came in tides of heat and cold on alternate days, dysentery and hunger. All these became the normal. (R. Braddon, cited in Wigmore 1957:584.)

All the more admirable was how despite all of these ordeals some remained aware of the needs of their fellow captives. The self-sacrificing work of countless medical officers has already been noted, and to this group should be added the male nurses, about whom Hamel wrote: 'Rarely did I see such heartfelt compassion, such practical charity, as among these people' (Hamel 1948:119). Also not to be forgotten is the comfort clergymen or lay clergy offered the sick and dying. Only a few of these pastors made such a deep impression on the prisoners of war as J.C. Hamel who, as mentioned, had reported voluntarily to a prisoner-of-war camp on Java. In February 1943, a Dutch prisoner of war wrote:[169]

[169]	A.H. Douwes, 'Persoonlijke herinneringen', 22 February 1943, p. 33 (NIOD IC, 81,315).

The stamina Hamel displays again and again is enormous: preaching daily in the hospital barracks and almost daily a new sermon: in the evening prayers; and personal visits throughout the day. In everyone's view this man, who twice turned down an offer of release because he feels it is his duty to be with the prisoners of war, whom he constantly accompanies as they move on, deserves a high royal honour.[170]

In spite of all of the problems, religious services were held both by Protestants and Catholics. In Rintin Camp a suggestion by the Protestants to hold joint gatherings was rejected by the Catholics; according to a Catholic in his diary, acceptance would 'constitute a danger for our weak'.[171]

Study sessions, as had been common in the camps on Java, were never held on the Burma Railway: there were no study books or writing materials, the moves were too frequent and no one had the energy. At the most, they could muster up the strength to play chess or cards. Moreover, some prisoners were able to provide diversion for their partners in adversity. For instance, as of the beginning of 1943, the accordionist Han Samathini along with several other people performed work written by Dolf Winkler in Thailand in a base camp serving as a hospital camp. And Wim Kan sang old and new songs in camps first in Burma and later in Thailand. On Queen's Day 1943 (31 August), when Mussolini's defeat in Italy was announced,[172] he sang a new song: 'Autumn in Europe' in which he had the fall of the 'man from the boot' (Mussolini) followed by that of the 'little man with your moustache' (Hitler):

Hear the wind drone through the forest,
Yonder falls something heavy and acute,
Look, the wind plays like a child
With the man from the boot,
Picks him up with a hiss
And drowns him then just so
Plucked from a palace of bliss
In his very own stinky Po!

Little man with your moustache,
Stay out of this wind,
For in the end it will blow you cold,
Straight in the direction of the scaffold!
Watch out, little man,
The storm is beyond your command!
For it is autumn in dictator land!

---

[170] Hamel was made an officer in the Order of Orange-Nassau in September 1946.
[171] Text of the diary in Brugmans 1960:365-6.
[172] In a few camps on the Burma Railway the prisoners of war had a clandestine radio, a crystal receiver; elsewhere, Chinese or Thai newspapers were received.

Wim Kan later wrote:

> I sang it in the middle of the wilderness on Queen Wilhelmina's birthday as the finale of a somewhat nationalistically coloured cabaret show. The audience was so exuberant that once it was finished they suddenly burst out with the strictly forbidden Wilhelmus [the Dutch national anthem]. Hans van Heusden, my accompanist, Jan van Bennekom, a lad with a good voice, and I stood rooted to the spot on the small, shaky stage. [...] At the end Van Heusden was able to get away, but Van Bennekom and I walked straight into the arms of the camp's Number One Japanese, who was in a state of hysterical rage. I had just enough time to rip 'Autumn in Europe' from my big songbook [...] before we instantly had to go to the Japanese office where, as luck would have it, there was just the one sergeant of the Nippon army who found the entire happening not the least bit important. (Kan and Vonk 1963:170.)

Queen's Day was celebrated in other camps as well. In the one where Hamel was stationed an improvised congratulations register was even allowed to be set out. According to the preacher, 'Allegedly, the Japanese sergeant, then the highest enemy commandant in the camp, owed his life to the courage of one of our young men who saved him from the water. Something he apparently never forgot.' (Hamel 1948:170.)

The camps along the Burma Railway were not closed, guards were few, and during the nightly marches the prisoners of war left behind frequently walked from one camp to the other without surveillance. In theory, thus, escape was not difficult – in practice it was virtually impossible. Those who did take that risk had to find their own way through hundreds of kilometres of jungle and sooner or later rely on the help of the local inhabitants, whose language(s) almost no one spoke and whose village headmen knew that punishment by the Japanese would be harsh should they fail to turn in the escaped prisoners of war. There was a somewhat better chance of receiving help in Burma than in Thailand because the railway route in Burma was not far from where the Karens lived: tribes traditionally opposed to the Burmese and who helped the British in the Second World War.

Five KNIL soldiers long succeeded in remaining at liberty in Burma. For four of them escape was linked to the fact that they refused to take the declaration of obedience required by the Japanese, which included a stipulation that prisoners of war promise not to flee. This demand created great commotion in the camps in Thanbyuzayat in September 1942, which at the time contained the Dutch, British and Australian prisoners of war who first had built the airfields in the far south of Burma. The Dutch senior officer, Major C.F. Hazenberg refused to sign, setting an example which was followed by the British and Australian senior officers. According to C. Mak, 'harassment, repeated roll calls, strict examination of the sick', and 'a great deal of trouble and misery' were the consequences.[173] At the end of September, the Kempeitai arrested the three senior officers. After being seriously mistreated they came to the conclusion that promising obedience under duress was not objectionable – they were brought back to their camps and modified their instruction.

Bearing in mind that this matter had preoccupied the KNIL prisoners of war for several weeks and that the resolve of all of the prisoners of war had only brought them grief, it is hardly surprising that several refused to follow Major Hazenberg's new directive. These were four Dutch Eurasians, namely Captain P.L. van Hemert and three soldiers: R.H. Hoffman, E.F. Portier and a certain Schuurman. Hoping to reach Tavoy and find a sailing boat there, they escaped dressed as simply as possible on 4 October.[174] During the first 12 days they covered a total of 40 kilometres in the tropical jungle in heavy rainfall, staying alive by eating young bamboo shoots, plants and some rice they had brought along, 'which, however', according to Portier later, 'was sour (everything was soaked through, naturally) and made us sick. Moreover, Captain Van Hemert contracted malaria, Schuurman Burma fever, and I got an infection in my leg'.[175] They met up with a Karen who brought them to a village headman. The latter spoke some English and even though the Japanese had posted a reward for their capture, he had guides take them to a Karen district where they were hidden in separate places. They lived there for more than six months, finally reuniting in July 1943. Knowing that the Japanese were hunting them down, in September they took the advice of Karen headmen and became members of a band of robbers numbering close to 300 men which undertook numerous sorties against the Japanese in which they participated. They were joined in December 1943 by a fifth KNIL soldier, Sergeant G. Knoester. Together with three other officers he had escaped at the end of November 1943. These three were caught several days later (and shot by the Japanese), but Knoester managed to save himself, joined a Karen guerrilla band and a year later succeeded in finding Captain van Hemert's small group. This was reduced even further because for unknown reasons Private Hoffman refused to recognize the captain's authority.

The Japanese increased pressure on the territories of the Karens in the first six months of 1944, which was also related to the fact that the British appeared to be in position to launch an offensive in Burma (one that failed). According to Portier, '*Kampong* headmen were tortured and executed; anyone owning a British gun was horribly murdered and burned along with his

---

[173] C. Mak, 'Dagboek', 29 September 1942, p. 94 (NIOD IC).
[174] Their escape resulted in a five-hour punishment muster in the camp in question. Moreover, everyone who had slept next to the four escapees had to stand at attention for the Japanese guard for 35 hours. Similar punishment was meted out after others escaped as well.
[175] E.F. Portier, 'Verslag', n.d., p. 1 (NIOD IC, 81,295).

house and property'.[176] Van Hemert, Portier, Schuurman and Knoester faced ever greater difficulties given that some Karen headmen wanted to hand them over. They were forced to flee in July 1944, 'the unrelenting rain, new bouts of malaria and the bad food aggravated our situation'.[177]

After a round up on 31 July, in which Burmese with dogs took part, they were arrested at the edge of a deep ravine, 'tied up with split bamboo, beaten by the livid Japanese corporal' and brought before a Japanese officer who 'refused to believe that he was dealing with Dutch escaped prisoners of war. He knew nothing about Hoffman'. Still alive in July 1944, Hoffman vanished without trace.[178]

The Japanese executed the Karen headman who had helped the four other escapees the longest ('he had even declared himself the owner of the rifle I had cast away'[179]). Van Hemert, Portier, Schuurman and Knoester were taken to the prisoner-of-war camp in Kanchanaburi in Thailand and in October sentenced by the Japanese court martial in Singapore: Captain van Hemert received a life sentence; the three lower lower-ranking soldiers were condemned to 15 years of forced labour. Van Hemert died in prison and the three others were freed in August 1945.

Another two KNIL soldiers, L.F. van der Worm and B.N. Tuinenburg, also managed to stay free, as did, finally, a group of 18 prisoners of war who only escaped when they were in a small camp in Bangkok after having worked on the Burma Railway.

Van der Worm, who lost all of his clothes[180] on the first day of his flight in mid-1943 (and so wore only a pair of pants made from plaited plants) was helped by a hermit and lived completely alone in the jungle for one and a half years until the Japanese collapse, 'by which time it was as familiar as the living room and the standard lamp'.[181] Tuinenburg had the advantage of having learned to speak Thai from his Thai mother. He drifted down the River Kwai, lived in a Buddhist monastery for a few months, subsequently joined a guerrilla group but distrustful of it returned to the monastery, where he found shelter until the end of the war.

The 18 who escaped from the camp in Bangkok, all dark-skinned Dutch Eurasians and indigenous KNIL soldiers,[182] did so on the grounds of the (incorrect) announcement that the British had penetrated northern Thailand.

---

[176] E.F. Portier, 'Verslag', n.d., p. 3 (NIOD IC, 81,295).
[177] E.F. Portier, 'Verslag', n.d., p. 4 (NIOD IC, 81,295).
[178] E.F. Portier, 'Verslag', n.d., p. 4 (NIOD IC, 81,295).
[179] E.F. Portier, 'Verslag', n.d., p. 5 (NIOD IC, 81,295).
[180] He had hung them up to dry and was bathing when a Japanese patrol approached.
[181] Cited by Gerth van Zanten in the Dutch daily, *De Telegraaf*, 21 March 1964.
[182] Among the KNIL prisoners of war deployed to work on the Burma Railway were about 500 indigenous people, mostly Ambonese.

They took to their heels in pairs and under the Ambonese sergeant J. Saimina set up a bivouac where they were able to sustain themselves as farmers with support from the Thais until the end of the war.

In addition to that of the three officers already mentioned, other attempts to escape also failed.

Between the attempts of Captain van Hemert and of the three officers, another three officers (in uniform) fled from the camp at Thanbyuzayat; they were found after three weeks and shot.

In February 1943 two KNIL soldiers managed to separate themselves from a group underway to Camp Rintin, and were shot in Thailand. The fate of two others, both sergeants who left Rintin in May, was just as tragic.

The first two roamed around the jungle for a month, received little support from the Thais, were turned over to the Japanese by a village headman, taken to Rintin and shot there three days later. The other two had maps of Burma and Thailand, additional clothing, a fair amount of food, money and even a gun – they had thus prepared themselves well for their attempt. Yet, the very first night out they ran into a Japanese patrol and were forced to abandon all of their possessions. One of them vanished without trace. The other hid near Rintin and snuck into camp every night where he was helped by a friend. A few weeks later he headed out to a larger camp where his captain was and where he could stay. However, during each muster he had to retreat into the jungle given that he fell outside of the number of men. This went well until the camp in question was to be evacuated. The captain asked Hamel for advice. He suggested that the captain quietly bury one of the people who had passed away in the sick bay one night, 'if necessary under another dead person' and have the escapee assume the place of the deceased. According to Hamel:

> The captain decided to act accordingly: time was pressing.
> Much later, when everything was over, I heard that the officers and medical officers had not been up to the task; the unfortunate sergeant was thus forced to report to the Japanese with the fatal result that he was executed by a firing squad. I do not wish to blame anybody, but lament the dearth of courageous, chivalrous fellows in the world! (Hamel 1948:157.)

The work teams that had begun in Burma reached Three Pagodas Pass in August 1943. Working further to the south, in mid-October they met up with the teams put to work in Thailand. The Burma Railway was finished. And, on time! According to Major Van Baarsel:

> The Japanese were deliriously happy. We were given three days leave. There had to be three days of celebration. We all had to fall in, and a pompous proclamation by the Japanese emperor to the effect that one of the greatest and most important works in the world had been finished was read out loud. We were given cigarettes

and even some pigs. [...] Wim Kan and a few other performers came to the camps (in turns) to give shows. We did not know what had hit us.[183]

The Japanese began using the entire railway in mid-November. Much of the rolling stock came from Java, as did the personnel working in the stations and passing places. According to Van Baarsel, 'Several of them tried to make contact with us, but were very afraid that the Japs would notice'.[184]

The Japanese intended the track to have a capacity of 3,000 tons a day in both directions. This was not reached. In 1944 (figures before and after are not available) only an average of about 500 tons a day was transported north via the Burma Railway, possibly more in the first than in the last months of that year. What was transported in those first months was not enough to give the Japanese army in Burma the necessary attacking power and the offensive they launched in March 1944 was a miserable failure. The Allies began bombing the Burma Railway at that time, killing several hundred prisoners of war. Not all of them had been moved out upon completion of the railway: five groups of about 3,000 men totalling close to 15,000 remained at the railway together with *romusha* to chop wood for the locomotives, load and unload freight wagons, dig air-raid trenches and air-raid shelters and repair damage to the railway sometimes due to errors (or sabotage) made during construction and sometimes due to the Allied bombings.[185] Initially the 15,000 or so men received enough food, but when the Japanese were cornered in Burma the prisoners of war were the first to feel the consequences: their food supply was disrupted and severe starvation was experienced on the Burma Railway from early 1945.

In late 1943 and early 1944 the prisoners of war not necessary for and on the railway were assembled in six large camps not far from its starting point in Thailand. As mentioned above, two large camps were established where the sick were concentrated. In some of them little good will existed between the officers and other ranks because only the former had money for additional food (no work was done and thus no fatigue money was paid out), and at best only a piddling amount of that was handed over to the kitty. According to Leffelaar and Van Witsen (1982:236), 'Many diaries by the rank and file note how serious discrepancies arose precisely upon completion of the railway',

---

[183] J. van Baarsel, 'Onder de Jappen', p. 73 (NIOD IC, 81,359).
[184] J. van Baarsel, 'Onder de Jappen', p. 86 (NIOD IC, 81,359).
[185] The degree to which sabotage was perpetrated is difficult to determine. Major Van Baarsel gave several examples: direction pickets were moved so that sections of track did not join up, also height pickets so that the track did not lie level. This all created delays. Wheelbarrows and wicker baskets vanished under the sand of the thrown up dike. 'Later, when the trains began to run and the rains had completely soaked through the track, there were repeated collapses' (J. van Baarsel, 'Onder de Jappen', p. 68 (NIOD IC, 81,359)).

and they found it 'striking that mention of this is made chiefly in the diaries kept by the KNIL, far more than in those of the British and the Australians'.

The movement of the prisoners of war destined to work in the mines and factories in Japan, who had to be transported out of Singapore or Saigon (transports during which many drowned), began in March 1944. No Dutch Eurasians, at least none with dark skin, were sent to work in Japan,[186] so that only some of the KNIL prisoners of war were embarked in Singapore or Saigon. Another roughly 3,600 Dutch prisoners of war were attached to the group of about 600 'technicians' (except for the officers, all Dutch Eurasians) working in Japan as of the beginning of 1943, and the 3,400 who left Java in September 1943.

The number of KNIL prisoners in Singapore grew to about 2,000.[187] The going got rough for them because in May 1944 the Japanese decided to use the large camp built near Changi Prison to house Japanese air force personnel and to cram the prisoners of war from the camp within the prison's walls. The buildings only had room for about 5,000 prisoners of war, the rest (initially about 7,000, but this number grew to about 9,000) were housed in bamboo huts. Naturally, hygiene in the crowded complex left much to be desired. Also in 1945 the rations were drastically reduced to about 2 ounces of rice and 1 ounce of vegetables per day and those who were sick got half of this. People stayed alive only through the hope of a speedy liberation and this hope was nurtured by the news of the war's progress received on the clandestine radios. The British senior officer was also able to secure important concessions from the Japanese commandant: groups were allowed to swim at the beach, there was a camp orchestra, there were plenty of books and according to Beets (1981:271), 'there was also an adult education centre with informed speakers on a range of subjects'. Every nationality (the Dutch group was led by the defender of Balikpapan, Lieutenant Colonel C. van den Hoogenband) had its own police – these units 'were not especially popular. [...] Disciplinary rules were sometimes enforced in a bewildering manner', namely very harshly. (Beets 1981:271-2.) There was also work to be done: within the camp by those who had fatigues, and outside by large groups assigned all manner of defence work. From mid-June to mid-July 1945 one group, also including KNIL prisoners of war, had to help with an airfield ('they're a sorry mess on extremely minimal rations')[188] and subsequently erect defences in the middle

---

[186] The reason for this may have been that the Japanese authorities who also pretended in their own country to 'have freed Asia' did not wish to have prisoners at work in Japan who could be seen as Asians.

[187] It should be remembered that in September 1944 about 750 prisoners of war, including many officers of the merchant navy considered prisoners of war by the Japanese, were transferred to Singapore to help dig a dry dock. They were later followed by other groups.

[188] F.B. Nijon, 'Aantekeningen', 14 June 1945.

of a large Chinese churchyard ('I see Chinese women weeping and begging. A lugubrious fatigue! It's very heavy work').[189] Also murderous was the work on the dry dock that had to be dug on a small island. Malaria and dysentery were rampant. The history of the Stoomvaart Maatschappij Nederland (Dutch Steamer Company) in wartime says:

> The latter was hardly surprising, for the drinking water there had to be drawn from a pit. In preparing the food at least it was still boiled. Making tea with it was the simplest thing in the world, for it only needed to be warmed up: it was already brown from the mud. (De Roever 1951:372.)

As mentioned above, only some of the KNIL prisoners of war were transferred from Burma to Japan, Singapore or Saigon. Others remained in the six large camps for quite some time, chiefly in Non-Pladuk II, where the KNIL group was by far the largest among a total of about 9,000 prisoners of war. The senior officer therefore was a KNIL captain, whose command according to Hamel became 'increasingly tyrannical' (Hamel 1948:181). Later, when after the arrival of new groups a lieutenant colonel became the senior officer, the captain – now as his adjutant – continued to run the show ('in his defence it should be mentioned that the men had virtually no discipline') (Hamel 1948: 186). Business flourished in this camp, 'prisoners received far more food, the location was reasonable, there was more free time' (Hamel 1948:186).

A second camp, Kanchanaburi III, was unfortunately surrounded by a two-metre high fence so that the men could see nothing of the world beyond. According to Major Van Baarsel, 'some men were so disturbed by this that they almost lost their minds'.[190] There was also a shortage of water.[191]

After four months, the KNIL prisoners in this camp were taken to Kanchanaburi I, which did have sufficient water but where they were tormented by bedbugs.

All of the patients, invalids and subsequently also the officers aged 50 and over were assembled in yet another camp, Nakompaton: it was spacious,

---

[189]   F.B. Nijon, 'Aantekeningen', 20 July 1945.
[190]   J. van Baarsel, 'Onder de Jappen', p. 92 (NIOD IC, 81,359).
[191]   A KNIL lieutenant, J.A. van Duyvendijk, who had to work outside of the camp with a team in Japanese storage areas was able to smuggle the *Bangkok Times* into camp every day in the false bottom of a rice barrel or in a hollowed-out bamboo pole. He received the newspaper from a Thai doctor. This doctor was betrayed by his assistant and tortured, whereupon he mentioned Van Duyvendijk's name, who was forced to divulge the names of those who were regularly informed of the translated news. Fifteen of them had previously agreed that they would turn themselves over to the Japanese should the news leak out. Van Duyvendijk and these 15 (including the senior officer, Lieutenant Colonel O. van Linden, and P.J. Koets) were subsequently transferred to Bangkok and sentenced to several years in prison in February 1945.The group was transferred to Singapore in July. One of them, Lieutenant Colonel R.B. van Dijken, perished there shortly after the liberation.

extending over about one square kilometre, with good barracks (virtually bedbug-free) to which the kitchen sent mess tins with food every day. 'We had never been treated better during the entire time in captivity,' according to Major Van Baarsel, 'here, we got [...] somewhat better food'. There was also 'a substantial canteen where a great deal of additional food could be purchased. [...] The day before you could submit a request for a pork chop, a steak, an egg with bacon or a *matasapi* [a fried egg]. [...] Compared to the railway it seemed like heaven.'[192] In the middle of that paradise there was also a closed barrack containing all of the prisoners of war found to be homosexual, whether in Burma or Thailand: 'several dozen so-called mental cases' the major noted.[193]

He then entered his next to last camp in Thailand, where he found himself with about 3,000 other KNIL prisoners of war – here, too, the circumstances were reasonable. The same applied to the last camp, again in Kanchanaburi, where in January 1945 the Japanese concentrated about 3,000 officers still in Thailand (including about 1,000 of the KNIL) as well as a few lower ranks for the fatigues.

Other KNIL prisoners of war who were not transported to Japan faced greater difficulties in 1944 and 1945 in that they were put to work. In Thailand they worked not only on the Burma Railway but also on a new road to Tavoy, in Burma, and in the east of Thailand on airfields and, finally, in French Indo-China where deep inland airfields had to be built by those for whom no room on ships bound for Japan had been found. At the time of the surrender of Japan there were 11,000 KNIL prisoners of war in French Indo-China and about 3,100 in Thailand.

The Pekanbaru Railway / Palembang

Yet a second railway had to be built in great haste in the Nampo region: the Pekanbaru Railway[194] on Central Sumatra (see Map 7) was to connect Pekanbaru on the River Siak, which was navigable for small cargo ships, with Muara, the starting point of the railway to Padang. The route was about 200 kilometres long. Two thirds of it ran south from Pekanbaru, partly through swamplands rife with malaria, before curving to the west, following a river valley into the Sumatra highlands. The laying of the railway (a single track)

---

[192] J. van Baarsel, 'Onder de Jappen', p. 106 (NIOD IC, 81,359).
[193] J. van Baarsel, 'Onder de Jappen', p. 109 (NIOD IC, 81,359).
[194] This general information is taken from the study published by H. Neumann and E. van Witsen in 1982, *De Pekanbaroe spoorweg*, as well as the third edition of Henk Hovinga's book published in the same year: *Eindstation Pakan Baroe 1944-1945; Dodenspoorweg door het oerwoud*.

had already been considered by the Dutch and detailed plans had been drawn up by the State Railways in 1920. The line, however, was not built because it did not appear to be financially profitable. The Japanese used this plan, though following a different route in the highlands, which in the Dutch plan had three tunnels.

Initially only *romusha* were put to work – about 4,000 who, as mentioned in the previous chapter, were seized during round ups on Java in March 1943. They and the first of about 18,000 other *romusha* who joined them began building a railway embankment southwards from Pekanbaru. They were driven mercilessly by the Japanese. Many died and fresh replacements were constantly needed. We know little about the transports of the *romusha*, but it is known that, apart from a number of transports from Belawan (in June, July and August 1944), there were three transports of prisoners of war from Java: the first in May 1944, the second in June, and the third in September (the *Junyo Maru*). The first one conveyed a little under 2,000 prisoners of war – Dutch, Dutch Eurasians, British, Australians and a few Americans – to Padang (as usual, an awful journey). From there they were first taken by train to Muara and then in trucks to Pekanbaru, where they were housed in old and filthy sheds belonging to the Dutch Pacific Petroleum Company. The second one conveyed 1,200 prisoners of war first to Singapore and then to Pekanbaru on a smaller ship. The troopship travelling from Belawan to Singapore in June was sunk by a British submarine; almost 180 of the more than 700 prisoners of war drowned. As mentioned above, the lives of almost 4,000 *romusha*, 270 Ambonese and Manadonese, and about 1,340 other prisoners of war were lost in the transport on the *Junyo Maru*. Upon arriving at the Pekanbaru line, the survivors of this disaster were greatly disadvantaged in having lost all of their belongings – they had nothing left with which to acquire additional food.

In the final stages, in July and August 1945, work on the Pekanbaru line had reached a feverish pitch, 36 hours at a stretch with only a two- to three-hour break. Here, too, resources were wanting but there were fewer beatings, at least by the Japanese (in contrast to the Koreans), than on the Burma Railway. The prisoners of war in various camps along the line (there were 14) were housed in primitive barracks and slept on boards: all of the barracks were leaky and there was no shortage of lice and rats. The food was insufficient for the hard labour required: a large amount of rice, but primarily also a great deal of meat was held back by the Japanese soldiers, the officials of the Manchukuo Railway (who supervised the work) and the Korean guards for their own use or for payment in kind to prostitutes – the prisoners of war received food that on average had a daily calorific value of only 1,720. Naturally, additional food suppliers were sought frantically, an endeavour in which chiefly the Ambonese and Manadonese were adept: 'born bushmen', according to F.F.E. von Fuchs, who was rescued from the *Junyo Maru*.

As military police on patrol in Aceh and elsewhere in the archipelago they had become accustomed to the life that awaited them in the jungle of Pekanbaru. Moreover, they had the advantage over their white friends that on the *pasar* and in the *kampong* they could move surreptitiously among the Sumatrans without actually being noticed by the Koreans or the Japanese.

They soon became the 'wealthy among the prisoners'[195] and thus the only ones able to buy extra food with a certain degree of regularity. Prices on the black market were steep. Here too special treatment was accorded the 'spike crew'. As always in all camps everywhere in the world, those involved with the preparation of food were also privileged, as were a number of the first prisoners of war in Pekanbaru I, near Pekanbaru. That camp, according to C. van Heekeren:

lay in a swamp and on a river [the Siak] which sometimes rose above its banks and flooded the campground. The barracks were built on dikes that had been erected in the swamp and the ground in between was planted with vegetables. [...] From the beginning a relatively small group in this camp had been able to hold their own and constituted the aristocracy. With each transport sent 'up the line', they were able to win more of the arable land so that by the time I arrived at the camp, the vegetable garden was in the hands of a few who by means of price fixing had control of the entire market, of which they made intensive use. They spoke contemptuously of the haggard, impoverished people who entered 'their' camp from the front camps, so poor that they couldn't even afford the fixed vegetable prices. (Van Heekeren 1964:141.)

Many became ill as a result of the hard work, scanty food and poor housing. In due course almost everyone suffered from malaria – about one third of all of the prisoners of war chronically. Pekanbaru II was the camp, again according to Van Heekeren (1964:138-9) 'where people came to recover and, in many instances, to die' ('in this camp you could smell death and fortunately you were numbed'). The other camps had hospital barracks, yet even though there were skilled and dedicated medical officers and nurses there were no good instruments, no bandages, and no medicine. As Neumann and Van Witsen (1982:48) wrote:

Old rags serve as bandages. Latex from the rubber trees is used as bandaid. Tropical ulcers are treated daily by being wiped out with a wet cloth or eaten clean by maggots. The maggots eat the decomposed tissue. Whoever gets a chance to go into the river allows his wounds to be eaten clean by the little fish. All of these methods of treatments are very painful.

Work progressed.

While work at Pekanbaru commenced around March 1943, the laying of the track at the other end, Muara, was begun only in March 1945. Rails were

[195]   F.F.E. von Fuchs, 'De torpedoramp van de *Joenio Maroe*', p. 74 (NIOD IC, 15,871).

brought in from Malacca and Java, as was the rolling stock supplemented with five locomotives from the Deli Spoorweg Maatschappij. From March 1945, the teams worked towards each other through the Sumatra highlands. They met up at the beginning of August 1945 – and the Pekanbaru Railway was finished on 15 August.

This was the day on which the Japanese capitulation was announced. They derived absolutely no benefit from the railway, whose construction cost the lives of about 17,000 *romusha* (four in five) and almost 700 prisoners of war (nearly one in seven).

There were other places on Sumatra where prisoners of war brought in from Java were put to work: airfields had to be built in the region of Palembang.

To this end, in early November 1943 about 2,000 prisoners of war (Dutch, Dutch Eurasian and British) in Priok were loaded into a ship as old as it was dirty. According to the notes of a reserve officer candidate:

> The journey is filled with despair and misery. We are [...] stowed in six scorching, unventilated holds. Cattle waste is still present. The trip is a nightmare. Three long nights are spent trying to sleep. Dozens of people have no place to lie down and sit dozing here and there. Our own condensed sweat drips down on us from the ceiling.[196]

Together with an unknown number of *romusha*, this group began building an airfield at Betung, about 80 kilometres southwest of Palembang, in the middle of the jungle. The work was backbreaking and food was scarce, which resulted in an ongoing struggle between the Japanese who demanded a maximum of labourers and the medical officer who did his best to keep as many patients as possible in the hospital barrack. To this end he divided the prisoners into five categories depending on their physical condition. Category 5 included those who were ill. Category 4, the 'borderline' cases, was, as Erik K. de Vries noted in his diary, divided into 5 subcategories: '4 *a* could, if need be, go outside; 4 *b* could still work in the camp; 4 *c* could do light chores in the camp; 4 *cz* could perform chores done seated; 4 *czs* could, seated, make sisal (hemp) rope' (De Vries 1980:382).

In May 1944 about 360 of the approximately 2,000 prisoners of war were transferred to Pangkalan Balai, a place just west of Palembang, to work on a second new airfield also begun in November 1943 – after a year of great hardship during which many perished (the rice ration was reduced to a mere 80 grams per day) they were moved to Singapore (that camp was 'heaven compared to Pangkalan Balai'[197]). When the airfield at Betung was finished,

---

[196]   F.B. Nijon, 'Aantekeningen', p. 11.
[197]   F.B. Nijon, 'Aantekeningen', p. 151.

others from the original group of about 2,000 remained in Palembang performing heavy labour, primarily in the harbour. The only privileged individuals here were the officers, about 200 in all: they organized the fatigues and received more to eat – the NCO's and other ranks, on the other hand, starved. Not counting those who died while working on the airfields at Betung and Pangkalan Balai (only a few at the first airfield, far more at the second), about 350 NCOs and other ranks (Dutch, Dutch Eurasian and British) died from mid-1944 to August 1945,[198] many from starvation. An accurate estimate may be that of the approximately 2,000 prisoners of war transported to Palembang in November 1943, one in four or five perished.

Proportionally, there were even more victims among the prisoners of war transferred from Java to the Moluccas and to Flores in April 1943, again to build airfields.

Flores / The Moluccas

In the last nine months of 1942, the Allied air forces operating from Australia were not in a position to be very active, but in early 1943 it became clear to the Japanese that this would change and that increasing numbers of American, Australian and Dutch bombers would attack targets in the Great East. The airfields that were located there in 1941 were known to the Allies and so the Japanese decided to build new ones: on the north coast of Flores near the capital Maumere (see Map 5), near Amahai on Ceram (see Map 11), on the island of Haruku to the east of Ambon, and on the northern tip of Ambon near Liang.[199]

The prisoners of war departed from Surabaya in mid-April 1943.

We will deal first with the group destined for Flores which was transported from Cimahi to Surabaya: almost 2,200 Dutch and Dutch Eurasians and two British mistakenly added to them. They were taken to the harbour by train from the camp in Surabaya where they had been accommodated after their arrival. According to one of the prisoners of war, the train moved slowly through the densely populated Indonesian neighbourhoods where:

> Something occurred that filled many of us with astonishment but also with great dismay. Along the tracks near the level stood hundreds of Indonesians, men, women and children, who [...] raised a deafening cheer, which degenerated into a flood of abuse. For a minute we thought that this jeering and shouting was meant for our guards [...] but with a shock we suddenly realized that this demonstration

[198] Only one officer died, from cancer which he had been suffering from for several years.
[199] The small airfield already there had to be significantly expanded.

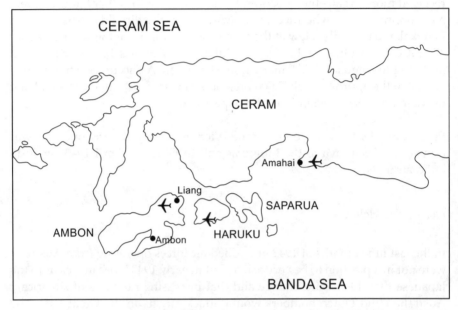

Map 11. Airfields in the Moluccas built by prisoners of war

was aimed against us, prisoners of war. That's how it was. Barely a year after we had had to strike our proud tricolour for brutal Japanese acts of war, the sentiments of a part of the Indonesian population had totally turned against us. (Cited in Veenstra et al. 1982:16.)

The convoy to Flores took almost three weeks – a horrible journey, primarily also because numerous prisoners of war had dysentery. No medicine was available on board, nor on Flores. The island was rife with malaria, from which many of the prisoners began to suffer.

What took place during work on the airfield is so eloquently recounted by one of the prisoners of war with respect to a 'random day in the month of August in the war year 1943', that it is worth quoting in its entirety. (Cited in Veenstra et al. 1982:150-3.)

After being woken early in the morning, the prisoners of war are herded to the airfield under construction where, divided into groups, they are handed their tools. They begin by working for about three hours, prodded by the Korean guards, under the approving supervision of the Japanese commandant of the airfield fatigue.

> A drawn-out *smèèèèè* [*Yasumi!* meaning 'rest!'] announces the first break which hardly lasts ten minutes, too short to rest, but long enough to smoke a hastily rolled cigarette. The Japanese fatigue commandant takes advantage of this intermezzo to complain about the work tempo. He quarrels with the Dutch fatigue commander, whom he blames for the lack of progress. The Dutch commander promptly replies that he will urge the boys to work faster and makes a demonstrative speech to the troop. 'Now listen, men. [...] Keep moving, even if you're only hitting air. These bastards will only look at the results. So chaps, do something. And for the rest, let them go to hell. Understood?' The troop shouts 'Hai!' [yes!] in unison.
>
> See, now the Japs are happy. They understand that the stupid *Oranda* [Hollanders] now get what they are saying. A loud screech, serving as the signal to stand up, is the sign for the men to resume work. [...] More work is done, at least the appearance thereof is created. Another hour and a half toiling in the scorching heat. Glistening bodies in a crowd bobbing up and down. Levelling the ground with shovel and pickaxe, bringing the soil from dug up hills to pits. The lads look repeatedly at the position of the sun. They are tired and their stomachs are growling from hunger. [...] They wait for the raising of the red flag, the signal for rest from twelve to two o'clock. During this break the midday meal is consumed. In the meantime the food is fetched by carriers from the camp and set in the shade of the large tree at the edge of the bush.
>
> Finally, the red flag is raised.

It takes a while before everyone gets his share.

> The malcontents think that the division of the food is too slow. They forget that they themselves are the cause of the slow process. And the corruption, which

has its friends among the distributors and the counters, always prevails. When everyone is considered to have had his helping, the captain comes to the conclusion that 16 helpings too many have been handed out. Sometimes a dozen men get nothing to eat. This evil cannot be rooted out as long as the men themselves remain corrupt.

The meal is consumed, standing or seated, in little groups. Here and there is a loner, wanting nothing to do with the cliques. There is no chair and no table, no tablecloth and no napkin, no glass and no finger bowl. The meal is consumed with a wooden spoon or simply with one's fingers. This is the primal condition. Eating to still hunger. Neither taste nor enjoyment are relevant. The food is nothing more than a stomach filler.

[...] It's time for the daredevils. They get up from their reclining position, carefully taking note of the outstretched pose of the guards, and cautiously steal away. Crossing the air strip they find the mercantile representatives of Flores' population deep within the bushes. A lively trade is conducted in fish and meat, eggs and vegetables, tobacco and cookies. The wares are certainly expensive, but worth the trouble. The men also exchange their surplus shirts and pants for goods. The risks involved in their little outings are very great. Therefore they do not take too long and return to the troop via a detour. Nonchalantly they stroll in and cautiously set themselves down. Fortunately, the Japanese notice nothing of their smuggling sortie. They slumber on, confident that the stupid *Oranda* would never dare run away.

[...] It's two o'clock in the afternoon, Japanese time. The red flag is struck and the white one raised. The *Oranda* stand up, sleepy and unwilling. The demi-gods begin to scream again, *'Lekas! lekas!'* [Quickly! quickly!]. The fatigue leader stands with his hands on his hips and a dissatisfied look passes over his gleaming face. The Dutch commander urges the group to make haste.

The Flores sun, at its zenith now, bathes the entire stage with a fierce and biting heat. For those without shoes, the radiation from the ground is sheer torture. The bent backs glisten from the sweat that eagerly escapes from every pore. The air hums in the white-grey hell. It is dead calm, not a breath of air to cool down with. Spirits slump.

[...] It is now three o'clock. Another 20 minutes of dragging and then another short ten-minute break. This span of time is just long enough to smoke a hastily rolled cigarette. Men run to the only tree in the vicinity and a few tall bushes, whose paltry shade still affords some kind of protection from the fierce rays of the sun. Once the signal to start work is given again and everyone gets ready to endure another sweat bath, the wind finally rises. First in feeble gusts, then powerful, blowing seawards. The wind is greeted with cries of joy, for it is everyone's friend and here a vital necessity.

A shout of hurrah, a loud roar. Hasty gathering of the tools. The end of the day's activities. Finally. Fall in. Right dress. Number off. March off. Just stopping on the way to hand in the tools.

When walking to work the men's pace is despondent. When they return to camp, it's spirited and even the Japanese can hardly keep up with the tempo. The troop now stands on the road in front of the camp. The sentry is informed that there is nothing unusual to report. Some guards come to count and frisk. 'The slowpoke' is duty officer and his relief corporal is 'The chubby sadist'. They have caught one of the labourers, stiff at attention and bashfully looking straight ahead. The Jap frisking him finds two eggs in his back pocket. He cuffs his ear soundly and asks him where they came from. With an anxious voice, the sinner answers that he has bought them. The Jap gives him a vicious kick in the shins and shrieks: *'Bakajaro! Tida bagoes!'* [Idiot! You're no good!] .

The offender is silent and stares at the ground. Then he is ordered to step out of line and come before the sentry. When 'The slowpoke' hears the punishable acts the *Oranda* is guilty of, he erupts in a terrible rage and snarls at him: *'Bakajaro! Bamboe motte koi!'* [Idiot! Get a piece of bamboo!]. The lad can choose the bamboo stick himself, a thick one naturally. It is wrenched from his hands and 'The slowpoke' then thrashes him. He groans with pain. Blood streams from four open wounds on his face and chest. Then 'The slowpoke' orders the interpreter to be fetched. When he has reported and heard the facts of the matter, 'The slowpoke' announces that the very next offender will be beaten to death. For this one time 'The slowpoke' will be merciful. He hits the boy in the face several more times and kicks him. With this the incident is over and the bugler can sound the call to fall out. *'Wakare!'* [Dismissed!]. The troop runs and bolts into camp. It is almost five thirty. Now we can bathe.

Not all of the prisoners were able to keep up this daily work. Rations were limited and could not be adequately supplemented. Many fell ill. The Japanese soldiers and the Korean guards had absolutely no sympathy for them: whoever was seriously sick in the first weeks had to be taken to a separate part of the camp and was left outdoors, exposed to the elements. The majority died – primitive hospital barracks were introduced only later. One Japanese did behave in a humane manner, a sergeant major who was in charge of about 300 prisoners working 60 kilometres from the main camp. In his diary, C. Binnerts (1947:67) noted in September that, 'It was good there, really good: [there was] decent food and hardly any beatings'. Moreover, the sergeant major 'and this is of the utmost importance, had told the Dutch command various things about the course of the war'.[200]

Unlike the inhabitants of Surabaya who had jeered at the prisoners of war, the indigenous people of Flores (about half of them were Catholic) displayed compassion. In his diary, a prisoner of war, who together with others had to collect bamboo with a truck in the mountains in the interior, wrote: 'The people were spontaneously friendly and waved at us everywhere. If there was a chance, all kinds of fruit was thrown on the loading platform. [...] Personally, I found the people on this island particularly brave and loyal.' (Cited in Veenstra

---

[200] Apparently no one knew anything about this in the main camp. In September, Binnerts, who kept the administration of the hospital barrack, wrote that many rumours were circulating, 'which became more improbable by the hour: the British had landed in Scheveningen and via Holland are already threatening the heart of Germany' (Binnerts 1947:67). Possibly the Japanese sergeant major reported (and this had also reached the hospital barrack) that Italy had capitulated.

et al. 1982:164-5.) Anticipating support from them may have prompted one of the prisoners of war to escape in May 1943. He was apprehended one week later 40 kilometres from the main camp; the Japanese shot him.

The airfield at Maumere was ready for use in October 1943; it was subsequently finished off and two other small airfields were built. At the end of this, only about 900 of those still alive on Flores were capable of working. They were taken to Batavia in June, August and September 1944, from where many were speedily sent on to Padang (with the *Junyo Maru*), or Singapore. Earlier, namely in January and May 1944, the ill and weak had been taken to Java in two transports – the worst-off were admitted to a hospital in Batavia.

As of 19 September 1944, 216 prisoners of war from the Flores transport had died (one in ten) – how many more perished after this date is not known.

Of the three transports to the Moluccas, one (to Liang on Ambon) contained only British prisoners of war, about 1,000; one (to Amahai on Ceram) almost exclusively Dutch and Dutch Eurasians, also about 1,000 (plus five Brits); and the third (to Haruku) was mixed, more than 1,700 British and 345 Dutch and Dutch Eurasians.

On 18 April 1943 all of these prisoners of war boarded four Japanese ships in Surabaya which, to start with, lay at anchor for four days: an ordeal in itself. They set sail on the 22nd. Crammed into the ever filthier holds, the prisoners were given very little to eat and dysentery, which had already begun in the camps in Surabaya, became virulent. They arrived in Ambon a week later. The group destined for Liang marched there, the two other groups had to unload whatever cargo there was for Ambon from the four ships. Having barely completed this work, the prisoners bound for Amahai and Haruku were loaded onto three of the four ships, which reached Ceram the next morning; many goods had to be taken ashore here as well. First they had to be removed from the hold and placed in proas and then hauled from the shore to a storage area about 800 metres away. No rest was granted before this work was finished, which took a total of 36 hours. According to one of the officers:

> Along the entire [...] transport road Japanese were deployed armed for the occasion with whipping canes, bamboo laths or thick wooden sticks. During the 36 hours of unloading these weapons were wielded frequently and whenever a white slave dared walk more slowly, a whipping, lashing blow communicated Nippon's insistence that the ships be unloaded as quickly as possible.
> [...] The first cases of utter exhaustion were not taken all too seriously. Buckets of water were dashed onto the collapsed drudges and the canes were expertly handled. The results were calves ripped to shreds and backs beaten raw. Sometimes a victim who had fallen down in exhaustion could be flogged into carrying his load a few hundred metres further, but after 24 hours even the Japanese understood that the fatigue was not simulated and that the physically feeble were on the verge of collapsing. They were temporarily left in peace, but at the expense of the

stronger ones who then had to assume the share of their weaker mates and work at an even faster pace and bear even heavier burdens. Gasping for breath and vomiting along the transport road from sheer exhaustion, the casualties realized this only too well and stood up as soon as they could. Tottering and tripping, with dull eyes and a determined expression they joined the row of drudges to lighten the burden of their hardier comrades, to the extent that they still could.

After 36 hours the freight proas arrived with completely debilitated loading crews which had been even harder pressed in the sweltering holds, meaning that finally the bottom of the transport ships had been reached. Nothing was eaten during this 36-hour long Herculean labour. Only a little was drunk. (Cited in Veenstra et al. 1982:35-6.)

Three days later, two of the ships that had reached Amahai sailed on to Haruku and this was the third island where the prisoners of war had first to unload and then move cargo.

Given that the group in Amahai was later taken to Haruku and later still transported to Ambon together with the group on Haruku, this sequence will be followed and a description of what took place on Amahai will be given first, followed by the events on Haruku and finally Ambon.

Following four months of labour on Amahai, the airfield was ready in early September 1943. During that time, 28 of the 1,017 prisoners of war perished (about 1 in 36). Moreover, the stay in Amahai cost the lives of three others who had escaped two weeks after their arrival. They were caught three days later only a few kilometres from the camp. The Kempeitai tortured them and several others who knew of their escape. One of the three escapees died: the two others were beheaded along with a fourth prisoner of war, but only in October when the group as a whole was moved to Haruku.

In building the airfield, the prisoners of war committed sabotage whenever they could, relying on information provided by the structural engineers among them. For instance, they filled the embankments of the aircraft pens with loose gravel and omitted several essential girders in the control tower and all of the edge girders in the covered shelter trenches for the Japanese. According to someone involved in this sabotage:

Later in Liang we heard what remained of the airfield at Amahai, at least after the first Allied bombing. A bomb fell about 30 metres from the control tower, and this was enough to make the 12-metre high tower collapse like a house of cards. Not much was left of the Japanese shelters [...] other than piles of sand with some girders sticking out; the aircraft pens crumbled like huge sand castles. (Cited in Veenstra et al. 1982:139.)

Exceptionally, permission was given for the Queen's birthday [then on 31 August] to be celebrated in the camp at Amahai: the prisoners of war were allowed to fall in for their own muster one half hour before the Japanese one. The senior officer and his deputy, Captain R. Korteweg, each gave a speech. Korteweg called Queen Wilhelmina 'a model from which we may derive strength because we realize that it will not be long now before that fine motto *Luctor et Emergo* [I struggle and escape] will come true'. He wished the queen 'strength, health, and a long life'. (Veenstra et al. 1982:156.) According to Korteweg:

> At the end of my speech, for the first time in 17 months we sang the two well-known verses of our glorious national anthem at the tops of our voices and we were unashamed of our tears. Then a roar of hurrahs to the queen. This was followed by an impressive silence and then, the greatest surprise for us all, outside of the camp an Ambonese flute ensemble played the Wilhelmus [the Dutch national anthem] just as the rising sun appeared over the horizon.
>
> Inexplicably, the Japanese left us alone the entire day. In the afternoon we were allowed to put on an 'Orange show' in an improvised open-air theatre.[201]

Five days later, on 5 September, there was more to celebrate, this time for the Japanese: the airfield was finished. In the afternoon a number of sporting events were held in which prisoners of war and Indonesians could participate. According to J.H.W. Veenstra, of the team competitions:

> The most exciting were the trials of strength between the Netherlands and Japan. In particular, the tug of war between the two nations drew upon the last remaining reserves of the undernourished. The Netherlands won under the maxim: 'Better a hernia or a stroke than lose!' The Japanese team was given a harsh scolding for this.[202] (Cited in Veenstra et al. 1982:158.)

About six weeks later the survivors of the Amahai group were transferred to Haruku.

As mentioned earlier, initially more than 1,700 British and 345 Dutch and Dutch Eurasian troops, including about 160 dysentery patients, disembarked on Haruku. All of them wound up in barracks that were not only too small but also carelessly constructed: bushes grew in them, coconut trees stuck through the roofs, which leaked, and beds were missing. The complex, through which flowed a little stream, had no drainage so that during a heavy downpour it became a quagmire and the water ran through the barracks at various places.

---

[201]   R. Korteweg, 'De 1000 van Amahai', 1946, p. 19 (NIOD IC, 28,919).
[202]   Indonesian events were also organized on this afternoon. According to Veenstra, 'a game involving children in school uniforms presented a striking spectacle. At a certain moment they were divided into four groups, distinguished by a red, a white, a blue and an orange ribbon. Oddly enough the latter group won all of the games!' (Veenstra et al. 1982:158.)

These living conditions did not prevent the Japanese camp commandant, a lieutenant, and his sergeant, 'Bamboo Mori' from imposing heavy fatigues: 1,200 men were to begin building the airfield immediately. This was difficult work because (this was also the case at Liang on Ambon) an area full of coral reefs had to be levelled to create a runway: the sharp rocks caused wounds which then turned into tropical ulcers. From the very start many were too weak to drag themselves to work. The consequence was that the company commanders of the prisoners of war were called together and beaten with a stick by Mori in the presence of the Japanese lieutenant. The British and Dutch medical officers lost the authority to declare prisoners of war unfit for fatigues – this was now done by a Korean soldier who toured all of the barracks driving anyone he deemed fit to work with blows from his stick.

One of the Dutch doctors, R. Springer, kept a diary. It gives us a picture of the desperate situation he faced, which must have mirrored that of his colleagues on Haruku and in many other places where, powerless, doctors were forced to witness how the Japanese made miserable wrecks of men who shortly before had been perfectly healthy. Historiography should permit the reader to 'see' the past – accounts by eyewitnesses can substantially contribute to this if they have sufficient visionary power, as is more than true of this report.

Doctor Springer:

10 May 1943 – Had a conference with the Japanese medical officer Shimada. He recognizes the difficulties: 'As a doctor I understand, but not as an officer'. He can offer little assistance because of the war. For us the situation appears hopeless, it has got completely out of hand. Currently 400 patients confined to their quarters and 150 patients whom we were finally able to bring together in one barrack.

One hour after the conference with the medical officer all of the patients confined to their quarters were checked by the Japanese under the command of the Japanese NCO *gunso* [sergeant] Mori. Forty of them were forced to work by being hit and kicked with the help of a bamboo [stick]. Various officers were also flogged because they were unable to assemble 1,200 men to work on the airfield.

12 May 1943 – Currently we have about 600 patients in this camp, where 2,000 men are quartered.

Ever more dysentery and diarrhoea. Conditions in the dysentery barrack are abominable. Water is lacking, as is the possibility of giving the dehydrated men tea in sufficient quantities. The patients suffer terribly and the male nurses and the doctors have a hugely demanding task which is aggravated by the fact that almost nothing effective can be done. Still [having] trouble with the lighting at night. The amount of Dagenan [a medicine for dysentery], made in Japan, we have on hand is only 400 tablets, while we need thousands. The patients remain outside the barrack lying in the mud because there are not enough tins for them to defecate in. To prevent soiling in the barracks they remain in the open air. The pollution of the camp ground is indescribable and the battle against this advancing epidemic is hopeless. This is all the more dangerous as the people are malnourished and

dehydrated because of insufficient food and insufficient fluids. In our view, the
dysentery is not virulent, yet the far too limited resistance will undoubtedly create
more victims. The Japanese nevertheless still demand 1,200 men for work on the
airfield and if necessary this number is reached by calling in patients confined to
their quarters. Many are sent back each day because they are simply exhausted.

17 May 1943 – The scale of the dysentery is increasing and now seems to be
worse. People who become ill at night have 15 to 20 watery bowel movements
with blood and mucus the next morning, which soon turns into only blood and
mucus.

The plague of flies is terrible. In the barracks, in addition to the moaning and
hiccuping of the dying one hears the endless buzzing of millions of flies; maggots
crawl over the fouled sleeping places and over the prostrate patients. They gratefully accept what little the nurses can do, yet this help is utterly ineffective. If the
weather doesn't break soon, the scale of the epidemic will increase greatly.

18 May 1943 – The epidemic is growing. All of the medicine has been used up,
the Norit [a medicine for diarrhoea] too.

According to the Japanese, it's our fault that the people are dying because we
haven't requested any medicine until now. Already on the boat we insisted on the
need for medicine and warned of the great danger of an imminent epidemic. It
is true that this happened only with the medical *gunso*, yet this was because we
had no contact with a Japanese doctor. At that time contact with a Japanese officer
was not possible. We requested medicine, in duplicate and even typewritten. Until
now, however, [we have] received nothing, even though this request was submitted via the Japanese doctor.

20 May 1943 – The scale of the dysentery is still growing along with the symptoms of avitaminosis. Many patients have large sores in the mucous membrane
of the mouth and on the tonsils. In two people this developed into large, putrid
wounds with severe swelling of the cheek: a noma. In our view the situation is
completely out of hand. We now receive some more food; however this is still too
little for the healthy and incorrect in composition for the people with full-blown
dysentery. The English prisoners especially are behaving more rudely to their
officers. There is virtually no discipline in the camp, and much swearing and
stealing take place.

21 May 1943 – There is still not enough water for the dehydrated patients: the
general picture in the dysentery barracks remains dismal and becomes grimmer
every day. The watery rice gruel is inedible, the patients do their best but throw it
up nevertheless. The soup or what passes as such looks unappetizing. Given the
existing persistent aversion to the food it's understandable that people can't keep
everything down.

We are desperate: we are not allowed to decide anything independently; permission must be asked of the Japanese for each measure we deem necessary. We
have no contact with the Japanese doctor; our recommendations appear to be
evaluated solely by Mori.

23 May 1943 – It remains a hopeless situation and in addition the healthy men
are disinclined to do anything extra for their 1,100 ill comrades. The water supplies
are still insufficient and that is certainly partly to blame on the camp inhabitants.
It should be possible to pay some attention to the diets in the kitchens. However,
we have no complaints about the work of our hospital assistants. Their number

has now been increased to 62. The majority are uneducated, yet so much needs to be done to help the patients that we are very happy to have at least received authorization for this expansion.

24 May 1943 – Conditions in the serious barracks are horrendous. The patients cannot be sufficiently cleaned because of the water shortage. They lie in their own excrement and that of others. They are too worn out to get to a bedpan in time or wait for one. The situation is out of control. Naturally the Japanese blame this on us: 'You are killing your own people'. The doctors' estimate of the number of deaths to be expected before the end of the epidemic still ranges from 50 to 400.

31 May 1943 – The situation is exceptionally grave and we see nothing of the cooperation of the Japanese doctors we had so hoped for. They still want to regulate everything themselves, even the diet of the patients, yet these people cannot stay alive eating rice gruel day in, day out. Their way of thinking differs enormously from ours. Those recovering suffer from chronic hunger; we can get nothing extra for them and gradually we are seeing an increase of people with avitaminosis and of extreme emaciation. One has the sense here of death on a vast scale.

The eyesight of quite a lot of people is deteriorating. The 'blurred vision' we noticed in Surabaya here turns into total blindness. Some have sores on their eyes, very painful and attributable to a lack of vitamins. Because they can no longer see anything, they cannot participate in catching flies. Every patient, no matter how sick, has to catch flies, otherwise they get no food! It is heart-rending to see the skeletons of these young chaps sitting inside the barrack or outside with an improvised fly swatter in one hand and a bag in which to put the dead bugs in the other.

1 June 1943 – The convalescent prisoners roam around the camp and our barracks in the hope of getting or, if need be, stealing a bite to eat somewhere. For the doctors and nurses, working in such circumstances is nerve-wracking. Here one can speak of a struggle for life in the saddest sense and it is hardly surprising that morale deteriorates more every day. In the barracks, even before a patient has died, attempts are made to take possession of his scanty valuables such as clothing or the remains of blankets. Before people are allowed to have their food they have to have killed 25 flies.

2 June 1943 – The compulsory fly catching has risen to 100! Mori will even give an egg to anyone who catches 200 flies.

On the order of the Japanese, today the rice ration was reduced from 500 grams of rice to 300 grams. Moreover, not enough work is being done! Salt is being reduced from 30 grams to 20 grams.

3 June 1943 – No one died in the night! Buning[203] finally succeeded in getting permission for us to have some *pisang* [...] and [...] vegetables for the sick. He was even able to buy two goats. Since this momentous event he has received the nickname 'the *haji*'. Getting something like this from the unpredictable Japanese requires a special kind of instinct for knowing just when to try. It seems quite peculiar, though, that from this the kitchen was only able to provide 100 men with a half cup of soup. The difficulties with the kitchen management have come to a

---

[203]   A fellow doctor, 'who', according to one of the prisoners, 'both through his attitude towards the Japanese and his sense of duty commanded everybody's respect'. (H.A. van Deinse, 'Verslag', 7 May 1947, p. 4 (ARA, Alg. Secr., Eerste zending, XXII, 45, 177).)

head and Buning – on behalf of the doctors and 1,300 patients – has asked them to step down. After consultation with the British camp commander, this finally took place.

[...] 7 June 1943 – Mortality is increasing rapidly, now, however, not so much because of the dysentery, but because of total prostration and extreme emaciation. It is awful to see these young people deteriorating. To the end they drag themselves to the cans to avoid fouling their sleeping places with excrement. In later stages everything runs over the *baleh-baleh* [sleeping places], they no longer have any control of their bowels. Everything is water with mucus, sometimes only pure blood.

Then they are too weak to do anything for themselves and have to be cleaned as best as possible by the overworked nurses. This has to be done with too little water and no towels or decent rags. Their minds become clouded; many have a sense of well-being, feel they are getting better, report less frequent bowel movements, sometimes become disoriented, claim to have eaten well, etc. Following this they lose consciousness and fall into a sort of peaceful delirium after which the end comes swiftly. In our view, the death rate from this kind of state of exhaustion will exceed by far that of dysentery. The people who enter this state can no longer be saved even if we had vitamin preparations and sufficient protein nutrition.

11 June 1943 – [...] People are coming down with more and more symptoms that clearly point to a general disorder of the central nervous system. The long-standing complaints of pain and weakness in the legs is extending now to the entire lower and middle abdomen. Without exception a feeling of tightness is experienced which spreads over the abdomen like a belt. People also repeatedly indicate severe pain. These symptoms suggest a disorder of the spinal cord known as B-2 avitaminosis. Signs of neuritis in the arms now occur regularly. Oedema, swelling of the arms and face, stomachs distended by many litres of fluid that impede breathing, enormously swollen legs as a result of subcutaneous fluid accumulation which causes small cracks in the skin from which fluid runs – all of the possible symptoms described for avitaminosis are present here. Combined with this are the signs of severe protein deficiency.

The skin symptoms as a result of pellagra [a kind of avitaminosis] rapidly present themselves the minute one has been in the sunlight for any length of time. After that scabies increases, with complications from the consequent skin infections. How can we combat this without medicine, with poor food, no salves, no bandages, no vitamin preparations, no protein? Naturally, the patients know the situation and it is amazing that they nevertheless appreciate the help of the doctors and the nurses!

The patient who fractured a vertebra in a fall in the hold of our ship has now been ordered back to work by the Japanese doctor. As proof of his recovery he was kicked in the back.

[...] 14 June 1943 – Today a young Japanese doctor came who passes as a pathologist. He will perform some post-mortem examinations of the deceased patients, if possible two a day. My colleague Bryan and I took him around in the course of the afternoon and were soon joined by the Japanese doctor Ishii and the camp commandant. The latter two gentlemen seemed to derive pleasure in making dents in the swollen lower legs of the beriberi patients. At least it gave rise to much laughter. They didn't go in the critical barracks. Perhaps the conditions there would have made them think differently: the appalling filth that prevails there, the large wounds of the patients with bedsores on the hard *baleh-baleh*, in which teem hundreds of fly maggots, the hiccuping of the dying, the stench of urine and faeces. Here there is human suffering no pen can adequately describe.[204]

16 June 1943 – Finally received some medicine, unfortunately not what we so desperately need. Only about 11 kilograms of Epsom salts, a few hundred tablets of Rivanol, 70 ampoules of 1,000 units of vitamin B-1 and 1,500 tablets of 25 units of B-1. All of this is not even enough to treat the patients in the two serious barracks for a single day!

Is this powerlessness or unwillingness?

21 June 1943 – [...] The eye complaints also increase in the sunlight; people devise the oddest creations to shut out the irritating sunlight: there are those who bind bamboo cases around their eyes with an opening in the centre in order to be able to see where they are going outdoors.

[...] 24 June 1943 – Another bad day for barrack I: wind and rain came through the roof at night. The patients were soaked to the skin and in the morning were huddled together in the few dry places. The dying and delirious patients lay among them, so that the entire scene made an indescribably chaotic impression. The whole barrack stinks again of dysentery excrement, which lies in numerous places on the *baleh-baleh*, the aisles and the blankets of the patients. The sparing illumination was blown out. Everything had to be done in pitch black. What this demands of the patients and the nurses is unimaginable![205]

These are entries spanning a period of six weeks up to 24 June. The situation had hardly improved one month later:

22 July 1943 – [...] The suffering of the dying is gruesome to see. Death comes slowly, the people lie all day long, usually conscious, waiting for the end, swallowing is virtually impossible because of the pain, the bedsores are full of fly larva, the wounds extend widely subcutaneously, faeces and urine run in the remains of the blankets and clothing. The Japanese doctor Morioka told me that the hospital should just be blown up because Nippon's goal was 'victory' and not the treatment of patients.[206]

Again a month later:

24 August 1943 – Ever more difficulties are being put in our way, even though the condition of the patients is becoming simply horrendous. Extreme emaciation to the bone, countless infected wounds, skin parasites, pellagra, mental aberration, extensive filth, chronic diarrhoea, motor disturbance to complete invalidity, pains due to neuritis, distended bellies and legs due to enormous water retention. This is human suffering as cannot be imagined in your wildest dreams. Many weep from the pain and general intense misery in these hopeless circumstances. That a young

---

[204] On the same 14 June, 'all walking sick', according to a British officer, Squadron Leader W.C. Pitts, 'were paraded and the Japanese sergeant [Mori] [...] viciously went among the parade hitting over the head those he thought were fit enough to work'. W.C. Pitts, 'Report on Haroekoe', 29 August 1945, p. 2 (NIOD IC, 1,646).
[205] R. Springer, 'Dagboek', pp. 39-60 (NIOD IC, 81,346).
[206] R. Springer, 'Dagboek', pp. 63-5 (NIOD IC, 81,346).

English soldier entreated me shortly before he passed away to tell his mother that he 'died like a soldier' speaks of a fortitude beyond comprehension.

There is no humanity here any more.[207]

This is what it was like.

A contributing factor to the filth and the dysentery was that the prisoners of war in their camp by the sea were not allowed to bathe in it or even use seawater for cleaning. The sea, Mori said, was Japanese property and should a latrine be built it would infect the water. An additional factor was that except for the medical officers, the British and Dutch officers provided little leadership. This only added to the chaos which Mori then attempted to curb, though exclusively with his own hard-handed methods. The camp exuded an atmosphere of doom which the men from Amahai, when they were transferred to Haruku in October, immediately sensed. One of them, a navy officer, wrote:

> When we enter this camp through the damp, steaming forest, we are overcome with clammy dread. There is something nameless and cruel in all of these trees, and creepers and liana growing on and over one another and proliferating into a green hell threatening to absorb the damp reed huts of the camp. (Cited in Veenstra et al. 1982:191.)

The airfield at Haruku was ready at the end of October 1943, the month in which the men from Amahai arrived – only then did Mori give leave to deploy more labourers for the improvement of the camp. Nevertheless, by mid-November there were still about 300 patients in the primitive hospital barracks – many of the others able to do fatigues were still suffering from dysentery, Doctor Springer noted in mid-November:

> If at all possible we let them work nonetheless, [...] so that they can at least buy some additional food and not sink further into avitaminosis. We are trying to get light assignments for these diminished men in the gardens or some work in the camp to improve the living conditions. Mori is sympathetic in this respect; he takes pride in the appearance of the camp and, indeed, it must be acknowledged that its present state cannot be compared to what it was a few months ago. But to achieve this at the cost of almost 400 dead is a heavy toll![208]

Upon completion of the airfield (it was soon bombed by the Allies from Australia, and prisoners of war were wounded and killed), the Japanese approved the return of the ill prisoners of war to Java. At the end of November 1943 a transport was put together on Haruku consisting, in addition to a

---

[207]   R. Springer, 'Dagboek', p. 70 (NIOD IC, 81,346).
[208]   R. Springer, 'Dagboek', 15 November 1943, p. 79 (NIOD IC, 81,346).

medical officer and a few dozen assistants, of almost 550 men from Haruku as well as more than 150 who had first worked at Amahai. Only one small troopship was available. The patients had to be squeezed into the holds, the floors of which were covered with coal dust; 11 men who were dying were returned to shore, while the rest first sailed to Ambon.

More than 1,000 British prisoners of war were first disembarked on Ambon in early May 1943 to build an airfield at Liang. Marching through Ambon, the British received a measure of support from the Ambonese: some made the V sign, called out words of encouragement or threw them packs of cigarettes. They sorely needed this succour for the conditions at their camp situated on a coral plateau were just as primitive as those at Haruku and the work was in no way lighter. Here too many prisoners of war became ill and died, in total about 200. When the ship with patients from Haruku arrived, the Japanese gave permission for 339 ill prisoners of war in the Liang group to be sent back to Java. Twenty of them drowned when the raft conveying them to the boat capsized; there was not enough room for the rest in the two holds covered with coal dust. A second Japanese ship was deployed which took on board about 540 prisoners of war. On the way to Java, this second ship was torpe-doed by an American submarine. A Japanese corvette rescued the Japanese. The surviving prisoners of war swimming around were machine gunned – all 540, including 131 Dutch and Dutch Eurasians, perished. About 110 prisoners of war on board the first ship also died before reaching Surabaya.

Following this there was a concentration of prisoners of war on Ambon: those who had not died on Haruku were transferred to Ambon in large groups in December 1943 and in April and August 1944, first to help com-plete the airfield at Liang and subsequently to work in the harbour in the city of Ambon. The camp at Liang was even worse than the one on Haruku. According to one of the officers:

> Having done service for a year, the barracks were on the verge of collapsing. The roofs were leakier than a sieve. Garbage and latrine pits were overfull and there was no more room for new pits on the plateau, so that garbage fatigues had to remove the waste. These fatigues, however, could not be sufficiently manned because anyone remotely able to stay on his feet was requisitioned for work on the airfield. Deathly ill wretches now lugged the waste from the camp or tried to.
> [...] The hospital barracks were overcrowded and in addition to the so familiar cases of dysentery and exhaustion there was an appalling number of patients with tropical ulcers. [...] Dreadful sores where the flesh had been eaten away right to the bone; hundreds of sores in which vermin crawled around and which gave off a nauseating stench were presented to our doctors and nurses daily for treatment, to the extent that one could still speak of treatment with the lack of medicine. All we had at our disposal were grubby bandages and cold tea. (Cited in Veenstra et al. 1982:262.)

When the airfield at Liang was completed (it too was soon bombed by the Allies), the prisoners of war were transferred to a camp in the city of Ambon, where the food rations were cut back and the job of loading and unloading ships was murderous, usually lasting 36 hours at a stretch. The advance of MacArthur's forces led the Japanese in mid-1944 to send all of the patients as well as the prisoners still able to work back to Java. By the end of September 1944, slightly over 400 prisoners of war remained and about 2,000 had departed:[209] 600 at the beginning of August 1944, 27 of whom died before arriving in Surabaya; about 800 at the end of August, among whom there were probably about 30 deaths; and two more troopships on 9 and 16 September – the first with 151 patients and nine assistants, the second with about 450 prisoners of war, half of whom were ill, and who included the most serious cases no one had dared evacuate earlier.

The first ship got no further than the island of Muna, where it was fired on by an American bomber and burst into flames. Eight prisoners of war died – 142 reached shore and awaited the arrival of the second ship.

That second vessel was one of the oldest Koninklijke Paketvaartmaatschappij (Royal Packet Shipping Company, KPM) ships, renamed the *Maros Maru* by the Japanese. Embarkation in the torrential downpours and in the dark was horrible. According to Veenstra:

> Lacking shoes, we have to walk barefoot to a jetty for a half hour on a hard, mud-covered coral road. The men transporting the patients on stretchers slip and slide and are driven by the guards with shouts and blows. At the jetty [...] we have to await further orders. A request by the doctors to place the patients in a few empty huts there is rejected. (Cited in Veenstra et al. 1982:297.)

Embarkation commenced after a three-hour wait. The holds of the *Maros Maru* were shut: all the prisoners of war had to remain on deck, exposed to the elements, and endure the journey sitting or lying on the sharp-edged pieces of wood used in the absence of coal to stoke the ship's furnaces. When the sun shone, it burned them mercilessly. They were given some rice gruel cooked in sea water twice a day and no more than a half a mug of water a day. Only after 30 patients had died did the Japanese commandant approve of a sort of sail being hung above the serious cases.

Five days after setting off from Ambon the *Maros Maru* reached the island of Muna, where the 142 survivors of the ship that had been shot at and caught fire came on board. According to one of them:

[209]   These 400 or so were shipped out in October 1944, but were unable to reach Java in the remaining ten months of the war when Allied submarines were active primarily in the Java Sea. They stayed put on the island of Muna south of Celebes (see Map 9) and from there more than 260 prisoners of war got no further than Makassar.

The legs criss-crossing one another constituted an inextricable tangle. The people lying there were clearly in a bad state. [...] At least half of them were English. [...] The majority just lay there apathetically staring straight ahead when we hesitated at the top of the stairs, not knowing where to go. But when we were forced by the Japanese to set foot on deck and began looking for a way through the intermingled bodies, the entire mass instantly turned into a single hostile block. They flailed at us with their stick-like arms or kicked with their badly swollen legs and cursing and threats were rife.

[...] To escape the lice and itching, some of them had rolled up the remains of their clothing and we saw many whose legs but also genitals [...] had swollen up to elephant-like proportions. Everything was all mixed together. Among those suffering from beriberi were others with severe wounds and dysentery patients who stank to high heaven because they had lost control. Fortunately, much of the waste fell below through the stacked up firewood. (Cited in Veenstra et al. 1982:300.)

Leaving Muna the ship sailed ever more slowly and stranded on the roadstead of Makassar: the engine needed to be repaired. The prisoners of war had to remain on board. According to one of the British officers:

Covered with awful blisters the men all lay in the tropical sun on the uneven piles of firewood. Tongues began turning black, bruised naked shoulders started to bleed, and many were nearing madness. The night was filled with the screaming and moaning of the dying, the cursing of the exhausted men unable to fall asleep and the incessant hiccuping of those about to die of beriberi. [...] A young man who lay raving as a result of sunstroke cried out all manner of gibberish for 30 hours until he was too feeble to utter a single word. (Cited in Veenstra et al. 1982:303.)

Corpses had to be cast overboard daily and the possessions of those who were dying were stolen; they could be traded for food from the Korean guards.

After three weeks the commandant relented. Mori was allowed to go to Makassar to buy vegetables, fruit, fish and eggs – he returned with nothing more than a small sack ('for the living' he said) and a bag with rocks and a coil of rope ('for the dead'). In the sack was tobacco – not surprisingly the commandant immediately banned smoking: the holds of the *Maros Maru* contained bombs and shells.

Half of these were unloaded with the help of the prisoners of war – after which everybody was locked up in the holds.

The *Maros Maru* set sail again after six weeks (during which almost 160 prisoners died) – not to Java, incidentally, but to somewhere on the west coast of Celebes. The ship remained there for two weeks – 90 deaths.

It only reached Surabaya on 26 December, two and a half months after its departure from Ambon. Of the approximately 600 men who embarked in Ambon on this ship and the one set afire, only 320 made it to shore.

As mentioned above, more than 4,100 prisoners were transported to the Moluccas to build the airfields on Amahai, Haruku and Ambon. Not counting those who died following their return to Java or after running aground on Muna (figures for this are missing), about 1,230 men, or three in ten, lost their lives.

Java, the second period

As of September 1942 large numbers of prisoners of war were transported elsewhere from Java: to Japan, Burma and Thailand, Sumatra, Flores and the Moluccas. Groups were sent back to Java only from Flores and the Moluccas. These were then divided into new groups: in September 1944 to be deployed on the Pekanbaru Railway, and in January 1945 to work in Singapore. As a result only a few prisoners of war remained on Java: at the time of the Japanese capitulation there were about 4,000, chiefly on West Java, and most of them on the Bandung plateau. The Japanese 16th Army had designated this plateau as the place where the Japanese battalions should withdraw in the event of an Allied landing on Java. At the same time, the Japanese had received orders from Tokyo to prevent their prisoners of war from being liberated by the Allies.

What may be called the 'second period' on Java (beginning with the mass removal of large groups of prisoners of war) can be divided into two sub-periods: one from October 1942 to February 1944 and one from February 1944 to August 1945. Generally speaking there was no serious shortage of food in the first sub-period, but there was in the second, which naturally was related to the catastrophic decline in food production on Java described in Chapter III, and the general indifference of the Japanese to the fate of the prisoners of war. While the Japanese had sufficient rice, famine was nevertheless experienced on Java. They could have made adequate supplies available to the prisoner-of-war camps (as well as those with the interned civilians) had they felt the need, or been willing to comply with their international obligations – this need was lacking and these obligations were honoured only on paper.

After the camps were closed at Malang, Cilacap and Surabaya (which had been the point of departure for the transports to Flores and the Moluccas) there were still prisoners of war in Batavia (the point of departure for the troopships to Burma, Thailand and Japan, later to Sumatra and Singapore) and on the Bandung plateau, namely in Bandung and in Cimahi.

Bandung had three camps: one for the Dutch and Dutch Eurasians (the former camp of the 15th Battalion); one for the British, Australians and Americans; and one for the Ambonese and Manadonese (who had refused to become *heiho*, or auxiliaries). The senior officer in the camp of the 15th Battalion, Lieutenant Colonel Poulus, was transferred to Cilacap in June 1942 and his position was taken over by Lieutenant Colonel S. de Waal. In February 1943 the Japanese imprisoned De Waal and some of his officers (on the suspicion that radio reports were circulating in his camp and that contact had been established with the camp of the Ambonese and the Manadonese).[210] In the meantime, Poulus had been brought back to Bandung and again became the senior officer. In his post-war report, he characterized the Japanese way of dealing with his camp as 'Jap-like', 'that is to say incalculable, violent, humiliating and slavish, with moments of relative freedom alternating with periods of veritable terror'.[211] The actual Japanese commandant was a sergeant for whom, according to Poulus, 'the thrashing of field officers [...] was a particular delicacy'.[212] These difficulties notwithstanding, Poulus and his aides organized their camp fairly well. The scanty rations were supplemented with food financed by a Food Fund. For this fund, which consisted partly of contributions from officers and men, Poulus (like the GESC in Batavia) clandestinely borrowed substantial sums from organizations and private individuals, presumably mostly Chinese. The fund also derived income from the profits of various businesses and *toko*, restaurants, and bars that were set up inside the camp. There were many sporting events and numerous theatrical, cabaret and musical performances were given, usually in collaboration with the British prisoners of war. 'Under the circumstances' the medical care 'could be called quite good'.[213]

Poulus's illicit loans were discovered in mid-December. He was beaten and the entire Food Fund was confiscated by the Japanese sergeant and had to be spent immediately (so that 'in a few days enormous amounts of food, tobacco, fruit and all manner of junk flooded the camp').[214] Poulus and several other officers were subsequently taken to Cimahi, where they were thrashed and incarcerated. Except for the British and the Americans, all of the prisoners of war from Bandung were transported to Batavia and confined in the former barracks of the 10th Battalion. The KNIL camp section was later used again as a civilian internment camp.

As Rob Nieuwenhuys later wrote, at the beginning of 1943 the camp in Cimahi, where Major Hoedt was the senior officer, was experienced by the incoming prisoners of war from Cilacap as:

> unbelievable. That something like this still exists! The first day we were welcomed with rice and pieces of meat and real *sajur* containing vegetables and spices and

---

[210]   De Waal and a few officers had to leave Java in September 1943 on their way to Formosa, where they were added to the Special Party.
[211]   H. Poulus, 'Verslag', p. 15 (NIOD IC, 2,031).
[212]   H. Poulus, 'Verslag', p. 16 (NIOD IC, 2,031).
[213]   H. Poulus, 'Verslag', p. 16 (NIOD IC, 2,031).
[214]   H. Poulus, 'Verslag', p. 16 (NIOD IC, 2,031).

even a drop of home-made banana liqueur. Cimahi appeared to be a camp over which a cornucopia had been emptied. (Nieuwenhuys 1979:87.)

Not that everyone shared equally in this bounty! Those who could acquire substantial quantities of additional food and regularly visit the camp restaurants and cafes fared much better than most of the others. According to Nieuwenhuys:

> There was no strong sense of solidarity and equality as in Cilacap. [...] The differences remained too great. That many of us were more irritated and exasperated by this inequality and the attitude of some of the 'privileged' than by the actions of the Japanese is understandable. (Nieuwenhuys 1979:87-8.)

As mentioned above, Cimahi had many camp businesses. There was a study room with a library of more than 2,000 titles;[215] there were theatrical and musical performances and cabaret shows. Many of the cabaret scripts were written by Erik K. de Vries, who sang a song, 'Kort verlof' (Short leave), in one of the revues. The refrain went as follows:

> The idea of power here on earth
> Never beats the power of the idea.
> If you poke just a little fun
> At the gravity of your fate,
> You will see for yourself: the future isn't so bad!
> (Nieuwenhuys 1979:91.)

A particularly attractive feature of the revues was the prisoners of war performing in drag,[216]

> The great star was Miss Mabel, actually a graceful and slender Indonesian boy always surrounded by admirers who indeed wanted for nothing. [...] No one could resist the singular world of eroticism which moved between performance and reality. (Nieuwenhuys 1979:91-2.)

In general the fatigues in Cimahi were not onerous: the largest working team, consisting of more than 100 prisoners of war, always worked in the vegetable

---

[215] Books from private collections and issues of the literary monthly *Groot Nederland* found in a camp office allowed a number of poetry-loving Dutchmen to compile an anthology of modern Dutch poets: *Onschendbaar domein* (Inviolable domain). Fifteen copies of this were each typed separately and illustrated with woodcuts (a barrack doorway was cannibalized for the wood) by among others Leo Vroman. This was a publication of the KKK Studio, and the three Ks stood for 'Kale Koppen Kampement' (Bald Heads Encampment). The volumes were sold for 15 guilders and the proceeds were deposited in the camp kitty.

[216] One of the revues was stopped by the Japanese who forced the hula-hula girls to undress: they thought that girls had been smuggled into the camp.

garden several kilometres away from the camp. This was not so bad. But would it last? It was doubtful: transports were occasionally assembled in Cimahi – one never knew under what circumstances one would be transported or what work would be assigned, only that American submarines were lying in wait. According to Nieuwenhuys (1979:95), every approaching transport was also 'a golden time for the dysentery patients. There were plenty who sold their blood and mucus.'

Similar events occurred in the 10th Battalion barracks in Batavia, where numerous prisoners of war moved from Bandung and Cimahi landed before leaving Java. The proximity of that departure could result in men taking extra risks: some would purposely crush a few fingers of their left hand during a fatigue, 'but the usual method', according to Nieuwenhuys, 'was the deliberate infection of wounds. [...] The morbid growth of a "tropical ulcer", which extended to the bone and was remarkably painful, was gratefully accepted as a sign of Providence.' (Niewenhuys 1979:102.)

A nurse, Nieuwenhuys was one of those who did not make it any further than the 10th Battalion barracks, which experienced hunger in 1944 and even famine in 1945, resulting in the death of many prisoners of war.

As of January 1944 only NCO's and soldiers were in that camp. The Japanese – evidently driven by the desire to gather prisoners of war deemed especially valuable by the Allies in a separate group (the same endeavour that earlier had led to the creation of the Special Party) – had confined all of the officers from the remaining camps in Struiswijk Prison in Batavia, from where the interned men, including many prominent figures, had vanished. The Dutch senior officer there was Lieutenant Colonel A. Doup (there was also a British one). Within the walls of the complex the prisoners of war enjoyed a certain degree of freedom (religious services were permitted on several occasions, and what was forbidden, such as lectures, was organized clandestinely – exams were even given, for example for helmsman and radio operator and even for Indonesian). Barring the shortage of vitamins, the food was reasonable because additional provisions could be bought and because the Japanese had allotted the members of the garden fatigue an additional 150 grams of rice per day – this rice was distributed among all of the prisoners. Struiswijk had a hospital division and serious cases could be transferred to two Catholic hospitals in Batavia. There was a secret radio in the prison: the progress of the war was thus known, and this gave them heart. Unpleasant, on the other hand, were the Japanese inspections: looting raids invariably accompanied by violence. Of the more than 1,000 officers confined in Struiswijk, 15 died while in detention (from January to October 1944).

The prison camp was discontinued at the end of October and the officers were transported inland to the encampment of the 1st Battalion in Bandung, where the officers from the camp at Cimahi had also ended up. The senior officer then was Colonel M. Vooren, who had been the territorial commander on South Celebes during the Japanese invasion and whom the Japanese had failed to include in the Special Party. Sent to his camp were a total of about 1,300 KNIL, more than 300 British officers, about 70 other ranks and even almost 100 civilians. All of these prisoners had far too little room at their disposal and were starving. As of April 1945 they had even less room and fewer rations when they were transferred to the Landsopvoedingsgesticht (LOG, National Reformatory), where they encountered about 2,000 lower ranks: roughly 1,300 from the KNIL and 650 British. The LOG, built to accommodate a maximum of 300 youthful delinquents, now housed a total of 3,700 prisoners of war within its walls: some slept in dormitories or other rooms, others in open galleries, still others outside the buildings in the open air. Naturally, there were too few faucets and toilets, but no shortage of lice and bedbugs.

At the end of July about 800 prisoners of war, including most of the British, were taken from the LOG to Batavia, specifically to the 10th Battalion camp. The Japanese needed all manner of labourers there, but chiefly technical experts. The Japanese used the General Motors assembly plant in Priok to convert passenger cars into semi-trucks. Qualified workers were not to be found among the Indonesians, hence their decision, contrary to their general policy, to bring a group of prisoners of war to the coast. At the LOG, the prisoners were required to report whether they had a driver's licence. According to a Dutch prisoner of war (he had earlier worked on Haruku):

> After virtually the entire camp answered the question with 'yes' [anything was better than staying in the LOG!], all of the eligible drivers had to come forward. Subsequently a division was made between those who had had their licence less than or more than eight years. The Japanese designated those belonging to the latter group as technicians: after all, anyone behind a wheel for eight years had to have some understanding of cars.[217]

There is no explanation for why, according to the camp statistics, almost exclusively British troops were transported to Batavia. Volunteers were requested there for work at the General Motors plant and according to the above-quoted Dutchman 'unfortunately there were more than enough people [in total, however, not many more than about 200 of the 800] prepared to work for the enemy for the sake of more food'.[218]

One circumstance ought now to be considered. At the time of the Japanese

---

[217]   H.A. van Deinse, 'Verslag', 7 May 1947, p. 5 (ARA, Alg. Secr., Eerste zending, XXII, 45, 177).
[218]   H.A. van Deinse, 'Verslag', 7 May 1947, p. 5 (ARA, Alg. Secr., Eerste zending, XXII, 45, 177).

capitulation and the proclamation of the Republic of Indonesia (17 August 1945) only a few thousand Dutch and other soldiers were being held as prisoners of war on all of Java: 3,700 at the most, the largest group was in Bandung, the smallest in Batavia.[219] Many, many more were removed and isolated group by group in Sumatra, Singapore, Thailand, French Indo-China, Manchuria (a large part of the Special Party) and finally also in Japan – the fate of the last of these groups will now be examined.

Japan

Mention has already been made of the fact that a total of about 37,000 prisoners of war had to work in Japan: Dutch and Dutch Eurasians, British, Australians, Canadians (brought in from Hong Kong), and Americans (primarily from the Philippines). This 37,000 included about 8,000 Dutch and Dutch Eurasians of whom 728 (one in eleven) died in Japan. Moreover, more than about 37,000 were shipped north – many (how many exactly is not known) drowned or lost their lives otherwise during the transports.

Of the Dutch and Dutch Eurasians sent to Japan, the survivors of the Battle of the Java Sea belonging to the group of about 500 that was removed from Celebes (this group was treated reasonably well in Japan), and the approximately 600 'technicians' designated in Cimahi were the first to arrive in May and in December 1942, respectively.[220] The other groups numbering more than 7,000 arrived later, that is at the end of 1943 and in the course of 1944, and consisted partly of prisoners of war from Java and partly of prisoners of war who had first worked on the Burma Railway. We know the kind of work the approximately 600 'technicians' (Dutch Eurasian soldiers with a small group of Dutch officers) had to do in Japan,[221] but similar information

---

[219]   According to the first report by the Japanese after their surrender, namely to Rear Admiral Patterson, there were about 3,360, that is about 1,500 Dutch and Dutch Eurasians, about 1,200 English, about 400 Australians, about 60 Americans and about 200 soldiers of other nationalities (they were probably primarily Indonesian).

[220]   Also arriving in Japan in December 1942 was the Navy hospital ship *Op ten Noort* that had been illegally seized by the Japanese. The European crew and the medical staff, including several nurses, totalling 44 people, were interned in a country house in the mountains not far from Hiroshima – they were well treated there.

[221]   They and the accompanying roughly 100 British, Australians and Americans were split into three groups: close to 300 worked in a blast furnace complex, about 200 in the related iron mine, and about 200 in a coal mine. In accordance with the Geneva Convention the officers in these groups were not required to work. According to one of those who worked in the coal mine, more than two years later they were 'ashen from the continual lack of sunlight' and 'moreover weak and thin as rails because the food was scanty and simply awful'; they were dressed in 'rags', which 'even the worst beggar in Holland [would have] thrown away long ago'. (J.W. le Comte, 'De laatste dienst', 28 August 1945, p. 1 (NIOD IC, 1,128).)

is lacking for the more than 7,000 who followed them. In Japan there were a total of 85 prisoner-of-war camps, none large, with the number of prisoners varying from 300 to 750. These camps differed enormously: some had decent barracks with adequate hygiene, others were primitive and squalid. The winters in Japan are cold (long periods of subzero temperatures are no exception) and the prisoners of war suffered terribly. But there were also camps where the barracks, especially in the winter of 1943-1944 and even that of 1944-1945 (when most of the Japanese civilians barely received any fuel), were well heated. In general the prisoners of war, and most of the Japanese civilians, had too little to eat, chiefly in 1945,[222] and the supply of clothing (most had arrived in lightweight garb – many died from pneumonia) and footwear was inadequate. Treatment in the camps differed greatly. Van Witsen wrote:

> There are camp commandants who [...] perform their work conscientiously, dutifully. The result is a decent camp, where abuse is limited and corruption remains within boundaries. [...] When the commandant [...] exercises sufficient control over his subordinates, looks into the complaints of the camp inhabitants, [...] does not allow punishment to be meted out by every guard, one can speak of a good camp. Theft from the stored Red Cross parcels then stays within reasonable limits. [...] There are indeed such camps, with a mortality of 5 per thousand a year. Unfortunately, they are the exception.[223]

Such relatively favourable conditions were not found in most camps. Van Witsen himself was fortunate: in November 1943 he was interned in a camp near Tokyo from where the prisoners were put to work in a blast furnace complex. He wrote:

> We arrived there with 364 men; in general, the Japanese behaved calmly. [...] Work, food, hygiene and housing were reasonable, which was reflected in the mortality rate: four men in one and half years! The prisoners of war, many former officers and NCOs and Landstormers [reservists], behaved decently to one another. [...] Only one incident took place in all this time: a KNIL adjutant stole a gold watch from a sublieutenant. The Japanese got wind of this and the guilty party was punished with 50 lashes on his bare back in view of all of the camp inhabitants. The camp commandant, a Japanese lieutenant, announced: 'The thief is a man who has tarnished the name of the Europeans, fortunately there is [only] one of his kind in the entire camp'.[224]

The prisoners of war had to work long and hard, usually 12 hours a day, but also in 8-hour shifts. There were few days off, as a rule only two a month. In

---

[222] In one of the camps servicing a coal mine, in March 1945 the daily ration had a calorific value of 3,012 (too low for mine workers), which dropped to 1,975 by the end of June.
[223] E. van Witsen, 'Over krijgsgevangenen in Japanse handen', pp. 388-9.
[224] E. van Witsen, 'Over krijgsgevangenen in Japanse handen', p. 592.

the coal mines (where 7,400 prisoners of war of various nationalities were working in March 1945) carts had to be loaded and pushed; buttressing material had to be hauled and rails laid, and above ground all manner of clearing work was required. In the factories as well simple but unpleasant tasks were assigned to the prisoners of war: shovelling out the ash, emptying basements, laying rails, loading and unloading ships and wagons, levelling the ground. There was much outdoor work and the chores performed with fairly primitive tools were monotonous. Disagreeable, chiefly in wintertime, were the roll calls following the day's work.

All in all, conditions were better than those, for example, on the Burma and Pekanbaru Railways and on Flores and the Moluccas. There was less hunger and more possibilities for nursing the sick. Moreover, in many camps it was possible to some extent to follow the course of the war; at least the reports relating to the great events (the fall of Mussolini, the surrender of Italy, the Allied landing in Normandy, the American landings in the Pacific, the surrender of Germany) penetrated most of the camps.[225] This was due to contact with Japanese guards and Japanese civilians. Most of the civilians were not hostile to the prisoners, except for the occasional youth incited to fanaticism. Writing in his diary following his arrival from the Burma Railway, Hamel noted that 'the youths were defiant, [and] the older public more curious'.[226]

Our general impression is that the prisoners of war who had to work in the coal mines were worst off. Minework is always hard and, moreover, most of the coal mines in Japan were relatively primitive (the shortage of fuel was so great that long abandoned mines were started up again) and they were ruthlessly exploited there and elsewhere: all of the labourers, including the prisoners of war, were mercilessly driven and no account was taken of the safety regulations. Rightly so, many prisoners of war feared that they would be struck by falling rocks deep under the ground or that a mine would explode.[227] Some even resorted to self-mutilation: according to Beets (1981: 259), 'tough Australians crushed their own toes with a boulder in order to, in God's name, escape having to work in the mine'. Some mines were not very deep and thus their entrance shafts were sometimes sloped, but there were also some with layers far below the surface without an elevator and accessible only by ladder, so that the men had to climb down storey by storey. In one

---

[225]   In the camps of the prisoners of war brought in from Java in December 1942, a copy of an English language Japanese daily was received until May 1943. After that, back issues several months old were received sporadically, and in the end no newspaper was received at all.
[226]   J.C. Hamel, 'Dagboek', 15-18 June 1944 (NIOD IC, Dagboek 12).
[227]   Prisoners of war were injured in mining accidents. According to one who had been a mining engineer in civilian life, 'It must be said that when accidents occurred, regardless of the victim's nationality, the Japs continued to work like horses'. (F.F.F.E. van Rummelen, 'Verslag', 18 September 1945, p. 2 (NIOD IC, 1,139).)

mine this meant that even before their eight-hour shift began, the prisoners of war had to clamber down for two hours and after their shift up for two and a half hours. According to one of the prisoners of war working in this mine, 'broken legs were considered a blessing'.[228]

There is little information concerning the relations among the prisoners of war from various backgrounds. Each camp had fatigues and the most coveted was kitchen duty. As a rule the first group of prisoners of war arriving at a given camp defended this fatigue tooth and nail from the following ones – not only those doing this fatigue profited, but their fellow countrymen as well. In the camp at the coal mine where Hamel found himself,[229] both the kitchen and the sick bay fatigues (nurses were not required to work in the mines) were run by the Americans who had first populated the camp. The Dutch minister wrote:

> It appeared as if America had sent the dregs of its society to the Philippines, for many of the internees exhibited truly criminal tendencies and were in no way hampered by scruples. [...] The American officers did nothing, literally nothing, to protect their men from themselves. No, and worse: many of these officers gambled along with them, themselves buying the food of the weak under their command. (Hamel 1948:209, 214.)

In April 1945, a KNIL prisoner of war noted that, 'The kitchen was in English hands, and thus extremely unfair'.[230] But another, a reserve officer candidate who arrived in June 1945 with 50 Dutch and Dutch Eurasian, 75 American and 25 British prisoners at a camp on the west coast of Japan ('entirely new buildings in excellent condition, good encampment, bath, latrines, officers' quarters, pharmacy with medicine, hospital [...] into which six patients were immediately admitted'),[231] wrote:

> It is worth noting that the attitude of the small group of British men without an officer put in our group was superlative. They stood out for their excellent discipline, cleanliness and willingness to cooperate in helping to run things smoothly.
>   In general, the composition of the camp population from three nationalities presented no special problems. Special praise is due to the Eurasian boys for the way in which they handled their captivity. They were outstanding in their helpfulness, solidarity and diligence.[232]

---

228   J.F. van West de Veer, 'Landstormsoldaat 1941-1945', p. 71 (NIOD IC, 81,314).
229   The mine was run by the Mitsui trust. The leadership of that concern had created a relatively good camp: they also saw to it that the prisoners of war received additional food.
230   J.D. Backer, 'Dagboek', 5 April 1945 (NIOD IC).
231   L. ter Braake, 'Verslag', September 1945, p. 1 (NIOD IC, 1,209).
232   L. ter Braake, 'Verslag', September 1945, p. 1 (NIOD IC, 1,209).

In 1944 the American long-range bombers began attacking Japanese industrial complexes from the Marianas. They changed their tactics in early 1945, repeatedly raiding Japanese cities with fire bombs. Naturally, these bombardments claimed victims among the prisoners of war, although not that many for their camps were not located in the city centres.

No Dutch or Dutch Eurasian prisoners of war were in the vicinity of Hiroshima when it was annihilated by the first American atom bomb on 6 August 1945, but this was not the case when the second atom bomb exploded near Nagasaki on 9 August (not above the centre, but about six kilometres to the north).[233] Located between that centre and the point above which the explosion took place, the so-called epicentre, was a shipbuilding complex owned by the Mitsubishi trust, including a shipyard that had been established by a Dutch naval officer in 1857. Initially the property of the Japanese government, it was later bought by the trust and at the time of the Second World War was one of the world's largest shipyards. Prisoners of war housed in a nearby military prison camp (Fukuoka 14) were working there as of May 1943. They suffered terribly from the cold during the winter of 1944-1945 and mortality was relatively high (more than 60 deaths among over 500 men), chiefly as a result of a dysentery epidemic. In addition, Nagasaki was bombed by the Americans on 1 August 1945: a 'conventional' bombardment.

On 9 August (at the time only 168 prisoners of war were still in Fukuoka 14; 128 Dutch and Dutch Eurasians, 24 Australians, 16 British), a team of prisoners of war had been busy since early that morning clearing rubble from the side of a factory building on the grounds of the Mitsubishi complex. There was a clear blue sky. The drone of an aeroplane was heard at 11 o'clock. Several people looked up (no alarm was sounded) and saw an object being cast from the American aircraft and floating down suspended from three balloons. Those who kept on looking up from this spot, less than two kilometres from the epicentre, were blinded by the flash of the exploding plutonium bomb and, to the extent that their bodies were exposed, covered with burns. Others immediately dropped to the ground and shut their eyes. A colossal muffled detonation followed: buildings collapsed and fires broke out everywhere.

That same morning some prisoners of war riveting cross beams on a ship under construction were so absorbed in their work that they never saw the explosion. 'Look there!' one of them heard. 'I turned my head around and looked', according to the report the latter wrote shortly thereafter:[234]

---

[233]   What follows is based on the work published in 1980 by J. Stellingwerff: *'Fat man'* [the code name of the second atom bomb] *in Nagasaki; Nederlandse krijgsgevangenen overleefden de atoombom.*

[234]   Text in Brugmans 1960:605-6.

I remained speechless for a few endless seconds. I saw an indescribably fierce white light comparable to that at the end of a welding torch, but it lasted much longer, unbelievably long. A reddish glow, which was far stronger than daylight then spread against the background of this bright white light. This began at the ground, surged up like a powerful fountain, and slowly, very slowly grew into an enormous mushroom.

Initially, there were very few casualties among the prisoners of war. The upper torso of one was covered with burns, a second broke a few ribs, a third, the Dutch senior officer, had a concussion. Other victims were discovered only later when, after having run back to the camp (all of the barracks were demolished), people then returned to the Mitsubishi complex. Large buildings were ablaze and presumably many who had been wounded, or lost consciousness, or been trapped were still in them. Indeed, many hundreds of Japanese girls, factory workers, in the top storey of the factory building mentioned above could not be reached. Nor could a prisoner of war also trapped there. Every possible effort was made to save him, 'he was still conscious', according to one of those trying to rescue him, 'then the boys had to abandon him when the roof was about to collapse above their heads. He burned alive.' (Stellingwerff 1980:110.) In the following days, while Nagasaki burned, the prisoners of war bivouacked in caves at the foot of the nearby hills. Those who had been blinded remained apathetic: 'with faces for the most past swollen on one side [the one facing the explosion] attracting swarms of mosquitoes, sitting expressionless staring straight ahead' (Stellingwerff 1980:107). The others still able to work (the atom bomb at Nagasaki killed nine Dutch and Dutch Eurasian prisoners of war) were summoned by the governor of the city to help collect the countless corpses which had to be cremated as quickly as possible. 'You had to pick up grievously mutilated body parts (the bodies disintegrated) with your bare hands – it was horrible' (Stellingwerff 1980:106).

This labour lasted four full days. On 16 August (the Japanese government had decided to capitulate on the 14th, Hirohito's radio address was broadcast on the 15th) the prisoners of war commenced a rest period and three days later, on 19 August at a quarter to five in the afternoon, they heard that the war was over.

Conclusion

Having reached the end of this chapter, there is no need to embark on a long general deliberation. The facts and figures presumably speak for themselves and only a few comments will be added to them.

The first is that, barring the reporting of the names of the prisoners of war, the Japanese in no way observed the provisions of the Geneva Convention

– provisions they had accepted in January 1942. There were Japanese, like General Murakami, head of the Prisoners of War Bureau in Tokyo, who occasionally referred to these obligations, and others who behaved humanely towards the prisoners of war, but they were exceptions (all instances of such conduct encountered in the course of our research are mentioned). As noted above, Lieutenant Colonel Poulus, senior officer at the camp of the 15th Battalion in Bandung, characterized the actions of the Japanese he had dealings with as 'incalculable, violent, humiliating and slavish, with moments of relative freedom alternating with periods of veritable terror'. And it should be borne in mind that these were qualifications being applied to a camp from where no hard work had to be done. When this labour was required, little was left of those 'moments of relative freedom'. A British Flight Lieutenant later reported on the terrible journey of the *Maros Maru* from Ambon to Makassar, from Makassar to the coast of Central Celebes and from there to Java: 'Throughout the experience I never met with any attitude on the part of the Japanese other than brutish cruelty, cynical indifference to needless suffering, unbelievable stupidity and utter incompetence'.[235] These qualifications must have applied to countless Japanese in any way involved with prisoners of war.

That the Japanese also took very bad medical care of their own low-ranking soldiers and worked them to a degree unthinkable in the armies of the European powers and of the United States, and that, in keeping with views shaped by their cultural patrimony, they considered virtually all of their prisoners of war as inferior, despicable creatures may explain their conduct to a certain extent, but in no way excuses it. In the Sino-Japanese War, the Russo-Japanese War and in the First World War, the Japanese authorities were aware that they were expected to treat their prisoners of war in accordance with the standards that applied in the prisoner's country of origin – standards known to the Japanese authorities. The same applied to the provisions of the Geneva Convention. Furthermore, the deceit carried out when delegates of the International Red Cross or representatives of the Protecting Powers were allowed to visit some camps, and the misleading footage shot on Java, on Formosa and in Singapore, prove that every Japanese involved knew there was a gap between the way in which Japan ought to treat its prisoners of war as expected by its adversaries and how they were treated in reality.

The second comment is that while all of the prisoners of war suffered, not all did so to the same degree. They all suffered in that they were robbed of their liberty, subjected to the whims and caprices, abuse and extortion of the Japanese soldiers and the Korean guards (who, due to their inferiority complex, usually behaved in a manner more 'Japanese' than the Japanese

[235] W.M. Blackwood, 'Report', n.d., p. 6 (NIOD IC, 1,605).

themselves), often starving, usually deprived of encouraging news, virtually always isolated from their family, and not just for a few weeks or months but for several years. Not all suffered to the same degree though because in almost every camp 'clever guys' were able to build up a privileged position; it made a difference whether one was a private or an officer; because it also made a difference whether one could stay on the island where one had been taken prisoner or had to endure the horror of the transports overseas; and because, finally, it made a difference to which area the men in the latter instance were transferred. Proportionally, there were fewest deaths among those transported to Japan before the end of 1943 and most (three in ten) among those who had to build the airfields on the Moluccas. But can the suffering of one ever be compared to that of another? Every anguish has its own duration and intensity; no comparison may be made between the agony of the many who were admitted to primitive barracks, enduring hunger, thirst and pain, who were tormented by lice and other insects, who were lonely and felt their strength ebb in the course of weeks or months, and that of the many others who desperately thrashed about in the waves of an all-powerful ocean knowing full well that they were doomed.

The third comment is that I am conscious that the overview presented exhibits lacunas. In general, too little is known about the relationships among the prisoners of war themselves and the corruption that took place in many a camp. Moreover, not enough is known about the way in which the transports were composed. Sometimes this was done by the Japanese, but usually they notified the senior officer of the number of labourers they needed, and it was the task of the senior officer and his assistants to select those who had to leave. As a rule everyone wanted to stay put. At least they knew the environment to which they had adapted to some degree – departure meant uncertainty, uncertainty meant fear. What criteria were applied in this selection? Only one example could be cited, that of Major Hoedt who assembled the sizeable transport of Dutch Eurasians in the large camp at Cimahi in 1942 of those (the 'worst elements [...] people from the lowest levels of East Indies society') he wished to be rid of, and there are indications that in other camps as well in the last months of 1942 senior officers initially selected those they wished to be rid of. What tensions, what contrasts, what conflicts were thus engendered? This is an important question, which cannot be answered due to a dearth of information.

The fourth and final comment is that soldiers captured by the Japanese had to endure ordeals immeasurably harsher than those borne by the prisoners of war (except for the Russians) taken by the Germans or Italians. Of the former, with respect to the British and American troops, no less than 27% died, of the latter only 4%. But then, generally speaking, the provisions of the Geneva Convention were indeed applied by the German and Italian rulers.

These also worked to the advantage of the Dutch in the occupied mother country who were transported to Germany as prisoners of war, whether in 1940 (a small group of regular officers who had refused to make a kind of declaration of obedience), in 1942 (most of the regular officers, midshipmen and cadets), or in 1943 (a small part of the reserve officers and of the lower ranks).[236] Until the Railway Strike on 17 September 1944[237] they were able to correspond with their relatives in occupied territory from where they received packages, and after that messages and packages from the Allied world. Aside from those who were prisoners of war for only a short while in May and June 1940 (they were given leave to return to occupied territory), a total of more than 13,000 Dutch soldiers were detained in Germany as prisoners of war: of them 300 to 400 died, or about 3%. There is not only a stark contrast between this 3% and the 19.4% who succumbed in Japanese captivity, but the vast majority of those who survived captivity at the hands of the Japanese were subjected to traumatic experiences that were spared virtually all of the prisoners of war of the Germans.

This constitutes a striking difference between the occupation history of the Netherlands and that of the Dutch East Indies.

---

[236] Of those who had to report, in total probably 240,000 soldiers, many stayed away and others were granted exemption; only about 11,000 were transported to Germany.
[237] The Allied operation Market Garden began in the Netherlands on 17 September 1944. The same day the Dutch government in exile in London made a radio appeal for railway personnel to call a general strike in order to hinder German transport as much as possible. In general this appeal was widely heeded.

CHAPTER V

Internees

Just as the men of the Dutch Navy and the KNIL suffered greater hardships during the Japanese occupation than the soldiers in the occupied
Netherlands, so too did the Dutch citizens (including Dutch Eurasians) in
the East Indies suffer greater hardships than the civilians in the Netherlands.
There, during five years of occupation, some *groups* in the population found
themselves in great need (the persecuted, those affected by the fighting and,
in the hunger winter, those living in non-agricultural areas in the west of the
country), but in the Indies this need was more widespread, lasted longer and
cost far more lives proportionally.

Because nearly all the Japanese documents relating to internment, and
many of the camp archives, have been lost, our information about the
number of internees is incomplete. The available material was gathered by
D. van Velden in her wide-ranging study of 1963 *De Japanse interneringskampen voor burgers gedurende de Tweede Wereldoorlog* (The Japanese internment
camps for civilians in the Second World War).[1] According to her figures, in
total about 96,300 Dutch and Dutch Eurasian civilians were interned in the
East Indies, and of them, during an internment which in most cases lasted for
three full years, about 13,120 died, or 13.6%.

These figures may be too low. After the war the Dutch government asserted
that there had been slightly over 100,000 internees in the Indies.[2] It is known
that during the war the Japanese told the International Red Cross[3] that there
were about 98,000 internees and that 16,800 of them had died, that is 17%.[4]

---

[1]   Most of the general information incorporated into this chapter is derived from her study.
[2]   *Report of the International Committee of the Red Cross on its activities during the Second World
War*, Vol. II (1948), p. 205.
[3]   In 1955, during the negotiations with Japan which led to 38 million guilders being paid
in compensation, the Dutch government worked on the assumption that there had been about
110,000 internees, one in five of whom had died. This account is based on the slightly lower
figures published by Van Velden eight years later. The compensation worked out at just over 30
cents for each ex-internee for each day of internment.
[4]   In his 1982 study, mentioned in the prevous chapter, S. Adachi published figures on the
internees on Java, Sumatra and Borneo based on reports in the Japanese army archives (he does
not deal with the internees in the area administered by the navy). He arrived at a total of at most

Perhaps it is best to assume that there were about 100,000 internees and that internment cost the lives of one in six.

For all the internees it meant a break in their normal life: instead of being individuals with freedom of movement and useful work they were inmates. The men were suddenly separated from their families and lost virtually all their possessions. All the internees faced a very uncertain future under Japanese rule. The conditions in which they had to endure internment were not the same everywhere: most of the camps were bad, but a few were better than the rest.

It was only in the Dutch East Indies that conditions became truly appalling. Was this inevitable? By no means. To underline this important point, we shall begin by describing the 'best' camp: the one in which Dutch and Dutch Eurasian women and children on southeast Celebes were confined in 1943.

Some of these women and children had been evacuated to Java in December 1941 and January 1942. Apart from a group of women doing war work in Makassar, those who were unable or unwilling to leave were moved at the end of January to two places in the mountains east of Makassar, Malino and Pakato (see Map 9). Here the KNIL commander had set up evacuation centres for them and for the wives and children of indigenous KNIL soldiers; they were accommodated in several dozen holiday cottages. About two weeks later the Japanese landed near Makassar. They gathered all the Dutch and Dutch Eurasian women and children together in Malino. To them were added in the middle of March 1942 the women from Makassar, who had come through a difficult time in the barracks of the indigenous police, followed a few months later by the Dutch and Dutch Eurasian women and children from all the Lesser Sunda Islands except Lombok[5] (Bali, Sumbawa, Sumba, Flores and Timor). In May 1943 they left Malino – the Japanese military administration (in this case the naval civil administration, the Minseibu) had decided to turn an empty sanatorium complex at Kampili, 25 km south of Makassar, into a new internment camp. In February 1943, 400 women and children were brought there from Ambon as the first internees; they also included a group from Dutch New Guinea.[6] The camp at Kampili accommodated a total of nearly 1,700 women and children, including several dozen of foreign nation-

---

78,000 internees. In comparison with Van Velden's figures based on reports by camp leaders and reliable information from internees, his total for these islands is too low: evidently, the Japanese army reports were incomplete.

5   The internees on Lombok were taken to Java.

6   On Ambon the Japanese had set up a munitions store near where the internment camps for men and women and the prisoner-of-war camp were. On 15 February 1943 this store exploded during an Allied air raid: 23 internees were killed as well as 9 Australian prisoners of war who immediately came to the aid of the internees (the KNIL prisoners of war had already been moved to Hainan).

ality. After some time Annie H. Joustra became the camp leader. She was a
45-year-old secondary school teacher from Makassar who had come to the
East Indies in 1920 and had taught there with a few interruptions, for example
for leave in Europe, ever since. A courageous and level-headed woman, she
was appointed by the Japanese commandant, Sergeant Tadashi Yamaji. She
worked together with camp officials who were no better off than the other
internees in any way, and she applied the sensible rule that all work should be
done in rotation, thus ensuring that there would be no privileged groups.

The complex consisted of 12 bamboo sheds in which each internee had
her own bed, and seven stone barracks in which there were a further 200
beds. There were seven fireplaces where the drinking water was boiled and
hot food cooked, and four eating areas with adequate, if primitive, tables and
benches. Of the three stone office buildings, the largest served as the camp
office, while the other two were used as sick bays and had about 50 beds
all together. Only these three stone buildings were connected to the water
mains; elsewhere water had to be drawn from wells or a nearby irrigation
channel. By these wells, 15 in total, there were bamboo-screened washing
and 'shower' facilities. There were a few classrooms: despite the difficulties
(there were hardly any teaching materials), young pupils were taught in the
morning and older ones in the afternoon. There were also ten so-called club
houses (small rooms), a church shed with a stage (it had benches for 800 people) and two sewing rooms – one room served as a carpenter's workshop.

All these buildings, except for those in stone, were quite basic. The church
shed, for instance, was twice destroyed by fierce gusts of wind; the stage was
not added until the third shed.

The interned women had not had to build all these sheds themselves. This
had been done by coolies, who later also dug the air-raid trenches inside the
fence. They were paid by the Japanese.

The camp had a cowshed, a large number of pigsties (the pigs were fed
with scraps from the Japanese barracks at Makassar), a chicken run and a
place for slaughtering. There was also a stretch of grass where football or korf-
ball could be played (there was one ball); tennis could be played occasionally
and swimming in the irrigation channel was allowed under Japanese supervision. The agricultural land that belonged to the camp covered 34 hectares.

The food they received was deficient in vitamins and fats, but there was
no serious hunger at Kampili. The gardens and *sawah* produced vegetables,
sweet potatoes, tuberous plants, bananas, papayas and rice. Sometimes additional food was brought from Makassar by lorry and the nearby *kampong*
occasionally supplied fruit, eggs, vegetables and water-buffalo milk. At the
end of 1943 the camp had 12 lean cows (together they produced only four
or five litres of milk a week). From the chicken run each internee received
one egg per month; sometimes there were duck eggs too (the ducks were

on the *sawah*). They did not benefit from the 500 pigs (whose meat went to the Japanese in Makassar), but they sometimes got meat from the goats that were also in the camp. Moreover, every once in a while a water buffalo was brought into the camp to be slaughtered.

As for clothing, many women brought into the camp whatever clothes they had, but some had been left behind in Malino. Camp commandant Yamaji gave permission for the clothes to be collected. When the camp was bombed (see below) the Japanese in Makassar sent towels, kimonos and shirts. In the end every internee received adequate working clothes. There were 18 sewing machines in the camp: ten for the sewing rooms, and eight that were used for altering and adding to the internees' own clothing. There were enough sun hats and clogs for working on the land. Boys and girls from the age of 12 upwards and women who were capable of heavy labour had to work on the *sawah* – other women had to knit socks for the Japanese and embroider decorations, and in the last phase of the camp they had to split mica. The wages applying to all these kinds of work were deposited by the Japanese in the fund from which the Japanese naval administration in Makassar financed the camp.

The money required for the support of the internees was provided initially by the internees themselves, as had happened in Malino, but when their reserves (the groups from Ambon and Timor, in particular, turned out to have quite a lot of money) were exhausted at the end of 1943, the Minseibu paid the various suppliers, probably up to a total of over 200,000 guilders (15 cents per internee per day was spent on food). In addition, the construction of extra sheds and the maintenance of the entire camp was paid by the Minseibu – this cost over 110,000 guilders in total.

Camp commandant Yamaji was always accompanied by one of three Japanese soldiers: 'Danny', 'Applecheeks' and 'Nine and a half' (who was missing half a finger). The last of these was a real hothead. The camp was guarded by Indonesian policemen. Yamaji himself was rather unpredictable and inclined to uncontrollable outbursts on occasion; it was characteristic of him to want to perform the task given to him perfectly. 'With him', said the camp leader, 'the interests of the camp and its inmates came above everything else. [...] In the everyday life of the camp he worked from early till late, giving up his meals and sleep if necessary.'[7] In the middle of July 1945 the camp was twice bombed and fired on by Allied aircraft (a Japanese airfield was about 10 kilometres away). Seven internees were killed and eight wounded, and the camp was severely damaged.[8] 'During both attacks', according to the

7   'Rapporten over Kampili', August 1945, pp. 5-6 (NIOD IC, 81,511).
8   After the second raid, which took place two days after the first, a Dutch flag was laid out on a patch of ground in the complex and the words 'Dutch women' painted in big letters in white. As

camp leader, 'Yamaji was where help was needed, regardless of the danger to himself'.[9]

Yamaji was remarkably accommodating to the internees in many ways. Admittedly, they had to line up every day to be counted in accordance with Japanese regulations, and to bow afterwards, but he agreed that this bow might be made not in the direction of the imperial palace in Tokyo but in that of the Netherlands and London, where Queen Wilhelmina was. At first lessons could only be given clandestinely, but Yamaji allowed kindergarten and secondary education to be given, as best it could be in the circumstances. In the church shed they were allowed to hang the Dutch flag above the stage, flanked by drawings of the Queen and William the Silent, one draped with the Dutch tricolour and the other with an orange flag. On the Queen's birthday verses from the national anthem could be read out and religious services were allowed every Sunday. On holidays a choir would sometimes perform: the camp had two, a general one and one consisting of nuns. After a while there were three men living in the camp: a doctor, a minister from Ambon (he was allowed to stay in Kampili because his wife was gravely ill) and a youth leader who had arrived with a group of boys from the men's camp on southwest Celebes. Yamaji agreed to the nuns' request for a priest to be sent (the youth leader then had to leave). According to the camp leader, the commandant 'really took trouble not to offend our religious sensibilities and not to interfere with customs and habits to do with our faith'.[10] Furthermore, at the beginning of 1945 he personally ensured that girls interned in the camp were not sent to Makassar to become prostitutes for Japanese officers. He repeated to his superiors an argument furnished by one of the internees: the Japanese emperor would never approve of such an act. This argument was accepted by the commander of the Japanese fleet in the Great East.

Thus the courteous behaviour of a Japanese commandant ensured that there was one camp where, whatever the uncertainties and fears (when would liberation come and would the men from whom almost nothing had been heard still be alive then?), conditions were not desperate, at least until July 1945. The deterioration that began then was the result of Allied bombing, not of the actions of the Japanese.

Of the nearly 1,700 women and children held in the camp, 28 or just over 1.5% died in the two years it existed, not counting the victims of the two air raids.

---

a result of the raids, a previously prepared 'emergency camp' had to be brought into use, which of course created many difficulties.

[9]   'Rapporten over Kampili', August 1945, p. 6 (NIOD IC, 81,511).
[10]   'Rapporten over Kampili', August 1945, p. 40 (NIOD IC, 81,511).

Kampili was an exception, not only in the East Indies but also on Celebes. On that same island, namely at Manado in Minahasa, from the first day, according to Van Velden, about 160 interned men and youths were given:

> filthy rice and the vegetable waste from the *pasar*. They had to work in the city and on the docks, for which they received nothing extra. From time to time they were given nothing to eat for several days. They had no camp doctor of their own and were allowed to appoint only one nurse. [...] The Japanese doctor did nothing and gave no medicines. There were frequent beatings and the camp was often given collective punishment. In this camp 44% of the men and youths died – a percentage that is much higher even than the average death rate among the prisoners of war. (Van Velden 1963:296.)

Beyond the East Indies

Dutch and Dutch Eurasian civilians were interned beyond the East Indies as well, that is, elsewhere in Japanese-controlled territory, during the war in the Pacific. There were not many of them: about 70 in Japan, 400 in Nanking China, slightly over 50 in Hong Kong, 150 on the Philippines, 5 in French Indo-China, 7 in Thailand and 80 in Singapore.

At the beginning of 1942 the Japanese government gave an undertaking to the governments of the United States, Great Britain and the Netherlands that it would treat both the prisoners of war and the internees in accordance with the provisions of the Geneva Convention. As regards the internees in Japan, the Japanese government kept to this undertaking; indeed, it went further than was required by the Convention by in principle housing, feeding and clothing the interned civilians (just under 700 in total) according to Western standards. 'All the buildings', says Van Velden, 'that they used for internees were built in Western style and healthy, and often beautifully located.' The internment complexes were often not even fenced off.

> Each month the internees could speak freely with the representatives of the Protecting Powers and they were in touch with the delegates of the International Red Cross. In many camps private visits were allowed. The internees could also leave the camp to go to the hospital or the dentist and sometimes to take a walk, go shopping or to visit their families.[11] They were allowed to write one letter of 100 words each month to a country outside Japan, plus as a rule one letter a week to a place in Japan. [...] The Japanese commandants and guards generally behaved correctly. The maintenance of the camps and the supply of food, soap, medicines and clothing were adequate, except in the last year. (Van Velden 1963:226.)

[11]   This last applied when only the husband in a family had been interned.

Also well cared for were the engineers of the radio laboratory at Bandung and their families, a group of 22 people who had been moved to Japan by the Sumitomo concern, as mentioned in Chapter I. The same was true of the medical staff and the non-indigenous crew members of the navy hospital ship *Op ten Noort*, which had been seized by the Japanese (in violation of the international rules). Curiously, in Japan not all the citizens of states with which it was at war were interned: about 350 were left at liberty.

In China, where over 9,000 Allied civilians were interned, most of them in the major commercial centre of Shanghai, conditions were less favourable. The internment complexes did not provide enough space and in 1944 and especially 1945 the rations were inadequate. On the other hand, the internees did not have to work for the Japanese and in general there was no ill-treatment. As in Japan, there were ample opportunities for study, worship and recreation. 'No wonder', according to Van Velden (1963:241), 'that after the Japanese surrender people said that the internees looked healthy and that the Dutch group in particular had come through it in fine shape'.

In Hong Kong and on the Philippines too, conditions were never desperate, and in French Indo-China and Thailand the French and Thai authorities made every effort to ensure that the life of the internees was as bearable as possible. At first in Singapore part of Changi Prison was used as an internment camp: women and children were put in a separate wing, and all were given enough food. When in 1944 all of Changi Prison came to be used for prisoners of war, the internees were moved to another camp, where there was hunger.

Finally, it is notable that, of all the areas we have mentioned so far, there was only one where the men and youths were separated from the women and other children. This was Singapore, which came under the authority of Field Marshall Terauchi. Men and women were always separated in the areas under his control. But in Singapore and in Burma (where no Dutch citizens were interned) and in British Borneo under the control of the Japanese army, men and women were held in the same camp complex. Van Velden writes:

> They knew a little about each other and occasionally caught a glimpse of one another in the distance, and sometimes the Japanese allowed an official meeting lasting several hours. They could help each other out: the women did sewing for the men, the men did the heaviest work for the women, such as digging and cutting wood, and sent them part of the crops from the gardens. In the camps in Burma and Singapore the men cooked for the women throughout their internment. (Van Velden 1963:283-4.)

On the Philippines, in Hong Kong, in Nationalist China and in Japan itself there was no question of families being separated. There was only one region where this separation was complete: the Dutch East Indies. Through this alone, the internees there had a harder time than those in the other areas controlled by Japan. Moreover, the number of internees in the East Indies was by far the greatest. In total over 125,000 civilians were interned in Japanese-controlled territory: about 100,000 in the Dutch East Indies, a little over 25,000 elsewhere. It should also be noted that, as became apparent in the chapter on the prisoners of war, the representatives of the Protecting Powers and the delegates of the International Red Cross had no freedom of movement in the Nampo region and could not send reports to their governments or Geneva except to a limited extent in French Indo-China and Thailand. The Dutch and East Indies authorities outside the Indies had no clear picture of what was happening to their citizens there. Van der Star, Stokhuyzen and Van der Veen sailed from Priok at the beginning of July 1942, when many of the men on Java had been interned, often in prisons, but not yet the women and children. De Haas, who left East Java with his group at the end of September, had read in a newspaper in Bandung that all Dutch men were to be interned and that the Japanese authorities were considering giving Dutch women and children 'the necessary protection'. He had also heard that on East Java large groups of Dutch and Dutch Eurasian men had been taken to a camp in Kesilir. He knew nothing more about the internment of women and children. In Japanese broadcasts, heard in Australia, all that was said on this point was that women and children had been placed in 'protected districts'. Were these districts closed off and guarded, and thus in fact internment centres? The Dutch and East Indies authorities suspected as much, but could not prove it, in part because in 1943 and 1944 they failed completely to establish secret communications with the Indies. The result was that, while of all internees those in the Indies were by far the worst off, the governments of the United States and Great Britain were responsible for the fact that a disproportionately small part of the few aid shipments permitted by the Japanese went to the East Indies. Thus when deciding how to divide up the large consignment sent to Vladivostok (and from there to Nakhodka) at the end of 1944, it was assumed that there were 33,000 internees in the Indies, whereas the true figure was three times that.

Two phases

There were two differences between the internments on the Outer Islands and those on Java. The first is that on the Outer Islands not only the Dutch but also as a rule many Dutch Eurasians were interned initially, whereas on Java most of the Eurasians were exempted. The second is that on the Outer Islands the internment process was soon completed, whereas on Java the internment of Dutch men did not really get under way until mid-1942, and the women and children did not have to move to the 'protected districts' until late 1942 to mid-1943. The beginning of these internments has been dealt with in Chapter I – here we shall confine ourselves to recalling that on Java on the orders of General Imamura in April 1942, after there had been earlier arrests in March in Batavia, all prominent Dutch and Dutch Eurasians were picked up. Many of the Eurasians and all who earned less than 300 guilders a month were released. From May 1942, starting in Batavia, men (and boys aged 17 and over) were rounded up in raids. The rest of the internment process took place in the second half of 1942 and later on the basis of the special registration whereby all 'foreigners' had to acquire an identity card.[12] The forced removal of women and young children occurred in Batavia in October 1942, and later elsewhere on Java, and the 'protected districts' and other internment centres on Java were not overcrowded in the beginning.

On Celebes and on Dutch Borneo[13] the internment camps at first came under the Japanese armed forces, that is, the navy, but from early 1943 they came under the navy civil administration, the Minseibu. On Java and Sumatra, however, the men's camps initially came under the army administration and the women's camps under the indigenous administration; but from April 1944 all camps came directly under the Japanese armies – on Java the 16th and on Sumatra the 25th. In the first, 'civilian', phase, the internment camps, insofar as they were not prisons, were guarded by the Indonesian police; in the second, 'military', phase, the guards were Japanese soldiers or members of the fiercely anti-Western, indigenous auxiliary corps set up by the Japanese. On Sumatra they were sometimes soldiers of the pro-Japanese 'Indian National Army', which consisted of several thousand troops from British India, most of whom had been captured during the Japanese conquest of the Malay Peninsula and Singapore. In the second phase the camp staff (the commandant and his assistants) was made up of soldiers from the Japanese army – Japanese, Koreans and Formosans.

The change in the administration of the camps on Java and Sumatra resulted from Japanese defeats. The advances of the forces under Nimitz and MacArthur led the Japanese authorities to decide[14] to increase the isolation of the internees; they were to have no contact at all with the indigenous population and the camps were to be run on military lines. In one of the women's camps on Central Java, one internee, H. Helfferich-Koch (1981:120-1), wrote in her diary:

[12]   Most of the Dutch were classified as *Belanda-totok*, most of the Dutch Eurasians as *Belanda-Indo*, but there were also cases in which Dutch people born in the East Indies were registered as *Belanda-Indo* and Eurasians born in the Netherlands as *Belanda-totok*.
[13]   That is to say, South and East Borneo, because, as mentioned, the internees from West Borneo were taken to British Borneo.
[14]   This is laid down in a decree signed by Emperor Hirohito and dated 7 November 1943.

> We've come out of the frying pan into the fire. The military authorities are now in
> charge. Consequently, we are to be treated just like soldiers. Roll call is at 6 am,
> followed by physical exercise and roll call again at 9.15 pm. [...] [We] hear that
> we're not allowed to cook anything ourselves, not even boil water to make coffee
> (which isn't real coffee of course) or tea, but that from now on everything will
> come from the central kitchen. Soldiers don't cook for themselves either. [...] All
> the curtains and screens around our sleeping areas [...] must go, together with
> all large cupboards. All the beds and small cupboards must be placed in a row:
> the beds in the middle of the rooms, the cupboards along the walls. So there is no
> longer any possibility of privacy.

Moreover, the Japanese authorities wanted to ensure that, in the event of
Allied landings, the internees could not assist the invading troops in any
way.[15] On Java, as described in the previous chapter, almost all the prisoners of war were assembled on the Bandung plateau, and the internees were
brought together in similar concentrations.

Some of the men interned on South Sumatra had already been moved in
September 1943 to the prison in the principal town on Bangka, Muntok. In
November 1944 the women and children from South Sumatra were moved
to the same place, where they were housed in barracks. All these internees
did not stay on Bangka. In March and April 1945 they were again moved,
this time to an abandoned rubber estate at Lubuklinggau (for all the places
on Sumatra mentioned, see Map 7), deep in the interior. The internees from
Sumatra's west coast were also taken into the hinterland, to Bangkinang, an
abandoned rubber estate on the road to Pekanbaru. Also transferred were
the internees from North and East Sumatra, most of whom had been brought
together in camps in the Alas Valley and near Medan, Belawan and Brastagi
in the course of 1942 and 1943. Not far from Rantauparapat the men found
themselves in Siringoringo Camp, which was located in a desolate, virtually
uninhabited area in a marshy valley. The women and children went to Aik
Pamienke Camp, surrounded by sombre rubber trees.

Even before the army was made responsible for the internment camps,
those on East Java had already been abandoned: the women and children
were all in camps on Central and West Java, and the men all on the Bandung
plateau on West Java. In 1944 and 1945 the army organized more moves.
The number of women's camps was reduced (thus those that remained were
more crowded); all men aged over 60 and all boys aged 11 and over were
sent (on West Java) to the men's camps or (on Central Java) to separate camps
in Semarang and Ambarawa (for all the places on Java mentioned see Map
8). Chronic and seriously ill patients were also sent from the camps on the

---

[15]   This same concern evidently lay behind the decision around September 1943 to end the
employment of nearly all Nippon workers.

Bandung plateau to Semarang and Ambarawa. Other patients were sent in May 1945 to hospital camps at Bandung and Batavia. Can a pattern be discerned in these movements? Perhaps this: the Japanese concentrated all the men who posed no threat on Java's north coast, where the women's camps also were, the largest in Batavia and Semarang; the men whom they saw as potential helpers of the Allies were held in the interior. From the outset they had treated the prominent figures among these men (civil servants with the rank of assistant resident or higher) as a special group. In 1942 they had been confined with others in Struiswijk Prison in Batavia and in mid-1943 in Sukamiskin Prison at Bandung; in 1944 they were put in the Baros (Cimahi) KNIL barracks, which had previously held prisoners of war. We shall return to this group of prominent figures.

Many of the internees were moved about a great deal, concludes Van Velden (1963:309):

> Every move [some are described below] was in itself a disaster. Everybody lost some of their belongings; lugging things about [...] sometimes used up their last strength; the sick could not be cared for. When they were finally ready for departure, they had to keep the children together, and stand for hours in the sun or the rain to be counted and recounted. On arrival in the new camp they were often searched and beaten. When they were at last inside, if the camp was unoccupied, they had to clean it first and find out for themselves how to get food. If there were other internees already in the camp, they would do their best to welcome the newcomers, but it took an effort to reorganize their own corner, and adapt to different rules and new companions. Every adjustment cost energy and many of them had none left. They often lost their best friend [...] during a move. And of all the costly things in an internment camp, a good friend was the most valuable.

It was not only because of the stricter confinement, the introduction of a more military regime and the frequent moves that the second, 'military' phase was an ordeal for those interned on Java and Sumatra; it must also be remembered that 1944 and 1945 were the years of the worst food shortages. In itself this need not have had disastrous consequences for the internees: the two Japanese armies had large stocks of food and could make available from them what was needed, as well as being able to buy any food or other goods that were required at the official, low prices. A precondition, however, was that the officers responsible for running the camps in the East Indies[16] had to be inclined, as the authorities in Japan and the commandant of Kampili, Yamaji, were, to take care of the internees as well as possible, or at least in accordance with international law. Most were not so inclined and from this arose the des-

---

[16]   It is not known under which field officer the internment camps (treated as the equivalent of prisoner-of-war camps) on Sumatra came. On Java it was the successor to General Saito (who was transferred to Singapore in March 1944), Colonel Masayuki Nakata.

perate conditions seen in the East Indies, and only there to that extent.

There were several hundred internment centres in the East Indies: shed complexes, prisons, city districts, coolie quarters, school buildings, barracks, bivouacs, forts, hospitals, asylums, orphanages, sanatoriums, hotels, exhibition halls, factories, monasteries, boarding schools, cinemas, stables, warehouses, churches, resthouses (pasanggrahan) – Van Velden was able to identify a total of 225 (Van Velden 1963:525-43). Many were used for only a short time, others for nearly three years. Each of these places has its own history, as do each of the German Konzentrationslager and each of the hundreds of Aussenkommandos belonging to them. This study provides a broad overview and so the general aspects of the internment camps will be described first, and only afterwards a few unusual camps or groups on the Outer Islands or Java. Each of the approximately 100,000 internees had his or her own history in the years of the Japanese occupation, although not perhaps consciously experienced by the youngest children. For almost all of them it meant a decline into a misery that they would previously have thought impossible, and some experienced this decline as a continuously descending line, while for others dramatic events punctuated life in the camps. Individual experiences will not be ignored in this account: on the contrary, they will illustrate, supplement and balance the overall view.

Before going on to that view, it is worth pointing out one factor that must always be kept in mind when reading the section 'General aspects' and indeed the other sections of this chapter. This is the tropical climate with its exhausting heat and no less exhausting humidity. Prior to their internment, the majority of the internees had been able to protect themselves in relatively cool, comfortable homes. In most of the camps, however, they were exposed to the elements: the burning sun, the heat, the clammy oppressiveness and the tropical downpours that turned the dusty ground into a quagmire in the monsoon months. Only in the mountains was there occasionally some relief from the heat. Not that life there was more pleasant! In July 1943 a woman in Ambarawa (in the mountains south of Semarang) wrote in her diary:

> There's a gale blowing and the wind howls through our thin frocks and along our bare legs. We're not exactly dressed for life in such a raw mountain climate. It seems that Ambarawa is notorious for its fall winds that [...] dance round here as if in a bowl. (Helfferich-Koch 1981:68.)

A month later:

> The heaviest rain showers alternate with oppressive heat, but the gales are the worst thing. [...] No one has clothing for this climate. Everyone spends their rare free moments trying to make better clothing, especially for the children, and we've all started knitting. But there's hardly any wool to be had. (Helfferich-Koch 1981:80.)

Thus the tropical climate – irritatingly unchanging in some places, irritatingly unpredictable in others – was for many internees (probably more for the old than the young) an additional ordeal. The camp diaries do not contain that many complaints about it: the climate was simply part of the natural environment which did not receive a great deal of attention.

Nor is there a great deal of complaining in the diaries about a second general factor: the duration of internment, which must also always be kept in mind. 'History', I wrote in the foreword to one of my books on the German occupation of the Netherlands, 'attempts to describe the past – but how can I express in words the *length*, the agonizingly slow passing of those five years of occupation?' The same applies to the three years of internment by the Japanese. Years are abstract: it is more real to speak of over a thousand days and over a thousand nights. Those years were very, very long, unbearably long.

Readers may notice that in illustrating our general view the words of women are more often used than those of men. This is easily explained: more women than men published an account of their camp experiences. Thus it can be stated here that, broadly speaking, the men faced two extra hardships. First, many of them were initially held in prisons. Second, only the women were allowed to take some furniture and other possessions with them, at least to some of the larger women and children's camps. The male internees generally had nothing with them except underwear. In most of the men's camps they did not have 'normal' tables, chairs, beds or cupboards. Thus life there was even more primitive than in the women's camps. The reader should bear this in mind.

General aspects

The internment camps were Japanese camps – what happened there cannot be separated from the mentality of the Japanese at that time. Here a distinction must be drawn between the higher authorities who issued the regulations and the lower ranks who enforced them.

The regulations (only those from the period in which the camps came under the Japanese army have been preserved) do not seem severe at first glance. At the beginning of November 1943 the Department of War in Tokyo issued a document (text in Van Velden 1963:562) that was in line with practice in Japan itself. The principal articles were as follows:

> Army internees shall be treated with justice, taking into consideration their customs and manners, and no insults or maltreatment shall be imposed upon them.
> The army internment camp shall be housed in buildings which are adequate

enough to prevent the escape or mischief of army internees and which are adequate for the maintenance of their health.

Army internees shall be put to practical use by giving them suitable work. However, they shall not be compelled to work except on work connected with administration, internal organization, and the maintenance of the camp.

As a rule the pay of army internees shall be the same as that received by prisoners of war who are non-commissioned officers.[17]

Adequate medical supplies will be furnished to the army internment camp.

From these principles laid down by Tokyo followed regional regulations. In discussing these documents, Van Velden rightly emphasized Article I of the regulations (text in Van Velden 1963:565-70) applying to army camps on Java, since it revealed most clearly 'the curious Japanese attitude' evident in all the regional regulations. Article I reads:

> The internees must be grateful for the special favour of being protected by the Japanese army and they must obey the orders of the chief commandant of the internment camps.[18] They must comply with the regulations and do their best to maintain order in the camp and to further their well-being.

Thus what came first was the obedience required of every member of Japanese society: the internees were not to do as they wished but to accept their fate with cheerful diligence. According to the regulations applying on Sumatra (text in Van Velden 1963:570-2), they were 'to lead an orderly life and exercise self-discipline in order to keep up morale. To achieve this they must carry out their work of their own free will.' This is a curious formulation, combining 'must' and 'free will', but for the Japanese this was not a contradiction: the 'must', the sense of duty, had been so drilled into them that what began as a regulation became the exercise of their own will.

The regional regulations also contained provisions dealing with the organization and daily routine in the internment camps. They were to be simply furnished; a roll call was to be taken in the morning and the evening; all Japanese soldiers and civilian officials were to be acknowledged in the prescribed way, that is, with a bow; declarations of obedience were to be made and confirmed by one fingerprint (in one of the women's camps on Sumatra this rule was applied to babies and infants);[19] guards were to be posted at night; the Japanese commandants were to designate camp leaders and permit religious gatherings (on Java they were forbidden); no diaries were to be kept and only approved books might be read; the internees were permitted

---

[17]   They generally received 15 or 25 cents for each day of fatigues.
[18]   In other words, Colonel Nakata.
[19]   In one of the women's camps on Java in April 1944 several women refused to swear obedience to the Japanese; they were punished by being locked up for a few days.

to cultivate vegetable gardens and keep chickens, goats, cows and pigs; cooking had to be done at a central kitchen; the internees were to be paid for their
work and were allowed to keep no more than 10 guilders of the money they
brought with them – whatever they had in excess would be saved; letters
would be censored, and so on. These were only the most important rules, but
one more must be mentioned. This was an article in the regulations for Java
which read: 'Everyday conversations must be conducted in Malay' – this rule
was nowhere applied.[20]

It was intended that the Japanese authorities would supply the camps
with sufficient food – nothing was said about clothing, footwear or household
articles such as soap. 'The reason was', according to Van Velden (1963:127),
'that the Japanese took the view that the internees had lived a life of luxury
and had enough of everything to last for years'. Nor was there any mention
of the right of complaint: it was not appropriate, thought the Japanese, for
internees to complain.

In this respect, as in others, the regulations revealed a mentality that was
alien to the internees, and the alienation was only underlined when high-
ranking Japanese appeared in the camps to explain to them why they must
be 'grateful for the special favour' granted them. Writing after the war, W.H.J.
Elias, who was interned from November 1942 in Bandung and from August
1943 in Cimahi, described what one of these explanations was like:

> The speaker begins by climbing on to a raised platform, for he is usually smaller
> than his audience. He folds his arms and peers round to see if everyone is neatly
> lined up and paying attention. Then he grasps his sword, comes down from the
> platform and walks along the rows to inspect his prospective audience, dealing
> out a kick or a blow here and there, before climbing back up and [...] beginning.
>   [...] After he has heard the sound of his own voice for about a quarter of an
> hour, the interpreter translates his speech into two or three short phrases. Then he
> resumes emitting his harsh monkey-noises. No one understands his words, which
> are underscored by the rolling of crossed eyes and foaming at the mouth. Short
> barks of monosyllables that bear scarcely any resemblance to a human language.
> (Elias 1946:165-6.)

These hate-filled words doubtless express the feelings of many internees on
such an occasion. But there is also no doubt that they ignore the fact that the
high-ranking Japanese was sincerely convinced that the worthless internees
who had lost their fatherland, and thus had no right to anything ('You are like
shreds of paper, blown away by the wind,' the Japanese commandant of the

---

[20]   Many of these rules did not apply on Sumatra: there it was forbidden to cultivate vegetable
gardens; no wages were paid for work; correspondence was not allowed; there was no electricity in the camps outside the towns; and there was no requirement to learn Japanese or sing the
Japanese national anthem.

Baros men's camp at Cimahi once said) (Van Velden 1963:223), ought to be grateful that he had deigned to address them.

Another telling account describes the speech by a Japanese colonel on 21 November 1942 in the Pulu Brayan camp for women and children near Medan. One of the internees, T. van Eijk-van Velzen (1983:49-50), wrote in her diary:

> Today we received a message to assemble at four o'clock at the office. The gentleman kept us waiting for nearly an hour. All that time we stood in the burning sun. Meanwhile the Jap in charge of us taught us how to bow. In the end we couldn't help laughing so much that he suddenly rushed off inside.
>
> [...] At last, at five o'clock, the colonel came. A table was brought out and then a smaller table on top of it, and the colonel and the interpreter, who spoke Dutch, stood on that. I can't write down all the comments, but we had great fun. It was like a stage play performed on top of a table. He began by saying he had heard that reports had reached us about the Americans. They were said to be carrying out landings and pushing back the Japanese. 'I'm sorry for you', he said, 'but that is impossible. The Americans will never come.' [...] We would remain interned for the duration of the war, and we must take good care of ourselves. 'Victory will be ours, of course', he said. Furthermore, our gratitude left a lot to be desired. Some ladies were grateful occasionally (how is that possible?), but not grateful enough, because we soon forget about it again.
>
> We had to restrain our laughter. They really are like children, but malign ones.

Two worlds, two cultures, confronted each other. The Japanese did not understand the internees, nor the internees the Japanese. Moreover, they did not understand each other's language – only rarely did a Japanese speak Dutch or an internee Japanese.[21] Nonetheless, relations were highly charged on both sides: the Japanese felt far superior to all the impoverished Whites, and nearly all the latter felt a deep hatred and contempt for the Japanese. Regulations that stemmed from Japanese culture seemed to them purely arbitrary. In Japan marriage partners were generally chosen by the family; affection played only a minor role in the relationship between husband and wife, and it was considered unseemly for married couples to have physical contact, for example kissing, in the presence of others. The Japanese could not abandon of these norms. In December 1942 in Batavia permission was granted for short visits to the men interned in Struiswijk and Bukit Duri Prisons and in Adek Camp (the visits did not, in fact, take place), but the wives, children, fathers, mothers and fiancées were told in advance that 'embraces and kisses were absolutely forbidden'.[22]

---

[21]   With some Japanese it was possible to communicate to a slight extent in English or Indonesian.

[22]   'Mededeling van de Commissie voor Ge nterneerden te Batavia', 4 December 1942, in Brugmans 1960:418.

When, as on British Borneo, men and women were in adjacent camps, they were not allowed to wave to each other or even nod. There or elsewhere, men might be permitted to enter a women's camp to do some work, but even if their wives were there, embraces were forbidden. In turn, some Japanese behaviour appeared to the internees to be improper. In Japan it was normal to undress in the presence of strangers before bathing, and Japanese men were used to going about nearly naked indoors when it was hot. Women internees were upset on being received by an almost naked Japanese commandant. 'They were miles apart', writes Van Velden (1963:419), 'in attitudes and customs, and neither party made an effort to understand the other'.

There were only a few exceptions to this general rule, in particular Kampili, where Commandant Yamaji did his best to respect the attitudes and religious beliefs of the internees.

There were very few Japanese staff in the camps. The smaller camps had one or two Japanese, the larger ones slightly more, but even in a women and children's camp like the Cideng district of Batavia, in which there were eventually over 10,000 inmates, the staff never numbered more than ten. How they behaved depended to a large extent on the character of the Japanese commandant.

The commandant of Kampili, Sergeant Yamaji, was not the only one to be favourably judged. The internment camps on British Borneo (which also held the internees from the west of Dutch Borneo) were under the command of a Japanese officer who behaved humanely.[23] From April 1943 to April 1944, Cideng had a commandant who, according to an ex-internee in April 1946, 'always ensured that all orders from Headquarters were interpreted as mildly as possible. In practice he always approved applications for permits. [...] He was always decent.'[24] The first commandant of the Unie *kampong* men's internment camp (at Belawan on Sumatra) was 'not so bad. He does no good and he does no harm. [...] We call him Dozy.' (Brandt 1947:42.) At the beginning of July 1945 the Glugur women and children's camp at Medan got a new commandant who was 'a decent fellow'. According to Van Eijk-van Velzen (1983:149):

> I've never heard a good word said about a Jap, but you can't possibly hold any-thing against this chap. [...] He really takes care of us and helps out everywhere. He even works with us. He's in high spirits all day long; he hurries you up, but in a nice way. He says that we must work hard, but he will make sure we get plenty of food. We've just been given extra rice.

---

[23] Out of a total of about 530 internees, 30 died, and on Dutch Borneo 30 out of about 240.
[24] Dutch D[isplaced] P[ersons] Camp Kandy (Ceylon), 'Verslag van verhoor van L. Perelaer', 2 April 1946, p. 3 (NIOD IC, 16,289).

Just over a year earlier, on the other hand, at that same Medan, one of the leaders at the Belawan Estate men's camp who had drawn the attention of a Japanese to the rising death rate was told: 'Let them kick the bucket' (Leffelaar 1963:224). It was the same in the camp at Ambarawa, where about 2,000 elderly men from West and Central Java were concentrated at the start of 1945. According to D.M.G. Koch (1956:245), the founder in 1938 of the journal *Kritiek en Opbouw* (Criticism and Advancement), the only European publication in the Dutch East Indies that was critical of the colonial government:

> From the outset the number of deaths was seven to eight a day, and it rose gradually to fourteen. At that point I went to the Japanese commandant to ask him to improve the food supply. He replied that when we got up to fifteen deaths a day he would think about providing better food. If the liberation had come three months later, the whole camp would have been dead.

In the women and children's camp Halmaheira (one of the camps at Semarang) a Japanese camp head arrived who struck so hard that according to one of the internees, Eliza Thomson (1965:52):

> he was immediately given the nickname *Satengah mati*, meaning 'half dead'. [He] was an intensely nasty type. Whenever he passed a woman, she ran the risk that he would stub out his cigarette in her nostril or between her fingers. He also often ran his finger over women's faces to see if they were powdered. If they were, he did not hesitate to beat his victims till they were half dead.

The commandant of Cideng from April 1944, Lieutenant Kenichi Sonei, became especially notorious. He had behaved highly erratically before as commandant of the prisoner-of-war complex in the former barracks of the 10th Battalion of the KNIL at Batavia. General Scholten, who was moved away in January 1943 as a member of the Special Party, called him 'the least malign Japanese camp commandant we encountered', but even he had noticed that from one moment to the next Sonei could get into a blind fury in that peculiar transformation so often seen in the Japanese:

> Sometimes you could start a normal conversation with him, and then he would suddenly burst out in anger, blaming us for not having committed harakiri. Once he swept the draught- and chessboards from the tables with his sword, broke up the chairs and benches, and screamed at us that we were loafing about as if there wasn't a war in which Japan was fighting for its very survival! (Scholten 1971:82.)

After Scholten's departure Sonei gave full reign to his anger on many occasions. He ill-treated Ambonese who were reluctant to become *heiho*, made healthy and sick prisoners of war stand for hours for roll calls (once for 18 hours), and often personally gave officers a beating. He also closed the camp canteen at the slightest excuse. As commandant of Cideng women and children's camp he was even more merciless. Punishment roll calls were the order of the day and once he allowed big monkeys to enter the camp and bite the women and children. At the end of September 1944 he ordered a roll call for all the women and children, including the sick, that lasted from 7 pm to midnight and the following day another from 1.30 to 11 pm. In June 1945, after having all the bread buried in the ground, he allowed no food to be distributed for three days. Later that month he was promoted to captain and appointed head of the office for all prisoner-of-war camps on Java. On the 20th he gave up his post in Cideng; he stayed on for a few days, probably to show his successor how to conduct himself. On 21 June a rumour spread in the camp that peace had come. Dozens of women went to the camp fence to exchange clothes for food with the indigenous people who had gathered there. Sonei was alerted by one of the interned women who lived in a house next to his with her daughter, his mistress. The first thing he did was to take two of the young women who had made the illegal contact and bang their heads together. Then he shaved off their hair brutally. They were put in the burning sun for hours, while the blood ran down their faces. Next he demanded that the barrack heads supply him with 300 women who had engaged in clandestine bartering. The 300, among them several volunteers, reported to him. They were mistreated for an evening and a whole night, while Sonei drank a bottle of whisky. More than 50 of them had their hair shaved off. It was cut by Indonesian *heiho* and then Sonei went over their bald heads with a pair of clippers. According to one internee, 'The screams of the women and Sonei's bellowing went on till morning.'[25]

It was best to suffer this abuse without making a sound. 'Hitting back', writes Van Velden (1963:430) 'was a disaster. It did happen on occasion, even in a women's camp. The culprit was so severely punished that he or she barely survived and the camp usually suffered collective punishment as well.'

As mentioned, in the 'civilian' phase the women and children's camps were guarded by Indonesian policemen. As a rule they were not ill-disposed to the internees – they turned a blind eye to a great deal. Later in 1943 the Japanese brought in younger Indonesians who had been recruited as *heiho* and they were stricter, but even then guards could be found who were ready to help smuggle all kinds of goods, principally food, for payment.

There was little physical abuse in the years 1942 and 1943, but more later on. These punishments were a routine part of the training of recruits to the Japanese army. Sometimes the victim's lower jaw or arm was broken. In the event of a punishment roll call (which could last many hours, as we have seen) cases of sunstroke were not uncommon.

Roll calls were a torment, even when not ordered as a punishment. They

[25]   M. Leatenua-van Os, 'Verslag', 27 May 1946, p. 12 (NIOD IC 47,538).

came to be a fixed element in the day when the army took over the camps.
As in the prisoner-of-war camps, the Japanese had problems counting. This
was done in the morning and the evening. The internees had to form up in
rows, make the prescribed bow, and were then usually counted by their own
barrack head (in Japanese!).[26] The figures were then reported to the Japanese
commandant; only when all was correct were the internees allowed to stand
up straight again. It was a twice daily annoyance that had to be borne with
inward resilience. A camp song[27] written in one of the women and children's
camps on West Java put it this way:

> We must bow to the Jap:
> Halt! Face front! And bend, bend!
> And if you don't bend, you're floored,
> Something inside must be broken!
> Will he ever succeed?
> We bend like the slender reed,
> We bend, but we don't break!

Another annoyance was the sentry duty which the internees were required
to do from time to time (once a week or a fortnight). This was especially irk-
some because when they encountered the Japanese sentry they had to explain
in Japanese that all was well. Many people had trouble remembering these
phrases in Japanese, and if they made a mistake in speaking them punishment might follow.

In the 'military' phase in the internment camps inspections were held as
often as in the prisoner-of-war camps. They were carried out by Japanese
soldiers who looked for money or goods, particularly the valuables that every
internee tried to conceal. Early in July 1944 a sudden inspection was held
in one of the camps at Ambarawa. H. Helfferich-Koch gave the following
description:

> It is 6.30 am. There is the normal busy scene of bringing out the bedding, tidying
> up and sweeping, while some of the people in our room get dressed behind the
> *klambu* [mosquito net] round their bed and the boys who have come over from
> their barracks walk in and out. Suddenly, above all the other sounds, we hear the
> thud of heavy shoes, rough voices, banging, stamping. Like a swarm of angry
> wasps a horde of Nippon soldiers force their way into the barrack, banging their
> short rifles against the door and hammering on the floor, yapping and making gut-

[26]   The men interned in Palembang were at first allowed to count in Dutch. Since the Japanese
did not understand, they turned 'one', 'two', 'three' and so on into 'heck', 'blast', 'damn' and so
on. 'Those of us who were not prepared for this', said an engineer from the merchant navy, 'had
terrible trouble not to burst out laughing. The Jap clicked his heels, saluted and made an about
turn.' (J.W. de Roever 1951:376.)
[27]   Text in Brugmans 1960:427.

tural noises. This time they really have caught us unaware. They chase us outside. Before we realize what is happening, we have all been driven out of the barrack towards the main road. But in that split second before they reach us, I snatch the tiny handkerchief containing a valuable ring and a bracelet from under my pillow; and pop it inside my dress. Whatever we're holding we have to drop. When we reach the road, we merge into the stream of slowly moving people going towards the end of the camp.

There they had to wait.

The sun gets steadily hotter, now it burns mercilessly. We wait and wait and thirst torments us, worse than hunger. And slowly the hours pass.

[...] Just when we think we can't stand it any more, there is movement on the other side of the crowd and word reaches us: 'We can go out, but first we have to be searched!' Slowly we press towards the opening where two Nippon soldiers and two of our women stand. One by one we have to go through the narrow gate, and watched closely by the Nips the women run their hands over us, patting and feeling to see if we've hidden anything. The tension among us is terrible, for everyone has hidden something in her clothes.

[...]. The Nips stand very close and I walk slowly, shuffling, so that the handkerchief I've now pinned as low as possible to my underwear will not be visible through my thin, worn dress. What if she feels it [...]? She does, but she gives me a wink and lets us pass quickly.

Everyone was allowed back into the barrack.

Here we find everything in indescribable chaos such as we have never experienced. The mattresses have been slit open, kapok is still swirling round everywhere, nothing is in its right place. Everything, absolutely everything, has been pulled out of the cases and thrown in all directions. Dirty soldier's boots have trampled all over the sheets we washed so carefully and laboriously. Portrait frames lie in fragments on the floor amid torn and smeared papers. My diary is a complete mess; the pages have been torn out. (Helfferich-Koch 1981:143-5.)

Inspections like this were more frequent in the 'military' than in the 'civilian' phase: the army had set stricter rules and enforced them more diligently. One of these rules, as mentioned above, was that cooking was no longer allowed in the barracks, but many did their best to hang on to their own gas or electric stove or simple chafing dish – these were confiscated during inspections. Receipts were often given for goods seized. Little faith was placed in them, but in many camps after a while some goods were returned on production of a receipt. They were not always permanently returned: later an order might come to hand everything in again. No one ever knew what lay ahead.

Just as the prisoner-of-war camps had a senior officer, so the internment camps had a camp leader. This was a difficult, even perilous post. If something went wrong, the leader was held responsible and might be punished on the spot.[28] He or she was sometimes appointed by the Japanese commandant and sometimes chosen by the internees. Normally, the leader set up committees to deal, for example, with the food supply, medical care, schooling, youth clubs, religious matters, recreation, finance and the division of labour. The heads of these committees, together with the leader, made up the camp executive. Their position was 'extremely difficult' according to Koch (1954:577-8.):

> If the executive refused to humble itself for the Japanese commandant, the whole camp often suffered the consequences. If it was more obliging than was consistent in the view of many with the demands of honour, then it was often possible to secure concessions which benefited all the internees. It was extremely difficult to strike the right balance between pride, which was dangerous, and compliance, which was seen as spineless and unprincipled. The camp leader needed to show a great deal of tact and personal courage, and far from all of them had these qualities. One might ignore justified complaints and requests out of fear, while another submitted them, was given a thrashing, and then presented the same request or complaint again.

'There was one camp leader', writes Elias (1946:149), 'who was stabbed through the arm with a bayonet, went off to get bandaged and came back to raise the matter again.' The Japanese concerned showed respect for this attitude, but he could also have treated it as a case of grave insubordination in which the Kempeitai would have to be involved.

One of the hardest tasks for every executive was keeping order in the camp: order among the children, who, in the absence of the fathers, soon became unruly in the special conditions of the camp (the isolation, the lack of space, the monotony of everyday life), but also among the adults, among whom there were always those who broke the rules, often to everyone's disadvantage. What punishments could be imposed? Sometimes the offenders were denied access to the camp shops (if there were any) for a certain period, or given extra fatigues, for example cleaning vegetables, or told to move within the camp. In the most serious cases, repeated theft for instance, the name of the thief was made known.[29] In Cihapit Camp at Bandung, which on occasion held about 14,000 women and children, punishments were decided by a supervisory body consisting of five women. According to a report by one of the leaders of this camp:

> In only two of the hundreds of cases that were dealt with [not that many in proportion] did the supervisory body call on the Japanese to enforce the punishment imposed. Both cases involved a move made necessary by the need to make room in the camp; a refusal jeopardized a whole chain of moves. It was characteristic of the

---

[28]	The interpreter present on such an occasion might also be punished, especially if he or she had dared to translate into Japanese a remark to which the camp commandant took offence.
[29]	In a few camps there were cells in which serious offenders were confined for a time.

disgraceful mentality of the women concerned that one word from the Japanese was enough to make them obey like lambs.[30]

There was a great deal of work to be done in the camps, in the first place for the camp itself. Work was allocated as fairly as possible by the camp leadership. In the 'civilian' phase indigenous workers could be brought in, but this was no longer allowed in the 'military' phase, which began in early April 1944. According to Van Velden (1963:332-3):

> This meant that all the work had to be done by the internees themselves, including in the women's camps. Thus, besides the ordinary housework [in itself a hard task that had to be done without the help of servants, to which most of the women had become accustomed], repairing houses and barracks, building central kitchens [cooking had to be done for the whole camp], collecting refuse, emptying cesspits and cleaning drains, moving chests and furniture, lugging 40-kilo bags of rice for the monthly rations. [...] Other tasks that were especially heavy for the women were chopping up tree trunks, stoking the primitive ovens of the kitchens, boiling and moving heavy drums of rice or porridge, digging graves for the dead, [...] digging air-raid trenches, and burning all the rubbish, which involved standing all day in the sun beside a fire that had to be out by dusk because of the blackout rules. Furthermore, there was the digging of waste ground full of stones for use as gardens, and carrying buckets of water for the kitchen or garden. Then there were the countless moves within the camp, not only when transports arrived or left, but also for the many internal reorganizations, for example when the camp hospital was moved (in Cihapit Camp this happened seven times) or expanded, or when the camp was reduced in size as a security or punishment measure, or when the Japanese staff needed more space. In addition, there were still the ordinary tasks in the kitchen and hospital.

The best overview of the types of work and the deployment of labour is provided by the figures for the Cihapit women and children's camp as of 27 February 1945, when the camp, after many had been moved away, still held 4,853 internees, including 1,210 children aged under 10. At that time 77 women were involved in the camp leadership and managing the various departments, and they had 27 orderlies to assist them. In total 2,877 women had a particular task in the camp (women aged over 55 and those with a child younger than 14 months were excused): 800 (the largest group) were assigned to child care, 240 to looking after infants, 305 to mess duties, 297 to cleaning vegetables, 112 to the medical service, 136 to street sweeping, and 410 were 'furniture women' (helping to move furniture left behind in the original homes). These were only the largest groups.[31]

---

[30]   M.H. Diepeveen-Lindner, 'Verslag van het vrouwenkamp Tjihapit', 1 February 1946, p. 8 (NIOD IC, 34,961).
[31]   M.H. Diepeveen-Lindner, 'Verslag van het vrouwenkamp Tjihapit', 1 February 1946, Appendix 5 (NIOD IC, 34,961).

Moving furniture about, though useful for the Japanese, was relatively innocent, but even in the 'civilian' phase the interned men were sometimes required to do work that directly aided the Japanese war effort, for example work on airfields that had to be carried out on pain of death. In the 'military' phase, when the work was paid for (the workers received 100 grams extra food per day and 15 cents[32]), from July 1945 men from the camps at Bandung and Cimahi had to build a new railway on the Bandung plateau. Prior to this railway work (there was a great deal of sabotage), a special team in Cimahi had to make bayonets and other military equipment. In 1944 in a camp at Bandung about 600 men were chosen for work on the Andir airfield; when it turned out that they had to build runways, on the second day some 60 internees refused to start work. The first to be questioned by the Japanese was one of the former controllers of the Kediri residency. Asked why he refused to work on Andir, he said, 'Since you want me to do military work, as a Dutchman I must refuse.' 'A brave and dignified answer' thought a fellow internee, J.M.J. Morsink, a former civil servant at the Office of the Advisor on Native Affairs.[33] The 60 who refused to work were beaten but their refusal was accepted. Morsink continued:

> That some 540 men quickly gave in to Japanese methods is understandable, but that a President of the High Court[34] should later put forward the theory that the enemy was entitled to demand this work falls short of what this observer considers acceptable.

In the 'military' phase the interned women were given work connected either with the construction of wooden ships – rope-making, producing wooden nails, peeling tree bark[35] – or with the troops' equipment – sewing clothes and gloves (according to Helfferich-Koch, the latter was 'a horribly fiddly job') (Helfferich-Koch 1981:164), knitting socks and belts, making caps or putting eyelets in them, embroidering insignia on uniforms, making mattresses. One case of a refusal to do such work is known (there may have been more). In Halmaheira Camp at Semarang in August 1944, nine women internees refused to make soldier's caps. They were first punched in the face, then interrogated for five days and beaten with clubs. They were held for four months – afterwards three of the nine died.

How was the food supply for the internees organized?

The camps were closed off: it was the responsibility of the Japanese to ensure that sufficient food was delivered. In Batavia they handed over this

---

[32]   This money was, it seems, often put in the camp fund – the internee did not actually receive any of it.
[33]   J.M.J. Morsink, 'Kort Verslag', p. 5 (ARA, Alg. Secr., Eerste zending, XXII, 45, 288).
[34]   The President of the High Court from 1937 was J. Elshout.
[35]   The bark was used to fill joints.

responsibility, as regards the closed districts for women and children (and men over 60), Kramat and Cideng, to the Gemeentelijk Europees Steuncomité (Municipal European Assistance Committee), the GESC. This committee arranged for food deliveries to be made by Indonesian and Chinese suppliers. Until late August 1943 Indonesian traders were allowed to go as far as the entrance to the two districts, and to that of a third district, Grogol, where in July 1943 the Japanese had concentrated all those from Kramat and Cideng, about 1,200 internees in total, who had no money of their own left – they were given 25 cents per person per day by the Japanese. Moreover, the GESC was allowed to set up camp shops in Kramat and Cideng and it also received permission to give every interned family of three persons 18 guilders a month (later 22.50 guilders). At the end of August 1943 the 2,500 women, children and elderly men in the Kramat camp were transferred to the Cideng camp (which at the same time was reduced to half its size and thus became considerably more crowded). Afterwards Kramat was used as an internment centre for about 3,400 men, women and children: Nippon workers and their families, women and children not of Dutch nationality (see below) and mentally ill patients. On Java at the end of August 1943, furthermore, Indonesian and Chinese traders were forbidden to go to the entrances to the camps. This was a setback but, at least as regards the camps in Batavia, not a serious one.

In general the food provided by the Japanese in the 'civilian' phase had a calorific value of about 1,600, at least on paper. In reality the internees got less: what was actually delivered was often 15 to 20% lighter than stated (thus the suppliers were swindlers or the Japanese had stolen supplies); moreover, the quality was poor or bad. Van Velden (1963:268) recounted:

> The rice and flour were full of dirt and vermin. As for vegetables, meat and fish, which were highly perishable, the quality was even more important than with rice and so the internees depended all the more on the good will of the Japanese camp authorities. In many places the vegetables sent to the camps by the Japanese were left over after the local market closed. These were of the poorest quality, and often 90% were rotten. It was the same with the meat and fish: the meat consisted largely of skin and bone, the fish was often bad.

On the other hand, in the 'civilian' phase the internees were free to buy extra food. This was arranged by the camp committees, which set up a central fund to which everyone who had been able to bring some money made a certain contribution. A great deal of food was also smuggled into the camp during the 'civilian' phase. The guards, at that time Indonesian policemen, often gave their help in return for payment, and so did the Japanese sometimes, in exchange for watches, fountain pens and jewellery. Many internees, however, negotiated directly with the local population: if they were working outside the camp they exchanged clothes for food; these exchanges also took place straight over the camp fence. There were internees who left the camp secretly at night to do business. Particularly in the women and children's camps during the 'civilian' phase, security was not tight.

This changed when the 'military' phase began in 1944. The Japanese army authorities imposed stricter checks. They also stipulated that, as mentioned, all cooking had to be done at central kitchens[36] and that all internees hand over whatever money they had (in Batavia the GESC was no longer allowed to make payments). The money thus collected (this did not happen everywhere) might be used to buy extra food, but in most camps only 4.50 guilders per month per internee could be spent in this way.[37] This amounted to 15 cents a day and, given the price rises there had been, not much could be obtained for that.

The Japanese armies had determined that from the army stocks per internee per day 100 grams of rice, 200 grams of various kinds of flour, 20 grams of sugar and 20 grams of salt should be made available. In many camps, however, sugar and salt were not seen for months, and the deliveries of rice and flour were generally 10 to 20% short of the amount laid down. This daily ration cost 8 cents. Tokyo had decided that the armies would be allowed to spend 25 cents per internee per day. The remaining 17 cents would be used for wood and additional food – vegetables (or rather vegetable waste), meat (often intestines), fish (often bad), beans, sugar and, for the babies and the sick, milk. All this meant that in most camps only about 40 cents (15 + 25) per day per internee could be spent on food and wood. The army authorities also ordered that the internees must grow as much extra food as possible for themselves. Every patch of ground that was suitable inside the camps was dug over (heavy work, especially for the women) and various vegetables were planted.

There was hunger in almost all the camps during the 'military' phase: what the army authorities supplied was too little, and the internees got less and less for the amount of money they were allowed to spend outside the camps. In most of the women and children's camps on Java in 1945 the calorific value of the food was not much above 1,000; there were also camps

---

[36]   Up to then internees had been able to cook their own extra food anywhere in the women and children's camps on gas stoves, electric appliances and charcoal burners. Later gas and then electricity were disconnected. As mentioned, cooking equipment was confiscated during inspections. 'In the end', according to one internee in the large Lampersari camp for women and children (a district of Semarang where there were about 8,000 internees), 'we were reduced to making fires. [...] The strangest things were burnt [...]: spare furniture, doors and window frames, old books and even gramophone records.' (Boissevain and Van Empel 1981:152.)
[37]   In Cideng Camp, however, the amount was 10 guilders. In Adek Camp (Batavia) in May 1944, 23 guilders per internee could be spent on additional food, and in June 1944, 16 guilders (no further information is available).

where the internees received no more than 800 calories a day. According to Van Velden (1963:349):

> The menu in many camps consisted of one meal a day made up of about 90 grams of dry rice with a sauce of vegetables mixed with herbs and grated coconut and, if available, a small fish or a spoonful of a paste made from intestines or beans. For the rest of the day they were given a piece of bread (most resembling a lump of hard rubber) or porridge made from flour or rice[38], or boiled maize, etc., depending on what the Japanese supplied. The stale maize and various kinds of beans were difficult to cook and make edible, and many could not stomach them. The additional food bought in centrally was carefully chosen for its nutritional value and consisted mainly of varieties of beans rich in protein, [...] sugar, fish, fruit and spices, but the camp suppliers often did not stick to the orders or sent poor quality produce.

The internees were powerless to do anything about such trickery. Moreover, in the 'military' phase smuggling became much more risky. The camps were now under Japanese troops and the Indonesian policemen had been replaced by Koreans and Indonesian auxiliaries, or *heiho* (who had been used previously here and there), indoctrinated with anti-Western attitudes. We shall return to the subject of smuggling.[39]

In most camps it was very difficult to make a meal out of the few provisions that were sent in. It was hard work in the kitchens! According to one internee in Lampersari camp (Semarang) (it was no different elsewhere):

[38] The greasy and stinking porridge (known in one of the women's camps on Java as 'Jap snot') normally had to be eaten without sugar or salt. 'It tasted (and smelt) so awful', according to an internee in one of the camps at Semarang, 'that we could hardly bear to gulp it down even in the worst periods of hunger. One of us usually counted to three and then we swallowed a mouthful while holding our nose.' (Vermeer-van Berkum 1980:130.) This porridge tended to promote water retention and thus contributed to the development of hunger oedema.

[39] It is worth noting that in the last week of April 1944 the Japanese authorities in Bandung granted permission to the local committee of Dutch Eurasians to take gifts to both the prisoners of war and the internees on the emperor's birthday, 29 April (a Saturday). 'It's short notice', observed Bouwer on Thursday 27 April, 'but word has spread throughout the city at fantastic speed. The shops have been overwhelmed since Wednesday. [...] Everything may be sent: clothes, rice, other foodstuffs, shoes, cigarettes, cigars, tobacco and so on. [...] The collection is turning into a fierce protest by the European population against the treatment the prisoners of war and internees have suffered at the hands of the Japanese. Those in charge of the organization are receiving floods of money from people who can't do any shopping themselves before 29 April. The loyal Indonesian and Chinese people [that is, loyal to the Dutch government] are openly making gifts. The shops are quickly emptying.' (Bouwer 1988:253.) After this collection, on 29 April, 48 carts with various gifts were driven to the camps: 24 to the prisoner-of-war camps and internment camps at Cimahi, and 24 to the internment camp for men at Bandung. The Japanese considered that the women's camp at Bandung needed no additional assistance. A few days later Bouwer wrote: 'A great deal of rice and sugar has been sent, items which were indeed the most badly needed. Over 4,000 guilders have been raised in cash. That is less than I expected. Moreover, it could not all be spent because there was simply nothing left to buy.' (Bouwer 1988:256.)

It was really an epic achievement. The women who worked there every day (and every night) beside the hot fires, normally on bare feet, and had to move the heavy cooking tanks and lift them on to shakily built walls that sometimes crumbled away, so that the boiling hot tank fell over and the hot porridge flowed over your bare feet, performed a superhuman task. Not forgetting the problem of a shortage of wood, or bad wood that wouldn't burn, and knowing that thousands of hungry women and children were waiting for the serving of the food to start – what these women and girls did was fantastic. With a minute quantity of meat and a few vegetables (usually cabbage) they managed to make an edible *sayur*. (Boissevain and Van Empel 1981:154.)

Despite these efforts there was increasing hunger.[40] This prompted the reactions seen in any confined community where there is not enough food. 'Everyone', Van Velden noted (1963:415-6),

copied out recipes; cookbooks went from hand to hand; the more exotic and peculiar the recipe, the better. People gave each other beautifully written recipe books, illustrated with drawings, as presents. […] It was, however, annoying that in most novels [several camps had a library of books brought in by internees] there was so much eating and drinking. We had never noticed this before, but now it sometimes made them unreadable.

'There were men', wrote H.L. Leffelaar (1959:87) on the basis of his experiences in various men's camps on Sumatra, 'who could lie motionless on their bed for hours with a page from *Life* in front of them with photographs of exquisite meals. […] Others kept meticulous lists of recommended eating places in Holland.' Of course there were also quarrels about food, especially if it was not shared out equally (those who regularly received proportionally more are discussed below). 'I can still see', wrote Leffelaar (1959:83):

the seance at which in Siringoringo [the camp where in the end about 2,000 men and boys from the Medan area were interned] the fish was divided. Since we no longer got any meat, this division was inordinately important. It took an entire afternoon. The contents of half a bucket were spread out on a large zinc plate. From this equal portions were made, crumb by crumb. And from their beds the men watched, furtively and as if they couldn't care less. In other barracks the portions were even weighed on a letter scale. The diary I've been keeping for the last two years is three quarters filled with notes of the grams of rice, sugar and salt we have been officially allocated. And almost every page has an account of a fierce quarrel about food.

Anything that was edible was regarded as additional food: dogs and cats, monkeys, snakes, snails, grasshoppers, bats, ants, mice and rats. A woman

---

[40]   And thirst! In many camps there was a shortage of drinking water either permanently or occasionally.

doctor interned on Sumatra found rat meat 'remarkably tender and easily digestible; the taste is good and comes somewhere between chicken and rabbit. You can safely eat the very young animals that are still bald, skin, hair and all; they are quite delicious.'[41]

Since most of the doctors and dentists practising in the East Indies were Dutch, there were certainly enough trained medical staff in the large internment camps, particularly when those who had originally not been interned were put in the camps in the second half of 1943. They were allowed to take some of their instruments (which in many cases, however, were later removed by the Japanese). There were also enough nurses, at least in the large women and children's camps, though not in the men's camps. All these trained doctors and nurses were unable to do very much, in the first place because of the shortage or complete absence of medicine, which could be only partly made up for with various herbs. In the worst camps hunger oedema and other deficiency diseases appeared as early as 1943. There was one camp, the women and children's camp high in the Alas Valley on Sumatra, where almost everybody soon caught malaria because the Japanese had completely neglected the anti-malaria measures in the region into which the Dutch colonial government had put a great deal of effort. In the 'military' phase, when the quantity and quality of the food decreased and hygiene became more difficult, many internees contracted infectious diseases such as dysentery and various liver conditions. In time in many camps around a third of the internees were officially ill – the true percentage was higher, because if you could still move about and did not have a fever the Japanese commandant did not consider you sick, no matter what the doctors said.

Nearly everyone lost weight, many to an extreme degree,[42] and often felt cold because of insufficient metabolism in the body, despite the tropical heat. Most women ceased to menstruate ('it only bothered the women in the beginning', Van Velden (1963:360) wrote, 'later it was seen as one thing less to worry about'). Children hardly grew at all. The shortage of food and above all the lack of vitamins led to the same illnesses as described in the chapter on the prisoners of war: burning feet, night blindness (almost exclusively among the men), and skin infections. Scabies was frequent and tropical ulcers were not uncommon. Many more patients suffered from dysentery and other con-

41   Letter, 10 December 1945, in Brugmans 1960:425.
42   Carla van Berkum, born in 1930, wrote in her diary after a period of illness at the end of June 1945: 'I'm so thin now. I'm like a washboard, the ends of my pelvis stick out in points and my trousers rest on them. The bones of my knees stick out. Nothing is left of my fat thighs. [...] At night I can' t lie comfortably.' Two days later: 'I had to laugh so much this morning. In the midst of a warm embrace we discovered that we were just hurting each other with our bones and that we ought to make special cushions, like violin pads.' (Vermeer-van Berkum 1980:160-1.)

tagious diseases (but not typhoid or cholera, because the Japanese armies usually had the internees vaccinated against these diseases every six months) – many children died of diphtheria. There were occasional epidemics of measles and whooping cough in the women and children's camps. The most dangerous, however, whether or not in combination with dysentery, was what came to be known in the hunger winter in the west of the Netherlands as 'the hunger disease', which took a great many lives in the Indies as well.

The large camps always had special barracks for the sick (and for the mentally ill),[43] but in 1944 the Japanese gave permission for seriously ill patients to be put in special departments in the large camps. In addition, in 1945 two monasteries on Java, one at Batavia and one at Bandung, were designated special hospitals, for women and men respectively. They were not properly equipped as hospitals: the patients lay on thin mattresses, prey to hunger and thirst and becoming increasingly dirty. Hundreds died there, separated from all who were dear to them.

It does not seem necessary to report the number of deaths and death rates for each individual camp in this general study (they are given in Van Velden 1963:366-9.). However, it should be remembered that in the East Indies about one in six internees died while interned and that mortality differed considerably from region to region and camp to camp. For instance, on Celebes there were only a few deaths in Kampili women and children's camp, while 44% of the men and boys in the men's camp at Minahasa died.

Such discrepancies are found elsewhere as well. In the camps on North Sumatra, almost 5% of the internees perished; on Central Sumatra the figure was 10%, and on South Sumatra 37%. The exact death rate for Java is not known but is presumably somewhere in the neighbourhood of 16%. Almost all of the deaths occurred in the 'military' phase (bearing in mind that there had already been serious malnutrition in the 'civilian' phase), and the death rate was highest among infants and toddlers and people aged 60 or older. Noteworthy, furthermore, is that two to three times more men than women died – significant in this respect may be that there were many professional nurses in the women and children's camp, but Van Velden (1963:372) calls it 'crucial that the women were more vital and better able to adapt'. An important observation which we will return to at the end of this section.

According to Van Velden (1963:374-5):

> When someone died, the Japanese authorities often devoted greater attention to him than before! They came to pay their respects on various occasions and with a show of bowing they laid flowers and fruit on the coffin. At least this was the case

[43]   The mentally ill from some camps were taken to Indonesian asylums; very few of them survived.

when the camps were under army control; prior to that, funerals were left entirely to the internees, who hired an undertaker. Relatives and clergymen were then allowed to go to the churchyard and one had to pay the costs of burial oneself. The army provided the funeral for free, but when the number of dead rose, the flowers and fruit were dropped. Burial took place in the general cemetery of the town and family members were no longer allowed to be present. If the camp was in the country, a cemetery was established in nearby woods; the internees dug the graves themselves and carried the dead out to burial, which was announced in the camp by hitting a bell or a piece of iron.

There were many camps in which that gloomy and baleful sound resounded daily in 1945.

It is an illusion to think that severe hardships draw people closer together. This may be true for small groups, cliques, whose members support one another to the best of their abilities, but when the normal struggle to make a living becomes an abnormal struggle to simply stay alive, the general differences are intensified and many (not all!) try to put themselves before others. This was the case in the 'hunger winter' in the occupied Netherlands, in the German prisons and concentration camps, and also in the internment camps in the East Indies.

To begin with, one source of inequality was that relatively 'rich' and relatively 'poor' individuals were interned together. In the men's camps the employees of large companies usually had a fair amount of money with them which at least in 1943 could still be clandestinely supplemented in those instances when the company directors had managed to keep cash resources out of Japanese hands. In contrast, interned civil servants had only a little money, and the families of soldiers and of people who had reached retirement age usually had no financial reserves at all. Any camp leadership keeping a firm grip on the situation immediately established a relief fund to assist the less wealthy. Thus, there were camps in which everything was divided more or less equitably: the money at hand, the incoming food, the work to be done. In other camps, however, the relatively wealthy contributed very little to the camp fund and the old social differences continued to exist. Those with nothing, that is to say only the daily 25 cents provided by the Japanese to buy additional food, had to borrow money on which, according to Van Velden, 100 to 500% interest was 'repeatedly' charged. 'This kind of egoism', she wrote,

> was detrimental to everyone because the Japanese knew full well that substantial amounts of money were still concealed and so resorted to house searches and collective punishments, such as cutting back permission for additional purchases and revoking other privileges. [...] The countless house searches conducted by the Japanese revealed that many fellow internees in every camp still had a good deal of money even though they swore they had none left. (Van Velden 1963:386-7.)

Conversely, there were instances of fraud, that is to say internees who appealed to the relief fund when, as investigation proved, they had no need of such assistance.

Stealing also took place in the camps: food, sometimes laundry. Sheets (this applied solely to the women and children's camps) could be traded over the enclosure, the *gedèk* (this trading was called *gedèkken*), primarily for foodstuffs. As Van Velden (1963:391) wrote,

> This greatly stimulated theft. Not so much the occasional smuggling, but the kind that was more or less organized by certain fixed cliques, who turned it into a business and sold the food smuggled in for inordinately high prices to people with financial resources, and in so doing did not shy away from all manner of deceit.

Were there such cliques in all of the camps? We do not know.

What is certain is that in general many, if not most, of the people involved in preparing food were better off than the average internee. 'The positions of those in charge of the kitchens, of supplies and of the camp shops [the men's camps had no such shops] were the most conducive to dishonesty', according to Van Velden (1963:383).

> This applied to everyone working in these sectors. Allow me to add immediately that these were also the areas in which temptation was particularly great. For who would miss a spoonful of rice from a large drum? In every camp accusations were levelled at the kitchen and shop staffs. Often the only "proof" was that they were fatter than the others. Undoubtedly, the majority sometimes weakened and took an extra mouthful.

Van Velden also warned against generalizing: there were 'innumerable camps where every internee vouched for the honesty of the kitchen and the shop' (Van Velden 1963:384). In others, however, supervisory teams had to be established and they had the greatest difficulty in doing their job. There was even one camp (*Kampong* Makassar just south of Batavia, in which about 3,600 women and children were interned as of January 1945) where those in charge of the kitchen and of supplies traded some of the supplies on the black market with the support of the Japanese camp staff.[44]

Van Velden wrote that 'the majority sometimes' took an extra mouthful. Elias was more critical of the camp inhabitants in general, about whom he writes (somewhat pessimistically it seems to me), '98% saw nothing wrong in

---

[44]   According to another internee in *Kampong* Makassar, speaking in April 1946, who had been able to observe the supply team: 'These people usually did not eat all of their food, even though everyone was hungry.

They traded it for jewels. [...] [They] gave each other fine presents when everyone was broke.

They regularly ate *nasi-goreng*, always made with "a bit of left-over oil".' (Dutch DP-Camp Kandy (Ceylon), 'Verslag van verhoor van L. Perelaer', 2 April 1946, p. 6. (NIOD IC, 16,289).)

stealing extra food from the community or procuring an additional portion in a devious fashion' (Elias 1946:153). As for all the camp officials working under the Japanese, he noted:

> It is simply acknowledging a plain fact: despite the nerve-wracking work of the camp administrations and the incessant threats of the Japanese there is virtually not a single administrator, nor one of the lesser gods, who has died from a deficiency of calories. The camp leaders never suffered from hunger oedema, nor did the management of the camp kitchens, technical services, foremen and the like. That tiny bit (or perhaps relatively large bit) of extra food they were able to obtain helped them get by. (Elias 1956:151.)

In the camp at Cimahi, the former prisoner-of-war camp, in which in 1944 more than 10,000 French, British, Iraqi Jews and 600 Chinese were interned (the latter were transferred from the old prison in Banten), there was a large kitchen department fenced in with barbed wire where water buffaloes were slaughtered occasionally. The butchers were called 'the cannibals' – 'rightly so', wrote one of the internees:

> for before the eyes of hundreds of people looking on in hunger, they did not hesitate to eat a piece of raw water buffalo meat now and then. [...] The entire camp began to complain that [...] there was almost no meat in the soup. The climax was reached when rumours began circulating that you could buy smoked meat from certain individuals. [...] They were always the same people and their friends. Finally things got out of hand. (Jalhay 1981:344-5.)

The camp leader, jonkheer C.H.V. de Villeneuve (during Dutch rule, president of the Federation of Industry and Commerce and a member of the College of Delegates of the Volksraad) finally intervened: with the camp police he raided the kitchen, established that large quantities of meat were hanging in the chimneys to be cured, and subsequently replaced the kitchen personnel with Chinese, whose chef stated that anybody doing wrong would be lynched, 'and, indeed, from that day on the food was a lot better' (Jalhay 1981:345).

Bad behaviour was also evident in Baros Camp in Cimahi, where in July 1944 about 1,700 men and youths were interned. A Dutch boy, then 14 years old, who in the camp was greatly helped by a Dutch Eurasian sailor, informed us in 1985 that of the 12 youth leaders in his barrack, 'all school inspectors, nurses, one professor, men you said 'sir' to', only two or three did not misbehave. These two or three men were sent to work on the railroad on the Bandung plateau. According to this account:

> The boys in the barrack had to work every day in an arrack factory. Dragging bottles from one building to the other. For this we received 170 grams of rice. We suspected that the barrack leaders stole from this. Five of us boys reported sick. Remained lying on our beds. A half hour before the workers returned, their rice

was brought. A cry of 'Food!'. Our fine leaders stuffed themselves. I was one of the five. We drew up a report, and signed it, all five of us. Took the report to the camp commander, the Dutch one, his name was Bos. The leaders were put on the carpet. Thereafter, at the following roll call, the barrack commander began to tell us off. What had we done now, etc. We were to consider him and the others as our fathers. Ernst Schoutendorp cried out: 'Our fathers wouldn't eat our food!', whereupon he was thrashed and the leader said: 'We'll do it until the war is over and you can all go to hell', or something to that effect.[45]

In Lampersari women and children's camp, the kitchen team gave offence. At the end of July 1944, Carla van Berkum wrote in her diary:

If you could see just how much the cooks and the leader take home: cauldrons of water, piles of pancakes, bowls of porridge and vegetables. It's the limit! Should one of us try to put a small pan of our own on the stove, we are kicked out of the cooking area! And then you are cursed at like nobody's business.

When the portions had been distributed, the people who supervised the dishing out of the portions ate again:

one cup of *sayur* after the other, alternating with dozens of cups of coffee. And when she goes below, she has a milk pot and a vegetable dish full of *sayur*. Great job. She isn't the only one, they're all like this!!! (Vermeer-van Berkum 1980:172.)

At the end of August 1944 matters reached a head in Brastagi Camp on Sumatra, then home to about 1,750 women and children internees, and according to one of the women, 'there was an awful row about the food. One third of the camp fatten themselves by stealing from the others.'[46] This report may have been somewhat exaggerated, but along with the 'dozens of camps' where the scarce resources were divided equitably, according to Van Velden, there were, indeed, others where some of the internees could arrogate all manner of privileges.

Privileges were also enjoyed by women and girls who had sexual relationships with the Japanese. The Japanese commandant in each of the women and children's camps had a white 'girlfriend' (sometimes he had more than one),[47] who was separately housed, while in others a small area serving as a brothel was set up next to the original camp. The camp brothel in Bandung was called 'the rabbit hole' (Elias 1946:157). At the end of 1943, a row of

---

45   Letter from S. Nieuwenweg, 9 January 1985.
46   Toeter-Teunisse, 'Dagboek', uittreksel, p. 3 (NIOD IC, dagboek 9).
47   Sexual relations between interned women (chiefly Dutch Eurasians) and indigenous guards occurred more often than with the Japanese, according to Van Velden (1963:420). This applied solely to the 'civilian' phase.

houses on the outskirts of Batavia was surrounded with a fence; here, according to the Dutch Eurasian (not-interned) journalist W.C.J. Bastiaans, 'blonde, white ladies from the camps', namely Cideng, were accommodated.

> [They] enjoy relative freedom, well dressed. Opening of nightclub on the night of 24 to 25 December 1943. Christmas eve! Exclusively for officers. [...] First nights quiet and noiseless; after that riotous. [...] Sad yet shameful sight, when a procession of *becak* [trishaws] takes these women for a medical examination to the Municipal Health Department. [...] Nightclub did not last long. Maybe about two months. After that [it] closed down. I don't know where the inhabitants went. Nippon mad about nightclubs. Such enclosures are everywhere in the city.[48]

As far as is known, no women and girls from the internment camps were housed in the other enclosed brothels.[49]

Relatively speaking, only very few of the interned women and girls were prepared to have sexual relations with the Japanese and it must be remembered that most of them had been prostitutes before their internment. That their numbers were few is evident from the fact that the Japanese military authorities repeatedly put pressure on the camp leaders to select the female internees necessary for their brothels and that in 1943 and 1944 they even began using force to this end.[50]

The Japanese long attempted to convey women and girls from the women and children's camp in Padang to the brothels in Fort de Kock, the Japanese administrative centre on Sumatra. In February 1943 the members of the camp leadership attempted to prevent the removal of several of the girls who had been selected. This led to a scuffle with indigenous policemen. According to the camp leader's report:

> The whole camp came out, many helped. Finally, the policemen were ordered to stop. The [camp] leaders were held responsible for this incident and summoned to go by car to explain the matter to the Japanese resident. The assembled camp

---

[48]   W.C.J. Bastiaans: 'Merkwaardige mensen in een merkwaardige tijd', n.d., pp. 11-2 (NIOD IC, 80,230 I).

[49]   Homosexual contacts also took place between the Japanese and interned youths. In Adek Camp in Batavia this was seen as so offensive that a minister and a priest lodged a protest with the Japanese camp commandant; both were horribly mistreated. 'No matter how justified the complaint had been, it was supposed', as an internee later stated, 'to be an affront to the Japanese Army which had thus lost face' (J.D. Thijs, 'Affidavit', 18 March 1955, p. 2 (NIOD IC 32,228)).

[50]   In Pontianak (West Borneo) the Japanese military police was charged with collecting the women needed for the brothels. They arrested women and girls (mostly Indonesian and Chinese) and brought them to the brothels. 'Women', according to a 1946 Nefis report, 'did not dare to escape from the brothels, as family members were then immediately arrested and severely maltreated' (J.H. Heybroek, 'Report on enforced prostitution in Western Borneo during Japanese Naval Occupation', 5 July 1946, p. 2, (IMTFE, Exhibit 1,702)).

inhabitants resisted this. Once again it looked as if there would be a fight. Finally, all of the Japanese drove away threatening to return that same evening.[51]

They only came back in October – again collective resistance was offered to prevent the girls from being taken away.

In the women's camp in Brastagi in May 1942 on two occasions eight women were told under threat that they had to agree to work in a residence for Japanese officers – two acquiesced, six resolutely refused.

At the end of 1943, the headquarter of the Japanese 16th Army on Java gave permission to the Japanese military authorities in Magelang and Semarang to collect 12 women and girls from each of several women and children's camps for a number of brothels about to be built, provided they state in writing their willingness to go as volunteers. This condition was ignored by the authorities in Magelang and Semarang – Japanese officers appeared in the camps in question, had all of the women and girls aged between about 18 and 30 line up, selected the 12 most attractive (to them), and simply informed the camp leader that they had to work elsewhere for a brief period. There were two camps, one in Semarang and one in Ambarawa, from where the Japanese did indeed succeed in removing the women in question. The camp leader at Ambarawa, where ten girls had to leave (two were ill), protested. According to an account from December 1945, she was told that if they resisted 40 internees would be shot.[52] According to a statement by one of the girls, the Japanese swore up and down that not a hair on her head would be harmed:

> One of the Japanese even told my mother that he knew what the women thought would happen to the girls, but that the Japanese were not as *boesoek* [depraved] as the *belanda*. He gave his Nippon sword to another lady, along with a handshake as a pledge that nothing would happen to the girls being taken away. The girls were then given 15 minutes to pack a bag. Heartrending scenes took place when they said goodbye, for a number of the girls did not want to let go of their mothers. However, they were wrenched apart by the Japanese and the native policemen and kicked into the bus.[53]

The ten were taken from Ambarawa to Semarang where they encountered a group that had been designated in one of the camps there and removed involuntarily, as well as another group consisting of volunteers. The young women who had been selected were given a choice between dying or working in one of the four Japanese brothels in Semarang. Five chose death – they were mistreated and told that their parents would pay for this if they did not

---

51   Verslag (n.d.) in Brugmans 1960:409.
52   Interview, with Jeanne Alida O'Herne, December 1945 (NIOD IC, 238).
53   Algemene recherche, proces-verbaal M.R., 8 January 1946, p. 4 (NIOD IC, 3).

change their minds. At the end of the evening, sometimes at gun or sabre point, they were driven into bedrooms and raped by Japanese officers. One girl tried to kill herself after this ordeal. All of the girls were divided among the four brothels.

In February 1944 the message finally penetrated the headquarters of the 16th Army (we do not know via what channel) that there were girls in Semarang who had been coerced into brothel life. The headquarters reported this fact by telegraph to Singapore and Tokyo. Singapore failed to respond, but at the end of April Tokyo ordered all of the brothels in which Dutch and Dutch Eurasian women and girls were working to be shut down. This took place at the beginning of May[54] – the women and girls in question were first interned in a special Nippon workers' district in Buitenzorg, and later in a closed part of Kramat Camp in Batavia. According to one of the girls who had been picked out in Semarang:

> In general no difference was made between the volunteers and the girls who had been coerced. The ladies outside of the area reserved for us treated us horribly, swearing and spitting at us, etc., because they were unwilling to believe that girls who had been forced were among the voluntary prostitutes. Our life there was hell.[55]

As mentioned above, heart-rending scenes took place upon the departure of the ten girls from Ambarawa Camp who, it was feared, would be forced to work in brothels. However, scenes like this were not infrequent, for in the internment camps in the East Indies forced separations occurred on a far more general scale. When they reached a certain age, growing boys were transferred from the women and children's camp to a men's camp. Initially, this age was set at 16, but in 1942 or early 1943 boys older than 16 arrived at various women and children's camps. In many camps on Java and later on Sumatra the age limit of 16 was lowered first to 14, then to 10, and in a few cases even to 9 or 8. What the motives of the Japanese were in introducing these reductions is not clear. They probably removed the older boys from the women and children's camps partly because in certain camps sexual relationships had developed between some boys and some women which was considered objectionable when it became known. That the Japanese nowhere set the limit lower than 8 years is probably related to the fact that in the Japanese culture of the time boys who had turned 8 were expected to adhere to the strict adult behavioural code. In Japan, however, these boys were not deprived of maternal care! Which is exactly what happened in the intern-

---

54   The 'nightclub' Bastiaans wrote about was probably also only closed then – it would have been in existence for over four months.
55   Algemeene recherche, proces-verbaal E.L., 7 January 1946, p. 6 (NIOD IC, 12).

ment camps. This separation was experienced as cruel and arbitrary.

Be that as it may, it was a disadvantage to the camp as a whole that boys 14 or older had to leave the women and children's camps where they had been interned for a few months or even a few years because they could help with the hardest work. Most mothers suffered terribly from the forced departure of the boys. They had already been separated from their husbands and as a rule did not even know where, let alone how, they were – and now a son was facing an unknown future with no assurance that he would be met by his father in the camp he was being sent to. If the father had been a soldier, this would certainly not be the case, for the soldiers were in prisoner-of-war camps. The younger the age set by the Japanese, the greater the sorrow of the women at the departure of their sons, and the greater, too, their concern. At the beginning of 1944 L. van Empel noted in Lampersari Camp (Semarang):

> We cheered, but with tears in our eyes, as 42 boys aged between 14 and 18 left the camp this afternoon. A difficult day for the mothers! It was very crowded at the gate. I also went to take leave of various boys. There were such kids among them. Departure was delayed a few times [...] but finally, after waiting endlessly, they left at 4:30 on two trucks. Both sides had resolved to keep a stiff upper lip and there was cheering, but for many it was too much, especially when one of the smallest boys burst into tears and could not be calmed down. (Boissevain and Van Empel 1981:124-5.)

Over nine months later, in mid-September 1944, when the Japanese decided to intern all of the boys and older men in one of the Ambarawa camps on Central Java, the boys who were much younger than 14 also had to leave Lampersari. This was:

> A heart-wrenching departure [...], which I will not soon forget. More than 400 boys and older men. They were issued numbers, then called off, and one by one walked through the gate. Small boys of 10. How could they possibly have done this? Children not yet able to take care of themselves! (Boissevain and Van Empel 1981:176.)

How did the boys who had to leave react? Here too we have only limited information. Presumably most tried to put on a good face. In one of the women's camps at Medan, the ten-year-olds who had to leave even said in December 1944 that they found the prospect 'really interesting', 'but', according to one of the women, 'if you see what toddlers they still are, it is really awful.' (Van Eijk-van Velzen 1983:124.) If there was a strong positive emotional bond between the son and his mother, that forced departure could engender a neurotic condition,[56] though how general this reaction was is not

---

[56]   Having just turned 14, in early 1943 H.L. Leffelaar had to leave the women and children's

known. It is worth mentioning, however, that it could be a great advantage for many of the boys separated from their fathers and mothers if they received care and protection from a so-called camp father in their new camp.[57]

There are only very few descriptions that answer the question of how young children experienced camp life. They all suddenly lost a part of their childhood and their father. Most mothers tried to keep the family together despite the great material shortcomings of camp life. Some succeeded better than others. One great difficulty was that many children suffered from the seclusion, originating from the puzzling world of the adults, which had suddenly come into their existence. 'You grew up', as Leffelaar (1980:104) wrote, who was 13 when he was interned (in a relatively small camp):

> but nothing much of any import happened. The lack of contact with the outside world was numbing. Nothing was added to the topics of conversation. Like beasts of burden walking around a well, it was always the same. When would it end? It was a spiritually impoverishing process. Treading water so as not to sink, but no forward movement.

'They had no recreation and no sport', according to Carla van Berkum (Vermeer-van Berkum 1980:155) talking about the children, 'no fun, only hunger, duties and worries.' Perhaps the factor of 'hunger' should be underlined: for children this could be a greater daily torment than for the adults. There were many mothers who gave their children something extra from their own meagre rations.

---

camp Pulu Brayan at Medan and was transferred to the Unie *Kampong* men's camp. 'I think', he wrote a generation later (1980), 'that the transport consisted of about 30, perhaps even 50 boys, and God help you should anyone see you crying. The women did cry. [...] In my official store of memories, that departure is entered as an adventure. Finally old enough to be sent to a men's camp! [...] Reality was different, and logically so. And I am now talking about the inner reality. In this reality I in no way wanted to leave my mother and I held her [...] responsible for this separation. She freely let me go and, worse, had given 'preference' to keeping my brother with her. I went to the men's camp [...] with a rancour which I harboured against her for years. [...] This also explained why in the first months in Unie *Kampong* Camp I often sat crying under a bush at night – not at all the reaction of someone who is proud to be counted prematurely as one of the 'adults', but rather the helplessness of a 14-year-old, tottering between dependence and anger about a supposed, deliberate banishment. [...] Looking back on those years, I am sure that my departure to the men's camp and the separation from my mother and brother was the most important and radical event in those 40 months of war.' (Leffelaar 1980:22-3, 92.)
[57]   The boys aged between 11 and 13 were taken from the women and children's camps in Ambarawa and Banjubiru to one of the Ambarawa camps where about 2,000 elderly men from West and Central Java were also concentrated. Not a single one could be welcomed by his father. Many of these old men died – it was a horror for the boys to be continually confronted with death. This group of lone boys had an exceptionally hard time of it.

For better or worse, the children received some education in most camps. In general this was better organized in the men's camps than in the women and children's camps, chiefly in the 'civilian' period, when less work for the Japanese had to be done. Only the boys aged 16, later 14 and older, were then interned in the men's camps, along with the Dutch teachers who had not been mobilized. According to Van Velden (1963:264), 'complete schools were organized with official final exams, sometimes under the supervision of the professors in the camp. Naturally, the internees had to provide their own books, paper and writing implements, yet many children had their schoolbooks with them.' Fewer teachers were interned in the women's camps – moreover the Japanese raised many obstacles in the women's camps on Java. Schools initially permitted were usually closed after some time. In Lampersari this happened in 1943. The indigenous police commandant (it should be remembered that the women and children's camps on Java were under the indigenous administration in the 'civilian' phase):

> Had heard Dutch being spoken, which is *sala besar* ('a big mistake'). It is a great disappointment but it is clear that the school has to go no matter what, even if we had sung *kroncong* songs[58] all day long. In any case we had the benefit for nine months. We closed the school by singing 'Een vaste burcht is onze God' ('A safe stronghold our God is still'). (Boissevain and Van Empel 1981:104.)

Presumably some primary education was given afterwards clandestinely in Lampersari and the same must have been true in other women and children's camps on Java, where teaching was forbidden before or after September 1943.

It should be stated that even though the Japanese permitted education in the men's camps this was certainly not made easy. The textbooks soon had to be handed in and writing materials were very scarce or lacking entirely. People then used slates and when these were no longer available, the backs of their dinner plates; the teachers also used charcoal or pieces of plaster to write or draw on the cement floors. One significant difficulty was that 'assemblies' were prohibited: lessons thus had to be given to very small groups. All this work was felt to be very worthwhile: people could practise their profession and, in terms of learning, the boys did not stand still. On the contrary, people contributed to their being given an education which, it was hoped, would help them take part sooner or later in rebuilding the post-war Indies.

The rebuilding, that is, of a Dutch East Indies. Especially in 1944 and 1945, when the death rate in almost all of the camps rose alarmingly, many internees began to doubt whether they would live to see the liberation (in numer-

---

[58]   This kind of music constituted a mixture of Indonesian and Western elements. The texts were usually in Malay, sometimes alternated with a few lines of Dutch.

ous camps it was also feared that the Japanese would simply kill the internees were the Allies to land in the Indies), but the majority of those robbed of their freedom were certain that Japan would lose the war and that Dutch authority would then be restored. People were interned because they were Dutch – and everything that was a symbol of Dutchness acquired additional value.

In Chapter I it was noted that as long as they were free, the Dutch (and Dutch Eurasians) on Java made a point of celebrating the birthdays of members of the Royal Family, that of Crown Princess Juliana on 30 April, Prince Bernhard on 29 June, and Queen Wilhelmina on 31 August. This was no different in the internment camps, though they gradually had to go about it more carefully. Carnations made of toilet paper were worn on Prince Bernhard's birthday in 1942 in the women and children's camp Pulu Brayan at Medan (Prince Bernhard, married to Crown Princess Juliana, always wore a white carnation in his buttonhole). The wearing of orange was forbidden in mid-August – a restriction which was ignored by some (and for which they were not punished). Two red, white and blue flags were flown in the women and children's camp in Palembang on the Queen's birthday in 1942. Everybody in Brastagi women and children's camp adorned themselves with a white paper or fabric flower on 19 January, the first birthday of Princess Margriet (whose name means daisy). According to one of the internees later:

> It was supposed to be a daisy. Naturally the Japanese noticed this immediately and the commandant asked [...] what it meant. The answer was: 'Oh, actually it is just like in Japan. As Japan has its cherry blossom day, Holland too has a day on which everyone wears a daisy. Just like in Japan it's a day of fertility.' [...] The commandant said that he found this sympathetic. So – the lights could stay on until 10 o'clock and we celebrated.

A revue was put on.

> To the tune of *Wings over the Navy*, we sang: 'We want to go home', forming first a V [for victory] and then a W [for Wilhelmina]. By chance that evening we were not bothered by a Japanese visit. Fortunately. (Gunning 1947:82.)

The Queen's birthday in 1943 in Lampersari women and children's camp:

> was an unforgettable day. This morning quickly did the washing and after that took a break. In the morning there were hockey matches for the schoolchildren with their sticks made of branches. At lunch all of the children received a bar of chocolate, a splendid treat nowadays. [...] After the prize giving, Mrs Van der Poel [the camp leader] made a short speech that ended with: 'Long live the Queen!' After our meal, including a cake, back to the craft school to sing four songs by Valerius.[59]

---

[59] The Dutch composer Adrianus Valerius (1575-1625) was actually a notary. After his death a collection of his songs was published in which the Dutch revolt against Spain was celebrated.

[...] The songs seemed to have been written for us. Unfortunately the performance was interrupted by Mrs Van der Poel, who came to say that remarks had been made about this demonstration and requested us to go home quietly. It was not the usual camp evening, and it gave us renewed courage and good cheer to last us quite some time. (Boissevain and Van Empel 1981:102-3.)

In that same camp a year later the Japanese commandant issued an order that no orange, or anything resembling it, be worn. He punished several women whom he felt had nevertheless put on some decoration (they were made to stand in the sun for hours on end) and he walked around the camp himself to make sure that no one was celebrating. But 'on the inside, we all have the same colour: orange' (Boissevain and Van Empel 1981:174).

In 1943 the large men's camp at Bandung clearly celebrated all of the birthdays of the members of the royal family, including a minute of silence on Queen's Day. According to one internee,[60] 'several members of the NSB' did not participate ('they even refused the potatoes given as our meal that evening').[61] In 1944 the men from Bandung, now interned in Cimahi, behaved more cautiously – only two verses from 'Wilt heden nu treden' ('We gather together to ask the Lord's blessing') were sung by a small choir on Queen's Day.

Presumably (there is no more information) similar celebrations also took place in other camps on the occasion of royal birthdays.[62] The 10th of May (on this day in 1940 Germany invaded the Netherlands) was also sometimes commemorated. According to Carla van Berkum (Vermeer-van Berkum 1980:28), interned in one of the smaller camps in Semarang, 'all together, on 10 May, we recited "Wien Neerlands Bloed" [the Dutch national anthem until 1932, when

---

[60] G.D. Bosman, 'Dagboek', uittreksel, 31 August 1943, p. 3 (NIOD IC).

[61] With respect to internment, the Japanese made no distinction between members and non-members of the NSB. In some men's camps the NSB members were put in a separate barrack or, if there were houses, accommodated in a separate room. Serious brawls took place in the large internment camp at Bandung: the anti-NSB people involved in this were removed by the Kempeitai – at their request the NSB members were then housed in a barrack near the indigenous police. On the occasion of Hitler's birthday on 20 April 1943 they sent a telegram and flowers to the German consul general in Batavia – other members of the NSB interned in Batavia were given the opportunity to send a deputation to this consul general offering him congratulations. When the men were transferred from Bandung to Cimahi, the NSB members remained together as a separate group – in their barrack hung the German and Japanese flags. These flags were also hung in the 'NSB barrack' in the LOG camp (National Reformatory in Bandung). Not all of the NSB groups stayed together: due to the many transfers NSB members sometimes landed in camps which led to more normal relations with non-NSB members. A small group first interned in the Kesilir colonisation camp was released at the end of 1943 – we will return to this later in this chapter.

[62] It is worth mentioning that a Christian Ambonese, D.A. Gaspersz, a tax official, appeared at the gate of one of the internment camps on South Sumatra together with his family on Queen's Day 1943 to offer his congratulations to the interned resident. He also brought along a large quantity of meat. He was locked up in the prison in Jambi and died there in July 1945.

it was replaced by the Wilhelmus]. Everyone was in tears.' Churchill's birthday, or the day of the Relief of Leiden,[63] or if there were American internees,
Independence Day, the 4th of July, were also celebrated.

And, naturally, primarily in the women and children's camps, Sinterklaas,
or the feast of St Nicholas[64] was not overlooked. The children had such an
impoverished existence! Simple presents were made with primitive means.
Incidentally, it was a rule that each interned child receive something extra
from the camp kitchen on his or her birthday, even if it was just a piece of fruit
or a rice cake – under the circumstances this could be a greater gift than any
luxury they had been given before.

In many internment camps religious holidays were also celebrated in such
a way that they contained an element of national protest – each celebration
during the internment recalled the times Easter or Christmas, for instance,
had been celebrated in freedom. In 1942 and 1943, in Pulu Brayan women
and children's camp Christmas songs were sung early Christmas morning by
a women's choir, 'I choked on my tears now and then' wrote one of the members of the choir in 1942 (Van Eijk-van Velzen 1983:55), and Leffelaar, who at
the time was still in the same camp, noted: 'Our emotion was great' (Leffelaar
1959:101). According to one of the internees in Lampersari in 1943:

> There was a poignant Christmas service. In a very crowded room we were singing:
> 'Daar is uit 's werelds duist're wolken / een der lichten opgegaan' ['Unto us a child
> is born'], when a policeman made a very noisy entrance. The singing continued
> [...] with redoubled force. When it was quiet, the Reverend Jannie Stegeman told
> us: 'The singing is forbidden, we will confine ourselves to preaching'. And even
> though outside of the room there was a lot of noise, the clumping of shoes and
> screaming on the part of the police [...], it was a wonderful service. I realized more
> than ever before that no one can keep the promise and the gifts of God from us.
> [...] I feel stronger than ever, for I am not alone. [...] I will never forget this day!
> (Boissevain and Van Empel 1981:177.)

Though the celebration of Christmas was not generally forbidden by the
Japanese, that of Easter and Pentecost usually was. Other religious gatherings
were also often banned, and in some camps there was no way around this.
In Cideng Camp the holding of religious assemblies was no longer allowed
at a certain point – an interned minister there, H.J. Kater, then circulated his
sermons in typescript. The Japanese caught wind of this and subsequently

---

[63] In the early stages of the Dutch revolt against Spain, the city of Leiden was long besieged
by Spanish troops. However, the city did not fall and on 3 October 1574 the siege ended. This day
is still celebrated annually in Leiden.
[64] In the Netherlands this is the principal family celebration, held on the name day of St
Nicholas (6 December) or the night before. Presents are given on this day, primarily to children.

demanded that all those who had received the typed texts step forward. According to the Reformed minister, J.A. Verkuyl:

> Hundreds stepped forward, and many who had never seen the sermons came forward out of a sense of solidarity. What were the Japs to do? The end of the story was that they removed 20 clergymen and women from the camp[65] and in so doing indeed struck back at the camp in a hurtful and subtle fashion.[66]

People pray in affliction. And, much praying was done by the many internees in the camps who felt the need. Many also had themselves baptized, 'hundreds', according to Verkuyl, as members of the Protestant or Reformed Church[67] – how many joined the Catholic Church is not known. Cooperation between the Protestant Church of the Dutch East Indies, the Reformed Churches and the Salvation Army was, according to the Reformed minister:

> Excellent. [...] In most of the camps, there were religious committees that jointly arranged the services, set up programmes for circles and lectures, organized welfare work, etc. In some camps there were camp church councils consisting of members of both churches who together dealt with ecclesiastical matters and even regarded making a confession of faith as being confirmed before the Camp Church. Other camps had separate church councils but in addition there were coordinating bodies.[68]

This ecumenical goal did not extend so far as to embrace the Catholics as well. In their turn, they tried to continue administering the sacraments as best they could. In Ambarawa, and possibly also elsewhere, this took place clandestinely in the 'military' phase. According to one of the internees:

> A ray of hope is when the priest [priests older than 60 were also interned in the large women and children's camps until 1945] lets it be known that some sacramental wine and a couple of wafers have been smuggled in again. Then he can celebrate mass, to which no one may come, but to which we nevertheless go very quietly while it is still dark and remain standing outside near the cubicle. The feeble light of a single candle shines through the boarded up window. We take turns going inside, kneeling by the little table[69] and when we have received Holy Communion, we move on quickly and go somewhere else and lean against a wall or a tree to contemplate this mighty Presence. [...] Not a word is spoken, only a few whispered benedictions go with us, what a day. (Helfferich-Koch 1981:163-4.)

---

65   That is to say, interned elsewhere; the same happened to a group of nuns. Kater's wife and three small children were locked up as punishment for this.
66   J.A. Verkuyl in *Zending*, November 1945, p. 5.
67   J.A. Verkuyl in *Zending*, November 1945, p. 5.
68   J.A. Verkuyl in *Zending*, November 1945, p. 7.
69   The priest of the Old Catholic Church interned in Struiswijk Prison in Batavia, whose ministry also extended to a group of Protestants and a group of Anglicans, used a ping-pong table as an altar.

Verkuyl believed that all of this religious work exerted 'a preservative and inhibiting influence against the demoralizing forces of camp life'.[70]

The demoralizing forces were also countered with meaningful recreation. Overcoming all material difficulties, theatre performances were given. As were camp cabarets – Corry Vonk, the wife of prisoner-of-war Wim Kan, did this once a week with a small company, first in Cihapit Camp (Bandung), later in *Kampong* Makassar Camp (in Batavia). In the first camp she did the laundry of the sickbay as a volunteer (and caught dysentery), and in the second she worked with the pig keepers and garbage removal service, yet, according to another internee, 'Corry brought such merriment everywhere she went'.[71] A great deal of music was listened to or performed in many a camp. When they were interned, women were usually allowed to bring along musical instruments and gramophones with records and in virtually all of the camps (this did not apply when prisons were used as internment centres) the Japanese commandant also permitted the presence of one or more pianos. Among the internees were both amateur and professional musicians,[72] and so ensembles were created and choirs set up.[73] Applause was not allowed at many of these performances. According to Elias (1946:163),

> The indigenous management [in the 'civilian' phase] and later the Japanese [in the 'military' phase] are afraid that because of this the outside world will have the impression that the prisoners are still cheerful and don't realize that they have been defeated. Instead, as a sign of applause each number is followed by loud hissing, like the sound of air escaping from a tyre.

We have addressed many of what are called 'the general aspects' of camp life: the change from the 'civilian' to the 'military' phase, the camp regulations, the clashes between Western and Japanese culture that occurred in the camps, the Japanese commandants, the camp guards, the inspections, the roll calls, the difficult position of the camp administrations, the work that had to be done, the poor provision of food that cost the lives of so many, the fact that there were privileged groups, the 'normal' and forced prostitution, the dif-

---

[70]   J.A. Verkuyl in *Zending*, November 1945, p. 5.
[71]   R.M. Meinders-De Boer, 'Dagboek', uittreksel, p. 4 (NIOD IC, dagboek 112).
[72]   On Java, the internationally famous duo pianist Lili Kraus and violinist Szymon Goldberg were given permission for a while to give recitals in the camps. In Batavia, in the 'civilian' phase the Japanese administrative officials under whom the camps fell would attend their recitals. Later, Goldberg stayed for some time in the same camp as his wife – he received preferential treatment, it would appear, because he had once performed in Japan for a brother of the emperor.
[73]   In the women's camp at Palembang a choir with 30 members hummed instrumental music; their first performance, at the end of December 1943, included passages from works by Chopin, Debussy, Dvorak, Händel and Mendelssohn.

ficult existence of the interned youths and the separation of boys from their mothers, and all of the attempts made to prevent demoralization: education of the young, the celebration of national and religious holidays, religious life in general, and recreation.

So far nothing has been written about one aspect that lay at the root of all the rest: the confinement of the internees, their isolation.

A separate section is devoted to this aspect.

Isolation

Initially, at least on Java, the women and children's camps were not closed and people could leave once or twice a week. As of March 1943, however, this was no longer possible. Indigenous tradesmen could then still appear at the camp but this was ended in August 1943. The camps were then enclosed, and the gate was shut and remained shut. In principle, contact with the outside world was no longer permitted, nor could the internees receive any mail. The situation could be somewhat more favourable only where men were interned in prisons, because then the normal prison regulations were sometimes applied. For instance, those who were interned in the prison on Werfstraat in Surabaya (these internees were transferred elsewhere in January 1944) – first once a month and later once every six months – could write family members who were not interned, primarily Dutch Eurasians, a post card in Malay of no more than 25 words. Later they had to choose from ten standard sentences. Furthermore, packages could be dropped off here three times a month: clothing, tobacco, medicines, toiletries. Packages could also sometimes be dropped off in some of the women and children's camps in the course of 1943, but this did not last long. Visits to doctors or dentists practising outside of the camp were also forbidden and all subscriptions to Indonesian dailies permitted earlier were cancelled.

In the 'civilian' phase women on Java could send a card written in block letters to other women interned on Java once a month, men to other men interned on Java once every six months (many of them never arrived). According to Van Velden (1963:262): 'writing to civilian internees in another area, for instance from Java to Sumatra, was just as impossible as corresponding with the moon'. With respect to the Outer Islands, all we know is that around the time of Japan's capitulation several men in Camp Siringoringo on Sumatra received Red Cross cards that had been written in 1943 by their wives interned in Medan. One of the men noted: 'They don't say much: "I am fine. Many kisses. Hang in there." But for many of us it opens up a world and gives new strength.' (Brandt 1947:199.)

In the 'military' phase the rules were altered in so far that mutual correspondence between the internees and correspondence with prisoners of war was allowed in the form of postcards written in Japanese or Malay (or, for destinations outside of the East Indies, in English). From 12 standard sentences, naturally several of them positive (for example: 'We have an excellently equipped hospital and also a rest home', 'Our camp is well set up and comfortably furnished', 'We enjoy working in the open air'), they had to select 3 and could add 20 words of their own. Much of this mail never arrived and postcards to or from prisoners of war that were indeed received had sometimes taken years to reach them.

Because spouses could only rarely send each other a postal message even when they were interned relatively close by, clandestine letters were sent via indigenous guards for money, and people sometimes took advantage of unexpected contacts, for instance in Surabaya. In 1943 a diphtheria epidemic broke out in the Darmo district, the internment centre for women and children, resulting in the transfer of numerous patients to the Central City Hospital. Next to this hospital was a men's internment camp. One of the patients in hospital received letters from men with notes for their wives; after memorizing the messages she chewed them up and swallowed them – she was able to pass them on after her recovery.

It was a burden that, in the absence of clandestine contact, for a long time most of the internees had no idea where their husband or wife was or how they were doing (this was worst in the 'military' phase when they saw so many perish in their own camp). However, in general they had faith that the internees they were close to had not vanished from the island in question – should they stay alive they expected to see each other again soon after the liberation (which was never doubted).

The situation was different for the prisoners of war. In most of the women and children's camps on Java and Sumatra it became known that large groups of prisoners of war had been transported elsewhere, even though it could take quite some time before the first reports to this effect came in. With regard to the prisoners of war transported from Belawan to Burma in May 1942, the women in Pulu Brayan received the first report in July. 'Our husbands are above Rangoon', noted Van Eijk-van Velzen (1983:28):

> They are not required to work hard and the climate is said to be reasonable. The message comes from workers who sailed with the boats and have now come back. We finally know for certain where they are.

All of this information was incorrect – just as incorrect as the news in Pulu Brayan at the end of December 1942 'that the prisoners of war are in Bombay. They were liberated by the Chinese.' (Van Eijk-van Velzen 1983:57.) The first postcards arrived nine months later, in September 1943 – they had been written one year earlier:

I cried and laughed at the same time. Others hugged me and were very happy for me. The card comes from Moulmein in Burma and is written in English in block letters and there is the signature to which one attaches the greatest significance. My husband is healthy and earns 10 cents a day. That is what he is working for. He writes that I must take good care of myself. The card was written last year. But, oh, I am so happy. He also mentions the names of our friends in Medan, thus they are together. I cannot describe how I feel. It is as though you are closer to me my darling. [...] There are also many ladies who have received nothing. This is so very hard. [...] What a happy day for us. I believe it is almost the happiest day of my life. (Van Eijk-van Velzen 1983:86.)

A second card arrived three months later at the end of December 1943 which had taken seven months to be delivered ('the whole day [...] you go to your friends to show it. Only it's really rotten for women who haven't yet received anything.' (Van Eijk-van Velzen 1983:95.)) A third one written in Thailand in January arrived at the beginning of August. Three messages thus in more than three years of separation. Was this about average? Van Velden calls it 'a remarkable exception.' The general impression is that it took quite a while before many women even became vaguely aware that their husbands had been taken away, from whom they subsequently heard nothing whatsoever. In Lampersari the message that the husbands of two of the interned women had died in Singapore in November 1942 was only received in July 1943 ('the entire camp is upset') (Helfferich-Koch 1981:98). In November 1943 one card came from Japan and 'all sorts of postcards from men presently in Thailand' ('it is a real shock now that it appears that men have actually been taken away from Java. Everybody is overwhelmed.') (Helfferich-Koch 1981: 112.) The first message from Carla van Berkum's father from Manchuria only arrived in March 1945.

Death announcements were not always believed. At the beginning of November 1943 messages were passed round in Cihapit Camp (Bandung) that countless men on Flores had died – 14 days later a clandestine letter arrived from the Cimahi prisoner-of-war camp: 'Don't believe the death announcements from Flores'. Somewhat later one of the internees who had been in touch with indigenous inhabitants at the fence heard that only the governor-general and a few other highly-placed officials from Java had been removed, 'but' noted an interned girl whose father was said to have perished on Flores, 'not the other prisoners of war; Thailand, Burma, etc, are invented names. A war of nerves?'[74]

'We don't talk much about our husbands, who are nevertheless so dear to our hearts', wrote H. Helfferich-Koch (1981:91) in Ambarawa:

---

[74]   H.S. Kabel, 'Dagboek', uittreksel, p. 4 (NIOD IC, dagboek 60).

For many of us having to live separately in perhaps the most difficult years of our lives is such a painful, harrowingly bitter task that we can barely cope with it. Having to be separated from one another when you promised to stand by, to help, to cherish the other in good times and in bad, in sickness and in health, until death do you part. It is something that goes against our sense of justice above all that it is better not to talk about it or even *think* about it. Sometimes it is far better not to even think much at all. However, you don't always have this under control. Sometimes one of us hesitantly begins talking about her husband, as if musing out loud. How he may change, after all, we're changing too, aren't we? Physically and mentally! Whether you can drift apart in these circumstances? Terrible thought. We dismiss all of this vehemently and immediately. This cannot be! But deep in our hearts the idea doesn't seem so strange, unfortunately. Is he healthy? Can he bear up to a harsh existence? And then: can he take care of himself and how will we ever find each other again? No, let's not think about it.

People tried to suppress frightening questions.

How were the families and friends of the internees in the occupied Netherlands?

Most internees never received a single message from them. Some received telegrams or Red Cross messages dating from 1942 in March 1945, others later still; these had arrived on Java in 1944 but the Japanese had been in no hurry to deliver them to the addressees. On rare occasions the mail arrived more swiftly – the shortest period found in the available information was one and a half years.

A few people could submit a telegram to be sent to the Netherlands in February 1945, but this favour was strictly rationed. In one of the camps in Banyubiru (south of Semarang), where about 1,000 women were interned at the time, 7 were allowed to submit a telegram, and in Lampersari 15 of the approximately 2,000 interned women were given leave to do the same. We do not know how the choice was made. Moreover, none of the telegrams seem to have reached the Netherlands.

It goes without saying that many internees attempted to break through their isolation: notes were smuggled out and foodstuffs smuggled into the camps. In the 'civilian' phase indigenous policemen often lent their assistance for payment in money or goods, and in the 'military' phase people were dependent on the paid help of the Japanese, Koreans or *heiho*. In addition (this has been mentioned previously) clandestine bartering was conducted with indigenous people right over the camp enclosure, called *gedèkken*, and internees sometimes crawled out of or dealers into the camp at night. All of this clandestine trade was more difficult in the 'military' than in the 'civilian' phase. In both phases the Japanese could impose harsh punishment either on the smugglers among the internees (quite often the entire camp was punished) or on the indigenous smugglers.

For instance, in Pulu Brayan in January 1944 a confession was forced from an indigenous gold smuggler by putting his hands and feet in boiling oil. One of the internees noted: 'Some of us saw him, he was carried in a chair by his friends. We're back in the Middle Ages.' (Van Eijk-van Velzen 1983:98.)[75]

In complete contrast to this, in October 1944, 200 interned men from the Medan area were brought to a camp in Aik Pamienke, that is to say the coolie barracks of a French rubber plantation where the corrupt camp commandant, a Korean, happily condoned camp smuggling. Klooster ('Willem Brandt') wrote:

> This man is friends with a Chinese dealer who comes every day to see whether the commandant has anything for sale: clothing, jewellery, suitcases, anything goes. The commandant has our camp leaders come and asks for bids. We [...] offer trousers and shirts, watches and bags and name a price. The Jap [meaning the Korean] adds a substantial percentage for himself and the articles go to the Chinese. He then pays us [...] in foodstuffs, tobacco, etc., at a rate that is not too high. And we can get virtually everything, even soap and toothbrushes. [...] The result of all of this is that we get more than enough food. (Brandt 1947:161.)

The haves allowed the have-nots a share.

There is some information about smuggling with respect to the internment camps in Bandung. One of the former civil servants there, A.F. Holm, who, as mentioned in Chapter I had succeeded in building up a large transport business as of April 1942, began smuggling notes out of and money, medicines and food into the camp he had had to report to in early December 1942. His contact outside the camp was a Mrs Van der Waals, a Dutch Eurasian. It became a full-fledged business in which the most trusted employees in his transport enterprise took part. Everything was done for payment: camp guards had to be bribed, messengers paid. According to Holm in his post-war report:

> We could get into the women's camps due to the fact that we were removers and also had to take care of moves within the camp. If by chance there were no moves, we always had our special 'climb-over boys'. We had really terrific boys,

---

[75]   Another incident took place in this camp at the end of 1943. With an eye to a camp inspection, the Japanese commandant of Pulu Brayan had a few wooden bathing cubicles erected (purely for show as there was no running water). When the inspection failed to take place, the women broke up the cubicles, using the planks to protect their scarce possessions from the rain. About 60 women found to be in possession of these planks were taken to Medan and confined in the small rooms of a department store. A number of them were 'interrogated' in the prison, some of whom were brought back to the camp, and others (18 women) sentenced to one year in prison in March 1944.

East Indian [that is Dutch Eurasian] and Ambonese, loyal, with a taste for adventure and afraid of nothing.[76]

Everything went well for six months: Holm managed to get countless goods into the camp, 'even bottles of wine for my birthday and, last but not least, every week a review of the foreign radio broadcasts'[77] – but this changed in early June. The PID arrested Mrs Van der Waals. Ten days later the Kempeitai picked up the employees from Holm's enterprise involved in the smuggling, Holm himself, and five of his most important messengers (four indigenous policemen and the indigenous warehouse manager of his camp). The five indigenous men received prison sentences. Most of the others (also Mrs Van der Waals who was helped in 'a brilliant fashion' by an indigenous police inspector)[78] were released after some time, while Holm was sentenced to two years in prison in February 1944 by an indigenous judge solely for disseminating false rumours.

This was how one smuggling operation was rounded up – others remained active, both in Bandung and in Cimahi, which became an internment camp in February 1944. Three months later, at the end of May, Bouwer (1988:264) wrote in his diary:

> Six distributors of clandestine notes from Cimahi Camp were betrayed to the Kempeitai by Indonesians and arrested. The matter threatens to snowball and if the majority of the detainees (and the others who will inevitably be arrested, for virtually every woman [namely Dutch Eurasian women] in the city has had clandestine contact with the camps) don't keep their mouths shut, half of the city will be thrashed. Accompanied by their Indonesian servant boys, the various Kempeitai thugs already drive through the city in handsome cars provided with complete lists. I could give a long list of names of European women who have been beaten up in the past few days. The Kempeitai appears to be pretty much aware of all of the branches of the clandestine contact with the camps and when they aren't this Gestapo takes the arrested distributors in the car through the city and finds a means of forcing them to point out the addresses. Even the pseudonyms under which the correspondence is conducted are known. [...] Three distributors of return mail from the city have also been arrested in the civilian camp at Cimahi. The 'submarine contact' with Sukamiskin [prison] also appears to have been discovered.

This intervention notwithstanding, smuggling for the sake of Cihapit women and children's camp was continued: bacon, oil, eggs butter and other foodstuffs continued to reach the camp. As noted by the report of the camp leader (from March 1944 to May 1945):

---

[76]   A.F. Holm, 'Verslag', 10 April 1947, p. 2 (ARA, Alg. Secr., Eerste zending, XXII, 45, 194).
[77]   A.F. Holm, 'Verslag', 10 April 1947, p. 2 (ARA, Alg. Secr., Eerste zending, XXII, 45, 194).
[78]   A.F. Holm, 'Verslag', 10 April 1947, p. 4 (ARA, Alg. Secr., Eerste zending, XXII, 45, 194).

Indonesians smuggled these articles in at night via the sewers and the enclosure. The prices were very high and so only a small wealthy group was able to profit from this.[79] The 'business' was in the hands of a few groups which did not tolerate interference; as a result, some serious clashes took place. The Japanese authorities continued to try to suppress this trade, but never entirely succeeded in doing so.

Here, too, there were Japanese who participated in this traffic: they 'repeatedly exchanged watches, fountain pens, tennis rackets and the like for foodstuffs'.[80]

The differences evident in Cihapit were also present in the large camp at Cimahi (the former barracks of the IVth and the IXth Battalions of the KNIL). A former assistant resident interned there, B. de Jong, believed that the camp leadership did little to distribute additional food according to need so that 'hundreds died from starvation'. On the other hand, he was annoyed that in combating the smuggling the leadership adopted Japanese threats. After the Kempeitai discovered large-scale smuggling in May 1945 that was conducted 'certainly with the knowledge of the Japs charged with supervision', the camp leadership had all of the private supplies, even the smallest, confiscated and made an announcement to the effect that every smuggler 'indeed deserved the death penalty'.[81] This punishment was not imposed in the few months of occupation left.

As mentioned above, when it was decided how Red Cross parcels were to be distributed among the prisoners of war and civilian prisoners of various nationalities in Japan and in the countries governed by Japan, due to a lack of information the Dutch government failed to have the internees in the Indies recognized as full-fledged prisoners. Consequently, in the few shipments allowed by the Japanese far too few parcels were destined for the internees in the Indies. There were only four shipments, as mentioned in the previous chapter: two via Lourenço Marques (one in July, one in September 1942); one via Goa (October 1943); and one via Vladivostock and Nakhodka (November 1944). Parcels arrived in the Dutch East Indies only from the first and second shipment via Lourenço Marques and the shipment via Vladivostock and Nakhodka. The first time part of about 10,000 food parcels (from the American, the Canadian and the South African Red Cross) initially delivered on shore in Singapore arrived. The second time about 56,000 food parcels (from the British, the South African and the Australian Red Cross) arrived.

[79] Women, thus, who had managed to withhold money or valuables.
[80] M.H. Diepeveen-Lindner, 'Verslag van het vrouwenkamp Tjihapit', 1 February 1946, p. 13 (NIOD IC, 34,961).
[81] B. de Jong, 'Verslag', 1 May 1947, p. 4 (ARA, Alg. Secr., Eerste zending, XXII, 45, 924).

The third time (the transport with the *Awa Maru*, which was sunk by an American submarine on its return journey) 49,000 food parcels (chiefly from the American Red Cross though partly financed by the Dutch government) were unloaded in Priok in March 1945. The arrival of these parcels did not mean that they were distributed to the prisoners of war and the internees: the Japanese appropriated by far the largest share, including the medicines. It could take years before the prisoners of war and the internees indeed received the parcels, and those from the *Awa Maru* made it no further than Java.

The first parcels were only distributed in the internment camps in the period May-August 1944, about two years after they had reached the Japanese: parcels from both the first and the second shipment. Parcels from the same two shipments were also distributed in March 1945. Subsequently, April and May 1945 were the two months in which parcels from the *Awa Maru* came into distribution. Make no mistake: parcels from all of these shipments only made it to some and not all of the internment camps. The camps on Borneo and Celebes received nothing, nor did the camps on Central and South Sumatra. Parcels from the second shipment were distributed in the camps on North Sumatra in July and August 1944 but only one four-person parcel to every ten, fifteen or (Aceh) twenty-four internees. In his camp at Belawan, Klooster ('Willem Brandt') wrote:

It's the first time we have heard anything from the Red Cross. So it still exists and it knows that *we* exist. Parcels arrive with chocolate, tins of cheese and butter and fish, dried prunes. They are parcels meant for four men, but we have to share a single parcel between ten men. The Japanese have stolen most of them. (Brandt 1947:149-50.)

According to one of the internees in Glugur women and children's camp at Medan:

We have received a wonderful present from the American Red Cross. [...] We were so happy we didn't know what to do. We could hardly control our nerves. Just imagine, after two years, receiving chocolate and tins of meat, butter, soap, powdered milk and jam – and for each of us a pack of Chesterfields (cigarettes) or Camels, 20 in a pack. We immediately began trading some of the items. [...] Tins have to be shared with three, four or seven people, but we are so grateful. [...] Oh, to drink coffee with milk again! We can hardly believe it. (Van Eijk-van Velzen 1983:114.)

In the men's camp on Bangka the American Red Cross parcels – or what was left of them – were distributed as late as October 1944.

We have information about the distribution of the parcels on Java only with respect to a few camps. In May 1944, in Lampersari women and children's camp (Semarang) every ten internees received one parcel ('There is feasting everywhere') (Boissevain and Van Empel 1981:148), and in Ambawara III, where 18 parcels had to be divided between about 800 internees, everyone got even less:

> A sixth of a tin of corned beef, half a tin of butter, two and a half square centimetres of cheese, three dried prunes, one square centimetre of chocolate, a tiny bit of paté, two sugar cubes – and some good, real coffee! [...] Oh, we are so happy! And instantly we are all a lot friendlier. (Helfferich-Koch 1981:133.)

At the end of May 1944 there were about 1,500 parcels for 14,000 internees in the large Cihapit women and children's camp in Bandung. According to one of them, it was 'an indoor party. We repeatedly said to each other: "If only they knew in America just how much these parcels mean to us!"'[82]

In the camp at Muntilan (between Magelang and Yogyakarta) with more than 4,000 women and children internees, the women acting as the camp leaders (including the wives of navy officers from Surabaya) appropriated so many parcels that when those from the *Awa Maru* arrived, a block leader demanded they all be divided in public view – which was then done.

In Cimahi men's camp there was one parcel for every eight internees; the Americans each received their own parcel, but they refused to accept this and shared them out equally. According to one of the men, 'Later on many appeared to have been stolen, first by the Japanese, then by the Indonesian police, then by our own men'[83] – it should be remembered, though, that by far the most were filched by the Japanese, who, as mentioned in the previous chapter, appropriated nine tenths of the first two shipments and five sixths of the *Awa Maru* shipment.

Sergeant Major De Haas, who left Java at the end of September 1942 and reached Australia in late December, was the first (and only) person who could report to the Dutch East Indies authorities there that the majority of Dutch men on Java were interned and that their families as well as the prisoners of war were facing grave material hardships. The Dutch government in London, which was already in a position to lend assistance to the small group of Dutch people interned elsewhere in the Japanese sphere of influence,[84] immediately

---

[82]   Verslag, 23 January 1946, in Brugmans 1960:413.

[83]   G.D. Bosman, 'Dagboek', uittreksel, p. 9 (NIOD IC).

[84]   In Japan the Dutch internees received sufficient pocket money via the Swedish Legation; in Nanking China via the Swiss consul general in Shanghai they received the equivalent of 50 guilders, later 15 guilders per month; on Hong Kong via the International Red Cross the equivalent of 75 guilders, later 35 guilders per month; and for a long time on the Philippines via the Swedish representative the equivalent of 100 guilders per adult and 50 guilders per child per month. In French Indo China the internees had access to their own money and in Thailand the Thai government took good care of them and the Swedish consul gave them an allowance.

began making efforts to transfer money to the East Indies for the interned men, their families and the families of prisoners of war and of the Indonesians (civil servants and a number of navy and army men) evacuated to Ceylon and Australia. It is estimated that about 15,000 men were interned, that these internees and the prisoners of war had about 40,000 wives and about 58,000 children and that there were about 600 family members of evacuated Indonesians who had been left behind – relief was thus to be extended to a total of 140,000 people. De Haas had said that each family needed 25 guilders in assistance per month – for 40,000 families a minimum of 1 million guilders a month would have to be transferred. However, were all of these families interned? This was assumed not to be the case and furthermore it was assumed that the internees were not required to pay for their food and housing. All of these uncertainties led to the decision to send both internees and non-internees 10 guilders a month per person: this amounted to more than 1 million guilders or (according to the last exchange rate of the East Indies guilder) over 150,000 pounds.

Had this plan actually been realized, the government would have provided all of the internees highly important assistance – however, the Japanese also obstructed this aid to the Indies. The proposal for a first trial transfer of 50,000 pounds was presented to Tokyo via the Swedish envoy in May 1943. Tokyo requested further information in June: how did the government wish to distribute this 50,000 pounds? The answer was prompt: four fifths on Java, the rest among the Outer Islands. After this nothing more was heard from Tokyo. Subsequently in February 1944, the government proposed transferring 50,000 pounds through the mediation of Sweden. Tokyo agreed and asked that the transfer be made in Swiss francs. The Dutch government had no objections to this – but insisted on receiving full disclosure on how the amount was spent: it wanted to be sure that the Japanese had indeed distributed it. The Swedish government received 50,000 pounds in June 1944 and forwarded the equivalent in Swiss francs to the Yokohama Specie Bank in Tokyo. Consequently, in August the Japanese authorities in the naval area and the army areas were authorized to distribute 50,000 pounds in Dutch East Indian guilders among the internees. Even though the Dutch government never received any information concerning this distribution, it nevertheless sent another 50,000 pounds to the Swedish government in April 1945. The money made it no further than Stockholm because the Japanese military authorities in the Nampo told Tokyo that the second 50,000 pounds would cause inflation to rise in the Indies. This was sheer nonsense – the military authorities evidently objected to once again following Tokyo's instructions, specifically those of the minister of foreign affairs.

In addition to the first 50,000 pounds more money was sent to the Indies through another channel, namely the Vatican. In March 1944 Tokyo had approved of the Vatican sending 23,000 pounds to the British internees in the Nampo – two months later the Dutch government received notification that 50,000 pounds in Swiss francs could be transferred for the benefit of Dutch internees via the Vatican. The Vatican received the 50,000 pounds in July – why the money only reached the Japanese authorities via the Apostolic Delegate in Tokyo in March 1945, that is eight months later, is not clear. During this time other plans for financial assistance were discussed in which the Swiss envoy in Tokyo was to play the central role, yet none were realized. In July 1945 Tokyo announced to the envoys of Sweden and Switzerland that financial aid to the internees (and prisoners of war) was no longer possible: there was, it was said, nothing left to buy on the open market in the Nampo region.

The financial aid was indeed disbursed in the Indies, albeit not equally. The women and children's camp at Banjarmasin on Borneo, where about 70 women and 90 children were interned, received 600 guilders; each internee in the two women and children's camps on Celebes (one was Kampili) received 50 guilders; and each internee in the two men's camps, 16 guilders. None of that money was allowed to be spent. In contrast, the Dutch internees on British Borneo received more than 150 guilders per person with which they could buy food. On Sumatra the monies paid out (from the first 50,000 pounds) varied from 8 guilders to 14 guilders per internee and these were followed later by 'collective' amounts drawn from the 50,000 pounds that the Vatican had received – foodstuffs could be bought from all this money except on Sumatra's east coast, where it was deposited in a Japanese bank. In the period November 1944-March 1945 internees in a number of camps on Java received 8 to 10 guilders per person, though in others they received nothing. Here the amount transferred via the Vatican was distributed, though many camps (in so far as is known only women and children's camps) did not receive money, but rather shoes, 'shoes from the Pope', they were called. In some camps large amounts became available; for instance on 1 August 1945, two weeks before the Japanese capitulation, Cideng women and children's camp received almost 130,000 guilders, or about 12 guilders per internee.

The Japanese did not appropriate the relief monies, as they had done with the relief goods. However, they did refuse to send a part of the financial assistance to the non-interned Dutch Eurasians. According to Van Velden, 'The reasons for this are obvious. Their number was so great and they were so widespread that the administration involved would have been quite out of proportion to the slight amount of the gift.' The Japanese had an even more important motive, however: their political ambition (evident from their attempt to involve Dutch Eurasians in the AAA campaign) to make the Dutch Eurasians Asians. 'Gifts from the Dutch government or the Red Cross would have emphasized their Dutchness and their "apartheid"' (Van Velden 1963: 163) – 'apartheid' (separateness) in an Asian milieu.

The internees thus did not receive much, but the psychological significance of the amounts that did arrive was equal to that of the parcels: they were seen as 'miracles', Van Velden (1963:158) wrote, 'as almost unbelievable proof that the outside world still existed, where they were still remembered'.

The isolation was temporarily interrupted.

This isolation was also experienced as painful chiefly because so little information was available about the course of the war. Initially radios could be taken to the women and children's camps on Java but they were 'castrated' and, moreover, soon had to be turned in. But did this take place with all of the sets? No. People were able to hold on to one or two in many a camp,[85] and as a rule in the men's camps there were a few technicians who succeeded in building a receiver with parts smuggled in. The internees were also frequently moved, making it difficult to take along a radio. For instance, when the camp of the IVth and IXth Battalions in Cimahi began to function as a men's internment camp initially there was no set, but some of the Chinese interned there put one together and hid it in the mortuary, which the Japanese, fearful as they were of infection, did not dare enter. On the basis of the messages thus received, Jacques de Kadt drafted a daily, concise news bulletin which was duplicated and sent on to certain intermediaries. The camp of the XVth Battalion in Bandung had a radio that was mounted in a chair.

It is furthermore assumed that news about the course of the war was also heard via clandestine contacts with Dutch Eurasians and Indonesians who were not interned. The Japanese afforded a limited news service: in 1943 on Java they first allowed indigenous newspapers into the camps and subsequently the weekly *Voice of Nippon*, which was mentioned in the previous chapter. As of the beginning of 1944 these were no longer sent to the women and children's camps. The *Voice of Nippon* reported Japanese victories but in 1943 it also mentioned that Italy had capitulated: in contrast, in 1944 the Allied landings in Normandy were concealed. This weekly was discontinued at the end of 1944 – after that copies of a Japanese newspaper published throughout the Nampo area, the *Nippon Times,* occasionally reached some camps both on Sumatra and on Java. In November 1944 it reported that the Germans had surrendered virtually all of France. Finally, in many camps people succeeded occasionally and sometimes regularly, even if only for a short while, in getting hold of a copy of the Japanese daily that was published on

---

[85]   A large set was kept in the big Lampersari women and children's camp (Semarang), a sizeable apparatus, which, whenever there was the threat of a Japanese inspection, the owners hid in the dark in a large chest on top of a pile of suitcases in a storage area; 'all very simple', according to one of the internees, 'just like the most ingenious plans, but it required a fair amount of courage [...] to execute this simple plan' (Boissevain and Van Empel 1981:225).

each of the large islands in the archipelago. It there was even one internee in the camp in question who could read Japanese, this was enough to get some idea of how the war was progressing. Of course, the Japanese asserted repeatedly that they had sunk the entire American Pacific fleet, first at the Gilbert and Marshall Islands, then at the Marianas, then at the Philippines – the only thing that could be inferred from this was that the liberators were approaching and thus gaining strength.

This could also be inferred from pamphlets dropped from bombers stationed in Australia. Many of these pamphlets were directed at the Indonesians, but on four occasions special propaganda flights were undertaken to drop pamphlets in Dutch. The first was carried out in the night of 9 to 10 November 1943 by a USAF plane over Surabaya. Subsequently there were three flights by bombers of the KNIL air force: at dawn on 24 September 1944 over Preanger, Buitenzorg and Batavia, in the morning of 28 January 1945 over Surabaya and Semarang, among other places, and finally on 21 June 1945 (from Morotai) over Southwest, Central and North Celebes.

As far as we know, the pamphlets dropped above Surabaya in November 1943 (pamphlets with a personal message from the second-in-command of Eastern Forces, Rear Admiral P. Koenraad, who had been navy commander in Surabaya until his departure to Australia)[86] did not reach the interned women and children in the Darmo district, though news of the flight definitely got through to them and the men interned elsewhere in the city.

The second propaganda flight, that of 24 September 1944, was successful. Two aircraft with red, white and blue stripes on their fuselage and under their wings dropped a total of 300,000 pamphlets above Preanger (Bandung and surroundings). Most of them gave news of the war – chiefly about the Allied airborne landings in the Netherlands that had begun on 17 September (Operation Market Garden, the Battle of Arnhem) – and some with messages from Lieutenant General Van Oyen and Van der Plas. The intention was that the parcels with pamphlets in Dutch would be dropped in and around Bandung above the large Cihapit women and children's camp and Sukamiskin Prison, and in Batavia above Cideng women and children's camp, the prisoner of war camp in the Xth Battalion barracks and two prisons. The aircraft destined for Bandung could not reach its goal because Japanese fighters were in the air, and so it dropped the pamphlets elsewhere in Preanger. However, the plane bound for Batavia was able to carry out all of its mission. The aircraft flew low to the ground; it was clearly seen by prisoners of war and internees and both groups were able to get hold of the pamphlets. Flying

[86] Koenraad himself flew with the bomber in question; it dropped about 50,000 pamphlets. 'Today' he said in his message 'I flew over our city: before long I hope to walk in the streets again and see my friends. Have patience!' (Text of the pamphlet in Zwaan 1981:173).

southward from Batavia, in Buitenzorg the aircraft fired at close range on the governor-general's palace – it almost caught a large Japanese flag hanging on a nearby mast when it climbed up again.

During the third propaganda flight, on 28 January 1945, pamphlets were dropped above many places: Surabaya, Madiun, Surakarta, Semarang, Magelang, Yogyakarta. The aircraft had almost 300,000 pamphlets on board. Underway to Semarang it passed the internment camps at Ambarawa: that such camps existed there (the first since as long ago as December 1942!) was unknown to the Dutch East Indies authorities in Australia, but the commander of the low-flying B-25 saw thousands of women and children flocking together and waving at him – he circled the camps for 20 minutes and dropped about 10,000 pamphlets in Dutch. 'The emotion, the joy, the excitement, the unbelievable feeling of happiness that welled up in our hearts,' as H. Helfferich-Koch (1981:181) described the reactions in Ambarawa VI, where more than 3,000 women and children were interned:

> make us forget *everything*. And suddenly the entire camp is a mass of singing, waving, cheering, even dancing and crying women with children on their arms, pointing: 'There, there, do you see it? A *Dutch* plane, a Hollander!' Hugging each other, patting each other on the shoulders, mothers calling out with high, breaking voices: 'Look, look, we haven't been forgotten, they know we're here! There's still a Dutch army, there are still Hollanders free. [...] Our papa will soon be here!'

The reaction was the same in Lampersari women and children's camp (Semarang), where as the pamphlets fluttered down ('we wanted to snatch them from the air') (Boissevain and Van Empel 1981:212) one could pick up copies of four different ones: in English, in Chinese, in Malay and in Dutch. Carla van Berkum (Vermeer-van Berkum 1980:102-3) noted that:

> They said that on landing [in MacArthur's region] they received great support from the natives, who were united behind them, and they asked if we would do the same, for this meant the liberation of *Indonesia*!

Terrific, wizard.

> All we know about the fourth propaganda flight, that of 21 June 1945, is that a few of the orange pamphlets landed in Kampili women and children's camp: they reported that the Netherlands was liberated and that Queen Wilhelmina had returned.

It should be added that presumably (again, there is no information about this) the Allied bombing raids on the oil installations in Palembang in December 1944 and January 1945 became known to the internees in that area. This was certainly the case with the attacks on Belawan and on shipping in the Strait of Malacca. The former, carried out on 4 January 1945, led one of the internees to note in her diary: 'Could this really be the beginning of the end?' (Van Eijk-van Velzen 1983:125.)

That end, liberation, was eagerly awaited.

Inevitably, the longing for liberation time and again engendered the most optimistic rumours. These are mentioned in various camp diaries.

For instance, on 14 June 1942 (1942, not 1943 or 1944!), a rumour that British armed forces had landed on the Dutch coast circulated in Pulu Brayan women and children's camp at Medan. One of the internees there noted:

> We don't quite believe it entirely, but are nevertheless full of hope. They make it sound even better, for it is said that The Hague has already been taken and that they are fighting in the province of Holland. It must be true.
> 15 June. [...] Suddenly I hear resounding through the house: 'Holland is free!' I jump up. We pale from the excitement. Could it really be true? I can't believe it. They tell me that they are already wearing orange in the camp and the children party hats. I think this is premature. After all, so many rumours make the rounds.
> [...] A smack in the face, the rumour that Holland is free proved not to be true. And everyone is now down. Fortunately, I did not believe it, so it isn't such a blow for me. (Van Eijk-van Velzen 1983:22-3.)

Five days later:

> A man wearing an armband who bicycled past [a Nippon worker] is supposed to have called out that the British were only 70 miles from Berlin.

Could this be true? And was it true that the prisoners of war removed from Belawan in May had come back?

> Wham, a kick in the teeth. For the umpteenth time, the reports are not true that our husbands are back and the British are only 70 miles outside of Berlin. This is the last time that I will get excited about such reports. (Van Eijk-van Velzen 1983: 24.)

Yet everyone who resolved to do this still caved in when a new optimistic rumour was doing the rounds. Two years later, at the end of April and beginning of May 1944, in this same camp it was reported for a week that: Sumatra was surrounded by 400 Allied warships; that the Allies had landed at Palembang and in Aceh; that there was an armistice in Europe; and that Hitler had fled to Switzerland. In Brastagi women and children's camp on the other hand, where as early as February 1943 it was said that Germany had ceased fighting, it was only put about in October 1944 that the Germans had 'really' capitulated (and in January 1945 that 'the United States of Europe had been established', that Queen Wilhelmina and Princess Juliana had 'stepped down' and that 'in Rome serious consultations' were taking place about the end of the war in the Pacific).[87]

In Lampersari, Carla van Berkum (Vermeer-van Berkum 1980:33-4) wrote in her diary on 14 June 1944 that the day before a report had been received to the effect that:

> There was a battle by Batavia. Afterwards a certain someone passed on something she had heard from the Nips themselves, so there's a 90% chance that it's true, about which everyone was terribly excited.

Exactly two months later, on 14 August 1944:

> Once again, the reports were tremendous. Europe free, Hitler dead, the Parindra caught,[88] etc. If it is all true, the predictions will have proven to be correct. Thanks to all this we are in a terrific mood. This morning I quickly made a sketch of the wooden bed, otherwise I won't have the chance, and Mom and I have begun working on our liberation outfits like busy bees. We all assume that we will be free at the end of August, beginning of September. Well, I certainly hope so. (Vermeer-van Berkum 1980:42.)

More than five months later, in early February 1945:

> The news is good. Madura is in our hands, also the airfield at Malang. Surabaya and Malang have been razed, etc. They are making good headway. We will be set free within this month. (Vermeer-van Berkum 1980:106.)

4 March 1945:

> Diary, we are free! I cannot say anything more, but it *is* true!! I hugged Aunt Cor. Oh, I just can't take it in. It is still a dark secret, but absolutely 100% [true]. I am bursting. [...] The rumour is that it will be announced to us on the 8th.[89]
>
> 5 March. R[oosevelt] spoke last night and congratulated us on the world peace![90] And that between 8 and 11 M[arch] the Nips will withdraw under safe-conduct. Just imagine that! Yet I am curious whether we will hear anything on the 8th. Oh goodness, I hope so.
>
> [...] 8 March. Yesterday there were ten high-ranking Nips in the camp. [...] And then the *hancho* [barrack heads] were summoned to Mrs Van der Poel's and told that all the rumours about the boys coming back [...] etc., were not true, etc. But that we are free, is true, they can't convince me otherwise, for that is 100% certain, not just a rumour. And precisely now that they have told us this, I believe it again. At first I wasn't sure, but now I am, I have no more doubts.

---

87   Toeter-Teunisse, 'Dagboek', uittreksel, pp. 1, 3, 5, 7 (NIOD IC, dagboek 79).
88   Presumably this means: the Indonesian nationalists were arrested by the Japanese.
89   That is 8 March 1945, the third anniversary of the capitulation of Kalijati.
90   Upon returning from the Yalta Conference, President Roosevelt addressed Congress on 1 March 1945 and voiced his expectation that the conference had established a safe basis for a harmonious post-war collaboration with the Soviet Union.

[...] 11 March. [...] The armistice (it was not peace) has fallen through again. (Vermeer-van Berkum 1980:121-2, 124.)

And so the morale of many internees went up and down: raised by a wave of optimistic rumours, they fell back into the abyss when these proved unfounded. Did these ups and downs have an unfavourable effect on their stamina? Probably not. Given the conviction that Japan would be vanquished, the highs were more important than the lows. Most simply could not live without the optimistic rumour: 'Intoxicating, giver of hope, saviour,' wrote Rudy Verheem (1979:42), 'issuing from the combination of isolation, despair, and hope; uncritically lapped up, an odourless gas that permeated everywhere' – odourless yet inspiring. 'I am certain', says Leffelaar, reviewing his more than three-year internment on Sumatra, 'that many more people would have died had we not continually been deluged with the most insane reports'. Others too expressed themselves in the same vein. According to D.M.G. Koch (1956:240-1):

> I saw fellow internees die from nothing other than homesickness for freedom. In my view the attitude of a few 'realists' who predicted at least a three-year loss of liberty was irresponsible,[91] because under the given circumstances all that mattered was keeping [our] spirits as high as possible, if necessary against all odds.

When asked how long the interment would last, Koch 'invariably' answered 'another three months'.

For most, internment lasted around three years and of those three, the last one, when starvation was so widespread and one saw so many internees die, was the most difficult by far. According to Van Velden (1963:411-2) in a more personal passage (she was interned in Cideng):

> After mid-1944 people began to lose their interest in most matters. If one now [her study appeared in 1963] look back on the internment, before then the days still had a certain shape to them, but everything thereafter has become a murky blur. For myself I can say that I remember nothing about when and in what sequence various events took place during the last 12 months. The last weeks must have seemed endless. Years later, when I looked at a list of the dead of Cideng in 1945 in search of the dates of the deaths of acquaintances and family members, they turned out not to have died in April or May, but all in the last weeks before the Japanese capitulation. Although I know this information is correct, in my memory their death took place months before the end.

Three years of hardship and filth, three years of isolation and lack of privacy, three years of forced togetherness with countless strangers – this demanded fortitude to adjust and carry on. In general it was more difficult for those

---

[91]   De Kadt was one of these realists.

who considered a Western existence as the only possible way of life than for those who had the capacity to adjust to an Oriental style of life. In general it was more difficult for intellectuals (according to Van Velden, 'a number of them were shattered completely') than for the 'uneducated' (who 'sometimes were towers of strength') (Van Velden 1963:397). In general men had a tougher time than women. Leffelaar, a keen observer young as he was, was transferred from a women and children's camp (Pulu Brayan) to a men and boys' camp (Unie *kampong*, later Belawan Estate, later still Siringoringo) and so in a position to compare the two. He wrote:

> Although the bearing of the women [...] in general evidenced more character than that of the men, the atmosphere in Pulu Brayan was less healthy than in the men's camp and the relationships worse. People were more envious. [...] It also seems to me that there was greater resentment. When a quarrel took place in the men's camp, it was over after an exchange of heated words or physical blows. In the women's camp, where a scuffle was a rarity, a disagreement often fermented for a long time and a trifling difference of opinion could take on the character of a long-drawn-out vendetta. (Leffelaar 1959:148.)

He found it 'striking' that the interned women indulged in a great deal of occultism, which in the men's camp he encountered only 'as a party game' (Leffelaar 1959:152).

> Reviewing the women's camps and summarizing my impressions, I arrive at the general conclusion that morale was less low there than among the men. Naturally, I remember plenty of women whose every other expression was 'God damn it', who stole or collaborated [with the Japanese], but nevertheless a certain reserve was maintained and, quite simply said now, a certain pride. This could be attributed to the children for whom they were responsible and for whom they had to keep up at least a semblance of decency. But there were also children in the men's camps. For them respect was lost there for things that we now hold high again. [...] If there was an obligation to maintain standards before the young, it should have weighed most heavily on the men. The women in any case adhered to normal standards as long as possible. They did this with great self-sacrifice and courage, with which the behaviour of many men paled in comparison. (Leffelaar 1959:161.)

It may be that 'an obligation to maintain standards before the young [...] should have weighed most heavily' on the men, but it ought to be remembered that the women had their own children with them, and that many boys found themselves in men's camps where strangers had to take care of them because their own fathers were prisoners of war. The presence of these young children gave meaning and substance to the lives of many interned women, and not only the mothers among them: in the internment camps they could pursue, albeit under great material difficulties, a large part of their 'regular' female duties. Moreover, at that time women in general were used to con-

forming to the wishes of their husbands – that subordination did not affect
their sense of self-respect, whereas many men found it difficult to bear the
subordination to the Japanese. And then domestic chores had to be done in
every camp – for most women the most normal thing in the world, for most
men something highly unusual. Women had an easier time than men keeping somewhat clean with the most primitive means and, in general, did not
slide into a state of neglect that could lead to apathy followed by death.

Perhaps to all of this should be added that in general the Japanese (and
the Koreans imitating them) behaved less harshly in the women and children's camps than in the men's camps.[92] According to Van Velden, there were
Japanese who 'both during and after the war (stated) that they were unable to
stand up well to the women and had no idea of how to deal with them'.

It is notable that protest demonstrations against the starvation rations
erupted in several women and children's camps. One such demonstration
in a camp at Medan during which a Japanese was hit with a stick led to the
confinement of 40 women without food and water until the name of the individual who had wielded the stick was divulged after three days – she was
still in jail at the time of the liberation. Once in Brastagi about 400 women
left the camp in protest – the Kempeitai brought them back and punished the
leaders with a thrashing and weeks of detention.

We do not know of similar demonstrations in the men's camps.

Did the women have more fighting spirit and did their distress cause
them to act with greater recklessness? Perhaps.

The fact remains – and this points in the direction of this greater fighting
spirit as well as the ability to adjust better – that, as stated, two to three times
fewer women than men died during internment.

While general aspects of camp life were sketched in the previous section of
this chapter, one highly important aspect is singled out here for closer analysis: the isolation. The internees received virtually no news about those dear
to them, and if messages did get through, they had been mailed at least one
and a half and sometimes three years earlier. Most welcome in and of themselves, Red Cross parcels were distributed only on rare occasions. As a consequence of the opposition of the Japanese authorities in the Nampo territory,
the financial assistance which the government had gone to some trouble to
establish at an early stage arrived very late – moreover, this support was only
a drop in the bucket. The internees had no clear idea of the war's progress,
giving cause for many to believe in absurd rumours time and again. This
notwithstanding, they maintained a certain resilience (the women generally
somewhat more than the men), albeit that in the last phase of internment

[92]   Some Japanese treated young children with a certain tenderness.

many became apathetic, primarily due to the alarming lack of food.

Approximately one in six internees perished and most of these deaths occurred in the last phase of internment. Naturally, people outside of the camps suffered from starvation as well. The point is that the Japanese military authorities who were responsible for the well-being of the internees – indirectly prior to 1 April 1944 and directly thereafter – because of their requisitions had sufficient food supplies at their disposal.

The reader is reminded that throughout the Indies there were 225 locations where internees were sequestered for longer or shorter periods of time. As noted above, each of these centres had its own history, just as each of the almost 100,000 internees in those bitter years had to bear his or her own fate. The aim of this general study was to offer a global idea of the situation, whereby developments and incidents in certain camps as well as the experiences and reactions of individual internees served a strictly illustrative function. Can this chapter be concluded here? The answer is no. A few camps in the Outer Islands deserving special attention, and developments in the Japanese internment policy on Java that could not be discussed in previous sections should be elucidated: the internment of groups that were not initially confined, the dissolution of the Kesilir 'colonization camp', the segregation of Jewish internees and the rounding up and isolation of prominent Dutchmen, including some of the highest-ranking administrative officials in internment.

These issues will now be addressed in greater depth.

Some particulars – the Outer Islands

This chapter opened with a description of what was without doubt the least odious internment camp in the Dutch East Indies: Kampili women and children's camp near Makassar. Now that the general misery of the camps has been discussed, it is all the more evident just how much depended on the Japanese commandants' interpretation of their tasks. The same instructions applied for the commandant of Kampili, Sergeant Yamaji, as for all other commandants – however, he wished to carry them out properly. Most of the other commandants, as well as their superiors elsewhere in the Great East and on islands such as Java and Sumatra, ignored these instructions in so far as they prescribed decent treatment (for example, the general regulation issued at the beginning of November 1943 by the department of War in Tokyo), and exhibited supreme indifference to the fate and suffering of the internees whom they so despised.

In the introduction to this chapter, it was noted that of the roughly 160 men and older boys in Minahasa, no less than 70 died.[93] While Kampili had

---

[93]   Twenty-eight of the approximately 400 women and children interned there died. Higher

few deaths, about 40 of the approximately 650 men and older boys interned on Southwest Celebes died. They were housed in barracks until October 1944 and subsequently in the filthy sheds of an abandoned hog farm where dysentery took the lives of about 25 internees. Finally, as of May 1945, when MacArthur's troops had landed on Tarakan, they were in a camp in a wet, chilly valley, high in the mountains, where there was far too little space (two square metres per person) and where the men suffered greatly from starvation. According to one of the internees,[94] 'the atom bombs saved us from an inevitable death by exhaustion'.[95]

As mentioned above, Sumatra had the greatest number of centres where internees were held for shorter or longer periods of time: 91 (Java 85).[96] Most of them were not in the least equipped to house such large numbers, though, as Van Velden (1963:285) noted, some were 'fairly decent and not all too full'. She specially mentions the women and children's camp in Pematang Siantar and the women and children's camp in Brastagi which, she wrote (1963:285), 'with the beautiful buildings and grounds of the agricultural school and its excellent mountain climate [was] long the star among the women's camps'.[97] Other camps were undeniably bad, such as the prison in Padang where about 1,000 men were initially interned, and where, after their departure in October 1943 to a camp in the mountains (the barracks of a rubber planta-

---

still than among the interned men and boys in the Minahasa was the relative mortality rate of the internees on Dutch New Guinea, some of whom were taken to Ambon though most remained behind: about 1,000 Dutch Eurasians and Indonesians (assistants of the Dutch administration) as well as about 200 clergymen and nuns from Australian New Guinea. In these groups (descriptions of their internment are lacking) no less than 800 people perished.

[94]   A very precise record of the various nationalities in this men's camp in February 1945 exists: at that time there were 417 Dutchmen, 108 Dutch Eurasians, 4 Indonesians, 20 Englishmen, 6 Australians, 2 Americans, 2 Canadians, 1 Italian, 1 German, 3 Belgians, 1 Dane, 2 Poles, 1 Rumanian, 1 Swiss, 4 Chinese, 16 Armenians, 1 Iraqi and 2 Arabs (A. Bikker, 'Verslag mannenkamp Zuid-Celebes', 4 October 1945, p. 2 (NIOD IC, 32,708)). This camp also experienced sharp contrasts; 'some', according to a Catholic brother in his post-war report, 'had ample clothing and money and others only the clothes in which they had been taken prisoner'. Much smuggling took place except for in the last camp, 'the most honest among them asked for 10% of the proceeds as their wages, but there were also those who took 40 to 50%. [...] All of this could have been much better and easier if there hadn't been so many selfish men who would rather see others die than do without their refreshments.' (Brugmans 1960:416).

[95]   J. Prins, 'Rondom de Japanse capitulatie in Celebes', n.d., p. 6 (NIOD IC, 81,580).

[96]   For all of the places mentioned, see Map 7.

[97]   Initially, the camp command here consisted of men. Moreover, in the first months there were a few dozen indigenous servants. In July 1942 appeared the first issue of a stencilled camp bulletin, *De lijdende vrouw* (The suffering woman), which was strikingly outspoken. One poem, 'Resurrection' read: 'The Japs rule here with harsh violence', and ended with the lines: 'With the image of our queen in mind/We can still tolerate a good deal of abuse/Deep inside we know with certainty/that in the end Victory is ours!' (NIOD IC, 36,416).

tion in Bangkinang), about 2,300 women and children were interned who had previously been housed in a mission complex. A few months later these women and children were also transported to Bangkinang, where 236 of the more than 6,400 internees died, that is almost 4%, while most of the others were extremely weak.[98]

Elsewhere on Sumatra the death rates were much higher.

This applied to the internees on Sumatra's East Coast and especially to those on South Sumatra.

The greatest number of deaths was among the internees on Sumatra's East Coast in the last year of occupation. Conditions in the women and children's camps in that region were already dire in 1944, but at the beginning of 1945 the Japanese decided to move all of the internees away from the areas where the Allied landings were expected. In the period from April to July 1945 approximately 4,000 interned women and children were consequently trans-ferred to Aik Pamienke at Rantauparapat, where primitive barrack complexes were set up in areas that had been cleared in the rubber forests – 40 died within just a few months. Except for two groups that were first moved to Aik Pamienke to build the barrack complexes for the women and children, the men who had long been crammed together in previously mentioned camps, such as the Unie *kampong* in Belawan and Belawan Estate, were transported to a new camp on the Bila River in October 1944. This was Sirigoringo – the two groups from Aik Pamienke ended up there as well.[99] Belawan Estate, an abandoned tobacco plantation whose housing for the coolies had already been condemned by the labour inspectorate under Dutch rule, was far worse than the Unie *kampong*. The so-called hospital, a shed with small rooms where married coolies had lived with their wives, was, according to an internee:

> Something atrocious. [...] The grim walls covered with a sinister mould and dirty streaks; on the ground vile mattresses and sheets which had not seen the likes of soap in years. The emaciated, mostly older men with their grey beards and uncombed hair, clothed in pyjamas in which their elbows stuck out, formed a deplorable mass of hopeless human misery. (Visser 1982:162-3.)

[98] Proportionally many more Dutch Eurasians were interned on Sumatra than on Java, but in several camps quite a few were released after some time. Nevertheless, in early September 1945 in Bankinang there were, of a total of 3,207 internees, 1,289 Dutch and 1,703 Dutch Eurasians (plus 85 Indonesians and 29 others, that is British, Australians, Canadians and Americans) ('Overzicht telegrammen van de RAPWI, Sumatra, naar Ceylon', p. 2 (NIOD IC, 81,411).) The first RAPWI commandant who came to this site, the South African major G.F. Jacobs, later wrote: 'The general living conditions in the Bangkinang camps were somewhat better and the spirits of the women internees higher than at some of the other camps. At the men's camp [...] however, the morale was low.' (Jacobs 1979:112.)
[99] The British internees and several prominent Dutch figures were incarcerated in a separate camp at Rantauparapat.

Siringoringo, however, likewise an abandoned rubber plantation, where ultimately about 1,500 men and 500 boys ended up, afforded even more misery. According to Leffelaar:

> It was in many respects a barbaric camp. By day the heat beat straight down from the sky on an open area in the middle of the forest. In the dry season the ground was as hard as rock and cracked. There was no shade to be found. The barracks were built of wood, with walls of woven bamboo through which the wind had free play.

When the first groups arrived there in October of 1944 following an excruciating one-and-a-half day train journey:

> The woods [nevertheless] were bowed from the rainfall and the earth squished under our feet. [...] With the voice of a cornered person, someone asked: 'Where is this leading to?' 'To Hell', responded someone next to him, 'to Hell, lad', and it was as though he summed up everyone's feelings. (Leffelaar 1959:120-1.)

As it turned out the internees in Siringoringo were guarded not by Koreans or Indians but by indigenous auxiliaries ('Scum. They lash out'). (Leffelaar 1959: 164.) According to Klooster ('Willem Brandt'):

> The menu is worse than it ever was in the camp at Belawan Estate. [...] You can't buy anything, not even through contraband, because smuggling is impossible here: there are no *kampong* in the vicinity. We are locked in between the river and the swamp. [...] The entire surroundings are permeated with the smell of faeces: largely the consequence of bacillary dysentery. [...] There are already 600 patients. They can't possibly all fit in the sick bays, so that most of those suffering from dysentery remain lying among the others and in their own excrement. 'We live here in a diluted solution of each other's excrement. This is a so-called faecal community,' so says the doctor. (Brandt 1947:174-5.)

As mentioned above, roughly 500 boys belonged to this community. The last group only arrived at the camp when it had already been in existence for quite some time: 'a long row of 200 little scrags', an administrative official later wrote (Van de Velde 1982:119), 'ten-year-old boys who had been taken away from their mothers [...] in the women's camps. They looked more like boys of six or seven, that's how small and gaunt they had stayed.'[100]

The hunger began to gnaw ever more fiercely. Some relief was experienced in the steady supply of crude, unrefined palm oil, 'the taste is disgusting, the product contains acids that not every stomach can tolerate. But for us',

---

[100]   But they were 'remarkably clever and independent'; they put field mice in boiling palm oil 'and then gobbled them up. I heard that they have already eaten the Japanese commandant's cat.' (Van de Velde 1982:120.)

according to Klooster, 'this oil is our salvation. We drink it, no, we guzzle it by the spoonful.' (Brandt 1947:187.) Not that this supply prevented theft from occurring with great frequency! Publicly announcing the names of the culprits did not help either.

In Siringoringo 120 internees died, most of them of malaria and jaundice. The only burial ground was a swampy terrain: one hour after a grave was dug there would be a foot of water in it.

Let us turn to the internees of South Sumatra. The internees in this region, about 900 of them (including approximately 120 oil technicians, who had first had to help repair the refineries at Palembang), were brought to the island of Bangka in September 1943, where they were locked up in the prison and quarantine station in the capital Muntok. This transfer presumably stemmed from the fact that the Japanese had got wind of the resistance being planned by the Ambonese, which is discussed in Chapter II. The living conditions in the prison and quarantine station were deplorable. Another approximately 200 starving internees who had first been incarcerated elsewhere on Bangka (including an Ambonese, Louhanapessie, who was set on being treated as a Dutchman), were also sent there. According to a survivor of the *Poelau Bras* disaster (the ship sunk by the Japanese on 7 March 1942 off the coast of South Sumatra):

> Many became ill with malaria, dysentery and avitaminosis. Selfishness was rampant [...] the number of deaths increased. [...] Some worked in the kitchen and thus earned some extra food. [...] Others took on fatigues for payment in order to be able to purchase some tobacco or a cup of coffee. Smuggling with the outside world, sometimes via the Japanese or the guards, was rife. A shirt went for 4 kilos of maize; watches, fountain pens, wedding rings or jewellery were very much in demand on the outside. (De Roever 1951:374-5.)

The survivors (259 had perished) were transported from Muntok back to Sumatra at the beginning of March 1945. They lived in coolie sheds on an abandoned rubber estate near Lubuklinggau, 'where', the survivor of the *Poelau Bras* wrote, 'we spent the last months of the war in a state of starvation' (De Roever 1951:375) – here another 96 men lost their lives.

A total of about 720 interned women and children had to cover the same routes. They, too, were transferred from various places to Muntok, though only in October 1944. Subsequently, in April 1945 – a month after the men thus – they were taken back to Sumatra and also ended up in the sheds of the rubber estate near Lubuklinggau. The transport in both cases was appalling. Little boats were used for the journey there. 'Some boats', wrote Van Velden (1963:308), 'had no toilet; one boat was so small that 100 women on board had to sit without moving a muscle for the duration of the crossing'. The transport back cost six lives. Furthermore, 67 women and children died in Muntok and 95 in Lubuklinggau.

In the camps on Central Sumatra, 10% of the internees perished, on North Sumatra 5%, and on South Sumatra (Bangka included) 37%. Little can be recounted here about the South-Sumatra group – too little in relation to the atrocities they were subjected to. Incidentally, the same applies to the internees on Dutch New Guinea and to the interned men in Minahasa. There were no Willem Brandts or Leffelaars in these latter groups and no extant camp diaries.

Some particulars – Java

As described in Chapter I, the internment process on Java was gradual. The first internments took place in Batavia, where in the first ten days of the Japanese occupation many eminent Dutchmen were incarcerated either in Struiswijk Prison or Glodok Prison, including administrative officials, police officials, teachers, members of the judiciary as well as the officers and the Dutch members of the Batavia Stadswacht. Months thereafter the internments were still limited to men: first the prominent figures, and then the others aged 17 to 60, of whom only the Dutch Eurasians and those Dutch who earned less than 300 guilders per month were released. Moreover, on East Java in July 1942 approximately 1,400 Dutch and about 1,000 Dutch Eurasian men were forced to move to Kesilir 'colonization camp', not far from Java's extreme southeastern tip.[101]

Action against the women and children, in so far as they were registered as 'pure' Dutch (*Belanda-totok*), began later: in October 1942 in Batavia, and subsequently also elsewhere, they had to move to certain centres, usually city districts. In Batavia these were the rather run-down districts of Kramat and Cideng, but in cities such as Bandung, Semarang, Surabaya and Malang relatively good districts were designated. Thus initially the women and children were accommodated in slightly better internment centres than the men, whose housing consisted primarily of 11 prisons in the beginning. It became more difficult for the women and children when from September 1943 to February 1944 they were concentrated in Batavia, Bandung, and Semarang as well as in Ambarawa and Banyubiru. On East Java they then had to leave the internment districts in Surabaya and Malang – the groups from Surabaya and Malang arrived in Lampersari Camp (Semarang) with stories that incited jealousy. L. van Empel (Boissevain and Van Empel 1981:131) noted:

---

[101] For all the places mentioned see Maps 1 en 8.

They were quite well off in Malang: plenty to eat (that is if you had any money left), a *pasar* in the camp where you could buy all sorts of goods, a fine hospital, numerous doctors, medicine, etc. [...] In Surabaya they were even better off than in Malang. Even to the very end they had money and therefore the possibility of buying sufficient food.

The establishment of Kesilir Camp was the first step towards the realization of one of General Imamura's ideas: to unite Europeans who had lost their income with their families in a region where they would be able to support themselves through agriculture. This step was limited to East Java where, incidentally, the designated region was unsuitable for colonization – the camp leader assigned by the Japanese, J.G. Wackwitz, had repeatedly and emphatically warned against this, but to no avail.

Kesilir began with about 2,400 colonists: close to 1,400 Dutch and 1,000 Dutch Eurasians. Was this number to remain stable? Wackwitz was soon informed that the Japanese wished to increase it to about 10,000 in the short term. In the end not 7,600 men were added, but a mere 800, the largest group of whom consisted of more than 500 Dutchmen who had first been interned in one of the prisons in Surabaya: they arrived in Kesilir in May 1943.

In the beginning, the colonization region was a cheerless sight to those arriving there. The Dutch Eurasian Rudy Verheem, who was brought to the camp in 1942, recorded the following impressions:

Abandoned bamboo huts loom up, a few collapsed, left in haste by the expelled Javanese population. [...] Our destination an empty bamboo house, the rooms formed by plaited walls, already occupied by fellow prisoners cast into this waste some weeks earlier. A silent reception, there is room for just a few men, in the distance there are still empty huts for the rest of us. Bamboo poles, walls, a roof of *atap* [dried palm leaves], floor of stamped clay, a bare compound, imperceptibly merging into the rolling, dry plain. [...] A mat on the floor, some clothes under one's head, one's sleeping place; life has been reduced to the level of existence of the original population, impoverished and toiling, spending their lives in a remote place.

How long would one have to stay in this godforsaken spot? Roaming around were:

Sombre men, their world violated, their lives disrupted, stunned by imprisonment and the loss of dominion, unaccustomed to bowing to oriental rulers. After years of issuing orders and being obeyed, now aimlessly staring, weak, limp, many finding a quick death in this place of exile due to resentment and sorrow. (Verheem 1979:24-5.)

The camp (where a total of 44 internees died) nevertheless became fuller and among the first additional groups were various men aged between 20 and 50 who, in spite of all the difficulties, wished to pitch in:

> The paralysis and desperation of the first weeks made way for industriousness. We worked for ourselves, for our own existence and well-being, the huts were repaired, the roads improved; we were allowed to keep the harvest for our own use. [...] The energy of the camp dwellers was transformed into health, and vigour and optimism returned and the desolate piece of land became a symbol of reclamation. (Verheem 1979:31, 34.)

Wackwitz's energetic leadership contributed greatly to the improved atmosphere. He did his best to maintain order. Among the internees, according to his report, there were 'many bad elements' and 'a lot of stealing took place'.[102] To combat this theft and other misbehaviour he set up a camp police and meted out punishments (up to a maximum of three weeks of house arrest). He ran the camp as democratically as possible: each housing unit could elect its own leader, above them were senior leaders and after some time every 500 internees could choose a member for an Advisory Council which assisted Wackwitz. There were also two assistant commanders: P. Cellarius, an official at the headquarters of the Handelsvereeniging Amsterdam (HVA, one of the largest agricultural concerns) in Surabaya, and the architect Lang from Malang.[103]

They set to work. Tools they lacked were brought in from Surabaya from time to time. Water buffaloes were also introduced to work the *sawah*. The harvest was good: to supplement the Japanese rations the men in Kesilir received more than sufficient rice. Meat, vegetables, sugar and coconut oil were amply supplied. To reach this point, however, took time – the first months were difficult. Subsequently, when the fear of starvation had disappeared, many internees mustered up the energy to participate in all kinds of recreational activities: there was soccer, draughts, chess and bridge; plays and concerts were given and much reading was done (there was a sizeable library). Moreover, every Sunday there were church services for Protestants and Catholics.

It was crucial that the internees were not entirely isolated. Copies of *Asia Raya* reached the camp (and a small group even had a clandestine radio at its disposal for quite some time) and correspondence with family members was permitted, albeit only in Indonesian. Moreover, the internees were allowed to receive goods from their families. 'It was surprising', Wackwitz noted, 'what actually came in this way: [...] hundreds of bicycles [these were sorely needed in the colonization region which covered about 2,500 hectares], as well as numerous pieces of furniture, even large cabinets'.[104] Better yet: visits were

[102] J.G. Wackwitz, 'Rapport inzake de kolonisatie-Kesilir', March 1946, p. 28 (NIOD IC, 28,991).
[103] The latter, as mentioned in Chapter II, was executed by a firing squp. ad as a member of the Koops Dekker group in mid-June 1943.
[104] J.G. Wackwitz, 'Rapport inzake de kolonisatie-Kesilir', March 1946, p. 33 (NIOD IC, 28,991).

sanctioned as often as the 10th of every month.

Yet this was no simple matter! Kesilir was located in a remote area and the train went no further than Benculuk, from where it was still 35 kilometres to the camp: too far to walk, but with little carts from Benculuk one could get within two kilometres of Kesilir. The day before the 10th a special train ran on East Java, which, according to a Dutch woman living in Malang, only 'the girlfriends of the Japs (and there were quite a few of them at that time)' did not have to take, 'because they rode in their boyfriends' private cars' (Moscou-de Ruiter 1984:61). For all of the others it was a long journey.[105] Frequently jeered at by Indonesians, sometimes also pelted with eggs and rotting fruit, they had to travel fourth class, the lowest, and arrived in Benculuk in the late afternoon. There they could eat and sleep in bamboo sheds and on the visiting day, still in the darkness of night, a long queue of carts was set in motion. Every visitor lugged a parcel with her, mostly containing foodstuffs the internees needed in the early period. The visit was very brief, lasting only 20 minutes. Many women returned to their carts weeping. 'Then too', according to the Dutch woman, 'we were ridiculed and pointed at by the natives along the road. [...] We were deeply struck by our husbands' appearance: dishevelled, weather-beaten, wild.' (Moscou-de Ruiter 1984:42.)

The women (there were many hundreds every time) were able to make the exhausting trip to Kesilir seven times. However, the visiting arrangement was suddenly cancelled on the day of the last visit, 10 February 1943, presumably because the Japanese became aware that numerous internees had received information from their visitors about the state of the war as reported by Allied radio broadcasts.

How did the Japanese hear about this?

In the camp, which was first guarded by Japanese soldiers and subsequently by about 250 young Indonesian policemen (commanded by two Japanese, 'two extremely ill-mannered and vicious individuals'),[106] were internees who – as mentioned in Chapter II – collaborated with Japan: about 40 NSB members and another group comprising pro-Indonesian Dutch Eurasians. The emergence of this latter group was related to the fact that the Japanese pursued the same course in Kesilir as elsewhere: they attempted to involve not the Dutch but the Dutch Eurasians in the AAA campaign (carried out in 1942 and underscoring Japanese leadership). In Bandung they had separated the Dutch and Dutch Eurasian prisoners of war. The same was done in Kesilir. When on 20 October 1942 the Japanese army transferred control of the

---

105   Some internees in Kesilir were from Central Java – their wives travelled first to Surabaya and then the following day via Malang to Benculuk.
106   J.G. Wackwitz, 'Rapport inzake de kolonisatie-Kesilir', March 1946, p. 11 (NIOD IC, 28,991).

colonization camp to the Japanese military administration, the new Japanese commandant, a colonel, gave a speech for which the internees had to line up in two separate groups: Dutch and Dutch Eurasians. Some time earlier, after conversing with several Japanese in his quarters, an internee suddenly disappeared from Kesilir. This man, Pieter Hendrik van den Eeckhout, returned to the camp at the end of October, thus after the Japanese colonel's speech, and mounted a campaign among the Dutch Eurasians which created a great deal of discord (and was a source of great concern for camp leader Wackwitz).

Van den Eeckhout was a native Indonesian from Makassar who had been adopted by a European, whose Dutch name and nationality he had thus received. He had served in the navy, and in 1933 had participated in the mutiny on board the *Zeven Provinciën*. Shortly before the war he was employed at the naval complex in Surabaya. He was transported from Surabaya to Kesilir and when he returned there at the end of October, he informed Wackwitz that he had conducted negotiations in Japanese (which he claimed to have learned on Borneo) with various Japanese, though he did not wish to say what exactly the contents of these talks had been. This, however, soon became clear: he had drafted a document in which those who signed it declared that they wanted to be released from internment and would be pleased to participate in the building of the 'Greater East Asian Co-Prosperity Sphere', and not as Dutch Eurasians: no, they wished to be accepted as Indonesians. About 300 Dutch Eurasians signed the document and it was submitted to the Japanese. It had no effect, however, for the gate of Kesilir remained locked also for those who had put their names to it. Consequently, Van den Eeckhout intensified his campaign: if the Japanese wanted proof of his new political persuasion, they would have it! He assumed an Indonesian name and began wearing Indonesian clothes: approximately 150 adherents followed his example. They spoke only Indonesian with each other, memorized Japanese songs and the *Indonesia Raya* and adorned themselves with white squares with a red ball – various badges of rank were also shown on these squares, from which it appeared that Van den Eeckhout had promoted himself to the rank of colonel. However, the group did not become larger but smaller – and more radical. In April 1943 it selected a name for itself: the Persaudaraän Asia Golongan Indonesia (Asian Fraternity, Indonesian Group), or Pagi (*pagi* means 'morning' in Indonesian). For the time being though, the sun did not rise on that morning, because the release of the Pagi members was out of the question.[107]

In mid-1943 the Japanese decided to close Kesilir. Through the efforts of

---

[107]   A total of 27 internees were released from Kesilir, but not because they belonged to the Pagi group. Furthermore, the Japanese allowed 35 internees who were declared medically unfit to return home.

the camp leadership and the internees the camp itself had become a tolerable centre under the circumstances, even though the colonization experiment had failed. The Japanese again, in principle, separated the Dutch and the Dutch Eurasians: in August almost 1,700 men, mostly Dutch, were transferred to the prison in Banyubiru (Central Java). From there in February 1944, after a period of starvation, they were moved to the former barracks of the XVth Battalion in Bandung. In September a group of more than 1,400, mostly Dutch Eurasians, including the 40 NSB members and about 100 followers of Van den Eeckhout (including eight who were Dutch) first ended up in the regular prison in Tangerang, just west of Batavia, and subsequently in the juvenile prison there. Wackwitz also arrived in Tangerang where, according to a fellow internee, he was 'thrashed by a dozen policemen plus the Japanese camp leader in a horrific way'.[108] He was not the only one to be abused, because various other men were betrayed by members of the Pagi group, for speaking Dutch for example, and subsequently were brutally punished by Indonesian guards.

In Tangerang too the Japanese tried to segregate the Dutch from the Dutch Eurasians across the board. They presented the latter with a questionnaire in which they could declare themselves in favour of the Greater East Asian Co-Prosperity Sphere, and hinted that whoever sided with them stood a chance of being released. About 80 Dutch Eurasians refused to fill in the questionnaire and were subsequently added to the Dutch group – the others, together with the members of the Pagi group and of the NSB, were taken to the internment camp in Cimahi. The arrogance of the Pagi group and the NSB members stirred up quite a lot of trouble, but even before year's end in 1944 the members of both groups were released. The Japanese assigned the NSB members to various posts in the economic sector and the members of the Pagi group were mobilized in September 1944 to coerce the Dutch Eurasian group as a whole into adopting a pro-Japanese stance. The extent to which many of them behaved badly is described in the following chapter.

The fact that increasingly fewer foodstuffs entered the camps complicated the internees' existence as of the second half of 1943. Moreover, the camps became more crowded, on the one hand by being combined and on the other hand because groups initially not interned were now being detained. A group of Dutch Eurasian women were confined in Cihapit Camp in Bandung for a few months. They had committed minor offences (some of the interned Dutch women there treated them with open contempt).[109] As of mid-1943

---

[108] H.P. Goudriaan, 'Rapport', 27 November 1946, p. 2 (NIOD IC, 60,779).
[109] Bouwer heard and recorded in April 1943 that they were called '*kampong* chickens'. 'Profanities were hurled over the camp enclosure at any passing Dutch Eurasian ladies. Even the

most Nippon workers were also interned (a fairly large group, though no statistics are available), then a group of Jews from the Near East, mainly Iraq, as well as the Hungarian and stateless Jews, and at the end of 1943 almost everyone with Belgian, French, Norwegian or Danish nationality. They were followed some time after Italy's capitulation (September 1943) by the Italians, though those who declared their solidarity with Mussolini were released. As far as is known, only the Germans (until Germany's capitulation in May 1945), the citizens of the countries allied with Germany such as Romania[110] and, in principle, nationals of neutral countries, remained at liberty – these neutrals, and especially the Swiss so mistrusted by the Kempeitai, were nevertheless subjected to numerous petty annoyances.[111]

Conversely, groups were also released from the camps: in September 1944 about 40 members of the NSB and the members of the Pagi group, and in other months of that year, when the Japanese were doing their best to win over the Dutch Eurasians, some Eurasian women who had wound up in the camps in the confusion marking the beginning of the internment. There is no clear picture of the increase and decrease in the numbers of internees, though what was written in Chapter I bears repeating: by far the majority of people interned at the time of Japan's capitulation had lost their freedom in 1942 or in the first months of 1943.

During the Japanese occupation there was no persecution of the Jews in the Indies, though special measures were taken against some who were interned on Java.

---

word "betrayer" was repeatedly used, while I notice daily [Bouwer's wife was a Dutch-Eurasian] how much effort the still free Indo-European ladies put into easing the fate of their interned fellow countrymen, how these women perform dangerous and valuable work.' (Bouwer 1988:174.) When those Dutch Eurasian women were allowed to leave Cihapit a few months later, Bouwer learned of details that shocked him deeply: 'The Indo-European ladies [...] were very unkindly received by the full-blooded women, who wondered what the "*kampong* chickens" thought they were doing being with the "pure-bred chickens". Other Indo-European women were called "niggers" and "blackies". Naturally, they were not the best and most intelligent specimens of full-blooded womanhood in the camp. The term "fishwife" would be more accurate. I myself am a *totok*, still I am ashamed [...] of these women who feel it necessary to display these divisions in the presence of the Japanese and Indonesian "directors". Many of these full-blooded European "ladies" have refused to be housed together with Indo-European women. Carts used for moving by Indo-European women were tipped over by full-blooded sisters at the entrance to the camp. Indeed, readers, this truly happened.' (Bouwer 1988:196-7.)
[110]   In Semarang a Dutch medical specialist remained at liberty by passing himself off as a member of the Rumanian nobility.
[111]   Living on Java were about 2,000 Swiss nationals, but according to Bouwer in mid-1944 'under all kinds of pretexts (usually Freemasonry) the Japanese authorities have arrested or interned most neutral businessmen and seized their businesses, placing them under the control of the Army' (Bouwer 1988:271-2).

In the 1920s and 1930s there were anti-Semitic groups in Japan in which a role was played by officers who – during Japan's failed campaign in Siberia, shortly after the Russian Revolution – had had contact with Tsarist officers who blamed this revolution on the Jews. This anti-Semitic agitation (it was usually coupled to agitation against the Freemasons) gained momentum during the Second World War and anti-Semitic articles frequently appeared in Japanese newspapers. This agitation had no effect on government policy – moreover there were commentators who contended that were it true that the Jews 'ruled the world', it was decidedly in Japan's interest to work with them. Be that as it may, the Japanese authorities were tolerant of the Jews living in Japan, Manchuria and China. There were not that many in Japan, but at the time of the outbreak of the war in the Pacific about 6,000 Russian Jews were living in Manchuria, and a colony of about 17,000 Jewish refugees from Germany and Austria and various other central and eastern European countries had formed in Shanghai. These two groups were left in peace. Incidentally, most of the Japanese understood nothing of what was written about 'the Jewish danger': for them, Jews were Europeans who practised a certain kind of Christianity. Naturally the government knew that the Jews were severely persecuted in Germany and the countries it had occupied, but most of the Japanese authorities turned a deaf ear to the German exhortations that such persecution should also be instituted in the Japanese sphere of influence. They did not see the sense of it and the exhortations were considered a form of unwarranted interference.

Several thousand Jews were living in the Indies at the time of the Japanese occupation. They were chiefly Dutch and the men moved in business, government and scientific circles, in education, journalism, the medical world and sometimes also in the army (rarely in the navy). These Jews belonged to the group of Europeans: this applied to those who had built up their own livelihood in the Indies as well as to the approximately 400 Jewish refugees who had arrived from England and Portugal in 1940 and 1941.[112] In addition to these Dutch Jews, also living on Java, chiefly in Surabaya, was an entirely different group consisting of several hundred Jewish traders and shopkeepers, including some very wealthy individuals, most of whom had come (via Bombay) from Iraq, chiefly from Baghdad, and spoke Arabic. They were called the 'Baghdad Jews' or 'Iraqis' or 'Armenians'.

The Japanese classified these 'Baghdad Jews' as Asians – 'fellow Asians' were exempt from all internment regulations in 1942.[113]

[112] Various German Jewish refugees who were allowed into the Indies as of 1933 were interned as Germans in May 1940, and removed with the other (German) internees to British India in December 1941 and January 1942.
[113] Much the same happened at the end of June 1942 in Adek Camp at Batavia. There a large group of Dutch men who had been rounded up were interned and upon their entry the Japanese

This situation changed in 1943. In early April a high Kempeitai official in Batavia spoke to journalists, arguing that the policies of the United States and of Great Britain were determined by the Jews and that there were also Jews on Java who were keeping a low profile. Later that month the Indonesian daily in Surabaya published the Nuremberg decrees[114] in extenso and the daily that appeared in Bandung published an entire series of anti-Semitic articles by the nationalist leader Soekardjo Wirjopranoto. Bouwer (1988:173-4) wrote about this as follows:

> I have fairly certain information from a reliable Indonesian source that this was instigated by Berlin, which has expressed its resentment of the fact that so far the Jews have been counted among the Asians and generally left in relative peace on Java.[115] It is, moreover, quite remarkable, for the Indonesians know nothing of the Jewish issue and therefore the entire campaign is completely artificial. [...] In any event, the fairly substantial Arabic population of the Indies is being vigorously pitted against the Jews.

Around the time of the first anti-Semitic campaign, the recently replaced German ambassador in Tokyo, Eugen Ott, who himself did not feel strongly about the matter, travelled throughout Java. After his departure, the propaganda was resumed in which it was suggested that President Roosevelt was a Jew of Dutch descent and moreover the head of international Freemasonry.

While actual regulations were not imposed after Ott's visit, they were after the visit begun at the end of July 1943 by three other Germans: the economic negotiator H. Wohltat, the consul general in Mukden, E. Ramm and the consul in Kobe, H. Bräunert. In mid-August in Surabaya, and somewhat later on Java, the 'Baghdad Jews', the Jews of German origin and, to the extent they were not already interned, the leaders of Freemasonry were rounded up, and in a number of internment (and some prisoner-of-war) camps Jewish internees were ordered to report separately.[116] As far as is known, the only

camp commandant, a Christian, told the Jews to stand apart. Several did so and were given their own barrack, the worst, until one of them went to the commandant and swore that the Jews came from Asia. An atlas was produced and the Japanese were shown where Palestine was located. Consequently, the worst barrack was exchanged for the best.
In Bandung all of the Jews (that is to say the women and the men not interned) had to register separately at the end of October 1942. Bouwer wrote, 'They received a sort of race certificate. So far the Japanese still consider them Asians.' (Bouwer 1988:136.)
[114] These decrees, dating from September 1935, forbade marriage and sexual intercourse between Jewish and non-Jewish Germans.
[115] This applied to the 'Baghdad Jews' and to the German Jews not interned in 1940 and the stateless Jews.
[116] On Flores the Japanese commandant of the prisoner-of-war camp compared a dozen Jewish prisoners of war with cartoons from the notorious German anti-Semitic weekly *Der Stürmer* and concluded that there was no resemblance.

internment centre to implement segregation was Struiswijk Prison in Batavia, where a separate group was formed of those internees who had reported their Jewish descent (not all had done so) – to their vexation they were added to the NSB group.

All was quiet for more than six months, but on 29 April 1944 (Hirohito's birthday) the new head of the Department of General Affairs of the Japanese Military Administration, Colonel Moichiri Yamamoto (the successor to Colonel Nakayama) gave a fierce anti-Semitic radio address (text in Benda, Irikura and Kishi 1965:112-3) in which he asserted that 'the slavery' to which a thousand million Asians had been subjected for centuries was the work of the Jews and that it was thus obvious 'that the Jews are the enemies of all Muslims'.[117] Segregation measures were introduced in the camps on West Java a few months later. The Jewish men in Cimahi were transferred to separate barracks, and as of 1 January 1945 they were made to wear a red triangle which indicated that they were highly dangerous (thus they could not do fatigues outside of the camp). They were subsequently put together with the Freemasons in separate barracks in Baros Camp in Cimahi, which was home to the large group of interned leading figures from the entire European community on Java, who were also required to wear the red triangle.

Furthermore, the juvenile prison in Tangerang was largely evacuated: people from the Kesilir group confined there were transferred to internment camps on the Bandung plateau, and the American, British and Australian women and children interned in the juvenile prison were sent to Cideng and Adek camp in Batavia – only the women and children of prominent Europeans remained behind in Tangerang. To this camp, in the last months of 1944 the Japanese then moved all of the Jewish women and children from the camps in Bandung and Batavia. Tangerang was abandoned in April 1945 – and all of the women and children from that centre were assigned to Cideng and Adek camps, in both of which the Jewish women and children were separately housed. There, on 14 August, just the day before the emperor announced the Japanese surrender, they received one final shock: they were again required to register separately, and that order was linked to rumours that the Japanese were planning to transport all of the internees to Borneo. Were they going to be the first? No, the registration had no effect whatsoever.

The above makes clear that on Java, just as elsewhere in the archipelago, groups of internees were frequently moved around. In early 1944 the situation

[117] This theme was promptly taken up in several Islamic periodicals. The Central Advisory Council, established in September 1943, included several anti-Semitic tirades in the session it held in May 1944, in response to questions posed by the Japanese military administration – these did not recur in later responses.

was that the women and children were together on Central and West Java and the men on the plateau at Bandung (namely in Bandung and Cimahi). The concentration was further increased in 1945, whereby a decisive factor was the Japanese expectation that the Allies would land on Java around October 1945. A small women and children's camp on Central Java was discontinued – the people in question were transferred to the camps in Ambarawa, Banyubiru and Semarang. Then there were the women and children from a few small camps on West Java, for example Tangerang, who were moved to the large camps in Batavia. The interned women and children in Bandung were also transferred, some to Semarang, Ambarawa and Banyubiru, others to Batavia where *Kampong* Makassar, which had served as a prisoner-of-war camp in 1942 and 1943, was now used to accommodate the approximately 3,600 women and children from Bandung, the overcrowded Cideng Camp and two other camps. Furthermore, everywhere the men older than 60 and the boys aged 10 and older were taken from the women and children's camps and transferred to the men's camps (on West Java) or to separate camps (on Central Java). Moreover, a large number of old men, chronically ill and seriously sick patients were moved from the camps in Bandung and Cimahi to these separate camps on Central Java or, after May 1945, to hospital camps at Batavia.[118] Finally the group of prominent individuals (those in Batavia were initially confined with others in Struiswijk Prison) was expanded and concentrated in a separate camp.

Was there any logic to all of these displacements? Indeed there was. According to Van Velden, the Japanese combined all of the old men and the ill with the women and children on the north coast (the presence of these groups would only hinder the Allied troops after their landing), and concentrated the more able-bodied men – evidently wishing to keep a close watch on the prominent individuals among them – on the plateau of Bandung, where they intended to offer resistance to the very end. It should be remembered that, as mentioned in the previous chapter, there were plans to kill these individuals should the liberators draw near.

The concentration carried out by the Japanese resulted in all of the camps still in use becoming inordinately full. The sun beat down mercilessly on

[118] A nurse in one of these camps kept a diary, from which the following is quoted:
'22 May 1945 - A thousand ill men [...] have arrived. Wearing rags, uncivilized, demoralized men. 25 May 1945 - Indescribable conditions. Filth, insufficient water! Food minimal.
14 June 1945 - Huge commotion. [...] Two men betrayed while trading over the *gedèk*. Tied to one another with a belt around their neck for the entire day. In the afternoon [...] they were beaten with a stick and belt and kicked before the entire camp.
20 June 1945 - The men are dying like rats, sometimes seven in a single day.
3 August 1945 - After two and a half months, about 130 of the 1,000 men have died.
14 August 1945 - One third of the nurses lie sick in bed.' (W. de Greve, 'Dagboek', uittreksel, p. 6 (NIOD IC, dagboek 129).)

filthy complexes where the internees had to share the tiny spaces they had been able to preserve with the new arrivals. There was little to eat, and often even less to drink. Shabbily dressed, hungry and thirsty, the elderly deathly tired from struggling for almost three years to keep their heads above water, the youths usually suffering more from the hunger and the thirst, they yearned for a liberation which many feared would come too late.

The writer Beb Vuyk arrived in *Kampong* Makassar (at that time many other camps were no better) in 1945. Years later she wrote:

> I will never forget the smell of baccillary dysentery, of blood and mucus. All of the very serious patients were taken to the overcrowded hospital; the rest remained in the hut in their 50-centimetre sleeping places, the sick and the healthy next to one another on only 50 centimetres. You ate your portion of rice and next to you a child fouled the mattress. You washed your plate in a bucket on the floor before you and less than a half meter away someone was sitting on a pot full of blood and mucus in a rotting stench of decay. And at night you slept on the same mattress in between a feverish, delirious, highly infectious child and your neighbour on the other side, also feverish, who was so close you could touch each other's elbows and knees any moment.
>
> You forced yourself to consider all of this normal, you did not want to allow yourself to realize just how critical was the situation of this undernourished throng, piled far too close together, without disinfectants and almost without *obat* [medicines], at the mercy of an infectious disease. If on occasion full awareness took hold, despair overwhelmed you. The two toddlers of a young woman lying across from me were running high fevers, one from malaria, the other from dysentery. The youngest was born when the father had already been gone for months and the woman had never heard from him again. She said: 'I stopped shedding tears long ago about the fact that my husband may never come back to me, but I can weep for nights on end about the aversion I now feel to the glowing, feverish little bodies of my own children'.
>
> We sat outside although it was way past time and Nippon kept a close watch on whether people left their huts. That night, a moonlit night of unreal beauty, the *banjir* of despair poured over us.
>
> And so we lay in clouds of death and decay, and daily the strongest helped drag the worst off to the hospital, and the weakest and the old and the young children died and were buried in a mat, because there was no more wood for a coffin in this country rich in trees.
>
> A short prayer, the truck driving closer and the hospital nurses who pushed the bier onto it and handed over the wooden cross. When the engine was started, the Nippon sergeant jumped onto the running board and so, guarded to the very end, our young children were driven to their soldier's grave.[119]

If liberation were still to happen in time, what then? To the extent that they were married and had children, the women wanted nothing so much as to

---

[119] Beb Vuyk, 'Boerderij Makassar', pp. 2-3 (NIOD IC, 81,277).

take care of their children under normal circumstances and to be reunited
with their husbands. Most did not worry about what would happen in the
liberated society – they did not have the energy for this and, moreover, everything related to political issues was seen as a male prerogative.

Among these men there was one group which was indeed much concerned with the measures to be taken once the Allies landed: the group consisting of prominent figures.

Virtually all of the internees hoped that they could simply resume
unchanged the life that had been disrupted by the arrival of the Japanese and
interrupted by internment. Women hoped for the restoration of normal family
life, men for the resumption of their careers. Whoever had held a leading position, whether in government or in the business community, wished for nothing other than to once again contribute as quickly as possible to the rebuilding
of East Indies society which, as could be inferred from the starvation rations,
had been critically undermined by the war and Japanese mismanagement.
The first priority was the swiftest possible restoration of Dutch authority.

It was primarily the group of prominent figures that gave this consideration. When Japan capitulated, almost all of the internees – isolated as they
were and in camps far removed from one another – were politically passive
and in no state to develop any general initiative beyond the immediate relief
effort. This did not apply to the group of prominent figures: immediately
after Japan's capitulation, on Java they attempted to regain control of the
general administration – the fact that this attempt failed should not prevent
us from devoting special attention to this group. Describing their experiences
has the additional advantage of allowing the reader to follow a single group
of internees and thus, in the last part of this chapter, gain an understanding
of the shifting circumstances that affected the lives of all of them.

First, we must return to the early days of the Japanese occupation of Java
and to the Indies' capital, Batavia.

On 9 March 1942, four days after the arrival of the Japanese advance guard,
the European officers of the municipal police were confined in Glodok
Prison, together with the European officers and some of the members of the
Stadswacht, in total about 450 men, along with the resident of Batavia, C.W.A.
Abbenhuis, and several civil servants. The next day the resident and the civil
servants were transferred to Struiswijk Prison: the others remained in Glodok
and were held for two weeks in this prison teeming with bedbugs.

On 25 March the officers of the municipal police and of the Stadswacht
also had to move to Struiswijk under armed escort. According to a police
inspector:

> We [walked] there with dirty, unshaven, ashen and emaciated faces. European
> women who saw our procession pass by burst into tears, even the Indonesian

population [...] was deeply moved and watched the procession pass by full of compassion. The Indonesian policemen stood at attention when they saw their superiors file by. Virtually the entire European community which we passed by during the march secretly tried to give or throw us something, such as cigarettes, fruit, clothes and other items. A few Indonesian fruit vendors also threw some fruit to us as we went by. [...] Fortunately we were not searched by the guard when we entered Struiswijk.[120]

Built in a horseshoe shape, Struiswijk was a modern prison with about 16 blocks. Each block of 15 single cells received 60 to 100 prisoners: initially, as far as the Dutch and Dutch Eurasians are concerned, the groups mentioned were the only inmates. Later some of those who, as described in Chapter I, were arrested in March, April, May or June were added. A large number of prominent figures from the European community in Batavia was then imprisoned there. At first they were required to stay in their own blocks during the day; however, after a few months they could move about the inner prison yard in the afternoon. The Japanese required each block to have its own leader and there also had to be a general leader. This was jonkheer H.A. van Karnebeek, who had been the representative of the Nederlandsche Koloniale Petroleum-Maatschappij (Dutch Colonial Petroleum Company) and one of the captains of the Stadswacht in Batavia. He had impressed the Japanese with his announcement that in the early 1920s, when his father was minister of Foreign Affairs, he had met Hirohito, then still crown prince, when he had visited the Netherlands.

In cooperation with Resident Abbenhuis, Van Karnebeek exercised resolute and sensible leadership: he saw to it that sufficient time was devoted to sport and education and that hygiene was not neglected. As soon as it was possible, matches were organized in the prison yard in the afternoons. Food was reasonable only in the beginning, when they were allowed to receive a canister of food from home twice a week; later it was insufficient. Contact with their families was not permitted, but Indonesian warders maintained a fairly extensive clandestine exchange of letters,[121] 'for money but nevertheless at great risk', as the official, L.G.M. Jaquet, formerly in the Department of East Asian Affairs, later wrote (Jaquet 1978:166). He learned Latin in Struiswijk and 'the presence of the entire legal and medical faculty was [...] taken advantage of to organize many lectures' (Jaquet 1978:167). Struiswijk also had a popular cabaret; a professional Hungarian band that had been arrested by the Kempeitai played there, and religious services were allowed as of the end of 1942.

In 1942 the people confined in Struiswijk, like so many still at liberty, were

---

[120]   J. Burer, 'Verslag', 1 February 1947, p. 2 (ARA, Alg. Secr., Eerste zending, XXII, 45, 100).
[121]   With help from the Japanese commandant's Indonesian houseboy, one of the wardens could even make use of the commandant's saddlebag to this end.

fairly optimistic. They had access there to several radios made from parts that had been smuggled in and they listened avidly to the Allied broadcasts. The reports and commentaries (which were not passed on to all of the internees) were amplified with optimistic rumours – many prisoners were convinced that the British and Americans would soon land on Java. And what then? People considered what would have to take place immediately and what at a later time. It was assumed that the Japanese would have to concentrate their armed forces on the landing points – in that case it might be possible to rapidly take Batavia or parts of it from Struiswijk; plans for this were worked out in which the internees, divided into groups, were given special tasks.[122] In addition, the interned administrative officials met to discuss the administrative measures that would need to be implemented directly after the arrival of the Allies. In this respect it was important that a number of high officials who had participated in the discussions at the Olcott Park Hotel (also aimed at the restoration of Dutch rule) which had been chaired by Spit, vice-president of the Council of the Dutch East Indies, had been transferred to Struiswijk Prison from Sukamiskin Prison in Bandung. Among them were J.M. Kiveron, head of the General Secretariat, and P.J. Idenburg, director of the governor-general's cabinet. Van Karnebeek was well informed about the discussions held in Struiswijk – a core was established of determined individuals who did not for a second doubt that Japan would be defeated and who had decided what they would undertake in Batavia the minute this defeat was near or was a fact.

This determination was reinforced when a crisis arose in Struiswijk around July 1942 because the Japanese demanded that the internees, who after all were considered 'foreigners', make the usual declaration of obedience to the Japanese army. Heated debates ensued. Some interned lawyers argued that a forced declaration was invalid and moreover that what the Japanese were asking for was in line with the *Aanwijzingen* (Directions) issued by the colonial government, but these arguments made no impression on five of the internees: Lieutenant Colonel B.H. Gronewold (commander of the Batavia Stadswacht), H.M.J. Hart (head of the Central Office of Statistics), A. Ritz (head of the Government Accounting Department), M. de Niet (the representative of the missionary bodies in Batavia) and jonkheer W. Strick van Linschoten (director of the KNIL farrier school). These five men refused to set

---

[122] Something similar took place in Bukit Duri Prison in Batavia, where, a member of the Internal Administration later noted, 'the absurd and irresponsible stories about Allied victories which had taken place, about fighting by Allied landing forces that had already progressed to Sukabumi and the like led to the setting up of commando and other units, which fully intended to go into action'. (J.M.J. Morsink, 'Kort Verslag', n.d., p. 2 (ARA, Alg. Secr., Eerste zending, XXII, 45, 288).)
The group from Bukit Duri was added to those in Struiswijk in July 1942.

their thumbprint under the declaration. As a consequence they were beaten, put in separate cells, placed on half rations, and were not allowed to receive any books or tobacco, nor to shave or bathe. A captain of the Stadswacht, K. Hoonstra, later noted: 'In general there was enormous respect for their firm stance' – 'the weak' drew courage from the example set by the five.[123]

The core group in Struiswijk was not the only one to emerge. A second was formed in Sukamiskin Prison in Bandung, where the Japanese concentrated the officials of the Internal Administration who had been taken in April 1942 and initially confined in or near where they were stationed.[124] Academics and leading business figures joined them, and in early September 1943 those who had participated in the deliberations at the Olcott Park Hotel came from Struiswijk, as well as all of the other high officials who had earned a monthly salary of 900 guilders or more. The Sukamiskin group numbered about 200 prominent figures and besides them there were approximately 150 other Dutch (and about 350 British) internees there.

Struiswijk and Sukamiskin Prisons were discontinued as internment centres for men in early 1944. Most of the internees from both prisons were transferred to the former camp of the XVth Battalion in Bandung. The prominent figures first went to the camp of the IVth and IXth Battalions at Cimahi and subsequently, in October 1944, to another camp in the same place, Baros III.

The XVth Battalion camp looked like a German concentration camp: not only were there barbed wire fences, but also watchtowers. It was a large camp – just walking around the inner periphery took one and a half hours. In the end about 10,000 men were interned here, 'the humblest of Indos from the *kampong*' wrote Rudy Verheem 'alongside top officials and millionaires; crammed together, emaciated, hungry, some still in possession of smuggled gems or gold, most desperately poor' (Verheem 1979:46). The poorest could earn a bit of money: 15 cents per day for whoever was willing to take part in fatigues organized by the Japanese outside of the camp: maintaining the roads, clearing out the internment camps from which the women and children had been moved, building the railroad embankment on the Bandung plateau.[125] According to Verheem (1979:53-4):

[123] K. Hoonstra, 'Verslag', 1 July 1946, p. 4 (ARA, Alg. Secr., Eerste zending, XXII, 45, 386).
[124] In Yogyakarta in September 1942, one administrative official who was seriously ill was allowed to go home to recover; he stayed there for 11 months (he was married to a Dutch Eurasian woman) and with a radio he had held on to, he listened to the Allied news broadcasts a few hours every day. After the war he recounted: 'The reports were relayed via doctors, ministers, some civilians and employees of sugar factories. To camouflage the comings and goings of all of these people my wife set up a cookie bakery in our house.' B. de Jong, 'Verslag', 1 May 1947, p. 3 (ARA, Alg. Secr., Eerste zending, XXII, 45, 924).
[125] One of the internees assigned to the railway fatigue, the civil servant R.C. Kwantes, wrote about this shortly after the war in letters to his family in the Netherlands: 'This railway fatigue, or Nip tour, was better than the other coolie work in the city of Bandung. You received twice the

In the morning lining up in rows of five before the camp gate, so the guards have a good view, ready to be counted. Trousers full of holes, the worn patches repaired with motley bits of cloth, a little singlet with tears, a ripped shirt. Bare feet or wooden clogs, a strip of leather around the foot, clattering like a Chinese pedlar. A food bowl and a spoon with a string around the middle. Count and count again. Bow. Very low, face turned in the direction of the son of the sun, the emperor of Japan. One last count, hoarse Japanese voices, a kick here and there, borne patiently and helplessly. Shuffling along, a disorderly, long chain of men, no military pace, as long as the men keep moving and the row of five, magical number for the sons of the sun, is maintained. Guards before, behind and at the side, surly and hostile looking Javanese *heiho*, all this under the command of a Japanese balancing on his little bicycle. The fresh air of the mountain city shortly after dawn, the once so elegant region unrecognizably mutilated by endless bamboo enclosures, barbed wire, weeds, dilapidated roads and buildings. At a distance the indigenous population, not betraying their thoughts with a single look, neither hostile nor friendly, looking on impassively, steadily pursuing their activities.

However, when such a column approached parts of the city where non-interned Dutch Eurasians lived, there was a reaction. From there came:

> The sounds meant specially for us, the prisoners, the column: often singing, a short song referring unmistakably to liberation, staying the course, not giving up hope, a piano with a continually repeated refrain: 'J'attendrai toujours [I will wait forever]'.

Sounds, affirmations of loyalty like these, were for some in the XVth Battalion camp – where some of the internees knew that Japan was being steadily driven into a corner (there were three clandestine radios) – all the more reason to continue preparations for taking over the general administration immediately after liberation. The group from Struiswijk, which had already drawn up 50 emergency ordinances there, acted cautiously. At the initiative of Captain Hoonstra they first established who was suspected of spying for the Japanese – after that the tasks, as already specified in Struiswijk, were again allocated. A retired colonel on the KNIL's General Staff, later a member of the Military Supreme Court, M.E.A. van Goor, was given command of a secret organization. According to Hoonstra, a magistrate, P.H.G.M. Brugman, 'in

amount of rice and bread and the soup was better. Moreover, oil, more sugar and tobacco. Line up in the morning at 7 Tokyo time (this was called 'stink time'). And then just stand, stand. To the train around 8:30, leave at 9, arrive at work around 10:30. Line up there at 5, leave at 6, arrive home around 7:15 or 7:30. Our motto was "See Preanger with the Nip tour". On the way serious trading was conducted with the *heiho*. Mostly clothes for money, sometimes also for eggs and coconut oil. The clothes were often pinched from the evacuated women's camp [in Bandung]. I sure got to know your average European Joe in the Indies! Pathetic. And not just the little man. Often the high-ups were morally bankrupt. I mean in the area of corruption. We called our camp Corruption Headquarters.'

consultation with Mr Hoven' (previously head of the department of general administration in the Internal Administration) discussed 'countless contingency measures that were to go into effect immediately after liberation or during an interim period'.[126] Captain Van Karnebeek was kept in the dark about the details: as camp leader here as well, he was too closely observed by the Japanese. But he did know the general scheme and maintained contact about it with Resident Abbenhuis, who was transferred from Struiswijk to Cimahi, specifically the camp of the IVth and IXth Battalions.

In August-September 1944, the secret organization in the XVth Battalion camp took a heavy blow: many able-bodied men on whom they were counting (most of them members of the Batavia Stadswacht and many merchant navy men) were transported to Batavia in order to be transferred on the *Junyo Maru* to Padang to work on the Pekanbaru Railway. Incidentally, Hoonstra and many others from the Struiswijk group were moved to Camp Baros III in October 1944. There they again encountered the prominent figures, who came from the camp of the IVth and IXth Battalions.

A few days after his arrival, Hoonstra reported to Resident Abbenhuis and A.S: Block, the interned Attorney General. He told them about the organization in the XVth Battalion camp. According to Hoonstra in his report on the matter, 'I was ordered to wait for the time being. I also discussed the matter with Hoven. His advice was: "Hoonstra, keep your eyes and ears open and wait."'[127] Was this a recommendation to remain passive? Hoonstra disregarded this. He began to build up a new secret organization, command of which was assumed by Block. He chose about 700 able-bodied men whom he split into sections and groups, all under subcommanders, established contact with the leader of the camp of the IVth and IXth Battalions, jonkheer De Villeneuve, and took 'measures ensuring that [at liberation or during the power vacuum] cooperation with contact persons could be fully realized within a few hours'.[128]

But on whose behalf would this secret organization be acting when the time came? This was unclear; at least there was no one who could give it any authorization. Therefore it was of cardinal importance that at the end of 1944 or beginning of 1945 Spit (who, as mentioned in Chapter II, was in Purwokerto for a long time on suspicion of having given instructions for railway sabotage) was brought to Baros III. In the absence of a governor-general or lieutenant governor-general, the vice-president of the Council of the Dutch

[126] K. Hoonstra, 'Rapport over het interneringstijdperk jan. 1944-okt. 1944', August 1946, p. 2 (ARA, Alg. Secr., Eerste zending, XXII, 45, 389).
[127] K. Hoonstra, 'Rapport over het interneringstijdperk 10 okt. 1944-15 sept. 1945', August 1946, p. 1 (ARA, Alg. Secr., Eerste zending, XXII, 391).
[128] K. Hoonstra, 'Rapport over het interneringstijdperk 10 okt. 1944-15 sept. 1945', August 1946, p. 1 (ARA, Alg. Secr., Eerste zending, XXII, 391).

East Indies was the highest representative of Dutch authority. Should it ever be necessary to assume authority from the Japanese in a situation in which the Dutch government had no authorized representative in place, there was only one person who could in law demand this transfer of power: Spit. According to Hoonstra, 'Everything was soon concentrated on this figure. The progress of the work was reported to him [...] and everything had his full approval. [...] At his request, Block stayed on as leader of the organization.'[129]

Hoonstra was unable to keep his 700 men together: in May and June 1945 a number of them were transferred yet again, and he retained only about 400 men who were 'medically examined and found to be able-bodied and fit for our organization'.[130]

No one in the Indies could foresee that a full month would elapse after the announcement of the Japanese capitulation, on 15 August, before the first Allied battleship, the British cruiser *Cumberland* would appear off Batavia. For the entire month Spit, Block, Hoonstra, the members of their secret organization and so many others were faced with a situation they had not anticipated. The Republic of Indonesia was proclaimed in Batavia and law and order were to be guaranteed by the Japanese, and this not by order of the Dutch but rather the British authorities. Spit and his secret group had only a legal claim which had been pushed aside without their knowledge – they had no means of enforcing it. They knew that as to the possible restoration of Dutch authority it was likely that nothing could be expected from the Dutch and Dutch Eurasian soldiers: most of them were widely dispersed. They also knew that internment had seriously weakened the Dutch civilians. What about the Dutch Eurasians, the great majority of whom were not interned?

Most of the other Europeans were not aware of what had happened to this group, neither the prisoners of war nor the internees.

[129]   K. Hoonstra, 'Rapport over het interneringstijdperk 10 okt. 1944-15 sept. 1945', August 1946, p. 2 (ARA, Alg. Secr., Eerste zending, XXII, 392).
[130]   K. Hoonstra, 'Rapport over het interneringstijdperk 10 okt. 1944-15 sept. 1945', August 1946, p. 2 (ARA, Alg. Secr., Eerste zending, XXII, 392).

CHAPTER VI

Dutch Eurasians under pressure

In previous chapters it has been noted more than once that the picture presented here is somewhat sketchy because of the lack of reliable information. This may not have applied to the account of the fate of the prisoners of war and the internees, but it certainly applies to the description of resistance and clandestine activity, and to the passages dealing with the Japanese mismanagement of the economy, the fate of the *romusha*, and the shocking impoverishment of the indigenous population. It also applies to what follows here on the subject of the Dutch Eurasians. This group faced its own special difficulties during the Japanese occupation, and indeed found itself in an increasingly desperate position. However, almost no authentic documents from this period have been preserved; there has been no historical study comparable to Van Velden's work on the internees, and there have been few published accounts by the victims themselves. Furthermore, what is true of this work as a whole is especially true in this area: much less is known about what happened on the Outer Islands than about what happened on Java.

A first general difficulty is that there is no firm statistical basis for any account. Officially, the Dutch and the Dutch Eurasians in the East Indies belonged to the same group, that of the Europeans. The legal system made no distinction between Dutch and Dutch Eurasian, who all had the same, Dutch, nationality. Nor did the statistics distinguish between them. As a result, and because no census had been held in 1940, it is not known exactly how many Dutch[1] and how many Dutch Eurasians were living in the East Indies at the beginning of the Japanese occupation. In an earlier work we put the figures (not without some hesitation) at approximately 80,000 Dutch and a little over 200,000 Dutch Eurasians. These were estimates – substantially higher figures for the Eurasians have also been suggested. While working on this book, it was discovered that according to a Japanese report 200,000 Eurasians were not interned on Java in 1944, and in view of this we now assume that at the time of the Japanese invasion there were about 280,000 Dutch Eurasians in the whole of the East Indies.

[1]   In the rest of this chapter the term 'the Dutch' refers exclusively to the *totok*.

More than 42,000 Dutch and Dutch Eurasian men were taken prisoner, and an estimated 100,000 of the remaining Dutch and Dutch Eurasian men as well as women and children were interned. In other words, about 220,000 of them, nearly all Eurasian, remained outside the camps, by far the majority on Java. The latter fact was due to two circumstances: first, before the arrival of the Japanese, the Eurasians were more highly concentrated on Java than the Dutch; second, as noted in Chapter I, in principle the Dutch Eurasian civilians on the Outer Islands were interned, while those on Java were not. The Japanese military administration on Java pursued a policy entirely of its own in relation to the Eurasians.

As for the Dutch Eurasian civilians on the Outer Islands, some figures were given in the previous chapter. In the men's camp on Southwest Celebes in February 1945 there were over 400 Dutch and over 100 Eurasian internees; and the group from Sumatra's west coast consisted of close to 1,300 Dutch and slightly over 1,700 Eurasian internees at the time of Japan's surrender. These figures appear to suggest that on Southwest Celebes some of the Dutch Eurasian men were not interned, or at least not for long (there is no further information about their fate outside the camps), and that most, if not all, of the Dutch Eurasian civilians on Sumatra's west coast were interned until the end of the war. It is known that some of the Eurasian women and children interned soon after the Japanese landed on Sumatra's west coast were released. We also know that Dutch Eurasian men living with their families in Medan in internment centres and employed as Nippon workers were offered the opportunity to leave those centres in June 1942 provided they made a declaration of loyalty to Japan. In one of the centres, the St Joseph School, 21 of the 45 men involved refused. The next day 24 were allowed to leave, but those who had refused were imprisoned and mistreated before, presumably, being interned again later.

What the Dutch Eurasians who were not interned went through elsewhere on Sumatra or the Outer Islands is unknown. It seems likely that they suffered the same hardships as the non-interned Dutch Eurasians on Java. This large group not only faced poverty but was also put under a great deal of political pressure.

Java – the refusal to accept Japanese rule

Why the Japanese on Java did not intern most of the Dutch Eurasians is not entirely clear. It is possible that they could not do without the many skilled workers in this group (it would have been difficult to replace them by Indonesians in the short term). It may also have been that they were daunted by the prospect of interning a further 200,000 in addition to the many who were designated to be interned. So did the Japanese simply make a virtue of necessity? This seems doubtful, and at the very least it is probable that a political motive played a role. The Dutch Eurasians were in part of Indonesian origin, thus in a sense fellow Asians – could they not be persuaded to put all their efforts into building the 'Greater East Asian Co-Prosperity Sphere'? Whatever may be the case, from an early stage the military administration on Java tried to find people among the Dutch Eurasians who were prepared to subscribe to the Japanese slogans and encourage others in the group to do the same.

Consequently, Dutch Eurasians were given an opportunity to join in the AAA campaign – a committee consisting of Eurasians was set up for this purpose. Who the members were is not known. We do know, however, that in December 1942, that is after the end of the AAA campaign, three Dutch Eurasians – E.G.G.R. Ellendt, E. Endert and H. van der Tas[2] – published an article in *Asia Raya* in which they called on all Eurasians to sign a declaration of political loyalty to the Japanese administration. There was evidently little response to this appeal: it has been pointed out above that most Dutch Eurasians felt a strong allegiance to the colonial government and the Netherlands. It may be that the failure of this call was one of the reasons why in January 1943 the Japanese military administration established an Office of Indo-European Affairs in Batavia and published a 'Warning to the Indo-Europeans'[3] which said that their position was 'extremely difficult':

> During the period of Dutch rule they were considered to be Dutch: they were given a Dutch education and a Dutch upbringing, and they adopted a Dutch lifestyle. Nonetheless, the full-blooded Dutch discriminated against them.[4] They were also kept at a distance by the [indigenous] population, not only because of their mixed blood but also because of their attitude. All this is indisputable.
>
> Considering their position, one is forced to feel sorry for them, especially since they know no other home than Java. The Japanese army aims to give each group a decent place. With this aim in mind, the Japanese administration [...] has shown magnanimity to the Indo-Europeans, assuming an attitude of watching and waiting. [...] Furthermore, the Japanese administration hoped that the group would of its own accord become aware of its present position in Greater East Asia and that it would do no harm. Some of the Indo-Europeans, however, have misunderstood the aims of the military administration and have let themselves be incited or used by hostile elements. There are also those who spread rumours and deliberately undertake actions aimed against the Japanese administration.[5] This truly is deeply disappointing.

---

[2]   Ellendt was a civil servant with the State Railways, Van der Tas a lawyer and prosecutor at Batavia; what post Endert held is unknown.

[3]   Text in Brugmans 1960:454.

[4]   What is meant is social discrimination.

[5]   It is worth remembering that, as was shown in Chapter II, there were no clandestine groups on Java in 1942 in which Dutch Eurasians did not play an important role, if not the leading one.

This is why the Japanese army now wishes to make clear its attitude to the Indo-Europeans, so that they will change their ways. The army is ready to accord them a position equal to that of the indigenous population, provided that they [...] are sincerely willing to cooperate with the Japanese administration. If, however, they are reckless and do not change their incorrect attitude and views [...], the army will abandon its magnanimity and not shrink from taking severe measures against them as if against an enemy people.

The last sentence was a barely veiled threat to introduce mass internment.

For the time being there was only one positive response from Dutch Eurasian circles. It came from P.F. Dahler, a 60-year-old Dutch Eurasian who had been a civil servant from 1908 to 1917 (among other posts he was a controller on Bali) and had then served until 1934 as an official of the Kantoor voor de Volkslectuur (Bureau for Popular Reading) before being given a post in the Government Publicity Department in 1941. Before the First World War he had been a supporter of the Indische Partij, which had been founded by E.F.E. Douwes Dekker and which advocated independence for the East Indies. Later he joined the Indische Sociaal-Democratische Partij and represented it in the Volksraad for six years during the 1920s and 1930s, finally becoming party secretary in the early 1930s. It has to be assumed that Dahler was in touch with Ellendt, Endert and Van der Tas: at all events, in an interview with the Japanese press agency Domei, which was published in at least one Indonesian daily, he too called for cooperation with the Japanese.[6] He said that he was 'very grateful' to the Japanese 'for their warning, since it once again shows how generous and right the government's judgement is'. 'Indo-Dutch society', he was quoted as saying,[7] 'should now be eliminated in this country, that is to say that an Indo-Dutch person should not only regard him- or herself as Indonesian but must also become purely Indonesian. Those who are not willing to do this must be forever foreigners.'

This statement did not accord with the aims of Ellendt, Endert and Van der Tas. They had pronounced in favour of a special declaration of loyalty, but Dahler – who had only visited the Netherlands once and did not feel at home there – had gone substantially further: he advocated giving up the Dutch Eurasian identity.

On 12 March 1943 in the 'radio camp' Jansen noted in his diary that 'nothing had come' of the call by the three men, except that 'some members of the IEV' (the Indo-Europeesch Verbond founded in 1918) continued 'to ask shyly

[6]   Text of the interview, as published in the Indonesian daily *Tjahaja* (Bandung) in Brugmans 1960:455 (in Dutch translation).
[7]   I have phrased it this way because during the war the Japanese published various interviews, with among others Governor-General Van Starkenborgh and General Ter Poorten, which were largely fabrications.

to be admitted'. What is probably meant here is admission to the Poetera, the political movement whose founding was announced by Sukarno on 9 March and which was only open to Indonesians.

A month later, in April, according to the Japanese, the attitude of the approximately 15,000 Eurasians in Bandung and the surroundings who were not interned still left much to be desired. The monthly report by the Japanese military administration there (the only report of this type to be preserved) says that in the home of one Eurasian that was searched the Japanese flag was found to be in use as toilet paper; that Eurasians said, 'that it was quite unnecessary to hang out the Japanese flag, given that Japan would be defeated'; and that the Japanese were increasingly referred to as 'the monkeys'.[8]

In the same month on Java a special registration of all Dutch Eurasians was introduced. In Bandung and its surroundings they were called up for this in June and divided into eight groups (as far as is known, this was done only in Bandung). Bouwer (1988:189), in hiding in his own house, described the system as follows:

> Group 1: *totok* father and Indo mother; Group 2: *totok* mother and Indo father; Group 3: Indo father and Indo mother; Group 4: *totok* father and Indonesian mother; Group 5 (oddly enough!) *totok* father and *totok* mother, but born in the East Indies[9]; Group 6: Indonesian father and *totok* mother; Group 7: Indonesian father and Indo mother, and Group 8: Indonesian father and mother of another Asian nationality.

Bouwer heard that those put in Groups 1, 2 and 5 would soon be interned. He wrote, 'What seems to be decisive is the colour of the eyes and hair. Pending the summons to give further information about the details filled in [the new registration cards had to be completed before 1 July], many ladies are having their hair dyed black to make their Indonesian descent more plausible.' (Bouwer 1988:189.) By this he meant the *partially* Indonesian descent which many had tried to 'prove' with made-up information, often provided by the National Archive in Batavia,[10] when it was announced in 1942 that Dutch women and children would be interned. Bouwer's Eurasian wife, Ivy, and his Eurasian mother-in-law did not dye their hair but they were all right anyway:

> Wednesday 7 July 1943. Ivy and my mother-in-law have been put in Group 3. Both have blond hair and light eyes and the Japanese who was in charge of the classification as the head of a forum of top Japanese civilian officials and Indonesian

---

[8] Japanese Military Administration Bandung, Monthly Report for April 1943, p. 3 (NIOD IC).
[9] This was not really that odd: after all, here and there in 1942 *totok* born in the Indies were registered as '*Belanda*-Indo'.
[10] The head of the National Archive, F.R.J. Verhoeven, was arrested in April 1943 and the archive was closed. After that the Japanese left it alone.

assistants clearly hesitated for a few seconds. So for the time being the danger is past. Ivy's statement that her husband had left her was not questioned. Both registration cards bear an impressive *tjap* [stamp] which reads in translation: 'This is a child of mixed parentage' – plus a figure 3 in blue pencil that can easily be turned into an 8. (Bouwer 1988:190.)

Those who, as indicated by the 8, had an Indonesian father and a mother of another Asian nationality did not need to fear being interned sooner or later.

Again, there was widespread cheating. The special registration of Eurasians had taken place in Malang (and perhaps elsewhere on East Java) in May. In Malang, according to M. Moscou-de Ruyter (a Dutch woman married to a Dutch Eurasian but not interned because she had a French mother): 'Many lied through their teeth. Suddenly they had a Javanese grandmother, because if you had an Indonesian relative in the first, second or third generation you were free. Several people also put in a Chinese person somewhere.' (Moscou-de Ruyter 1984:124.) As we have seen, the registration in Bandung had a similar effect. Bouwer wrote in 1945 that '90% of the Indo-Europeans [say, by far the majority] had a (usually fictitious) family tree' (Bouwer 1988: 332). We assume that these were the documents drawn up in 1942 or 1943.

After this special registration, the second to which the Dutch Eurasians had been subjected,[11] the Japanese went a step further. In a second warning to the Eurasians, issued on 19 September 1943,[12] they referred to the first and announced that some Eurasians had been guilty of espionage or involved in 'drawing up secret plans to restore the previous regime, and other similar acts'. This meant that the group was 'on the wrong path':

> The Indos [Dutch Eurasians] must not forget that they were born and raised on Java and have no other fatherland than Java. [...] So let the Indos appreciate the intentions of the army of *Dai Nippon* and let them, as inhabitants of Java, put all their efforts into building the new Java that is their fatherland too.

Now it did not stop at words. As a group the Eurasians were, so to speak, officially recognized by the Japanese administration. Dutch Eurasian children were admitted to state primary schools; Eurasians with bank accounts were allowed to withdraw part of their funds. Dahler was appointed head of department of a continuation of the Office of Indo-European Affairs mentioned above; this was the Office for People of Mixed Descent, the Kantor Oeroesan Peranakan or KOP. The significance of all this was explained in a radio address by the head of the Department of General Affairs, Colonel M. Yamamoto, the successor to Colonel Nakayama (among other things he said that the Japanese military administration would look favourably

---

[11]   The first had been part of the issuing of identity cards, the *pendaftaran*.
[12]   Text in Brugmans 1960:455-6.

at requests for the release of interned Eurasian men). There was a further radio address by Dahler on 27 September[13] in which he recalled the work of '[E.F.E.] Douwes Dekker, who made our group aware of the position we occupied in Western imperialist society and argued that we are Asians like the Indonesians'. Alas, the newspapers had 'poisoned' the Eurasians: they wanted to see the Netherlands as their fatherland. However, 'thanks to the Holy War in Greater East Asia, the Dutch state and Dutch imperialism' had been swept away. Admittedly, 'the majority' had not yet been 'disillusioned' by this, but that could change – what the Japanese military administration had now done was an 'act of benevolence, springing from a noble heart'.

New 'acts of benevolence' were to follow. In the last days of September Dutch Eurasian internees with seven Eurasian or Indonesian great-grand-parents were released and those with only one were interned. In October the third registration of Dutch Eurasians took place. This was a registration by family, whereby the head of the household had to fill in new forms for himself and for all the family members. Forgeries would be punished by a maximum of three months in jail or a fine of up to 100 guilders. Why this new registration? 'It is thought', noted Bouwer (1988:217), 'that the Japanese are looking for a large number of false registration cards, with false stamps, false names and everything else false'. At the same time the Japanese announced that in future money would be made available to help Eurasians in need. There was, however, a price to be paid: the whole assistance scheme (to which we shall return below) had to come under the KOP, the Kantoor Oeroesan Peranakan.

The third registration was accompanied by a great deal of bickering, inso-far as Indonesian personnel was involved. This had to do with the fact that in general the Indonesians were not at all inclined to recognize the Dutch Eurasians as Asians. 'A survey across all levels of the Indonesian popula-tion', reported one Indonesian to the Japanese military administration at the end of September 1943,[14] 'has shown that no one supports the plans outlined in the various speeches. The differences between the Indo-Europeans and the Indonesians are too great for them to be simply brushed aside.' In turn, according to this report, the Dutch Eurasians had also rejected the plans. A nurse had told her Indonesian seamstress, 'I don't want to be treated the same as the Indonesians. I'd rather die.' One Dutch Eurasian, 'who might possibly be persuaded to support the government plans' took the following view:

> Dahler is not popular with the Indos, so we don't trust him that much. There is almost no contact between Indos and Indonesians. [...] It upsets us that we have

---

13   Text in Brugmans 1960:457-9.
14   Text of the report dated 29 September 1943 in Brugmans 1960:460-1.

to send our children to the state school, where the Indonesian children make fun of them.

For two years the Japanese have regarded us as enemies. The government did not care when our women were put in brothels or hotels. Of the Indo-European men 80% are prisoners of war[15] and 10% are interned as civilians. For whom are the speeches intended? [...] If Indos are released from the camps, but there is no work for them, what kind of a life will they have?

This last point was one of the reasons why, at least in Batavia, not many took advantage of the offer made by Colonel Yamamoto whereby interned Eurasian men[16] (the prominent figures among them had been detained in April 1942) could be released if a request was submitted. This concession was repeated at a gathering of Eurasians held at the zoo in Batavia in December 1943. 'Large crowd attended', noted the journalist W.C.J. Bastiaans.

> Blustering promise by Nippon to release confined *Peranakan* [Indo-Europeans], of their own accord and on request, but promise only goes for civilian internees. Few requests received for release of relatives, friends and acquaintances. 'Let them stay there,' was the tender motto. Evidently because the wife and/or daughter were occupied with other matters for which the presence of hubby, father, brother etc. was not required?[17]

Is Bastiaans's analysis correct? It seems unlikely. As explained above, there were not that many Dutch Eurasian women or girls who had sexual relations with the Japanese. Dutch Eurasian men would indeed have found it difficult to keep their head above water after being released. Moreover, at the end of 1943, thus still in the 'civilian' phase, the living conditions of the interned men were not as bad as they later became. Lastly, it is probable that many people gave absolutely no credence to Japanese promises.

In this they were quite right. Not until July 1944 were Eurasian men in Batavia released from internment. There were seven of them in all, and they were immediately put to work in the already notorious youth department of the KOP.

What is known about the Kantor Oeroesan Peranakan, the Office for People of Mixed Descent?

Not a great deal. Set up in August 1943, the KOP had a Japanese, one

---

[15]   The true percentage was lower, perhaps around 60%.
[16]   One of them was E.D. Wermuth, member of the board of the Indo-Europeesch Verbond and of the Volksraad. In April 1942 he had been imprisoned in Sukamiskin, but shortly thereafter he was told he could go, because he had been wrongly thought to be Dutch. Another internee who was present during the conversation informed us in 1982 that Wermuth had refused to be released, saying 'I'm going back to my cell because I am Dutch'. (J. Morra, 18 October 1982.)
[17]   W.C.J. Bastiaans, 'Verslag', n.d., p. 18 (NIOD IC, 80,230 I).

Hamaguchi, as its head and another Japanese as his deputy. The staff consist-ed of Dutch Eurasians and Dahler acted as their spokesman. In his absence, this function was taken over by the former deputy burgomaster of Batavia, A.T. Bogaardt, who was mentioned in Chapter I as one of the leading figures in the GESC (Municipal European Assistance Committee). Dahler was head of the KOP department responsible for promoting Japanese policy; Bogaardt was in charge of the department that supervised the assistance scheme for Eurasians. There were also departments for legal affairs and for registering the Eurasians and assessing their mood.

Just why the Japanese military administration had set up the KOP was explained to the staff on the day it was inaugurated by the head, Hamaguchi, in a circular in poor English:[18]

> The problem that need to be settled first is not about material matters, but the way of thinking, mentality of Eurasians. The worst defect of them is that they are not active. They have no initiative, always looking for the easiest way, expecting help from others, excusing themselves by searching faults on the other side. Their circumstances should never be said to be easy in any meaning of it, but they must notice that their way of thinking and their active attitude toward the new situation is the only means to open a new life.

Hamaguchi wrote in English because, as mentioned, the use of Dutch was officially prohibited – in fact he had a good command of Dutch, having stud-ied at the School of Law in Batavia. But even if he had not spoken Dutch, his staff certainly did, and the language was used in the departments that had most to do with Eurasians: the assistance and the registration departments. Bastiaans became a member of the staff of the registration department. There the record of every Dutch Eurasian family was kept up to date and when required this information had to be given to the Kempeitai and the PID. Writing after the war, Bastiaans said:

> Public not fond of KOP. The first workers at the office, specially selected by Nippon, encouraged this by their unfriendly and obstructive attitude. Level of the personnel improved later. Old staff, having done the damage, got rid of by Nippon. Difficult to correct the public's wrong ideas about the office. Nippon ensures that this does not happen. Public forgets this. No appreciation of the many good things that come from this office, or at least contribute to less harsh implementation of inevitable punishments and irritating measures.[19]

Bastiaans gave some examples of the latter in some observations on Dahler, to whom he referred people who came to him with complaints.

---

[18]   Text in NIOD IC, 80,230 II.
[19]   W.C.J. Bastiaans, 'Verslag', n.d., p. 18 (NIOD IC, 80,230 I).

Mr Dahler, in charge of propaganda and political matters at Peranakan office. Feels more Indonesian than European. Have never discussed 'politics' with His Lordship. Knows many Indonesian languages. Curious figure, who sticks to his convictions through thick and thin. In ordinary relations he is friendly and helpful. Experienced the following cases.

A young lady, smartly dressed, well turned out, enters the office in a state of agitation. Tears in her eyes, can barely speak. Offered a glass of water to revive her. Following conversation:

'Are you feeling better? Tell us what's happened.'

'Sir, my sister has been arrested. She'd just got back from Bandung and went to the PID to return her travel permit. There she was treated roughly and detained.'

'On what grounds, Miss?'

'My sister was wearing a Van Galen brooch[20] and the PID tore it off her dress'.

'Rather unwise of your sister to enter the lion's den wearing that'.

'She didn't think. She's just been ill and back home her children are waiting for their mother. A good friend of mine, a high-ranking Nippon officer I went to first, can't help me. He referred me to this office.'

Took the young lady to see Mr Dahler. After hearing her story he rang the PID. Married sister was released.

Another young lady, *Peranakan* but very blond, while shopping at Senen,[21] was stopped by a young detective, evidently a recent graduate of the police academy and thus very active, and ordered to report to the Koningsplein police station. Matter raised with Mr Dahler, who added a signed note to the blond lady's *Peranakan* card that she was indeed a *Peranakan*. No more trouble from police.

T.W., young lady, just turned 17, reported to the Council for *pendaftaran*. Could not produce a birth certificate. Young lady in sackcloth and ashes. Without *pendaftaran* risk of internment. Mr Dahler rang the council department concerned and proposed a note on *Peranakan* card that, since the young lady was born of an unmarried Indonesian mother and unknown father, and was not recognized by European foster parents, she should follow the mother's nationality and thus, despite bearing a European name, be exempted from obtaining and paying for the council *pendaftaran*.'[22]

These are telling examples, not of resistance but of attempts to apply the Japanese measures without unnecessary harshness.

By establishing the KOP, the Japanese military administration had marked out a path that the Kempeitai was also supposed to follow. Not without misgivings! Here again is what the February 1944 report on resistance on Java had to say about the Eurasians:

[20]   This was a brooch available in the Indies in 1940 which commemorated the destroyer *Van Galen* sunk by the Luftwaffe near Rotterdam in May 1940.
[21]   This was an Indonesian market in Batavia.
[22]   W.C.J. Bastiaans, 'Merkwaardige mensen in een merkwaardige tijd', n.d., pp. 10-1 (NIOD IC, 80,230 I).

Next to the Dutch, the Eurasians are the most dangerous. Their speech and actions indicate that they do not differ from the Dutch in their anti-Japanese ideas. It is necessary to supervise rigidly those insubordinate groups which do not understand the true intentions of our benign military administration. However, in view of the recent tendency of the people to cooperate more and more with the Japanese, it is necessary to exercise strict guidance and to bring the people enlightenment. It is likewise necessary to eliminate with one stroke all pro-Allied feeling.

The last aim was an impossibility and so for the Eurasians the year 1944 brought contrasting developments: a small concession (in May 1944 they and the Chinese were exempted from having to pay a fee when applying for an identity card), but on the other hand an intensification of the campaign to make them toe the line politically.

In all the cities on Java where there were large numbers of Dutch Eurasians, new committees were set up under the auspices of the KOP to further their interests. These *Kaoem*-Indo committees (committees for the Indo people) decided which of the Dutch Eurasians would have a function in the *tonarigumi* system when it was introduced throughout Java in 1943-1944. Each neighbourhood was given a leader, the *kumicho*, who had eight helpers or *hancho*. Together the neighbourhoods formed districts, *aza*, headed by *azacho*, and each month all the inhabitants of a neighbourhood had to attend a meeting at which the *kumicho* passed on the orders given to him at an *aza* meeting. Sometimes the Dutch Eurasians lived in neighbourhoods where there were also Indonesians, but usually they were in separate neighbourhoods in which they had to carry out all the functions belonging to the *tonarigumi* system. These were not unimportant posts. The *tonarigumi* system was used for rationing and for work allocation, to mention just two areas.

In Malang (and probably elsewhere) the *Kaoem*-Indo began by issuing new registration forms (this was the fourth registration!) on which one had to again fill in the information about descent but also answer two questions: 'Have you renounced the Dutch government?' and 'Do you feel Asian?' 'Simple questions at first sight', wrote M. Moscou-de Ruyter, who lived in the Tuindorp district of Malang where there were many Dutch Eurasians. But of course there was more to it than that.

> There were quarrels and divisions. It was said, even by members of the *Kaoem*-Indo, that if you answered these questions with 'no', you would be picked up and shipped off with 10 guilders and a small suitcase. You would be taken to a small island and left to fend for yourself. It got worse when a Javanese, the *azacho* [...] of a complex of neighbourhoods in Tuindorp, said, 'There's always room for the Indo, if only on the high seas [...]'. Many risked everything and filled in 'no', others put 'yes' out of fear. Others still, including me, put *'Tidah mengapa'* (indifferent). This registration took months and months. They kept pushing back the deadline by which you could change your answer. (Moscou-de Ruyter 1984:141-2.)

It goes without saying that the *Kaoem*-Indo in a city like Malang chose those who had been the first to answer 'yes' to both questions for the posts to be allocated under the new system. In Tuindorp, which was divided into eight neighbourhoods, an Indonesian was made *azacho* and Indonesians were appointed *kumicho* (in Indonesian *ketua*, 'elder'). They chose deputies, (*fuku*), who did much of the work and in Tuindorp most of them were Eurasian women. To quote M. Moscou-de Ruyter (1984:149-50) once more:

> The *ketua* spent most of the day at the office, so all sorts of jobs – distributing food, signing papers and settling disputes – were left to the *fuku*. If there was a meeting and the *ketua* could not attend or was not in the mood (this happened quite often with the Javanese), the *fuku* had to go and woe be it if the report was not in order.
> [...] The *ketua* were absolute rulers. [...] They were given their orders by the *azacho*, but they could make changes as they saw fit. Once a month there was a meeting of the *ketua* at the *azacho*'s and the day after at every *ketua*'s, each in his own neighbourhood; the inhabitants had to attend. [...] The *ketua* had a note delivered to every house stating the day and hour of the meeting at his house. [...] Each time [we] had to learn yet again (for it was never right) how to bow Japanese-style and to greet: stand in rows with faces turned towards Tokyo, bow, pray for the fallen (not the Europeans, of course, but the Indonesians and Japs), bow and sit down again, after which the meeting opened.

In addition to the *tonarigumi* system, the Japanese military administration on Java had founded a new mass organization with a Japanese name, the Djawa Hokokai or Organization for Service to Java. In early May 1944 a large gathering of Dutch Eurasians was organized in Batavia. Here Dahler, who had been on the organizing committee, called on the Dutch Eurasians to work together with the Djawa Hokokai. For most of those present his words went in one ear and out the other – they had come to know Dahler as someone who sided with the Japanese but was never personally aggressive, and thus presented no particular danger. At the beginning of September 1944, however, such danger became apparent. Van den Eeckhout and several like-minded figures, newly released from the big internment camp at Cimahi, settled in Batavia, and this meant that the KOP in general and the assistance scheme in particular were largely under the control of the Pagi group.

The first to feel the effects were the Dutch Eurasian youths in Batavia. As elsewhere on Java, in early 1944 the *Kaoem*-Indo had confronted them with the two questions: 'Have you renounced the Dutch government?' and 'Do you feel Asian?' Around four fifths of the youths had refused to answer 'yes'. In Batavia at the end of April two groups were arrested by the PID and held for some time. After that the recalcitrant attitude of most of the young people was simply noted. To the great annoyance of Van den Eeckhout! In September 1944 in Batavia he ordered that all the Dutch Eurasian youths aged between 16 and 23 be brought together – one by one they were to state whether they were pro- or anti-Japan. Most of the first group, assembled on 13 September, refused to declare in favour of Japan and were subjected to all manner of insults from Van den Eeckhout's supporters. It was obvious that there might be uproar the next day, when the second group was to assemble. Bogaardt had meanwhile been arrested; his successor as head of the assistance department of the KOP was the retired KNIL Lieutenant Colonel O. Peltzer. He went to the KOP office, where he heard Van den Eeckhout remark in a speech that the Dutch Eurasian youths need not be afraid of being forced to join the Japanese army (this fear had been a factor in the refusal of most members of the second group to declare themselves pro-Japan) since 'the Indo was a coward and thus useless as a soldier'.[23] The youths were outraged. When on the next day, 15 September, the third group gathered – about 300 youths, many accompanied by their mother – feelings were running high. Hamaguchi addressed the mothers, claiming that the military administration wanted nothing but to teach the young men discipline: agricultural colonies would be set up for them, like the ones already established here and there on Java. He was still speaking when elsewhere in the KOP compound disturbances broke out and several Japanese and Indonesian flags (after the speech by Prime Minister Koiso on 7 September in Tokyo it was permitted to fly the red and white flag from official buildings) were torn from the front gallery of the KOP building. Dahler alerted the PID, but when Indonesian detectives arrived it was all quiet again. This incident led to several arrests; how many is not known.

It was not to remain calm. After 15 September several youths who had declared in favour of Japan were assaulted on the street by others who wanted to stay loyal to the Netherlands come what may. When a last group was assembled on 23 September, there was again uproar: one youth leapt on to a table and shouted, 'Lads, let's not deny our Indonesian blood, but not our *Blanda* [Dutch] blood either!'[24]

The Japanese again stepped in. Four days later, on 27 September, scores of youths were arrested and put in the old and filthy Glodok Prison.[25]

---

[23]   O. Peltzer, 'De Japanse bezetting tot 16 december 1944', 30 August 1946, p. 11 (NIOD IC, 80,321).
[24]   I.M. Pool, 'Dagboek', uittreksel, p. 6 (NIOD IC, dagboek 76).
[25]   This incident contributed to the complete failure of a 'fraternity meeting' for the youth of various ethnic groups which was organized by the Djawa Hokokai in Batavia on 10 October. The Indonesian youths accused the Dutch Eurasians of insulting the Indonesian flag and thus the Indonesian people on 15 September. According to a report by one of the Indonesians present (text in Brugmans 1960:462-3), 'When neither the chairman nor any of those present came up with a proposal to make up for this insult, the Indonesians were very dissatisfied. [...] When the chairman suggested they should shake hands, no one responded.'

New arrests followed at the end of January 1945. On the 25th about 200 Eurasian youths were picked up, taken to Indonesian police stations (where their mothers, sisters and girlfriends gathered, many in tears) and then held in Glodok Prison. A little later they were joined by youths who had been arrested that day in Sukabumi and Buitenzorg.

In Bandung on the 25th a raid was carried out and over 180 Dutch Eurasian men, women and boys ended up in Sukamiskin Prison. Bouwer (1988:318) observed:

> In general the Indonesian police were fairly flexible and gave those arrested time to pack a suitcase, although they were not allowed (with very few exceptions) to take a mattress. Young lads and men were also taken from offices and workplaces, and later in the afternoon relatives were permitted to bring clothes for them to the PID. [...] Those arrested include two members of the local Indo Committee.
>
> [...] Without doubt, this is an ordinary internment of people believed to be hostile to the Japanese regime. Once they've worked their way through this list, a second and a third will of course follow, until in the end there isn't a single European man left in the city. Then the Japanese will start on the women.

Two weeks later in Bandung, on 8 and 9 February, they indeed worked their way through a second list (this time of those to be taken to Banceuy Prison). According to Bouwer (1988:321):

> They included some very old and sick men, people who were getting on for 80, 'hostile subjects'. This act has caused enormous indignation, among the Indonesians and Chinese too. No one will easily forget the scenes that [...] took place everywhere in the city. Old people [...] being taken away on trucks in the pouring rain (among them an old gentleman who had suffered a stroke a few days before). Not one of them will survive this, even if the Japanese occupation ends a month from now. [...] A number of Ambonese have been arrested as well. [...] The old folks showed great pluck. Mr Niemeyer, 76 years old, put on a clean white suit with the words, 'If at my age I'm to be dragged off to jail on a truck, I want to look my best. The Japanese mustn't get the idea they can break us.' Other detainees included 78-year-old Mrs Van der Wissel, the almost completely paralyzed Mrs Binkhorst, and the gravely ill TB patient Mr Termeulen, whose wife voluntarily went with him to prison.

On 25 January about 700 Eurasian men and youths were arrested on Central and East Java (they were held in the fort at Ngawi) together with an unknown number of women who were taken to 'ordinary' internment camps. Among the latter were three elderly aunts of the journalist W.C.J. Bastiaans who all died during their internment.

Certainly in the case of those held in Glodok Prison, great pressure was put on them by Van den Eeckhout and his followers to declare themselves pro-Japanese. Most if not all refused.

How many of those picked up before and on 25 January 1945 died in detention is known only in the case of the group in Ngawi and that in Glodok Prison. In Ngawi about 300 (probably) out of 700 died; in Glodok Prison (and in Cipinang Prison, where the sick ended up) about 80 out of 350. No details are known about what was endured by those in Ngawi and in Glodok and Cipinang Prison and by later detainees (raids continued to take place after 8 and 9 February 1945). Some of the losses due to detention are known, but not a single account survives. It is likely that these prisoners in particular suffered severely at the hands of the Indonesian prison staff – presumably many starved to death.

The Dutch Eurasians should not be thought of as a homogeneous group in all respects. Indeed, what has been said above confirms this. In Batavia there was a circle around Dahler; initially Van den Eeckhout had quite a few followers in Kesilir (about 300, of which he kept just under 100), and the KOP had representatives in several cities who often made life very difficult for the local Dutch Eurasians. In all these cities differences of opinion between three groups emerged: those who cooperated with the Japanese (in Surabaya those were about 300 Eurasians who were admitted to the Djawa Hokokai), those who rejected any form of cooperation with the Japanese and, in between these two, others who, like the Chinese, adopted an outward show of cooperation to protect the Dutch Eurasian community against greater dangers. Advocates of this kind of outward cooperation secured influential positions, especially in Surabaya and Semarang. Did they sometimes have to make concessions that others disapproved of? Did that lead to fierce arguments, feuds even? It is all too likely, but no details can be given because the information is missing.

One thing is clear: remembering that on Java some 200,000 Dutch Eurasians were not interned, the group that sided with Japan out of conviction was no bigger proportionally than the pro-German group during the occupation of the Netherlands. The Japanese attempt to get the Dutch Eurasians on their side was a failure. During years in which it was very difficult for them to keep their heads above water they remained loyal to the Netherlands, and many paid for this loyalty with their lives.

Java – struggling to avert disaster

Just as we lack reliable data on the number of Dutch Eurasians, so too do we lack information about the level of prosperity they had achieved before the Japanese invasion. Dutch employees, *totok*, generally started on a higher salary than equally well qualified Dutch Eurasians. This was one of the factors which gave many Eurasians the feeling that, even though they were Dutch citizens and several of them had risen to the highest positions, there was still social discrimination in the East Indies. There were wealthy Eurasians just as there were wealthy *totok,* but it was characteristic of the Dutch Eurasian group that, unlike the 'full-blooded' Dutch community, it also included a fairly large number of people in impoverished circumstances, ordinary folk always living in fear of sinking to the level of the *kampong.*

Be this as it may, under the Japanese occupation the Dutch Eurasians were a threatened group from the outset. The approximately 42,000 KNIL and navy prisoners of war included perhaps as many as 30,000 Eurasians; nearly all their families were left to fend for themselves.[26] The payment of all government pensions and allowances had been stopped as of 1 April 1942; most European businesses had closed; the Japanese had reduced all salaries, including those paid by the government, by a third on average. Numerous Dutch Eurasians lost their government jobs; it was only in the government-run services that many were kept on.

Further information about the income and expenditure of Dutch Eurasians is available only in the case of Batavia, and there is very little of it. Contained in two policy documents from the Central Office of Statistics (Batavia) dating from September 1946,[27] it relates to the sources of income of 11 families between March 1942 and August 1945, and to the prices in four months (June 1942, July 1943, April 1944 and November 1944) remembered by 15 families (these prices were not recorded at the time but given from memory in 1946).

Let us begin with the incomes. In one of the 11 families over 500 guilders a month was being earned at the time of the Japanese invasion (this one family forms a statistical exception and is therefore otherwise disregarded). Seven families had incomes of between 250 and 500 guilders a month, and three families had incomes below 250 guilders (how much below is not known). During the occupation these three families had had to manage on 118.10 guilders a month on average. This amount was earned as follows: from salaried work 69.09 guilders, from trade 10.50 guilders, from assistance 15.60 guilders and from the sale of possessions 22.91 guilders. The seven families which had previously earned between 250 and 500 guilders had to get by on 245.18 guilders a month on average. This amount was raised as follows: from salaried work 74.22 guilders, from trade 41.21 guilders, from the sale of possessions

---

[26]   As mentioned in Chapter IV, on Java from about September 1942 to November 1943 the wives of captured officers with the rank of captain or higher could withdraw 15 guilders per month per family member from a Japanese bank, but it is doubtful whether this rule was widely applied.

[27]   NIOD IC, 14,638 and 14,614.

122.25 guilders and from loans 7.50 guilders. The group of three families had not taken out any loans; the group of seven families had not received any assistance. Assuming that prior to the Japanese invasion the families in these two groups had derived their income chiefly if not entirely from salaried work, it is immediately clear how difficult their position became when the salary was reduced to an average of 69.09 and 74.22 guilders a month. They had to find supplementary income. For both groups of families the sale of possessions produced the most, on average 22.91 and 122.25 guilders per month (on average the group of seven families derived one and a half times as much income from selling possessions as from salaried work!). For the group of seven trade (in anything and everything) was also important: they earned an average of 41.21 guilders a month by this means.

The sale of possessions would not have yielded much if what was being sold was furniture, refrigerators, ovens or radios (before the end of 1943 they would not have fetched more than a third to a fifth of the original price). However, much more than the original price could be obtained for textiles, tableware and jewellery: in a time of inflation and uncertainty jewellery is always in demand, and textiles and tableware had become particularly scarce. According to a description in 1982 of the life of Eurasian women under the Japanese occupation:

> The war years in Semarang [it was no different elsewhere] were a time of extreme poverty. [...] They sold everything, absolutely everything, to stay alive – the husband's wedding suit and the bedspread her mother had bought for her trousseau. They split the threads of the bedspread in three and wound them on spools. They sold them. [...] Every cloth and every spool of thread could be traded for food.[28]

Now for the prices. In the document in question the Central Office of Statistics gives relative rather than absolute figures, with 1938 being set at 100. The 15 Dutch Eurasian families which provided information had incomes ranging from 50 to 500 guilders a month in 1942. In June 1942 as a whole the prices known to them turned out to have risen on average by 39% compared with 1938, in July 1943 by 170%, in April 1944 by 426% and in November 1944 by 1,275%. Taking food alone, the increase was less marked: compared with 1938, an average rise of 50% in June 1942, 74% in July 1943, 168% in April 1944, and 729% in November 1944. In the case of clothes and shoes the price rise was much greater: in November 1944 prices were more than 70 times those in 1938.

As was to be expected, an ever larger part of the spending of the 15 families went on food: on average 44% in 1942, 59% in 1943, 68% in 1944 and 77% in 1945. This study also revealed that expenditure per person per month

---

28   I. Harms and T. Pollmann in *Vrij Nederland*, 15 May 1982, supplement, p. 6.

varied widely, from 10 to 49 guilders a month in the families consisting of more than one person in 1942, and from 17 to 150 guilders a month in 1944 (and one person living alone had spent 223 guilders a month in 1942 and 216 guilders in 1944).

May one draw conclusions from these figures? Only the general conclusion (given that the statistical base is so narrow) that the Dutch Eurasians had the greatest difficulty in avoiding a complete social breakdown and that, where they succeeded, the sale of possessions and trade in all manner of goods (a trade that was sometimes on the verge if not part of the black market) made an essential contribution, while the poorest among them could not have managed without the assistance provided.

In Chapter I ('The elimination of the Netherlands') the beginning of the system of assistance was described. It was an impressive form of social work to which many devoted themselves as early as 1942 – the churches, private committees, and on East Java the Red Cross. At that time there was only one urban municipality – Batavia – where it was possible to set up a city committee. There, at the end of June, the Gemeentelijk Europees Steuncomité, the GESC, had been founded. By August 1942 it had given assistance to some 9,000 Dutch and Dutch Eurasians (about a quarter of the European population of the city) and by the beginning of 1943 to 11,000 (then almost exclusively Eurasians), as well as to around 1,500 indigenous people, namely the families of former KNIL soldiers. As described earlier, up to mid-1943 the GESC borrowed nearly 100,000 guilders clandestinely, mainly from wealthy Chinese (these loans were guaranteed by the Dutch government and repaid after the war on the gold basis). The executive of the committee consisted of F. Kramer, H.J. Manschot, department head at the Javasche Bank, and the diamond dealer A. Gutwirth – these three were also on the GESC's financial subcommittee.

In describing how the system of assistance on Java got into ever greater difficulties, we shall begin with Batavia. There, at the end of December 1942, the GESC suffered a blow when Kramer was arrested. The Kempeitai in Bandung had discovered that he had given financial aid to Welter's group. At the start of January 1943 two other prominent figures in the GESC were picked up, Manschot and Bogaardt; both were suspected of knowing about Kramer's clandestine activity. They were interrogated (that is, tortured) by the Kempeitai in Buitenzorg but denied everything. When they were confronted with Kramer, he confirmed their denial. Manschot, a *totok*, was interned; Bogaardt, a Eurasian, was released and was later able to resume his work for the GESC.

A few months later, in May 1943, the Japanese changed the name of the committee: it was too 'Dutch' for their taste and, moreover, now that virtually all the Dutch men and women were interned, the work was done by Dutch Eurasians, whom they liked to view as 'fellow Asians'. The committee was renamed Pertoeloengan Orang Blanda-Indo Miskin (Assistance for poor Indo-Europeans) or POBIM. Bogaardt became the chairman; Gutwirth continued to take care of the finances. This was crucial because the Batavia municipality had reduced the assistance it gave to the needy from 35 cents a week per person to 28 cents, despite the steep price rises. Gutwirth found the money needed for supplementary assistance, and for the parcels sent to the women and children's camps at Batavia (this was still possible in this 'civilian' phase).

This did not last long: Gutwirth was interned in August. How were the funds required to be raised now? With the permission of the Japanese, Bogaardt found a solution: the POBIM was allowed to take over a French wholesale business in pharmaceutical products, and this produced 20,000 guilders a month.

A new measure followed in November 1943. This was three months after the KOP, the Kantor Oeroesan Peranakan (Office for People of Mixed Descent), had been founded; as noted above, it had a department, headed by Bogaardt, which oversaw the provision of assistance for Eurasians. The name of the POBIM was changed to Pertoeloengan Orang Peranakan (Assistance for People of Mixed Descent) or POP, and it was placed under the KOP. This meant that the assistance system lost much of its independence, since the KOP, a political, purely Japanese creation, was closely watched by both the Kempeitai and the PID.

Early in December 1943 the Japanese demanded that Dahler and Bogaardt should make pro-Japanese speeches for the second anniversary of Pearl Harbor on 8 December. Dahler readily agreed, but Bogaardt, knowing the dangers full well (he was familiar with the methods of the Kempeitai in Buitenzorg), refused. To the delight of the Kempeitai, who had continued to see him as a conspirator, he was arrested.[29] He was succeeded by a retired KNIL lieutenant colonel, O. Peltzer, who has already been mentioned; after Kramer and Bogaardt he became the third person to be in charge of the assistance scheme in Batavia.

That assistance was drastically reduced. Despite the price rises, the allowances per person per week were lowered to 12 cents for families consisting

---

[29]   In February 1944 it was stated in the Kempeitai report on the resistance on Java that Bogaardt had been 'instructed' by General Ter Poorten 'that the IEV Society [the Indo-Europeesch Verbond] should be continued in order to collect military information on the Japanese army to assist the Allied armies at the time of their counterattack'; a diagram showed how Bogaardt and the IEV were linked to the KNIL (Kempeitai report, p. 10 and Diagram II).
It is not clear why Bogaardt was never put on trial; according to unconfirmed reports, the Kempeitai officers who were supposed to prepare the case against him were bribed.

of no more than five persons and 10 cents for families of six or more; for children under the age of 10 these amounts were halved. Moreover, it was laid down that a family was only eligible for assistance if it had been given a certificate of destitution by the Indonesian *kumicho*, and the *kumicho* took the view that Dutch Eurasians did not need assistance until they reached the standard of living of poor Indonesians. Anyone who still had a bicycle or a superfluous piece of furniture or had treated themselves to a ride by *becak* (tricycle-taxi) was firmly refused assistance. The number of people receiving assistance in Batavia, which had risen to about 17,000 (or four fifths of all the Dutch Eurasians living in the city!), was reduced to 6,000.

These measures, which had very serious consequences for numerous Dutch Eurasians, originated in the new policy adopted by the Japanese in 1944: they wanted to get as many Eurasians as possible working. In August 1944 this policy was made stricter in that it was decided that the POP could only give assistance to the 3,000 who were most in need.

The employment scheme was not a success, because the rates paid by the Japanese were too low. A woman who sewed 100 money bags received 4 cents; a day of rope-making produced 10 cents; knitting a pair of socks paid 1 guilder.[30] Men and boys had to do other work (for example, making nails needed to build wooden ships, and collecting scrap metal); it is not known what rates they were paid, but those concerned thought it was far too little. Many stopped claiming assistance because they were confident they could make a little more money in more or less clandestine trade. The whole situation contributed to the process whereby the adolescent Dutch Eurasians, as we have seen, became a turbulent element in society.[31] The Japanese had a solution for this: they were to be removed from Batavia and put to work in agricultural colonies.

[30] Slightly higher amounts were paid by a shop which the Roemer Visscher Society (a society for the advancement of women and girls, founded in Batavia in 1904) had been allowed to continue operating. This shop (in 1944 the turnover was nearly 50,000 guilders and in 1945 nearly 70,000 guilders) protected numerous Dutch Eurasian women and girls from the danger of prostitution. It should be added that Indonesian Protestants and Catholics in Batavia (and in other cities) were able to give some help to their Dutch Eurasian co-religionists right up to the end of the occupation.
[31] To keep his own son and some other lads off the street, the journalist W.C.J. Bastiaans set up a library which began with 400 books – later it had 4,000. 'Son, three friends and two girls', he wrote later, 'in charge of library. Arranged for official council permit, granted after inspections by the fire brigade, health department and PID. All books first examined by me, to avoid banned material. Administration and lending rules drawn up, announcements and warnings written out to prevent gatherings in the library: no commentary on newspaper articles, no political discussions, etc. so that the boys run no risks. Then let them get on with it. The boys are protected from being picked up. [...] Girls didn't stay, could earn more from Nippon. Warned them, in vain. One of the girls now the mother of a fatherless child. Pity!' (W.C.J. Bastiaans, 'Korte schets levenswijze gedurende Nippon overheersing', n.d., p. 3 (NIOD IC, 80,230 I).)

In December 1944 Peltzer was arrested (the reason is not known). The assistance scheme was now given its fourth, this time Japanese, name: the Konketsu Jumin Linkai (the Committee for Inhabitants of Mixed Blood). It was also given its fourth management: six Dutch Eurasians, only three of whom did their best despite all the difficulties to achieve something, that is to say to retain the assistance for the very poorest and to address the numerous problems arising from the arrests of several hundred youths and the sending of others to agricultural colonies.

The latter process began in Batavia in the first months of 1945 – the Van den Eeckhout supporters left behind in the internment camp at Cimahi were made overseers in the agricultural colonies. The course of events was the usual one: Japanese fanfares proclaiming a successful start followed by a fiasco. Bastiaans later recalled:

> At the beginning good, adequate food and clothing provided. Photos taken and exploited as propaganda material. Second transport follows. Things going down-hill. Food poorer, work hard. Many run away. Foraged on surrounding *kampong* because of too little food. Colony eventually abandoned.[32]

The Japanese could not tolerate this. In Batavia in May 1945 large numbers of young Dutch Eurasians were again rounded up and taken under guard to the deserted colony. Their fate was no better than that of the group that preceded them, but no further information is available.

Can a clear trend be discerned in these developments in Batavia? We believe so.

The assistance scheme began there as a more or less autonomous European affair. In 1943 it was brought under the control of Dahler and his supporters, who cooperated with Japan. In 1944 it was drastically reduced in scale and made part of the *tonarigumi* system. Finally, its scope was further limited because the Japanese military administration wanted to make use of the Dutch Eurasians as cheap labour, with the young men among them in agricultural colonies where they could be kept under control in the event of an Allied invasion.

The same trend was apparent elsewhere on Java, although here and there Dutch Eurasians who officially came under Dahler's KOP were able to retain something of their autonomy in practice.

In May 1944 in Semarang the committee of Eurasians incorporated into the KOP obtained permission to open a primary school for Dutch Eurasian children (similar schools were also opened elsewhere, for instance in Surabaya). There was no agricultural colony. Instead, the committee itself

---

[32] W.C.J. Bastiaans, 'Verslag', n.d., p. 23 (NIOD IC, 80,230 I).

took the initiative by planting cassava on the former golf course, but not until April 1945; about 2,000 Dutch Eurasians were set to work there.

In Surabaya all that was demanded of the Dutch Eurasians was that they should promise to cooperate with the Japanese administration. They did so at a mass gathering held at the beginning of February 1944 – after that, as far as is known, they had little trouble from the Japanese. This may have had to do with the fact that the Surabaya residency was administered by the Japanese navy, which tended to ignore as much as possible whatever the army ordered and implemented on the rest of Java.

In Surakarta, where few Dutch Eurasians lived, assistance was given by a group of Nippon workers. They were interned in November 1943; after that, assistance continued to be given on a smaller scale by Chinese.

In Malang J. Soesman, mentioned in Chapter I, was able to maintain the level of assistance given by his Red Cross Committee in 1943 and early 1944. Through gifts from private individuals and companies (some of them from Chinese circles) he raised a total of 150,000 guilders. The churches were also able to continue their welfare efforts. In April 1944 the *Kaoem*-Indo took over Soesman's work and decided that assistance should be given only to those who had answered 'yes' to the two questions 'Have you renounced the Dutch government?' and 'Do you feel Asian?' From then on the churches managed only with the greatest difficulty to provide some help to those who had answered 'no'. Around April 1944 several hundred young Dutch Eurasian men were put to work on an estate some 50 kilometres from Malang – when they returned to the city three months later many had to be admitted to hospital. In August 1944 a second group of young men was called up. About half returned to Malang ill and seriously undernourished; some were missing from the other half. They were accused of setting fire to a rubber store. Severe sentences followed: imprisonment for most, death for a few. The executions took place on 22 August 1945, a week after the announcement of Japan's surrender.

Bandung is the only city in which we are on firm ground when describing the assistance given to the Dutch Eurasians in 1944 and 1945. This is thanks to the diary entries for 4 January 1944 to 7 September 1945 of the former geography teacher and reserve naval officer F.J. Suyderhoud.[33] He was actually in charge of the assistance scheme, although officially it was run by J. Douwes Dekker-Mossel, the wife of E.F.E. Douwes Dekker, who had been sent to Surinam. These diary entries are particularly important because the number of Dutch Eurasians living in Bandung was substantial. Bouwer received information on this point several times from an Indonesian acquaintance who had been able to investigate the municipal register and who reported in May 1944 that

---

[33]   F.J. Suyderhoud, 'Dagboek', p. 163 (NIOD IC).

in Bandung nearly 16,700 Eurasians were not interned and in July 1945 over 15,300 (Bouwer 1988:359). At the beginning of January 1945 Bouwer (1988: 313) noted that 'in all Bandung there are only about 5,000 male Eurasians left'. This may indicate that at that time the Dutch Eurasians on Java, when not interned, consisted of about two thirds women and girls and one third men (chiefly elderly men) and boys.

In Bandung the Japanese resident appointed a new committee on 1 January 1944 to take charge of caring for the Dutch Eurasians: the Badan Oeroesan Golongan Indo (Committee for Promoting the Interests of the Indos) or BOGI. It had an executive of five Dutch Eurasians and Suyderhoud was made the chairman. He was equally courageous and tactful: courageous because he hid a navy officer in his house for a long period during the occupation,[34] and he had hung onto a radio and passed on news to a very select circle; and tactful because he held a position in which he was highly vulnerable but emerged with his reputation untarnished.

He was paid by the Japanese: all the members of the executive of the BOGI received the same salary, namely 70 guilders a month. This money was made directly available by the Japanese residency office; in 1944 this office reserved 40,000 guilders for the BOGI. Not all of these funds could be distributed directly to the needy – money was also needed for the administration of the BOGI and employment projects had to be financed. It is in fact possible that in 1944 the BOGI received only part of the 40,000 guilders reserved.[35] It is known that the BOGI was short of money for the assistance scheme. This is why regular collections were made. Unfortunately, there is only one month, September 1944, when Suyderhoud noted how much the BOGI had collected – 1,150 guilders – and how much it had paid out in assistance –650 guilders. These collections were almost always made up of small amounts but on one occasion, in March 1945, there was a large single contribution of 1,700 guilders – the amount one Dutch Eurasian had won at roulette.

These figures suggest that the BOGI was not able to assist a great many, but its efforts were important nonetheless. From the start the BOGI tried to find work for women and girls (knitting socks, spinning thread, making leggings, indeed entire uniforms) – work for which the Japanese had to provide the raw materials and, where needed, the machines and which had to be paid for by them. However, the wages were low and there was little enthusiasm for this kind of work in Bandung. For young men employment was sought

[34]   This officer was betrayed and arrested. Suyderhoud's wife managed to maintain that she and her husband knew nothing about his presence.
[35]   On 9 April 1945 Suyderhoud noted that between 1 April 1944 and 1 April 1945 he had received 4,500 guilders from the Japanese. In December 1944 he heard from Hamaguchi in Batavia that in that year the Japanese had spent 200,000 guilders on 'the Indos in the employment projects'.

in agriculture, rope-making and technical workshops, for women and girls in shops. Work permits were required for these jobs and the BOGI acted as the intermediary.

In general the BOGI formed the link between the Dutch Eurasians on the one hand and the Japanese and Indonesian administration (including the government enterprises) on the other. Every day housing problems had to be solved (the poorest Dutch Eurasians and a number of Ambonese were accommodated in buildings rented by the BOGI). It also had several outpatient clinics of its own; it referred people to hospitals and distributed what little medicine there was. The BOGI helped with applications for travel permits and for places in schools (in Bandung there were four state schools which would admit Dutch Eurasian children). The committee was responsible for the care of orphans and in February 1945 it took over a soup kitchen previously run by the council, again for the very poorest.

Contact with the Japanese was important whenever Dutch Eurasians found themselves in jail – via the BOGI they could sometimes be helped. Furthermore, Suyderhoud could make proposals to the local Japanese police chief for the release of certain interned Eurasians. At the end of November 1944 he actually managed to secure the release of 18 men, plus six women held in the Banceuy Prison.

In return the BOGI was required to make political concessions, but Suyderhoud was able to keep these to a minimum. At the end of May 1944 the Kempeitai told him that the BOGI must ensure that within a week no Dutch Eurasian would speak Dutch any more, not even at home. Suyderhoud confined himself to sending a circular to all Dutch Eurasians holding a post as *hancho* in the *tonarigumi* system (over 200 in Bandung and the surroundings) in which he asked them to speak Indonesian. The BOGI also organized some afternoon courses in which one could learn Indonesian. Suyderhoud made sure that an enthusiastic article about them appeared in the *Tjahaja* daily paper, although it also said, 'It is expected that the authorities will show moderation in their actions'.[36] A year later, in June 1945, Suyderhoud was informed that the largest possible number of Dutch Eurasians must attend monthly lectures which would be given under the auspices of the Djawa Hokokai. He provided the names of about 40 people 'who will be there to listen'[37] – listen, and no more than that.

Suyderhoud politely took note of the desire of the Japanese for the Dutch Eurasians to show understanding of the development towards 'independence' of the Indies. On 12 September 1944, five days after Prime Minister Koiso's announcement that 'independence' would be granted to the East

---

36   F.J. Suyderhoud, 'Dagaanteekeningen', 17 June 1944 (NIOD IC).
37   F.J. Suyderhoud, 'Dagaanteekeningen', 4 June 1945 (NIOD IC).

Indies, a mass gathering was held in Bandung to celebrate this happy news. Suyderhoud had one of his fellow members of the executive make a short speech (a speech was compulsory) but did not speak himself. In mid-October he let several Dutch Eurasians attend a reception in honour of Sukarno, but Suyderhoud was conspicuous by his absence. He agreed to a request from the Japanese resident in mid-July 1945 for 'one or two Indos to come to the meeting hall for a speech by M. Hatta',[38] but did not go himself.

He also kept Dahler, the POP and Van den Eeckhout's Pagi group at a distance. At the end of July 1944 Dahler asked him to come to Batavia for a meeting – he sent a replacement. Then at the end of September 1944 he received a written request from Dahler for a list of prominent Eurasians, which it took him two months to provide. He did not think he could avoid attending a meeting of heads of *Kaoem*-Indo groups from all the cities on Java organized by Dahler on 12 December 1944 in Batavia. But he limited himself to calling for separate schools for Dutch Eurasian children to be opened everywhere, and made no objection to Dahler being the representative of the Dutch Eurasians in the Central Advisory Council. He also urged Hamaguchi to release more Eurasians from internment (the answer was 'not for the time being'). When Van den Eeckhout asked him at the beginning of July 1945 'whether I could come to Jakarta regularly for discussions with Mr Dahler', he replied that 'as a civil servant I am very tied up'.[39] He left it at that.

Nevertheless, he could not prevent the Japanese from pursuing their policy in Bandung. In January 1945 the BOGI was told to designate 200 Dutch Eurasian men, 'chiefly the unemployed', who together with 100 family members were to go to an estate in the mountains about 40 kilometres west of Bandung. The first group – 50 men and five women with babies – left on 12 January. Bouwer heard that:

> They were all cheerful and in good spirits. A lot of food went with them; it was bought with the proceeds of collections for those leaving that were held among the Indo community all over the city. (Bouwer 1988:314.)

In addition to the first agricultural colony, Gununghalu, a second, Pasir Benteng, was established. Under the supervision of the Bandung PID (a fairly mild supervision because the inspector in charge was Raden Joesoef, a son of the great expert on Islam, Snouck Hurgronje),[40] the colonists on both enter-

---

[38] F.J. Suyderhoud, 'Dagaanteekeningen', 19 July 1945 (NIOD IC).
[39] F.J. Suyderhoud, 'Dagaanteekeningen', 3 July 1945 (NIOD IC).
[40] Christiaan Snouck Hurgronje (1857-1936) was a Dutch Arabist and expert on Islam. Because of his expertise in the languages and cultures of the Indonesian archipelago, he was an important government adviser. Snouck twice made a secret Islamic marriage. He did not have his two wives and children recognized as Dutch, and forbade them to come to the Netherlands, but he did ensure that the children were given a good education.

prises had to plant vegetables – they were given rice, sugar and salt, sometimes after a delay, by the Bandung council. Work on the two colonies did not
please everyone for long. In April 1945 Suyderhoud became aware 'that there
are lads in P[asir] B[enteng] who [...] bite on stones to get a toothache so that
they can go to Bdg [Bandung]'.[41] It was not uncommon for people who had
been sent to the two colonies to return to Bandung without leave, thus creating a huge problem for Suyderhoud, and indeed his entire committee. The
whole of Bandung had been divided into neighbourhoods, and the Dutch
Eurasians were in a minority of perhaps 1 in 20. Many Dutch Eurasians were
conspicuous by their appearance, and the *kumicho*, all Indonesian, felt themselves obliged to check carefully to see if there were any 'foreigners' in their
neighbourhood who ought to be elsewhere according to their identity card
and the observations on it.

The importance of the last point should be underlined. Not only in
Bandung but in every city on Java the Dutch Eurasians were daily subjected
to the strict checks carried out by the Indonesian administrative bodies,
by the Indonesian police, by the Indonesian auxiliary corps set up by the
Japanese, and by all Indonesians who wanted to curry favour with the occupying power.

Mood

There is very little specific information about the mood in which the Dutch
Eurasians (in this section Dahler and Van den Eeckhout and their followers
will not be considered) who were not interned endured the years of Japanese
occupation, or rather the more than 1,000 days and nights written about
earlier. Bouwer gives a few indications as regards Bandung, which above all
reveal the devotion to the Netherlands and to the House of Orange, and it
seems best to begin by quoting him.

It should be remembered that as early as 1942 on several occasions wild
rumours that the Allies had landed on Java circulated in Bandung. This happened again in April 1943. 'The city', noted Bouwer (1988:175) on 18 April,
'was in turmoil once more when *widely credited* [my italics] rumours went
round that Allied troops had landed at 17 points in the archipelago. The joy
was soon over ...'.

At the end of April, on 30 April, it was the birthday of Princess Juliana, the
daughter of Queen Wilhelmina (and her successor as head of state in 1948).
Her birthday had been fairly openly celebrated in 1942, but since then the
mass internment of the Dutch had taken place. 'In general people no longer

[41]   F.J. Suyderhoud, 'Dagaanteekeningen', 21 April 1945 (NIOD IC).

dared to hold Orange demonstrations. It was exceptionally quiet on the streets.' (Bouwer 1988:178.) It may be that people had been given the word to stay indoors. Prince Bernhard's birthday was also 'silently celebrated', but 'prisoners of war foraging in the city wore African marigolds on their uniforms' (Bouwer 1988:190). It was notable that on the Queen's birthday, 31 August, when Bouwer's wife went to do some shopping (and thus saw quite a lot), various Dutch Eurasians did show their feelings in public:

> More than last year (according to many), people have openly observed the special character of this day. Thank God it has not gone as far as excesses or demonstrations. Orange dominated inconspicuously. Gerbera or stefanotis in vases on window ledges. Ladies' dresses in the Dutch colours, here and there an orange bandeau round the hair, even the odd orange cycle flag.
> Ivy had a curious experience this morning when she went to do some shopping at the big Japanese department store Tjioda. While she was being served by an Indonesian assistant, the latter surreptitiously gave her a bottle of Eau de Cologne and told her to tuck it away quickly: 'Pop it in your bag, madam'. When Ivy protested the assistant said, 'It's the Queen's birthday today!' Then he hurried off to serve another customer. Picture the scene! (Bouwer 1988:205.)

Bouwer made no mention in his notes of the birthdays in 1944 of Princesses Margriet, Beatrix, or Irene or of that of their mother, Crown Princess Juliana, or their father Prince Bernhard. But he did have something to say about Queen Wilhelmina's birthday:

> After two and a half years of Japanese terror, still Orange today. Displaying it is now very dangerous. The European community in the city has gradually become so small that the Japanese know almost everyone by sight and certainly have all our addresses. (Bouwer 1988:284.)

A few days after the Queen's birthday, in early September 1944, there were rumours that Allied broadcasts had signalled a speedy liberation of the Netherlands. Thursday 7 September:

> The rumours are true, and we're all sick with emotion. We don't know the details, but they don't really matter anyway. We have this one, glorious fact that fills us with deep gratitude: the Netherlands is about to rise from the ashes! [...] Our joy knows no bounds, even though we can't show it. The arrival of Allied troops in the mother country has inspired us all with new courage and strength. Our suffering is far from over, nor is that of our fellow countrymen in the Netherlands, but we have been given new strength to bear it, despite the knowledge that the suffering we shall have to endure in the coming months will be many times greater than it has been up to now. (Bouwer 1988:285.)

There must have been similar reactions when around 17 September reports came of large-scale airborne landings by the Allies in the Netherlands. Did anything of this penetrate to the Japanese residency office? Possibly, and it is in any case notable that this office obliged some of the Dutch Eurasians to take part in a demonstration on Sunday 8 October which was intended to show that for them there would be no question of liberation. Three days later Bouwer observed:

> Last Sunday the Indo-Europeans from various districts were ordered by the local authorities to take part in a 12-kilometre walk to the war museum in Villa Isola and back. [...] All Indos aged between 12 and 45, women as well as men, had to join in the walk, and all attempts by the Indo committee [the BOGI] to dissuade resident Kihara from inflicting this humiliation on the Europeans failed. When they arrived at Isola, all the participants had to bow three times to the Japanese flag, then immerse their hands in a sort of holy water and with wet hands pay homage to some Japanese shrine. This was followed by a tour of Japanese war trophies collected on Java, including the official uniform of the Governor-General and his decorations. At 1 pm the walkers were back in the city.
>
> The local authorities intend to make each district go on such a walk one by one. (Bouwer 1988:294.)

It is not known whether this plan was carried out. In any event, the reports later in October of MacArthur's first landing on the Philippines must have given heart to the Dutch Eurasians in Bandung and elsewhere.

Would the Dutch East Indies, including Java, be the next target of the American offensive? Bouwer doubted it. The Australians and a few KNIL units formed in Australia landed on Tarakan on 1 May 1945. Two days later he noted:

> More than any other recent event [the Allies had driven deep into Germany, the Russians were fighting in Berlin, Hitler had committed suicide] this news has affected us. This is not the first campaign on Dutch East Indies territory. New Guinea and Morotai came earlier.[42] We were happy and enthusiastic about them, but our joy was tempered by the knowledge that both campaigns were part of a strategy for the recapture of the Philippines and not for the liberation of the Dutch East Indies. And while it is far from certain (and in my personal view highly unlikely) that this operation is the prelude to a campaign to liberate Java and the other islands, nonetheless our chances have improved. (Bouwer 1988:337.)

As far as MacArthur was concerned, those chances were rather better than Bouwer suspected. Knowing (not through the activities of secret agents but through the decoding of Japanese telegrams) that the Japanese had very few troops on Java, and feeling himself obliged to liberate the territory of his Dutch ally as soon as possible, MacArthur had informed the Combined Chiefs of Staff that he proposed to make the leap from southeast Borneo to

---

[42]   MacArthur's troops had landed here on 22 April and 10 September 1944 respectively.

Java at the end of June 1945. He intended to land near Batavia. The Combined Chiefs of Staff vetoed this plan. The American and Allied forces were to head straight for Japan, leaving far behind the Dutch East Indies with their Dutch Eurasians yearning for liberation.

They had lived for liberation through years in which their position had become steadily more difficult. The familiar Dutch authority had been replaced by Japanese rule with astounding speed. A society that had offered them opportunities to get ahead had given way to one in which they, as a small minority, felt increasingly threatened. Right from the beginning of the occupation, they suffered severe blows: many of the men made prisoners of war, mass internments on the Outer Islands, and on Java internment of all the prominent figures in their community. Their organizations were disbanded, their schools closed, their newspapers and magazines banned, their radios first 'castrated' then confiscated. In their own country (as they felt) they were branded 'foreigners': forced to register, forced, if aged over 16, to always carry the expensive identity card, the *pendaftaran*, forced to obtain a permit for every journey. On Java most were not interned, but their standard of living was affected. As early as 1942 serious poverty began to be seen: the payment of pensions had been stopped and many had lost their job. It was telling that in Batavia, where about 25,000 Dutch Eurasians were not interned, close to 11,000 of them were reliant on assistance after only one year of occupation. Furthermore, one gets the impression that in this city the position of the Dutch Eurasians was even more difficult than elsewhere on Java; during the rest of the occupation several hundred thousand Indonesians, who were fleeing the desperate conditions in the *desa*, tried to find accommodation in Batavia. Consequently, the Dutch Eurasians were hit extra hard by the drastic cuts in the assistance scheme described above.

How did these tens of thousands of families, from which the husband had often disappeared, keep their heads above water, especially in the last months of the occupation, when many of the men and youths who were still working were dismissed?[43] How did they find the resources, on the few occasions when it was permitted and the many when it was not, to give assistance to the prisoners-of-war, the internees, the prisoners in the 'ordinary' jails? No general survey of this exists. The scarce data cited here suggest that, as prices constantly rose, many could only stay alive and give help to others by selling some of their possessions and by deriving a little extra income from improvised

---

[43]   Bouwer reports this as happening in Bandung; it seems reasonable to assume that it happened elsewhere too. At the beginning of 1945 he noted: 'The Indo-European personnel at the Post Office have suddenly been transferred to administration. In most garages nearly all of the young Indos have been summarily dismissed; those that are left have been put into big teams of Indonesians, where they are strictly supervised.' (Bouwer 1988:338.)

retail trading. 'How my wife made ends meet,' E.B.L. van der Worm, a Dutch Eurasian who lived through the occupation in Bandung, reported to us in 1985, 'is a mystery to me. You couldn't call it housekeeping, it was magic.'[44]

In addition to impoverishment, the quality of life in general deteriorated. According to Van der Worm, 'You moved in loosely connected circles that were quite small. Being involved in more or less organized groups of any size could make the combined police forces suspicious.'[45] Cultural events or opportunities for relaxation were no longer possible: at best, performing artists could appear clandestinely for a small audience on occasion, or the young people, who had a hard time because their life was so circumscribed, could enjoy a little sport.

Then there was the fear: fear as to the fate of the prisoners of war who had disappeared into thin air, so to speak; fear of new measures by the Japanese, who were regarded as completely unpredictable; fear above all of the Kempeitai, who with the aid of the PID had made many arrests among the Dutch Eurasians on real or imaginary charges. 'Of all the aspects of life outside the camps', wrote Van der Worm, 'the constant threat and fear of Kempeitai practices were the most oppressive. Every evening when you went to sleep you kept in mind that you might be taken from your bed, and every morning that you woke up in your own bed you counted as a blessing from above.'[46]

This fear created unease, as did the multiple forced removals which began as early as 1942, when families moved in with each other in an attempt to save money. Later, as in Bandung, the neediest families were accommodated in the larger houses, with all the inevitable discomfort, tension and quarrels. People might also be forced out of their own home by the Japanese and left to find accommodation somewhere. Van der Worm had to move five times with his wife and baby from one outbuilding or garage 'room' to another 'because the main tenants had to leave their house' (which had been requisitioned by the Japanese).[47]

Nor should we forget the anger at those who publicly sided with the Japanese or, in the eyes of many, misbehaved in other ways. There were Dutch Eurasian girls and women who had sexual relations with Japanese.[48]

---

[44] E.B.L. van der Worm, 'Herinneringen aan een vogelvrij verleden. Bandoeng 1942-1945' (1985), p. 30.
[45] E.B.L. van der Worm, 'Herinneringen aan een vogelvrij verleden. Bandoeng 1942-1945' (1985), p. 26.
[46] E.B.L. van der Worm, 'Herinneringen aan een vogelvrij verleden. Bandoeng 1942-1945' (1985), p. 25.
[47] E.B.L. van der Worm, 'Herinneringen aan een vogelvrij verleden. Bandoeng 1942-1945' (1985), p. 28
[48] A few scattered figures suggest that in the occupied Netherlands the Germans fathered between 8,000 and 10,000 illegitimate children. Given that at the time there were a little over

In 1944 in Batavia some of them took up with members of the crews of the German U-boats that had entered Priok harbour. And, some acted as spies for the Kempeitai. In this connection it should be noted that, to the extent that there was any fear of betrayal, it focused primarily on the Indonesians. In general the lower-ranking Indonesian officials and the police officers treated the Dutch Eurasians with a remarkable rudeness that did not bode well.

It was, of course, clear to the Dutch Eurasians from the outset that the Japanese were trying to get the Indonesians onto their side. On Java this was already evident in 1942 from the AAA campaign, and the founding of the Poetera in March 1943 was part of the same effort. Later in the occupation, ever more semi-military and military auxiliary corps set up by the Japanese appeared in public – large groups of youths indoctrinated with fiercely anti-Western beliefs. What dangers loomed from them? Traditionally, there was more tension in relations between the Dutch Eurasians and the Indonesians than in those between the Dutch, the *totok*, and the Indonesians. The 'ethical policy' adopted at the beginning of the twentieth century was the product of the political thinking of the Dutch in the Netherlands, not those in the East Indies. The education of Indonesians introduced as a result of this policy had become a threat to the social position the Dutch Eurasians had built up at such great effort. Living more closely to the Indonesians than the *totok*, many Dutch Eurasians, in addition, believed more strongly than the *totok* that the Indonesians lacked the ability to run the complex society of the Indies in an acceptable fashion. This conviction was strengthened when during the Japanese occupation Indonesians took over posts held by the Dutch or Dutch Eurasians and showed themselves to be incompetent or corruptible. According to the Eurasian A.W.F. de Roock writing in 1957, when as Agus Daruch he was an Indonesian citizen:

> The chaotic state of affairs created in the management of the country as a result of the incompetence of the Japanese and the Indonesians' complete lack of experience of administration inspired derision and contempt among the Indos (civil servants for centuries).[49] Treachery, advocated by the Japs at every opportunity, and the use they made of the worst elements of Indonesian society, ensured that, if anything, the Indo-Europeans' hate for the 'older brother' deepened.
>
> The fact that in a confidential or drunken mood the Japanese had little good to say about the Indonesians they raised so high, and even called them 'dumb animals' and so on, did not alter the Indo's feelings. (Daruch 1957:66.)

4.5 million women and girls in the Netherlands and on Java less than 100,000 Dutch Eurasian women and girls, and that there were more Germans in the occupied Netherlands than Japanese on Java, it seems safe to assume that no more than a few hundred illegitimate children were born from these sexual relations with the Japanese.
[49]   For a few generations actually.

W.F. Wertheim (1946:280-1) expressed a more or less similar view in 1946 based on his memories of many discussions he had held during his internment and those at which he had been present:

> In many camps the Dutch colonial mentality dominates. We'll teach those Natives! What gives them the idea they can treat us whites as a negligible quantity! Just wait, it'll be our turn soon!
> [...] This is what the Indos in the camps think too. They normally keep some distance from the *totok*. Relations are often tense – the wretched conditions, the struggle to survive and the constant contact exacerbate the differences. Among the Indo-Europeans there's a mood of 'We'll teach them!' From their wife, their brother, their aunt they've heard how appallingly that one Native policeman, that Native who lives at the corner, that Native doctor at the hospital, has behaved towards them. The Indo's traditional hate for the Native (a hate stemming from the insecurity of the intermediate group which takes its lead from the upper group) [...] flourishes as never before. The Dutch were far too ethical. They should never have set up schools for the Natives. The Japs have shown how to treat the Natives. Keep them on a tight rein. And if they give you any lip, beat them. That's the only way to keep them down.

Is the term 'hate' used by De Roock and Wertheim not too strong? One wonders. There was certainly considerable animosity among many. As Wertheim rightly points out, this arose from the position of the group as a whole: while seeking to belong to the Netherlands and the Dutch (but not accepted as social equals by many *totok*), they had educated Indonesians close behind them.

Anyone inside or outside the internment camps who thought in this way, anyone who felt this, must have been particularly disturbed by what was heard (and also seen outside the camps) of Japanese attempts to indoctrinate the Indonesian masses and, though in a rather primitive fashion, militarize them. As mentioned in Chapter I, some Dutch and Dutch Eurasians were shouted at by Indonesians in the first phase of the occupation. This also happened later on (take the abuse in Surabaya of prisoners of war leaving for Flores and of Dutch Eurasian women from East Java on their way to and from Kesilir), but our impression is that it did not become a general phenomenon. There is no doubt that, as conditions deteriorated the longer the occupation lasted and the Japanese made themselves more hated, a large part of the Indonesian population on Java developed a strong preference for the vanished Dutch regime. On the other hand, the groups indoctrinated by the Japanese (including the youth labour corps Seinendan) displayed an aggressiveness that caused deep concern on the part of many Dutch Eurasians. In Bandung Bouwer (1988:297) devoted an important passage to this matter at the end of October 1944:

> It now appears that the Japanese are trying to turn the Indonesians against the Indo-Europeans. The Seinendan is being used as a tool for this. The Seinendan

leaders have been told to spread the rumour in the *kampong* that the Indo-European community is preparing an operation against the Indonesians and that therefore they must be on their guard. Of course this story is too silly for words. How could the tens of thousands of Indo-Europeans on Java (most of them women on their own) contemplate action against the millions of Indonesians, many of whom have been armed by the Japanese? What this is really about is the Japanese sowing the seeds of large-scale massacres that will take place as soon as they have to withdraw or are defeated in some other way.

Now suddenly I understand what is the cause of the abuse hurled by Indonesian street youths at passing Europeans that has been noticeable in recent weeks. Now I also understand why so many Indonesian youths go about with chains, truncheons and so forth and try to provoke fights with young Indo-Europeans at every opportunity. By an indirect route I have passed on this information from reliable Indonesian sources to the local Indo committee [the BOGI], and asked them to issue a warning that the Eurasian youths should not under any circumstances let themselves be provoked into fights. After all, they're bound to lose and it will only end in internment.

The chairman of the BOGI, Suyderhoud, makes no mention of such a warning in his daily notes, but, knowing that they were regularly examined by the Japanese, he exercised great caution when writing them. The warning may thus have been issued after all.

Be this as it may, Bouwer was right when he said that as long as the Japanese occupation lasted, the millions of Indonesians had nothing to fear from the Dutch Eurasians, even though their number was substantially larger than the 'tens of thousands' he spoke of. They indeed formed a group dominated by women on their own (that is, women whose husbands were not with them, but who often had growing children to look after). Moreover, they were dispersed. Assuming that there were relatively strong concentrations in Batavia, Bandung, Semarang, Surabaya and Malang (incidentally, most Dutch Eurasians lived outside these cities), it must be remembered that the distances from Batavia to these other cities, by road or by rail, were about the same as those from Amsterdam to Antwerp, Paris, Avignon and Marseilles. These distances must have played an important role in the thinking of the Dutch Eurasians, even though they never wrote about them. What were their larger and numerous smaller communities but islands in a restless sea?

Dispersed, discriminated against, powerless, weakened, many of them in need of help, they too were painfully surprised by the proclamation of the Republic of Indonesia in Jakarta on 17 August 1945.

Glossary

(I: Indonesian words; J: Japanese words)

adat (I)	Indonesian customary law
alang-alang (I)	a type of grass with long, narrow plumes
Asia Raya (I)	Great Asia
atap (I)	dried palm leaves
aza (J)	city district
azacho (J)	district chief
babu (I)	Indonesian nanny
balai-balai (I)	bench
banjir (I)	high tide, deluge
bataten	sweet patatoes
Belanda (I)	(I)Dutchman
Belanda-Indo (I)	Dutch Eurasian
Beppan (J)	Japanese military intelligence service
beras (I)	husked rice
becak (I)	trishaw
bibit (I)	seedlings
cap (I)	stamp
Dai Nippon (J)	Great Japan
desa (I)	country villages
Djawa Hokokai (J)	Organization for Public Service to Java
Domei (J)	Japanese press agency
fuku (J)	deputy neighbourhood chief
gaplek (I)	cassava
gedek (I)	camp enclosure
gedèkken	trading over the enclosure with people outside the camp
Great East	the eastern part of the Indonesian archipelago: Celebes, the Lesser Sunda Islands, the Moluccas and Dutch New Guinea
gunso (J)	sergeant
hai (J)	yes
hancho (J)	barrack heads (in an internment camp) or neighbourhood helpers (in a city)
heiho (J)	indigenous auxiliaries under the command of the Japanese army

Indo (I)	Dutch Eurasian
Indonesia Raya (I)	Great Indonesia (the battle song of the Indonesian national movement)
jagung (I)	maize
kali (I)	river
Kaoem-Indo (I)	committee for the Indo people
kasihan (I)	pity
Keibodan (J)	indigenous auxiliary police force
Kempeitai (J)	Japanese military police
ketan (I)	sticky rice
ketua (I)	ëelder (neighbourhood chief)
kiai (I)	Islamic leader
klambu (I)	mosquito net
kokki (I)	Indonesian cook
Konketsu Jumin Linkai (J)	Committee for Inhabitants of Mixed Blood
kumiai (J)	Japanese business corporations
kumicho (J)	neighbourhood chief
lekas (I)	quick
lombok (I)	hot pepper
lurah (I)	village headman
mandur (I)	supervisor
Minseiboe (J)	naval civil administration
Nampo (J)	South Pacific area (South East Asia)
nasi goreng (I)	fried rice
Nippon (J)	Japan
Nippon workers (J)	Dutch who continued to do their normal work under Japanese orders
nyonya (I)	madam
obat (I)	medicine
Oranda (J)	Hollanders
Outer Islands	the Indonesian islands beyond Java and Madura
padi (I)	unhusked rice
pasar (I)	market
pendaftaran (I)	registration certificate
peranakan (I)	people of mixed descent
pesantren (I)	Islamic seminary
pisang (I)	banana
raden/raden mas ario (I)	Javanese titles of nobility
rami (I)	hemp
romusha (J)	work soldiers (indigenous labourers who were put to work under Japanese military supervision)
sayur (I)	vegetable soup
sambal (I)	hot dishes made from peppers
sawah (I)	rice paddies
Seinendan (J)	youth labour corps
shimbun (J)	newspaper, magazine
Tenno Heika (J)	emperor of Japan
teuku (I)	an aristocratic title in Aceh

Tokkeitai (J)	military police of the Japanese navy
toko (I)	Indonesian shop
tonarigumi system (J)	the grouping of all of the inhabitants in small neighbourhoods
totok (I)	Dutch born in the Netherlands
ubi (I)	sweet patato
ulama (I)	Islamic scholar
wakare (J)	dismissed
warung (I)	stall
wedono (I)	district chief
yasumi (J)	rest

Abbreviations

AAA	Asia tjahaja, Asia pelindoeng dan Asia pemimpin (Japan the light of Asia, the protector of Asia and the leader of Asia)
Aneta	Algemeen Niews- en Telegraaf-Agentschap (General News and Telegraph Agency)
Bogi	Badan Oeroesan Golongan Indo (Committee for Promoting the Interests of the Indos)
Fiwi	Federatie van Ex-Illegale Werkers in Indië (Federation of Former Clandestine Workers in the East Indies)
GESC	Gemeentelijk Europeesch Steuncomité (Municipal European Assistance Committee)
GG	Governor-General
IEV	Indo-Europeesch Verbond (Indo European Association)
KNIL	Koninklijk Nederlandsch-Indisch Leger (Royal Dutch East Indian Army)
KOP	Kantor Oeroesan Peranakan (Office for People of Mixed Descent)
KPM	Koninklijke Pakketvaartmaatschappij (Royal Packet Shipping Company)
Nefis	Netherlands Forces Intelligence Service
Nica	Netherlands-Indies Civil Administration
NIROM	Nederlandsch-Indische Radio-Omroep Maatschappij (Dutch East Indies Radio Company)
NSB	Nationaal-Socialistische Beweging (National Socialist Movement)
Pagi	Pesaudaraan Asia Golongan Indo (Asian Fraternity, Indonesian Group)
PID	Politieke Inlichtingendienst (Political Information Department)
POBIM	Pertoeloengan Orang Blanda-Indo Miskin (Assistance for Poor Indo-Europeans)
Pop	Pertoeloengan Orang Peranakan (Assistance for People of Mixed Descent)
Rapwi	Recovery Allied Prisoners of War and Internees
VOC	Vereenigde Oost-Indische Compagnie (Dutch East Indies Company)

Bibliography

Adachi, Sumio
1982   'Unprepared regrettable events; A brief history of Japanese practices on treatment of Allied war victims during the Second World War', *The Studies of Cultural and Social Sciences* 45:257-332.

Backer, Dam
1995   *Buigend riet; Dagboek van een krijgsgevangene in Japan en Mantsjoerije 1944-1945.* Amsterdam/Antwerpen: Veen.

Beets, N.
1981   *De verre oorlog; Lot en levensloop van krijgsgevangenen onder de Japanner.* Meppel: Boom.

Benda, Harry J., James K. Irikura and Koichi Kishi (eds)
1965   *Japanese military administration in Indonesia; Selected documents.* New Haven, Conn.: Southeast Asia Studies, Yale University. [Translation Series 6.]

Bezemer, K.W.L.
1967   *Verdreven doch niet verslagen; Verdere verrichtingen der Koninklijke Marine in de Tweede Wereldoorlog.* Hilversum: De Haan.

Binnerts, C.
1947   *'Alles is in orde, heeren...!'; Een dagboek van het eiland Flores uit het jaar 1943.* Amsterdam: Swets en Zeitlinger.

Boissevain, Gon and Lennie van Empel
1981   *Vrouwenkamp op Java; Een dagboek.* Amsterdam: De Boekerij.

Bouwer, Jan
1988   *Het vermoorde land.* Franeker: Van Wijnen.

Braak, Menno ter and E. du Perron
1967   *Briefwisseling 1930-1940; Deel IV.* Amsterdam: Van Oorschot. 4 Vols.

Brandt, Willem [pseudonym of W.B. Klooster]
1947   *De gele terreur.* 's-Gravenhage: Van Hoeve.

Brugmans, I.J. (ed.)
1960   *Nederlandsch-Indië onder Japanse bezetting; Gegevens en documenten over de jaren 1942-1945.* Franeker: Wever.

Burger, D.H.
1975   *Sociologisch-economische geschiedenis van Indonesia.* Wageningen: Landbouwhogeschool Wageningen, Afdeling Agrarische Geschiedenis, Amsterdam: Koninklijk Instituut voor de Tropen, Leiden: Koninklijk Instituut voor Taal-, Land- en Volkenkunde. 2 Vols.

Cohen, J.B.
1949   *Japan's economy in war and reconstruction.* Minneapolis: University of Minnesota Press.
Daruch, Agus
1957   *De nationalistische beweging onder de Indo-Europeanen.* N.p.: n.n.
Doel, H.W. van den
1996   *Het rijk van Insulinde; Opkomst en ondergang van een Nederlandse kolonie.* Amsterdam: Prometheus.
Dubois, A.
1946   *De muren spreken.* Den Haag: Voorhoeve.
Elias, W.H.J.
1946   *Indië onder Japanschen hiel.* Deventer: Van Hoeve.
Enquêtecommissie regeringsbeleid
1956   *Enquêtecommissie regeringsbeleid 1940-1945; Militair beleid 1940-1945; Verslag houdende de uitkomsten van het onderzoek; Deel 8c-I. Verhoren.* Den Haag: Staatsdrukkerij- en Uitgeverijbedrijf.
Eijk-van Velzen, Truus van
1983   *Vrouwen op Sumatra achter Japans prikkeldraad.* Den Helder: Dinky Druk.
Frankfurther, A.
1961   *In klinkende munt; Herinneringen van een bankier.* Amsterdam: De Brug - Djambatan. [Van Gisteren tot Morgen 4.]
Gandasubrata, S.M.
1953   *An account of the Japanese occupation of Banjumas residency; Java, March 1942 to August 1945.* Ithaca, NY: Cornell University. [Data Paper 10.]
Gedenkboek vereniging ambtenaren
1956   *Gedenkboek van de vereniging van ambtenaren bij het Binnenlands Bestuur in Nederlands-Indië.* Utrecht: Oosthoek.
Goor, J. van
1987   *Indië/Indonesië; Van kolonie tot natie.* Utrecht: HES.
Grift, C. van der [pseudonym of C.C. van der Star]
1946   *Vier maanden onder de Jappen op Java en mijn ontsnapping.* Den Haag: Van Goor.
Gunning, C.P. (ed.)
1947   *Gedenkboek 1940-1945 van het Amsterdams Lyceum.* Amsterdam: Door-geven.
Hamel, J.C.
1948   *Soldatendominee.* 's-Gravenhage: Van Hoeve.
Heekeren, C. van
1964   *De 'Atjeh-party': 18 maart tot 3 november 1944; Een relaas.* Den Haag: n.n.
1968   *Rode zon boven Borneo; West-Borneo 1942.* Den Haag: Bert Bakker/Daamen.
Hees, G. van et al. (eds)
n.d.   *Velden 1940-1945.* Eindhoven: Mercurius.

Helfferich-Koch, H.
1981   *Een dal in Ambarawa*. Alphen aan den Rijn: Sijthoff.
Helfrich, C.E.L.
1950   *Memoires; Deel II: glorie en tragedie*. Amsterdam: Elsevier.
Hovinga, Henk
1982   *Eindstation Pakan Baroe 1944-1945; Dodenspoorweg door het oerwoud*.
               Third edition. Franeker: Wever.
Jacobs, Gideon François
1979   *Prelude to the monsoon*. Maidstone: Mann.
Jalhay, S.M.
1981   *Jalhay's kleine oorlog*. Den Haag: Thomas en Eras.
Jansen, L.F.
1988   *In deze halve gevangenis; Dagboek van mr dr L.F. Jansen, Batavia/Djakarta
               1942-1945*. Franeker: Van Wijnen.
Jaquet, L.M.G.
1978   *Aflossing van de wacht; Bestuurlijke en politieke ervaringen in de nadagen
               van Nederlandsch-Indië*. Rotterdam: Donker.
Jong, J.J.P. de
1998   *De waaier van fortuin; Van handelscompagnie tot koloniaal imperium: de
               Nederlanders in Azië en de Indonesische archipel 1595-1950*. Den Haag:
               SDU.
Jong, L. de
1984   *Het Koninkrijk der Nederlanden in de Tweede Wereldoorlog; Deel 11a; Neder-
               lands-Indië I*. Leiden: Nijhoff. 2 Vols.
1985   *Het Koninkrijk der Nederlanden in de Tweede Wereldoorlog; Deel 11b; Neder-
               lands-Indië II*. Leiden: Nijhoff. 2 Vols.
1991   *Het Koninkrijk der Nederlanden in de Tweede Wereldoorlog; Deel 14; Reac-
               ties*. Edited by J.Th.M. Bank and P. Romijn. Den Haag: SDU. 2 Vols.
Kadt, J. de
1978   *Jaren die dubbel telden; Politieke herinneringen*. Amsterdam: Van Oor-
               schot.
Kan, Wim and Corry Vonk
1963   *Honderd dagen uit en thuis*. Utrecht: Bruna.
Kanahele, George Sanford
1967   *The Japanese occupation of Indonesia; Prelude to independence*. [PhD thesis
               Cornell University, Ithaca.]
Keizer-Heuzeveldt, H.E.
1982   *En de lach keerde terug; Mijn Indische kampjaren en daarna*. Franeker:
               Wever.
Keizer, Madelon de (ed.)
1995   *'Een dure verplichting en een kostelijk voorrecht'; Dr. L. de Jong en zijn
               geschiedwerk*. Den Haag: SDU.
Koch, D.M.G.
1954   'De Japanse bezetting van Indonesië', in: J.J. van Bolhuis et al. (eds.),
               Onderdrukking en verzet; Nederland in oorlogstijd; Deel IV, pp. 535-87.
               Arnhem: Van Loghum Slaterus.

1956   *Verantwoording; Een halve eeuw in Indië.* Den Haag/Bandung: Van
                Hoeve.

Leffelaar, H.L.
1959   *Leven op rantsoen.* Amsterdam: De Arbeiderspers.
1963   *Through a harsh dawn; A boy grows up in a Japanese prison camp.* Barre,
                Mass.: Barre.
1980   *De Japansche regeering betaalt aan toonder; Een oorlog die niet verdween.*
                Alphen aan den Rijn: Sijthoff.

Leffelaar, H.L. and E. van Witsen
1982   *Werkers aan de Burmaspoorweg.* Franeker: Wever.

Locher-Scholten, Elsbeth
1999   'After the "Distant War"; Dutch public memory of the Second World
                War in Asia', in: Remco Raben (ed.), *Representing the Japanese occupation
                of Indonesia; Personal testimonies and public images in Indonesia, Japan, and
                The Netherlands.* Zwolle: Waanders, Amsterdam: Netherlands Institute
                for War Documentation.

Lubis, Mochtar
1975   'Van dingen die ik me nog herinner', *Tirade* 19-209:518-40.

MacGillavry, Annemie
1975   *Je kunt niet altijd huilen; Een Nederlands gezin in de laatste periode van
                Nederlands-Oostindië.* Baarn: De Boekerij.

Manschot, H.J.
1946   *Het geld-, bank en credietwezen in Nederlandsch-Indië in de bezettingsjaren
                1942-1945.* Rotterdam: n.n. [Reprint from *Economische-Statistische
                Berichten* 1507 (27 March 1946) and 1508 (3 April 1946).]

Melis, Ed. (ed.)
1984   *Eresaluut boven massagraf; Junyo Maru: de vergeten scheepsramp.* Nijme-
                gen: Stichting Herdenking Junyo Maru - Sumatra.

Min, Th.
1979   *Dagboek van een krijgsgevangene.* Gennep: Janssen.

Moscou-de Ruyter, M.
1984   *Vogelvrij; Het leven buiten de kampen op Java 1942-1945.* Weesp: Fibula-
                Van Dishoeck.

Nakamura, Mitsuo
1970   'General Imamura and the early period of Japanese occupation', *Indo-
                nesia* 10:1-26.

Neumann, H. and E. van Witsen
1982   *De Pekanbaroe spoorweg; Documentatie.* Amstelveen: Studio Pieter
                Mulier.

Nieuwenhuys, R.
1979   *Een beetje oorlog; Java, 8 december 1941 - 15 november 1945.* Amsterdam:
                Querido.

Poeze, Harry A.
1976   *Tan Malaka; Strijder voor Indonesië's vrijheid; Levensloop van 1897 tot
                1945.* 's-Gravenhage: Nijhoff. [KITLV, Verhandelingen 78.]

Reid, Anthony
1979   *The blood of the people; Revolution and the end of traditional rule in northern Sumatra.* Kuala Lumpur: Oxford University Press.

Roever, J.W. de
1951   *De 'Nederland' in de Tweede Wereldoorlog.* Amsterdam: Stoomvaart Maatschappij 'Nederland'.

Scholten, P.
1971   *Op reis met de 'Special Party'; Oorlogs- en kampherinneringen.* Leiden: Sijthoff.

Sjahrir, Soetan
1949   *Out of exile; Letters by Soetan Sjahrir, rewritten and edited by Maria Duchâteau-Sjahrir.* New York: Day.

Stellingwerff, J.
1980   *Fat man in Nagasaki; Nederlandse krijgsgevangenen overleefden de atoombom.* Franeker: Wever.

Thomson, Eliza
1965   *Setengah mati (halfdood).* Amsterdam: Van Ditmar.

Tjarda van Starkenborgh
1978   *Jhr.mr.dr. A.W.L. Tjarda van Starkenborgh Stachouwer; Bijdragen tot een kenschets, verzameld door mr. D.U. Stikker.* Rotterdam: Donker.

Veenstra, J.H.W.
1947   *Diogenes in de tropen.* Amsterdam: Vrij Nederland. [Noesantara Reeks 2.]

Veenstra, J.H.W. et al.
1982   *Als krijgsgevangene naar de Molukken en Flores; Relaas van een Japans transport van Nederlandse en Engelse militairen 1943-1945.* 's-Gravenhage: Nijhoff

Velde, J.J. van de
1982   *Brieven uit Sumatra: 1928-1949.* Franeker: Wever.

Velden, Doetje van
1963   *De Japanse interneringskampen voor burgers gedurende de Tweede Wereldoorlog.* Groningen: Wolters.

Verheem, Rudy
1979   *Bevrijding zonder bevrijders; De 'sinjo' tussen Indië en Nederland.* Baarn: Hollandia.

Vermeer-van Berkum, Carla
1980   *Kon ik maar weer een gewoon meisje zijn; Dagboek uit Japanse kampen '44-'45.* Amsterdam: Elsevier.

Visser, A.
1982   *Een merkwaardige loopbaan; Herinneringen van een bestuursambtenaar in Nederlands-Indië/Indonesië (1932-1950).* Franeker: Wever.

Visser, Frank
1976   *De schakel; Een documentaire uit de Tweede Wereldoorlog; Een selectie van authentieke verhalen van Nederlandse Engelandvaarders aan de hand van dagboeken, rapporten, brieven en uitgebreide persoonlijke interviews.* Baarn: Zuid-Hollandsche Uitgeversmaatschappij.

Vries, Erik K. de
1980		'Notities in Japanse krijgsgevangenschap', *De Gids* 143-6:371-406.

Vromans, A.G. and Rodney de Bruin
n.d.		*Het Indisch verzet.* [Unpublished manuscript, Nederlands Instituut voor Oorlogsdocumentatie, Amsterdam.]

Vuyk, Beb
1962		'Uit een Indisch dagboek', in: Mathieu Smedts (ed), *Den vaderland getrouwe; Een boek over oorlog en verzet*, pp. 247-58. Amsterdam: Arbeiderspers.

Wertheim, W.F.
1946		'Nederland op den tweesprong; Tragedie van den aan traditie gebonden mensch', *De Nieuwe Stem* 1-4:262-95.

Wigmore, Lionel
1957		*The Japanese thrust.* Canberra: Australian War Memorial.

Witsen, E. van
1971		*Krijgsgevangenen in de Pacific-oorlog (1941-1945).* Franeker: Wever.

Zwaan, Jacob
1981		*Nederlands-Indië 1940-1946; II: Japans Intermezzo 9 maart 1942 - 15 augustus 1945.* Den Haag: Omniboek.

Zwitzer, H.L.
1978		'Enkele gegevens over krijgsgevangenen en gesneuvelden onder de Europese militairen van het Koninklijk Nederlands-Indisch Leger gedurende de oorlog in de Pacific (1941-1945)', *Mededelingen van de Sectie Krijgsgeschiedenis Koninklijke Landmacht* 1-1 :5-23.

Index of personal names

Index of geographical names